I0813946

Christians who examine Revelation only as a collection of raw materials for their timetables of the last days or, worse, their theories about where exactly we find ourselves in that timetable are missing out on its far richer and more reliable contributions to our understanding of God, his Christ, the many facets of the cosmic rebellion against God, and the broad scope of God's redemption of his creation. Duvall masterfully lays out these greater riches and communicates about them in clear, winsome prose, all buoyed up by the spirit of devotion that drives him to this work. This is a book that helps us focus on what is truly at the heart of John's message and purpose—his own congregations' and *our* congregations' wholehearted commitment to worship, discipleship, and witness.

—*David A. deSilva,* Trustees' Distinguished Professor of New Testament and Greek, Ashland Theological Seminary

This latest addition to the Biblical Theology of the New Testament series does not disappoint! Scott Duvall offers a well-written and well-researched overview of Revelation's rich and deep theology. An extensive discussion of the historical and literary context lays a solid foundation for an extended literary-theological reading of Revelation that draws one into the grand sweep of Revelation's theological and doxological richness. Especially helpful are his "interpretive principles for reading Revelation responsibly." This clear, balanced approach is much needed in the study of Revelation! The ensuing discussion of nine key theological themes spotlights various facets of Revelation's mysterious beauty. This volume will serve both those unfamiliar with the challenges and delights of Revelation as well as those who have spent decades studying this "canonical capstone" to the Bible. This book also offers an in-depth survey of the vast scholarship on Revelation. I highly recommend this comprehensive and engaging work!

—*Dana Harris,* Professor and Chair of the New Testament Department, Trinity Evangelical Divinity School

Duvall argues that the Revelation of Jesus Christ centers on the Triune God and his glorious plan of redemption and restoration, inspiring his people to persevere in witness and worship. With scholarly excellence, pastoral insight, and an accessible style, this volume offers a sure guide for all teachers and students of the final book of sacred Scripture.

—*Brian Tabb,* President and Professor of Biblical Studies, Bethlehem College and Seminary

The biblical book is aptly titled "The Revelation of Jesus Christ," yet for many readers, it has often functioned more as an enigma, sealed with seven seals. The difficulty lies, in part, in its apocalyptic genre—a literary form brimming with evocative symbolism that depicts a storyline that seems distant both spatially and temporally. One hallmark of apocalyptic literature is the presence of a guide who leads the seer through the intricacies of their visionary experience. In this work, Scott Duvall assumes that role for modern readers, expertly illuminating the path through John's apocalypse. This volume is not only a masterful literary and theological engagement with the biblical text but also an unparalleled resource of historical and biblical insight. With scholarly precision and pastoral sensitivity, Duvall weaves together a robust biblical theology that is both erudite and accessible, making the once-mysterious vision of Revelation profoundly relevant for the contemporary church.

—*Robby Waddell,* Professor of New Testament and Early Christianity, Southeastern University

Scott Duvall provides readers with an accessible, comprehensive, and coherent reading of Revelation with attention to its historic context, literary structure, and, in particular, its theological themes. He interacts with a broad range of scholarship and this volume provides both a theology of Revelation and a gateway to further research for interested students. Theological insight and interpretive wisdom are evident on every page. Highly recommended.

—*Alexander E. Stewart,* Professor of New Testament and Vice President of Academic Services, Gateway Seminary

Simply put, Scott Duvall's *A Theology of Revelation* is a masterpiece. This marvelous literary-theological study of John's apocalypse invites us to focus our attention on the majestic work of the Triune God from creation to consummation. This clearly written and deeply engaging volume not only provides thoughtful insight regarding the meaning of the biblical canon's complex capstone, but warmly and persuasively invites all of us to renewed commitments in our followship, discipleship, and worship of the Lord Jesus Christ, our Redeemer and coming King. Heartily and warmly recommended!

—*David S. Dockery,* President and Distinguished Professor of Theology, Southwestern Baptist Theological Seminary

Revelation is a book that is rich in theology, far beyond the narrow eschatological focus of some treatments. Part of the problem is how to do theology in a unique book like Revelation. Scott Duvall effectively treats the major theological themes in Revelation, while modeling how to do theology in this unique book. Duvall demonstrates that Revelation makes a distinct contribution to all the major theological themes found throughout Scripture. He leads the reader skillfully through the intricacies of the book of Revelation and its theological message. More than just skillfully synthesizing the major biblical theological emphases of Revelation, Duvall offers the reader a complete orientation to reading and interpreting the book of Revelation in light of its literary genre and first-century historical background, to which Revelation's theology is a response. Duvall's work will become a standard theology of Revelation and the largest and most complete treatment of its theology to date. This book could be a 'one-stop' detailed guide to reading the book of Revelation. The serious student of Revelation will want to add this book to his/her library!

—*David Mathewson,* President and Distinguished Professor of Theology, Southwestern Baptist Theological Seminary

Highly readable and grounded in contemporary scholarship, Duvall's volume is more than a theology—it is also an introduction and commentary. Theological insights from Revelation are presented in a clear and comprehensive way. This book should be read by everyone interested in Jesus's message through John to the Seven Churches of Asia and to the Church today.

—*Mark Wilson,* Director, Asia Minor Research Center

This volume fills a gaping void in Revelation scholarship by offering a robust and comprehensive theology of Revelation. Duvall's writing is clear, crisp, engaging, and well researched. He judiciously and thoughtfully pulls together all the historical, literary, and theological threads to present a vibrant tapestry of the theology of John's Apocalypse as a whole. The overall breadth of content and topics he covers not only makes Revelation's theology beautifully accessible, but it also provides a one-stop shop for everything a serious student of Revelation may need to plunge its depths.

—*Alan Bandy,* Professor of New Testament and Greek,
New Orleans Baptist Theological Seminary

Duvall provides a worthy addition to the excellent Biblical Theology of the New Testament series, covering important issues clearly and competently, while interacting with a wide range of views on debated passages. He is a seasoned interpreter of Revelation who has taught and written extensively on the book, and this volume complements those works nicely. His work is well-organized and indexed, with a deft focus on central interpretive questions and key theological themes. It is comprehensive and detailed, but very readable. Highly recommended for students, pastors, and teachers of this controversial but rewarding book.

—*Buist Fanning,* Senior Professor Emeritus, New Testament Studies,
Dallas Theological Seminary

Scott Duvall's comprehensive volume on the theology of the "canonical capstone," with its focus on the Triune God, is highly accessible and unfailingly insightful. The balanced discussions of introductory issues, interpretive strategies, individual passages, and especially theological motifs—all supplemented with robust bibliographies—make this book an extremely helpful guide for students and an essential resource for scholars. An impressive contribution.

—*Michael J. Gorman,* Raymond E. Brown Chair in Biblical Studies
and Theology, St. Mary's Seminary & University

Scott Duvall's *A Theology of Revelation* is an outstanding resource for anyone seeking to understand the Bible's most complex book. While addressing essential introductory topics such as authorship, date, and setting, Duvall further explores Revelation's unique literary genre and interpretive challenges. With a focus on theological themes—God, Christ, the Spirit, salvation, discipleship, and new creation—this book serves as an invaluable guide, blending academic rigor with pastoral insight. Highly recommended!

—*Rob Dalrymple,* Director,
DetermineTruth.com

A THEOLOGY OF REVELATION

A THEOLOGY OF REVELATION

God's Grand Plan to Defeat Evil, Rescue His People, and Transform His Creation

BIBLICAL THEOLOGY OF THE NEW TESTAMENT

J. SCOTT DUVALL

Andreas J. Köstenberger,
General Editor

ZONDERVAN ACADEMIC

A Theology of Revelation

Published in Grand Rapids, Michigan, by Zondervan. Zondervan is a registered trademark of The Zondervan Corporation, L.L.C., a wholly owned subsidiary of HarperCollins Christian Publishing, Inc.

Requests for information should be addressed to customercare@harpercollins.com.

Zondervan titles may be purchased in bulk for educational, business, fundraising, or sales promotional use. For information, please email SpecialMarkets@Zondervan.com.

ISBN 978-0-310-29151-0 (hardcover)
ISBN 978-0-310-55551-3 (ebook)

Cover design: Rob Monacelli
Cover image: © Tuul and Bruno Morandi / Alamy Stock Photo
Interior design: Kait Lamphere
Interior typesetting: Sara Colley

Printed in the United States of America

25 26 27 28 29 30 31 32 33 34 35 36 37 38 39 40 /TRM/ 20 19 18 17 16 15 14 13 12 11 10 9 8 7 6 5 4 3 2 1

With deep gratitude to members of the Great Multitude who have mentored me along the way:

Bob and Peggy Duvall (parents)

Mrs. Laughingwell (first- and second-grade teacher)

Truman Parker (Minister to Students, FBC Crowley)

Don Purdy (Coach, Crowley High School)

Elmer Goble (Campus Minister, OBU)

Mark Baber (Pastor, Richwoods Baptist Church)

Dr. Tommy Lea (Professor, SWBTS)

Dr. Bruce Corley (Professor, SWBTS, doctoral supervisor, former president of B. H. Carroll Theological Institute)

Dr. Ben M. Elrod (former president, OBU)

My friends and co-workers in the Pruet School of Christian Studies at OBU

C. S. Lewis, John R. W. Stott, Philip Yancey, Eugene Peterson, Robert H. Mounce, Richard Bauckham, Grant Osborne (Christian writers)

And most of all, my amazing wife Judy, for whom I will be forever grateful!

Contents

PART 5: *Final Matters*

CONTENTS (DETAILED)

PART 3: *Literary-Theological Foundations for the Theology of Revelation*

PART 4: *Major Theological Themes in Revelation*

PART 5: *Final Matters*

SERIES PREFACE

THE BIBLICAL THEOLOGY of the New Testament series consists of eight distinct volumes covering the entire New Testament. Each volume is devoted to an in-depth exploration of a given New Testament writing, or group of writings, within the context of the theology of the New Testament, and ultimately of the entire Bible. While each corpus requires an approach that is suitable for the writing(s) studied, all volumes include:

(1) a survey of recent scholarship and of the state of research
(2) a treatment of the relevant introductory issues
(3) a thematic commentary following the narrative flow of the document(s)
(4) a treatment of important individual themes
(5) discussions of the relationship between a particular writing and the rest of the New Testament and the Bible

While biblical theology is a relatively new academic discipline and one that has often been hindered by questionable presuppositions, doubtful methodology, and/or flawed execution, the field is one of the most promising avenues of biblical and theological research today. In essence, biblical theology engages in the study of the biblical texts while giving careful consideration to the historical setting in which a given piece of writing originated. It seeks to locate and relate the contributions of the respective biblical documents along the lines of the continuum of God's salvation-historical program centered in the coming and salvific work of Christ. It also endeavors to ground the theological exploration of a given document in a close reading of the respective text(s), whether narrative, discourse, or some other type of literature.

By providing in-depth studies of the diverse, yet complementary perspectives of the New Testament writings, the Biblical Theology of the New Testament series aims to make a significant contribution to the study of the major interrelated themes of Scripture in a holistic, context-sensitive, and spiritually nurturing manner. Each volume is written by a scholar who has written a major commentary or monograph on the corpus covered. The generous page allotment allows for an in-depth investigation. While coming from diverse academic backgrounds and institutional affiliations, the contributors share a commitment to an evangelical faith and a respect for the authority of Scripture. They also have in common a conviction that the canon of Scripture is ultimately unified, not contradictory.

In addition to contributing to the study of individual New Testament writings and to the study of the New Testament and ultimately of Scripture as a whole, the series also seeks to make a methodological contribution, showing how Biblical Theology ought to be conducted. In each case, the way in which the volume is conceived reflects careful consideration of the nature of a given piece or body of writings. The complex interrelationships between the three so-called "Synoptic Gospels"; the two-volume nature of Luke-Acts; the relationship between John's Gospel, letters, and the book of Revelation; the thirteen letters making up the Pauline corpus; and the theologies of Peter, James, and Jude, as well as Hebrews, all present unique challenges and opportunities.

In the end, it is hoped that the volumes will pay tribute to the multifaceted nature of divine revelation contained in Scripture. As G. B. Caird puts it:

> The question we must ask is not whether these books all say the same thing, but whether they all bear witness to the same Jesus and through him to the many splendoured wisdom of the one God. . . . We shall neither attempt to press all our witnesses into a single mould nor captiously complain that one seems at some points deficient in comparison with another. What we shall do is rejoice that God has seen fit to establish His gospel at the mouth of so many independent witnesses. The music of the New Testament choir is not written to be sung in unison.[1]

In this spirit, the contributors offer their work as a humble aid to a greater appreciation of the magnificent scriptural symphony of God.

Andreas J. Köstenberger, series editor
Wake Forest, NC

1. G. B. Caird, *New Testament Theology*, compl. and ed. L. D. Hurst (Oxford: Clarendon, 1995), 24.

AUTHOR'S PREFACE

REVELATION is a wonderfully complex book. In this canonical capstone we find an epic story with numerous layers and multiple dimensions. There are various actors and audiences. The dangers and the victories are real. Readers may be shocked or frightened, but they will never get bored. It has been a daunting task to attempt a theology of Revelation. I hope many will read it, but if few do, it has been worth the labor just because of what I have learned. This academic exercise has also been personal. God has used this portion of his word to change me in deep and lasting ways. It has been a long journey, and I have not made the trip alone. There are many who deserve thanks.

I want to thank Ouachita Baptist University and the Pruet School of Christian Studies in particular for the encouragement, research support, and time to write. We have an environment that values scholarship and encourages us to invest in the ministry of study and writing. We are blessed because of it, and our leaders deserve thanks, particularly my current and former Vice Presidents for Academic Affairs, Dr. Justin Hardin and Dr. Stan Poole, and my current and former deans in the Pruet School, Dr. Jeremy Greer and Dr. Danny Hays. I am also extremely thankful for the students at OBU who have taken the Revelation class and given me encouragement along the way. It is fun to watch the lights go on as they realize all that God has done, is doing, and is going to do for his people. I am grateful too, to my former student assistant, Hannah Tullos, and my current assistant, Brooklyn Perkins, for all your help.

I offer special thanks to Janice Cockerham, our librarian responsible for interlibrary loan services until her recent retirement. Janice, you were tenacious and fearless and very patient in finding all those articles and books that I needed for my big project. At a small college like ours, without you, research would not be possible. I am deeply grateful for your hard work on my behalf and for your wonderful, Christ-like spirit along the way. Happy retirement!

I will be forever grateful to Katya Covrett, the vice president and publisher at Zondervan Academic, for having confidence in me as an author and inviting me to contribute this volume. Thanks also to Andreas Köstenberger, the editor of this series, for his exemplary scholarship and valuable insights as an editor and fellow laborer.

To my wife, Judy, thank you for the wonderful marriage we have. I am beyond blessed. In terms of this project, thanks for consistently telling me that it would be worth it!

May our Triune God receive all the praise and glory and be pleased with this work. May the people of God be encouraged to follow the Lamb!

Abbreviations

2 Bar.	2 Baruch (Syriac Apocalypse)
3 Bar.	3 Baruch (Greek Apocalypse)
1 En.	1 Enoch (Ethiopic Apocalypse)
2 En.	2 Enoch (Slavonic Apocalypse)
4 Ezra	4 Ezra
1QM	Milḥamah or War Scroll
AB	Anchor Bible
ABD	*Anchor Bible Dictionary*. Edited by David Noel Freedman. 6 vols. New York: Doubleday, 1992
ACCS	Ancient Christian Commentary on Scripture
ACNT	Augsburg Commentary on the New Testament
ACT	Ancient Christian Texts
Aen.	Aeneid (Vergil)
AGJU	Arbeiten zur Geschichte des antiken Judentums und des Urchristentums
AJEC	*Ancient Judaism and Early Christianity*
ANF	*Ante-Nicene Fathers*
Ann.	*Annales* (Tacitus)
ANRW	*Aufstieg und Niedergang der römischen Welt: Geschichte und Kultur Roms im Spiegel der neueren Forschung*. Part 2, Principat. Edited by Hildegard Temporini and Wolfgang Haase. Berlin: de Gruyter, 1972–
Ant.	*Jewish Antiquities* (Josephus)
ANTC	Abingdon New Testament Commentary
ANTF	Arbeiten zur neutestamentlichen Textforschung
Antichr.	*De antichristo* (Hippolytus)
AOTC	Apollos Old Testament Commentary
Apoc. Dan.	Apocalypse of Daniel
Apoc. Zeph.	Apocalypse of Zephaniah
Apol.	*Apologeticus* (Tertullian)
Ascen. Isa.	Martyrdom and Ascension of Isaiah (chs. 6–11)
ATJ	*Ashland Theological Journal*
Att.	*Epistulae ad Atticum* (Cicero)

AUSS	*Andrews University Seminary Studies*
AYB	Anchor Yale Bible
Barn.	Barnabas
BBC	Blackwell Bible Commentaries
BBR	*Bulletin for Biblical Research*
BCW	*Bible in the Contemporary World*
BDAG	Danker, Frederick W., Walter Bauer, William F. Arndt, and F. Wilbur Gingrich. *Greek-English Lexicon of the New Testament and Other Early Christian Literature.* 3rd ed. Chicago, 2000
BDF	Blass, F., A. Debrunner, and R. W. Funk. *A Greek Grammar of the New Testament and Other Early Christian Literature.* Chicago, 1961
BECNT	Baker Exegetical Commentary on the New Testament
Bib	*Biblica*
BibInt	*Biblical Interpretation*
BJRL	*Bulletin of the John Rylands University Library of Manchester*
BMW	Bible in the Modern World
BNTC	Black's New Testament Commentary
BR	*Biblical Research*
BRev	*Bible Review*
BRS	Biblical Resource Series
BSac	*Bibliotheca sacra*
BT	*Bible Translator*
BTB	*Biblical Theology Bulletin*
BTCB	Brazos Theological Commentary on the Bible
BTL	*Biblical Theology for Life*
BTNT	Biblical Theology of the New Testament Series
BZNW	Beihefte zur Zeitschrift für die neutestamentliche Wissenschaft
Carm.	*Carmina* (Horace)
CBQ	*Catholic Biblical Quarterly*
CBQMS	Catholic Biblical Quarterly Monograph Series
CCT	Contours of Christian Theology
CH	Church History
ChrF	Christian Foundations
Comm. Jo.	*Commentarii in evangelium Joannis* (Origen)
Comm. Matt.	*Commentarii in evangelium Matthaei* (Origen)
ConJ	*Concordia Journal*
CRINT	Compendia rerum iudaicarum ad Novum Testamentum
CSB	Christian Standard Bible
CT	*Christianity Today*

CTJ	*Calvin Theological Journal*
CTR	*Criswell Theological Review*
CurBR	*Currents in Biblical Research*
DBI	*Dictionary of Biblical Imagery.* Edited by John Hayes. 2 vols. Nashville: Abingdon, 1999
DBT	Discovering Biblical Texts
Dial.	*Dialogus cum Tryphone* (Justin Martyr)
Did.	Didache
DJG	*Dictionary of Jesus and the Gospels.* Edited by Joel B. Green, Scot McKnight, and I. Howard Marshall. 2nd ed. Downers Grove, IL: InterVarsity Press, 2013
DLNT	*Dictionary of the Later New Testament and Its Developments.* Edited by Ralph P. Martin and P. H. Davids. Downers Grove, IL: InterVarsity Press, 1997
DNTB	*Dictionary of New Testament Background.* Edited by Craig A. Evans and Stanley E. Porter. Downers Grove, IL: InterVarsity Press, 2000
Dom.	*De domo suo* (Cicero)
Dom.	*Domitianus* (Suetonius)
DRA	Douay-Rheims 1899 American Edition
DSS	Dead Sea Scrolls
EAC	*Evangelistae Apocalypsin Commentarij*
EBS	Encountering Biblical Studies
EDNT	*Exegetical Dictionary of the New Testament*
Ep.	*Epistulae* (Pliny the Younger)
ESBT	Essential Studies in Biblical Theology
ESEC	Emory Studies in Early Christianity
ESV	English Standard Version
ETS	Evangelical Theological Society
EvQ	*Evangelical Quarterly*
EVV	English versions
ExAud	*Ex auditu*
ExpTim	*Expository Times*
Fam.	*Epistulae ad familiares* (Cicero)
FET	Foundations of Evangelical Theology
Fr. Matt.	*Fragmenta ex commentarii in evangelium Matthaei* (Origen)
GBS	Gorgias Biblical Studies
Georg.	*Georgica* (Vergil)
Gk. Apoc. Ezra	Greek Apocalypse of Ezra
GNTE	Guides to New Testament Exegesis
Haer.	*Adversus haereses* (Irenaeus)
HBT	*Horizons in Biblical Theology*

Hist. eccl.	*Ecclesiastical History* (Eusebius)
HTR	*Harvard Theological Review*
IBR	Institute for Biblical Research
ICC	International Critical Commentary
Idol.	*De Idolotaria* (Tertullian)
Ign. *Eph.*	Ignatius, *To the Ephesians*
Ign. *Magn.*	Ignatius, *To the Magnesians*
Ign. *Phld.*	Ignatius, *To the Philadelphians*
Inst.	*Institutio oratoria* (Quintilian)
Int	*Interpretation*
ITC	International Theological Commentary
ITSS	Invitation to Theological Studies Series
IVP	InterVarsity Press
IVPNTC	InterVarsity Press New Testament Commentary
J.W.	*Jewish War* (Josephus)
JATS	*Journal of the Adventist Theological Society*
JBL	*Journal of Biblical Literature*
JEPTA	*Journal of the European Pentecostal Theological Association*
JETS	*Journal of the Evangelical Theological Society*
JohSt	Johannine Studies
JPT	*Journal of Pentecostal Theology*
JPTSup	Journal of Pentecostal Theology Supplement Series
JSFSC	*Journal of Spiritual Formation and Soul Care*
JSJSup	Supplements to the Journal for the Study of Judaism
JSNT	*Journal for the Study of the New Testament*
JSNTSup	Journal for the Study of the New Testament Supplements Series
JSOT	*Journal for the Study of the Old Testament*
JTI	*Journal of Theological Interpretation*
JTS	*Journal of Theological Studies*
Jub.	Jubilees
LBS	Linguistic Biblical Studies
LEC	Library of Early Christianity
LNTS	Library of New Testament Studies
L&N	Louw, Johannes P., and Eugene A. Nida, eds. *Greek-English Lexicon of the New Testament: Based on Semantic Domains.* 2nd ed. New York: United Bible Societies, 1989
LXX	Septuagint (Greek translation of the Old Testament)
LSJ	Liddell, Henry George, Robert Scott, Henry Stuart Jones, and Roderick McKenzie. *A Greek-English Lexicon.* Oxford: Clarendon, 1996

Marc.	*Adversus Marcionem* (Tertullian)
MSJ	*Master's Seminary Journal*
MT	Masoretic Text
NAC	New American Commentary
NASB20	New American Standard Bible 2020
Nat.	*Ad nationes* (Tertullian)
Nat.	*Naturalis historia* (Pliny the Elder)
NCB	New Century Bible
NCBC	New Cambridge Bible Commentary
NCC	New Covenant Commentary
NDBT	*New Dictionary of Biblical Theology.* Edited by T. Desmond Alexander and Brian S. Rosner. Downers Grove, IL, 2000
NEB	New English Bible
Neot	*Neotestamentica*
Nero	*Nero* (Suetonius)
NET	New English Translation
NETS	*A New English Translation of the Septuagint.* Edited by Albert Pietersma and Benjamin G. Wright. New York; Oxford: Oxford University Press, 2007
NIBC	New International Biblical Commentary
NICNT	New International Commentary on the New Testament
NICOT	New International Commentary on the Old Testament
NIDB	*New Interpreter's Dictionary of the Bible.* Edited by Katharine Doob Sakenfeld. 5 vols. Nashville: Abingdon, 2006–2009
NIDNTT	*New International Dictionary of New Testament Theology.* Edited by Collon Brown. 4 vols. Grand Rapids: Zondervan, 1975–78
NIGTC	New International Greek Testament Commentary
NIV	New International Version
NIVAC	NIV Application Commentary
NJB	New Jerusalem Bible
NLT	New Living Translation
NovT	*Novum Testamentum*
NovTSup	Novum Testamentum Supplements
NPNF^2	*Nicene and Post-Nicene Fathers,* Series 2
NRSVue	New Revised Standard Version, Updated Edition, 2022
NRTh	*La nouvelle revue théoligique*
NSBT	*New Studies in Biblical Theology*
NTL	New Testament Library
NTM	New Testament Message
NTMon	New Testament Monographs

NTS	*New Testament Studies*
NTSI	The New Testament and the Scriptures of Israel
NTTSD	New Testament Tools, Studies and Documents
OHBR	*Oxford Handbook on the Book of Revelation*. Oxford: Oxford University Press, 2020
OpenTh	*Open Theology*
Or. Bas.	*Oratio in laudem Basilii* (Gregory of Nazianzus)
OTM	Oxford Theological Monographs
P.Oxy.	Oxyrhynchus papyri
Paed.	*Paedogogus* (Clement)
Paideia	Paideia Commentaries
Pan.	*Panarion* (*Adversus haereses*) (Epiphanius)
PC	Proclamation Commentaries
Pneuma	*Pneuma: Journal for the Society of Pentecostal Studies*
PNTC	Pillar New Testament Commentary
Praescr.	*De Praescriptione haereticorum* (Tertullian)
PRSt	*Perspectives in Religious Studies*
PSBSup	*Princeton Seminary Bulletin Supplement*
PTMS	Princeton Theological Monograph Series
PW	Preaching the Word
Quis div.	*Quis dives salvetur* (Clement)
RBS	Resources for Biblical Study
RefR	*Reformed Review*
Res.	*De resurrectione* (Methodius)
ResQ	*Restoration Quarterly*
RevExp	*Review and Expositor*
Rom. Hist.	*Roman History* (Cassius Deo)
RTR	*Reformed Theological Review*
SBAL	Studies in Biblical Apocalyptic Literature
SBG	Studies in Biblical Greek
SBJT	*Southern Baptist Journal of Theology*
SBL	Society of Biblical Literature
SBLDS	Society of Biblical Literature Dissertation Series
SBLMS	Society of Biblical Literature Monograph Series
SBLSP	Society of Biblical Literature Seminar Papers
SBLSymS	Society of Biblical Literature Symposium Series
SBT	Studies in Biblical Theology
SCDS	Studies in Christian Doctrine and Scripture
Scr	*Scripture*

ScrB	*Scripture Bulletin*
Semeia	*Semeia*
SemeiaSt	Semeia Studies
SHBC	Smyth & Helwys Bible Commentary
Sib. Or.	Sibylline Oracles
SJT	*Scottish Journal of Theology*
SNTSMS	Society of New Testament Studies Monograph Series
SP	Sagra Pagina
Spect.	*De spectaculis* (Tertullian)
SSBT	Short Studies in Biblical Theology
ST	Second Temple
StBL	Studies in Biblical Literature
Strom.	*Stromata* (Clement)
StScrBT	Studies in Scripture and Biblical Theology
Symp.	*Symposium* (*Convivium decem virginum*) (Methodius)
T. Ab.	Testament of Abraham
T. Reu.	Testament of Reuben
TBT	*The Bible Today*
TCS	Text-Critical Studies
TDNT	*Theological Dictionary of the New Testament*
Them	*Themelios*
THNTC	The Two Horizons New Testament Commentary
ThPG	Theology for the People of God
ThTo	*Theology Today*
TNTC	Tyndale New Testament Commentary
Tob	Tobit
TOTC	Tyndale Old Testament Commentary
TPI	Trinity Press International
TrinJ	*Trinity Journal*
TS	*Theological Studies*
TTC	Teach the Text Commentary
TynBul	*Tyndale Bulletin*
VE	*Vox Evangelica*
Vir ill.	*De viris illustribus* (Jerome)
VR	*Vox reformata*
WBC	Word Biblical Commentary
WTJ	*Westminster Theological Journal*
WUNT	Wissenschaftliche Untersuchungen zum Neuen Testament

WW	*Word & World*
ZECNT	Zondervan Exegetical Commentary on the New Testament
ZIBBC	Zondervan Illustrated Bible Backgrounds Commentary
ZNW	*Zeitschrift für die neutestamentliche Wissenschaft und die Kunde der älteren Kirche*

Part 1

INTRODUCTORY ISSUES

Chapter 1

INTRODUCTION

BIBLIOGRAPHY

Alexander, T. Desmond. *From Eden to the New Jerusalem: An Introduction to Biblical Theology.* Grand Rapids: Kregel Academic, 2008. **Bauckham, Richard J.** *The Climax of Prophecy: Studies in the Book of Revelation.* London: T&T Clark, 1993. ———. *The Theology of the Book of Revelation.* Cambridge: Cambridge University Press, 1993. **Duvall, J. Scott.** *The Heart of Revelation: Understanding the 10 Essential Themes of the Bible's Final Book.* Nashville: B&H Academic, 2019. **Duvall, J. Scott, and J. Daniel Hays.** *God's Relational Presence: The Cohesive Center of Biblical Theology.* Grand Rapids: Baker Academic, 2019. **Flemming, Dean.** *Foretaste of the Future: Reading Revelation in Light of God's Mission.* Downers Grove, IL: IVP Academic, 2022. **Gorman, Michael J.** *Reading Revelation Responsibly: Uncivil Worship and Witness: Following the Lamb into the New Creation.* Eugene, OR: Cascade, 2011. **Helyer, Larry R.** *The Witness of Jesus, Paul and John: An Exploration in Biblical Theology.* Downers Grove, IL: InterVarsity Press, 2008. **Köstenberger, Andreas J.** *A Theology of John's Gospel and Letters: The Word, the Christ, the Son of God.* BTNT. Grand Rapids: Zondervan Academic, 2009. **Köstenberger, Andreas J., L. Scott Kellum, and Charles L. Quarles.** *The Cradle, the Cross, and the Crown: An Introduction to the New Testament.* 2nd ed. Nashville: B&H Academic, 2016. **Koester, Craig R.**, ed. *OHBR.* **Kraybill, J. Nelson.** *Apocalypse and Allegiance: Worship, Politics, and Devotion in the Book of Revelation.* Grand Rapids: Brazos, 2010. **Rainbow, Paul.** *The Pith of the Apocalypse: Essential Message and Principles for Interpretation.* Eugene, OR: Wipf & Stock, 2008. ———. *Johannine Theology: The Gospel, the Epistles and the Apocalypse.* Downers Grove, IL: InterVarsity Press, 2014. **Tabb, Brian J.** *All Things New: Revelation as Canonical Capstone.* NSBT 48. Downers Grove, IL: IVP Academic, 2019. **Tõniste, Külli.** *The Ending of the Canon: A Canonical and Intertextual Reading of Revelation 21–22.* LNTS 526. London: T&T Clark, 2016.

1.1 INTRODUCTION

Revelation is perhaps the most colorful, complicated, engaging, and awe-inspiring book in the Bible. It is certainly the strangest with its bizarre imagery, intriguing plot, and captivating characters. What draws readers is the possibility—dare we say the hope—that this story spells out in some way our future. As a result, people respond to Revelation in two very different ways, as almost any informal survey will demonstrate.[1] On the one hand, you find people who are obsessed with Revelation, focusing their attention on mapping out a timeline of future events. They are apocalyptic junkies who have read all the novels and watched all the movies. Other people, however, want absolutely nothing to do with the book and wish it would disappear from their Bibles, never to be mentioned again. It appears that all of Christendom is divided between fanatical preoccupation or intentional ignorance. Surely appearances can be deceiving.

I hope and pray this volume will continue the renewed interest in the responsible interpretation of John's Apocalypse, taking seriously its historical, literary, and theological contexts. The church desperately needs the good, beautiful, and true message of this canonical capstone, and we neglect it to our own spiritual peril. In the end, Revelation deals with us but is not all about us or even primarily about us (e.g., how we avoid the mark of the beast or prepare for the rapture or return of Christ). The message of Revelation centers on the Triune God and his majestic plan of redemption and restoration. Nevertheless, and thankfully, the book does concern us, especially as it gives hope to the suffering saints, repeatedly calls them to enduring obedience, and inspires their witness to God's faithfulness.

1.2 Revelation as Canonical Conclusion

Many Christian readers, even experienced readers, often miss the significance of Revelation's location in the Bible—the final book.[2] Bauckham famously describes Revelation as the "climax of prophecy," gathering up the meaning of the Old Testament as fulfilled in Jesus Christ for the purpose of stressing the final coming of God's kingdom.[3] Tabb rightly contends that Revelation is the "canonical capstone," the final, climactic chapter of the grand story of the Bible.[4] The climactic vision of Revelation (chs. 21–22) completes the story of Scripture that began in the original garden. God's determined purpose to live among his people will not be denied and in the end, we return to the garden, now a garden city, where God's people enjoy his presence for eternity.[5] Tõniste notes that "the early church assigned to the Apocalypse a particular canonical location (the end) and literary function (to be an ending)" and, as a result,

1. J. Scott Duvall, *The Heart of Revelation: Understanding the 10 Essential Themes of the Bible's Final Book* (Nashville: B&H Academic, 2019), 1–3.

2. See section 6.3 for more on the canonicity of Revelation.

3. Richard Bauckham, *The Climax of Prophecy: Studies in the Book of Revelation* (London: T&T Clark, 1993), xi, xvi.

4. Brian J. Tabb, *All Things New: Revelation as Canonical Capstone*, NSBT 48 (Downers Grove, IL: IVP Academic, 2019).

5. J. Scott Duvall and J. Daniel Hays, *God's Relational Presence: The Cohesive Center of Biblical Theology* (Grand Rapids: Baker Academic, 2019); Dean Flemming, *Foretaste of the Future: Reading Revelation in Light of God's Mission* (Downers Grove, IL: IVP Academic, 2022), 186–207.

we should read the book as the final chapter of the entire canon of Scripture.[6] This has profound implications for the church's reading of Revelation. An awareness of Revelation's location provides a corrective to both irresponsible popular readings that often fixate on how end-time predictions fit with contemporary world events to the neglect of the book of Revelation and to academic readings that relegate the book's message to ancient history. As the canonical capstone, Revelation has ongoing relevance and value for the life and faith of the church.[7]

Andreas Köstenberger, Scott Kellum, and Charles Quarles survey the primary ways Revelation contributes to the New Testament canon:

- The worship of God and of Jesus Christ
- The Lion of Judah who is also the slain Lamb reveals the future for God's people
- The call to uncompromising faithfulness to Christ
- The vindication of God's righteousness (theodicy) and of Christ's followers who suffer opposition from the world system
- The glorious return of Jesus as King of kings and Lord of lords
- The ultimate victory of Christ
- The restoration of all things in the new heaven and new earth[8]

As we take the long journey through an extensive study of Revelation it will be interesting to see how we affirm or modify these observations, but these provide a good starting point when thinking about Revelation's overall contribution.

1.3 Theologies of Revelation and Other Conversation Partners

One of the most surprising discoveries is how few dedicated "theologies of Revelation" have been written—that is, volumes that provide a biblical theology of the entire book of Revelation. Although fairly brief, Bauckham's *Theology of the Book of Revelation* packs a powerful punch and offers interpretive wisdom at every turn. Brian Tabb's *All Things New* in the New Studies in Biblical Theology series is also a valuable contribution to the field. The present volume will offer a comprehensive theology of John's Apocalypse and, alongside Köstenberger's *Theology of John's Gospel and Letters*, will provide a theology of

6. Külli Tõniste, *The Ending of the Canon: A Canonical and Intertextual Reading of Revelation 21–22*, LNTS 526 (London: T&T Clark, 2016), 1.

7. Robert W. Wall, "Apocalypse of the New Testament in Canonical Context," *The New Testament as Canon: A Reader in Canonical Criticism*, ed. Robert W. Wall and Eugene E. Lemico, JSNTSup 76 (Sheffield: JSOT Press, 1992), 274–98.

8. Andreas J. Köstenberger, L. Scott Kellum, and Charles L. Quarles, *The Cradle, the Cross, and the Crown: An Introduction to the New Testament* (Nashville: B&H Academic, 2016), 992, slightly rephrased.

the entire Johannine corpus. Thomas Schreiner's *The Joy of Hearing* offers a theology of Revelation for a wider audience, as do T. Desmond Alexander's *From Eden to the New Jerusalem*, Paul Spilsbury's *The Throne, the Lamb & the Dragon*, and my own *The Heart of Revelation*.

Then we find a host of insightful works that feature a dedicated section on the theology of Revelation. These include Paul Rainbow's *The Pith of the Apocalypse*, Larry Helyer's *The Witness of Jesus, Paul and John*, and William Dumbrell's *The End of the Beginning*. I have also benefited enormously from a group of books offering a rich theological reading of Revelation although not necessarily claiming to be a "theology of Revelation." These include Michael Gorman's *Reading Revelation Responsibly*, Dean Flemming's *Foretaste of the Future*, J. Nelson Kraybill's *Apocalypse and Allegiance*, Graeme Goldsworthy's *The Gospel in Revelation* (now published in his *The Goldworthy Trilogy*), and Joseph Mangina's volume on Revelation in the Brazos Theological Commentary on the Bible series. Paul A. Rainbow's work, *Johannine Theology*, is one of the few single volumes that treats all of John's theology, including the Gospel, the Epistles, and the Apocalypse.

There are also numerous special studies that investigate Revelation's theology although, again, not claiming to be a biblical theology of the entire book. The focus here is on works usually devoted to a particular theme or section of Revelation. There are too many to provide an exhaustive list so I simply offer a few examples: Richard Bauckham's *The Climax of Prophecy*, G. K. Beale's *The Temple and the Church's Mission*, Rob Dalrymple's *Revelation and the Two Witnesses*, David deSilva's *Seeing Things John's Way*, Scott Duvall and Daniel Hays's *God's Relational Presence*, Steven Grabiner's *Revelation's Hymns*, Craig Koester's edited volume, *The Oxford Handbook of the Book of Revelation*, Pilchan Lee's *The New Jerusalem in the Book of Revelation*, David Mathewson's *A New Heaven and a New Earth*, Stephen Pattemore's *The People of God in the Apocalypse*, Olutola Peters's *The Mandate of the Church in the Apocalypse of John*, Andrea Robinson's *Temple of Presence*, Brandon Smith's *The Trinity in the Book of Revelation*, Alexander Stewart and Alan Bandy's *The Apocalypse of John among Its Critics*, Robby Waddell's *The Spirit of the Book of Revelation*, and Mark Wilson's *The Victor Sayings in the Book of Revelation*. Again, numerous other entries could have been mentioned here.

You will also find short sections in some of the major commentaries dedicated to the theology of Revelation. See, for example, G. K. Beale, *Revelation*, NIGTC (171–77); Buist Fanning, *Revelation*, ZECNT (567–75); Grant Osborne, *Revelation*, BECNT (31–49); Ian Paul, *Revelation*, TNTC (45–48); and Stephen Smalley, *Revelation to John* (16–19). Sadly, not many commentaries contain such a section.

Likewise, there are brief discussions on the theology of Revelation in some of the standard volumes on biblical theology, New Testament theology, dictionaries of biblical theology, and New Testament introductions. See, for example, T. Desmond Alexander and Brian Rosner's *New Dictionary of Biblical Theology*, G. K. Beale's *New Testament*

Biblical Theology, G. K. Beale and Benjamin Gladd's *The Story Retold*, Craig Blomberg and Darlene Seale's *From Pentecost to Patmos*, Darrell Bock's *A Biblical Theology of the New Testament*, D. A. Carson and Douglas Moo's *Introduction to the New Testament*, David deSilva's *Introduction to the New Testament*, Walter Elwell's *Evangelical Dictionary of Biblical Theology*, Peter Gentry's *God's Kingdom through God's Covenants*, John Goldingay's *Biblical Theology*, James Hamilton's *God's Glory in Salvation through Judgment*, Andreas Köstenberger and Gregory Goswell's *Biblical Theology*, Andreas Köstenberger, L. Scott Kellum, and Charles Quarles's *The Cradle, the Cross, and the Crown*, Michael Kruger's *A Biblical-Theological Introduction to the New Testament*, G. E. Ladd and D. A. Hagner's *A Theology of the New Testament*, I. Howard Marshall's *New Testament Theology*, Ralph Martin and Peter Davids's *Dictionary of the Later New Testament and Its Developments*, Udo Schnelle's *Theology of the New Testament*, Thomas Schreiner's *The King in His Beauty* and his *New Testament Theology*, Charles Scobie's *The Ways of Our God*, Frank Thielman's *Theology of the New Testament*, Daniel Trier's *Evangelical Dictionary of Theology*, and Geerhardus Vos's *Biblical Theology*.

Finally, we are left with a mass of scholarly articles in journals and volumes of collected essays that are simply too numerous to mention. I have provided examples of these valuable works in the bibliographies attached to each chapter.

The above survey gives the reader a sense of my primary conversation partners when writing this volume. One of the most fascinating things about studying John's Apocalypse is that there is always something new to learn. How fitting that the book reflects its main topic, the Triune God, in this way!

1.4 An Overview of This Study

Biblical theology rests upon the foundation of what Köstenberger calls the "hermeneutical triad"—biblical-theological reflection built upon the study of the historical-cultural context of a particular text and the investigation of the literary and linguistic nature of that revelation.[9] In other words, Revelation's theology emerges from God's revelation of himself in history and the record of that revelation in Scripture, responsibly interpreted. Especially when it comes to the Apocalypse, ignoring the historical and literary contexts can have disastrous consequences for the life of the church. Unfortunately, this has sometimes been the case.[10] The present volume takes the hermeneutical triad seriously as the book's organization will demonstrate.

9. See Andreas J. Köstenberger, *A Theology of John's Gospel and Letters*, BTNT (Grand Rapids: Zondervan Academic, 2009), 42–45.

10. I would place "Left Behind" eschatology in this category. For more on how this theological agenda has affected the church, see Barbara R. Rossing, *The Rapture Exposed: The Message of Hope in the Book of Revelation* (Boulder, CO: Westview, 2004); Craig L. Blomberg and Sung Wook Chung, eds., *A Case for Historic Premillennialism: An Alternative to "Left Behind" Eschatology* (Grand Rapids: Baker Academic, 2009); and D. Mark Davis, *Left Behind & Loving It: A Cheeky Look at the End Times* (Eugene, OR: Cascade, 2011).

Part 1 explores the historical framework of Revelation. This begins in Chapter 2 with the important question of authorship. What does Revelation say explicitly about its author? Where does the early church evidence point? Is John the apostle the one responsible for this majestic work or could it be another John? We explore the options. In Chapter 3 we turn our attention to the question of when Revelation was written. The issue of date is tied to the issue of the persecution of Christians in the first century. Was the book written during the reign of Roman Emperor Nero or perhaps later under Emperor Domitian? There are several related issues in the text itself to consider as well as the earliest church traditions about the book's dating. Finally, we look at the occasion and purpose of Revelation. What was John's situation? What was happening in the churches and in the surrounding society at the time? What pressures were being put upon the church, and how was the church responding? These issues are all connected to the book's situation and purpose.

Part 2 is a deep dive into the literary-theological foundations we need to grasp in order to understand our subsequent discussion of the primary theological themes of Revelation. In Chapter 5 we consider the genre of Revelation as a prophetic-apocalyptic letter. In Chapter 6 we investigate the text and canonicity of the book. This is one of the more detailed Chapters, in which we look carefully at Revelation's textual history and consider how to practice textual criticism when it comes to Revelation. We then look at the question of Revelation's place Scripture, both the history of the book's acceptance into the canon and its function within the canon. Chapter 7 investigates important linguistic features of Revelation, including the book's idiosyncratic but intentional grammar, possible explanations for its grammatical peculiarities, and its verbal aspect. This chapter also explores the book's symbolic language—its nature and use in Revelation—along with a discussion of how to best understand the book's fantastic imagery. Chapter 8 considers the use of the Old Testament in Revelation, including the form and type of Old Testament references, the most influential Old Testament books, and how John uses the Old Testament.

Chapter 9 focuses on the literary structure of the book. Revelation is a complex but unified book, and its literary nature proves crucial to grasping its message—the book's oral/aural nature, its chief literary phrases/markers, the role of interludes, the use of numbers, the function of interlocking transitions. Does Revelation progress chronologically or does it recapitulate? At the end of this chapter, we provide an overall outline of the book. In Chapter 10 we consider how to interpret Revelation responsibly. What are the traditional approaches to the book in terms of how one understands the millennium in Rev 20? I am convinced that this "millennium-driven" hermeneutical approach to Revelation falls short of the balanced, holistic interpretive method that is needed. As a result, we then turn our attention to what such an interpretive method involves. We give special attention to reading Revelation's metaphorical language responsibly. Chapter 11 provides a short commentary on the entire book of Revelation. This literary-historical-theological reading of the book incorporates the conclusions of the previous chapters and paves the way for the more detailed study of theological themes to follow.

Part 3 gets at the heart of this volume with a more in-depth theological reflection on the major themes of Revelation. As to the particular themes selected, I chose themes that appear frequently throughout the book and occupy a central role in the overall storyline (e.g., God, Jesus Christ, the people of God). In addition, I chose themes that, while not appearing frequently, nevertheless play a significant role in the book's theological message (e.g., the Holy Spirit, discipleship). They may not be mentioned explicitly numerous times, but they play a crucial role as the supporting cast. To neglect these themes would result in a distorted picture of Revelation's overall theological message. In the end nine such themes were chosen. We begin in Chapter 12 with God, the sovereign Creator and Ruler of the world. As the God who speaks, loves, judges, and who is coming, he is worthy of worship. Chapter 13 highlights Jesus Christ, the Lion and the Lamb, the Faithful Witness and Firstborn from the dead who will return as Victor and Judge. Chapter 14 explores the identity and role of the Holy Spirit in Revelation, a much-neglected theological theme. The Spirit plays a key role and, together with Jesus the Lamb of God and God the Father, reflects how the Triune God stands as the central figure throughout the book.

From the Triune God we turn to how the book portrays God's salvation in Chapter 15—God's mission to the nations, the work of Christ, God's commitment to judge evil, how God's people participate in his mission, and the hope of future restoration. In Chapter 16 we consider the people of God, people identified through a host of powerful images and descriptions. This imagery reveals who God's people are and what they are called to do from Revelation's perspective. Some have said that Revelation is the Psalms of the New Testament with its rich and abundant emphasis on worship, the topic of Chapter 17. We explore the book's worship terminology along with the numerous hymns placed throughout. All this is set in contrast to the counterfeit worship context presupposed by the text. Chapter 18 treats the topic of Christian discipleship, of following the Lamb in a context of suffering and evil. What does enduring faithfulness look like? What does it mean to be devoted to the prophetic mission? In this way, chapters 16–18 offer a window into Revelation's robust ecclesiology and missional context.

Two additional chapters bring the third part to a close. Chapter 19 explores God's judgment of evil. What is the basis of divine judgment? How does God's judgment play out in Revelation? Who are the enemies of God and God's people? Where is God's justice in all the suffering? What role do God's people play in judgment? We end, appropriately, not with judgment but with hope. Chapter 20 looks more closely at the new creation. First, we provide an overview of this theme in Rev 1–20 and then explore the more detailed section of chapters 21–22. Next, we look closely at how Revelation describes the new creation—as place, people, provision, absence, and relational presence. In the concluding chapter for the entire project, we consider the overarching theological contribution of Revelation to the New Testament canon and to the grand story of Scripture as a whole. What is the lasting significance of the final vision of the Christian canon? I add a few concluding personal remarks to close out this volume.

Part 2

The Historical Framework of Revelation

Chapter 2

THE AUTHORSHIP OF REVELATION

BIBLIOGRAPHY

Bauckham, Richard. *Jesus and the Eyewitnesses: The Gospels as Eyewitness Testimony*. Grand Rapids: Eerdmans, 2006. **Böcher, Otto.** "Johanneisches in der Apokalypse des Johannes." *NTS* 27 (1981): 310–21. **Boxall, Ian.** *The Revelation of Saint John*. BNTC. Peabody, MA: Hendrickson, 2006. **Charles, R. H.** *A Critical and Exegetical Commentary on the Revelation of St John*. 2 vols. ICC. Edinburgh: T&T Clark, 1920. **deSilva, David A.** *An Introduction to the New Testament: Contexts, Methods and Ministry Formation*. Downers Grove, IL: InterVarsity Press, 2004. ———. "The Social Setting of the Revelation to John: Conflicts Within, Fears Without." *WTJ*. 54 (1992): 273–302. **Eusebius.** *Eusebius: Church History, Life of Constantine the Great, and Oration in Praise of Constantine*. Pages 81–404 in vol. 1 of *Nicene and Post-Nicene Fathers*, Series 2. Edited by Philip Schaff and Henry Wace. 1886–1889. 14 vols. New York: Christian Literature Company, 1890. **Ford, J. Massyngberde.** *Revelation*. AB 38. Garden City, NY: Doubleday, 1975. **Frey, Jörg.** "Erwägungen zum Verhältnis der Johannesapokalypse zu den übrigen Schriften des Corpus Johanneum." Pages 326–429 in Martin Hengel, *Die johanneische Frage: Ein Lösungversuch*. Tübingen: Mohr Siebeck, 1993. **Gundry, Robert H.** *Matthew: A Commentary on His Literary and Theological Art*. Grand Rapids: Eerdmans, 1982. **Gunther, John J.** "The Elder John, Author of Revelation." *JSNT* 11 (1981): 3–20. **Guthrie, Donald.** *New Testament Introduction*. 4th rev. ed. Downers Grove, IL: InterVarsity Press, 1996. **Hembold, Andrew.** "A Note on the Authorship of the Apocalypse." *NTS* 8 (1961): 77–79. **Hengel, Martin.** *The Johannine Question*. London: SCM, 1989. **Köstenberger, Andreas J.** *A Theology of John's Gospel and Letters: The Word, the Christ, the Son of God*. BTNT. Grand Rapids: Zondervan, 2009. **Köstenberger, Andreas J., L. Scott Kellum, and Charles L. Quarles.** *The Cradle, the Cross, and the Crown: An Introduction to the New Testament*. 2nd ed. Nashville: B&H Academic, 2016. **Leithart, Peter J.** *Revelation*. ITC. London: Bloomsbury T&T Clark, 2018. **Menzies, Allan, ed.** *The Gospel of Peter, the Diatessaron of Tatian, the Apocalypse of Peter, the Visio Pauli, the Apocalypses of the Virgil and Sedrach, the Testament of Abraham, the Acts of Xanthippe and Polyxena, the Narrative of Zosimus, the Apology of Aristides, the Epistles of Clement (Complete Text), Origen's Commentary on John, Books I–X, and Commentary on Matthew, Books I, II, and*

X–XIV. Vol. 9. *ANF.* New York: Christian Literature Company, 1897. **Ozanne, C. G.** "The Language of the Apocalypse." *TynBul* 16 (1965): 3–9. **Schüssler Fiorenza, Elizabeth.** *The Book of Revelation: Justice and Judgment.* 2nd ed. Minneapolis: Fortress, 1998. **Shanks, Monte A.** *Papias and the New Testament.* Eugene, OR: Pickwick, 2013. **Smalley, Stephen S.** *Thunder and Love: John's Revelation and John's Community.* Eugene, OR: Wipf & Stock, 1994. **Victorinus of Petovium et al.** *Latin Commentaries on Revelation.* Edited by Thomas C. Oden. Translated by William C. Weinrich. ACT. Downers Grove, IL: IVP Academic, 2011. **Wallace, Daniel B.** *The Basics of New Testament Syntax,* Grand Rapids: Zondervan, 2000. **Weinrich, William C., ed.** *Revelation.* ACCS NT 12. Downers Grove, IL: InterVarsity Press, 2005. **Whale, Peter.** "The Lamb of John: Some Myths about the Vocabulary of the Johannine Literature." *JBL* 106 (1987): 289–95. **Wilson, Mark.** "John of Ephesus: A Case of Multi-Personality Identification Disorder." Paper presented at the ETS annual meeting, New Orleans, November 19, 2009. **Yarbrough, Robert W.** "The Date of Papias: A Reassessment," *JETS* 26 (1983): 181–91.

2.1 INTRODUCTION

The authorship of Revelation merits fresh consideration, as does the authorship of any canonical book. Although a majority of contemporary scholars reject John the apostle as the author, the issues involved turn out to be more complicated than they might first appear. We begin by looking at what Revelation itself says (and does not say) about its author. What conclusions can be drawn from the text itself? Next, we consider additional evidence from the early church testimony, both for and against apostolic authorship. Is the early Christian tradition divided or somewhat united in ascribing authorship to a particular person? Finally, we lay out the central arguments for and against apostolic authorship. What is the best reasoning available to the question of who wrote the Apocalypse attributed only to "John"?

2.2 WHAT REVELATION EXPLICITLY SAYS ABOUT THE AUTHOR

The author of the Apocalypse identifies himself simply as "John," three times at the beginning of the book (1:1, 4, 9) and once at the end (22:8). In 1:1 this "John" is described as "his" (Christ's or possibly God's) "servant" (τῷ δούλῳ αὐτοῦ). John's self-designation as a "servant" or "slave," as Osborne notes, promotes no special title or authority but stresses an identification with his fellow believers previously referred to as "servants" (1:1).[1] John further connects with his readers on a deep level when he speaks

1. Grant R. Osborne, *Revelation*, BECNT (Grand Rapids: Baker Academic, 2002), 55.

as their "brother and companion (ὁ ἀδελφὸς ὑμῶν καὶ συγκοινωνὸς) in the suffering and kingdom and patient endurance that are ours in Jesus" (1:9).

John, the servant, bears the burdens of his readers and companions by holding fast to "the word of God and the testimony of Jesus Christ" (1:2), in spite of the accompanying tribulation (1:9: θλῖψις, NIV "suffering"). As Aune notes, the repeated use of first-person singular verb forms throughout stresses John's role as a witness to the visions he narrates.[2] John serves as an important eyewitness to God's message mediated to him, testifying to what he saw (1:2; cf. 1 John 1:1–3). His role as witness appears again at the end of the book: "I, John, am the one who heard and saw these things" (Rev 22:8).

John, the servant and faithful witness, also presents himself (not formally but implicitly) as a Christian prophet.[3] The self-description "I, John" (1:9; 22:8) matches the standard designation used in prophetic writings (e.g., "I, Daniel").[4] John apparently sees himself as a prophet in the tradition of the Old Testament prophets.[5] He identifies with true Christian prophets in 10:7; 11:10, 18; 16:6; 18:20, 24; 22:6, and especially in 22:9: "I am a fellow servant with you and with your fellow prophets and with all who keep the words of this scroll." He vigorously opposes false prophets (e.g., 2:6, 14–15, 20). He participates in the prophetic vision as do some Old Testament prophets (e.g., 10:8–11; cf. Ezek 3:1–3). According to Bauckham, John fits the profile of an early Christian prophet who would receive a visionary revelation from the Lord in private and would later report the vision to the church in a worship setting (e.g., Acts 10:9–11:18; Hermas, *Vis.* 1–4).[6] Whatever else John is, he certainly views himself in the tradition of the Old Testament prophets.

We can also conclude with Aune that John was almost certainly a Palestinian Jew.[7] In addition to the name "John" (Ἰωάννης being the Greek transliteration of the Hebrew name יוֹחָנָן, *yôḥānān*, meaning "Yahweh is gracious"), Aune notes that the author (1) had an impressive familiarity with the Old Testament, (2) used the genre of apocalypse which was at home in Palestine, (3) was familiar with the Jewish temple and cult in Jerusalem, (4) knew the areas of Palestine, and (5) had a distinctive type of semitizing Greek suggesting he was a native Aramaic or Hebrew speaker.[8]

R. H. Charles has argued convincingly that the Apocalypse was not pseudonymous, pointing to the identification of the author, "John" (1:1, 4, 9; 22:8), his description as a

2. David E. Aune, *Revelation 1–5*, WBC 52A (Dallas: Word, 1998), xlix. He notes the frequency of the first-person singular phenomenon in other Jewish apocalypses (Dan 7:2, 15; 8:1; 9:2; 10:2; 4 Ezra 2:33, 42; 3:1; 3 Bar. 1:1, 7; 4:1, 9; 5:1).

3. See the summary of evidence in Köstenberger, Kellum, and Quarles, *Cradle, Cross, and Crown*, 929–30.

4. Köstenberger, Kellum, and Quarles, *Cradle, Cross, and Crown*, 929. See, e.g., Daniel (Dan 7:15; 8:15, 27; 9:2; 10:2, 7; 12:5), Baruch (2 Bar. 8:3; 9:1; 10:5; 11:1; 13:1; 32:8; 44:1), Ezra (4 Ezra 2:33).

5. Richard Bauckham, *The Theology of the Book of Revelation* (Cambridge: Cambridge University Press, 1993), 4–5.

6. Bauckham, *Theology*, 4.

7. Aune, *Revelation 1–5*, xlix–l.

8. Aune, *Revelation 1–5*, 1, 18. See, e.g., 2 Kgs 25:23; 1 Chr 26:3; Ezra 10:6; Neh 6:18; 12:22; Jer 40:8. Aune concludes that John was a refugee from Palestine following the Jewish revolt of AD 66–73.

partner in the reader's sufferings (1:9), his banishment to Patmos due to his eyewitness account of the word of God and testimony of Jesus (1:9; 22:8), the lack of appeal to an "apostle" as one might have expected with a pseudonymous work, and the new age of the Spirit in which voices other than those codified in the law were heard afresh. Charles concludes that there is "not a single *a priori* reason for regarding the Apocalypse as pseudonymous," nor is there "a shred of evidence, not even the shadow of a probability," for such a hypothesis.[9]

Revelation itself leaves us with some critical parameters for identifying the book's author: John's name, his self-designation of "servant," "brother," and "companion" in suffering, his role as a faithful witness to God's message and as a Christian prophet, plus the likelihood of him being a Palestinian Jew. Even though we have narrowed the possibilities, we are still left with multiple candidates. To come to a conclusion regarding authorship, we must widen our search a bit to consider additional evidence from the early church.

2.3 EARLY CHURCH EVIDENCE

2.3.1 Evidence Supporting John the Apostle as Author

The identification of the author of Revelation with John the apostle was "virtually universal in the early church."[10] Justin Martyr (d. ca. 165) writes about "a certain man with us, whose name was John, one of the apostles of Christ, who prophesied, by a revelation that was made to him."[11]

Irenaeus (ca. 180) introduces a quotation from Revelation with this statement: "John also, the Lord's disciple, when beholding the sacerdotal and glorious advent of His kingdom, says in the Apocalypse . . ."[12] Irenaeus, as many have observed, was from Smyrna and as a young man likely listened to the preaching of Polycarp, a disciple of the apostle John.

The Apocryphon of John (ca. 120–180) also serves as an early witness for the apostolic authorship of Revelation. This gnostic document cites Rev 1:19 and claims to have been written by "John, the brother of James, these who are the sons of Zebedee." Helmbold dates the Apocryohon as early as the end of the first century but certainly not much later than AD 150 and concludes, "Either date establishes the Apocryphon

9. R. H. Charles, *A Critical and Exegetical Commentary on the Revelation of St John*, vol. 1, ICC (Edinburgh: T&T Clark, 1920), xxxviii–xxxix. Koester observes that "if 'John' is a pseudonym, one would expect the author to call himself an 'apostle' and weave in purported memories of Jesus's ministry, as is done in the *Apocalypse of Peter*." See Craig R. Koester, *Revelation: A New Translation with Introduction and Commentary*, AB 38A (New Haven: Yale University Press, 2014), 67.

10. William C. Weinrich, ed., *Revelation*, ACCS NT 12 (Downers Grove, IL: InterVarsity Press, 2005), xvii.

11. Justin Martyr, *Dial.* 81 (*ANF* 1:240). See also Eusebius, *Hist. eccl.* 4.18.8.

12. Irenaeus, *Haer.* 4.20.11 (*ANF* 4:491).

as an early witness, alongside the secondary testimony of Papias and Justin Martyr in Eusebius, for the Apostolic authorship of the Apocalypse."[13]

Clement of Alexandria (d. ca. 215) refers to the coming judgment using the language of Revelation as something "John says in the Apocalypse."[14] Likewise, Tertullian (ca. 220) refers multiple times to John the apostle as the author of Revelation.[15] And Hippolytus (ca. 235) labels Revelation's author as the "blessed John, apostle and disciple of the Lord," as well as "the prophet and apostle."[16]

Although Revelation was more widely used in the Western church than the Eastern church, it was known in the east and the early church leader Origen affirms its apostolic authorship. When commenting on the Logos of John 1, Origen introduces a supporting comment from Revelation referring to "this same John in the Apocalypse" and later identifies him as "the Apostle and Evangelist (and the Apocalypse entitles him to be styled a prophet, too)."[17]

We also see apostolic authorship affirmed in the Muratorian Fragment (late 2nd c.) and arguably by Papias of Hierapolis (ca. 110), who knew the apostle John personally (see 2.3.2 below). In addition, the earliest extant commentaries on Revelation affirm apostolic authorship.[18] Weinrich concludes that "the view that the Revelation was from John the apostle became the universal opinion of the broad catholic tradition."[19] Smalley likewise says, "There is no significant reason to question the relatively early ascription of the Apocalypse to John the apostle."[20]

2.3.2 Evidence Supporting a Different Author

The few who denied apostolic authorship in the early church did so more on theological rather than historical grounds. The second-century gnostic Marcion, who rejected all non-Pauline writings because of the Jewish influence (except an edited version of Luke), denied the apostolic authorship of Revelation as well. In the late second or early third century a group of heretics in Asia Minor, labeled the Alogoi,[21] who rejected both the Gospel of John and Revelation, seem to have attributed Revelation to the gnostic Cerinthus: "these are not of John but of Cerinthus and . . . are not worthy to exist in the church."[22]

13. Andrew Helmbold, "A Note on the Authorship of the Apocalypse," *NTS* 8 (1961): 77–79. Both quotations are from Helmbold.

14. Clement of Alexandria, *Strom.* 6.13 (*ANF* 2:504). See also *Paed.* 2.119; *Quis div.* 42.

15. Tertullian, *Praescr.*, 33; *Marc.*, 3.14.3; 3.24.4.

16. Hippolytus, *Antichr.* 35–36, 50 (*ANF* 5:211, 214–215).

17. Origen, *Comm. Jo.* 2.4 (*ANF* 9:325–26); cf. 1.1; 1.2; 1.14.

18. Victorinus of Petovium (11.1), Apringius of Beja (1:1), Caesarius of Arles (*Exposition*), and Bede the Venerable (*Versicle, Prefatory Letter*). See Victorinus et al., *Latin Commentaries on Revelation: Victorinus of Petovium, Apringius of Beja, Casearius of Arles and Bede the Venerable*, ed. Thomas C. Oden, trans. William C. Weinrich, ACT (Downers Grove, IL: IVP Academic, 2011).

19. Weinrich, *Revelation*, xix.

20. Stephen S. Smalley, *Thunder and Love: John's Revelation and John's Community* (Eugene, OR: Wipf & Stock, 1994), 39.

21. Epiphanius, *Pan.* 51.1.3–6; 51.32.2–33.3.

22. Epiphanius, *Pan.* 51.3 (ACCS, 12:xviii). See Weinrich, *Revelation*, xviii.

In a similar vein, the Roman presbyter Gaius in the early third century argued that the heretic Cerinthus wrote Revelation. Eusebius quotes Gaius:

> But Cerinthus also, by means of revelations which he pretends were written by a great apostle, brings before us marvelous things which he falsely claims were shown him by angels; and he says that after the resurrection the kingdom of Christ will be set up on earth, and that the flesh dwelling in Jerusalem will again be subject to desires and pleasures. And being an enemy of the Scriptures of God, he asserts, with the purpose of deceiving men, that there is to be a period of a thousand years for marriage festivals.[23]

Both the Alogoi and Gaius were also probably motivated to choose Cerinthus as the author "in order to undercut its [Revelation's] credibility because it seemingly supported the Montanist movement, which they opposed."[24]

The more influential detractor appears in the middle of the third century in one Dionysius of Alexandria (d. ca. 264). As it turns out, Eusebius is dependent on Dionysius, and a majority of modern scholars may have uncritically followed Eusebius when it comes to the authorship question. Dionysius posits that the apostle John wrote the Fourth Gospel and the Epistles of John but vehemently denies that John wrote Revelation.[25] Dionysius does not follow Gaius in attributing Revelation to Cerinthus but opts for a second John he supposes lived in Ephesus at the same time as the apostle John.[26] He moves this direction seemingly for three main reasons. First, the John of Revelation never identifies himself as the apostle John as one might expect.[27] Second, he considers the linguistic and stylistic differences between the Gospel and the Apocalypse too great to overcome. Third, he wants to put space between the millennial teachings of Revelation, which he rejects, and the Gospel of John, which he believes was written by the apostle John.[28] Dionysius greatly influenced later Eastern church leaders to reject apostolic authorship of Revelation (e.g., Cyril of Jerusalem, Chrysostom, Theodore of Mopsuestia, and Theodoret of Cyrus).[29]

The most persuasive evidence against apostolic authorship comes from Papias, bishop of Heiropolis, by way of Eusebius (d. ca. 340), but this evidence is much debated. Papias (ca. 70–163) wrote sometime between AD 95–110 and later died as a martyr in Pergamum.[30] He was a contemporary and "companion" (ἑταῖρος) of Polycarp, bishop

23. Eusebius, *Hist. eccl.* 3.28.2 (*NPNF*² 1:160).
24. Koester, *Revelation*, 67.
25. Eusebius, *Hist. eccl.* 7.25.22.
26. Eusebius, *Hist. eccl.* 7.25.7. See Weinrich, *Revelation*, xviii.
27. Eusebius, *Hist. eccl.* 7.25.8–9, 11–12.
28. Koester, *Revelation*, 68; Osborne, *Revelation*, 23–24.
29. Osborne, *Revelation*, 23–24.
30. Robert W. Yarbrough, "The Date of Papias: A Reassessment," *JETS* 26 (1983): 181–91; Richard Bauckham, *Jesus and the Eyewitnesses: The Gospels as Eyewitness Testimony* (Grand Rapids: Eerdmans, 2006), 14; Monte A. Shanks, *Papias and the New Testament* (Eugene, OR: Pickwick, 2013), 65, 103–104.

of Smyrna (ca. 69–156). According to Eusebius, Papias believed there were two Johns in Ephesus, John the apostle (the author of the Gospel of John) and John the Elder (the author of Revelation):

> (4) And if by chance someone who had been a follower of the elders should come my way, I inquired about the words of the elders—what Andrew or Peter said, or Philip, or Thomas or James, or John or Matthew or any other of the Lord's disciples, and whatever Aristion and the elder John, the Lord's disciples, were saying. For I did not think that information from books would profit me as much as information from a living and abiding voice.
>
> (5) Here it is worth noting that he lists the name of John twice. The first he mentions in connection with Peter and James and Matthew and the rest of the apostles, clearly meaning the Evangelist, but he classes the other John with others outside the number of the apostles by changing the wording and putting Aristion before him, and he distinctly calls him "elder."
>
> (6) Moreover, by these remarks he confirms the truth of the story told by those who have said that there were two men in Asia who had the same name, and that there are two tombs in Ephesus, each of which even today is said to be John's. It is important to notice this, for it is probably the second, unless one prefers the first, who saw the Revelation that circulates under the name of John.
>
> (7) And Papias, of whom we are now speaking, acknowledges that he had received the words of the apostles from those who had followed them, but he says that he was himself a hearer of Aristion and John the Elder. In any event he frequently mentions them by name and includes their traditions in his writings as well. Let these statements of ours not be wasted on the reader.[31]

Koester is likely correct to conclude that Eusebius develops the view of Dionysius of Alexandria who wanted to separate the millennial outlook of Revelation from the Gospel of John, which he believed to have been written by the apostle. He did so by taking Papias's reference to "apostle" and "elder" to refer to two different Johns and by mentioning two tombs in Ephesus for two people named John.[32]

2.4 ARGUMENTS AGAINST APOSTOLIC AUTHORSHIP

Although early-church evidence clearly stacks up in favor of apostolic authorship, a majority of contemporary scholars deny that John the apostle wrote Revelation. First,

31. Eusebius, *Hist. eccl.* 3.39.4–7; translation from Michael William Holmes, *The Apostolic Fathers: Greek Texts and English Translations*, updated ed. (Grand Rapids: Baker, 1999), 565.

32. Koester, *Revelation*, 68. Also, Aune, *Revelation 1–5*, liii.

they note that the author never claims to be an apostle or even implies such. The assumption is that the apostle John would certainly have identified himself as an apostle. DeSilva observes: "The author does not make any explicit or implicit claims to have known Jesus in the flesh or to have been one of the Twelve; in fact, he looks on the circle of the apostles from the outside (Rev 21:14). His 'brothers' are the 'prophets' (Rev 22:9), not the apostles."[33]

Second, the primary reason many scholars reject apostolic authorship goes back to Dionysius—the stylistic, linguistic, and theological differences between the Fourth Gospel and Revelation.[34] Dionysius concludes, "The Apocalypse is different from these writings and foreign to them; not touching, nor in the least bordering upon them; almost, so to speak, without even a syllable in common with them."[35] Koester notes that Revelation and the Gospel of John differ in terms of how they use similar language (e.g., "Word," "I am," "Lamb," imagery of shepherding, water and light) as well as in their vocabulary and linguistic style.[36] Scholars have also noted important theological differences (e.g., love vs. judgment, realized vs. futurist eschatology, Christology, soteriology, pneumatology).

In light of these objections, many contemporary scholars have opted for one of three major alternatives to apostolic authorship with a bit of overlap between the options. First, some see a Johannine "school" or "circle" or "community" composing the book of Revelation, with composition often occurring in stages, perhaps greatly influenced or crystalized by a person named John.[37]

Second, some have opted for John the Elder as the author.[38] This goes back to Eusebius's interpretation of Papias to refer to a John the Elder distinct from John the apostle. Gunther argues that John was an "ascetic Palestinian millenarian prophet-teacher-apostle who functioned as the intercessory high priest and tradition-bearing chief elder."[39] He had been a member of the early Jerusalem Church, where the apostle John was martyred. There are a host of variations of this proposal, including the identification of this John the Elder with "the Beloved Disciple, the author of the other Johannine documents."[40] Hengel says John the Elder may have written Revelation just before AD 70 and that it was modified by his disciples in the late first century.[41]

33. David A. deSilva, *An Introduction to the New Testament: Contexts, Methods and Ministry Formation* (Downers Grove, IL: InterVarsity Press, 2004), 894. See also Charles, *Revelation of St. John*, 1:xlii–xliv; Aune, *Revelation 1–5*, li.

34. Eusebius, *Hist. eccl.* 7.25.8, 17–18, 21–22, 24, 26. The linguistic comparison has been explored thoroughly by Charles, *Revelation of St. John*, 1:xxix–xxxiv, and more recently by Jorge Frey, "Erwägungen zum Verhältnis der Johannesapokalypse zu den übrigen Schriften des Corpus Johanneum," in Martin Hengel, *Die johanneische Frage: Ein Lösungversuch* (Tübingen: Mohr Siebeck, 1993), 326–429.

35. Eusebius, *Hist. eccl.* 7.25.22 (*NPNF*[2] 1:311).

36. Koester, *Revelation*, 81–83.

37. J. Massyngberde Ford, *Revelation*, AB 38 (Garden City, NY: Doubleday, 1975); Elizabeth Schüssler Fiorenza, *The Book of Revelation: Justice and Judgment*, 2nd ed. (Minneapolis: Fortress, 1998).

38. John J. Gunther, "The Elder John, Author of Revelation," *JSNT* 11 (1981): 3–20. Martin Hengel, *The Johannine Question* (London: SCM, 1989).

39. Gunther, "Elder John," 3.

40. John Christopher Thomas and Frank D. Macchia, *Revelation*, ed. Joel B. Green and Max Turner, THNTC (Grand Rapids: Eerdmans, 2016), 43.

41. Hengel, *Johannine Question*, 127.

Third, the most common alternative to apostolic authorship is to attribute the book to an early Christian prophet named John. Koester argues this option admirably. He concludes, "The most plausible view is that John was the real name of the author and he was a Jewish Christian prophet active in Asia Minor."[42] His self-identification as a Christian prophet provides the major evidence for this view (Rev 1:1–3, 10–19; 4:1–2; 10:11; 17:1–3; 21:9–10; 22:6–7, 9–10, 18–19). Koester sees John as best understood within the social context of Jewish Christianity in Asia Minor rather than linking him to Palestine.[43]

2.5 ARGUMENTS SUPPORTING APOSTOLIC AUTHORSHIP

The strong evidence in support of apostolic authorship from Justin Martyr, Irenaeus, the Apocryphon of John, and other early Christian leaders makes it probable (from the vantage point of external evidence) that the apostle John authored Revelation.[44] Eusebius's interpretation of Papias remains a key sticking point in the debate. Smalley, however, argues that Papias (quoted in Eusebius, *Hist. eccl.* 3.39.4) is referring to only one disciple named John rather than two, using two different descriptors: "first, among the disciples of Jesus who had died; and secondly, among those who were still alive (of whom Aristion alone is mentioned)."[45] That is, Papias refers to the Twelve using the terms "elders," "apostles," and "disciples of the Lord."[46] Shanks demonstrates that the use of an article before "elder" (ὁ πρεσβύτερος Ἰωάννης) suggests that "Papias actually meant to identify 'the presbyter John' as the same John from among the previously mentioned group of presbyters."[47] By following Dionysius in rejecting apostolic authorship, Eusebius also conveniently removes the apostle John from the futurist eschatology of Revelation, a theological emphasis Eusebius detested.[48] Perhaps this gives us a clue as to his motivation.

42. Koester, *Revelation*, 66. Aune, *Revelation 1–5*, liii–liv seems to follow suit.

43. Koester, *Revelation*, 69. While Beale concludes that John the apostle might have written the book, he believes John "should be socially identified with a group of early Christian itinerant prophets." G. K. Beale, *The Book of Revelation: A Commentary on the Greek Text*, NIGTC (Grand Rapids: Eerdmans, 1999), 35–36. See also David A. deSilva, "The Social Setting of the Revelation to John: Conflicts Within, Fears Without," *WTJ* 54 (1992): 273–302.

44. Peter J. Leithart, *Revelation*, ITC (London: Bloomsbury T&T Clark, 2018), 74. Leithart says it is "highly speculative to go off, as scholars have long done, searching for alternatives."

45. Smalley, *Thunder and Love*, 38; Osborne, *Revelation*, 3–4; Robert H. Gundry, *Matthew: A Commentary on His Literary and Theological Art* (Grand Rapids: Eerdmans, 1982), 611–12. Gundry argues that Papias, writing at the turn of the first century, is referring to first-generation witnesses rather than second-generation elders.

46. Ian Paul, *Revelation: An Introduction and Commentary*, TNTC (London: InterVarsity Press, 2018), 8.

47. Shanks, *Papias*, 19. He cites Daniel B. Wallace on the anaphoric use of the article to denote a previous reference. See Wallace, *The Basics of New Testament Syntax* (Grand Rapids: Zondervan, 2000), 98.

48. Shanks, *Papias*, 287. Shanks writes (p. 291) that "Eusebius was theologically biased and politically committed to an eschatology that no longer saw a need for Papias's brand of chiliasm, but instead attempted to apply a 'now more than ever' realized eschatology based upon a belief that the kingdom of God had come to earth through the reign of Constantine."

Also, Dionysius's conjecture that two tombs = two Johns was in reality two tombs = two memorials to the one apostle John.[49] To push back even more, Mark Wilson, an expert on both Ephesus and Revelation who has also lived in Turkey for many years, concludes that "only one burial site has ever existed. The location of John's interment, first in the ancient necropolis, was preserved over the centuries by Christians in Ephesus. . . . Local traditions from antiquity relate to only one John; there were never two tombs of John in Ephesus."[50] So one tomb = one John, the apostle John. Because of serious flaws in his methodology as well as his theological bias against chiliasm, Eusebius should not be considered a credible witness for understanding Papias and should not be uncritically relied upon as such.[51] Irenaeus (ca. 180) provides a witness equal or superior to Eusebius since he knew of Papias and his writings.[52] Irenaeus is clear that John, the beloved disciple and author of the Fourth Gospel, lived in Ephesus and also wrote the book of Revelation.[53]

The differences between the Gospel of John and Revelation have also been granted too much weight in the authorship debate.[54] The key issue comes down to this, according to Ian Paul: "Whether we think the two texts were written by the same person will depend on the extent to which we expect an author to use a common style in different documents, written at different times, in different genres for different purposes."[55] The substantial differences of genre, occasion, purpose, emphasis, time, and perhaps amanuensis offer sufficient and reasonable explanation for the stylistic, linguistic, and theological differences between the two books.[56] While some scholars have uncritically focused on R. H. Charles's list of linguistic differences between the two books, Whale's study of key terms (e.g., "lamb," "call," "nation," "world," "feed," "until," "witness") demonstrates that such differences have no significant effect on the authorship issue.[57]

---

49. Shanks, *Papias*, 282.

50. Mark Wilson, "John of Ephesus: A Case of Multi-Personality Identification Disorder" (paper presented at the ETS annual meeting, New Orleans, November 19, 2009). Polycrates, bishop of Ephesus (ca. AD 125–196), said, "For in Asia also great lights have fallen asleep, which shall rise again on the day of the Lord's coming, when he shall come with glory from heaven, and shall seek out all the saints. Among these are Philip, one of the twelve apostles, . . . and, moreover, John, who was both a witness and a teacher, who reclined upon the bosom of the Lord. . . . He fell asleep at Ephesus" (Eusebius, *Hist. eccl.* 5.24.1–3).

51. Shanks, *Papias*, 278, 291.

52. Shanks, *Papias*, 283.

53. *Haer.* 3.1.1; 4.20.11; 4.30.4; 5.35.2.

54. Rainbow has produced one of the few critical and comprehensive Johannine theologies and reaches this conclusion regarding authorship: "On the question of authorship there seems little reason to be swayed by the prevalence of excessive caution in academe rather than by the internal evidence of the books supported by the Fathers. . . . Therefore my working hypothesis will be that the Johannine literature, including the Apocalypse, more probably than not stems from a single mind." See Paul A. Rainbow, *Johannine Theology: The Gospel, the Epistles, and the Apocalypse* (Downers Grove, IL: IVP Academic, 2014), 50–51.

55. Paul, *Revelation*, 10.

56. Gordon D. Fee, *Revelation*, NCC (Eugene, OR: Cascade, 2011), xix, declares, "Even though it has several linguistic and grammatical differences from the Gospel and Epistles that bear John's name, these differences are no more severe than those between Galatians and Romans, both of which almost all living scholars assume to be Pauline. And with regard to the Revelation, one could argue further that the small differences between it and the Gospel of John can easily be attributed to John's exile on Patmos, where he probably had to write on his own without an amanuensis." On the role of an amanuensis in Greco-Roman antiquity, see E. Randolph Richards, *Paul and First-Century Letter Writing: Secretaries, Composition and Collection* (Downers Grove, IL: InterVarsity Press, 2004).

57. Peter Whale, "The Lamb of John: Some Myths about the Vocabulary of the Johannine Literature," *JBL* 106 (1987): 289–95.

Then there is the often-neglected matter of similarities between John's Gospel and Revelation.[58] Wilson observes numerous theological and thematic parallels between Revelation and John.[59] Köstenberger identifies a list of twenty-two major Johannine style characteristics and concludes that the list "underscores impressively the unity of style that pervades the entire gospel and extends also to the Johannine letters and, when proper allowance is made for the differences in genre and context, even to the book of Revelation."[60] Ozanne also recognizes certain words and phrases that are common to the Johannine writings that suggest common authorship.[61] Smalley argues that the beloved disciple, the apostle John, wrote Revelation on the basis of similarities such as the ethos of both books, their parallel theology (e.g., cosmology, Christology, eschatology), their language and structure, and their use of early testimony traditions.[62]

On a personal and pastoral level, we should also note that the author of Revelation had enormous influence and authority over the churches of Asia Minor that went beyond that of an itinerant preacher/prophet. Mounce concludes that "although he wrote as a prophet, he functioned among his churches as an apostle."[63] Ian Paul contends that while John does not describe himself as an apostle, he puts himself in the chain of transmission (1:1; 22:6) and thereby functions as an apostle.[64] In contrast to most Jewish apocalypses where a pseudonym was used to bolster the writer's authority, Keener notes that John "seeks no famous name from earlier centuries, instead openly stating his identity. That he does not need to qualify which John he is may suggest that he is the most obvious John among the early Christians, namely, John the apostle, son of Zebedee, who had personally known Jesus in the flesh (cf. John 21:22)."[65] Due weight should be given to John's inherent authority allowing him to write in his own name with the clear expectation that the churches would

58. A number of Revelation scholars have identified substantial similarities between the Gospel and the Apocalypse. See e.g., Paul, *Revelation*, 8–9; Osborne, *Revelation*, 4–5; Robert H. Mounce, *The Book of Revelation*, rev. ed., NICNT (Grand Rapids: Eerdmans, 1997), 14; Benjamin E. Reynolds, *John among the Apocalypses: Jewish Apocalyptic Tradition and the 'Apocalyptic' Gospel* (Oxford: Oxford University Press, 2020), 39–48; and the overall work by Rainbow, *Johannine Theology*.

59. Mark Wilson, *Charts on the Book of Revelation: Literary, Historical, and Theological Perspectives* (Grand Rapids: Kregel Academic, 2007), 38–39. These parallels are related to Jesus Christ (witness, atoning blood, "I am," victor, unity with God, lamb, shepherd, judge, Word, temple), to the Holy Spirit (speaks to congregation, witness to Jesus), to angels (servants of God, live in heaven), to Satan (devil, ruler and general), to the church (witnesses, hates evil, true Jews, characterized by love, sheep and lambs, bride of the Messiah), to eschatology (present eschatology, future eschatology), and to other imagery (unnumbered sevens, manna/living bread, God/Jesus as truth, door, living water, childbearing, wine, vine, bride and groom, God/Jesus as light).

60. Köstenberger, *Theology of John's Gospel and Letters*, 133–35.

61. See C. G. Ozanne, "The Language of the Apocalypse," *TynBul* 16 (1965): 3–9. He concludes (p. 9), "So marked are these parallels that even those who deny community of authorship have been obliged to assume some connection between the respective writers. However, now that the stylistic problem can be disposed of, there no longer seems to be adequate reason for denying that the Apostle John was the sole author of Gospel, Epistles and Apocalypse."

62. Stephen S. Smalley, "John's Revelation and John's Community," *BJRL* 69 (1987): 568: "Revelation was the first document in the Johannine corpus to be written, not the last, and . . . it was composed by John the apostle."

63. Mounce, *Revelation*, 9.

64. Paul, *Revelation*, 11.

65. Craig S. Keener, *Revelation*, NIVAC (Grand Rapids: Zondervan, 1999), 54–55.

acknowledge his leadership.[66] What is more, using the more empathetic terms "servant," "brother," and "companion" rather than the more authoritative term "apostle" reveals John's pastoral concern to suffer with those who suffer by aligning himself with the recipients in this important way. It would certainly motivate his readers to join him in being a faithful witness, a concern of utmost importance even to a prophet.

2.6 CONCLUSION

In the introduction to his Ancient Christian Commentary on Revelation, Weinrich concludes: "Although nowhere in the Revelation is this John identified with the apostle and evangelist John, this identification was virtually universal in the early church."[67] The already strong case for apostolic authorship based on external evidence becomes even stronger if we reject Eusebius's misreading of Papias as spurious. The only detractor is Dionysius. Guthrie sums up a reasonable response to Dionysius: (1) his conclusions are "not based on ancient testimony, but on subjective judgment," (2) his observations about the Greek of Revelation "tend to be misleading," and (3) his "alternative suggestion [taken up by Eusebius] does not inspire confidence for his 'second John' has remarkably flimsy testimony to his existence."[68] It is also important to remember that the vast majority of early church leaders disagreed with Dionysius's minority view.

The internal evidence, on the other hand, remains inconclusive about authorship. John was certainly a Christian prophet and quite possibly also the apostle and one of Jesus's twelve disciples. However, without denying John's prophetic role, certainly Köstenberger, Kellum, and Quarles are correct to suggest that "claiming John was *only* a prophet constitutes an undue inference. It is certainly possible, if not plausible, that one man could function in both roles at the same time. Thus, John's identity as a prophet does not necessarily obviate his status as an apostle."[69]

While John never identifies himself as an apostle, there are subtle hints that John is an apostle (e.g., his inherent authority, his presence in the chain of transmission, the departure from the normal use of a pseudonym). And the similarities between Revelation and the other Johannine writings also point to common authorship. Again, the differences in genre, occasion, purpose, emphasis, time, and so forth sufficiently account for the stylistic, linguistic, and theological variations between Revelation and John's Gospel. In light of the strong external evidence and debatable internal evidence,

66. Guthrie says this kind of departure from pseudonymous devices is favorable to apostolic authority, although the argument is not conclusive. See Donald Guthrie, *New Testament Introduction*, 4th rev. ed. (Downers Grove, IL: InterVarsity Press, 1996), 935.

67. Weinrich, *Revelation*, xvii.

68. Guthrie, *New Testament Introduction*, 934.

69. Köstenberger, Kellum, and Quarles, *Cradle, Cross, and Crown*, 931.

we conclude that it is entirely plausible, indeed probable, that John the apostle wrote Revelation. More and more Revelation scholars are deciding that "the simplest and most satisfactory solution . . . is to preserve the ancient church tradition" and see John the apostle, the beloved disciple and prophet (and by this time also elder) as the author of Revelation.[70]

70. Wilson, "John of Ephesus." See also Ian Boxall, *The Revelation of Saint John*, BNTC (Peabody, MA: Hendrickson, 2006), 6–7; Fee, *Revelation*, xix; Keener, *Revelation*, 54–55; Leithart, *Revelation*, 74–75; Mounce, *Revelation*, 15; Osborne, *Revelation*, 6; Paul, *Revelation*, 8; Smalley, *Thunder and Love*, 39; Stephen S. Smalley, *The Revelation to John: A Commentary on the Greek Text of the Apocalypse* (Downers Grove, IL: InterVarsity Press, 2005), 4.

Chapter 3

THE DATE OF REVELATION

BIBLIOGRAPHY

Barnard, L. W. "Clement of Rome and the Persecution of Domitian." *NTS* 10 (1964): 251–60. **Bell, A. A.** "The Date of John's Apocalypse: The Evidence of Some Roman Historians Reconsidered." *NTS* 25 (1979): 93–102. **Carson, D. A., and Douglas J. Moo.** *An Introduction to the New Testament.* 2nd ed. Grand Rapids: Zondervan, 2005. **Cook, John Granger.** *Roman Attitudes Toward the Christians: From Claudius to Hadrian*, WUNT. Tübingen: Mohr Siebeck, 2010. **DeSilva, David A.** "The Social Setting of the Revelation to John: Fears Within, Conflicts Without." *WTJ* 54 (1992): 273–302. **Downing, F. G.** "Pliny's Prosecutions of Christians." *JSNT* 34 (1988) 105–23. **Friesen, Steven J.** *Imperial Cults and the Apocalypse of John: Reading Revelation in the Ruins.* Oxford: Oxford University Press, 2001. ———. *Twice Neokoros: Ephesus, Asia and the Cult of the Flavian Imperial Family.* Leiden: Brill, 1993. **Guthrie, Donald.** *New Testament Introduction.* 4th rev. ed. Downers Grove, IL: InterVarsity Press, 1990. **Holmes, Michael William.** *The Apostolic Fathers: Greek Texts and English Translations.* Updated ed. Grand Rapids: Baker, 1999. **Jobes, Karen H.** *1 Peter.* BECNT. Grand Rapids: Baker Academic, 2005. **Jones, Brian W.** *The Emperor Domitian.* London: Routledge, 1992. **Klauck, Hans-Josef.** "Do They Never Come Back? Nero Redivivus and the Apocalypse of John." *CBQ* 63 (2001): 683–98. **Kraybill, J. Nelson.** *Imperial Cult and Commerce in John's Apocalypse.* JSNTSup 127. Sheffield: Sheffield Academic, 1996. **Mucha, Robert.** "Ein flavischer Nero: Zur Domitian-Darstellung und Datierung der Johannesoffenbarung." *NTS* 60.1 (2014): 83–105. **Price, S. R. F.** *Rituals and Power: The Imperial Cult in Asia Minor.* Cambridge: Cambridge University Press, 1984. **Robinson, John A. T.** *Redating the New Testament.* London: SCM, 1976. **Rojas-Flores, Gonzalo.** "The Book of Revelation and the First Years of Nero's Reign." *Bib* 85.3 (2004): 375–92. **Scott, Kenneth.** *The Imperial Cult under the Flavians.* New York: Arno, 1975. **Schnabel, Eckhard J.** "The Persecution of Christians in the First Century." *JETS* 61 (2018): 525–47. **Slater, Thomas B.** "On the Social Setting of the Revelation to John." *NTS* 44 (1998): 232–56. **Victorinus of Petovium et al.** *Latin Commentaries on Revelation.* Edited by Thomas C. Oden. Translated by William C. Weinrich. ACT. Downers Grove, IL: IVP Academic, 2011. **Warden, Duane.** "Imperial Persecution and the Dating of 1 Peter and Revelation." *JETS* 34/2 (1991): 203–12. **Wilson, J. Christian.** "The Problem of the Domitianic Date of Revelation." *NTS* (1993): 587–605. **Wilson, Mark.** "The Early Christians in Ephesus and the Date of

Revelation, Again." *Neo* 39.1 (2005): 163–193. **Yarbro Collins, Adela.** *Crisis and Catharsis: The Power of the Apocalypse*. Philadelphia: Westminster, 1984.

3.1 INTRODUCTION

With regard to the date of Revelation, there are two major possibilities—an early date (ca. AD 69) or a late date (ca. AD 95). Throughout the nineteenth century, the prevailing view was the earlier date: Revelation was written just after Nero's death during the short reign of Emperor Galba (AD 68–69).[1] With the publication of the influential commentaries by R. H. Charles, H. B. Swete, and I. T. Beckwith in the early part of the twentieth century, however, the scholarly tide turned in favor of a date near the end of Domitian's reign (ca. AD 95).[2] At present, most New Testament scholars prefer the late date with a minority holding to the early date. One's view on the dating of Revelation could affect how one understands the overall occasion of the book and, as a result, how one interprets particular details. Colin Hemer, who holds to a late date, goes so far as to suggest that the date of the book is "a crucial factor in the historical *Sitz im Leben*."[3] Yet, as Beale notes, "one can in fact affirm the early date or the late date without the main interpretative approach being affected. Under either dating position the book could be understood as a polemic against Rome and especially against compromise with ungodly Roman culture."[4] The key points of evidence used by advocates of both positions will be surveyed below.

3.2 THE PERSECUTION OF CHRISTIANS

3.2.1 What Revelation Says about Believers Suffering Persecution

We find evidence within the book itself that believers were suffering persecution, and the source of the persecution varies (see also 4.3.3).[5] John has been banished to Patmos "because of the word of God and the testimony of Jesus" (1:9) and relates to his readers as their "brother and companion in the suffering [θλῖψις] and kingdom and patient endurance that are ours in Jesus" (1:9). In the messages to the seven churches, we also see evidence of persecution. The church in Ephesus has "persevered and endured hardships" for the sake of Jesus's name (2:3). The Lord assures the believers in Smyrna,

1. J. Christian Wilson, "The Problem of the Domitianic Date of Revelation," *NTS* (1993): 587.

2. Charles, *Revelation of St John*; H. B. Swete, *The Apocalypse of St John* (London: Macmillan, 1917); I. T. Beckwith, *The Apocalypse of St John: Studies in Introduction with a Critical and Exegetical Commentary* (New York: Macmillan, 1919). See J. Christian Wilson, "Problem of the Domitianic Date," 587–88, who also notes a similar shift in German New Testament scholarship.

3. Colin J. Hemer, *The Letters to the Seven Churches of Asia in Their Local Setting*, BRS (Grand Rapids: Eerdmans, 2001), 3.

4. Beale, *Revelation*, 4.

5. See the summary in Eckhard J. Schnabel, "The Persecution of Christians in the First Century," *JETS* 61 (2018): 544–45.

telling them, "I know your afflictions [θλῖψις] and your poverty [πτωχεία]" (2:9). He continues, "I know about the slander [βλασφημία] of those who say they are Jews and are not, but are a synagogue of Satan. Do not be afraid of what you are about to suffer [πάσχω]. I tell you, the devil will put some of you in prison to test [πειράζω] you, and you will suffer persecution [θλῖψις] for ten days. Be faithful, even to the point of death, and I will give you life as your victor's crown" (2:9–10). The church in Pergamum is applauded for not renouncing their faith in Jesus, "not even in the days of Antipas, my faithful witness, who was put to death in your city—where Satan lives" (2:13). The believers in Philadelphia have kept Jesus's word and not denied his name (3:8), implying a testing of their faith.

Some references to persecution throughout the book are presented without a time frame, although the recent past remains a distinct possibility. With the opening of the fifth seal, John says he saw "under the altar the souls of those who had been slain because of the word of God and the testimony they had maintained" (6:9). They cry out for the Sovereign Lord to "judge the inhabitants of the earth and avenge our blood" (6:10). They are told to wait a little longer until "the full number of their fellow servants, their brothers and sisters, were killed just as they had been" (6:11). In chapter 16 God judges those who have "shed the blood of [his] holy people and [his] prophets" (16:5–6). Babylon the Great, the mother of prostitutes, is said to be "drunk with the blood of God's holy people, the blood of those who bore testimony to Jesus" (17:6). The use of the name "Babylon" as a symbol for Rome was common and suggests persecution as a recent occurrence.[6] In this woman/city/empire was found "the blood of prophets and of God's holy people" (18:24), and as she has judged believers, so God will judge her (18:20). God will condemn the great prostitute and avenge on her "the blood of his servants" (19:2). Some believers have been "beheaded because of their testimony about Jesus and because of the word of God," testimony which included refusing to worship the beast or its image or receive its mark of allegiance (20:4).

Other references to suffering trials take on an almost timeless quality that makes it difficult to nail down in terms of historical referent. In Rev 7:14 the great multitude is described as those "who have come out of the great tribulation [τῆς θλίψεως τῆς μεγάλης]." We see this usage also in the war between God's people and Satan. Although the great dragon "accuses [κατηγορέω]" believers before God constantly, they have triumphed over him "by the blood of the Lamb and by the word of their testimony; they did not love their lives so much as to shrink from death" (12:10–11). This same dragon wages war against the rest of the woman's offspring, described as those who "keep God's commands and hold fast their testimony about Jesus" (12:17). Finally, at

6. Cf. 1 Pet 5:13; 2 Bar. 11.1; 67.7; 79.1; Sib. Or. 5.143, 159; 4 Ezra 3:2.

the end of the book the voice from the throne reassures believers that God will "wipe every tear from their eyes. There will be no more death or mourning or crying or pain, for the old order of things has passed away" (21:4). This verse indicates more than the everyday hardships of life in a fallen world.

Some allusions to persecution refer to future events (from the reader's perspective), although whether the near or distant future is not always clear. In 6:11 we find a reference to the upcoming martyrdom of fellow believers: "until the full number of their fellow servants, their brothers and sisters, were killed just as they had been." In chapter 11, the outer court of the temple is not measured, "because it has been given to the Gentiles" who will "trample on the holy city for 42 months" (11:2). The two witnesses, whether two individuals or a symbol of the witnessing church, are attacked, overpowered, and killed by the beast from the Abyss (11:7). The beast blasphemes God and slanders "his name and his dwelling place and those who live in heaven" and has the power to "wage war against God's holy people and to conquer them" (13:6–7). The proverbial saying of 13:9–10, likely an allusion to Jeremiah 15:2, calls God's people to "patient endurance and faithfulness," including a willingness to suffer persecution: "If anyone is to go into captivity, into captivity they will go. If anyone is to be killed with the sword, with the sword they will be killed." In addition, the second beast is allowed to inspire the image of the first beast so that all who refuse to worship this image will suffer death (13:15) or economic deprivation (13:16–17). Following the messages of the three angels in chapter 14, John calls the people of God (i.e., those "who keep his commands and remain faithful to Jesus") to "patient endurance" (14:12). A voice from heaven responds with the second of seven beatitudes in the book: "Blessed are the dead who die in the Lord from now on," to which the Spirit adds an amen (14:13).

All this is to say that Revelation reflects not merely the potential for persecution, but the present reality of trials with the underlying expectation that things could get much worse. The source of such trouble, of course, is not always the Roman emperor, but he (and his agents) certainly factor in. John has been exiled, likely for political reasons. Some of the believers in the seven churches are now enduring tribulation (θλῖψις), slander (βλασφημία), poverty (πτωχεία), suffering (πάσχω), and testing (πειράζω). Antipas and others have been martyred (2:13; 6:9–10; 11:7; 16:5–6; 20:4). Christians are challenged to stay faithful unto death (12:11; 13:9–10), with martyrdom remaining a real possibility (6:11; 14:12–13). Witherington notes that the term μάρτυς in Revelation (1:5; 3:14 [of Jesus]; and 2:13; 11:3; 17:6 [of believers]) involves a "reference to the violent death of someone who was a faithful witness."[7] He adds that the term πιστός when used of believers (e.g., 2:10, 13, and perhaps 1:5) often implies a faithfulness unto death.[8]

7. Ben Witherington III, *Revelation*, NCBC (Cambridge: Cambridge University Press, 2003), 8.

8. Witherington, *Revelation*, 8.

The harlot Rome has shed "the blood of God's holy people" (17:6; cf. 18:24; 19:2) and her beastly agents are persecuting the saints (13:6–7, 9–10, 15–17). The great multitude is said to have come out of tribulation (7:14). There is no doubt that Christians in Asia Minor were experiencing some persecution, but the level of antagonism does not appear to be universal (e.g., only one named martyr in Antipas). As Beale notes, "the internal evidence of the book points toward a situation of relative peace and selective persecution, with an imminent expectation of intensifying persecution on a widening and programmatic scale."[9] With this picture in mind, we will now explore which date best matches the kind of persecution that Revelation describes.

3.2.2 Persecution of Christians under Nero

The persecution of Christians under Nero has been well documented.[10] Tacitus (ca. 110–120) writes about Nero using Christians as scapegoats for the great fire in Rome in AD 64.[11] The emperor arrested and convicted huge numbers of Christians and proceeded to mock and torture them. He covered them in animal skins and subjected them to dogs. He crucified some. He made human torches of others and used their burning bodies to light his gardens at night. Suetonius (ca. 110–120) also contends that Christians suffered persecution under Nero but does not mention specifics related to the great fire.[12] Eusebius cites Melito of Sardis (ca. 160–170) to say that Nero and Domitian alone brought slanderous accusations against Christians.[13] Tertullian observes that Nero was the first emperor to wield the sword against Christians.[14] In addition, Christian tradition holds that both Peter and Paul were martyred during the Neronian persecution. What is still debatable is whether Nero's intense persecution extended beyond Rome to the seven churches in Asia Minor in a manner that fits with the evidence in Revelation.[15]

3.2.3 Persecution of Christians under Domitian and Afterward

The persecution of Christians under Domitian and later is a matter of no small debate. In spite of some who say there is absolutely no evidence of any persecution whatever under Domitian, we do have some evidence from Christian and Roman sources that Domitian opposed Christians, although certainly not to the extent of his predecessor Nero. Persecution under Domitian *may* be reflected in 1 Clement 1.1 (AD 94–97) when

9. Beale, *Revelation*, 12.

10. See John Granger Cook, *Roman Attitudes Toward the Christians: From Claudius to Hadrian*, WUNT 261 (Tübingen: Mohr Siebeck, 2010), 29–111. See Eusebius, *Hist. eccl.* 2.25.

11. Tacitus, *Ann.* 15.44. See also a similar accusation against Nero in Sulpicius Severus, *Chronicle* 2.29, who also notes the martyrdom at this time of Peter and Paul.

12. Suetonius, *Nero* 16.2

13. Eusebius *Hist. eccl.* 4.26.9.

14. Tertullian, *Apol.* 5.3–4. Cf. *Nat.* 1.7.8–9.

15. D. A. Carson and Douglas J. Moo, *An Introduction to the New Testament*, 2nd ed. (Grand Rapids: Zondervan, 2005), 709.

Clement refers to the "sudden and repeated misfortunes [calamities] and reverses which have happened to us" that delayed his writing to the Corinthians.[16] Barnard explains,

> The universal Christian tradition that this Emperor was a second Nero may not be true in strict historical fact; yet in another sense it is true, for the Christians no less than others suffered mental torture as they were left in an agony of suspense in many ways harder to bear than direct persecution. . . . Domitian was not a wholesale "persecutor" of the Church in the sense that Nero was; rather he singled out individual Christians who were prominent members of the Church of Rome, among them his kinsmen Flavius Clemens and Domitilla. Domitian's persecution was a succession of short, sharp, assaults—the series of sudden and repeated misfortunes which had prevented Clement, on behalf of his Church, from writing to the Church in Corinth.[17]

As mentioned above, Melito of Sardis includes Domitian as an emperor hostile to Christians. Tertullian also refers to persecutions under both Nero and Domitian.[18] Eusebius likewise indicates that Domitian was a "successor of Nero in his hatred and enmity toward God" and "the second [emperor] that stirred up a persecution against us," although the persecution appears selective rather than systematic and widespread.[19]

Christians were clearly persecuted for refusing to worship the emperor during the reign of Trajan (AD 98–117). Pliny the Younger, imperial magistrate under Trajan, wrote a letter to the emperor asking about legal examination of Christians who were Roman citizens.[20] Those who admitted to being Christians after repeated questioning were imprisoned. He discharged those who recanted their faith or cursed Christ since they were obviously not true believers. Pliny refers to some who had abandoned their faith as long as twenty years back (ca. AD 90–92), possibly under social pressure.[21] Pliny subjected two deaconesses to torture to determine the exact nature of the faith and found only what he called a "depraved, excessive superstition" (Pliny, *Ep.* 10.96.8, my translation). He writes to Trajan because so many were involved in the Christian movement, which had negatively affected temple worship.

Roman historian Dio Cassius (ca. AD 155–235) confirms that Domitian executed the aristocrat Flavius Clemens and banished his wife Flavia Domitilla, one or both of whom were likely Christians since they were persecuted because of "atheism."[22] Dio Cassius defines "atheism" as a movement affiliated with Judaism, and this is quite likely

16. Holmes, *Apostolic Fathers*, 29. Holmes observes (p. 24), "At the time of writing, the church in Rome appears to be facing some sort of persecution; in fact, the letter to Corinth has been delayed because of it (1.1; cf. 7.1)." Cf. Beale, *Revelation*, 9, 13.

17. L. W. Barnard, "Clement of Rome and the Persecution of Domitian," *NTS* 10 (1964): 258, 260.

18. Tertullian, *Apol.* 5.

19. Eusebius, *Hist. eccl.* 3.17. In *Hist. eccl.* 3.20 Eusebius notes that Domitian did not persecute Jesus's relatives living in Rome because they posed no political threat to his reign.

20. Pliny, *Ep.* 10.96.

21. Hemer, *Letters to the Seven Churches*, 10.

22. Dio Cassius, *Rom. Hist.* 67.14.

a Roman reference to Christianity. He adds that some atheists were put to death while others had their property confiscated.[23]

To sum up, early scholarship assumed a widespread, intense persecution of Christians under Domitian and later, while recent scholarship has raised serious doubts that Christians were being persecuted as Christians during this time.[24] Wilson concludes, "No Roman historian . . . ever gives so much as a hint that he [Domitian] persecuted Christians. No Christian historian before Eusebius ever clearly states that he did. Eusebius writes fully two centuries after the events which he describes."[25]

Most recently, others have sought to balance out the extremes between total persecution and no persecution under Domitian. Beale interacts extensively with the arguments of Leonard Thompson and others and makes the following points. (1) Internal evidence shows that some Christians were being persecuted as Christians during this time. (2) The letters in Revelation suggest that some believers were seeking to avoid pressure either by identifying more closely with Judaism or by compromising with the trade guild or emperor cults, and both situations were more likely to have happened toward the end of the first century than earlier. (3) Christianity began to emerge (in the Roman view) as an illegitimate Jewish sect and was thus vulnerable to the charge of "atheism," and this took time. (4) The Romans became increasingly intolerant toward Christians for not participating in the political and religious life of Greco-Roman society, embodied in the imperial cult. And (5) "a date during the time of Nero is possible for Revelation, but the later setting under Domitian is more probable."[26]

Roman persecution of Christians as Christians certainly occurred during the time of Nero and may have occurred sporadically under Domitian.[27] Internal evidence indicates that persecution of Christians in Asia Minor was more intense in those cities that were centers of Roman civil and religious power: Ephesus, Smyrna, and Pergamum. This brings us to explore the role of emperor worship on the dating of Revelation.

3.3 Emperor Worship

"The imperial cult," writes Price, "along with politics and diplomacy constructed the reality of the Roman empire."[28] The imperial cult constituted an entire system of

23. Dio Cassius, *Rom. Hist.* 67.14.

24. Leonard L. Thompson, *The Book of Revelation: Apocalypse and Empire* (Oxford: Oxford University Press, 1990), esp. 95–115; Adela Yarbro Collins, *Crisis and Catharsis: The Power of the Apocalypse* (Philadelphia: Westminster, 1984), 69–73; Brian W. Jones, *The Emperor Domitian* (London: Routledge, 1992), 117: "No convincing evidence exists for a Domitianic persecution of Christians."

25. J. Christian Wilson, "Problem of the Domitianic Date," 589.

26. Beale, *Revelation*, 9; cf. Hemer, *Letters to the Seven Churches*, 7–12.

27. Robert Mucha perceptively contends that the absence of systematic, widespread persecution under Domitian does not necessarily mean that Revelation was not written during the reign of Domitian, since he was viewed as a second Nero and both emperors were chief persecutors of the church. See "Ein flavischer Nero: Zur Domitian-Darstellung und Datierung der Johannesoffenbarung," *NTS* 60 (2014): 83–105.

28. S. R. F. Price, *Rituals and Power: The Imperial Cult in Asia Minor* (Cambridge: Cambridge University Press, 1984), 248.

worship that involved almost every aspect of Roman society, including the Roman emperor, the traditional gods, political and economic systems, altars, temples, priests, festivals, processions, statues, coins, sacrifices, shrines, sanctuaries, inscriptions, and so on.[29] It was not so much an activity or event as much as a comprehensive religious system to honor the emperor as the personification of the empire. And the emperor cult was alive and well in Asia Minor.[30] It is also easy to see how this multifaceted polytheistic system came into conflict with the Christian faith with its worldview of the Triune God ruling over all.

By the end of the first century, Asia had three provincial imperial cult temples. The first was established in Pergamum in connection with Emperor Augustus, the second in Smyrna associated with Tiberius, and the third was the temple of the Sebastoi ("revered ones," used with reference to emperors) in Ephesus. This final temple was dedicated in AD 89–90 during the reign of Domitian and shows strong connections to him. Numerous inscriptions featuring a dedication to Domitian have been discovered, and the remains of a colossal statue of either Domitian or Titus have been found, illustrating the prominence of such public symbols encouraging emperor worship.[31] Friesen notes that the "provincial temples served as crucial symbols of the cosmology that supported imperial rule, that defined the evolving identity of the province, and that promoted provincial obedience at various levels of society."[32]

Friesen also points out that one of the most important developments in Asia Minor at the end of the first century was the use of the term *neokoros*[33] to describe "a city with a provincial imperial cult temple."[34] *Neokoros* became the most coveted civic title for a city in the provinces. This innovation, Friesen says, "was explosive," changing "the public rhetoric of the empire of Asia."[35] To be a city where the emperors were worshiped was the most prestigious honor a city could achieve. While this development cannot be used to date Revelation definitively, it seems to fit better with a late first-century date since it allows time for a fully developed system of emperor worship.

Revelation assumes that Christians were under pressure to worship the Roman emperor.[36] We see clear evidence pointing to the imperial cult in the text of Revelation, especially in the two beasts of Rev 13, with the beast from the sea symbolizing the power of Rome personified by the emperor and the beast from the earth representing the imperial cult. Beale notes that during Nero's reign Christians were not persecuted primarily because they refused to worship the emperor, but because they were

29. See Leonard Thompson, *Book of Revelation*, 158–64.

30. In addition to Price, see also Steven J. Friesen, *Imperial Cults and the Apocalypse of John: Reading Revelation in the Ruins* (Oxford: Oxford University Press, 2001).

31. See Friesen, *Imperial Cults*, 25–55, for a lengthy discussion of the three provincial temples.

32. Friesen, *Imperial Cults*, 55.

33. I.e., "warden of a temple"; see "νεωκόρος," LSJ 1172.

34. Friesen, *Imperial Cults*, 55.

35. Friesen, *Imperial Cults*, 150.

36. Beale, *Revelation*, 5, notes examples in Rev 13:4–8, 15–16; 14:9–11; 15:2; 16:2; 19:20; 20:4.

a convenient scapegoat for the great fire of Rome. In contrast, persecution arises in Revelation because Christians devoted themselves to Christ rather than to Caesar.[37] DeSilva also concludes that the "likelihood for persecution of Christians as Christians thus appears greater in the province [of Asia Minor] than in the capital."[38]

There is ample evidence that Domitian embraced divine honor without hesitation.[39] Roman writers such as Pliny the Younger (ca. AD 60–115), Suetonius (ca. AD 70–135), Tacitus (ca. AD 55–120), and Dio Cassius (ca. AD 155–235) all speak of Domitian negatively and some acknowledge his claims to deity.[40] For example, Suetonius writes, "With equal arrogance, when he [Domitian] dictated the form of a letter to be used by his procurators, he began it thus: 'Our lord and god commands so and so;' whence it became a rule that no one should style him otherwise either in writing or speaking."[41] Quintilian (ca. AD 35–100), a contemporary of Domitian, although not using the phrase *dominus et deus noster* ("our lord and god"), describes Domitian as worthy of divine honors.[42] While emperor veneration occurred from the time of Augustus on (especially after their deaths), it was especially strong during the lifetime of Domitian, moving toward what we see reflected in Pliny's letter to Trajan just a short time later. In and of itself the evidence related to emperor worship cannot determine the date of Revelation, but the later date seems a better match for the province of Asia Minor at this time. We conclude with deSilva that "the growing sense of forthcoming persecution centered on the imperial cult," along with other factors, "points to conditions known during the later first century."[43]

3.4 THE CONDITION OF THE CHURCHES IN ASIA MINOR

What hints do we see in the seven messages related to the condition of the churches at the time of writing, and do these conditions suggest an earlier or later date? To begin with, Christianity had spread to the seven cities addressed by Revelation, four of which are not mentioned elsewhere in the New Testament. DeSilva notes that this "presupposes

37. Beale, *Revelation*. 5.

38. DeSilva, "Social Setting," 277.

39. Beale notes that Kenneth Scott, *The Imperial Cult under the Flavians* (New York: Arno, 1975), finds passages from Martial (numerous), Statius (pp. 100, 107, 137), Juvenal (pp. 117, 125), and Silius Italicus (pp. 96–97), as well as inscriptional and numismatic evidence from Asia Minor "that attest to people addressing Domitian as a deity" (*Revelation*, 10). See also Steven J. Friesen, *Twice Neokoros: Ephesus, Asia and the Cult of the Flavian Imperial Family* (Leiden: Brill, 1993), 146–52.

40. Leonard Thompson, *Book of Revelation*, 95–115, catalogs the primary Roman sources regarding Domitian, although, Beale rightly argues, he has overstated his case that all the Roman sources were consistently biased against Domitian (see Beale, *Revelation*, 6–12).

41. Suetonius, *Dom.* 13. Notice also in this same passage Domitian recalling his wife to his "divine couch" (a pulvinar or consecrated bed on which images of the gods reclined) and his delighting when the crowds shouted, "Good Fortune attend our Lord and Mistress." See also Dio Cassius, *Rom. Hist.* 67.13.4.

42. Quintilian, *Inst.* 4; see also preface, 2, and 5. See Thomas B. Slater, "On the Social Setting of the Revelation to John," *NTS* 44 (1998): 236–37.

43. DeSilva, *Introduction to the New Testament*, 898.

a period of growth well past the death of Paul."[44] Several of the churches appear to have deteriorated spiritually by the time Revelation was written (i.e., Ephesus, Sardis, Laodicea). Two of these churches are known to have been either planted or influenced by Paul, and such deterioration would seem to require "a considerable interval since the foundation of the church," according to Guthrie.[45] Pergamum and Thyatira had also been heavily influenced by false teaching (2:14–15, 20–24), one established enough to be widely known by name (i.e., the Nicolaitans). The Laodicean church is described as self-sufficient and, we presume, wealthy even after the destructive earthquake of AD 60. Hemer mentions several building inscriptions from Laodicea from the period of earthquake reconstruction that date firmly to AD 79.[46]

After investigating the local setting extensively, Hemer concludes:

> We accordingly reaffirm the Domitianic date of the letters in the light of the kind of evidence here considered, while recognizing that many of these indications are uncertain. Cumulatively they align themselves with the case widely accepted on other grounds that the Revelation was written about AD 95.[47]

The later date would allow more time for these conditions to develop and makes better sense of the internal evidence but does not rule out the earlier date.

3.5 THE NERO MYTH

In Rev 13 and 17 John quite possibly makes use of a popular myth circulating at the time that Nero, who committed suicide in AD 68, would one day return to Rome. The main form of the legend was that Nero never actually died but escaped to the East (Parthia) and would later return to the West (Nero *redux*). Over time, the legend also took the form that Nero had died and would return from the dead (Nero *redivivus*). Bauckham considers the term *redivivus* to be misleading since the sources attest to the belief, at least to the end of the first century, that Nero had not actually died but was in hiding and would one day return.[48] Many scholars contend that if John alludes to this Nero legend, then a later date is more likely because it would have taken time for the myth to develop and circulate after Nero's death in AD 68. Wilson, on the other hand, argues that the myth arose as early as July AD 69 in Ephesus and therefore a later date for Revelation is not required.[49]

Bauckham discusses three known imposters during the first century who claimed to

44. DeSilva, *Introduction to the New Testament*, 897.
45. Guthrie, *New Testament Introduction*, 954.
46. Hemer, *Letters to the Seven Churches*, 194–95.
47. Hemer, *Letters to the Seven Churches*, 5.
48. Bauckham, *Climax of Prophecy*, 421.
49. Mark Wilson, "The Early Christians in Ephesus and the Date of Revelation, Again," *Neot* 39.1 (2005): 167.

be Nero.[50] The first appeared only about a year after Nero's death (July 69) in Greece where he gathered some support and sailed for Syria. He was captured and killed on the island of Cynthos during his journey, and his body was taken to Rome. The second "Nero" appeared in AD 80 in the province of Asia and gathered some support before fading. The last pretender dates to AD 88–89 during the reign of Domitian. Apparently, he gained the support of the Parthian king Pacorus II and presented a more serious threat to Rome. Bauckham observes, "On the most probable dating of Revelation [mid-90s AD], these events would have been fresh in the memory of John and his readers."[51] Bauckham argues that John uses two forms of the Nero legend in Rev 13 and 17. In chapter 13 he portrays the power of the Roman Empire to persecute the people of God. Chapter 17 paints a different picture. John is here concerned to show the coming fall of Rome (Babylon) and the destruction of the beast at the parousia. Therefore, Nero is depicted as an enemy of Rome bent on destroying her. To sum up, although there may have been earlier expectations that Nero would return to power, Bauckham goes to great lengths to demonstrate that the literary development of the legend and John's use of it supports the later date for Revelation.[52]

3.6 The Name "Babylon"

John refers to "Babylon" in 14:8; 16:19; 17:5; 18:2, 19 ("great city"), and 21, and identifies it in 17:9 with "seven hills," an allusion everyone in the ancient world would connect with Rome.[53] Adela Yarbro Collins notes that the occurrences of "Babylon" as a symbolic name for Rome in Jewish literature make it clear that the name was chosen because Rome had destroyed Jerusalem and its temple.[54] Regarding the impact of this symbol on the dating of Revelation, she concludes: "The use of the name is a weighty internal indication of the date. It is highly unlikely that the name would have been used before the destruction of the temple by Titus. This internal evidence thus points decisively to a date after 70 C.E."[55]

Wilson argues, however, that John is more dependent on Old Testament traditions such as Jeremiah than on later Jewish sources. He also points out that Peter uses "Babylon" as a symbolic name for Rome in 1 Pet 5:13, most certainly a pre-AD 70 letter. If 1 Peter and Revelation were both written pre-70 with Peter being martyred during

50. Bauckham, *Climax of Prophecy*, 413–14.

51. Bauckham, *Climax of Prophecy*, 414.

52. Bauckham, *Climax of Prophecy*, 407–450, esp. 429–30. See also Hans-Josef Klauck, "Do They Never Come Back? Nero Redivivus and the Apocalypse of John," *CBQ* 63 (2001): 683–98.

53. E.g., Vergil, *Georg.* 2.535; *Aen.* 6.738; Horace, *Carm.* 7; Cicero, *Att.* 6.5; Suetonius, *Dom.* 4; *Sib Or.* 2.18; 13.45; 14.108.

54. Yarbro Collins, *Crisis and Catharsis*, 58; J. Nelson Kraybill, *Imperial Cult and Commerce in John's Apocalypse*, JSNTSup 127 (Sheffield: Sheffield Academic, 1996), 33–34. See 4 Ezra 3.1–2, 28–34; 2 Bar. 10.1–3; 11.1; 67.7; Sib. Or. 5.143, 159–60.

55. Yarbro Collins, *Crisis and Catharsis*, 58.

the Neronic persecution of AD 65–66, then perhaps John is reminded of "Babylon" through 1 Peter or contact with the Roman Christians.[56]

Assuming 1 Peter predates the destruction of the Jerusalem Temple in AD 70, we need to look more closely at what Peter meant by his use of "Babylon" in 1 Pet 5:13. Jobes sees several parallels between the opening greeting in 1 Pet 1:1–2 and the letter closing in 5:12–14. One of those relates to the "Diaspora" in 1:1 ("exiles scattered," NIV) and "Babylon" in 5:13. Since Peter does not equate Rome or "Babylon" with evil in his letter, he appears to be using the term in 5:13 to signify a place away from their home, a place of exile. Jobes sees this *inclusio* of "Diaspora" and "Babylon" as identifying both the author and his readers as believers in exile. Therefore, "Babylon" in 1 Peter does not designate a specific location (e.g., the "waters of Babylon" in Ps 137:1) so much as any place in the world where God's people live (i.e., a state of exile). For Peter, Rome could still be his particular place of exile. Jobes concludes:

> The reference could be intended as a comparison. Just as God's people had been driven out of Jerusalem and sent into exile in Babylon, the capital city of their oppressors centuries before, Peter himself has been driven from Jerusalem by the Roman powers and is sojourning in exile in the capital city of his oppressors.[57]

Friesen also emphasizes the theme of imperial domination in John's use of "Babylon."[58] John uses "Babylon" not only because of the first destruction of the temple but also to shift his audiences' attention to broader theological matters such as imperial oppression and the need to persevere in the place of exile. Friesen concludes that the use of Babylon imagery requires a date after the destruction of the temple in AD 70 and more likely in the late first century "because that takes into account the aspect of domination that was the logical consequence of the destruction."[59] This becomes more likely in light of Rev 18 where John draws on Jer 50–52 and its description of the destruction of the temple and the deportation into exile.

3.7 THE JERUSALEM TEMPLE

Some argue that John's measuring of the temple in Rev 11:1–2 presumes the existence of the Jerusalem temple and thus supports a pre-AD 70 date for Revelation.[60] They see

56. Mark Wilson, "Early Christians in Ephesus," 165–66.

57. Karen H. Jobes, *1 Peter*, BECNT (Grand Rapids: Baker Academic, 2005), 323.

58. Friesen, *Imperial Cults*, 138–40.

59. Friesen, *Imperial Cults*, 140.

60. E.g., John A. T. Robinson, *Redating the New Testament* (London: SCM, 1976), 238–42; Smalley, *Thunder and Love*, 48–49; Mark Wilson, "Early Christians in Ephesus," 168–69; J. Christian Wilson, "Problem of the Domitianic Date," 604, who interestingly points out how the prophecy is wrong on two counts: (1) the whole temple and not just the outer court was given over to the gentiles, and (2) the Romans trampled over the temple much longer than forty-two months. This appears to be indirect evidence for a symbolic view of the temple in Rev 11.

connections between 11:1–2 and prophetic passages in the Gospels such as Luke 21:24: "Jerusalem will be trampled on by the Gentiles." If Revelation is a prophecy against Jerusalem, they contend, then this must be a literal temple and, as a result, evidence for an early date for Revelation.

But a literal reading of Rev 11:1–2 assumes a literal reading of the rest of chapter 11, which can be problematic. Most likely the temple imagery in chapter 11 is intended to symbolize God's people being surrounded by an unbelieving world rather than a literal temple (see 11.4.4.3).[61] As a result, the reference to the temple in 11:1–2 does not provide clear evidence for dating the book.

3.8 The Seven Kings

The primary internal evidence for dating Revelation, at least according to those who subscribe to the early date, centers around Rev 17:9–11 and the identity of the seven kings as seven Roman emperors:

> The seven heads are seven hills on which the woman sits. They are also seven kings. Five have fallen, one is, the other has not yet come; but when he does come, he must remain for only a little while. The beast who once was, and now is not, is an eighth king. He belongs to the seven and is going to his destruction.

What appears to be an apocalyptic riddle features five kings (emperors?) who have fallen + one who is now reigning + one who is yet to come but will only remain for a little while + one who is the beast (the eighth king). A list of Roman emperors through Domitian will help:

Julius Caesar (44 BC)
Augustus (31 BC–AD 14)
Tiberius (14–37)
Caligula (37–41)
Claudius (41–54)
Nero (54–June 68)
Galba (June 68–January 69)
Otho (January 69–April 69)
Vitellius (April 69–December 69)
Vespasian (69–79)
Titus (79–81)
Domitian (81–96)

There are important questions associated with how to identify the kings (e.g., whether to begin counting with Julius or Augustus and whether to count the three

61. See Koester, *Revelation*, 74; Beale, *Revelation*, 20–21; Mounce, *Revelation*, 213; Osborne, *Revelation*, 408–15; Keener, *Revelation*, 287–89.

emperors who only reigned for a few months during the chaos of AD 69—Galba, Otho, and Vitellius). Those backing an early date tend to begin with Julius Caesar and include the three civil war emperors so that Nero is the current king ("who is") or begin with Augustus so that Galba is the emperor at the time at the time Revelation was written.[62] This would mean "the beast" (the eighth king) is either Otho or Vitellius, two of the three emperors with extremely short reigns. Those favoring a late date begin with other emperors and often omit emperors in order to arrive at Domitian as the sixth and current king. Scholars have proposed numerous historic reconstructions in an attempt to solve this problem (see 11.5.3).

Yet there are also problems for those trying to make the historical reconstruction fit with the list of emperors, even with Nero as the sixth king.[63] And Ian Paul raises the question about whether John ever intended that his vision report be interpreted as a one-to-one correspondence between the kings and specific historical figures.[64] In other words, should we force a historical reconstruction on the riddle? For example, if we count emperors as kings, we end up with an emperor present even though the "beast" is not present since we are told in 17:8 that the beast "will come up out of the Abyss" in the future.[65] Such questions should give pause to the enterprise of trying to solve the riddle using the list of Roman emperors.

A symbolic approach seems to fit better with how numbers are used throughout Revelation. John often groups rulers, calamities, visions, and so on using specific numbers.[66] As Friesen concludes, "in this case the fact that there are seven heads is more important than the attempt to identify each one."[67] The number seven often conveys the idea of completion or even perfection and here points to the fullness of the beast's power (cf. 12:3; 13:1–2). The final wicked king/kingdom is described as an "eighth king" (17:11).[68] Of course, in John's day the specific embodiment of the beast is Rome (and her personification in the emperor). Again, those pursuing a historical reconstruction using specific Roman emperors tend to support an early date, but a symbolic reading of this apocalyptic riddle offers an even better approach in my view. As a result, we conclude with Friesen that "the value of Revelation 17 for determining the date of composition has been exaggerated."[69]

62. Robinson, *Redating the New Testament*, 242–53; J. Christian Wilson, "Problem of the Domitianic Date," 599–602; Mark Wilson, "Early Christians in Ephesus," 170–74. Smalley, *Thunder and Love*, 45–48, argues for an early date (during the reign of Vespasian [AD 69–79]) but begins with Augustus and omits the three civil war emperors.

63. Beale, *Revelation*, 22–23.

64. Paul, *Revelation*, 284–87.

65. Friesen, *Imperial Cult*, 141.

66. Friesen, *Imperial Cult*, 141, supports this claim with an example from 4 Ezra 11–12, and Beale, *Revelation*, 868–72, uses parallels from biblical texts (e.g., Dan 7; Rev 12:3; 13:1–2).

67. Friesen, *Imperial Cult*, 141.

68. J. Scott Duvall, *Revelation*, TTC (Grand Rapids: Baker Books, 2014), 227–28. For a more symbolic interpretation in addition to Beale and Paul, see also G. R. Beasley-Murray, *The Book of Revelation: Based on the Revised Standard Version*, rev. ed. (Eugene, OR: Wipf & Stock, 2010), 256–57; G. B. Caird, *Revelation of St John*, BNTC (London: A. & C. Black, 1966), 218–19; Mounce, *Revelation*, 315; and esp. David E. Aune, *Revelation 17–22*, WBC (Dallas: Word, 1998), 946–49.

69. Friesen, *Imperial Cult*, 140.

3.9 THE EARLIEST CHURCH TRADITIONS ABOUT THE DATE OF REVELATION

When dealing with matters of date, external evidence also plays an important role, and here the early church tradition is virtually unanimous—Revelation was written during the reign of Emperor Domitian. Irenaeus (ca. AD 130–202) locates John's banishment and his apocalyptic visions toward the end of Domitian's reign:

> We will not, however, incur the risk of pronouncing positively as to the name of Antichrist; for if it were necessary that his name should be distinctly revealed in this present time, it would have been announced by him who beheld the apocalyptic vision. For that was seen no very long time since, but almost in our day, towards the end of Domitian's reign.[70]

Irenaeus's testimony should be taken seriously given his relationship with Polycarp, bishop of Smyrna (Irenaeus's hometown), who claimed to have known the apostle John.[71] Numerous other early church leaders also place the writing of Revelation during the reign of Domitian, including Clement of Alexandria (ca. 150–215), Origen (ca. 185–254), Eusebius (ca. 260–340), Victorinus (d. 304) and Jerome (ca. 354–420).[72] Those favoring an early date point to the prefaces of the Old Syriac versions of the Apocalypse (sixth century?) and of Theophylact of Bulgaria (twelfth century) as evidence that John was exiled during the reign of Nero.[73]

3.10 CONCLUSION

Good arguments can be made for both the early and late dates for the writing of Revelation. The choice as to date does not affect the overall interpretive approach or theology of the book in a major way.

As we have looked carefully at the key pieces of internal evidence, we have seen

70. *Haer.* 5.30.3. Eusebius (ca. AD 260–340) concurs by favorably quoting Irenaeus in *Hist. eccl.* 3.18.1–3; 5.8.6.

71. See Eusebius, *Hist. eccl.* 14.3–8; 5.20.4–8; Guthrie, *New Testament Introduction*, 269–70; Paul, *Revelation*, 13. Schaff and Wace observe that if John had been banished during Nero's reign rather than Domitian's, then we have "the remarkable phenomenon of an event taking place at an earlier date than that assigned it by tradition, an exceptional and inexplicable thing. We have too the difficulty of accounting for the erroneousness of so early and unanimous a tradition" (*NPNF*^{2} 1:148).

72. Clement of Alexandria, *Quis div.* 42; Origen, *Fr. Matt.* 16.6. Clement and Origen date Revelation to the reign of "the tyrant," likely referring to Domitian. See also Eusebius, *Hist. eccl.* 3.1–3; Victorinus et al., *Latin Commentaries*, 13–14, 17; Jerome, *Vir. ill.* 9. Victorinus of Petovium, the first to write a commentary on Revelation, perhaps as early as AD 258, concludes: "When John saw this revelation, he was on the island of Patmos, having been condemned to the mines by Caesar Domitian. There, it seems, John wrote the Revelation." See Victorinus et al., *Latin Commentaries*, 13.

73. Theophylact of Bulgaria, *Praef. In Ioann.* Yet Köstenberger, Kellum, and Quarles, *Cradle, Cross, and Crown*, 941, note that in *Fr. Matt.* 20:22 Theophylact says John wrote during the reign of Trajan.

the scales tip in favor of the late date, around AD 95 during the reign of Domitian. To begin with, Revelation reflects a situation where Christians are being persecuted to a limited degree with the expectation that the trials could quickly intensify. This kind of selective persecution in Asia Minor fits better with Domitian than with Nero, who systematically and viciously persecuted Christians in Rome. The pressure under Domitian was felt most keenly in Ephesus, Smyrna, and Pergamum, places of Roman civil and religious power centered around the imperial cult. The more developed condition of the Asian churches in the late first century makes better sense of the internal evidence. In addition, the use of the Nero myth and the name "Babylon" better supports the later date. The reference to the temple in Rev 11:1–2 does not provide clear evidence for dating the book, and the reference to the seven kings in 17:9–11 supports the early date only if a historical reconstruction is the preferred way of reading this text. When looking at external evidence, the early church tradition overwhelmingly favors the late date.

The issue of date is closely tied to authorship, as Wilson observes.[74] We accept the early external testimony of Irenaeus in both cases. A later date also fits well, perhaps even better, with the internal evidence. To sum up, our conclusion is that the writing of Revelation dates to the time of Domitian (ca. AD 95), and this conclusion is consistent with early and well-attested external evidence in addition to a critical mass of internal evidence.

74. Mark Wilson, "Early Christians in Ephesus," 164–65, although in siding with Irenaeus in both cases, we are siding with the scholarly majority on date and with the minority on authorship.

Chapter 4

THE OCCASION AND PURPOSE OF REVELATION

BIBLIOGRAPHY

Bandy, Alan S. "Persecution and the Purpose of Revelation with Reference to Roman Jurisprudence." *BBR* 23.3 (2013): 377–98. ———. *The Prophetic Lawsuit in the Book of Revelation.* NTMon 29. Sheffield: Sheffield Phoenix, 2010. **Barclay, John M. G.** *Jews in the Mediterranean Diaspora from Alexander to Trajan (323 BCE–117 CE).* Edinburgh: T&T Clark, 1996. **Barr, David.** *Tales of the End: A Narrative Commentary on the Book of Revelation.* Santa Rosa, CA: Polebridge, 1998. **Beagley, Alan J.** *The "Sitz im Leben" of the Apocalypse with Particular Reference to the Role of the Church's Enemies.* BZNW 50. Berlin: de Gruyter, 1987. **Boxall, Ian.** *Patmos in the Reception History of the Apocalypse.* Oxford: Oxford University Press, 2013. ———. "Reading the Apocalypse on the Island of Patmos." *ScrB* 40 (2010): 22–33. **Carroll, Scott T.** "Patmos (Place)." Pages 178–79 in *ABD*. Edited by David Noel Freedman. New York: Doubleday, 1992. **De Jonge, Henk Jan.** "The Apocalypse of John and the Imperial Cult." Pages 127–41 in *KYKEON: Studies in Honour of H. S. Versnel.* Edited by H. F. J. Horstmanshoff. Leiden: Brill, 2002. **DeSilva, David A.** "Honor Discourse and the Rhetorical Strategy of the Apocalypse of John." *JSNT* 71 (1998): 79–110. ———. "The Social Setting of the Revelation to John: Fears Within, Conflicts Without." *WTJ* 54 (1992): 273–302. ———. *Unholy Allegiances: Heeding Revelation's Warning.* Peabody, MA: Hendrickson, 2013. **Downing, F. Gerald.** "Pliny's Prosecutions of Christians: Revelation and 1 Peter." *JSNT* 11 (1988): 105–23. **Duff, Paul B.** *Who Rides the Beast? Prophetic Rivalry and the Rhetoric of Crisis in the Churches of the Apocalypse.* Oxford: Oxford University Press, 2001. **Dunn, James D. G.**, ed. *Jews and Christians: The Parting of the Ways, 70–135 A.D.* Grand Rapids: Eerdmans, 1999. **Duvall, J. Scott.** "Revelation: The Transforming Vision." Page 255–77 in C. Marvin Pate et al., *The Story of Israel: A Biblical Theology.* Downers Grove, IL: InterVarsity Press, 2004. **Friesen, Steven J.** "Satan's Throne, Imperial Cults and the Social Settings of Revelation." *JSNT* 27.3 (2005): 351–73. **Harland, Philip A.** "Honouring the Emperor or Assailing the Beast: Participation in Civic Life among Associations (Jewish, Christian and Other) in Asia Minor and the Apocalypse of John." *JSNT* 22 (2000): 99–121. **Kraybill, J. Nelson.** *Imperial Cult and Commerce in John's Apocalypse.* JSNTSup 127. Sheffield: Sheffield Academic, 1996.

Maier, Harry O. *Apocalypse Recalled: The Book of Revelation after Christendom.* Minneapolis: Fortress, 2002. **Mayo, Philip L.** *"Those Who Call Themselves Jews": The Church and Judaism in the Apocalypse of John.* PTMS 60. Eugene, OR: Pickwick, 2006. **Price, Simon R. F.** *Rituals and Power: The Roman Imperial Cult in Asia Minor.* Cambridge: Cambridge University Press, 1984. **Ramsay, William M.** *The Letters to the Seven Churches.* Edited and updated by Mark Wilson. Peabody, MA: Hendrickson, 1994. **Royalty, Robert.** *The Streets of Heaven: The Ideology of Wealth in the Apocalypse of John.* Macon, GA: Mercer University Press, 1998. **Schüssler Fiorenza, Elizabeth.** *The Book of Revelation: Justice and Judgment.* Philadelphia: Fortress, 1985. **Thompson, Leonard.** *The Book of Revelation: Apocalypse and Empire.* Oxford: Oxford University Press, 1990. **Tonstad, Sigve K.** *Revelation.* Paideia. Grand Rapids: Baker Academic, 2019. **Yarbro Collins, Adela.** *Crisis and Catharsis: The Power of the Apocalypse.* Philadelphia: Westminster, 1984.

4.1 INTRODUCTION

So much of the "answer" that is the book of Revelation finds meaning in the "question" that is the book's historical context. In this section we will explore John's historical situation to get a better grasp of how the author's context may have shaped his writing. We will investigate the occasion that called for Revelation, most especially the setting of the churches in Asia Minor and the surrounding society. In this interplay between the book's prophetic-apocalyptic message and the religious and social forces at work in that culture, we begin to see why the church desperately needed (and continues to need) to hear and heed the words of this prophecy. We will attempt to sort out the nature of persecution faced by these churches and the extent to which they were tempted to adjust the faith to accommodate to their pagan surroundings. Finally, in light of the historical situation, we will consider John's purpose in writing.

4.2 JOHN'S SITUATION

John introduces his vision with these words: "I, John, your brother and companion in the suffering and kingdom and patient endurance that are ours in Jesus, was on the island of Patmos because of the word of God and the testimony of Jesus" (1:9). Several items deserve attention, and we begin with the place. Patmos is a tiny volcanic island in the Aegean Sea off the coast of Asia Minor, measuring almost thirty miles in circumference. It was one of the Sporades Islands located about forty miles west of Miletus and almost sixty miles southwest of ancient Ephesus. The three islands of Patmos, Lipsos, and Leros were designated the "fortresses" (φρούρια) of Miletus and protected the city on the Aegean side. In the first century, Patmos was populated by an army garrison from Miletus and included other civic features such as a gymnasium and a temple.[1] Boxall notes that Patmos was heavily influenced by Miletus, where the goddess Artemis along with her brother Apollo and mother Leto were influential religious figures.[2] Consequently, we should not imagine John alone on a nearly deserted island.

According to early church tradition, John was exiled during the reign of Domitian to Patmos. There he experienced the prophetic vision and lived in exile until Domitian's death, at which time he returned to Ephesus.[3] Roman prisoners and rebels were often exiled, and these three islands in the Sporades were ideal spots for banishment.[4] John reports that he was on Patmos "because (διά) of the word of God and the testimony of Jesus" (1:9). The use of the preposition διά with the accusative case in Revelation always expresses "cause" or "reason" and here indicates that his exile was punishment for proclaiming the gospel.[5] The terms "suffering" or "tribulation" (θλῖψις) and "patient endurance" (ὑπομονή) used earlier in verse 9 make clear that John did not travel to Patmos to evangelize or even to receive the revelation but rather found himself there as a consequence of staying faithful to the Christian message.

John was probably exiled for political reasons stemming from legal punishment. There were two types of banishment. Those facing a permanent sentence (*deportatio*) could also experience a loss of rights such as citizenship and property. Others faced a less severe and temporary sentence (*relegatio*).[6] Tertullian refers to John's exile as an *insulam relegatur* ("banishment to an island"), likely referring to a temporary exile.[7] Provincial governors held the power to enact such a punishment. The most likely scenario is that John came into conflict with the provincial authorities by refusing to conform to the local imperial cult worship practices. He could have been denounced before authorities by one of the opposition groups mentioned in the seven messages and, as a result, he was banished to Patmos.[8] As Irenaeus says, John was later released and lived into the reign of Trajan (AD 98–117).[9]

1. Aune, *Revelation 1–5*, 76–77, who notes that an inscription from the second century AD "reveals the presence of a cult and temple of Artemis on Patmos, complete with a public feast, a procession, and the recitation of hymns in honor of the goddess."

2. See Ian Boxall, "Reading the Apocalypse on the Island of Patmos," *ScrB* 40 (2010): 22–33, and his more comprehensive work, *Patmos in the Reception History of the Apocalypse* (Oxford: Oxford University Press, 2013). Boxall notes that in archaeological and inscriptional evidence, Delos, west of Patmos is remembered as the birthplace of Apollo, and Patmos is associated with Apollo's sister, Artemis, as "the most illustrious island of the daughter of Leto" (*Patmos in the Reception History*, 19, 233).

3. Eusebius, *Hist. eccl.* 3.18–20, 23; Pliny, *Nat.* 4.23; Irenaeus, *Haer.* 5.30.3; Jerome, *Vir. ill.* 9; Clement of Alexandria, *Quis div.* 42; Origen, *Comm. Matt.* 16.6; Victorinus et al., *Latin Commentaries*, 13–14, 17.

4. Scott T. Carroll, "Patmos (Place)" *ABD* 1:179.

5. Alan S. Bandy, "Persecution and the Purpose of Revelation with Reference to Roman Jurisprudence," *BBR* 23.3 (2013): 381. For διά with the accusative of cause, see Rev 1:9; 2:3; 4:11; 6:9; 7:15; 12:11, 12; 13:14; 17:7; 18:8, 10, 15; 20:4). The combination of "word" and "testimony" occurs in 1:2 in connection with the prophetic vision itself and in 6:9 and 20:4 explaining why the martyrs had been slain.

6. Bandy, "Persecution," 382; Aune, *Revelation 1–5*, 79.

7. Tertullian, *Praescr.* 36.

8. Bandy, "Persecution," 383. Bandy (pp. 383–87) observes that later when Pliny writes to Trajan to get advice about how to prosecute Christians, he notes that he had heard of such procedures for trying Christians at least twenty years earlier, during the reign of Domitian (Pliny, *Ep.* 10.96.6–7). And although Pliny did not have firsthand knowledge of prior procedures against Christians, this is not proof that such practices did not exist.

9. Irenaeus, *Haer.* 2.22.5.

John's setting on Patmos likely affected how he processed the visionary experience. Whether Patmos was just the location for John's vision and he later penned the Apocalypse from the mainland or whether he both experienced the vision and wrote while on Patmos, the island context would have provided at least some raw material for his prophetic imagination.[10] This could still be true while holding simultaneously that "the operative *Sitz im Leben* is that of the churches in Asia."[11] Multiple inscriptions indicate the strong presence of the Artemis cult on the island.[12] Along with the imperial cult, traditional polytheism formed an important part of the worldview that John fiercely opposed. Perhaps the most significant influence for John from Patmos would have been his experience as an exiled prophet. This surely heightened his awareness of the history of God's people and their prophets in exile (e.g., the Babylonian exile and Ezekiel and Daniel as exiled prophets). We see the prophetic influence of Ezekiel and Daniel even in John's introductory statement of 1:9.[13]

John's exile on Patmos falls in line with previous prophetic exiles. In addition, the Old Testament consistently associates islands with the "nations," which also plays into the contrast in Revelation between pagan empires and God's kingdom.[14]

4.3 THE OCCASION

4.3.1 The Composition of the Churches

John addresses his prophetic-apocalyptic letter to seven specific congregations in Asia Minor.[15]

Ephesus was the port of entry to the mainland of the province of Asia, and the rest of the seven churches were located in a circular route through the interior. Hemer notes that these seven cities had by this time acquired importance as "organizational and distributive centres for the church of the area."[16] Bauckham sees Revelation as a circular letter "probably named in the order in which a messenger would visit them starting from Patmos and travelling on a circular route around the province of Asia."[17] The messages

10. David Barr, *Tales of the End: A Narrative Commentary on the Book of Revelation* (Santa Rosa, CA: Polebridge, 1998), 62, interestingly describes islands as "transitional places," participating in both land and sea without belonging completely to either, so that a journey from "ordinary reality" to "transhistorical reality" seems appropriate.

11. Hemer, *Letters to the Seven Churches*, 29.

12. Boxall, "Reading the Apocalypse," 24–27.

13. See the chart on p. 15 of Boxall, *Patmos in the Reception History*, comparing the formal features of Rev 1:9–11, Ezek 1:1–4, and Dan 10:2–5.

14. Boxall, *Patmos in the Reception History*, 17–18, who briefly presents the biblical uses of νῆσος in the Old Testament.

15. The attempt to take the local setting seriously in reading the book has been led especially by William M. Ramsay, *The Letters to the Seven Churches* (London: Hodder and Stoughton, 1904); Hemer, *Letters to the Seven Churches of Asia*; and Jeffrey A. D. Weima, *The Sermons to the Seven Churches of Revelation: A Commentary and Guide* (Grand Rapids: Baker Academic, 2021). Mark Wilson has edited and updated the Ramsay volume in W. M. Ramsay, *The Letters to the Seven Churches*, updated ed. (Peabody, MA: Hendrickson, 1994).

16. Hemer, *Letters to the Seven Churches*, 15. He notes that "the use of the article in ταῖς ἑπτὰ ἐκκλησίαις (Rev. 1:4) . . . implies that the grouping was recognized, but not necessarily that these were the only churches in the province."

17. Bauckham, *Theology*, 12.

vary from church to church but should not be viewed as seven independent letters. Rather, these seven messages form a lengthy introduction to the rest of the book. In addition, the number seven indicates completeness and Bauckham rightly concludes that "by addressing seven churches John indicates that his message is addressed to specific churches as *representative* of *all* the churches."[18]

These Christian communities were likely mixed, composed of some followers of Jesus from a Jewish background with the majority coming from a gentile background.[19] No doubt some from the gentile background had been previously associated with the Jewish synagogue as well. These churches would have met in homes and been less than about forty in number. Of course, we would expect multiple house churches in most of the cities. Some subgroups within these communities would have developed their own identities that sometimes presented social and theological challenges to the primary identities of the church (e.g., the Nicolaitans and the followers of Jezebel and Balaam). Many Christians, both Jew and gentile, likely participated in the civic life of these cities (at least to some degree) through involvement in trade guilds, associations, civic networks, business endeavors, and entertainment.[20] As Koester says, "Christian communities faced the challenge of maintaining their distinctive beliefs and identity while their members lived and worked in Greco-Roman society."[21] The specific challenges centered around the complex interrelationships of politics, economics, and religion in that society. Another layer adding to the complexity was the relationship between the synagogue and the church and the resulting tensions among the followers of Jesus.

4.3.2 The Churches and the Surrounding Society

4.3.2.1 Traditional Religions and the Imperial Cult

Traditional Greco-Roman deities such as Zeus, Asclepius, Artemis, Dionysius, and Athena were worshiped widely throughout Asia, and devotees were not limited to just one particular god. Loyalties were not exclusive. Price describes the scene during the first three centuries AD in Asia Minor as a complex and powerful relationship of religion, politics, and power. "The imperial cult," he writes, "along with politics and diplomacy [and we might add, the Roman military], constructed the reality of the Roman empire."[22] To be sure, the worship of the emperor mixed and mingled with the worship of traditional deities. This reinforced the belief that Roman rule was being

18. Bauckham, *Theology*, 16, emphasis original.

19. This summary is drawn primarily from Koester, *Revelation*, 86–91.

20. For a full discussion, see Philip A. Harland, "Honouring the Emperor or Assailing the Beast: Participation in Civic Life among Associations (Jewish, Christian and Other) in Asia Minor and the Apocalypse of John," *JSNT* 77 (2000): 99–121.

21. Koester, *Revelation*, 93.

22. Price, *Rituals and Power*, 1, 248. Price has a revealing series of maps detailing the location (and thus widespread influence) of imperial altars, temples, priests, and non-imperial temples and theaters in Asia Minor (*Rituals and Power*, xxi–xxvi).

blessed by the gods.[23] Rome had been divinely chosen to bring the rule of law, peace, and well-being to the world and Rome was personified in her emperor.

Religious devotion was bolstered by a whole series of cultural institutions, landmarks, and practices. Many cities competed for permission to build shrines, altars, and temples dedicated to certain deities or emperors.[24] A temple dedicated to Augustus and the goddess Roma was erected in Pergamum in 29 BC. In AD 26 during the reign of Tiberius a second provincial imperial temple was built in Smyrna. A third imperial temple to the Flavian emperors was built in Ephesus during the reign of Domitian (ca. AD 89). By the end of the first century, thirty-five cities in Asia Minor possessed the title of "temple warden" (νεωκόρος) of an imperial cult site.[25] All seven of the churches in Revelation had cultic sites, with six (all but Thyatira) having an imperial temple and five (all but Philadelphia and Laodicea) having imperial altars and priests.[26] In addition, there were various kinds of shrines and sanctuaries and altars and icons that evoked divine attributes of the Roman emperor far beyond what a personal appearance of the emperor could have accomplished.[27]

Imperial images played an important role in the culture of the seven churches. Images appeared consistently on coins to remind citizens of the power and influence of Rome and her gods. Numismatics reinforced almost every aspect of Roman ideology—the peace of Rome, the divine emperors, military power, the relationship between the emperors and the traditional gods, worship rituals such as animal sacrifices, landmarks such as the Roman Coliseum, the goddess Roma, and so on. People were also surrounded by other images such as inscriptions, paintings, and busts or statues. Some of the statues could be quite large, such as the statue of Domitian (or perhaps Titus) in the temple of the "revered ones" (*sebastoi*) at Ephesus that stood almost eight meters tall. Inscriptions honoring emperors and public figures were located throughout the cities and reinforced the need for public devotion to these powerful figures. These in essence functioned as public literary images of the empire. Sensory images such as incense, lamps, speeches, and music added another layer to the pervasive influence of the imperial cult.[28]

Along with fixed displays of the imperial cult and traditional religions, people participated in religious festivals and celebrations. Price refers to imperial festivals as "the key manifestation of the cult in action" and "the essential framework of the imperial

23. For a clear introduction to the "public story" or worldview of the society in which the seven churches lived, see "Chapter 2—Divine Emperor, Eternal Rome: The Public Story about Roman Imperialism" in David A. deSilva, *Unholy Allegiances: Heeding Revelation's Warning* (Peabody, MA: Hendrickson, 2013).

24. Mark Wilson, *Charts on the Book of Revelation*, 115, shows a map of the imperial cult temples of Asia Minor.

25. Price, *Rituals and Power*, 66–67.

26. David A. deSilva, *Seeing Things John's Way: The Rhetoric of the Book of Revelation* (Louisville: Westminister John Knox, 2009), 41.

27. Leonard Thompson, *Book of Revelation*, 162–63.

28. J. Nelson Kraybill, *Apocalypse and Allegiance: Worship, Politics, and Devotion in the Book of Revelation* (Grand Rapids: Brazos, 2010), 60, notes that "music was a prime index of praise in the emperor cult."

cult."[29] Religion came alive in these communal celebrations, which included lavish ritual dress, processions through the city with people carrying images and busts of important political and religious figures, choirs, hymn singing, sacrifices, and athletic games. The whole city would participate in these events, and they often lasted for several days. What is more, they were repeated throughout the year in a regular cycle of celebrations.[30] The Roman Empire was very religious indeed, and it was certainly expected that everyone would participate in these public rituals since they demonstrated support for the emperor and the rule of Rome. Such pagan extravaganzas troubled Christians and their general response was to withdraw. In the late second century Tertullian characterized such spectacles as idolatrous and demonic and strongly urged Christians to avoid them.[31] The book of Revelation seems to agree. This supplies the context, at least in part, to the conflict within some of the seven churches and Jesus's rebuke of certain groups (e.g., the Nicolaitans and the followers of Jezebel and Balaam).

Trade guilds and local associations also flourished, and normally included a religious dimension through devotion to a specific deity. Guilds were, according to Hemer, religiously based, rooted in the local community, and persistent in their influence.[32] Guilds were formed around crafts and industries such as woolworkers, leatherworkers, fullers and dyers, parchment production, coppersmiths, silversmiths, woodworkers, physicians, teachers, architects, builders, tanners, potters, lawyers, entertainers, and more.[33] Normally each trade guild had a patron deity, and guild meetings often involved meals, banquets, and other rituals that paid homage to their patron deities as well as to the Roman emperor. The unusually strong presence of trade guilds in Thyatira provides the primary background for that letter. The influential woman Jezebel likely argued that Christians could join trade guilds and participate in their (often idolatrous and immoral) activities without compromising the faith. But when Christians separated from expected routines in society such as participating in trade guild activities, most people would have viewed such a retreat as "unpatriotic and atheistic," resulting in investigation, harassment, or persecution (e.g., John's exile and Antipas's death?).[34]

To say that first-century Asia Minor was an irreligious environment would be a huge mistake. Rather, it was extremely religious, and this setting affected almost every dimension of life, from the images people repeatedly saw to the institutions they interacted with to the powers they worshiped. Revelation was written to people thoroughly immersed in a religious milieu with enormous political, economic, and social consequences. There was no separation of "church" and state in the first-century Roman world.

29. Price, *Rituals and Power*, 101–2.

30. Price, *Rituals and Power*, 101–32.

31. Tertullian, *Spect.* 13–17; *Idol.* 13, 15.

32. Hemer, *The Letters to the Seven Churches*, 108–9.

33. Leonard Thompson, *Book of Revelation*, 152–54.

34. Michael J. Gorman, *Reading Revelation Responsibly: Uncivil Worship and Witness: Following the Lamb into the New Creation* (Eugene, OR: Cascade, 2011), 32.

4.3.2.2 Economic Prosperity Associated with Idolatry and Complacency

Rome was characterized as an empire of ostentatiousness and consumption.[35] John describes the Roman economic system as luxurious (e.g., Rev 18:3, 7, 9—with terms such as στρῆνος, στρηνιάω, and πλουτέω). Rome's consumerism extended its imperial reach into the provinces where natural resources were plentiful and goods were produced. This allowed people in those regions to partner with Rome, become wealthy, and raise their social status (e.g., the merchants and ship owners mentioned in Rev 18:3, 15 as those who "grew rich" or "gained their wealth"). But such prosperity came at a high price. One consequence was to drain the provinces of their natural resources and inflate prices (e.g., Rev 6:5–6 refers to this gross price inflation). Yet an even more lethal effect was the spiritually seductive power of Rome's wealth. Christians were sometimes lulled into complacency and accommodation with pagan culture through material attachment. Kraybill observes that the "urgent message of Revelation is that idolatry not only pervades the political and economic structures of the Empire but has also taken root within the churches of Asia Minor."[36]

This seems to be the chief problem at Laodicea where numerous Christians had "acquired wealth" and "become rich" (πλουτέω in 3:17–18). Perhaps surprisingly to them, Jesus says they are, in reality, "wretched, pitiful, *poor*, blind and naked" (3:17, emphasis added). The Laodiceans are "living on the surface, a superficial life, without a sense of the deep struggle that is going on."[37] In contrast, he reassures the materially poor Christians in Smyrna, "I know your afflictions and your poverty—yet you are *rich*!" (2:9, emphasis added).

Participating in the Roman economic system also meant joining in Rome's idolatrous religious practices, illustrated through a number of cultural arrangements (e.g., the temple of Artemis in Ephesus also served as the principal bank of the province of Asia).[38] The pursuit of wealth encouraged religious adultery since the very pursuit included the worship of other gods, including the emperor. Kraybill concludes:

> Here in the realm of harbors, guild halls, trade offices and banks we find mundane expression of what John saw as Roman arrogance, greed and idolatry. In the sphere of economic activity John found a virulent hybrid of materialism, social pressure and imperial cult that threatened the very essence of Christian faith.[39]

35. See the thorough treatment of the economic context in Kraybill, *Imperial Cult and Commerce*, 17. Kraybill reminds us that John was not against commerce and trade in itself but rather is warning "*Christians to sever or to avoid economic and political ties with Rome because institutions and structures of the Roman Empire were saturated with unholy allegiance to an Emperor who claimed to be divine (or was treated as such)*" (emphasis original).

36. Kraybill, *Imperial Cult and Commerce*, 38.

37. Yarbro Collins, *Crisis and Catharsis*, 132, Cf. deSilva, *Seeing Things John's Way*, 47.

38. DeSilva, *Seeing Things John's Way*, 47–48. DeSilva writes (p. 48), "Roman imperialism, with its seductive economy and blasphemous imperial cult, is the main challenge John identifies in Revelation 4–22."

39. Kraybill, *Imperial Cult and Commerce*, 102.

The trade guilds also reinforced the link between economic prosperity and idolatry. Christians' refusal to participate in the guild's immoral and idolatrous activities often led to their being excluded from the guild, resulting in the forfeiture of a trade and its income. As Keener says, to withdraw from the guilds was in many cities "economic suicide."[40]

A thorough reading of Revelation leads to the conclusion that spiritual apathy and compromise constitute one of the central problems facing the Christians of Asia Minor, and much of this stems from the partnership between economic prosperity and idolatry. Koester also notes that the pursuit of wealth undermines the cohesiveness of the Christian community as some members become more devoted to acquiring wealth, causing loyalties to their faith community to fade.[41]

4.3.3 Conflict and Compromise

4.3.3.1 Pressure and Persecution

The book of Revelation is a prophetic-apocalyptic response to a crisis. The key question is, What is the nature and extent of this crisis? And, as you might expect, on this question interpreters disagree. The issue of persecution (or lack of persecution) matters because it colors our understanding of the situation behind the book as well as John's response.[42] The leading options are as follows:[43]

- There was no crisis, real or perceived. Christians were simply not singled out for persecution by either civic or Roman authorities.[44]
- Hostility was more of a perceived crisis rather than an absolute or objective crisis. These Christians were not actually oppressed. Rather, they felt oppressed.[45]
- There was some persecution under Domitian as articulated in Revelation and other New Testament writings, but the evidence from official Roman historiography is weak.[46]
- The crisis related more to compromise with the all-powerful Roman system rather than persecution per se.[47]
- The crisis resulted not from without, whether from Rome or the Jews, but from within the churches themselves due to prophetic rivalry.[48]
- There was a real crisis, due both to pressure from Rome, especially related to the imperial cult, and to Jewish opposition. This persecution, however, was

40. Keener, *Revelation*, 353.

41. Koester, *Revelation*, 103.

42. Osborne, *Revelation*, 10.

43. See Paul B. Duff, *Who Rides the Beast? Prophetic Rivalry and the Rhetoric of Crisis in the Churches of the Apocalypse* (New York: Oxford University Press, 2001), 5–14; Sigve K. Tonstad, *Revelation*, Paideia (Grand Rapids: Baker Academic, 2019), 8–29.

44. Leonard Thompson, *Book of Revelation*.

45. Yarbro Collins, *Crisis and Catharsis*, 84–107.

46. Schüssler Fiorenza, *Book of Revelation*, 8.

47. Kraybill, *Imperial Cult and Commerce*; Kraybill. *Apocalypse and Allegiance*.

48. Robert Royalty, *The Streets of Heaven: The Ideology of Wealth in the Apocalypse of John* (Macon, GA: Mercer University Press, 1998); also, Duff, *Who Rides the Beast?*

> not systematic or widespread, although the threat of impending intensification persisted. In addition, the earthly situation should be seen in light of the larger reality of the cosmic conflict between God and the forces of evil. In this sense Revelation should be seen as a timeless prophetic narrative.[49]

We believe the final option best summarizes the actual situation. We have previously catalogued references to pressure and persecution within the book itself (see 3.2). But regarding the specifics, Koester helps by identifying three main levels of hostility, all of which were local and sporadic.[50] First, Christians encountered verbal harassment due to their beliefs and way of life. Second, Christians were denounced before the Roman authorities as troublemakers, leading to more formal investigations. Third, hostility sometimes rose to the level of arrest, interrogation, and sentencing, including imprisonment and even death.

Koester observes that believers at Philadelphia were likely experiencing the first level of hostility due to harassment by members of a local synagogue, with the threat of second-level persecution hanging over them. The Christians at Smyrna, however, were facing second-level hostility. Both Antipas (death) and John (banishment) suffered at the final level.

We have already seen how the Roman imperial cult provided a major source of hostility toward Christians (see 4.3.2). Revelation also stresses the Jewish community in Asia Minor as another significant source of opposition. It is helpful to remember that the first Christians were Jewish, and that Christianity grew out of Judaism. Jews had lived in Asia Minor since the second, perhaps even the third century BC.[51] Christians and Jews had much in common over against their Greco-Roman neighbors: they worshiped the God of Israel, shared the Jewish Scriptures, and rejected the idolatry and immorality common in most cities. They differed regarding their meeting place (the συναγωγή vs. the ἐκκλησία), their day of worship (the sabbath vs. the first day of the week), and certain practices such as circumcision, food laws, and sabbath observances. But most significantly, they differed regarding the identity and importance of Jesus as Messiah, though the churches in Asia Minor certainly included non-Jewish followers of Jesus as well.

When Judaism and Christianity officially split in Asia Minor is a complicated question.[52] There were many factors involved in the separation, and it seems to have

49. With some variation among scholars, this is the leading evangelical option. See, e.g., Osborne, *Revelation*, 10–12; Beale, *Revelation*, 28–33; deSilva, *Seeing Things John's Way*, 37–59; Witherington, *Revelation*, 5–10; Bandy, "Persecution."

50. Koester, *Revelation*, 96–98. It is important to remember that the "levels" are for the purposes of describing the situation and do not represent the trauma persecution would have brought at any level. Verbal abuse can be just as cruel and damaging as imprisonment.

51. John M. G. Barclay, *Jews in the Mediterranean Diaspora from Alexander to Trajan (323 BCE–117 CE)*. Edinburgh: T&T Clark, 1996.

52. See James D. G. Dunn, ed., *Jews and Christians: The Parting of the Ways, 70–135 A.D.* (Grand Rapids: Eerdmans, 1999).

happened for good by the early part of the second century,[53] but our concern here is with the nature of Jewish hostility toward Jesus followers in the seven churches of Asia Minor. Believers in Smyrna and Philadelphia were experiencing persecution originating to some degree from the local Jewish community. In the letter to Smyrna, Jesus speaks about his followers encountering the "slander of those who say they are Jews and are not, but are a synagogue of Satan" (2:9), while in Philadelphia he refers to "the synagogue of Satan who say that they are Jews and are not, but lie" (3:9, ESV).

A number of scholars see a connection between Jesus's statements in these messages and the results of the temple's destruction in AD 70, after which the emperor demanded that the annual Jerusalem temple tax be diverted to the temple of Jupiter Capitolinus in Rome.[54] By cooperating, the Jews in Asia Minor could maintain their status as *religio licita* ("legal religion") and enjoy the accompanying freedoms (e.g., exemption from pagan cults and freedom to practice their own religion). But such cooperation came at a high price. The money that once supported the worship of Yahweh would now sustain pagan worship in Rome (i.e., a synagogue now supporting Satan by contributing to Caesar or a "synagogue of Satan"?).[55] But what is the specific connection to the persecution of Christians?

Jews in Asia Minor walked a thin line between living as faithful Jews and catering to Roman power. Increasingly, Jews found the Christian movement to be a hindrance to maintaining this delicate balance. With Christians swearing allegiance to Jesus as Lord (rather than Caesar), Jews began to realize the religious, economic, and political advantages of disassociating themselves from this offshoot movement that could jeopardize their standing with Rome.

Consequently, by notifying the authorities that Christians were not in fact Jews, the status of those Jews was not compromised. Cooperating with the Roman authorities by informing on this minority movement of Jesus followers is likely what is meant by the term "slander" (βλασφημία) that describes the pseudo-synagogue in 2:9.[56] Informers were designated *delatores* (denouncers or accusers) who would formulate an *accusatio* (accusation), allowing the Romans to prosecute the case. When these Jews notified the pagan magistrates that these Christians were not Jews, the Christians would become vulnerable to the accusation of atheism (from a Roman point of view) since they were unwilling to worship the local gods. Hemer notes that Jews informing against Christians may partially explain the "book of life" reference in the letter to

53. See Philip L. Mayo, *"Those Who Call Themselves Jews": The Church and Judaism in the Apocalypse of John*, PTMS (Eugene, OR: Pickwick, 2006), esp. 27–76.

54. Josephus, *J.W.* 7.6.6, §218; deSilva, *Seeing Things John's Way*, 56–58; Kraybill, *Imperial Cult and Commerce*, 183–84.

55. DeSilva, *Seeing Things John's Way*, 56.

56. deSilva, *Seeing Things John's Way*, 57–58; Hemer, *Letters to the Seven Churches*, 9–10; Mayo, *"Those Who Call Themselves Jews,"* 34–36, 65–67; Bandy, "Persecution," 389; Keener, *Revelation*, 116; Witherington, *Revelation*, 100–101; Beale, *Revelation*, 240; Koester, *Revelation*, 274.

Sardis (3:5)—synagogues may have provided lists of their bona fide members to the authorities, thus excluding Christians.[57] Bandy reminds us that "Jewish hostilities against Christians expressed in the form of legal denunciation commonly occurred in the early church" (e.g., the martyrdom of Stephen, Paul's persecution of the church, the persecution Paul endured as a Christian, and the martyrdom of Polycarp).[58] This scenario best explains the context of Christian persecution addressed in Revelation.

4.3.3.2 The Temptation to Compromise

When the conversation shifts to the book of Revelation in popular circles, almost always the focus turns to persecution (or escape from persecution) but rarely to the subject of compromise with the prevailing culture. Yet, perhaps surprisingly, the messages to the seven churches place more emphasis on compromise than on persecution. As Maier puts it, "the problem the Apocalypse addresses is not too much persecution, but too little."[59] As we have seen in this chapter, the three main threats facing these believers included (1) the fear of being accused before the Roman authorities (often by Jews) and the negative consequences to follow (e.g., exile, imprisonment, death), (2) the enticement of material prosperity connected to partnership with the Roman system and the resulting spiritual complacency, and (3) the seduction of false teaching by professed believers that assured adherents they could remain faithful to Jesus *and* simultaneously enjoy the benefits of the world system. Hemer argues that "Christians in Asia faced a dilemma in which their safety [not only personal but also economic and social] was assured only by accommodation either to pagan society or to Judaism."[60] Beale astutely observes a chiastic structure in the presentation of the situation of the seven churches: the first and last are on the verge of losing their Christian identity (2:5; 3:16), the second and sixth are standing firm with no weaknesses, while the third, fourth, and fifth are in a mixed condition with some commendation and some criticism. This structure reveals that the churches are faced with "the challenge of witnessing in the midst of temptations to compromise with idolatry."[61]

Throughout the book John warns his readers against the idolatrous nature of secular power, against partnering with the pagan world, and against compromising the faith in order to gain personal wealth and security. The lure of compromise came most forcefully from the false teachers who claimed to be genuine believers. They claimed to have access to deep spiritual realities, which John labels "Satan's so-called deep secrets" in 2:24.[62] Most scholars view the named groups in the seven messages as false teachers

57. Hemer, *Letters to the Seven Churches*, 9–10, and n23.

58. Bandy, "Persecution," 389.

59. Harry O. Maier, *Apocalypse Recalled: The Book of Revelation after Christendom* (Minneapolis: Fortress, 2002), xiii, 34.

60. Hemer, *Letters to the Seven Churches*, 92.

61. Beale, *Revelation*, 32–33.

62. Beale, *Revelation*, 265: "This expression implies the view that it was possible for Christians to participate to some degree in idolatrous situations, thus having some experience with the demonic-satanic realm, and yet not be harmed spiritually by such participation."

who urged accommodation to pagan society: Jezebel and her followers (2:20–24), and the Balaamites and Nicolaitans (2:6, 14–15). There appears to be a connection between the false teachers and the participation in idolatrous and immoral meals and feasts, all undergirded by economic concerns.[63] Whether the occasion was a private meal that involved honoring a god, trade guild feasts featuring idolatrous and immoral religious rituals, or public feasts and banquets, all involved spiritual compromise and revealed a deep-rooted complacency. We see the threat of complacency repeated throughout the letters. For example, those at Ephesus had forsaken their first love (2:4), some at Pergamum and Thyatira are following these false teachers (2:14–15, 20), Sardis has a reputation for being alive but is in reality dead (3:1), and Laodicea remains lukewarm (3:16–17).

The spiritual activities connected to such meals (e.g., eating food offered to idols, worship of a particular god) appear to be the social occasion for such compromise, and wealth seems to be the ultimate motivator.[64] Yarbro Collins rightly concludes: "At stake here was the question of assimilation: What pagan customs could Christians adopt for the sake of economic survival, commercial gain, or social acceptability?"[65] So often in history, the love of money has proven to be the root of various kinds of evil (1 Tim 6:10). Kraybill notes how emperor worship permeates commerce, that imperial priests were powerful business figures, and that coins carried the mark of the beast, with everything held together by an incredibly strong system of patronage.[66] In other words, economic currents ran together with religious, social, and political forces to form the mighty Roman river in which Christians were challenged to swim upstream. John is not against wealth since, as deSilva notes, "the new Jerusalem is every bit as opulent as Babylon," but he is "deeply concerned about the compromises necessary to obtain wealth . . . not just compromising with idolatry, but also with a self-glorifying, violently repressive, economically exploitative system."[67]

4.3.4 Summary of the Occasion

John writes to these seven specific churches in Asia Minor as representatives of all the churches. His prophetic-apocalyptic letter confronts believers whose social setting tightly intertwines politics, economics, and religion. More specifically, this setting presents the church with two dominant challenges: pressure and persecution on the one hand or assimilation and compromise on the other. Both the Roman religious

63. Hemer, *Letters to the Seven Churches*, 91.

64. On the larger issue of wealth in the book of Revelation, see Kraybill, *Imperial Cult and Commerce*.

65. Yarbro Collins, *Crisis and Catharsis*, 88.

66. Kraybill, *Apocalypse and Allegiance*, ch. 9: "The Economics of Worship." Koester, *Revelation*, 101–3, identifies four levels at which John engages the question of wealth: (1) one's desire to obtain it (Rev 3:17), (2) how wealth makes people blind (3:17; 18:7–8), (3) how the desire for wealth draws people into the worship of the emperor and the gods (17:1–2; 18:3), and (4) how the pursuit of wealth undermines the cohesiveness of the Christian community.

67. DeSilva, *Seeing Things John's Way*, 59.

context, most especially the imperial cult, and the relationship between Christians and Jews left believers feeling pressured to participate in ways that would compromise their faith. The pressure only intensifies as some Christians (whom John characterizes as false believers) encourage others to accommodate the faith to welcome cultural religious practices. Beale rightly concludes that "in essence, the false teachers, such as the Nicolaitans, probably redefined the apostolic tradition so that it could be easier for Christians to live more peaceably and profitably within the surrounding society."[68] Believers, who for whatever reason opted to modify their faith in order to fit in or avoid trouble, found themselves in a position of spiritual compromise. Even when they appear to have won at the game of relating to their surroundings, as is the case with Laodicea, Jesus is particularly harsh on these compromising believers (see his words to the believers in Pergamum, Thyatira, Sardis, and Laodicea).

Yet Christians who stand firm in the faith would have experienced social pressure, economic loss, and mistreatment (e.g., imprisonment, banishment, or death). Jesus describes such experiences in the seven messages using terms such as "hardships," "afflictions," "poverty," "suffering," "persecution," "trial," "testing," and "death." Although not systematic and widespread during the time of Domitian, pressure and persecution were nevertheless existential threats to the church during this time. As a result, John's purpose in writing features twin challenges for the church: pressure/persecution and compromise.

4.4 THE PURPOSE

The overarching purpose of Revelation is to answer the most foundational of all questions: Who is Lord of all? In the first century, the Roman emperor/empire claimed such lordship in a variety of ways—military might, client kingdoms, taxation, trade guilds, temples, and a host of symbols like statues, coins, and public inscriptions. But Revelation contends that Jesus Christ is Lord! God is on his throne and Jesus rather than Caesar is Lord.[69] Revelation offers an alternative vision of reality and power and destiny, that of the enthroned God and the slain but risen Lamb and the ever-present Holy Spirit, and the Triune God's plan for his creation.[70] Revelation reassures disciples that, in spite of how things appear in the visible world of the Roman (or any earthly) empire, the decisive spiritual battle has been won at the death and resurrection of Jesus, who will one day return to establish his eternal kingdom. Consequently, the book offers the deepest level of hope for those remaining faithful in the face of mounting pressure.

This vision of hope critiques the Roman Empire or any anti-Christ empire

68. Beale, *Revelation*, 30.

69. Duvall, *Revelation*, 4.

70. J. Scott Duvall, "Revelation: The Transforming Vision," in C. Marvin Pate et al., *The Story of Israel: A Biblical Theology* (Downers Grove, IL: InterVarsity Press, 2004), 255–77.

throughout history, but it also critiques the church. Disciples are exhorted to remain faithful in their witness to Christ in the midst of an idolatrous and immoral world.[71] Will believers follow the one true Lord or the puppet rulers of this world? Gorman summarizes:

> The fate of empire is certain; what is *un*certain is the fate of those who currently participate in the cult of empire. The most significant critique is the critique of the church, and specifically of its participation in the idolatry of the imperial cult, the civil or national religion. Will the churches repent? For the churches, one main question emerges: "Beast or Lamb?[72]

Once again, "Who is Lord of all?" John has a twofold reason for confronting his readers with this question: to encourage/comfort those standing strong in the face of pressure and persecution but also to alert and warn those compromising by calling them to repentance. Revelation calls believers to "conquer" or "overcome" (νικάω) the social and spiritual forces that "conspire to defeat [them] in their contest to keep the commandments of God and to keep faith in Jesus."[73] John's ultimate hope is that believers will walk in faithfulness to Jesus (Rev 14:4) and enjoy God's relational presence eternally in the new heaven and new earth.[74]

Revelation accomplishes its purpose by, as Bauckham argues, providing a set of "prophetic counter-images," which impress on the reader a radically different vision of reality, a heavenly vision.[75] Greg Carey notes that Revelation provides a "counter-imperial script" to confront its audience with a contrasting choice between Beast power and Lamb power.[76] Overall, Revelation provides a transforming vision of God's plan for his enemies, his world, and his people:

> Revelation answers the question, "Who is Lord?" During times of oppression and persecution, the righteous suffer and the wicked seem to prosper. This begs the question, "Is God still on his throne?" Revelation says that in spite of how things appear, Caesar is not Lord and Satan is not Lord, but Jesus is Lord and he is coming soon to restore his creation and establish his eternal kingdom. Satan, sin, and death will not have the final word. The main message of this grand finale of the biblical story is "God wins!" Those who are being persecuted have their hearts and minds immersed in hope and their eyes opened to see God's future. Those who are selling

71. Beale, *Revelation*, 33.
72. Gorman, *Reading Revelation Responsibly*, 56.
73. DeSilva, *Seeing Things John's Way*, 70.
74. See Duvall and Hays, *God's Relational Presence*, 303–23.
75. Bauckham, *Theology*, 17.
76. Greg Carey, "The Book of Revelation as Counter-Imperial Script," in Richard A. Horsley, ed., *In the Shadow of Empire: Reclaiming the Bible as a History of Faithful Resistance* (Louisville: Westminster John Knox, 2008), 170.

> their souls to the pagan powers are shown God's future so as to shock them into repentance. One way or the other Revelation is indeed a transforming vision.[77]

As hearers/readers are immersed in Revelation's heavenly vision, they encounter reality as God intends, where he defeats the powers of darkness, judges evil, rescues his people, and restores creation. As a result, the ever-present images of empire fade and lose their grip, no matter the consequences. Believers are empowered to live out eternal, heavenly realities even as they are confronted daily with the rulers of this world and their propaganda. Having their thinking and affections reoriented, God's people are now able to persevere faithfully to Jesus Christ, the one, true Lord of all. Tabb sums up Revelation's purpose well: "Revelation's symbolic visions *challenge* readers to resist worldly compromise, spiritual complacency and false teaching. They also *encourage* embattled believers to persevere in faithful witness and hope in the present and future reign of God and the Lamb."[78]

77. Duvall, "Transforming Vision," 257.

78. Tabb, *All Things New*, 8, emphasis original.

[illegible] to the [illegible] powers, and show us [illegible] future so as to strengthen our [illegible] resistance. This way, [illegible] other Revelation, is indeed a transforming vision.

[illegible] the [illegible] of [illegible] of our reality [illegible] and [illegible] the [illegible] of [illegible], judgment, [illegible] the [illegible] the [illegible] gap [illegible] the [illegible], [illegible] reality [illegible] the [illegible] people are [illegible] symbolic [illegible] to [illegible] "spiritual" [illegible] also teaching. They also [illegible] believers to [illegible] hope in the present [illegible] God and the Lamb.[8]

[illegible] [8]. [illegible]

Part 3

LITERARY-THEOLOGICAL FOUNDATIONS FOR THE THEOLOGY OF REVELATION

Chapter 5

THE GENRE OF REVELATION: AN APOCALYPTIC PROPHETIC LETTER

BIBLIOGRAPHY

Arndt, William, et al. *A Greek-English Lexicon of the New Testament and Other Early Christian Literature*. Chicago: University of Chicago Press, 2000. **Aune, David E.** "The Apocalypse of John and the Problem of Genre." Pages 65–96 in *Early Christian Apocalypticism: Genre and Social Setting*. Edited by Adela Yarbro Collins. *Semeia* 36. Atlanta: Society of Biblical Literature, 1986. ———. "Apocalypse Renewed: An Intertextual Reading of the Apocalypse of John." Pages 43–70 in *The Reality of the Apocalypse: Rhetoric and Politics in the Book of Revelation*. Edited by David L. Barr. SBLSymS 39. Atlanta: Society of Biblical Literature, 2006. ———. *Apocalypticism, Prophecy, and Magic in Early Christianity*. Grand Rapids: Baker Academic, 2008. ———. "The Form and Function of the Proclamations to the Seven Churches (Revelation 2–3)." *NTS* 36 (1990): 182–204. ———. *Prophecy in Early Christianity and the Ancient Mediterranean World*. Grand Rapids: Eerdmans, 1983. **Aune, David E., T. J. Geddert, and Craig A. Evans.** "Apocalypticism." Pages *DNTB* 45–58. **Blackwell, Ben C., John K. Goodrich, and Jason Maston,** eds. *Reading Revelation in Context: John's Apocalypse and Second Temple Judaism*. Grand Rapids: Zondervan, 2019. **Charles, R. H.** *Studies in the Apocalypse*. Edinburgh: T&T Clark, 1923. **Collins, John J.** "Introduction: Towards the Morphology of a Genre." *Semeia* 14 (1979): 1–20. **Duvall, J. Scott.** "Revelation: The Transforming Vision." Pages 255–77 in *The Story of Israel: A Biblical Theology*. Edited by C. Marvin Pate et al. Downers Grove, IL: InterVarsity Press, 2004. **Fletcher, Michelle.** "Apocalypse Noir: How Revelation Defined and Defied a Genre." Pages 115–34 in *The Book of Revelation*. Edited by Garrick V. Allen, Ian Paul, and Simon Woodman. WUNT 411. Tübingen: Mohr Siebeck, 2015. **Hanson, Paul D.** "Apocalypses and Apocalypticism: The Genre." *ABD* 1:279–80. ———. *The Dawn of Apocalyptic*. Philadelphia: Fortress, 1975. **Helyer, Larry R.** *Exploring Jewish Literature of the Second Temple Period: A Guide for New Testament Students*. Downers Grove, IL: InterVarsity Press, 2002. **Hill, David.** "Prophecy and Prophets in the Revelation of St John." *NTS* 18 (1972): 401–18. **Koch, Klaus.** *The Rediscovery of Apocalyptic*. London: SCM, 1972. **Köstenberger, Andreas J., L. Scott Kellum and Charles L. Quarles.** *The Cradle, the Cross, and the Crown: An Introduction to the New Testament*. 2nd ed. Nashville: B&H Academic,

2016. **Kreitzer, Larry J.** "Apocalyptic, Apocalypticism." *DLNT* 55–68. **Ladd, George Eldon.** "Why Not Prophetic-Apocalyptic?" *JBL* 76 (1957): 192–200. **Linton, Gregory L.** "Reading the Apocalypse as Apocalypse: The Limits of Genre." Pages 9–41 in *The Reality of the Apocalypse: Rhetoric and Politics in the Book of Revelation*. Edited by David L. Barr. SBLSymS 39. Atlanta: Society of Biblical Literature, 2006. **Mathewson, David L.** "Revelation in Recent Genre Criticism: Some Implications for Interpretation." *TrinJ* 13 (1992): 193–213. **Mazzaferri, F. D.** *The Genre of the Book of Revelation from a Source-Critical Perspective*. BZNW 54. New York: de Gruyter, 1989. **Michaels, J. Ramsey.** *Interpreting the Book of Revelation*. GNTE. Grand Rapids: Baker Books, 1992. **Morris, Leon.** *Apocalyptic*. London: Tyndale, 1973. **Paul, Ian.** "The Genre of Revelation." Pages 36–50 in *The Apocalypse of John Among Its Critics: Questions & Controversies*. StScrBT. Edited by Alexander S. Stewart and Alan S. Bandy. Bellingham, WA: Lexham Academic, 2023. **Reddish, Mitchell.** "The Genre of the Book of Revelation." *OHBR* 21–34. Edited by Craig Koester. Oxford: Oxford University Press, 2020. **Russell, D. S.** *The Method and Message of Jewish Apocalyptic*. London: SCM, 1964. **Smith, Morton.** "On the History of ΑΠΟΚΑΛΥΠΤΩ and ΑΠΟΚΑΛΥΨΙΣ." Pages 9–20 in *Apocalypticism in the Mediterranean World and the Near East*. Edited by David Hellholm. Tübingen: Mohr Siebeck, 1983. **Yarbro Collins, Adela.** *The Apocalypse*. NTM 22. Wilmington, DE: Glazier, 1979.

5.1 INTRODUCTION

A literary genre refers to "a group of texts which exhibit a coherent and recurring pattern of features constituted by the interrelated elements of form, content and function."[1] Paul notes that genre matters because if affects interpretation, reveals much about the relationship between the author and the intended audience, and contributes to our understanding of the authority and inspiration of Scripture.[2] But when it comes to Revelation, identifying the genre is not as straightforward as it seems. The book opens and closes like a New Testament letter (1:4–6; 22:10–21) and early on features seven messages or sermons to specific churches in Asia Minor. Yet Revelation's very first word identifies it as an "apocalypse" (ἀποκάλυψις in 1:1), or at least that appears to be the case. John also labels the book a "prophecy" (προφητεία) multiple times (1:3; 22:7, 10, 18, 19). In addition, a number of other literary forms are used throughout: hymns, lists, speeches, narrative, reports, prophetic oracles, warnings, exhortations, proclamations,

1. David E. Aune, *Apocalypticism, Prophecy, and Magic in Early Christianity* (Grand Rapids: Baker Academic, 2008), 39. See also David E. Aune, "The Apocalypse of John and the Problem of Genre," in Adela Yarbro Collins, ed., *Semeia* 36 (Atlanta: Society of Biblical Literature, 1986): 65–96 (see 5.2 below). Paul notes that the well-known 1979 Collins/*Semeia* definition of genre faces three sets of problems: (1) whether it is possible to define *genre* in this way, (2) the unlikelihood that Revelation fits this definition, and (3) the numerous ways in which Revelation is distinct from most of the Second Temple Jewish apocalypses. See Ian Paul, "The Genre of Revelation," in *The Apocalypse of John among Its Critics: Questions & Controversies*, StScrBT, ed. Alexander E. Stewart and Alan S. Bandy (Bellingham, WA: Lexham Academic, 2023), 38–42.

2. Paul, "Genre of Revelation," 36–38.

woe oracles, laments, and so on.[3] Based on what we surmise from the text itself, we conclude, with the majority of scholars, that Revelation is a mixed or hybrid genre. Carson and Moo note that in Revelation "elements of prophecy, apocalypse, and letter are combined in a way that has no close parallel in other literature."[4]

Understanding genre is important because the meaning of a text is closely tied to its literary form. Authors and readers communicate clearly when they share expectations about how the message is being shared. Readers tend to make sense of works they are reading by relating them to similar works they have read in the past. Such genre identifications call for certain reading strategies that will allow them to understand the author's message clearly. But with its unique blend of literary forms, Revelation presents a formidable challenge. As Linton observes, "the Apocalypse of John is a text that overruns its [genre] boundaries to a high degree."[5] Are prophecy and apocalyptic literature mutually exclusive? Is one more dominant? What priority should the interpreter give to eschatology? Is the letter format simply an added garnishment or does it carry substantial weight? What about the abundance of hymns? Do we always know when one genre is moving to the foreground while others are receding to the background or perhaps being excluded entirely? These and many other questions confront the interpreter of Revelation regarding genre. The way forward is to look more closely at Revelation as an apocalypse, a prophecy, and a letter before drawing final conclusions.[6]

5.2 REVELATION AS AN APOCALYPSE

Revelation is the first known ancient composition "to be designated an 'apocalypse' by its author"—Ἀποκάλυψις Ἰησοῦ Χριστοῦ ("The revelation of/from Jesus Christ").[7] After a comprehensive study of the etymology of the word group ἀποκαλ-, Morton Smith concludes:

> Remarkable is the rarity of the words in works now commonly called "apocalypses." I do not know any such text prior to the New Testament Apocalypse which either

3. Paul, "Genre of Revelation," 45, observes, for example, seven "micro-genre" changes in Rev 1:1–9: apocalyptic (v. 1), benediction (v. 3), epistle (v. 4), doxology (vv. 5–6), apocalyptic (v. 7), prophecy (v. 8), and epistle (v. 9). Paul also advocates for "doxology" or "praise" as a fourth major genre in Revelation, and this merits further consideration. See our discussion of worship in chapter 17.

4. Carson and Moo, *Introduction to the New Testament*, 716. Similarly, Beale, *Revelation*, 37–43; Köstenberger, Kellum, and Quarles, *Cradle, Cross and Crown*, 955; Aune, *Revelation 1–5*, lxxi–xc; David L. Mathewson, "Revelation in Recent Genre Criticism: Some Implications for Interpretation," *TrinJ* 13 (1992): 206. Schüssler Fiorenza, *Book of Revelation*, 138, warns that the "scholarly alternative—either prophetic or apocalyptic, as derived from the discussion of Jewish apocalyptic origins—should not be applied to Rev" (cf. also 168–69).

5. Gregory L. Linton, "Reading the Apocalypse as Apocalypse: The Limits of Genre," in David L. Barr, ed., *The Reality of the Apocalypse: Rhetoric and Politics in the Book of Revelation*, SBLSymS 39 (Atlanta: Society of Biblical Literature, 2006), 10.

6. For an overview of the apocalyptic, prophetic, and epistolary aspects of Revelation's genre, see Mitchell Reddish, "The Genre of the Book of Revelation," *OHBR* 21–34.

7. Aune, *Revelation 1–5*, lxxvii.

describes itself or the proceedings in it as ἀποκαλύψεις or even uses the verb ἀποκαλύπτω for the whole of the revelation.[8]

As a result, interpreters are immediately faced with the challenge of interpreting the Apocalypse of John as apocalyptic literature when John's work is the very first known document with the title "apocalypse." Certainly, an apocalyptic genre could (and apparently does) exist apart from the content of any formal title, but the fact that no such documents exist with a title that includes "apocalypse" raises a caution flag about how this opening title should be understood with respect to the literary genre of Revelation.

Even the terminology related to "apocalyptic" and "apocalypse" can be confusing. Scholars normally distinguish between various pertinent terms.[9] *Apocalypse* usually refers to a particular genre or literary form or to a work that exhibits this form. *Apocalyptic* is normally understood as an adjective referring to either the literary genre or to the worldview essential to it. *Apocalypticism* often refers to a social movement, theology, or ideology embraced by the group that produced the apocalyptic writings.

In spite of the complicated history of attempts to understand this type of literature, most scholars now recognize a body of writings that can be classified as "apocalyptic," writings generated between about 200 BC and AD 200. Examples of Jewish texts that are considered apocalypses include Daniel, 1 and 2 Enoch, 2 and 3 Baruch, 4 Ezra, the Sibylline Oracles, the Testament of Moses, the Apocalypse of Abraham, the Apocalypse of Zephaniah, and sections of Jubilees, the Testament of Levi, and the Testament of Abraham. Examples of early Christian apocalypses include Revelation, the Shepherd of Hermas, the Apocalypse of Peter, and the Ascension of Isaiah. The question remains, however, as to John's direct dependence on this body of literature when writing Revelation.

The scholarly guild's attempt to define the genre "apocalypse" began in earnest when the Society of Biblical Literature's Apocalypse Group published their research in *Semeia* 14 (1979).[10] They observed a "master paradigm" of thirteen characteristics (with many subdivisions), taking into consideration both form and content.[11] The same group

8. Morton Smith, "On the History of ΑΠΟΚΑΛΥΠΤΩ and ΑΠΟΚΑΛΥΨΙΣ," in David Hellholm, ed., *Apocalypticism in the Mediterranean World and the Near East* (Tübingen: Mohr Siebeck, 1983), 14.

9. See Larry J. Kreitzer, "Apocalyptic, Apocalypticism," *DLNT* 55–56; Paul D. Hanson, "Apocalypses and Apocalypticism: The Genre," *ABD* 1:279–80; Köstenberger, Kellum, and Quarles, *Cradle, Cross and Crown*, 953.

10. Notable pioneers include R. H. Charles, *Studies in the Apocalypse* (Edinburgh: T&T Clark, 1923); and Charles, *Revelation of St. John*; D. S. Russell, *The Method and Message of Jewish Apocalyptic* (London: SCM, 1964); Klaus Koch, *The Rediscovery of Apocalyptic* (London: SCM, 1972); Leon Morris, *Apocalyptic* (London: Tyndale, 1973); and Paul D. Hanson, *The Dawn of Apocalyptic* (Philadelphia: Fortress, 1975).

11. John J. Collins, "Towards the Morphology of a Genre," *Semeia* 14 (1979): 5–9: (1) medium (often visionary) by which the revelation is communicated, (2) an otherworldly mediator who communicates the revelation, (3) a human recipient, (4) matters that deal with the beginning of history, (5) a review of history, (6) present salvation through knowledge (in gnostic texts), (7) eschatological crisis, (8) eschatological judgment and/or destruction, (9) eschatological salvation, (10) otherworldly elements, (11) paraenesis by the mediator to the recipients, (12) instructions to the recipient, (13) narrative conclusion.

then formulated a well-known comprehensive definition of the genre: "'Apocalypse' is a genre of revelatory literature with a narrative framework, in which a revelation is mediated by an otherworldly being to a human recipient, disclosing a transcendent reality which is both temporal, insofar as it envisages eschatological salvation, and spatial insofar as it involves another, supernatural world."[12]

In 1983 the Uppsala Colloquium on Apocalypticism published its results, arguing that along with form and content, function should play an important role in defining apocalyptic genre. The group highlighted important aspects of the genre including its hortatory function, the differences (and not just the similarities) between Revelation and Jewish apocalyptic texts, and the role of the social setting.[13]

In 1986 the Seminar on Early Christian Apocalypticism, another Society of Biblical Literature research group, published their findings. They embraced the form, content, *and function* triad of genre definition and amended the 1979 statement to include: "[Apocalypse is a genre] intended to interpret present, earthly circumstances in light of the supernatural world and of the future, and to influence both the understanding and the behavior of the audience by means of divine authority."[14]

The Jewish literature that came to be known as apocalyptic is characterized by several features. Taken together these elements carry the basic meaning of the word ἀποκάλυψις—i.e., to "unveil" or "disclose" or "reveal."[15] First, all of the writings except Revelation are pseudonymous, perhaps explained by a crisis of authority and the "need to legitimize the revelation given" by assigning a famous name from Israel's past to the work (e.g., Abraham, Moses, Isaiah).[16] Second, the primary mode of communication is visionary, often cast within a first-person narrative framework. The visions normally focus on heavenly or otherworldly realities and are mediated by angelic or divine guides, usually in cooperation with a human seer or prophet. Third, apocalyptic literature is characterized by symbolic language such as figures of speech, metaphors, images, and other literary devices utilized in unusual ways with the result that the message is both revealed and concealed. Fourth, these writings disclose a transcendent, normally eschatological, perspective related to the salvation and judgment of human beings. Thus, they sometimes fulfill a hortatory or parenetic function in relation to the recipients who are confronted with end-time expectations. Fifth, apocalyptic works are marked

12. Collins, "Morphology of a Genre," 9.

13. Adela Yarbro Collins, "Introduction: Early Christian Apocalypticism," *Semeia* 36 (1986): 1–11.

14. Yarbro Collins, "Introduction: Early Christian Apocalypticism," 7.

15. William Arndt et al., *A Greek-English Lexicon of the New Testament and Other Early Christian Literature* (Chicago: University of Chicago Press, 2000), 112. Our term "revelation" comes from the Latin translation of this Greek noun: *revelatio*.

16. See Aune, *Revelation 1–5*, lxxxii–lxxxviii; Larry R. Helyer, *Exploring Jewish Literature of the Second Temple Period: A Guide for New Testament Students* (Downers Grove, IL: InterVarsity Press, 2002), 117; D. E. Aune, T. J. Geddert, and Craig A. Evans, "Apocalypticism," *DNTB* 48; Köstenberger, Kellum, and Quarles, *Cradle, Cross, and Crown*, 953.

by a dualism between heavenly and earthly realities where the sin and rebellion and suffering of this temporary world are contrasted with God's expected intervention to establish his eternal kingdom. In connection with this dualism, apocalyptic works often feature otherworldly journeys and mediators, along with reviews of human history.

Linton rightly questions the circular reasoning of the process of genre definition sketched above.[17] Revelation is set up as a prototype for all other apocalypses without first clearly establishing that it belongs to the genre of apocalypse. As a result, we must proceed with caution and resist the temptation to assign Revelation exclusively (or perhaps even primarily) to the genre apocalypse. The Jewish apocalyptic tradition appears to be quite varied. Bauckham doubts John's direct literary dependence on Jewish apocalyptic works, pointing instead to his familiarity with a common tradition that took many different forms.[18] With that caveat, John did not write in a vacuum and was aware of and likely influenced by the prophetic and apocalyptic traditions of his time.

It is important to keep in mind that Revelation "defines as well as defies" the genre of apocalypse.[19] In addition to similarities, there are also notable differences between Revelation and Jewish apocalyptic writings.[20] As Fletcher concludes, "Whilst Revelation lies at the heart of scholarly apocalypse understanding, it does not sit comfortably alongside other apocalypses. It is *different*."[21] A few major differences should be kept in mind. Revelation is not pseudonymous but, as Aune points out, "is one of the only apocalypses for which the author, audience, and setting are generally known because they are not concealed in the work itself."[22] John's prophetic (and perhaps apostolic) persona certainly plays a role in the book's significance. Bauckham comments on the importance of John writing in his own name:

> Since he [John] stands at the culmination of the whole [prophetic] tradition, on the brink of the final eschatological fulfillment to which all prophecy had ultimately pointed, his authority is if anything greater than that of his predecessors. Of course, the authority really resides not in himself but in the revelation of Jesus Christ to which he bears prophetic witness (1:1–2). But his prophetic consciousness is such that, like Isaiah or Ezekiel, he feels no need of pseudonymity but writes in his own name (1:1, 4, 9; 22:8) and relates his own commissioning to prophesy (1:10–11, 19; 10:8–11).[23]

---

17. Linton, "Reading the Apocalypse," 33–34.

18. Bauckham, *Climax of Prophecy*, 39, 54, 83.

19. Michelle Fletcher, "Apocalypse Noir: How Revelation Defined and Defied a Genre," in Garrick V. Allen, Ian Paul, and Simon Woodman, eds., *The Book of Revelation*, WUNT 411 (Tübingen: Mohr Siebeck, 2015), 115–34.

20. Notably, the recent collection of essays in Ben C. Blackwell, John K. Goodrich, and Jason Maston, eds., *Reading Revelation in Context: John's Apocalypse and Second Temple Judaism* (Grand Rapids: Zondervan, 2019), 27, exposes not only theological similarities between Revelation and Jewish apocalyptic literature but theological differences as well. Cf. also Bauckham, *Climax of Prophecy*, xii.

21. Fletcher, "Apocalypse Noir," 116, emphasis original.

22. David E. Aune, "Apocalypse Renewed: An Intertextual Reading of the Apocalypse of John," in Barr, *Reality of Apocalypse*, 70.

23. Bauckham, *Theology*, 9.

Revelation also lacks an outline of history, lists of revealed things, and journeys through heavenly worlds.[24] And while Jewish apocalypses are characterized by visual imagery, the extent to which Revelation uses visual symbolism far exceeds what is typical. Also, in Revelation the apocalyptic tradition of interpreting visions is "virtually absent" since John is rarely puzzled by what he sees (exceptions being 7:13–17; 17:7–18).[25] Revelation is basically one long vision where John "creates a single symbolic universe in which its readers may live for the time it takes to read (or hear) the book."[26] In addition, Revelation's complicated structure and epistolary framework are also unique. The pessimistic view of history that one meets quite often in Jewish apocalypses is replaced in Revelation with the belief that the future has been inaugurated in the person of Jesus Christ, leading to a much more optimistic outlook. Likewise, one encounters a parenetic urgency in Revelation that stands apart.

John's use of the apocalyptic traditions represented in the Jewish writings noted earlier has important interpretive significance. We will address interpretive approaches later in chapter 10, Interpreting Revelation, but we offer a couple of observations here. First, understanding the living traditions in which John shared can shed much light on his context for writing. John certainly draws on the world of the Roman Empire, but the Jewish background with its apocalyptic traditions has often been neglected.[27] Yet these influenced all that went into John's composing Revelation. A second major takeaway for interpreting Revelation in light of its Jewish apocalyptic background is to highlight how the book *differs* from its antecedents. Such departures call attention to the uniqueness of John among the apocalypses and remind us that the book is first and foremost a "revelation *of/from Jesus Christ*" (1:1). Sometimes this crucial modifying phrase is omitted from the discussion. But Revelation as an apocalypse is more than a "what" that is being revealed; it is a "who." Revelation is personal theology, or better, Christological theology at its core. We will explore more of what is imbedded in these opening lines later in the section on theology (11.1.1; 12.2). Now, to add another layer to our understanding of Revelation's genre, we turn our attention to the prophetic nature of the book.

5.3 Revelation as a Prophecy

The relationship between apocalyptic and prophecy is complex and intertwined to the extent that it is often difficult to distinguish clearly between the two. Apocalyptic was

24. Schüssler Fiorenza, *Book of Revelation*, 168.

25. Smalley, *Revelation*, 7.

26. Bauckham, *Theology*, 10.

27. Thankfully, Blackwell, Goodrich, and Maston, eds., *Reading Revelation in Context*, provides an excellent collection of essays that demonstrate the value of reading Revelation in light of its Second Temple Jewish context. See also Bauckham's chapter, "The Use of Apocalyptic Traditions," in *Climax of Prophecy*, 38–91, where he explores how these traditions might affect our understanding of four specific texts in Revelation: 14:20b; 6:9–11; 20:13; 8:1.

originally understood as prophecy and grew out of prophecy. Beale labels apocalyptic an "intensification of prophecy."[28] John likely would not have made this distinction between these two genres since he would have regarded Daniel and any post-biblical apocalypses he knew as "a form of prophecy."[29] For us to cast prophecy and apocalyptic as exclusive alternatives would be a mistake, and any sharp dichotomy between them is a false one.[30] Bauckham concludes: "John was writing what he understood to be a work of prophetic scripture, the climax of prophetic revelation, which gathered up the prophetic meaning of the Old Testament scriptures and disclosed the way in which it was being and was to be fulfilled in the last days."[31]

Those scholars who see prophecy as the dominant genre of Revelation have good internal evidence for coming to that conclusion. John refers to the book as a "prophecy" (προφητεία) five times (1:3; 22:7, 10, 18, 19), and this comes as close to a clear genre designation as one will find in Revelation. John's prophetic call or commissioning to proclaim the oracles of God described in 10:8–11 uses the verb "prophesy" (προφητεύω) and resembles that given to various Old Testament prophets (e.g., Jer 1:4–19; Ezek 2:1–3:15). John also clearly uses the biblical language of the Prophets throughout the book. Instead of quoting their words directly, he often "weaves the biblical language into his own visionary text, with the result that the older prophetic words become a vehicle for communicating a contemporary message."[32] Revelation lives and breathes the words of the Prophets. For example, John's description of the heavenly throne room echoes Ezekiel 1–2 and Isaiah 6, the description of the four horsemen recalls Zechariah 1 and 6, and his own commissioning resembles that of Ezekiel, who ate a scroll with writing on both sides (Rev 5:1; 10:1–11; Ezek 2:1–3:3; cf. also Jer 1:9–10).[33] Examples abound, but what we see in Rev 10 is particularly telling.[34] In 10:7 John hears that "the mystery of God will be accomplished, just as he announced to his servants the prophets," likely an allusion to Amos 3:7 as a reference to the Old Testament prophets. But John then proceeds to record his own prophetic call reminiscent of Ezekiel's call. As a result, we know that John views himself as a prophet who serves the churches

28. Beale, *Revelation*, 37. He points to the term "apocalypse" (ἀποκάλυψις) in 1:1 as less of a genre identifier and more an allusion to Dan 2, where the term is used of "the prophetic revelation communicated from God to the prophet Daniel" (Dan 2:22, 28, 29, 30, 47).

29. Bauckham, *Climax of Prophecy*, xi; Beale, *Revelation*, 37, sees apocalyptic as "an intensification of prophecy." Cf. also Adela Yarbro Collins, *The Apocalypse*, NTM 22 (Wilmington, DE: Glazier, 1979), 5; Osborne, *Revelation*, 13; Buist M. Fanning, *Revelation*, ZECNT (Grand Rapids: Zondervan Academic, 2020), 31–32; Schüssler Fiorenza, *Book of Revelation*, 138; Hanson, *Dawn of Apocalyptic*; David Hill, "Prophecy and Prophets in the Revelation of St John," *NTS* 18 (1972): 401–18.

30. Aune, *Revelation 1–5*, lxxv, who notes that we have "a spectrum of texts composed over centuries"; see also the classic article by George Eldon Ladd, "Why Not Prophetic-Apocalyptic?" *JBL* 76 (1957): 192–200. A minority of scholarship sides with prophecy altogether to the exclusion of apocalyptic—e.g., F. D. Mazzaferri, *The Genre of the Book of Revelation from a Source-Critical Perspective*, BZNW 54 (New York: de Gruyter, 1989).

31. Bauckham, *Theology*, 5.

32. Koester, *Revelation*, 109.

33. Koester, *Revelation*, 109.

34. See Bauckham, *Theology*, 4, for this example.

of Asia Minor via a prophetic ministry that in many ways brings to fulfillment the ministry of his Old Testament prophetic predecessors (Rev 10:11; 22:6, 9). He is truly a prophet of Christ the long-awaited Messiah (cf. "the revelation of Jesus Christ" in 1:1). Throughout the book, "the prophets" are highlighted as playing an important role in God's plan (e.g., 16:6; 18:20, 24). No doubt John's view of his own prophetic ministry should influence our understanding of what he has written (10:11; cf. 11:3).

From the start we learn that the revelation was given by God and passed on by Jesus to his angel and to John, who testifies to "the word of God and the testimony of Jesus Christ" (1:2). The phrase "the testimony of Jesus" occurs six times in Revelation (1:2, 9; 12:17; 19:10 [2x]; 20:4, ESV) and is usually paired with "the word of God" (1:2, 9; 6:9; 19:9, 13; 20:4; cf. 17:17), a phrase that carries prophetic echoes. Most scholars take these expressions to refer to the content of Revelation. In 22:16 Jesus reminds John that he sent his angel to give him (and other believers—ὑμῖν) "this testimony for the churches." In this context, 19:10 connects some dots for us. John hears the voice of a great multitude praising the Lord God Almighty for the arrival of the wedding of the Lamb and is told (likely by an angel) to write, "'Blessed are those who are invited to the wedding supper of the Lamb!' And he added, 'These are the true words of God'" (19:9; cf. 21:5; 22:6). In response to the divine revelation, John falls down in worship. But the "fellow servant" who also holds to "the testimony of Jesus" rejects such worship, which is rightly reserved only for God. Then the angel explains, "For the testimony of Jesus is the Spirit of *the* prophecy" (19:10, translation mine). The witness from and about Jesus is the same as what the Spirit now speaks in this prophecy, that is, in the book of Revelation (cf. 22:6). Indirectly but powerfully, Revelation is identified here as a prophetic work.

Another indication that Revelation is a prophecy relates to its many oracles.[35] Revelation includes vision reports, where John receives revelations to pass on to others, and oracles—messages coming from God or spoken in the name of God that deal especially with salvation and judgment.[36] Such oracles of salvation and judgment are familiar to us from Israel's prophetic tradition. When it comes to detecting oracles in Revelation, David Aune says, "The single reliable feature whereby the oracles embedded in the Apocalypse may be confidently identified is the first-person singular speech of a divine revealer, whether the risen Jesus, an angel, or God."[37] He then lists Rev 1:7–8, 17–20; chapters 2–3; 13:9–10; 14:13; 16:15; 18:21–24; 19:9; 21:3–4, 5–8; 22:7, 12–14, 18–20 as prophetic oracles. Related to oracles, some see the pattern of uttering prophecy in Christian worship as reflected in the way John's voice blends with God's voice throughout.[38]

35. See the extensive treatment of the basic features of Christian prophetic speech in David E. Aune, *Prophecy in Early Christianity and the Ancient Mediterranean World* (Grand Rapids: Eerdmans, 1983), 317–38. For more on the seven messages as Christian prophetic speech, see pp. 274–79.

36. Bauckham, *Theology*, 3.

37. Aune, *Prophecy*, 279–80.

38. Koester, *Revelation*, 109; Aune, *Prophecy*, 280–88.

The seven prophetic messages of Rev 2–3 serve as clear examples of oracles.[39] Smalley divides the entire book into seven text units and sees the first scene, the seven prophetic messages of chapters 2–3, as corresponding to the last scene, the "seven prophecies" of 21:2–22:17.[40] In this way the entire book is framed by prophetic oracles. Aune appropriately concludes that the seven messages of Rev 2–3 should be identified as "parenetic salvation-judgment oracles," a genre which puts a strong emphasis on ethical and behavioral exhortation motivated by the promise of salvation or the threat of judgment.[41]

We find still other indications that Revelation is a prophecy. The prophetic message to each church begins with the formula "these are the words" or "thus says" (τάδε λέγει), and ancient readers would certainly have associated this phrase with prophetic messages.[42] The "thus says the Lord" phrase occurs over 250 times in the LXX and is regularly used to introduce prophetic speech (cf. the use in a prophetic address in Acts 21:11). Also, the command to "write . . . and send" (Rev 1:11), which is a variation of the "go and tell" prophetic commissioning formula, is the "functional equivalent to the sending of prophetic messengers in the OT."[43] Beale specifies that this command to write reflects Yahweh's commands to his prophetic servants (LXX of Exod 17:14; Isa 30:8; Jer 37:2; 39:44; Tob 12:20).[44] Also, the directive to "hear" (ὁ ἔχων οὖς ἀκουσάτω τί τὸ πνεῦμα λέγει ταῖς ἐκκλησίαις) that occurs at the conclusion of each of the seven messages functions as a "prophetic signature" similar to "Hear the word of Yahweh," which often introduces prophetic oracles in the Old Testament (e.g., Jer 29:20; 42:15; Amos 7:16).[45]

Reading Revelation as a prophecy means that we should expect the forthtelling (proclamation) and foretelling (prediction) of the fulfillment of God's redemptive plan, including both salvation and judgment. Christian prophets played an important role as "guardians and preservers of Christian behavior, beliefs and customs," especially in light of the constant pressure believers faced while living in the Roman Empire.[46] And if Revelation is indeed the "climax of prophecy" as noted above, the foretelling aspect of the book should not be surprising.[47] There is one final piece to the genre puzzle, and that is Revelation as a letter.

39. David E. Aune, "The Form and Function of the Proclamations to the Seven Churches (Revelation 2–3)," *NTS* 36 (1990): 182–204. Weima argues that the seven messages are definitely not "letters" and finds "sermons" a more modern, user-friendly designation for a prophetic oracle. See Weima, *Sermons to the Seven Churches*, 2–5.

40. Smalley, *Revelation*, 7–8, identifies the "seven prophecies" as 21:2–4, 5–8, 9–21, 22–27; 22:1–5, 6–9, 10–17, with each emphasizing an aspect of life in God's new creation: "new covenant, new life, new Jerusalem, new temple, new relationship, new advent, and new testimony."

41. Aune, "Proclamations to the Seven Churches," 183, 198; Aune, *Prophecy*, 275, 277, 326.

42. Aune, "Proclamations to the Seven Churches," 197–204; Aune, *Prophecy*, 274–79.

43. Aune, *Prophecy*, 275. The command to "write" appears in this sense in Rev 1:11, 19; seven times in 2–3; 14:13; 19:9; 21:5; and the one time he is told not to write in 10:4.

44. Beale, *Revelation*, 203.

45. Aune, "Proclamations to the Seven Churches," 193.

46. Aune, *Prophecy*, 277–78.

47. Fanning, *Revelation*, 31.

5.4 REVELATION AS A CIRCULAR LETTER

Verse 4 of Revelation's opening chapter has the recognizable format of a Greco-Roman letter, complete with the identification of the sender, the recipients, a greeting that includes a blessing (in this case a full description of the Triune God who gives the blessing), and a doxology (cf. Gal 1:4–5):

> John, To the seven churches in the province of Asia: Grace and peace to you from him who is, and who was, and who is to come, and from the seven spirits before his throne, and from Jesus Christ, who is the faithful witness, the firstborn from the dead, and the ruler of the kings of the earth. To him who loves us and has freed us from our sins by his blood, and has made us to be a kingdom and priests to serve his God and Father—to him be glory and power for ever and ever! Amen. (Rev 1:4–6)

Then at the very end of the book, we find a concluding benediction similar to one of Paul's letters: "The grace of the Lord Jesus be with God's people. Amen" (Rev 22:21). This epistolary framing causes us to consider the entire book of Revelation, and not just the seven prophetic messages of chapters 2–3, as a letter. What are some key implications of the whole of Revelation as a letter?

Revelation is a circular letter addressing seven churches in the order in which a courier would visit them. This means from the start that we must come to grips with the message to the first readers/hearers. And while circular letters would normally be a bit more general, John includes seven messages to seven particular congregations in the early going. This allows him to address his audience specifically in light of their particular context. He can then address larger issues but still be relevant to specific local churches.[48] The entire book of Revelation then is about "the way the Christians of the seven churches may, by being victorious within the specific situations of their own churches, enter the New Jerusalem."[49] But the fact that John addresses *seven* congregations shows that the book's message goes beyond these particular locations. In other words, John intends the entire book to apply to all churches since these seven specific churches are "*representative* of *all* churches."[50] This assumption is confirmed by the conclusion to each of the seven messages: "Whoever has ears, let them hear what the Spirit says to the churches" (2:7, 11, 17, 29; 3:6, 13, 22).

The recipients were expected to read aloud any communication from an important Christian leader with the gathered community, and this would have been in a worship setting. Aune even suggests that John may have utilized the "epistolary guise to facilitate

48. Bauckham, *Theology*, 13–15.

49. Bauckham, *Theology*, 14.

50. Bauckham, *Theology*, 16, emphasis original.

its reading within the setting of Christian worship."[51] This explains to some degree the prominence of the first of seven beatitudes: "Blessed is the one who reads aloud the words of this prophecy, and blessed are those who hear it and take to heart what is written in it, because the time is near" (1:3). With all seven congregations hearing every message read aloud and not just the one directed to them comes a spiritual challenge. Koester comments on the rhetorical force of the public character of Revelation as a letter to seven churches: "The text will communicate reproof and encouragement to individual congregations, yet what is said to one will be read by all. Recipients have incentive to heed the message because their reputations are at stake among the churches throughout the region."[52] For instance, the hearers would have recognized that the book's message of judgment would be for their enemies to be sure, but also for them if they decide to follow the beast (e.g., the false prophet Jezebel at Thyatira).[53] And they would have noticed that the book's message of salvation was not just about the future but also very much concerned with their present situation. Osborne concludes, "The book is not just a casebook for identifying future events but more a theological workbook addressing the church in the present through the prophecies of the future. John expected his readers to see themselves and their current situation through the lens of this book and to realize that as the church of the last days, they were corporately identified with the church at the end of the age."[54]

5.5 CONCLUSION

A more in-depth look at the genre of Revelation confirms a mixed or hybrid genre. Bauckham sums it up nicely: "Revelation seems to be an apocalyptic prophecy in the form of a circular letter to seven churches in the Roman province of Asia."[55] Powerful literature often breaks the bounds of neat, clean genre categories, as Michaels observes:

> Many literary theorists have suggested that good, and especially great, works never quite belong to a single genre. They are highly individual creations that expand the categories to a breaking point. This is certainly true of the Book of Revelation. If a letter, it is like no other early Christian letter we possess. If an apocalypse, it is like no other apocalypse. If a prophecy, it is unique among the prophecies.[56]

Revelation is the first known document with the title "apocalypse." The book is a revealing or unveiling about or by Jesus Christ and, as such, features visionary

51. Aune, *Revelation 1–5*, lxxii.
52. Koester, *Revelation*, 110.
53. Bauckham, *Theology*, 15.
54. Osborne, *Revelation*, 12–13.
55. Bauckham, *Theology*, 2.
56. J. Ramsey Michaels, *Interpreting the Book of Revelation*, GNTE (Grand Rapids: Baker Books, 1992), 31–32. Carson and Moo, *Introduction to the New Testament*, 716, note that in Revelation "elements of prophecy, apocalypse, and letter are combined in a way that has no close parallel in other literature."

communication through an abundance of symbolic language. It opens up an alternative spiritual reality intended to transform the readers so that they can live faithfully in their present contexts.[57] The apocalyptic dimension of Revelation intensifies the prophetic.

As we have noted, John is writing the climax of prophetic revelation. Often using the language of the Old Testament prophets, John writes as a prophet of Christ, who brings to fulfillment God's redemptive plan. Combining oracles of salvation and judgment in an apocalyptic narrative, John foretells and forthtells the received message. The prophetic aspect of Revelation develops and strengthens the apocalyptic.

This apocalyptic prophecy is then circulated to the churches in the form of a letter. The message is intended to be believed and lived in the crucible of this world. As the churches hear the prophetic revelation in the context of worship, they are inspired and equipped to live faithfully in this world.

Smalley links each genre with John's identity. He is a seer who participates in the "revelation" and writes an apocalypse. He is also a prophet of Christ who portrays God's words of salvation and judgment to the churches.[58] And, some might add, he is also an apostle who writes a letter under Christ's authority but nevertheless refers to himself not as a seer or a prophet but as a servant (δοῦλος in 1:1).

57. See Duvall, "Transforming Vision," 255–77.

58. Smalley, *Revelation*, 8.

Chapter 6

THE TEXT AND CANONICITY OF REVELATION

BIBLIOGRAPHY

Aland, Barbara, and Klaus Wachtel. "The Greek Minuscule Manuscripts of the New Testament." Pages 43–60 in *The Text of the New Testament in Contemporary Research: Essays on the* Status Quaestionis." Edited by Bart Ehrman and Michael W. Holmes, Studies and Documents. Grand Rapids: Eerdmans, 1995. **Allen, Garrick V.** "The Apocalypse in Codex Alexandrinus: Exegetical Reasonings and Singular Readings in New Testament Greek Manuscripts." *JBL* 135 (2016): 859–80. ———. *The Future of New Testament Textual Scholarship: From H. C. Hoskier to the Editio Critica Maior and Beyond.* WUNT 417. Tübingen: Mohr Siebeck, 2019. **Allen, Garrick V., Ian Paul, and Simon Woodman,** eds. *The Book of Revelation.* WUNT 411. Tübingen: Mohr Siebeck, 2015. **Allert, Craig D.** *A High View of Scripture: The Authority of the Bible and the Formation of the New Testament Canon.* Grand Rapids: Baker Academic, 2007. **Bandy, Alan S.** "Should John's Apocalypse Be in the Canon?" Pages 9–35 in *The Apocalypse of John among Its Critics: Questions & Controversies.* StScrBT. Edited by Alexander E. Stewart and Alan S. Bandy. Bellingham, WA: Lexham Academic, 2023. **Comfort, Philip W.** *Encountering the Manuscripts: An Introduction to New Testament Paleography and Textual Criticism.* Nashville: B&H Academic, 2005. **Daley, Brian E.** *The Hope of the Early Church: A Handbook of Patristic Eschatology.* Grand Rapids: Baker Academic, 2002. **Elliott, J. K.** "Recent Work on the Greek Manuscripts of Revelation and the Consequences for the *Kurzgefasste Liste.*" *JTS* 66 (2015): 574–84. **Gallagher, Edmon L., and John D. Meade.** *The Biblical Canon Lists from Early Christianity: Texts and Analysis.* Oxford: Oxford University Press, 2017. **Gurry, Peter J.** "How Your Greek NT Is Changing: A Simple Introduction to the Coherence-Based Genealogical Method (CBGM)." *JETS* 59 (2016): 675–89. **Head, Peter M.** "Editio Critica Maior: An Introduction and Assessment." *TynBul* 61 (2010): 131–52. **Hernández, Juan, Jr.** "The Apocalypse in Codex Alexandrinus: Its Singular Readings and Scribal Habits." Pages 341–58 in *Scripture and Traditions: Essays on Early Judaism and Christianity in Honor of Carl R. Holladay.* Edited by Patrick Gray and Gail R. O'Day. NovTSup 129. Leiden: Brill, 2008. ———. "The Greek Text of Revelation." *OHBR* 343–60. ———. "Nestle-Aland 28 and the Revision of the Apocalypse's Textual History." Pages 71–81 in *Studies of the Text of the NT* *and Early Christianity: Essays in Honor of Michael W. Holmes*. Edited by Daniel M. Gurtner, Juan Hernández Jr., and Paul Foster. NTTSD 50. Leiden: Brill, 2015. **Kruger, Michael J.** *Canon Revisited: Establishing the Origins and Authority of the New Testament Books*. Wheaton, IL: Crossway, 2012. ———. "The Reception of the Book of Revelation in the Early Church." Pages 159–74 in *Book of Seven Seals*. Edited by Thomas J. Kraus and Michael Sommer. WUNT 363. Tübingen: Mohr Siebeck, 2016. **Maier, Gerhard.** *Die Johannesoffenbarung und die Kirche*. WUNT 25. Tübingen: Mohr Siebeck, 1981. **McDonald, Lee Martin.** *The Biblical Canon: Its Origin, Transmission, and Authority*. Peabody, MA: Hendrickson, 2007. **Metzger, Bruce M.** *The Canon of the New Testament: Its Origin, Development, and Significance*. Oxford: Clarendon, 1987. **Metzger, Bruce M., and Bart D. Ehrman.** *The Text of the New Testament: Its Transmission, Corruption, and Restoration*. 4th ed. Oxford: Oxford University Press, 2005. **Nicklas, Tobias.** "The Early Text of Revelation." Pages 225–38 in *The Early Text of the New Testament*. Edited by C. E. Hill and M. J. Kruger. Oxford: Oxford University Press, 2012. **Oecumenius and Andrew of Caesarea.** *Greek Commentaries on Revelation*. Edited by Thomas C. Oden and Gerald L. Bray. Translated by William C. Weinrich. ACT. Downers Grove, IL: IVP Academic, 2011. **Parker, D. C.** *An Introduction to the New Testament Manuscripts and Their Texts*. Cambridge: Cambridge University Press, 2008. **Porter, Stanley E.** *How We Got the New Testament: Text, Transmission, Translation*. Grand Rapids: Baker Academic, 2013. **Schmid, Josef.** *Studies in the History of the Greek Text of the Apocalypse: The Ancient Stems*. Edited and translated by Juan Hernández Jr., Garrick V. Allen, and Darius Müller. Atlanta: Society of Biblical Literature, 2018. **Tõniste, Külli.** *The Ending of the Canon: A Canonical and Intertextual Reading of Revelation 21–22*. LNTS 526. London: T&T Clark, 2016. **Victorinus of Petovium et al.** *Latin Commentaries on Revelation*. Edited by Thomas C. Oden. Translated by William C. Weinrich. ACT. Downers Grove, IL: IVP Academic, 2011. **Weinrich, William C.**, ed. *Revelation*. ACCS 12. Downers Grove, IL: InterVarsity Press, 2005. **Williams, Peter J.** "P^{115} and the Number of the Beast." *TynBul* 58 (2007): 151–53.

6.1 INTRODUCTION

Like other aspects of studying Revelation, our look at the text and canon of this remarkable book takes its own interesting twists and turns. Revelation has a fascinating textual history since textual decisions seem always connected to the theological persuasions of the critic.

Because the Montanists (2nd c.) used Revelation in their debates, some early church leaders wanted nothing to do with it. But in spite of this chiliastic baggage, the book was generally well received. Koester writes, "Christians in the west generally valued Revelation and assumed that John the apostle wrote the work, along with the Fourth Gospel and one or more of the Johannine Epistles. Christians in the east held similar views until the late third century, when questions were raised about the book's authorship in the wake of controversies about its message."[1] In this chapter we will unpack Revelation's distinctive textual history, survey its most important witnesses, and discuss what it looks like to do textual criticism in the Apocalypse. In addition, we will examine the canonicity of Revelation, including its early and consistent acceptance in the West and struggle for acceptance in the East.[2]

6.2 THE TEXT OF REVELATION

6.2.1 Revelation's Distinctive Textual History

Along with its genre distinctives, Revelation features an intriguing textual history. The book circulated widely in the early church as is evidenced by Irenaeus's (late 2nd c.) familiarity with the reading of Rev 13:8 that claimed the number of the beast was 616 rather than 666.[3] But there are fewer manuscripts of Revelation compared to other New Testament books because it was copied less and often copied separately from other New Testament works, likely due to its unique character and challenging theology.[4]

Revelation is also a text-critical outlier because the book was often inserted later into existing New Testament manuscripts, most likely to complete the collection.[5] Revelation is frequently preserved with nonbiblical writings, a rarity for other New Testament books, and this probably speaks to what the Byzantine Church thought about the book.[6] When Revelation is included with other New Testament books, it is often added much like an appendix.[7] Hernández concludes: "The late insertions, non-canonical companions, and liturgical exclusion merge into a trifecta of textual exile. The book appeared problematic. The regular juxtaposition of commentaries and scholia alongside it underscored the need to regulate the work's meaning. Guidance was necessary."[8] So, Revelation has always been an interpretive challenge. Nothing new there. But in spite of these peculiarities, the Greek text of Revelation is comparatively well attested when it comes to the earliest period of transmission.

At present there are about 310 manuscripts of Revelation preserving the Greek text, compared to about 1,700 Greek copies of portions of the Gospels, 800 copies of Paul's letters, and 600 of Acts and the General Letters.[9] Of these 310, seven are papyri, twelve uncials, and 291 are minuscules. There are no lectionary texts since Revelation

1. Koester, *Revelation*, 30.

2. For an excellent recent treatment of the text and canon issues related to Revelation, see Alan S. Bandy, "Should John's Apocalypse Be in the Canon?," in Stewart and Bandy, eds., *The Apocalypse of John*, 9–35.

3. Irenaeus, *Haer.* 5.30.1.

4. Fanning, *Revelation*, 49–50.

5. Juan Hernández Jr., "Greek Text of Revelation," *OHBR* 344.

6. Joseph Schmid, *Studies in the History of the Greek Text of the Apocalypse*, trans. and ed. Juan Hernández Jr., Garrick V. Allen, and Darius Müller, TCS (Atlanta: SBL Press, 2018), 35–36.

7. Schmid, *History of the Greek Text of the Apocalypse*, 37–38.

8. Hernández Jr., "Greek Text of Revelation," 344–45.

9. Hernández Jr., "Greek Text of Revelation," 344; D. C. Parker, *An Introduction to the New Testament Manuscripts and Their Texts* (Cambridge: Cambridge University Press, 2008), 232–236; Fanning, *Revelation*, 50.

was never included in the liturgical readings of the Greek Church. In addition, there are quotations and allusions to Revelation in the writings of ancient church leaders.[10] Plus we have Latin, Armenian, Georgian, Coptic, Ethiopic, and Syriac versions, as well as a number of early Christian commentaries on Revelation from both the Greek and Latin traditions.[11] Oecumenius's commentary (early sixth century) is the first complete commentary on Revelation in Greek.

The first Greek New Testament to be printed was the Complutensian Polyglot (1514), but Erasmus was the first to publish a Greek New Testament (1516). For the book of Revelation, he had only one mediocre manuscript dated to the twelfth century. In this Codex 2814 the text of Revelation was combined with the commentary by Andrew of Caesarea (early 7th c.). It omits words throughout, occasionally has wording unique in the Greek tradition, and lacks the last six verses of the book (22:16–21). Erasmus corrected the manuscript and translated those last few verses from the Latin Vulgate back into Greek. Erasmus's Greek text went through multiple editions and eventually became the basis for the Textus Receptus or "received text," the standard printed Greek text for centuries to come.[12]

In the 1800s, Lachmann (1831), Tischendorf (1841), Tregelles (1844), and Westcott and Hort (1881) broke with the received text and produced critical editions of the Greek New Testament. As manuscripts were discovered, research on the Greek text of Revelation continued to develop and advance.[13] Herman C. Hoskier's *Concerning the Greek Text of the Apocalypse* provides "the most comprehensive collection of manuscript data for the Greek text of Revelation published to date."[14] Hoskier's contribution was as an effective collator rather than a textual critic. Josef Schmid's *Die Studien zur Geschichte des griechischen Apokalypse-Textes* is considered to be the twentieth century's most influential reconstruction of the Greek text of Revelation.[15] In a multi-volume study that spanned twenty-five years of research, Schmid broke new ground. He provided a comprehensive history of text-critical research on Revelation from the beginning to 1955 and identified four major textual groupings: A C, $\mathfrak{P}^{47}$ S, *Av*, and K.[16] Although

10. See Aune, *Revelation 1–5*, cxlviii–cl.

11. See Aune, *Revelation 1–5*, cli–clvi; Parker, *New Testament Manuscripts*, 236–40; Schmid, *History of the Greek Text of the Apocalypse*. On the commentaries, see Victorinus et al., *Latin Commentaries*; Oecumenius and Andrew of Caesarea, *Greek Commentaries on Revelation*, ed. Thomas C. Oden and Gerald L. Bray, trans. William C. Weinrich, ACT (Downers Grove, IL: IVP Academic, 2011).

12. Bruce M. Metzger and Bart D. Ehrman, *The Text of the New Testament: Its Transmission, Corruption, and Restoration*, 4th ed. (Oxford: Oxford University Press, 2005), 137–45; Parker, *New Testament Manuscripts*, 227–228. On p. 148, Metzger and Ehrman note that in Erasmus's fourth edition, he altered the text of Revelation in about ninety passages on the basis of the Complutensian text.

13. For more detail on the early textual history of Revelation, see Parker, *New Testament Manuscripts*, 227–32; Hernández Jr., "Greek Text of Revelation," 345–51.

14. Hernández Jr., "Greek Text of Revelation," 349; see also Garrick V. Allen, *The Future of New Testament Textual Scholarship: From H. C. Hoskier to the Editio Critica Maior and Beyond*, WUNT 417 (Tübingen: Mohr Siebeck, 2019).

15. Hernández Jr., "Greek Text of Revelation," 350–51; see the English translation of Schmid, *History of the Greek Text of the Apocalypse*.

16. For an explanation of each text type or form, see Schmid, *History of the Greek Text of the Apocalypse*, xxix–xxxi.

the overall structure of Schmid's work remains in place today, the twenty-first century has seen his work modified in significant ways. Perhaps most importantly, the dating of the *Av* tradition has now shifted from the fourth century, as Schmid had concluded, to the seventh century. Also, newly discovered or previously unexamined manuscripts have come into play (e.g., Codex 2351, 2433, 2846, $\mathfrak{P}^{98}$, and $\mathfrak{P}^{115}$).

In terms of more recent developments, Hernández Jr. notes that the "greatest promise toward laying a new foundation for the Greek textual tradition [for Revelation] rests with the work of the *Text und Textwert* (*TuT*) volume published in 2017."[17] This volume contains the collation results of 123 test passages of Revelation and the evaluation list of all available Greek manuscripts.

Eventually the Coherence-Based Genealogical Method (CBGM) will offer a comprehensive genealogical analysis of the entire manuscript tradition of Revelation and will appear in the forthcoming *Editio Critica Maior* (*ECM*) of Revelation, produced by the Institut für neutestamentliche Textforschung in collaboration with other institutes.[18] The *ECM* aims to investigate all Greek witnesses, ancient versions, and patristic citations through the first millennium.[19] Future editions of the Nestle-Aland Greek New Testament (NA) will feature this text, as the NA^{28} already does for the Catholic Letters.[20]

6.2.2 The Most Important Witnesses to Revelation

In this section we will comment on a few of the most important manuscripts for studying Revelation.[21] The earliest witnesses are papyrus manuscripts, and the oldest extant witness is $\mathfrak{P}^{98}$ dating to the second century, but it only includes the text of Rev 1:13–20. The most important papyrus is $\mathfrak{P}^{47}$ (3rd c.), the Chester Beatty papyrus, which contains Rev 9:10–17:2. Koester notes, however, that "the scribe was careless about orthography, and the text may include up to eighty readings that are not supported by other manuscripts. None of the unique readings appears to preserve the earliest text. Overall, the readings often correspond to those in א."[22] The other

17. Hernández Jr., "Greek Text of Revelation," 352. See Markus Lembke, Darius Müller, and Ulrich B. Schmid, with Martin Karrer, eds., *Text und Textwert* der griechischen Handschriften des Neuen Testaments VI: Die Apokalypse; Teststellenkollation und Auswertungen, ANTF 49 (Berlin: de Gruyter, 2017).

18. The *ECM* of Revelation is under development at the Institut für Septuaginta- und biblische Textforschung at Kirchliche Hochschule Wuppertal/Bethel and is directed by Martin Karrer.

19. For more insight into CBGM and *ECM*, see Peter J. Gurry, "How Your Greek NT Is Changing: A Simple Introduction to the Coherence-Based Geneaological Method (CBGM)," *JETS* 59 (2016): 675–89; Peter M. Head, "Editio Critica Maior: An Introduction and Assessment," *TynBul* 61 (2010): 131–52.

20. While the text of the NA^{28} has only been revised for the Catholic Letters, this edition does update the manuscript data in the apparatus of the entire New Testament. See Juan Hernández Jr., "Nestle-Aland 28 and the Revision of the Apocalypse's Textual History," in Daniel M. Gurtner, Juan Hernández Jr., and Paul Foster, eds., *Studies of the Text of the NT and Early Christianity: Essays in Honor of Michael W. Holmes*, NTTSD 50 (Leiden: Brill, 2015), 71–81.

21. See the surveys of the manuscript tradition in Aune, *Revelation 1–5*, cxxxvi–clx; Koester, *Revelation*, 144–51; Parker, *New Testament Manuscripts*, 232–41; Tobias Nicklas, "The Early Text of Revelation," in *The Early Text of the New Testament*, ed. C. E. Hill and M. J. Kruger (Oxford: Oxford University Press, 2012), 225–38.

22. Koester, *Revelation*, 146–147.

significant papyrus manuscript is 𝔓[115], which was published in 1999. It contains portions of Rev 2; 3; 5–6; and 8–15, and plays an important role in assessing readings, as we will see below.

The oldest complete copies of Revelation are uncials. Codex Sinaiticus (א, 01) dates to the fourth century, while Codex Alexandrinus (A, 02) and Codex Ephraemi (C, 04) come from the fifth century. Codex Vaticanus (B, 03) does not include Revelation. Sinaiticus provides the oldest complete copy of Revelation, but the quality of Revelation's text (unlike the rest of the New Testament) is mixed due to scribal errors, omissions, and about two hundred singular readings. On Revelation, Sinaiticus (א) is considered inferior to the text of Codex Alexandrinus (A) and Codex Ephraemi (C). The most valuable complete manuscript of Revelation is A, which was copied by a single scribe and provides a high-quality reading that generally corresponds to C, another very valuable early witness to portions of Revelation (text from Rev 1; 3–5; 7–11; 16–18; 19–21). Codex C is the most important New Testament palimpsest. Both A and C are considered the best surviving witnesses to Revelation. Other fourth-century uncials include 0169, 0207, and 0308, which contain portions of Revelation 3:19–4:3, 9:2–15, and 11:15–18 respectively. Minuscules 2053, 2062, and 2344 also play an important role in connection with the commentary by Oecumenius.

6.2.3 Textual Criticism in Revelation

The goal of textual criticism remains that of reconstructing the "published" text—the final edited form released by the biblical author for circulation in the Christian community.[23] These final forms were eventually collected as authoritative Scripture and "came to be recognized as the authorized 'original' text of a given book."[24] The same goal remains for Revelation.

While the familiar text types of Alexandrian, Western, Byzantine, and Caesarean may be relevant for textual criticism in other parts of the New Testament (although these groupings are becoming outdated even there), the same rules do not apply to Revelation. The latest text-critical approaches rely on text-type categories less and less, but those forms will still prove useful while scholarship works out a better methodology. Schmid identifies four major textual groupings and most Revelation scholars continue to follow his lead. The two more ancient types were represented by A, C, Oecumenius, and 𝔓[115] (the primary type) and 𝔓[47], א and Origen (the secondary type). The two more

23. Philip W. Comfort, *Encountering the Manuscripts: An Introduction to New Testament Paleography and Textual Criticism* (Nashville: B&H Academic, 2005), 11–17.

24. Stanley E. Porter, *How We Got the New Testament: Text, Transmission, Translation* (Grand Rapids: Baker Academic, 2013), 32–36. Porter rightly cautions against a wholesale abandonment of seeking the "original" published text as the goal of textual criticism in favor of seeking the "initial text." These may or may not be the same, and the "initial text" concept potentially allows for a good bit of movement away from the biblical author. Contra Hernández Jr., "Greek Text of Revelation," 355, who claims that "the quest for the original has essentially been abandoned."

modern text types include the Andreas text (*Av*)[25] and the Koine (K) text.[26] Yet these two modern text types are edited versions of an earlier text and could be early enough (perhaps 4th c.) to represent the original reading. For example, in Rev 4:3 they correctly describe a rainbow (ἶρις), rather than priests (ἱερεῖς), around the throne.[27] For Schmid, no single text form dominates the *Urtext* and the original reading may be found in any one of the four types.[28]

What are some general guidelines for making reliable text-critical decisions in Revelation?[29] Text critics give priority to the two old text groupings (A, C, Oecumenius, 𝔓115 and 𝔓47, ℵ, Origen), and when these two agree that reading is normally to be preferred. When the two old groups differ, 𝔓115 carries extra weight. When there is no clear agreement among the groups, internal evidence will play a more important role. Fanning makes several important observations about the role of internal evidence. (1) Although singular readings (readings found in only one witness) are normally not given as much weight because of the smaller number of manuscripts for Revelation, readings supported by only a few witnesses sometimes need to be given more weight.[30] (2) The "shorter reading is always better" rule does not always apply since some scribes deleted rather than added material. (3) Some scribes tended to smooth out or correct Revelation's unusual grammar so such corrections may be less likely to be original. And similarly, (4) theological adjustments (e.g., toward a higher Christology) are sometimes evident and may indicate a secondary reading.[31]

An interesting case in point regarding textual decisions relates to the number of the beast in Rev 13:18. The NA28 text reads ἑξακόσιοι ἑξήκοντα ἕξ (i.e., 666). This reading is supported by the 𝔓47/ℵ text, A, P, 046, 051, 𝔐 (in Revelation the agreement of the *Av* and K texts), most minuscules, many early versions. Irenaeus (2nd. c.) knew and accepted 666 and knew but did not accept 616 apparently. The leading variant reads εξακοσιαι δεκα εξ (616) and is supported by C and now by the oldest surviving manuscript with that reading—𝔓115 (late 3rd or early 4th c.). Both numbers can produce the same connection to "Nero(n) Caesar" written in Hebrew characters

25. This text is represented by some seventy-five copies of the Revelation commentary of Andreas of Caesarea ca. AD 563–614 (David Aune, *Revelation 1–5*, clvi).

26. The K text is a group of manuscripts within the Byzantine tradition and dating to the 9th to the 10th centuries (Barbara Aland and Klaus Wachtel, "The Greek Minuscule Manuscripts of the New Testament," in *The Text of the New Testament in Contemporary Research: Essays on the* Status Quaestionis," ed. Bart Ehrman and Michael W. Holmes, Studies and Documents [Grand Rapids: Eerdmans, 1995], 44).

27. Koester, *Revelation*, 143.

28. Schmid, *Studies in the History of the Greek Text of the Apocalypse*, xxiv.

29. For the suggestions to follow, see Parker, *New Testament Manuscripts*, 241–45; Fanning, *Revelation*, 51–53; Koester, *Revelation*, 50.

30. Fanning, *Revelation*, 52, gives as examples the singular readings from Codex A that are "almost universally accepted as original: 12:10 (κατήγωρ); 13:10 (ἀποκτανθῆναι); 21:4 (ἀπῆλθαν)." See also Garrick V. Allen, "The Apocalypse in Codex Alexandrinus: Exegetical Reasonings and Singular Readings in New Testament Greek Manuscripts," *JBL* 135 (2016): 862–66.

31. On scribal tendencies, see also Juan Hernández Jr., "The Apocalypse in Codex Alexandrinus: Its Singular Readings and Scribal Habits," in Patrick Gray and Gail R. O'Day, eds., *Scripture and Traditions: Essays on Early Judaism and Christianity in Honor of Carl R. Holladay*, NovTSup 129 (Leiden: Brill, 2008), 342–52.

(נרון קסר [*nrwn qsr*]—666 with and 616 without the final consonant ן [*n*] on the first word). Also, the Greek word "beast" in the genitive as it is in 13:18 (θηρίου) equals 616 when transliterated into Hebrew (תריו [*tryw*]), while the nominative form (θηρίον) transliterated into Hebrew (תריון [*trywn*]) equals 666.

Koester rightly prefers the reading ἑξακόσιοι ἑξήκοντα ἕξ (666) due to the breadth of attestation and the probability that a symmetrical number like 666 (rather than 616) would match better with 144,000 in Rev 14:1.[32] Furthermore, the second century church father Irenaeus was familiar with both readings and said that 666 was found "in all the most approved and ancient copies" by men "who saw John face to face."[33] But Aune, Metzger, and other reliable text critical guidebooks who opted for 666 were written prior to the publication of 𝔓[115], so the alternate reading of 616 now becomes a more serious contender. Peter J. Williams adds another reason why 616 may deserve more serious consideration.[34] In 𝔓[115] the number of the beast is written in digits as χιϛ (indicated by a line over them). Elsewhere in the manuscript such a line indicates a *nomen sacrum*, and χιϛ is visually similar to the *nomina sacra* χϛ [with line] "Christ" and ιϛ "Jesus." Williams suggests the possibility that the number could have been "a deliberate mimicking of the appearance of these *nomina sacra*."[35]

Textual criticism in Revelation, as our short discussion notes, is more complicated than in the rest of the New Testament. Although the text is well established in the Western church, the limited number of manuscripts means that typical patterns reflected in New Testament textual criticism may need modification when it comes to the Apocalypse. Other considerations such as the author's established style, scribal habits, the influence of the Old Testament, and so on. may often play a significant role in these decisions.

6.3 THE CANONICITY OF REVELATION

6.3.1 Early Acceptance in the West

Revelation was accepted as Christian Scripture from the beginning in the Western church. The first explicit mention of Revelation is by Justin Martyr in the middle of the second century, who attributed authorship to John the apostle.[36] But even earlier we know that Papias (late 1st–early 2nd c.) comments on Rev 12:7–8, as Andrew of Caesarea notes in his commentary (early 7th c.).[37] Ignatius (AD 110–117) and the

32. Koester, *Revelation*, 599.

33. Irenaeus, *Haer.* 5.30.1 (*ANF* 1:558).

34. Peter J. Williams, "P115 and the Number of the Beast," *TynBul* 58 (2007): 151–53.

35. Williams, "P115 and the Number of the Beast," 153.

36. Justin, *Dial.* 81.15.

37. Andrew of Caesarea, *Commentary on the Apocalypse* 34.12. Bandy observes that Gerhard Maier, who has produced the most thorough investigation of Papias and the book of Revelation, concludes that Papias knew John the apostle (the "Elder" in Asia Minor) and attributed the book to him. See Gerhard Maier, *Die Johannesoffenbarung und die Kirche*, WUNT 25 (Tübingen: Mohr Siebeck, 1981), 62–63; Bandy, "Should John's Apocalypse Be in the Canon?," 12.

Epistle of Barnabas (AD 130–131) may also allude to Revelation, though these connections are questionable.[38] Revelation was likely used by the Shepherd of Hermes (ca. AD 140) and by Melito of Sardis (ca. AD 165). In the prologue to his commentary, Andrew of Caesarea also refers to other proponents of Revelation: the early church leaders Papias, Irenaeus, Methodius, and Hippolytus, along with the later leaders Gregory of Nazianzus and Cyril of Alexandria.[39] Irenaeus (late 2nd c.) makes frequent use of Revelation, as do Tertullian and Cyprian. Other influential church leaders such as Clement of Alexandria, Jerome, and Augustine also affirm its canonical status.

Revelation is included in the earliest list of canonical books, the Muratorian Canon (late 2nd c. or, more recently dated, 4th c.), Eusebius, *Ecclesiatical History* 3.25 (late 3rd c.), and in Athanasius's thirty-ninth festal letter, written for Easter in AD 367, where he lists the now familiar twenty-seven New Testament books. Revelation was also included in the official canonical list at the Council of Carthage in AD 397. The earliest known commentary on the Apocalypse is that of Victorinus, bishop of Petovium, (late 3rd century).[40]

The book was opposed by the heretic Marcion, who also rejected any New Testament book that was sympathetic to the Old Testament or Judaism, which certainly included Revelation with its plethora of Old Testament allusions. It was also rejected by Gaius (a church leader in Rome at the beginning of the 2nd c.) and by the group known as the Alogoi, probably because they associated it with Montanist movement. In the early third century Hippolytus (ca. AD 170–235) quotes Revelation extensively in refuting Gaius's criticism of both the Gospel of John and Revelation.[41] Carson and Moo rightly conclude that "these scattered rejections of Revelation in the Western church did not affect its canonicity, and from this point forward there is no hint of doubt about Revelation's full canonical status in the West."[42]

6.3.2 The Struggle for Acceptance in the East

Revelation's canonical status in the East, however, was a mixed bag. Although accepted and used by early leaders such as Theophilus of Antioch (d. ca. AD 183), Clement of Alexandria (d. ca. AD 215), and Origen (d. AD 254), Revelation was for all practical purposes dismissed by Origen's student Dionysius, the bishop of Alexandria from AD 248–264. Dionysius said John the Apostle wrote the Gospel, but Revelation

38. Osborne, *Revelation*, 23. For Ignatius, see Ign. *Eph.* 15.3 = Rev 21:3; Ign. *Phld.* 6.1 = Rev 3:12, and for the Epistle of Barnabas, see Barn. 6.13 = Rev 21:3; Barn. 21.3 = Rev 22:10.

39. Oecumenius and Andrew of Caesarea, *Greek Commentaries*, 114. He cites the following as those who "testified to the trustworthiness of the book": Gregory of Nazianzus, *Or. Bas.* 29.17; 42.9; Cyril of Alexandria, *Adoration and Worship of God in Spirit and Truth* 6; Irenaeus *Haer.* 1.26.3; 4.14.2; 4.17.6; 4.18.6; 4.20.11; 5.26–34; Methodius, *Res.* 2.28; *Symp.* 1.5; 5.8; 6.5; Hippolytus, *Antichr.*, where Revelation is used often.

40. Victorinus et al., *Latin Commentaries*.

41. Craig D. Allert, *A High View of Scripture: The Authority of the Bible and the Formation of the New Testament Canon* (Grand Rapids: Baker Academic, 2007), 135–36.

42. Carson and Moo, *Introduction to the New Testament*, 717.

was written by another person named John. This authorship distinction diminished Revelation's credibility and raised serious doubts about it in the East for a period. Dionysius was motivated, it seems, by his anti-chiliastic position. In addition, certain Eastern church leaders refused to acknowledge Revelation as canonical (e.g., Cyril of Jerusalem). It is also missing from the Apostolic Canons, the Syriac Peshitta, and was not included in the lectionaries of the Eastern church. In addition, other Eastern church leaders such as Theodore of Mopsuestia, John Chrysostom, and Theodoret of Cyrus never quote from Revelation.

Yet several influential Eastern church leaders did accept the book as canonical. It is listed in the catalogues of Epiphanius and Athanasius and is accepted and referenced by Origen, Basil of Caesarea, and Cyril of Alexandria.[43] No doubt support by influential leaders such as Jerome (c. 414) and Augustine (c. 426) paved the way for greater acceptance. Due in part to the Greek commentaries on Revelation by Oecumenius and Andreas in the sixth and seventh centuries, Revelation gained favor in the East and the Council of Constantinople in AD 680 granted it canonical status.[44]

Revelation was likely rejected in the East largely because of its eschatological focus. It would not be the last time that Revelation would be rejected for theological rather than historical reasons. Martin Luther gave it a backseat to other New Testament books saying, "My spirit cannot accommodate itself to this book. There is one sufficient reason for this small esteem in which I hold it—that Christ is neither taught nor recognized" (in preface to Luther's 1522 Bible). Carson and Moo rightly respond, "One might wonder at this point whether Luther was reading the same book that we have in our Bibles, the book that makes 'the Lamb that was slain' the linchpin in God's plan for history and the end of history."[45] Kruger notes several reasons why Revelation gained acceptance in the end: (1) the connection to Papias in the early second century, (2) the belief that the apostle John was the author, and (3) those who accepted the book early on included both chiliasts and non-chiliasts.[46]

6.3.3 Revelation's Canonical Function

Aside from contributing to our knowledge of the history of the canonical reception afforded Revelation, the book serves a larger canonical purpose, first in relationship to the rest of the New Testament and then in connection with the grand story of Scripture.[47] As a New Testament letter, Revelation focuses on the Christian community,

43. Weinrich, *Revelation*, xx.

44. Osborne, *Revelation*, 24. See also Michael J. Kruger, *Canon Revisited: Establishing the Origins and Authority of the New Testament Books* (Wheaton, IL: Crossway, 2012), 273–74.

45. Carson and Moo, *Introduction to the New Testament*, 718.

46. Michael J. Kruger, "The Reception of the Book of Revelation in the Early Church," in Thomas J. Kraus and Michael Sommer, eds., *Book of Seven Seals*, WUNT 363 (Tübingen: Mohr Siebeck, 2016), 173.

47. Much of this section is drawn from Duvall, "The Transforming Vision"; Tõniste, *Ending of the Canon*; Thomas and Macchia, *Revelation*, 15–16; and the monograph by Tabb, *All Things New*. See also Duvall and Hays, *God's Relational Presence*, esp. 279–323.

the foundation of her ultimate hope in Christ, the false teachings and powers that threaten her, and the need for faithful perseverance—similar emphases to what we encounter in Paul's letters, for example.

Because Revelation is Christocentric, it also offers continuity and fulfillment in relationship to the Gospels. Some ancient manuscripts even place Revelation just after the Gospels to highlight this connection.[48] Revelation shows the fulfillment of Messiah's salvific mission to the Jewish people and the nations (e.g., the 144,000 and the great multitude).[49] There is also a link between the Fourth Gospel and Revelation, made even stronger if apostolic authorship is granted as we have argued; for example, the continuity and fulfillment in the portrayals of Jesus as the Lamb of God and the work of the Holy Spirit.[50]

Revelation also serves as the "climax of prophecy," as Richard Bauckham has so forcefully argued:

> John was writing what he understood to be a work of prophetic scripture, the climax of prophetic revelation, which gathered up the prophetic meaning of the Old Testament scriptures and disclosed the way in which it was being and was to be fulfilled in the last days . . . because in the revelation made to him by Jesus Christ was disclosed the secret of the divine purpose for the final coming of the kingdom of God.[51]

In the Apocalypse we find the "canonical capstone," the final, climactic chapter of the grand story of the Bible. Tabb writes, "Revelation brings the scriptural narrative concerning God, his people and his world to its grand conclusion in the already-not-yet reign of Christ and the glorious new creation."[52] As the concluding chapter to God's story, Revelation uses colorful language and powerful imagery to show how God reverses the curse of sin, restores his creation, and lives among his people forever. There are numerous parallels between the opening chapters of Genesis and the closing chapters of Revelation.[53] Humanity's rebellion has been conquered through judgment and salvation. God's reign has been established on earth as in heaven. God's creation has been redeemed as originally intended. And it all comes back to the garden, this time the garden of the new creation where God's people worshipfully enjoy his presence for eternity.

48. Bruce M. Metzger, *The Canon of the New Testament: Its Origin, Development, and Significance* (Oxford: Clarendon Press, 1987), 295.

49. Thomas and Macchia, *Revelation*, 16.

50. Thomas and Macchia, *Revelation*, 16. For more details of this relationship, see Duvall and Hays, *God's Relational Presence*, 279–323.

51. Bauckham, *Climax of Prophecy*, xi, xvi.

52. Tabb, *All Things New*, 24; cf. also 227.

53. Duvall, "Transforming Vision," 270–72.

6.4 CONCLUSION

The early church wrestled with Revelation on a canonical-textual level as well as on a theological level. Yet the Greek text of Revelation is well attested. As a vast improvement on Erasmus's Greek text of the Apocalypse, we have multiple critical editions produced in the 1800s. The work of Josef Schmid (mid-20th c.) stands as a landmark contribution to the study of Revelation's text. More recent developments include the recently published *Text und Textwert* (*TuT*) volume and the ongoing *Editio Critica Maior* (*ECM*) project. For Revelation, presently the most valuable manuscripts include $\mathfrak{P}^{115}$, Alexandrinus (A), Ephraemi (C), and Oecumenius, with $\mathfrak{P}^{47}$, Sinaiticus (א), and Origen also offering valuable contributions. But we are quick to add that relying strictly on a single manuscript or textual grouping in Revelation is not as important as looking carefully at each textual decision in the context of other important factors such as the author's style, scribal habits, the influence of the Old Testament, and so on.

In terms of Revelation's place in the canon of Scripture, the Western church accepted the book early on without reserve. From Papias to Justin Martyr to Irenaeus and beyond, Revelation was accepted in the West. However, the book struggled for acceptance in the East due in large part to the influence of Origen's student Dionysius. In spite of being rejected or, more commonly, ignored by Eastern leaders, Revelation was not without its influential advocates in both the East and West (e.g., Origen, Jerome, Augustine). Kruger rightly concludes that "with such broad support for Revelation, along with its very early attestation and reception, the confusion in the East eventually dissipated, and the book was once again universally acknowledged."[54]

And as we attempt to discern the details of Revelation's textual and canonical past, we must not lose sight of its canonical contribution on a theological level—as the climactic chapter of God's great story. The book's canonical function will be expanded in Chapter 11, A Literary-Theological Reading of Revelation.

54. Kruger, *Canon Revisited*, 274.

Chapter 7

THE GRAMMAR AND SYMBOLIC LANGUAGE OF REVELATION

BIBLIOGRAPHY

Bandy, Alan S. "The Hermeneutics of Symbolism: How to Interpret the Symbols of John's Apocalypse." *SBJT* 14.1 (2010): 46–58. **Callahan, Allen Dwight.** "Language of the Apocalypse." *HTR* 88 (1995): 453–70. **Campbell, Constantine R.** *Basics of Verbal Aspect.* Grand Rapids: Zondervan, 2008. ———. *Verbal Aspect, the Indicative Mood, and Narrative: Soundings in the Greek of the New Testament.* SBG 13. New York: Peter Lang, 2007. ———. *Verbal Aspect and Non-Indicative Verbs: Further Soundings in the Greek of the New Testament.* SBG 15. New York: Peter Lang, 2008. **Decker, Rodney.** *Temporal Deixis of the Greek Verb in the Gospel of Mark with Reference to Verbal Aspect.* SBG 10. New York: Peter Lang, 2001. **Deissmann, Adolf.** *Light from the Ancient East: The New Testament Illustrated by Recently Discovered Texts of the Graeco-Roman World.* 2nd ed. Translated by Lionel R. M. Strachan. London: Hodder & Stoughton, 1911. **DeSilva, David A.** *Seeing Things John's Way: The Rhetoric of the Book of Revelation.* Louisville: Westminister John Knox, 2009. **Evans, Craig A., and James A. Sanders,** eds. *Early Christian Interpretation of the Scriptures of Israel: Investigations and Proposals.* JSNTSup 148. Sheffield: Sheffield Academic, 1997. **Fanning, Buist M.** *Verbal Aspect in New Testament Greek.* Oxford: Clarendon, 1990. **Guffey, Andrew R.** *The Book of Revelation and the Visual Culture of Asia Minor: A Concurrence of Images.* Lanham; London: Lexington Books; Fortress Academic, 2019. **Hays, Richard B.** *The Moral Vision of the New Testament: A Contemporary Introduction to New Testament Ethics.* New York: HarperSanFrancisco, 1996. **Huber, Konrad.** "Imagery in the Book of Revelation." *OHBR* 53–67. **Mathewson, David L.** *Revelation: A Handbook on the Greek Text.* Waco, TX: Baylor University Press, 2016. ———. "Revelation's Use of the Greek Language." *OBHR* 101–14. ———. "Verbal Aspect in the Apocalypse of John: An Analysis of Revelation 5." *NovT* 50 (2008): 58–77. ———. *Verbal Aspect in the Book of Revelation: The Function of Greek Verb Tenses in John's Apocalypse.* LBS 4. Leiden: Brill, 2010. **McKay, K. L.** *A New Syntax of the Verb in the New Testament.* SBG 5. New York: Peter Lang, 1994. **Metzger, Bruce M.** *Breaking the Code: Understanding the Book of Revelation.* Nashville: Abingdon, 1993. **Mussies, G.** *The Morphology of Koine Greek as Used in the Apocalypse of St. John: A Study in Bilingualism.* NovTSup 27. London: Brill, 1971. **Ozanne,**

C. G. "The Language of the Apocalypse." *TynBul* 16 (1965): 3–9. **Paul, Ian.** "The Book of Revelation: Image, Symbol and Metaphor." Pages 131–47 in *Studies in the Book of Revelation*. Edited by Steve Moyise. Edinburgh: T&T Clark, 2001. **Porter, Stanley E.** "The Language of the Apocalypse in Recent Discussion." *NTS* 35 (1989): 582–603. ———. *Verbal Aspect in the Greek of the New Testament, with Reference to Tense and Mood*. SBG 1. New York: Peter Lang, 1989. **Poythress, Vern S.** "Genre and Hermeneutics in Rev 20:1–6." *JETS* 36 (1993): 51–54. **Schmid, Joseph.** *Studies in the History of the Greek Text of the Apocalypse*. Translated and edited by Juan Hernández Jr., Garrick V. Allen, and Darius Müller. Atlanta: SBL Press, 2017. **Schmidt, Daryl D.** "Semitisms and Septuagintalisms in the Book of Revelation." *NTS* 37 (1991): 592–603. **Stewart, Alexander E.** "*Ekphrasis*, Fear, and Motivation in the Apocalypse of John." *BBR* 27 (2017): 227–40. **Thompson, Steven.** *The Apocalypse and Semitic Syntax*. SNTSMS 52. Cambridge: Cambridge University Press, 1985. **Turner, Nigel.** *Style*. Vol. 4 of *A Grammar of New Testament Greek*. 4 vols. Edited by James H. Moulton. Edinburgh: T&T Clark, 1976. **Ureña, Lourdes García.** *Narrative and Drama in the Book of Revelation: A Literary Approach*. SNTSMS 175. Cambridge: Cambridge University Press, 2019. **Wallace, Daniel B.** *Greek Grammar beyond the Basics: An Exegetical Syntax of the New Testament*. Grand Rapids: Zondervan, 1996. **Watt, Jonathan M.** "Some Implications of Bilingualism for New Testament Exegesis." Pages 9–27 in *The Language of the New Testament: Context, History, and Development*. Edited by Stanley E. Porter and Andrew W. Pitts. LBS 6. Leiden: Brill, 2013. **Yarbro Collins, Adela.** "Numerical Symbolism in Jewish and Early Christian Apocalyptic Literature." *ANRW* II/21/2 (1984): 1221–87. ———. "Pergamon in Early Christian Literature." Pages 163–84 in *Pergamon: Citadel of the Gods*. Edited by Helmut Koester. Harrisburg, PA: Trinity Press International, 1998.

7.1 INTRODUCTION

The language of Revelation is stimulating and challenging both at a grammatical and at a symbolic level. It is simply unlike any other New Testament book. In this chapter we will explore the idiosyncratic grammar of Revelation in more detail, looking specifically at what marks it out as peculiar and why. Was John simply a bad grammarian or is something more intentional at work? Does the grammar result from John writing in a second language or is there a better explanation? In addition, we will address the issue of verbal aspect in Revelation and see how this sheds light on the ways this remarkable book communicates.

Next, we will investigate Revelation's symbolic language. How does Revelation use picture language to communicate? What is the nature of this symbolic language and what is John trying to accomplish through the use of such vivid and fantastic imagery? And where do we turn to grasp the meaning and significance of the imagery? We will save the issue of interpreting Revelation's symbolic language for later (see Ch. 10).

7.2 THE GRAMMAR OF REVELATION

7.2.1 Revelation's Idiosyncratic but Intentional Grammar

Revelation's grammatical peculiarities are well known.[1] The same Dionysius of Alexandria who denies apostolic authorship also had a strong opinion about the Greek of the Apocalypse: "his dialect and language are not accurate Greek, but . . . he uses barbarous idioms, and, in some places, solecisms."[2] Such idiosyncrasies include lack of agreement in case and gender with nouns and participles, improper case usage, redundant pronouns, word order, unusual use of prepositions and conjunctions, and odd lexical choices.[3]

The classic example of John's peculiar grammar appears in portions of the greeting in 1:4–5 (CSB): "Grace and peace to you from the one who is, who was, and who is to come, and from the seven spirits before his throne, and from Jesus Christ, the faithful witness" (χάρις ὑμῖν καὶ εἰρήνη ἀπὸ ὁ ὢν καὶ ὁ ἦν καὶ ὁ ἐρχόμενος καὶ ἀπὸ τῶν ἑπτὰ πνευμάτων ἃ ἐνώπιον τοῦ θρόνου αὐτοῦ καὶ ἀπὸ Ἰησοῦ Χριστοῦ, ὁ μάρτυς, ὁ πιστός . . . ὁ ἄρχων). The preposition ἀπό normally takes the genitive case, but here God is identified using the nominative case (ὁ . . . ὁ . . . ὁ). In this description of God, John puts a definite article before the participle, which is common (ὁ ὢν), but then also uses the article as the subject of the verb (ὁ ἦν), which is not expected. Then in verse 5 John describes "Jesus Christ" in the genitive case (Ἰησοῦ Χριστοῦ) using three appositional terms in the nominative case, when one would expect the genitive for agreement—"the faithful witness," "the firstborn," and "the ruler." John does not play by the rules at times, and this results in a peculiar style that sometimes violates conventional grammatical patterns. Copyists would often correct the grammar to bring it into line with standard practice.[4]

Fanning is surely correct, however, to caution against concluding that John's grammar is simply "bad" or "incorrect," preferring instead to admit that it is nonstandard, nonnormal, unexpected, unusual, and the like.[5] John can play by the rules when he wants to, so there must be valid reasons for his peculiar usages. We will explore these options below (see 7.2.2), but first a couple of helpful clarifications. Fanning notes

1. See Charles, *Revelation of St John*, 1:cxvii–clix; Schmid, *History of the Greek Text of the Apocalypse*, 183–263; G. Mussies, *The Morphology of Koine Greek as Used in the Apocalypse of St. John: A Study in Bilingualism*, NovTSup 27 (London: Brill, 1971); Steven Thompson, *The Apocalypse and Semitic Syntax*, SNTSMS 52 (Cambridge: Cambridge University Press, 1985); and more recently, see the comprehensive treatment of the syntax of Revelation in Aune, *Revelation 1–5*, clix–ccvii, where he addresses the use of the article, pronouns, adjectives, cases, prepositions, verb tenses, the participle, the infinitive, particles and parataxis, coordinate and subordinate clauses, Semitic interference, and issues of agreement. See also the overview of apparent grammatical incongruities in David L. Mathewson, "Revelation's Use of the Greek Language," *OHBR* 102–3, 108–11.

2. Eusebius, *Hist. eccl.* 7.25.26 (*NPNF*[2] 1:311).

3. See Charles, *Revelation of St John*, 1:cxlii–cliv; Nigel Turner, *Style*, vol. 4 of *A Grammar of New Testament Greek*, ed. James Hope Moulton, 4 vols. (Edinburgh: T&T Clark, 1908–1976), 145–58; BDF §§136–37.

4. Koester, *Revelation*, 139.

5. Fanning, *Revelation*, 53–54.

two significant qualifications.[6] First, linguistic patterns vary from person to person and from language to language, and usage varies depending on the audience, the social purpose, the intended message, and so on. Linguistic competence includes the ability to adapt to the situation as needed and John certainly does this. Second, John's nonstandard usage rarely if ever obstructs or hinders the effective communication of his message. Readers struggle with interpreting Revelation for a lot of reasons, but failing to grasp John's grammatical oddities is not one of them.

As we said, John can play by the rules when he wants to. In other words, his peculiar grammar is intentional. The grammatical rules that are set aside in some places are observed elsewhere.[7] Rather than John being careless, incompetent, or linguistically inadequate, Callahan argues that John's "language is due not to intellectual deficiency, but to an idiolectical peculiarity that is both intentional and insurgent."[8] Looking briefly at the 1:4–5 example, we find several reasonable explanations for John's unusual grammar. First, ἀπό takes the description of God in the nominative rather than the Genitive likely because of the connection to the name of God in the LXX of Exodus 3:14 (Ἐγώ εἰμι ὁ ὤν). John goes out of his way to honor God's name, and here this clause functions as a divine title. Wallace notes that nowhere else does John use a nominative immediately following a preposition and even uses ἀπό thirty-two times with a genitive immediately following.[9] Second, the use of the article with the verb (ὁ ἦν) may also serve to get the reader's attention by expressing something about God in an unusual way, but in a way that preserves what may have been a general title for God in Judaism.[10] Third, the link between Jesus Christ in the genitive with the three appositional terms in the nominative may also preserve the grammatical case of the Old Testament allusion (Ps 88:38 LXX [EVV 89:37; MT 89:38]: καὶ ὁ μάρτυς ἐν οὐρανῷ πιστός). The point in this brief example is not to provide a detailed exegesis of Rev 1:4–5 but to show that John was intentional with his unusual grammar rather than incompetent, uninformed, or just mistaken. While each grammatical departure from the norm will need to be analyzed in its own context, there are some general explanations.

7.2.2 Possible Explanations for the Grammatical Peculiarities

A position popular in the past is famously summarized by Charles's quip that while John "wrote in Greek he thought in Hebrew."[11] John was at home in Hebrew (and Aramaic) because of his Palestinian heritage but, as this explanation goes, never truly

6. Fanning, *Revelation*, 53–54.

7. C. G. Ozanne, "The Language of the Apocalypse," *TynBul* 16 (1965): 3–9.

8. Allen Dwight Callahan, "Language of the Apocalypse," *HTR* 88 (1995): 454.

9. Daniel B. Wallace, *Greek Grammar beyond the Basics: An Exegetical Syntax of the New Testament* (Grand Rapids: Zondervan, 1996), 63. Wallace insightfully suggests that 1:4 "may function paradigmatically for many of the solecisms" by telling the reader to pay careful attention to his words, words rooted in the Old Testament (*Grammar*, 64). For John it seems that at times theological emphases trump grammatical formalities.

10. Beale, *Revelation*, 187–88.

11. Charles, *Revelation of St John*, 1:x, xxi, xliv, cxliii.

mastered Greek, so he translated his idioms literally into Greek. The grammatical peculiarities of Revelation, then, are attributable to Semitic syntax, primarily biblical Hebrew and Aramaic.[12] This is what Thompson deems "Jewish Greek" and Turner calls "Biblical Greek": "Especially is this so in that book which closes the canon and which is, I think, the most characteristic example of this kind of Greek, the chief glory of this hieratic tongue. The Book of Revelation is the sublimest icon of them all."[13] This explanation suggests that in Revelation the Greek serves as a thin covering for a thoroughly Semitic framework. Grammatical solecisms tend to be viewed as "Semitisms"—"a non-Greek construction produced by an overly literal rendering either of a Hebrew or Aramaic oral or written source."[14] But as Porter has demonstrated, the most we can argue for is "Semitic enhancement" at points, and even that remains doubtful.[15]

An alternative explanation sees John's primary language as Greek, but his grammatical style comes not from Hebrew or Aramaic but primarily from Septuagintal influence.[16] According to Schmidt, a "Septuagintalism" is a syntactical peculiarity that results from rendering Semitic constructions into Greek in one of the translation styles of the Greek Old Testament (vs. idiomatic Greek or the translation of Semitic grammatical structure).[17] Callahan notes, for example, that the nominative and infinitive construction of Rev 12:7 is "barbaric," but the construction has a precedent in the LXX (Hos 9:13; 1 Chr 9:25; Ps 24:14 [EVV, MT 25:14]; Eccl 3:15) and so "any Greek speaker familiar with the Septuagint would have encountered this construction simply by reading the Greek Bible and being influenced by its language."[18] But while the influence of the Greek Old Testament on John's grammar and style would account for some irregularities, it would certainly not explain them all, especially those not characteristic of the LXX.[19]

Beale has argued that John's unusual grammar intentionally calls attention to the Old Testament.[20] Many of these irregularities occur, Beale contends, when John alludes to the Old Testament because "John is carrying over the exact grammatical forms of

12. Steven Thompson, *Apocalypse and Semitic Syntax*, 1, 47–50, 102–8; cf. also Nigel Turner, *Grammatical Insights into the New Testament* (Edinburgh: T&T Clark, 1966), 183. See Aune, *Revelation 1–5*, cxcix–cciii, for examples of what he labels "Semitic interference." See Stanley E. Porter, "The Language of the Apocalypse in Recent Discussion," *NTS* 35 (1989): 582–603, for a convincing critique of Thompson and others taking this view.

13. Steven Thompson, *Apocalypse and Semitic Syntax*, 108; Turner, *Grammatical Insights*, 188, respectively.

14. Beale, *Revelation*, 103.

15. Porter, "Language of the Apocalypse," 587, 599–600.

16. See Daryl D. Schmidt, "Semitisms and Septuagintalisms in the Book of Revelation," *NTS* 37 (1991): 592–603.

17. Schmidt, "Semitisms and Septuagintalisms," 594, 596, 602.

18. Callahan, "Language of the Apocalypse," 456. See David L. Mathewson, *Revelation: A Handbook on the Greek Text* (Waco, TX: Baylor University Press, 2016), 161, for an explanation of the grammatical difficulties of this verse.

19. Fanning, *Revelation*, 56.

20. See Beale, *Revelation*, 77–99 for "The Use of the Old Testament in the Apocalypse" and 100–103 for "The Solecisms as Signals for the Presence of Old Testament Allusions," in addition to his fuller treatment, "Solecisms in the Apocalypse as Signals for the Presence of Old Testament Allusions: A Selective Analysis of Revelation 1–22," in *Early Christian Interpretation of the Scriptures of Israel: Investigations and Proposals*, ed. Craig A. Evans and James A. Sanders, JSNTSup 148 (Sheffield: Sheffield Academic Press, 1997), 421–46.

the allusions, often from the various versions of the Greek OT and sometimes from the Hebrew."[21] Since John does not change the grammatical form to fit the surrounding context in Revelation, it becomes quite obvious. This creates what Beale calls "syntactical dissonance," which focuses John's readers sharply on the Old Testament allusion.[22] It creates a kind of "biblical effect" to show the solidarity of his message with the Old Testament.[23] But Fanning cautions that while Old Testament allusions occasionally help explain Revelation's grammatical irregularities, they generally do not (e.g., Rev 1:5; 2:13; 4:1; 8:9; 9:14; 11:15; 12:7; 14:7).[24]

Some take a more sociolinguistic view by contending that John's peculiar grammatical style stems from his attempt to subvert the dominant language of the empire. Koester seems sympathetic to this view when he observes that "at points the writer deliberately flouts the accepted forms of grammar, which fits the idea that neither the writer nor the God to whom he bears witness is held captive by social convention."[25] Callahan is more direct when he says that John's deviations from standard Greek syntax "alter the language, defamiliarize it, and subvert it."[26] He labels Revelation a "solecistic liturgy," a text that "asserts anew the authenticity of subaltern voices." And every time its words are repeated, the Greek language ceases to be "an imperialist prison" as its readers "participate in the emancipation of discourse itself."[27] Yet this polemical view falls short of adequately explaining John's peculiar grammar. That John is relying on scattered grammatical irregularities as a means of rebelling against the empire is simply not persuasive as a primary strategy. Such an approach may even serve to undermine his already understandable subversive message.

Perhaps the most realistic explanation is that John's peculiar grammar results not from one but from several factors. To begin with, he was multilingual. While his first language was Aramaic or Hebrew, he was still quite capable in Greek.[28] Revelation was not written in Hebrew and then translated badly into Greek, contends Fanning, nor did John struggle to express himself in Greek so that we should question his competence.[29] But his first linguistic instincts were drawn from the Semitic languages he knew and used most naturally and these affect his Greek linguistic choices. Some of John's expressions would surely have been a bit awkward in a second language, but these can be viewed positively. Watt writes, "Bilinguals have a tremendous capacity for communicative diversity and creativity" since their "mental lexicon permits flexibility

21. Beale, *Revelation*, 101. Beale cites Rev 1:4, 5, 10–11, 12, 15; 2:13, 20; 3:12; 4:1; 5:6a, 12; 7:4, 8, 9b; 8:9; 9:14; 10:2, 8; 11:4, 15; 12:5, 7; 14:7, 19; 19:6, 20; 20:2 as examples. See also Bauckham, *Climax of Prophecy*, 270–271 and 286, where he writes, "Unusual and difficult phrases in Revelation frequently turn out to be Old Testament allusions."

22. Beale, *Revelation*, 101.

23. Beale, *Revelation*, 103.

24. Fanning, *Revelation*, 56–57.

25. Koester, *Revelation*, 141.

26. Callahan, "Language of the Apocalypse, 466.

27. Callahan, "Language of the Apocalypse, 470.

28. This seems to be the position of Fanning, *Revelation*, 53–58.

29. Fanning, *Revelation*, 54–55.

of meaning that exceeds the monolingual's possibilities."[30] As a result, John would have possessed a "diverse arsenal of competencies" to communicate effectively as he saw fit.[31]

In addition to his multilingual capabilities, surely the role of Old Testament allusions, the influence of the LXX, the "abnormal" subject matter of prophetic-apocalyptic, and his theological/spiritual and social contexts would best account for his grammatical idiosyncrasies. Also, if apostolic authorship holds, as we contend, John was a Palestinian Jew who had for some time (probably decades) lived in Asia Minor. This older man had been (or still was) a prisoner on Patmos. He was also thoroughly immersed in the Greek translation of the Old Testament and was writing to churches in Asia Minor. At times, John seems to use peculiar grammatical forms simply for emphasis, especially in connection with the Old Testament (e.g., identifying God in the nominative in 1:4 to preserve God's self-identification in Exod 3:14 and emphasize his absoluteness). These various factors can account for John's irregular grammar at points, and each context must be studied carefully to tease out the particular influence. Nevertheless, John's Greek, as Mathewson argues, "falls within the range of acceptable first-century Greek."[32] One more recent approach to understanding John's grammar, especially his variation of verb tenses, is that of verbal aspect.

7.2.3 Verbal Aspect in Revelation

Grammarians have traditionally understood Greek verbs in terms of time (tense) and/or kind of action (*Aktionsart*). More recently, there is increasing recognition that the Greek verb system relies even more on "verbal aspect," which speaks to how the author chooses to view or portray the action. Most simply, verbal aspect refers to the viewpoint of the author or speaker.[33] The theory and practice of verbal aspect has been the topic of much debate and discussion over the past forty years or so.[34] But surprisingly the insights gleaned have not yet filtered into the leading commentaries.[35]

30. Jonathan M. Watt, "Some Implications of Bilingualism for New Testament Exegesis," in *The Language of the New Testament: Context, History, and Development*, ed. Stanley E. Porter and Andrew W. Pitts, LBS 6 (Leiden: Brill, 2013), 21, 23.

31. Watt, "Bilingualism," 24.

32. Mathewson, "Revelation's Use of the Greek Language," 111, 113.

33. Constantine R. Campbell, *Basics of Verbal Aspect* (Grand Rapids: Zondervan, 2008), 19.

34. The leading contributors to the discussion of verbal aspect and biblical studies include Stanley E. Porter, *Verbal Aspect in the Greek of the New Testament, with Reference to Tense and Mood*, SBG 1 (New York: Peter Lang, 1989); Buist M. Fanning, *Verbal Aspect in New Testament Greek* (Oxford: Clarendon Press, 1990); K. L. McKay, *A New Syntax of the Verb in the New Testament*, SBG 5 (New York: Peter Lang, 1994); Rodney Decker, *Temporal Deixis of the Greek Verb in the Gospel of Mark with Reference to Verbal Aspect*, SBG 10 (New York: Peter Lang, 2001); Constantine R. Campbell, *Verbal Aspect, the Indicative Mood, and Narrative: Soundings in the Greek of the New Testament*, SBG 13 (New York: Peter Lang, 2007); Constantine R. Cambell, *Verbal Aspect and Non-Indicative Verbs: Further Soundings in the Greek of the New Testament*, SBG 15 (New York: Peter Lang, 2008). Other scholars give more weight to the role of time in their understanding of verbal aspect—e.g., Steven E. Runge, *Discourse Grammar of the Greek New Testament: A Practical Introduction for Teaching and Exegesis* (Peabody, MA: Hendrickson, 2010); Chrys C. Caragounis, *The Development of Greek and the New Testament: Morphology, Syntax, Phonology, and Textual Transmission* (Grand Rapids: Baker Academic, 2007).

35. One exception is Aune, who comments on verbal aspect throughout his three-volume work.

David Mathewson has done the lion's share of the work on verbal aspect related to Revelation.[36]

In Revelation, John uses a variety of Greek tense forms to portray the action within the narrative. In many cases he changes tenses even though he is referring to the same temporal framework.[37] Scholars have explained this shifting of tenses in two main ways. First, some say that the tense changes relate to John recounting his apocalyptic visionary experience.[38] Second, others point to Semitic influence.[39] But because John shifts within the same temporal sphere, this suggests he is not trying to communicate temporal information.[40] Instead, verbal aspect helps us understand that John is saying something through the way he portrays the action in these episodes. And these insights from recent research into the Greek verb could be significant for exegesis.

Again, verbal aspect relates to the author or speaker's viewpoint and offers insight into how they want to depict the action. Tense forms can be used to signal prominence. The respective tense forms generally carry the following significance:[41]

- Aorist—the basic form to narrate the main events and carry the central storyline; often presents events in summary fashion from a distance.
- Imperfect—narrates background information that is often supplemental; portrays action that is remote.
- Present—presents foreground information and often appears in discourse; readers are drawn into the story as proximity is increased.
- Perfect—signals prominence as proximity is heightened even more so than with the present; Campbell describes the perfect as the "*super-present*."[42]

A common illustration to describe verbal aspect is that of a reporter tasked with reporting on a street parade.[43] To put it simply (and generally), the aspect of the aorist is when the reporter is in a helicopter above the parade, viewing it from afar. The imperfect is when the reporter is on the street viewing it as an insider but still viewing it from a distance. The present is when the reporter is also in the parade, but now seeing the action up close. And the perfect is when the reporter is on the street and face to face with the action (a close-up view).

36. David L. Mathewson, *Verbal Aspect in the Book of Revelation: The Function of Greek Verb Tenses in John's Apocalypse*, LBS 4 (Leiden: Brill, 2010); David L. Matthewson, "Verbal Aspect in the Apocalypse of John: An Analysis of Revelation 5," *NovT* 50 (2008): 58–77; and his more recent *Handbook on the Greek Text*.

37. Mathewson, "Verbal Aspect in the Apocalypse of John," 59.

38. Mussies, *Morphology of Koine Greek*, 333–34.

39. Steven Thompson, *Apocalypse and Semitic Syntax*, 47–50. Yet Mathewson, *Verbal Aspect*, 175, has demonstrated that "for verb tenses, direct Semitic influence plays little, if any, role in the author's selection of tense forms."

40. Mathewson, *Handbook on the Greek Text*, xxvi.

41. Mathewson, *Handbook on the Greek Text*, xxvi–xxvii; Campbell, *Basics of Verbal Aspect*, 34–52.

42. Campbell, *Basics of Verbal Aspect*, 51.

43. Campbell, *Basics of Verbal Aspect*, 19–21; Porter, *Verbal Aspect*, 91.

Mathewson has examined the scene of the investiture of the Lamb in Rev 5, for example, from the vantage point of verbal aspect.[44] He distinguishes between background (aorist), foreground (imperfect and present), and frontground (perfect and pluperfect). In Rev 5 the aorist verbs do indeed summarize key events in John's vision and provide the skeletal structure of the narrative. The present and imperfect verbs highlight or foreground main characters and key events or features of the vision. The perfect then focuses attention on (i.e., frontgrounds) two of the most important aspects of the narrative: the scroll and the Lamb. There are seven perfect forms in Rev 5: "writing" (v. 1), "sealed" (v. 1), "slain" (v. 6), "standing" (v. 6), "sent" (v. 6), "took" (v. 7), and "slain" (v. 12), and all are participles except the one in verse 7. Mathewson is surely correct to conclude that the perfect tense in Rev 5 is used to frontground or highlight in bold the main character of the vision, the Lamb, and his primary task at this stage of the story, taking the scroll from the right hand of God. The story becomes utterly hopeless unless the Lamb takes the scroll, as John's weeping indicates (5:5). Through the lens of verbal aspect, we can see that the transfer of the scroll from the right hand of God to the Lamb is the central narrative event of this chapter.[45]

Having looked at the grammar of Revelation with its peculiarities, we now turn our attention to the book's symbolic language. Here we will discuss the nature of Revelation's symbolic language, how it functions, and the primary contexts for properly grasping its meaning. Much of the mysterious beauty and power of the book flows from its extraordinary use of language.

7.3 THE SYMBOLIC LANGUAGE OF REVELATION

Richard Hays rightly observes that "interpreters have strained to make sense of the phantasmagoric imagery of the Apocalypse."[46] In simplest terms, Revelation uses "picture language" to draw in the audience, inform them about what is real and what is a lie, and persuade them to live in faithful discipleship to Jesus. The reader sees, hears, and experiences the drama through a complex, multicolored literary creation. To appreciate fully the picture language of Revelation, the reader must understand how Revelation proposes to communicate truth, the nature of the book's symbolic language and how it functions, and the primary contexts for grasping this type of language.

44. Mathewson, "Verbal Aspect in the Apocalypse of John," 62–74.

45. Mathewson, "Verbal Aspect in the Apocalypse of John," 70–71, 74.

46. Richard B. Hays, *The Moral Vision of the New Testament: A Contemporary Introduction to New Testament Ethics* (New York: HarperSanFrancisco, 1996), 170. See also Konrad Huber, "Imagery in the Book of Revelation," *OHBR* 53–67.

7.3.1 The Way Revelation Communicates

In Rev 1:1, John's terminology suggests he is using picture language as the primary means of receiving and communicating the vision: "The revelation (ἀποκάλυψις) from [or "of"] Jesus Christ, which God gave him to show (δείκνυμι) his servants what must soon take place. He made it known (σημαίνω) by sending his angel." Beale has developed the connection with Dan 2 (LXX) to demonstrate that the primary manner of communication in Revelation is symbolic, in both John's reception and communication of the vision:

> The symbolic use of σημαίνω in Daniel 2 defines the use in Rev. 1:1 as referring to symbolic communication and not mere general conveyance of information. Therefore, John's choice of σημαίνω over γνωρίζω ("make known") is not haphazard but intentional. Regardless of which Aramaic or Greek word or version is in view, however, the allusion to Dan. 2:28–30, 45 indicates that a symbolic vision and its interpretation is going to be part of the warp and woof of the means of communication throughout Revelation.[47]

John also adds that God gave Jesus the revelation to "show" (δείκνυμι) his servants what is to come (Rev 1:1; cf. the seven uses of the term elsewhere in 4:1; 17:1; 21:9–10; 22:1, 6, 8). As we will see below, this term carries the idea of communicating through the senses, and this is confirmed by John's testimony that he "saw" the heavenly vision.[48] Just as God communicated to Daniel through symbols, so he communicates to (and through) John in the same manner.

We will explore in a later chapter how to interpret symbolic language (see Ch. 10) but here we conclude with Beale that Revelation's picture language should be taken seriously. *While some interpreters presume a literal reading unless the context demands that we interpret symbolically, this cluster of terms in the opening verse and the connection to Daniel encourages us to take the opposite approach.* In Beale's words, "we are told in the book's introduction that the majority of the material in it is revelatory symbolism (1:12–20 and 4:1–22:5 at the least). Hence, the predominant manner by which to approach the material will be according to a nonliteral interpretative method. Of course, some parts are not symbolic, but the essence of the book is figurative."[49]

Since John communicates in picture language, it stands to reason that he is passing on what he has seen and heard in his vision. Visual and auditory language pervades the Apocalypse (e.g., 22:8: "I, John, am the one who *heard* and *saw* these things. And when

47. Beale, *Revelation*, 51; cf. also 152–54; 181–83. The noun form of this term (σημεῖον, "sign") is featured in John's Gospel, where Jesus's seven signs figure into the organization of the first half of the book.

48. Beale, *Revelation*, 52.

49. Beale, *Revelation*, 52.

I had *heard* and *seen* them, I fell down to worship at the feet of the angel who had been *showing* them to me"). Revelation primarily uses three verbs to express John's experience of seeing: βλέπω (13x), θεωρέω (2x), and especially ὁράω (61x).[50] John, who has been "shown" the vision, now "sees" it. John is a visual witness who testifies faithfully to "everything he saw" (1:2). Interestingly, Ureña notes that John avoids verbs that have the opposite meaning (e.g., "to conceal," "to hide," "to disappear," etc.) unless they are needed to make a specific point (e.g., the "hidden manna" of 2:17).[51]

Guffey highlights the book's visuality.[52] It is a vision and within this vision we find a multitude of images. It is indeed "a work of visual theology."[53] He argues that John uses images in ways similar to the three uses of *ekphrasis* in the ancient world with *ekphrasis* being defined as "the verbal representation of visual representation."[54] The uses include making a reality present, grounding the orator's authority, and captivating the audience emotionally.[55] This leads naturally into the function of Revelation's symbolic language, which uses imagery to combine cognitive and emotional appeals for the reader to experience and participate in the reality of the vision.[56] Visual imagery plays a significant role in the divine author's attempt to dramatically transform the audience's perception of spiritual reality.

But Revelation does not just engage the visual senses; it also engages our sense of hearing. Mangina writes:

> The Apocalypse is a book of auditions. Trumpets sound, thunderclaps boom, angels cry out—almost always "with a loud voice." The absence of sound can be equally important. Silence in heaven marks a period of expectant waiting for fresh revelation (8:1), and the death of Babylon will later be denoted by the sound of silence—musicians, singers, the voices of the bridegroom and the bride all strangely quieted (18:22–23). But for the most part Revelation is a very loud book, situating us in the midst of an extraordinary aural universe.[57]

Revelation was both a spoken and a heard revelation: "to his servant John, who *testifies* to everything he saw—that is, the *word* of God and the *testimony* of Jesus Christ. . . . I, John, am the one who *heard* and saw these things. And when I had

50. For more on the use of these lexemes in Revelation, see Lourdes García Ureña, *Narrative and Drama in the Book of Revelation: A Literary Approach*, SNTSMS 175 (Cambridge: Cambridge University Press, 2019), 51–55.

51. Ureña, *Narrative and Drama in the Book of Revelation*, 54.

52. Andrew R. Guffey, *The Book of Revelation and the Visual Culture of Asia Minor: A Concurrence of Images* (Lanham; London: Lexington Books; Fortress Academic, 2019).

53. Guffey, *Visual Culture*, 207.

54. Guffey, *Visual Culture*, 96. See also Alexander E. Stewart, "*Ekphrasis*, Fear, and Motivation in the Apocalypse of John," *BBR* 27 (2017): 227–40.

55. Guffey, *Visual Culture*, 103–6, 206.

56. Bruce M. Metzger, *Breaking the Code: Understanding the Book of Revelation* (Nashville: Abingdon, 1993), 13.

57. Joseph L. Mangina, *Revelation*, BTCB (Grand Rapids: Brazos, 2010), 37.

heard and seen them . . ." (1:1–2; 22:8, emphasis added). Forms of the verb ἀκούω ("I hear") occur almost fifty times in Revelation and emphasize its auditory nature.[58] In addition, messengers speak, choruses sing and recite, prophetic instructions are given, instruments play, voices voice and sound abounds in the Apocalypse.

We should always remember that Revelation was originally meant to be read aloud and heard by a group of believers gathered for worship. The first of seven beatitudes is pronounced on "the one who reads aloud the words of this prophecy" and "those who hear it and take to heart what is written in it" (1:3). Rather than individuals reading alone silently, we should imagine a corporate audience hearing the book read aloud. As a result, we must attend to auditory elements of the book whenever possible—verbal repetitions, rhythmic patterns, alliteration, silence, and so on.

To be sure, the auditory power of Revelation can be just as transformative as its visual:

> The auditors who came together to hear the Apocalypse were summoned to a transformative experience. Those first ancient auditors of the Apocalypse came together not merely to be informed, but to be transformed, to undergo a collective change in consciousness, an aspiration that makes modern individual and group reading practices trivial by comparison, with the possible exception of the reading of wills. Reading the Apocalypse aloud, and hearing the Apocalypse read aloud, was effectual: through exhortations and exclamations, threats and thunder, the reading of the Apocalypse moved its hearers, effected them; the text *did* something to them.[59]

While Revelation uses picture language to appeal to the senses, it also communicates through a nuanced and complex series of literary expressions that narrative and rhetorical approaches are designed to notice. Along with metaphor and simile, Koester notes the use of antonomasia, hyperbole, metonymy, and polysyndeton in Revelation.[60] James Resseguie has a lengthy discussion of the more common literary terms and narrative devices used in Revelation, including metaphors and similes, progressions, verbal threads, chiasm, *inclusio*, numbers and numerical sequences, setting, characters, point of view, plot, narrator, and structure.[61] DeSilva has argued extensively for a rhetorical reading of Revelation that considers the many ways John seeks to persuade his audience.[62] At this point we need to explore further the nature of Revelation's symbolic language.

58. Ureña, *Narrative and Drama in the Book of Revelation*, 126–87, explores in great detail the auditory nature of Revelation.

59. Callahan, "Language of the Apocalypse," 460.

60. Koester, *Revelation*, 141–44.

61. James L. Resseguie, *The Revelation of John: A Narrative Commentary* (Grand Rapids: Baker Academic, 2009), 17–59. Cf. also Barr, *Tales of the End*.

62. See, e.g., deSilva, *Seeing Things John's Way*; cf. also Witherington, *Revelation*.

7.3.2 The Nature of Symbolic Language

All these means of communication shows that Revelation is communicating at several different levels. Drawing on Poythress, Beale identifies four such levels:

- Linguistic—the textual record itself
- Visionary—John's actual visionary experience (i.e., what John saw)
- Referential—the historical identification of what is seen in the vision (i.e., what the vision refers to in history)
- Symbolic—what the symbols in the vision say about the historical referent[63]

Interpreters are often clear about what John saw but are not always clear about what it refers to or what the symbols say about the referent. At times interpreters even collapse the referential and symbolic in a more literalistic interpretive approach so that the visions are direct representations of historical events.[64] To unpack the nature of Revelation's symbolic language we begin with what lies at the heart of symbol—comparison.

Symbols are "figurative comparisons."[65] Revelation uses three basic forms of comparison. Beale explains: "Formal metaphor [is comparison] in which the literal subject is connected to the figurative subject by a form of 'to be' ('*The Lord is my shepherd* who loves me'). Simile is when the two subjects are linked by 'like' ('*The Lord is like a shepherd* who loves me'). Hypocatastasis occurs when the literal subject is not stated but assumed ([The Lord who is like] '*The shepherd* loves me')."[66] Sometimes these comparisons have one clear referent (e.g., 1:20: "the seven lampstands are the seven churches"), while at other times more than one point of comparison seems intended (17:9–10a: "The seven heads are seven hills on which the woman sits. They are also seven kings").[67] Yet even those symbols with a single referent can be just as evocative and powerful as those with multiple referents (e.g., Jesus Christ as the slain but risen Lamb).

The comparison at the heart of symbolic language is essential in Revelation where John is attempting to convey spiritual realities to his audience. He is moving from what we know to what we have never experienced or perhaps never even heard about. In essence, this is what happens anytime we attempt to do Christian theology. Can we really say anything about God without using metaphorical language? Ian Paul writes,

63. Vern S. Poythress, "Genre and Hermeneutics in Rev 20:1–6," *JETS* 36 (1993): 51–54; Beale, *Revelation*, 52–55.

64. Beale, *Revelation*, 53–54, cites Walvoord's commentary as a prime example of this approach. See John F. Walvoord, *The Revelation of Jesus Christ* (Chicago: Moody, 1966).

65. Beale, *Revelation*, 55.

66. Beale, *Revelation*, 57.

67. Scholars have labeled symbols denoting a single referent as "steno symbols," while "tensive symbols" cannot be restricted to a single referent. See Ian Paul, "The Book of Revelation: Image, Symbol and Metaphor," in Steve Moyise, ed., *Studies in the Book of Revelation* (Edinburgh: T&T Clark, 2001), 135–136. Yet this classification seems to oversimplify Revelation's use of symbolic language.

"Metaphor is the centre of all Christian theology, and in that sense Revelation is the most Christian text in the New Testament."[68]

In Revelation we see symbolic language applied noticeably to colors and numbers. Gorman notes that in the Apocalypse "colors function more like images than adjectives, and the numbers more like adjectives than numbers."[69] The following table highlights the symbolism of colors often observed by scholars:[70]

Color	Symbolism	References
White	Victory, purity/cleanness, resurrection, heaven/divinity, radiance, splendor	1:14; 2:17; 3:4–5, 18; 4:4; 6:2, 11; 7:9, 13–14; 14:14; 19:11, 14; 20:11
Golden	Splendor, divinity, incorruptible wealth	1:13; 15:6
Rainbow	Omnipotence	4:3; 10:1
Bright red	Blood, slaughter, war, violent power	6:4; 12:3
Fiery red	Judgment	9:17; 10:1; 11:19
Scarlet	Royalty	17:3–4; 18:12, 16
Purple	Royalty	17:4; 18:16
Black	Disaster, famine, death	6:5, 12
Pale greenish grey	Death	6:8; 8:7; 9:4
Blue	Smoke	9:17
Yellow	Sulfur	9:17

As was common in the ancient world, John's audience would have also understood numbers to carry symbolic significance. The table on the next page shows some of the symbolic values noted by scholars.[71]

But Revelation goes beyond simply using numbers in the text to signify completeness or imperfection or the like. John uses numbers in several other important ways in his carefully crafted literary masterpiece. First, certain words or events occur with particular frequencies, thus giving them added significance. For instance, the divine title consists of a present, past, and future dimension: "who is and who was and who is to come" (1:4, 8; 4:8; cf. 11:17; 16:5). We also see the Lord God Almighty described as "Holy, holy, holy" (4:8). God is often praised in threes (e.g., 4:11; 12:10; 19:1). Christ and his work are sometimes described using threes (1:5; 22:13).[72]

68. Paul, *Revelation*, 31.

69. Gorman, *Reading Revelation Responsibly*, 17, who credits his student Brian McLoughlin for the observation.

70. See Gorman, *Reading Revelation Responsibly*, 17–18; Mark Wilson, *Charts on the Book of Revelation*, 49; Ureña, *Narrative and Drama in the Book of Revelation*, 39–41.

71. See Gorman, *Reading Revelation Responsibly*, 18–19; Mark Wilson, *Charts on the Book of Revelation*, 49; Resseguie, *Revelation*, 28–32.

72. Resseguie, *Revelation*, 28.

Number	Symbolism	References
1/4, 1/3, 1/2	Limited scope or time, short, brief	6:8; 8:1, 7–12; 9:15, 18; 12:4
1	Exclusiveness, primacy, excellence	17:12; 18:8, 10, 17, 19
2	Plurality	11:3–4, 10; 12:14; 13:11; 19:20
3	Sufficiency; divinity or false divinity	1:4–5; 6:6; 8:13; 9:18; 16:13, 19; 21:13
3 1/2	Limited time (half of 7)	11:2–3, 9, 11; 12:6, 14; 13:5
4	Cosmic completeness, universality especially related to creation	4:6–8; 5:6, 8, 14; 6:1, 6–7; 7:1–2, 11; 9:10, 14–15; 14:3; 15:7; 19:4; 20:8
5	Limited	9:5, 10
6	Incompleteness, imperfection, false divinity	4:8; 13:18
7	Completeness, fullness, perfection	1:4, 11–12, 16, 20; 2:1; 3:1; 4:5; 5:1, 5–6; 6:1; 8:2, 6; 10:3–4; 12:3; 13:1; 15:1, 6–8; 16:1; 17:1, 3, 7, 9–11; 21:9
10	Completeness, fullness	2:10; 12:3; 13:1; 17:3, 7, 12, 16
12 (and multiples: 24, 144)	Completeness, number of God's people, God's presence, cosmic fullness	**12:** 12:1; 21:12, 14, 21; 22:2 **24:** 4:4, 10; 5:8; 11:16; 19:4 **144:** 7:14; 14:1, 3; 21:17
1,000 and its multiples	Large number with enhanced symbolism	5:11; 7:4, 5–8; 11:13; 14:1, 3; 20:2–7
144,000	12 × 12 × 1000	7:4; 14:1, 3

The same applies to the number four with four corners, four winds, four living creatures, a four-plus-three pattern to the judgments, a fourfold formula drawn from the related terms *tribe*, *language*, *people*, *multitudes*, *kings*, and *nation* (a formula which occurs seven times: 5:9; 7:9; 10:11; 11:9; 13:7; 14:6; 17:15), a cargo list of twenty-eight items (4 × 7), and certain names of God and Christ are repeated four times, along with four references to the seven spirits.[73]

The number seven is used extensively in this manner. There are seven beatitudes, seven "sickles" in Rev 14, seven times God is titled "Lord God Almighty," and seven occurrences of "Christ," "testimony of Jesus," "prophecy," "I am coming," "sign," "endurance," and "cloud." There are seven times that "elders" and "living creatures" are named together, while Jesus and the Spirit and the saints are all mentioned fourteen times (2 × 7).[74] In addition, there are seven messages to the churches and three series of seven judgments. Doxologies may also be threefold, fourfold, or sevenfold.

We also see a similar pattern with the number twelve. There are twelve tribes of Israel and twelve apostles of the Lamb. Twelve is also the number of God's people, "squared for completeness, multiplied by a thousand to suggest vast numbers" (i.e.,

73. Bauckham, *Climax of Prophecy*, 29–37.

74. Paul, *Revelation*, 35.

144,000).[75] Twelve is also mentioned twelve times in the description of the New Jerusalem in 21:9–22:5, a reminder of the completeness of the people of God in the new creation. These examples show that John used numerical composition carefully and intentionally throughout the book.

Second, Revelation draws on the mathematical significance of square, triangular, and rectangular numbers. John consistently uses square numbers to represent the things of God, especially the people of God (e.g., 144 and 1,000), while he uses triangular numbers to designate the opponents of God (e.g., 666).[76] Bauckham applies this mathematical reality to the number 666 (a rare doubly triangular number) in support of identifying Nero as the beast.[77]

Third, we also see the use of isopsephism or gematria, which refers to calculating the numerical value of words and names by adding up the value of their letters.[78] For example, the number of the beast, 666 in 13:18, can quite naturally be viewed as reference to Nero Caesar (*NRON KSR* calculated in Hebrew). Interestingly, using gematria, the name of Jesus (*IESOUS*) is calculated as 888, a number often associated with abundant and overflowing blessings. Such a practice was not uncommon in the ancient world, and John's readers would have been familiar with it.

John's symbolic language, including his use of colors and numbers, clarifies his story and enhances its rhetorical power and realism, while theologically reminding the reader that God is in control and his victory over evil is certain. For example, Beale notes that four, seven, and twelve "figuratively convey the notion of God's ordering of the world and his sovereignty over it."[79] Yarbro Collins concludes that John uses these numbers to represent the divine "net in which the Satanic forces are captured, surrounded and confined on all sides," thereby showing God's ultimate victory over evil.[80]

7.3.3 The Purpose and Function of Symbolic Language

Revelation's picture language creates a "symbolic world which readers can enter and thereby have their perception of the world in which they live transformed."[81] Creating a symbolic world was necessary because the Roman world was full of images with enormous transformative power. In a typical Greco-Roman city, believers were surrounded by statues, inscriptions, temples large and small, image-bearing coins, rituals, festivals, altars, friezes, and various other iconography supporting the empire

75. Bauckham, *Climax of Prophecy*, 36.

76. Paul, *Revelation*, 36–37.

77. Bauckham, *Climax of Prophecy*, 384–452.

78. Paul, *Revelation*, 37–38. See Mark Wilson, *Charts on the Book of Revelation*, 85–86, for a list of the numerical value of Greek and Hebrew letters and ways to calculate the number of the beast.

79. Beale, *Revelation*, 59.

80. Adela Yarbro Collins, "Numerical Symbolism in Jewish and Early Christian Apocalyptic Literature," *ANRW* II/21/2 (1984): 1286.

81. Bauckham, *Theology*, 17.

as ultimate reality. This does not even include the "verbal imagery" such as speeches, songs, prayers, pledges, and the like.

As believers gathered in house churches to hear the book of Revelation read (and all who have heard it since), they would enter a rival symbolic world with its own set of "Christian prophetic counter-images."[82] The purpose was to purge the Christian imagination, "refurbishing it with alternative visions of how the world is and will be."[83] Bauckham explains:

> [Revelation with its imagery] tackles people's imaginative response to the world, which is at least as deep and influential as their intellectual convictions. It recognizes the way a dominant culture, with its images and ideals, constructs the world for us, so that we perceive and respond to the world in its terms. Moreover, it unmasks this dominant construction of the world as an ideology of the powerful which serves to maintain their power. In its place, Revelation offers a different way of perceiving the world which leads people to resist and to challenge the effects of the dominant ideology. Moreover, since this different way of perceiving the world is fundamentally to open it to transcendence it resists any absolutizing of power or structures or ideals within this world. This is the most fundamental way in which the church is called always to be counter-cultural.[84]

The prevailing Greco-Roman culture with its plethora of idolatrous images simply could not be debated out of existence; it had to be overpowered by an alternative vision that was even more captivating. This alternative vision then provides believers with more peace, hope, perspective, truth, and courage than the existing cultural vision. One vision of ultimate reality triumphs over another. Above all, as a counter vision, Revelation points people to the true worship of the one true God, under whom all of reality fits into place.[85]

Revelation's symbolic language accomplishes its purpose by appealing in a unique way to the human imagination.[86] By using language that is evocative and expressive, Revelation appeals to more than the intellect; it appeals to the whole person, emotions included.[87] The entire affective dimension is engaged and transformed. Revelation does not just say something to us; it does something to us as well. Schüssler Fiorenza summarizes the evocative rhetorical strategy of Revelation:

> [Revelation] seeks to persuade and motivate by constructing a "symbolic universe" that invites imaginative participation. The strength of its persuasion for action lies not in the theological reasoning or historical argument of Rev. but in the "evocative"

82. Bauckham, *Theology*, 17.
83. Bauckham, *Theology*, 17.
84. Bauckham, *Theology*, 159–60.
85. Gorman, *Reading Revelation Responsibly*, 55.
86. Metzger, *Breaking the Code*, 11; Koester, *Revelation*, 139.
87. Gorman, *Reading Revelation Responsibly*, 20–21.

> power of its symbols as well as in its hortatory, imaginative, emotional language, and dramatic movement, which engage the hearer (reader) by eliciting reactions, emotions, convictions, and identifications.[88]

We are quick to add that there is no need for an either/or between theology and history on the one hand and the evocative nature of symbolic language on the other, between the meaning of the text and its meaningfulness or function.[89] The two work together beautifully.

Both Bauckham and Koester use the example of John's vision of the woman in Rev 17 to illustrate the transformative power of images.[90] In John's world, Rome was personified through various images as a noble lady, a city seated on seven hills, the goddess Roma in all her splendor and glory. According to the visual and auditory narrative of the day, she was worthy of devotion and worship. But John portrays her as a drunken whore sitting on a seven-headed beast. This seductively arrogant harlot amasses extravagant wealth and power in the process of deceiving and corrupting her devotees. Through the use of vivid imagery Revelation thus transforms the reader's vision of ultimate reality and draws the reader deeper into faithful discipleship to Jesus.

It is important to keep in mind that the purpose of the imagery in the end is to reveal rather than conceal. Picture language provides a way of seeing spiritual reality—God, his character and his ways, the condition of the world, the church's situation, and so on. Even more, such picture language calls the readers into obedient action. Hays writes, "The ethical staying power of the Apocalypse is a product of its *imaginative richness*."[91] The overall function is to exhort and encourage the audience to faithful discipleship.[92] The symbols are not merely timeless objects for contemplation. This transforming vision confronts as well as comforts by engaging the whole person with the ultimate reality of the Triune God and his plans to make all things new. Readers are engaged by the imagery for the purpose of responding righteously in the world as followers of the Lamb. This helps us understand the opening beatitude: "Blessed is the one who reads aloud the words of this prophecy, and blessed are those who hear it and take to heart what is written in it" (1:3).

7.3.4 The Primary Contexts for Grasping Revelation's Imagery

In subsequent chapters we will discuss further how to interpret Revelation's imagery and the use of the Old Testament in Revelation (see Chs. 8 and 10). Here we simply

88. Schüssler Fiorenza, *Book of Revelation*, 187.

89. See Beale, *Revelation*, 65–69, for an appropriate critique of the new hermeneutic for concluding that symbols do not point to objective reality or even to doctrinal truth but are merely evocative. To be sure, arguing for both the meaning and function of the text's symbolic language also need not drive us to excessive literalism when attempting to identify potential referents, or when determining whether referents are even identifiable in certain cases.

90. Bauckham, *Theology*, 17–18; Koester, *Revelation*, 138.

91. Hays, *Moral Vision*, 184, emphasis original.

92. Beale, *Revelation*, 69.

note that there are two primary contexts for grasping the images and symbolism of the book, and neither is the contemporary context of modern readers. Both contexts are ancient. We have to begin with what it meant to them before we proceed to what it means to us.

First, John draws much of his imagery from the Old Testament and Jewish tradition. Revelation is saturated with Old Testament allusions that "frequently presuppose their Old Testament context and a range of connexions between Old Testament texts which are not made explicit but lie beneath the surface of the text of Revelation."[93] For example, John's identification of the two witnesses in 11:4 with two olive trees and two lampstands points to the two anointed ones, Joshua and Zerubbabel, in Zech 4:1–14. As he sometimes does, however, John modifies the Old Testament allusion to suit his purposes. John sees two lampstands instead of one and he equates the trees with the lampstands. For John lampstands denote churches (Rev 1:20) and the imagery of the two witnesses likely refers to the Spirit "empowering his people with prophetic authority as a testimony against the nations."[94] Examples abound in virtually every paragraph of the Apocalypse as John draws on the Old Testament to give his picture language substance and authority.

John also mines the contemporary Greco-Roman context for his imagery, and this provides the second context for grasping his picture language. The churches of Asia Minor would have been able to pick up on such references. For example, Keener points to the Parthians and their reputation as fierce mounted archers as the likely background for the rider on the white horse in Rev 6:2 (cf. 9:14; 16:12 for other possible Parthian connections).[95] Some interpreters associate "Satan's throne" (2:13, ESV) with the altar of Zeus Soter in Pergamum.[96] Other examples surface in the process of exegesis and interpreters would be wise to consider the possibility that the image derives from its local setting.[97]

7.4 CONCLUSION

Without a doubt John sometimes violates standard grammatical practice. After weighing the explanations for his unusual grammar, we have argued that a number of factors contribute. His peculiar grammar does seem intentional rather than arbitrary. So why does he take this route? John's grammatical idiosyncrasies stem from a combination

93. Bauckham, *Theology*, 18.

94. Alan Bandy, "The Hermeneutics of Symbolism: How to Interpret the Symbols of John's Apocalypse," *SBJT* 14.1 (2010): 51.

95. Keener, *Revelation*, 202.

96. Adolf Deissmann, *Light from the Ancient East: The New Testament Illustrated by Recently Discovered Texts of the Graeco-Roman World*, 2nd ed., trans. Lionel R. M. Strachan (London: Hodder & Stoughton, 1911), 280; Adela Yarbro Collins, "Pergamon in Early Christian Literature," in *Pergamon: Citadel of the Gods*, ed. Helmut Koester (Harrisburg, PA: Trinity Press International, 1998), 163–84.

97. See the excellent works by Weima, *Sermons to the Seven Churches*, and Hemer, *Letters to the Seven Churches*.

of his multilingualism, the role of Old Testament allusions, the prophetic-apocalyptic topic, and his theological, spiritual, and social context and purpose. Interpreters must carefully study each grammatical context to determine the most viable explanation and, more importantly, to see through the construction to John's larger emphasis.

We have also considered briefly how verbal aspect or the analysis of the viewpoint of the author or speaker can shed light on the Greek of Revelation. Typically, John signals prominence (background, foreground, and frontground) through particular tense forms. Verbal aspect often reveals the inner workings of a passage and displays what is most significant.

The final portion of this chapter treated Revelation's symbolic language—its picture language sets the book apart as unique in the New Testament canon. We observed the book's claim to be communicating through symbols and the implication that we should approach the book with an interpretive framework that honors figurative language as primary. We explained John's utilization of visual and auditory language and its power to transform the reader. We found Beale's four levels of language paradigm useful for making sense of Revelation's symbolic language. We also looked more closely at how John uses colors and numbers to clarify and enhance the rhetorical power of the message.

John's purpose in using symbolic language is to create an alternative reality to the prevailing idolatrous cultural narrative so that readers may be transformed by a true and lasting vision of God. Revelation appeals to the whole person, mind and imagination included, in calling readers deeper into discipleship to Jesus. As we pay attention to both the Old Testament and the first-century local contexts, the meaning of the imagery will come more clearly into focus. We are now in a position to move forward with an investigation of John's use of the Old Testament before looking more closely at the structure of the book and how it should be interpreted.

Chapter 8

THE USE OF THE OLD TESTAMENT IN REVELATION

BIBLIOGRAPHY

Allen, Garrick V. "Scriptural Allusions in the Book of Revelation and the Contours of Textual Research 1900–2014: Retrospect and Prospects." *CurBR* 14 (2016): 319–39. ———. "Textual Pluriformity and Allusions in the Book of Revelation: The Text of Zechariah 4 in the Apocalypse." *ZNW* 106.1 (2015): 136–45. **Beale, G. K.** *Handbook on the New Testament Use of the Old Testament: Exegesis and Interpretation*. Grand Rapids: Baker Academic, 2012. ———. *John's Use of the Old Testament in Revelation*. LNTS 166. London: T&T Clark, 2015. ———. "Revelation." Pages 318–36 in *It is Written: Scripture Citing Scripture*. Edited by D. A. Carson and H. G. M. Williamson. Cambridge: Cambridge University Press, 1988. ———. *The Use of Daniel in Jewish Apocalyptic Literature and in the Revelation of St. John*. Eugene, OR: Wipf & Stock, 1984. ———. "Thirty-Five Years of Research on John's Use of the Old Testament in Revelation." Pages 188–246 in *The Apocalypse of John among Its Critics: Questions and Controversies*. StScrBT. Edited by Alan S. Bandy and Alexander E. Stewart. Bellingham, WA: Lexham, 2023. **Beale, G. K., and Sean M. McDonough.** "Revelation." Page 1081–1161 in *Commentary on the New Testament Use of the Old Testament*. Grand Rapids: Baker Academic, 2007. **Decock, Paul B.** "Scriptures in the Book of Revelation." *Neot* 33 (1999): 373–410. **Fekkes, Jan, III.** *Isaiah and Prophetic Traditions in the Book of Revelation: Visionary Antecedents and Their Development*. JSNTSup 93. Sheffield: Sheffield Academic, 1994. **Hays, Richard B.** *Echoes of Scripture in the Letters of Paul*. New Haven: Yale University Press, 1989. **Hieke, Thomas.** "The Reception of Daniel 7 in the Revelation of John." Pages 47–67 in *Revelation and the Politics of Apocalyptic Interpretation*. Edited by Richard B. Hays and Stefan Alkier. Waco, TX: Baylor University Press, 2012. **Jauhiainen, Marko.** "The Minor Prophets in Revelation." Pages 155–71 in *The Minor Prophets in the New Testament*. Edited by Maarten J. J. Menken and Steve Moyise. LNTS 377. London: T&T Clark, 2009. ———. *The Use of Zechariah in Revelation*. Tübingen: Mohr Siebeck, 2005. **Kowalski, Beate.** "Transformation of Ezekiel in John's Revelation." Pages 279–311 in *Transforming Visions: Transformations of Text, Traditions, and Theology in Ezekiel*. Edited by W. A. Tooman and M. A. Lyons. Cambridge: James Clark, 2010. **Mathewson, David L.** "Assessing Old Testament Allusions in the Book of Revelation." *EvQ* 75:4 (2003): 311–25. ———. "Isaiah in Revelation." Pages 189–210 in *Isaiah in the New Testament.* Edited by Steve Moyise and Maarten J. J. Menken. London: T&T Clark, 2005. ———. *A New Heaven and a New Earth: The Meaning and Function of the Old Testament in Revelation 21.1–22.5.* JSNTSup 238. Sheffield: Sheffield Academic, 2003. **Mealy, J. Webb.** *After the Thousand Years: Resurrection and Judgment in Revelation 20.* JSNTSup 70. Sheffield: JSOT Press, 1992. **Michaels, J. Ramsey.** "Old Testament in Revelation." *DLNT,* 850–55. **Moyise, Steve.** "Genesis in Revelation." Pages 166–79 in *Genesis in the New Testament.* Edited by Maarten J. J. Menken and Steve Moyise. LNTS 466. London: T&T Clark, 2012. ———. "The Language of the Old Testament in the Apocalypse." *JSNT* 76 (1999): 97–113. ———. "The Psalms in the Book of Revelation." Pages 231–47 in *Psalms in the New Testament.* Edited by Steve Moyise and Maarten J. J. Menken. London: T&T Clark, 2004. ———. *The Old Testament in the Book of Revelation.* JSNTSup 115. London: Bloomsbury T&T Clark, 2015. ———. *The Old Testament in the New: An Introduction.* 2nd ed. London: Bloomsbury T&T Clark, 2015. **Mulzac, Kenneth.** "The 'Fall of Babylon' Motif in the Books of Jeremiah and Revelation." *JATS* 8.1–2 (1997): 137–49. **Paul, Ian.** "The Use of the Old Testament in Revelation 12." Pages 256–76 in *The Old Testament in the New Testament: Essays in Honour of J. L. North.* Edited by Steve Moyise. JSNTSup 189. Sheffield: Sheffield Academic, 2000. **Paulien, Jon.** "Criteria and Assessment of Allusions to the Old Testament in the Book of Revelation." Pages 113–29 in *Studies in the Book of Revelation.* Edited by Steve Moyise. Edinburgh: T&T Clark, 2001. **Wilcox, Max.** "Text Form." Pages 193–203 in *It Is Written: Scripture Citing Scripture.* Edited by D. A. Carson and H. G. M. Williamson. Cambridge: Cambridge University Press, 1988.

8.1 INTRODUCTION

No other New Testament text draws from the Old Testament more than the book of Revelation, but it often does so in a subtle and complicated manner. Michaels notes that Revelation never mentions "the Scriptures" or cites as "Scripture" any specific passage or uses the expressions "it is written" or "to fulfill," yet John is repeatedly told to "write" and refers to his finished work as "the things written" (1:3; 22:18–19).[1] You can find the Old Testament in every nook and cranny of this book, and while John never formally cites the Old Testament with an introductory formula, the Apocalypse is filled with informal quotations and allusions.

John alludes to the Old Testament in almost every verse of Revelation. In the NA^{28} critical apparatus, we can see that John draws on more than thirty Old Testament books and, if each reference is counted each time it is used, there are around 750 Old

1. J. Ramsey Michaels, "Old Testament in Revelation," *DLNT* 850–51.

Testament allusions in Revelation. The exact number is difficult to pin down since it depends on the criteria used to identify the reference, whether to include general parallels, and John's use of composite allusions (i.e., where he combines two or more Old Testament texts into a single allusion).[2]

Bauckham concludes that "Revelation's use of the Old Testament scriptures is an essential key to its understanding."[3] But rather than John randomly or haphazardly using Old Testament language just because of familiarity, Bauckham rightly sees an intentional method to John's madness:

> It [Revelation] is a pattern of disciplined and deliberate *allusion* to specific Old Testament texts. Reference to and interpretation of these texts is an extremely important part of the meaning of the text of the Apocalypse. It is a book designed to be read in constant intertextual relationship with the Old Testament. John was writing what he understood to be a work of prophetic scripture, the climax of prophetic revelation, which gathered up the prophetic meaning of the Old Testament scriptures and disclosed the way in which it was being and was to be fulfilled in the last days.[4]

In this chapter we will first examine the form and type of references along with the key contribution of several Old Testament books. Next, we will focus specifically on ways John uses the Old Testament in Revelation to advance his theological purposes.

8.2 THE FORM AND TYPE OF OLD TESTAMENT REFERENCES IN REVELATION

8.2.1 The Issue of Text Form in John's Old Testament References

When it comes to John's use of the Old Testament perhaps the most basic question is Which form of the Old Testament does he use? While earlier scholarship acknowledged that John had the knowledge and ability to interact with both Hebrew and Greek sources, they tended to push for one or the other. For example, H. B. Swete believed John was more heavily influenced by the LXX,[5] while R. H. Charles and others emphasized his dependence on Hebrew sources.[6] More recent scholarship has shown

2. G. K. Beale and Sean M. McDonough, "Revelation," in *Commentary on the New Testament Use of the Old Testament* (Grand Rapids: Baker Academic, 2007), 1082.

3. Bauckham, *Climax of Prophecy*, x.

4. Bauckham, *Climax of Prophecy*, xi. Other scholars who hold to John's use of the Old Testament in a manner consistent with its context include Beale, Vogelgesang, Paulien, Fekkes, Wei Lo, Rogers, Kowalski, Brueggemann, Tõniste, and Mathewson, while the following seem to prefer a reader-response approach: Schüssler Fiorenza, Decock, Ruiz, Royalty, Moyise, and Fletcher. See for the extensive "Afterward" by G. K. Beale, "Thirty-Five Years of Research on John's Use of the Old Testament in Revelation," in *Apocalypse of John Among Its Critics*, StScrBT, ed. Alexander E. Stewart and Alan S. Bandy (Bellingham, WA: Lexham Academic), 188–246.

5. Swete, *Apocalypse of St. John*.

6. Charles, *Revelation of St. John*. For a thorough overview of the history of scholarship on the text forms used in Revelation, see Garrick V. Allen, "Scriptural Allusions in the Book of Revelation and the Contours of Textual Research 1900–2014: Retrospect and Prospects," *CurBR* 14.3 (2016): 319–39.

that John's textual situation was, shall we say, a bit more complicated. Allen warns that "the textual culture in which the NT works were composed was complex and simple a priori assertions pertaining to textual form can no longer be tolerated."[7] This applies especially to Revelation. In fact, some Old Testament references in Revelation agree with the MT, while others favor the LXX. John knew and used both. He seems to have preferred the OG/LXX forms of certain books (e.g., Genesis, Ezekiel, Isaiah, Daniel, and Psalms), while favoring a Hebrew form of others (e.g., Zechariah).[8]

This calls for a fresh evaluation of the form of the biblical text John is using, a technical task that is beyond the scope of this study. We can expect research into this specialized area to continue to grow in years ahead, especially with the completion of the *Editio Critica Maior* on Revelation. For now, we know that John knew and used both Greek and Hebrew, and each reference must be analyzed individually with this is mind.[9] This meshes well with John's habit of weaving together words and phrases from various Old Testament references rather than formally citing single references. When possible, then, we begin by identifying the particular textual form referenced by John in each context.[10] We also need to be alert to the type of reference John is making.

8.2.2 The Type of Old Testament References in Revelation

Often scholars classify the Old Testament references in the New Testament as either quotations or allusions. Quotations are easy to spot since they are normally introduced by a formula, such as "it is written" (e.g., Matt 4:4) or by using some form of the word "fulfill" (e.g., Matt 8:17), and there is clear verbal parallelism between the Old and the New Testaments. Scholars tend to agree about the number and location of these direct citations. They also note that Revelation includes few, if any, of these formal citations or quotations, and even the most likely quotations lack any typical introductory formula (e.g., Rev 1:7; 2:26–27).

The less formal allusions, on the other hand, are a different matter. Such allusions abound in Revelation and are much more difficult to pin down in part because scholars do not always agree about how to define and identify an allusion.[11] To muddy the waters

7. Garrick V. Allen, "Textual Pluriformity and Allusions in the Book of Revelation: The Text of Zechariah 4 in the Apocalypse," *ZNW* 106 (2015): 145.

8. Allen, "Textual Pluriformity," 145. Allen contends that multiple textual forms were circulating at the time: "The textual evidence from the Judean Desert suggests that multiple textual exemplars of certain books of the Hebrew Bible and its early Greek versions (OG/LXX) circulated concurrently in Jewish and early Christian communities in the first century CE" (Allen, "Textual Pluriformity," 137).

9. In his article on "Textual Pluriformity," Allen does this very thing with Zech 4 in Revelation using two test cases: "seven spirits" (1:4; 3:1; 4:5; 5:6) and "two witnesses" (11:1–13). Beale, *Revelation*, 78, rightly concludes that "the likelihood is that John draws from both Semitic and Greek biblical sources and often modifies both." See also Steve Moyise, "The Language of the Old Testament in the Apocalypse." *JSNT* 76 (1999): 112–13.

10. See Max Wilcox, "Text Form," in D. A. Carson and H. G. M. Williamson, eds., *It Is Written: Scripture Citing Scripture* (Cambridge: Cambridge University Press, 1988), 193–203.

11. The total number of allusions ranges from the three hundreds to upward of one thousand. See the discussion by G. K. Beale, "Revelation," in Carson and Williamson, eds., *It Is Written*, 318–36.

even more, some scholars add the category "echo." Since it is almost impossible (or at least a bit artificial) to distinguish between an allusion and an echo, we place them in the same category, while recognizing that there are different types of allusions, and some of them can be very subtle and indirect.

Beale defines an allusion as "a brief expression consciously intended by an author to be dependent on an OT passage."[12] Moving beyond the definition to the validation of an allusion is the more difficult task. The much-quoted work of Richard Hays provides a good starting point, offering criteria for validating allusions: (1) availability, (2) volume, (3) recurrence, (4) thematic coherence, (5) historical plausibility, (6) history of interpretation, and (7) satisfaction.[13] Hays's work offers a reliable foundation on which to build, and Revelation scholars have done just that.

Beale uses five main criteria (theme, content, specific construction of words, structure, and explanation of authorial motive) to put the allusions in Revelation into one of three categories: (1) *clear allusion*—the wording is almost identical to the Old Testament source, shares some common core meaning, and could not likely have come from anywhere else, (2) *probable allusion*—the wording is not as close but still contains an idea or wording that is uniquely traceable to the Old Testament text or exhibits a structure of ideas uniquely traceable to the Old Testament passage, or (3) *possible allusion*—the language is generally similar to the source, echoing its words or concepts.[14] This remains a helpful way of understanding the type of Old Testament references found in Revelation.

Paulien argues that we need a more objective method of determining these Old Testament allusions. His work rests on the differentiation between direct or intentional allusions on the part of the author and echoes, where Old Testament language and themes are used but without any intentional reference to any particular text.[15] While this distinction sounds nice in theory, we continue to prefer the single category "allusions" even as we admit to numerous types of allusions. Paulien uses authorial intention to draw the line between allusion and echo but, as Ian Paul notes, "he provides no clear criteria for discerning whether something was in the author's mind or not."[16]

While rightly affirming authorial intention as a guide to the meaning of a biblical

12. G. K. Beale, *Handbook on the New Testament Use of the Old Testament: Exegesis and Interpretation* (Grand Rapids: Baker Academic, 2012), 31. Beale notes that an allusion will bear "an *incomparable or unique parallel in wording, syntax, concept or cluster of motifs in the same order or structure*" (31, emphasis original).

13. Richard B. Hays, *Echoes of Scripture in the Letters of Paul* (New Haven: Yale University Press, 1989), 29–32. Beale, *Handbook*, 32–35, slightly modifies the explanation of Hays's criteria.

14. Beale, *Revelation*, 78. See G. K. Beale, *The Use of Daniel in Jewish Apocalyptic Literature and in the Revelation of St. John* (Eugene, OR: Wipf & Stock, 1984), 307–9, for a discussion of the five criteria.

15. Jon Paulien, "Criteria and Assessment of Allusions to the Old Testament in the Book of Revelation," in *Studies in the Book of Revelation*, ed. Steve Moyise (Edinburgh: T&T Clark, 2001), 119.

16. Ian Paul, "The Use of the Old Testament in Revelation 12," in *The Old Testament in the New Testament: Essays in Honour of J. L. North*, ed. Steve Moyise, JSNTSup 189 (Sheffield: Sheffield Academic Press, 2000), 260. Paulien, "Criteria and Assessment," 128, admits that "certainty regarding an author's intention will remain somewhat elusive." To use this "elusive" criterion for distinguishing between an allusion and an echo remains problematic. I do, however, appreciate Paulien's acknowledgment of the importance of the author's intention in the entire process.

text, Mathewson recognizes the limitations of always being able to discern John's conscious intentions when it comes to studying Old Testament allusions in Revelation. A better approach, says Mathewson, is to evaluate potential Old Testament allusions based on how they cohere with the text itself, the author's final communicative act. Interpreters should focus on how the possible allusion functions within the text of the Apocalypse. While classifying allusions may be helpful to an extent, Mathewson is surely correct to say we should focus on their interpretive and theological significance.[17]

8.3 THE MOST INFLUENTIAL OLD TESTAMENT BOOKS

John pulls from a range of Old Testament books in Revelation, more than thirty in all, but he concentrates on a select group: Genesis, Exodus, Deuteronomy, Psalms, and five prophetic books—Isaiah, Jeremiah, Ezekiel, Daniel, and Zechariah. From the Pentateuch we find around one hundred allusions, with most coming from Genesis, Exodus, and Deuteronomy.

8.3.1 Genesis, Exodus, and Deuteronomy

John alludes to Genesis in large part to shape Revelation's grounding theological narrative.[18] Images such as the garden of God, the tree of life, the ancient serpent, the great city, fire and sulfur (judgment and death), and the Lion of Judah are drawn from Genesis and figure prominently in the overall plot of Revelation (e.g., Rev 2:7; 12:9).

We see a similar pattern in Deuteronomy. John emphasizes the theme of judgment, and more specifically plagues of judgment, using texts from Deuteronomy (e.g., Deut 28:35, 59–60; 32:17, 28–33, 40). But he also confronts his readers with the need to persevere in obedience using images such as the camp of the saints, protection in the wilderness, and the call to witnesses (e.g., 2:7; 8:3, 15–16; 17:9; 19:15; 23:14; 29:5; 32:10). He emphasizes God's faithful deliverance and restoration of his people, often connected to the Song of Moses (e.g., 31:19, 22, 30; 32:44), resulting in the ongoing call to live obediently (e.g., Rev 22:18–19; cf. Deut 4:2; 12:32).

Perhaps surprisingly, there are more than twice the number of allusions to Exodus compared with Genesis and Deuteronomy. With its epic battle between the Lord and the forces of darkness, personified by Pharaoh, Exodus lends itself to John's description of the climactic battle between God and the powers of evil. The sovereign and Almighty "I AM WHO I AM" (Exod 3:14; cf. Rev 1:4, 8; 11:17; 16:5) confronts the powers of evil using a series of judgments, patterned after the plagues inflicted by God on the Egyptians (see the chart in 11.4.4.2)

17. David L. Mathewson, "Assessing Old Testament Allusions in the Book of Revelation," *EvQ* 75.4 (2003): 311–25.

18. See the helpful essay by Steve Moyise, "Genesis in Revelation," in *Genesis in the New Testament*, ed. Maarten J. J. Menken and Steve Moyise, LNTS 466 (London: T&T Clark, 2012), 166–79; cf. also Michaels, "Old Testament in Revelation," 852.

Little wonder that the song of praise for God's deliverance is described as the "song of God's servant Moses and of the Lamb" (15:3; cf. 11:15; 19:6). The eschatological exodus has fulfilled the original deliverance from evil powers, so the song rooted in the celebration of Exod 15:1–18 seems fitting. God's powerful appearance on Mount Sinai recorded in 19:16–25 is one of the most important events in the entire Old Testament and provides the backdrop for describing God's awesome presence in Revelation (Rev 4:5; 8:5; 11:19; 16:18).[19]

8.3.2 The Psalms

John alludes to the Psalms about one hundred times, focusing on God's character, judgment, and salvation. Moyise offers the following summary (with modifications) of how John uses the Psalms in Revelation (Psalm citations below are given based on EVV; where different, LXX and MT citations are placed in brackets):[20]

1. Judgment:
    - God defeats the raging nations (Pss 2:1–2; 99:1 [LXX 98:1] in Rev 11:15–18)
    - the nations' opposition is smashed like clay pots (Ps 2:8–9 in Rev 2:26–27)
    - judgment according to works (Ps 62:12 [MT 62:13, LXX 61:13] in Rev 2:23)
    - the wicked drink the wine of God's wrath (Ps 76:7 [MT 76:8, LXX 75:8] in Rev 14:10)
    - plagues patterned after the exodus (Ps 78:44 [LXX 77:44] in Rev 16:4)
    - condemnation of idolatry (Ps 115:4–6 [LXX 113:12–14] in Rev 9:20)
    - Babylon is judged for her cruelty (Ps 138:7 [LXX 137:8] in Rev 18:6)
2. Salvation:
    - all nations come and worship God (Ps 86:8–10 [LXX 85:8–10] in Rev 15:4)
    - led to springs of living water (Ps 23:1–2 [LXX 22:1–2] in Rev 7:17)
    - not having names erased from the book of life (Ps 69:29 [MT 69:30, LXX 68:30] in Rev 13:8; 17:8; 20:12, 15; 21:27)
    - blessing on those who fear God (Ps 115:13 [LXX 113:21] in Rev 11:18; 19:5)
    - prayers rising like incense (Ps 141:2 [LXX 140:2] in Rev 5:8)
    - singing a new song (Pss 40:3 [MT 40:4, LXX 39:4]; 98:1 [LXX 97:1]; 144:9 [LXX 143:9]; 149:1 in Rev 5:9; 14:3)

19. Duvall and Hays, *God's Relational Presence*, 29–32, 318–22.

20. See Steve Moyise, "The Psalms in the Book of Revelation," in *Psalms in the New Testament*, ed. Steve Moyise and Maarten J. J. Menken, NTSI (London: T&T Clark, 2004), 231–47.

3. Attributes of God and his Anointed
    - searches the human heart (Pss 7:9 [MT, LXX 7:10]; 62:12 [MT 62:13, LXX 61:13] in Rev 2:23)
    - judges in righteousness (Ps 96:13 [LXX 95:13] in Rev 19:11)
    - true and just judgments (Ps 119:137 [LXX 118:137] in Rev 15:3; 16:7)
    - God's anointed is the firstborn of the dead, the ruler of the kings of the earth (Ps 89:27 [MT 89:28, LXX 88:28] in Rev 1:5)

8.3.3 The Prophets

John's primary intertextual connection is with the Prophets, notably Isaiah (145x), Jeremiah (70x), Ezekiel (100x), Daniel (80x) and Zechariah (30x).[21] If you add the allusions for the other prophetic books (about 60x) to these five books, we find that about 65 percent of John's Old Testament allusions are to a prophetic book. This makes good sense because John is writing a prophecy (Rev 1:3; 19:10; 22:6–7, 9–10, 18–19; cf. 10:7, 11). It is almost as if John needs to breathe in the Old Testament prophetic air in order to properly exhale his apocalyptic vision.

Fekkes makes a helpful classification of thematic categories for John's allusions to Isaiah.[22] First, John uses the language of Isaiah (along with Ezekiel) to describe his visionary experience (Isa 6:2–3 in Rev 4:8). Second, John uses Isaiah to shape Christological titles and descriptions such as judge, sovereign Lord, promised descendent of David, faithful and true witness (e.g., Isa 11:1 in Rev 5:5; 22:16; Isa 11:4 in Rev 19:11; Isa 22:22 in Rev 3:7; Isa 44:6; 41:4; 48:12 in Rev 1:8, 17; 21:6; 22:13; Isa 63:1–3; 11:4; 49:2 in Rev 19:13, 15; Isa 65:16 in Rev 3:14). Third, John draws from Isaiah to portray God's eschatological judgment. He does so by referencing the coming day of the Lord (Isa 2:10–20; 34:4; 50:3 in Rev 6:12–17; Isa 63:1–3 in Rev 14:19–20), and by highlighting God's judgment on the nations, chiefly Babylon. In Rev 14–19 John uses Isaiah repeatedly (along with Jeremiah and Ezekiel) to paint the picture of God holding the nations accountable.[23] Fourth, John uses the language of Isaiah to depict God's eschatological salvation, with the greatest concentration of allusions occurring in Rev 21–22 as one might expect. These references are too numerous to discuss here, but most are drawn from Isa 40–66 with its emphasis on the renewal of creation and the New Jerusalem.[24]

---

21. These numbers are approximate and are based on the NA[28] critical apparatus.

22. Jan Fekkes III, *Isaiah and Prophetic Traditions in the Book of Revelation: Visionary Antecedents and Their Development*, JSNTSup 93 (Sheffield: Sheffield Academic Press, 1994), 282. See also David L. Mathewson, "Isaiah in Revelation," in *Isaiah in the New Testament*, ed. Steve Moyise and Maarten J. J. Menken, NTSI (London: T&T Clark, 2005), 189–210, who interacts in detail with Fekkes's classification.

23. See the summary chart on p. 198 of Mathewson, "Isaiah in Revelation."

24. See Mathewson, "Isaiah in Revelation," 200–209, for a detailed exploration of these allusions.

Allusions to Jeremiah are sprinkled throughout the Apocalypse, but they play an especially significant role in how John depicts the fall of Babylon.[25] Jeremiah 50–51, a prophecy against Babylon, provides fitting language for portraying the fall of the great center of pagan power described in Revelation. Babylon is God's enemy and the enemy of God's people, a powerful kingdom full of arrogance, deception, and the murdering of the saints (e.g., Rev 14:8; 17:2–4; 18:3, 5, 24; cf. Jer 50:11, 14; 51:7–9, 49). She will fall suddenly under God's judgment (Rev 18:8; cf. Jer 50:31–32) and will be condemned according to her evil deeds (Rev 18:6, 21; cf. Jer 50:15, 29; 51:63–64). As a result, God's people are called to separate from Babylon and her ungodly ways (Rev 18:4; cf. Jer 51:6, 9, 45; cf. also Isa 52:11). God's people rejoice at her downfall as God judges the great prostitute and avenges the blood of his servants (Rev 18:20; 19:2; cf. Jer 51:25, 48).

John makes thorough use of the prophet Ezekiel as well, especially at the structural level.[26] There are several important parallels between Revelation and Ezekiel worth noting. First, John's vision of God on his throne in Rev 4–5 corresponds in striking ways to Ezekiel 1 (e.g., brilliant light, precious stones, rainbow, crystal sea, four living creatures, multiple eyes, figure like a man). Second, the sealing or protection of the saints in Rev 7 parallels the marking of those who grieve over the sins of the people in Ezek 9–10. Third, the description of the prostitute Babylon in Rev 17 draws on the portrayal of Jerusalem, the adulterous wife, in Ezek 16 and 23. Fourth, the lament over Tyre in Ezek 26–27 with its lists of trading partners and products corresponds to the lament over the fall of Babylon/Rome in Rev 18. Fifth, and the most remarkable connection, is that between the establishment of the New Jerusalem in Rev 20–22 and Ezek 37–48 (see the chart on the next page).[27]

This does not mean that John follows his Old Testament sources slavishly since even in this last parallel John sees no temple in the heavenly city (Rev 21:22), whereas Ezekiel speaks of a restored temple (Ezek 40–44). John's tendency is to transform these images in light of his eschatological situation—for instance, the measuring and filling of the temple in Ezekiel becomes the measuring and filling of the entire temple-city, the whole of the new creation, in Revelation (cf. Ezek 40:5; 43:2; Rev 21:15, 23).

Swete notes that "in proportion to its length the Book of Daniel yields by far the greatest number" of Old Testament references in Revelation.[28] Beale has written more than anyone on John's use of Daniel and he suggests that Revelation is a midrash on

25. Kenneth Mulzac, "The 'Fall of Babylon' Motif in the Books of Jeremiah and Revelation," *JATS* 8.1–2 (1997): 137–49.

26. See Steve Moyise, *The Old Testament in the Book of Revelation*, JSNTSup 115 (London: Bloomsbury T&T Clark, 2015), ch. 4, on "John's Use of Ezekiel," and Steve Moyise, *The Old Testament in the New: An Introduction*, 2nd ed. (London: Bloomsbury T&T Clark, 2015); see also Beate Kowalski, "Transformation of Ezekiel in John's Revelation," in *Transforming Visions: Transformations of Text, Traditions, and Theology in Ezekiel*, ed. W. A. Tooman and M. A. Lyons (Cambridge: James Clark, 2010), 279–311 (see pp. 302–7 for a comprehensive list of allusions to Ezekiel in Revelation at both the lexical and structural levels).

27. Cf. Moyise, *Old Testament in the New*, 193; J. Webb Mealy, *After the Thousand Years: Resurrection and Judgment in Revelation 20*, JSNTS 70 (Sheffield: JSOT Press, 1992), 131–35.

28. Swete, *Apocalypse of St. John*, cxlviii.

Daniel, especially Dan 7, as John sees his own situation as the fulfillment of Daniel's prophecies.[29] This influence occurs, according to Beale, even at the structural level as Daniel provides the conceptual framework for Revelation.[30] Yet recently, and after decades of writing and reflection, Beale concludes, "After thirty-five years of reflection, I think it is better to say that Daniel is a secondary model (or at least a major influence) for Revelation but that Ezekiel is a more explicit model."[31]

Ezekiel 37–48	**Revelation 20–22**
Revival of the dry bones (37:1–14)	First resurrection (20:5)
Reunited kingdom under Davidic Messiah (37:15–28)	Messianic millennial kingdom (20:4–6)
Final battle against Gog & Magog (38–39)	Final battle against Gog & Magog (20:7–10)
	Second resurrection (20:11–15)
Vision of the new temple/Jerusalem (40–48) • High mountain (40:2) • Temple measured (40:5) • Temple full of God's glory (43:2) • River of life (47:12)	Descent of heavenly Jerusalem (21–22) • High mountain (21:10) • City measured (21:15) • City full of God's glory (21:23) • River of life (22:2)

Moyise discusses the primary sections of Daniel that Revelation alludes to: (1) the Nebuchadnezzar material (Dan 2–4), (2) the vision of the "beasts" and the "one like a human being" (Dan 7), (3) the interpreting angel (Dan 10, 12), and (4) Dan 5:23 (writing on the wall scene) and 8:10 (the little horn incident). Chiefly, John draws on Dan 2; 4; 10; 12; and especially 7. In addition, Moyise notes several important ways that John uses Daniel.[32] He models some of his vision descriptions on the visions of Daniel (e.g., Rev 1; cf. Dan 7; 10). He often uses the language and imagery of Daniel (e.g., Babylon of Dan 4 in Rev 14), even when it is interwoven with other Old Testament texts. He uses Dan 2:28–29 as a structural marker in Rev 1:1, 19; 4:1; 22:6, and he also uses Daniel to heighten the eschatological outlook of his readers (e.g., "the time of the end" in Dan 12:4 becomes "the time is near" in Rev 1:3; 22:10).

John sees what Daniel had previously seen but now sees these initial prophecies fulfilled with the coming of Christ, the Son of Man (i.e., the "one like a human being").

29. Especially Beale, *Use of Daniel*, and throughout his commentary on *Revelation* for specifics. On the role of Dan 7 on Revelation, see also Thomas Hieke, "The Reception of Daniel 7 in the Revelation of John," in *Revelation and the Politics of Apocalyptic Interpretation*, ed. Richard B. Hays and Stefan Alkier (Waco, TX: Baylor University Press, 2012), 47–67.

30. Beale, *Use of Daniel*, 275–85, 297.

31. See Beale, "Thirty-Five Years of Research," in *Apocalypse of John among Its Critics*, 239–40.

32. Moyise, *Old Testament in the Book of Revelation*, 56–58.

It is John's high Christology based on the revelation of Jesus Christ that now drives him to see his own time as the inauguration of the last days spoken of by Daniel.[33] Just as Daniel envisioned (1) the judgment of rebellious nations and the establishment of God's kingdom, (2) God's absolute sovereignty over all earthly rulers, and (3) the saints undergoing trials at the hands of worldly powers, so Revelation trumpets these same themes.[34] This congruence of themes is the primary reason why John alludes to Daniel so extensively.

Revelation also references the minor prophet Zechariah more than one might expect.[35] In the opening of his letter (1:7), John describes Christ's return using language from Zech 12:10 (cf. Dan 7:13; Matt 24:30). Jesus (the "firstborn"; cf. Rev 1:5) assumes Yahweh's role and his coming will result in the people's repentance (or perhaps judgment). John again promotes a high Christology as he links the "seven eyes" of Yahweh from Zech 4:10 with the seven eyes of the Lamb in Rev 5:6 (cf. Zech 3:4, 9).[36] As Beale and McDonough observe, "It is only by the Spirit of Yahweh's 'Servant the Branch,' the messianic lamb, that iniquity has been removed from the world (Zech 3:9) and resistance to the kingdom overcome (cf. Zech 4:6–7)."[37] The four horsemen of Rev 6 are often linked to Zechariah's vision of the horses in 1:8–11 and the four chariots with different colored horses in 6:1–8. In Zechariah the groups of horses are told to patrol the entire land, perhaps signifying God's vast authority. In contrast to "the whole world at rest and in peace" reported in Zechariah (1:11) stands the judgment tied to the horses in Revelation. In both cases, the images communicate that "God's sovereign plan of judgment and salvation will be accomplished in all the earth."[38] The question of "how long" in Zech 1:12 is alluded to in Rev 6:10 as the martyrs ask the Lord when he will judge the guilty. In 11:4 the figures of the olive trees and lampstand come from Zech 4:1–14, where the priest and king, the two "anointed ones," are empowered by the Spirit and represent God's presence in the temple and among the people. In Revelation the two witnesses symbolize the Spirit-empowered witnessing church, the locus of God's presence.[39] Finally, John alludes to Zech 14:11 when saying that in the heavenly city "no longer will there be any curse" (Rev 22:3). The hoped-for safety and security of the earthly Jerusalem in Zechariah finds its ultimate fulfillment in the complete absence of destruction and curses in the new Jerusalem.

33. Hieke, "Reception of Daniel 7," 65–66.

34. Beale, *Use of Daniel*, 272–73.

35. See the helpful works of Marko Jauhiainen, *The Use of Zechariah in Revelation* (Tübingen: Mohr Siebeck, 2005); Marko Jauhiainen, "The Minor Prophets in Revelation," in *The Minor Prophets in the New Testament*, ed. Maarten J. J. Menken and Steve Moyise, LNTS 377 (London: T&T Clark, 2009), 155–71.

36. Jauhiainen, "Minor Prophets," 159–60.

37. Beale and McDonough, "Revelation," 1102.

38. Fanning, *Revelation*, 240.

39. Jauhiainen, "Minor Prophets," 165–67.

8.4 HOW JOHN USES THE OLD TESTAMENT

Beale's identification of the various ways John uses the Old Testament throughout Revelation proves helpful.[40] To begin with, John uses sections of the Old Testament as *literary models or prototypes*. Here, John patterns his writings after particular Old Testament contexts, themes, sequences, catch phrases, and the like because they serve as models for what he is trying to communicate. For instance, Beale sees Dan 2 and 7 providing the broad patterns for Rev 1; 4–5; 13; and 17.[41] And Decock points out the structural influence of Ezek 40–48 on the vision of the New Jerusalem in Rev 21–22.[42] John is even more radical than Ezekiel in his vision of the newness of creation. Whereas Ezekiel sees God dwelling in a new temple (Ezek 43:1–5), John sees the whole of the new creation as throne, temple, and holy of holies. God's relational presence replaces these symbols of presence. Most scholars agree that the trumpet and bowl judgments (Rev 8, 16) are patterned after the plagues reported in Exod 7–14 (see 11.4.4.2). Beale notes that Revelation often serves to expand on the Old Testament prototype by further explaining past and present eschatological fulfillment (e.g., the Roman emperor as a beast in Rev 13 and 17) and further defining and predicting future eschatological fulfillment.[43]

Sometimes John develops specific Old Testament *themes* in Revelation. These can be broad themes such as judgment, salvation, and covenant, or more specific themes such as Daniel's "abomination of desolation" or the eschatological earthquake. At times even particular genres are used in a thematic way. For instance, John makes use of hymns throughout with special dependence on the Servant Songs of Isa 40–55.

John also uses the Old Testament *analogically*. He employs Old Testament persons, places and events (with some creative freedom) to "convey principles of continuity between the OT and NT."[44] Behind this continuity lies John's belief that both Testaments reflect God's one story and reveal his plans to judge evil and save his creation. Analogies relating to judgment, persecution of God's people, idolatrous teaching, God's protection, God's people winning the battle over evil, and the Spirit empowering God's people serve as examples of how John links his message with the Old Testament.

At times John *universalizes* Old Testament realities that once applied only to Israel to a much larger group. For example, the description of Israel as "kingdom of priests" in Exod 19:6 is now applied to the whole people of God, the church, in Rev 1:6 and 5:10.

40. The survey below, with slight modifications, is drawn from Beale, *Revelation*, 86–99; for more detail, see ch. 2 in G. K. Beale, *John's Use of the Old Testament in Revelation*, LNTS 166 (London: T&T Clark, 2015).

41. Beale, *John's Use of Daniel*.

42. Paul B. Decock, "Scriptures in the Book of Revelation," *Neotestamentica* 33 (2) (1999): 379–86. On Ezekiel's pervasive influence, see also Moyise, *Old Testament in the Book of Revelation*, 64–84.

43. Beale, *Revelation*, 88.

44. Beale, *Revelation*, 89.

The reference to Israel (i.e., "house of David and inhabitants of Jerusalem") in Zech 12:10 becomes "all the tribes of the earth" in Rev 1:7. Likewise, the "leaves of healing" of Ezek 47:12 becomes "the leaves of the tree are for the healing of the nations" in Rev 22:2. Often the period of Israel's persecution (e.g., ten days and three-and-a-half years in Dan 1:12; 7:25; 12:7) is extended to the persecution of the whole people of God, "the eschatological, true Israel—throughout the world."[45] Beale notes that the "primary reason for the extended applications is the NT's and John's assumption concerning the cosmic dimensions of Christ's lordship and death."[46]

Sometimes John alludes to Old Testament texts to indicate present or future *prophetic fulfillment*. The question of when such a fulfillment has occurred or will occur—John's day, later in church history, or in our future—remains a matter of debate but all reveal John's reliance upon the Old Testament. Beale notes several examples from Daniel: John's substitution of "quickly" (ἐν τάχει) in Rev 1:1 for Daniel's "in the last days" (ἐπ ἐσχάτων τῶν ἡμερῶν) in Dan 2:28; the book sealed until the end of time in Dan 12:4, 9 now becomes an unsealed, open book in Rev 22:10 because "the time is near" (ὁ καιρὸς γὰρ ἐγγύς ἐστιν); and others (e.g., the new name of Isa 62:2; 65:15 referring to Israel's future status is now fulfilled in the new name written on all believers in Rev 2:17; 3:12; 22:4; the wiping away of tears in Isa 25:8 and Rev 21:4; the new heaven and new earth in Isa 65:17; 66:22 and Rev 21:1). There are many other examples of the fulfillment use.

There are times when John's use of the Old Testament seems like a *reversal* of the original context and meaning. This inverted use of the Old Testament often makes use of irony and indicates God's bigger plan that moves beyond original expectations. For example, in Rev 3:9 we read that God will make those who pretend to be Jews but are not come and bow down at the feet of his church. This runs contrary to the expectation that the nations would bow down to Israel (e.g., Isa 45:14; 49:23; 60:14). Again, in Dan 7:14 the "one like a son of man" is given authority by the Ancient of Days over all nations. He receives an everlasting kingdom that will never be destroyed, but in Rev 13:7–8 the beast is given authority to wage war against God's people and to conquer them. Beale observes that "the point of these kinds of ironic uses is to mock the enemy's proud attempt to overcome God and his people and to underscore the fitting justice of the punishment."[47]

Many of the ways Beale observes John using the Old Testament above often overlap with each other and fall broadly into the more overarching category known as *typology*. Typology may be defined as "the study of analogical correspondences among revealed truths about persons, events, institutions, and other things within the historical

45. Beale, *Revelation*, 91.

46. Beale, *Revelation*, 92. Other examples of universalization include lampstands (1:12–13, 20), manna (2:17), prostitute (17:1–18), bride (19:7), and Jerusalem (3:12; 21:2).

47. Beale, *Revelation*, 95.

framework of God's special revelation, which, from a retrospective view, are of a prophetic nature and are escalated in their meaning."[48] The later parallel offers a deeper realization or finalization of God's revelation of himself and his ways. Fanning notes the three basic elements included in typology: "(1) a shared pattern or correspondence in historical fact; (2) a divinely intended anticipation; and (3) an escalation or intensification in the later part of the correspondence."[49]

For one example—and there are many to choose from—, the plagues on the Egyptians connected with the Exodus event provide a type or pattern of God's judgment of evil that appears in the seal, trumpet, and bowl judgments of Revelation. Similarly, Pharaoh is a type of the Roman emperor who may also serve as a type of future beasts. God's deliverance of Israel from captivity and his provision for her in the wilderness corresponds to the spiritual protection God provides for his people on their "wilderness" journey to the new creation. At its core this new exodus corresponds to the cross and resurrection of Jesus. Typology assumes a coherence to the overall message of Scripture but also indicates a progression so that what God has said and done in earlier times finds its ultimate fulfillment later, especially in relationship to Christ and God's design for consummating the kingdom and living forever among his people. Whereas verbal prophecy might be seen as directly fulfilled, typological prefigurings can be viewed as "indirect" prophecy; both are equally fulfilled.[50]

Fanning wisely offers several clarifying principles for understanding typology and its use in Revelation.[51] First, typology is not limited to the common topics of Christology and soteriology, but includes other areas such as God's judgment, the final battle characteristics of good and evil, and so on. Second, typology does not always mean a shift from physical, geographic, or historic realities to spiritual realities. For example, the typology of sacrifice does not call for a merely "spiritual" crucifixion and resurrection of Jesus. Likewise, the physical descriptions of the new creation in the Old Testament are to be fulfilled in a new heaven *and* a new earth. Third, the type is not necessarily annulled by the fulfillment. For instance, Adam as the one who bears God's image and rules over creation (Gen 1; Ps 8) is not abolished for subsequent redeemed humanity but restored in Christ (Heb 2; Rev 2:26–27; 20:4, 6; 22:5). Fourth, it is possible for the Old Testament pattern to find more than one future fulfillment on the road to its ultimate fulfillment. We see this with the Egyptian Pharaoh and ancient Babylon, the Roman emperor/Rome as Babylon, subsequent empires/beasts and the final anti-Christian empire/beast. Typology allows us to understand how John's imagery can relate to the first-century world, to subsequent Christian history, and to the final climactic period of history.[52]

48. Beale, *Handbook*, 14.

49. Fanning, *Revelation*, 46.

50. Beale, *Handbook*, 15–18; Fanning, *Revelation*, 47.

51. Fanning, *Revelation*, 47–48.

52. Fanning, *Revelation*, 49.

8.5 CONCLUSION

In this chapter we have looked carefully at the forms and types of Old Testament references in Revelation, the most influential books alluded to by John, and the variety of ways in which he uses the Old Testament. It is no exaggeration to say that Revelation is consumed with the Old Testament. John seems convinced that the language of the Prophets was the best way to express his visions.[53] But the Old Testament is not only a "servant" for John; it is also a "guide," using Beale's terms:

> For John the Christ-event is the key to understanding the OT, and yet reflection on the OT context leads the way to further comprehension of this event and provides the redemptive-historical background against which the apocalyptic visions are better understood; the New Testament interprets the Old and the Old interprets the New.[54]

As the above survey shows, John uses the Old Testament in a variety of ways. But the most significant way is that it seems to provide "a symbolic world or conceptual framework" enabling his readers to see their own situation in light of the climactic Christ event and how that shapes their own eschatological expectations.[55] In other words, the Old Testament and John's Christian commitments play into the single redemptive story of promise and fulfillment that runs through both Testaments. This one biblical metanarrative brings it all together for John and provides him the resources to articulate God's overarching purposes for his people in the last days. In short, John believed he was writing the culmination of biblical prophecy, and the Old Testament is an integral part of that project.[56]

53. Beale, *Revelation*, 96.

54. Beale, *Revelation*, 97.

55. David Mathewson, *A New Heaven and a New Earth: The Meaning and Function of the Old Testament in Revelation 21.1–22.5*, JSNTSup 238 (Sheffield: Sheffield Academic Press, 2003), 224–25.

56. Bauckham, *Climax of Prophecy*, xi; Bauckham, *Theology*, 153–54.

Chapter 9

THE LITERARY STRUCTURE OF REVELATION

BIBLIOGRAPHY

Bandy, Alan S. "The Layers of the Apocalypse: An Integrated Approach to Revelation's Macrostructure." *JSNT* 31.4 (2009): 469–99. **Barr, David L.** "The Apocalypse of John as Oral Enactment." *Int* 40 (1986): 243–56. ———. *Tales of the End: A Narrative Commentary on the Book of Revelation*. 2nd ed. Salem, OR: Polebridge, 2012. **Bauckham, Richard.** "Structure and Composition." Pages 1–37 in *The Climax of Prophecy: Studies in the Book of Revelation*. Edinburgh: T&T Clark, 1993. **Dalrymple, Rob.** *Revelation and the Two Witnesses: The Implications for Understanding John's Depiction of the People of God and His Hortatory Intent*. Eugene, OR: Wipf & Stock, 2011. **DeSilva, David A.** "Rhetorical Features in the Book of Revelation." *OBHR*, 69–83. ———. "X Marks the Spot? A Critique of the Use of Chiasmus in Macro-Structural Analyses of Revelation." *JSNT* 30 (2008): 343–71. **Hall, Mark Seaborn.** "The Hook Interlocking Structure of Revelation: The Most Important Verses in the Book and How They May Unify Its Structure." *NovT* 44.3 (2002): 278–96. **Koester, Craig R.** *Revelation and the End of All Things*. 2nd ed. Grand Rapids: Eerdmans, 2018. **Korner, R. J.** "'And I Saw . . .': An Apocalyptic Literary Convention for Structural Identification in the Apocalypse." *NovT* 42 (2000): 160–83. **Osborne, Grant R.** "Recent Trends in the Study of the Apocalypse." Pages 473–504 in *The Face of New Testament Studies: A Survey of Recent Research*. Edited by Scot McKnight and Grant R. Osborne. Grand Rapids: Baker Academic, 2004. **Perry, Peter S.** *The Rhetoric of Digressions: Revelation 7:1–17 and 10:1–11:13 and Ancient Communication*. WUNT 2.268. Tübingen: Mohr Siebeck, 2009. **Resseguie, James L.** "Narrative Features of the Book of Revelation." *OBHR*, 37–52. **Smalley, Stephen S.** *Thunder and Love: John's Revelation and John's Commentary*. Eugene, OR: Wipf & Stock, 1994. **Smith, Christopher R.** "The Structure of the Book of Revelation in the Light of Apocalyptic Literary Conventions." *NovT* 36 (1994): 373–93. **Tavo, Felise.** "The Structure of the Apocalypse: Re-examining a Perennial Problem." *NovT* 47 (2005): 47–68. **Victorinus of Petovium et al.** *Latin Commentaries on Revelation*. Edited by Thomas C. Oden. Translated by William C. Weinrich. ACT. Downers Grove, IL: IVP Academic, 2011. **Waddell, Robby.** *The Spirit of the Book of Revelation*. JPTSup 30.

Blandford Forum: Deo, 2006. **Wendland, Ernst R.** "The Hermeneutical Significance of Literary Structure in Revelation." *Neot* 48.2 (2014): 447–76. **Wright, Brian J.** *Communal Reading in the Time of Jesus: A Window into Early Christian Reading Practices.* Minneapolis: Fortress, 2017. **Yarbro Collins, Adela.** *The Combat Myth in the Book of Revelation.* Eugene, OR: Wipf & Stock, 2001.

9.1 INTRODUCTION

As many scholars have opined, there seems to be as many outlines of Revelation as there are people writing about it! David Barr just might be right: "How you arrange the material depends on what you are looking for."[1] At this point, no clear consensus exists regarding the overall literary structure of the book. Nevertheless, structure remains an important concern and one worth wrestling with because how the book is organized and presented relates directly to its theological message. In fact, John uses a complex literary structure to communicate theology with even greater persuasive appeal and dramatic impact.[2] Wendland concludes, "The *artistry* to be found in the Apocalypse is also eminently *functional*—an outstanding case of art created in support of the divinely intended 'message' (*form* as well as *content*) that it was designed to serve."[3]

In this chapter, we are first reminded of the importance of literary structure and how to evaluate the various proposals related to Revelation, a complex but unified work. Next, we explore the literary nature of Revelation, including the leading reasons why a consensus related to structure remains so elusive. In this context we discuss the much-debated issue of chronological progression versus recapitulation. Finally, we present our own outline and reiterate our hope to arrive at a better understanding of the book's structure so that we can be more alert to its carefully nuanced theology.

9.2 A COMPLEX BUT UNIFIED WORK

Perhaps as much as anyone, Bauckham has researched and written on Revelation's structure and composition. He concludes that the book is "extraordinarily complex" but also "one of the most unified works in the New Testament."[4] Revelation is not an accidental hodgepodge of religious reflections, but a carefully structured,

1. Barr, *Tales of the End*, 15.

2. Ernst R. Wendland, "The Hermeneutical Significance of Literary Structure in Revelation," *Neot* 48.2 (2014): 464.

3. Wendland, "Hermeneutical Significance," 465, emphasis added.

4. Bauckham, *Climax of Prophecy*, 1.

multilayered work of literary and theological artistry.[5] Bandy is surely correct when he observes that "the book of Revelation represents an intricately woven literary masterpiece exhibiting a cohesive unity."[6] Again, as we have noted, the literary unity grows out of its theological unity, as Smalley observes: "the proposed structure should be directly related to the theological and eschatological content of the book, and indeed arise from it."[7]

Yet, the unity displays a rich complexity due to several important factors. In no particular order these include the book's various literary genres, the complex narrative movements within the story, the location and roles of the interludes, the abundance of symbolism and the use of numbers, Revelation's intertextuality and intratextuality, the repetition of events and themes, the variation of viewpoint, the level of chronological progression, and so on.[8] This complex unity keeps us diligently searching for a consensus regarding its literary structure.

When evaluating the various options related to the book's structure, the following guidelines prove useful.[9] First, structure rests upon sound biblical exegesis. Second, structural outlines that are more concrete are better—that is, outlines that rest on actual lexical features rather than semantic content alone. Third, we should rely more on formal features than on other matters when it comes to evaluating structure. Fourth, outlines that provide the most coherence prove better than those that have less coherence. Fifth, linear structures that follow the flow of the discourse take priority over chiastic arrangements. Sixth, one aspect of the proposed outline must fit well with other aspects (i.e., it must have congruence). Although the purpose of this chapter is not to evaluate all the competing outlines in terms of the criteria above, these guidelines play an important role in constructing our own outline.

9.3 THE LITERARY NATURE OF REVELATION

Revelation has a carefully crafted literary-rhetorical structure that incorporates various features at multiple levels. In this section we will discuss the oral/aural nature of Revelation, particular literary phrases and markers that play a prominent role in the

5. Wendland, "Literary Structure," 464–65, identifies eight examples, all found in Rev 19, that betray the well-crafted artistry that is Revelation: structural shaping, genre diversity, morphosyntactic rhetoric, semantic density, contrastive imagery, engaging enigma, dramatic direct discourse, and pervasive intertextuality.

6. Alan S. Bandy, "The Layers of the Apocalypse: An Integrated Approach to Revelation's Macrostructure," *JSNT* 31.4 (2009): 471.

7. Smalley, *Thunder and Love*, 103.

8. Cf. Grant R. Osborne, "Recent Trends in the Study of the Apocalypse," in Scot McKnight and Grant R. Osborne, eds., *The Face of New Testament Studies: A Survey of Recent Research* (Grand Rapids: Baker Academic, 2004), 497–98.

9. Wendland, "Literary Structure," 461–62.

book, the interludes and their importance, as well as the place of numbers, especially the number seven.

9.3.1 The Oral/Aural Nature of Revelation

John makes it clear that Revelation was meant to be read publicly (oral) and heard by the community (aural):

> He made it known by sending his angel to his servant John, who *testifies* to everything he saw—that is, the word of God and the *testimony* of Jesus Christ. Blessed is the one who *reads aloud* the words of this prophecy, and blessed are those who *hear* it and take to heart what is written in it, because the time is near (Rev 1:1–3, emphasis mine).

John's work is a "testimony" or a witness (μαρτυρία) as he bears witness (μαρτυρέω) to what he has seen in the visions. A testimony or witness would have been both spoken (later written) and heard. The first of seven beatitudes is pronounced on those who hear and obey the spoken message. In the letter closing John repeats the emphasis on the oral/aural nature of the book:

> "I, Jesus, have sent my angel to give you this *testimony* for the churches. . . . I warn everyone who *hears* the words of the prophecy of this scroll: . . . He who *testifies* to these things says, "Yes, I am coming soon." Amen. Come, Lord Jesus (Rev 22:16, 18, 20; cf. 22:8, emphasis mine).

The sixth beatitude is pronounced in 22:7 as a blessing on those who keep (both hear and obey) "the words of the prophecy written in this scroll." The angel commands John not to seal the scroll because "the time is near," implying that "everyone needs to have the opportunity to hear it read communally (22:10)."[10]

The seven churches are also instructed to "hear what the Spirit says to the churches," presumably by hearing and obeying the written prophecy of Revelation as it is read in the context of corporate worship (2:7, 11, 17, 29; 3:6, 13, 22). The church in Sardis is specifically told to "remember, therefore, what you have received and heard," likely referring to the proclaimed gospel message (3:3; cf. 14:6 and the angel with the "eternal gospel to proclaim").

Bauckham observes that the essential macrostructure of Revelation would have been apparent and clear for the hearer: "in a text intended for oral performance the structure

10. Brian J. Wright, *Communal Reading in the Time of Jesus: A Window into Early Christian Reading Practices* (Minneapolis: Fortress, 2017), 199.

must be indicated by clear linguistic markers."[11] Consequently, we would expect the macrostructure of Revelation to be simple and clear enough that those listening could understand and remember it.[12] This is not to deny that Revelation is also a complex literary composition and that subtle details will be understood upon further study and reflection. Both are likely true. As a result, we should expect oral/aural markers throughout and this is what we find, as the survey in 9.3.2 indicates.[13]

9.3.2 Important Literary Phrases/Markers

Many scholars identify specific literary markers as the key to understanding the structure of the book. The phrase "in the Spirit" (ἐν πνεύματι) occurs in 1:10; 4:2; 17:3 and 21:10 and serves as the primary marker of macrostructure.[14] Bandy notes that this phrase "indicates a shift of setting from Patmos (Rev 1:9), to the heavenly throne room (Rev 4:1–2), into a desert (Rev 17:3) and finally to a great, high mountain (Rev 21:10)."[15] "In the Spirit" is also used in close connection with the expression "I will show you" (δείξω σοι in 4:1; 17:1; 21:9) to signal a major structural transition.[16] Using these markers, we are left with four primary visions constituting the macrostructure of Revelation:

- 1:10–3:22—the risen and glorified Christ who speaks to the churches
- 4:1–16:21—the heavenly throne room vision and resulting judgments
- 17:1–21:8—the destruction of Babylon the Great and the final victory
- 21:9–22:5—the new creation: God's presence among his people

The phrase "and I saw" (καὶ εἶδον) often signals minor transitions within the major units.[17] Aune says that this phrase functions in three ways in Revelation:

> (1) It introduces a new vision narrative (8:2; 10:1; 13:1; 14:1, 6, 14; 15:1; 19:11, 17; 20:1, 4, 12; 21:1; cf. Acts 11:5; Dan 8:2; 10:5; 12:5; Ezek 1:4; 3:13; 8:2; 13:1). (2) It

11. Bauckham, *Climax of Prophecy*, 3. Likewise, David L. Barr, "The Apocalypse of John as Oral Enactment," *Int* 40 (1986): 243–45.

12. Felise Tavo, "The Structure of the Apocalypse: Re-examining a Perennial Problem," *NovT* 47 (2005): 57–58.

13. For further study of the oral nature of Revelation, see Barr, "Apocalypse of John as Oral Enactment," 243–56. He lists the following as techniques used in such oral/aural settings: numbering, combinations of place and image (e.g., seven letters written to seven places featuring images unique to that place), and scrolls (of letters, liturgy, and heavenly signs). He concludes (p. 256): "The orality of the Apocalypse is an essential element in its interpretation, for its oral presentation within the liturgy mediates the coming of Jesus to his congregation in salvation and judgment enabling them to carry on the divine service, that is, the realization of God's rule in their midst.

14. Bauckham, *Climax of Prophecy*, 3–4; Robby Waddell, *The Spirit of the Book of Revelation*, JPTSup 30 (Dorset, UK: Deo, 2006), 138–50.

15. Bandy, "Layers of the Apocalypse," 475.

16. Bandy, "Layers of the Apocalypse," 475. Cf. Bauckham, *Climax of Prophecy*, 3–7.

17. This phrase occurs in Rev 5:1, 2, 6, 11; 6:1, 2, 5, 8, 12; 7:2; 8:2, 13; 9:1; 10:1; 13:1, 11; 14:1, 6, 14; 15:1, 2; 16:13; 17:3, 6; 19:11, 17, 19; 20:1, 4, 11, 12; 21:1, 2 (καὶ . . . εἶδον).

introduces a major scene within a continuing vision narrative (Rev 5:1; 6:1; 8:13; 13:11; 15:2; 19:19; 21:2; 21:22; cf. Ezek 2:9). (3) It is used to focus on a new or significant figure or action that occurs within a continuing vision narrative (Rev 5:2, 6, 11; 6:2, 5, 8, 12; 7:2; 9:1; 16:13; 17:3, 6; cf. Acts 11:6; Dan 12:5; Ezek 37:8; 44:4).[18]

Occurring thirty-three times, this phrase marks out many of the important sections in Revelation and proves useful for adding detailed structure to the four main visions. See, for example:

5:1	The slain Lamb
6:1	Seal judgments
7:2	Sealing of God's people
8:2	Trumpet judgments
8:13; 9:1	First woe
10:1	John's recommissioning
13:1	Beast from the sea
13:11	Beast from the earth
14:1	The Lamb and the 144,000
14:6	Proclamation of the eternal gospel
14:14	Grain harvest
15:1, 2	Bowl judgments
19:1	Warrior Messiah
20:1	Imprisonment of Satan
20:4	Millennial reign
20:11	Final judgment scene
21:1	Vision of the new creation
21:2	Vision of the new Jerusalem

Another phrase—"After this I saw" (μετὰ ταῦτα εἶδον) in 4:1; 7:9; 15:5; 18:1—also indicates important transitions in the book.[19] Interestingly, most of the important phrases used to mark structure relate directly to the overall purpose of the book as a Spirit-inspired, prophetic vision ("in the Spirit" and expressions related to seeing or being shown).

To this point we have seen the overarching macrostructure of four visions and many of the key transitions marked by particular literary phrases. There are three more elements that play an important role in discerning the structure of Revelation: interludes, the use of the number seven, and interlocking transitions.

18. Aune, *Revelation 1–5*, 338.

19. Bandy, "Layers of the Apocalypse," 477.

9.3.3 The Role of Interludes

John often uses interludes (sometimes called digressions or parentheses or intercalations) to accomplish his literary and theological purposes in Revelation.[20] Among other things, interludes offer heavenly viewpoints, supply flashbacks to grounding events, answer important theological questions, give insight into current circumstances, provide examples of previous faithful witnesses, specify the responsibilities of God's people, explain the conflict between good and evil, allow for a dramatic pause in the action before the next push forward, and preview God's coming victory through judgment.[21] The key interludes in Revelation include 7:1–17; 10:1–11:14; and 12:1–14:20, although this last unit is sometimes described differently.

Revelation 7:1–17 includes two visions: the protective sealing of the 144,000 (i.e., God's people on earth [7:1–8]) and the celebration of the great multitude (i.e., God's people in heaven [7:9–17]). When the sixth seal is broken in 6:12–17, the result is the shaking of the entire cosmos (i.e., a great earthquake, the sun turning black and the moon blood red, stars falling and the heavens receding like a scroll, plus the removal of the mountains and islands). The day of God's wrath has arrived, and the only question is, "Who can withstand it?" (6:17). This first interlude answers the question—only God's people who are sealed and destined for eternal salvation will be protected from his wrath. In this way the interlude offers perspective, consolation, and hope.

The second interlude in 10:1–11:14 also features a pair of visions: the mighty angel and the little scroll in 10:1–11 and the two witnesses in 11:1–14. This interlude clarifies the role of God's people in the present and offers perspective and encouragement to endure faithfully. The theme of prophecy unites both visions, including John's role as a prophet and the church's role as witness.[22] This interlude also creates a literary delay in God's judgments that both heightens the drama and highlights the challenge for God's people.[23]

The third interlude of 12:1–14:20 is much longer and details the cosmic conflict between the false trinity and God and his people. John uses this grand interlude to explain the underlying cause of the hostility against the church. The spiritual warfare that affects the saints is part of a much bigger conflict, a cosmic holy war. The essential battle is explained in chapter 12, whose visions "form the theological heart of the entire book."[24] In chapter 13 we see the defeated dragon's chief agents for attacking God's people: the sea beast and the earth beast. Chapter 14 offers God's response to the actions of the unholy trinity: the triumph of the Lamb and

20. See Peter S. Perry, *The Rhetoric of Digressions: Revelation 7:1–17 and 10:1–11:13 and Ancient Communication*, WUNT 2.268 (Tübingen: Mohr Siebeck, 2009), esp. 209–41.

21. Cf. Fanning, *Revelation*, 62.

22. Smalley, *Revelation*, 254, who notes: "The verb προφητεύειν (*prophēteuein*, 'to prophesy') occurs in 10:11; 11:3 (and only there in Revelation); the noun προφήτης (*prophētēs*, 'prophet') appears in 10:7; 11:10; and the noun προφητεία (*prophēteia*, 'prophecy') is used in 11:6."

23. See Koester, *Revelation*, 356; Rob Dalrymple, *Revelation and the Two Witnesses: The Implications for Understanding John's Depiction of the People of God and His Hortatory Intent* (Eugene, OR: Wipf & Stock, 2011), 78–79.

24. Mounce, *Revelation*, 230.

his followers (14:1–5), the proclamations of coming judgment (14:6–13), and the harvests of judgment (14:14–20).[25] This entire unit introduces the bowl judgments that follow in chapter 16.

All along, the saints are reassured that God protects and vindicates his people, even as they are called to faithful endurance.

Overall, the interludes offer God's people heavenly perspective about God's purposes, a perspective that encourages them to stay faithful in the midst of tribulation by enduring in their faithfulness to Jesus.

9.3.4 The Importance of the Number Seven

The number "seven" (ἑπτά) is used fifty-five times in Revelation in a variety of important ways, one of which is to mark structure, although interpreters can easily become overly fascinated with the arrangement. The term ἑπτά appears in reference to seven churches (1:4, 11, 20 [2x]), seven spirits (1:4; 3:1; 4:5; 5:6), lampstands (1:12, 20 [2x]; 2:1), stars (1:16, 20 [2x]; 2:1; 3:1), lamps (4:5), seals (5:1, 5; 6:1), horns (5:6), eyes (5:6); angels (8:2, 6; 15:1, 6, 7, 8; 16:1; 17:1; 21:9), trumpets (8:2, 6), thunders (10:3, 4 [2x]), 7,000 (11:13), heads (12:3; 13:1; 17:3, 7, 9), crowns (12:3), hills (17:9 [2x]), last plagues (15:1, 6, 8; 21:9), bowls (15:7; 16:1; 17:1; 21:9), and kings (17:9, 11). The adjective "seventh" (ἕβδομος) is also used five times (8:1; 10:7; 11:15; 16:17; 21:20). In addition, there are also series of seven items that are not explicitly numbered: seven beatitudes (1:3; 14:13; 16:15; 19:9; 20:6; 22:7, 14), seven messages (2:1, 8, 12, 18; 3:1, 7, 14), seven hearing formulae (2:7, 11, 17, 29; 3:6, 12, 22), seven attributes of the Lamb (5:12), seven categories of people (6:15), seven descriptions of the nations (5:9; 7:9; 10:11; 11:9; 13:7; 14:6; 17:15), seven terms of doxology (7:12), and perhaps others.[26]

While there is no doubt that John uses series of sevens strategically, we must, as Osborne wisely notes, "balance text-linguistic considerations (introductory formulas, grammatical phrasing, etc.) and thematic indicators (the way ideas develop as the narrative continues)."[27] Bauckham cautions against finding series of sevens where John has not clearly numbered them since those listening to an oral performance would have not counted visions in this way.[28] At the very least, we should be cautious about allowing unnumbered series of sevens to play a major role in determining the structure

25. Duvall, *Revelation*, 190.

26. See Tavo, "Structure of the Apocalypse," 65, and Wendland, "Literary Structure," 449, 454, 466, 471, who also observes seven references to the second coming of Christ (1:7; 11:17–18; 14:14–20; 16:15; 19:11–16; 21:2–8; 22:12–20), seven "sights" (19:11, 17, 19; 20:1, 4, 11, 12), and seven admonitions of the book's conclusion (22:6, 8, 10, 12, 17, 18, 20).

27. See Osborne, *Revelation*, 453, who believes thematic concerns outweigh formulas like καὶ εἶδον and καὶ ἰδού in determining structure.

28. Bauckham, *Climax of Prophecy*, 17, who is responding to Yarbro Collins's view that 12:1–15:4 comprise an unnumbered series of seven visions. See Adela Yarbro Collins, *The Combat Myth in the Book of Revelation*, HDR 9 (Missoula, MT: Scholars Press, 1976; repr., Eugene, OR: Wipf & Stock, 2001), 14.

of Revelation. All that said, the number seven does play an important role in the literary structure of the book.

John begins with the messages to the seven churches (2:1–3:22). As many have observed, the number seven symbolizes completeness or perfection so that the messages from the risen Christ are not simply intended for these few congregations in Asia Minor but for the whole people of God. In the most complex section of the book (chs. 6–16), John has given helpful structural clues using series of sevens: seven seals (6:1–17; 8:1), trumpets (8:2–9:21; 11:15–19), and bowls (15:1–16:21). As a result, the interludes and the three series of sevens help to clarify the structure of this center section of the book. John often uses interlocking transitions to stitch together larger units.

9.3.5 Interlocking Transitions

John often makes use of interlocking or interweaving units to maintain continuity between units while allowing for narrative progression. For example, the seal judgments of 6:1–17 conclude with heavenly silence (8:1) that leads to a liturgical setting before the throne (8:2–6). But in 8:2 the trumpet judgments are introduced and begin officially in 8:7. The next set of judgments will be even more intense as the narrative progresses. We see much the same thing in 15:1–8 when the bowl judgments are introduced.[29]

These interlocking transitions connect to the previous unit, introduce the following unit, and often make an important theological reference (e.g., to God's throne). Tavo identifies six important transitions that follow this same pattern: 4:1–5:14; 8:1–5; 11:15–19; 15:1–8; 16:17–19:10; and 21:1–8.[30] We would modify this by suggesting that chapters 4–5 are less transitional and more grounding, and that 19:6–10 serves as the transitional unit rather than 16:17–19:10. The following units seem to function as interlocking transitions: 8:1–5; 11:15–19; 15:1–8; 19:6–10; 21:1–8; and perhaps 22:6–9. These important units refocus the hearer on the throne-room vision grounded in the worship of God in Rev 4–5 and move the narrative forward while staying connected to what has come before.

The presence of these interlocking units helps to explain some details in the text that have puzzled interpreters when it comes to identifying structure. For example, Bandy observes the *inclusio* between 11:19 and 15:5 related to the phrase "the temple was opened" (ἠνοίγη ὁ ναὸς), the only two times that phrase occurs in the book.[31] This reaffirms the interlude of 12:1–14:20 and links the conclusion of the trumpet judgments and the beginning of the bowl judgments. Or, for instance, note how 19:6–10 links chapters 17–19 with 21–22 since, as Bauckham points out, "announcement of the

29. Koester, *Revelation*, 114.
30. Tavo, "Structure of the Apocalypse," 61–62.
31. Bandy, "Layers of the Apocalypse," 479.

Lamb's marriage to his bride [occurs] at the end of the rejoicing over the fall of Babylon (19:7–9a)."[32] This connection is reinforced by John's thematic agenda of contrasting two cities/people/destinies portrayed as women:

> In 17:1–19:10 he sees the harlot of Babylon and her fall; in 21:9–22:9 he sees the bride of the Lamb, the New Jerusalem, which comes down from heaven. Together these two sections form the climax toward which the whole book has aimed: the destruction of Babylon and her replacement by the New Jerusalem.[33]

The presence of interlocking transitions also explains why scholars are divided about where to place particular units. Oftentimes the answer is that they are transitional and could work in either place. For example, many place 21:1–8 at the conclusion of God's judgment (e.g., Aune, Fanning, Moloney), while others place it at the beginning of the new heaven and new earth section (e.g., Mounce, Osborne, Smalley, Fee). Aune's labeling of some of these units as "transitional" seems to reflect their interlocking nature accurately (e.g., 21:1–8; 22:6–9).[34]

9.4 CHRONOLOGICAL PROGRESSION OR LITERARY RECAPITULATION?

A key structural question in Revelation concerns how the events in the book relate to one other. Does the action progress in a linear way or does it repeat itself as the same events are described over and over? Chronological progression or literary recapitulation? And is this entirely an either/or issue? Typically, a futurist reading of the book prefers chronological progression, while idealists seem more comfortable with some form of recapitulation. In addition, theology is often (but not always) tied to conclusions about structure. For example, the literary progression view does not necessitate a popular futurist reading.

Chapters 6–16 and 19–21 are the main sections up for debate. In the first section, the question is how do the seal, trumpet, and bowl judgments relate?[35] Fanning summarizes the arguments for each view.[36] The chronological progression view finds support in the following: (1) the numbering within each series (first, second, etc.), (2) the typological connection to the Egyptian plagues that themselves indicate sequence as they get progressively worse, (3) the intensification within each series, (4) the bowl judgments are called "the last plagues" that "complete" God's judgment (15:1; 21:9),

32. Bauckham, *Climax of Prophecy*, 5.

33. Bauckham, *Climax of Prophecy*, 4–5.

34. Aune, *Revelation 1–5*, civ; cf. Beale, *Revelation*, 150.

35. See 11.6 for more on chs. 19–21.

and (5) the contents of the seventh seal and seventh trumpet are not specified but are tied directly to the next series.

The recapitulation view, on the other hand, finds support in the following: (1) thematic parallels among the seal, trumpet, and bowl judgments, (2) problems with a literal reading (e.g., the first trumpet burns all the green grass but the locusts in the fifth trumpet are told not to harm it—8:7; 9:4), (3) the trumpets and bowls seem to end at the same place—the consummation of God's judgment, (4) a storm theophany comes at the end of each series (8:5; 11:19; 16:18–21), and (5) the sixth seal (6:12–17) describes events that must occur immediately prior to Christ's return.[37]

Fanning's observations suggest that this might not strictly be an either/or issue. With the recapitulationists, as Beale suggests, the strongest argument for this view is "the observation of repeated combined scenes of consummative judgment and salvation found at the conclusions of various sections throughout the book."[38] The fact that all arrive at the end simultaneously must signal some form of repetition in the cycles of judgment. We also see repeated references to the fall of Babylon scattered throughout (14:8; 16:19; 17:16; 18:2, 10, 17, 19–21; 19:2–3).[39] In addition, you have the inconsistencies of a strictly linear reading of the contents of the judgment series.

Yet, the progressionists are right to see some degree of intensification. As Resseguie puts it, the seals, trumpets, and bowls refer to "similar events but with important variations that up the ante."[40] Such intensification appears even in the storm theophanies that conclude each series and the very place where they seem to repeat themselves. The display of light and sound and effect demonstrates this intensification (compared to the first occurrence of light and sound in 4:5); see the chart on the next page.[41]

For this reason, Resseguie finds the recapitulation theory not entirely convincing. Again, the linear view does not mean that one must hold to a neat chronological progression sought by some popular approaches but instead that Revelation features some degree of literary progression.[42]

It seems best on this question of progression or recapitulation to see elements of both in the structure of Revelation. The actual way Revelation is structured shows forward movement but not in a strictly linear fashion. Rather, Revelation seems to spiral

36. Fanning, *Revelation*, 60–62.

37. As far as we can determine, the recapitulation view goes back to Victorinus, bishop of Petovium (modern Ptuj in Slovenia), who wrote in the second half of the third century. He seems to be the first to have interpreted Revelation "not as a continuous and successive sequence of visions but as repetitive, the trumpets and the bowls portraying the same events under different images." Victorinus writes, "We ought not pay too much attention to the order of what is said. For the sevenfold Holy Spirit, when he has passed in revue [the events] to the last time, to the very end, returns again to the same times and supplements what he had said incompletely. Nor ought we inquire too much into the order of the Revelation. Rather, we ought inquire after the meaning" (*On the Apocalypse* 8.2). See Victorinus et al., *Latin Commentaries*, xxiv.

38. Beale, *Revelation*, 121.

39. Dalrymple, *Revelation and the Two Witnesses*, 71.

40. Resseguie, *Revelation*, 54.

41. Cf. Resseguie, *Revelation*, 58–59.

42. Resseguie, *Revelation*, 59.

forward as events are repeated to some degree but with ever increasing intensification.[43] Even the fractions in the three judgments series show this kind of forward moving spiral (1/4 → 1/3 → 1). Mounce concludes: "There is progress in the book, but it is a progress that moves the reader to a fuller experience of the divine plan for victory rather than a progress that ticks off the minutes of an eschatological clock. Each new vision intensifies the realizing of coming judgment."[44] Fanning likewise comments, "In summary, a basic chronological progression with embedded flashbacks, previews, or contemporary glimpses is the most satisfactory way to read the central section of Revelation (chs. 6–16, most of the second major vision)."[45]

Rev 4:5	Rev 8:5	Rev 11:19	Rev 16:18–21
From the throne came flashes of lightning, rumblings and peals of thunder. In front of the throne, seven lamps were blazing. These are the seven spirits of God.	Then the angel took the censer, filled it with fire from the altar, and hurled it on the earth; and there came peals of thunder, rumblings, flashes of lightning and an earthquake.	Then God's temple in heaven was opened, and within his temple was seen the ark of his covenant. And there came flashes of lightning, rumblings, peals of thunder, an earthquake and a severe hailstorm.	Then there came flashes of lightning, rumblings, peals of thunder and a severe earthquake. No earthquake like it has ever occurred since mankind has been on earth, so tremendous was the quake. The great city split into three parts, and the cities of the nations collapsed. God remembered Babylon the Great and gave her the cup filled with the wine of the fury of his wrath. Every island fled away and the mountains could not be found. From the sky huge hailstones, each weighing about a hundred pounds, fell on people. And they cursed God on account of the plague of hail, because the plague was so terrible.
Light—flashes of lightning, Sound—rumblings, thunder	Light—Fire, flashes of lightning Sound—thunder, rumblings Effect—fire from altar, earthquake	Light—flashes of lightning Sound—rumblings, thunder Effect—Temple opened and ark visible, earthquake, severe hailstorm	Light—flashes of lightning, Sound—rumblings, thunder Effect—uniquely severe earthquake, city split in three parts, cities collapsed, God's wrath on Babylon, islands and mountains removed, huge hailstones, people affected curse God

43. Koester, *Revelation*, 114–15; Craig R. Koester, *Revelation and the End of All Things*, 2nd ed. (Grand Rapids: Eerdmans, 2018), 38–40; Smalley, *Revelation*, 19. Tavo refers to this dynamic as "progressive recapitulation" in "Structure of the Apocalypse," 56.

44. Mounce, *Revelation*, 33.

45. Fanning, *Revelation*, 62.

9.5 AN OUTLINE OF REVELATION

To this point, we have noted important literary phrases/markers, interludes, the number seven, and interlocking transitions to arrive at the following macro-outline of Revelation:

1:1–8	Prologue
1:1–3	Opening
1:4–6	Greeting and Doxology
1:7–8	Prophetic Confession
1:9–20	John's Introductory Vision: The Risen and Glorified Christ
1:9–11	The Setting of John's Vision and His Commission
1:12–16	John's Vision of Jesus
1:17–20	Jesus Confronts John
2:1–3:22	The Messages to the Seven Churches
4:1–16:21	Heavenly Throne Room Vision and Resulting Judgments
4:1–5:14	The Grounding Vision: The Heavenly Throne Room
4:1–11	God on His Throne as Sovereign Creator
5:1–7	Worthy Is the Lamb Who Was Slain
5:8–14	God and the Lamb Are Worthy of Worship
6:1–7:17	The Seal Judgments
6:1–17	The First Six Seal Judgments
7:1–17	The First Interlude
7:1–8	God's People Protected on Earth
7:9–17	God's People Celebrating in Heaven
8:1–11:19	The Trumpet Judgments
8:1–6	Transition: The Seventh Seal and Preparation for the Seven Trumpets
8:7–9:21	The First Six Trumpets
8:7–12	The First Four Trumpets
8:13–9:11	The Fifth Trumpet (First Woe)
9:12–21	The Sixth Trumpet (Second Woe)
10:1–11:14	The Second Interlude
10:1–11	John Recommissioned to Prophesy
11:1–14	The Church's Role as Witness
11:15–19	Transition: The Seventh Trumpet

12:1–14:20	The Third Interlude: The Cosmic War between God and the Forces of Evil
12:1–13:18	The False Trinity Versus God and His People
12:1–6	The Woman, the Son, and the Dragon
12:7–12	The War in Heaven
12:13–17	The Earthly War between the Dragon and the Woman and Her Children
13:1–10	The Beast from the Sea
13:11–18	The Beast from the Earth
14:1–5	The Lamb and the 144,000
14:6–13	Proclamations of Judgment and Reward
14:14–20	The Harvest of the Earth
15:1–16:21	The Bowl Judgments
15:1–8	Transition: Seven Angels with Seven Last Plagues
16:1–21	The Bowl Judgments
17:1–19:5	The Destruction of Babylon the Great
17:1–6a	The Vision of the Great Prostitute and the Scarlet Beast
17:6b–18	The Interpretation of the Vision
18:1–8	The Coming Judgment Calls for the Saints to Leave Babylon
18:9–19	Three Funeral Laments over Babylon the Great
18:20–19:5	God's Judgment of Babylon Calls for Rejoicing and Praise
19:6–20:15	The Final Victory
19:6–10	Transition: The Announcement of the Wedding of the Lamb
19:11–21	The Warrior Messiah Conquers the Two Beasts and Their Followers
20:1–3	The Temporary Imprisonment of Satan
20:4–10	The Millennial Reign and Satan's Judgment
20:11–15	The Final Judgment
21:1–22:5	The New Creation: God's Presence among His People
21:1–8	Transition: The New Heaven and New Earth
21:9–22:5	A Vision of the New Jerusalem
21:9–21	A Description of the Heavenly City
21:22–27	The Internal Features of the Temple City
22:1–5	The Garden City as Paradise Transformed
22:6–21	Epilogue
22:6–7	Blessings for Those Who Obey the Authentic Revelation from God
22:8–11	The Angel's Commands
22:12–16	Christ Speaks

22:17	Exhortations to Come to Christ
22:18–19	A Warning against Adding to or Subtracting from the Book
22:20	A Final Promise and Prayer for Christ's Return
22:21	Concluding Benediction

Again, there are about as many outlines of Revelation as there are scholars trying to discern its structure.[46] The outline above sees Revelation spiraling forward with a basic progression that makes use of recapitulation. In our view, it best fits the guidelines proposed by Wendland (see 9.2 above).

9.6 CONCLUSION

In the end John's vision will not be easily captured by a simple outline. Revelation is a complex but unified work of theological and literary artistry. This deep, rich, multilayered vision report with its abundant symbolism resists oversimplication. We find here a composition intended for oral performance and, therefore, its essential macrostructure would have been clear enough to be understood and remembered by those listening. John also adds specific literary markers to indicate structure, such as "in the Spirit" or "and I saw." Interludes too play a significant role since the dramatic tension cannot continue to mount without pause, reflection, added viewpoints, answers to important questions, and further instruction. Many of the key theological themes for the listeners can be found in the interludes (e.g., 7:1–17; 10:1–11:14; 12:1–14:20). Perhaps above all, interludes offer perspective about the larger conflict and clarify God's calling of his people to obedience in the spiritual battle. John has also given important structural clues using the number seven. Finally, he stitches together this grand vision report using interlocking transitions. These units bind together larger sections and provide important transitions as the narrative moves forward.

On the issue of chronological progression or literary recapitulation, we have answered "both/and" rather than "either/or." There is repetition as we encounter cycles that repeat what has come before. But the plotlines also spiral forward through the vision cycles. Koester is on target with his summary of the situation:

46. Osborne, "Recent Trends," 498–504, offers six typical kinds of outlines of Revelation with representative scholars: chiastic structure (Lund, Schüssler Fiorenza, Beale), dramatic (Bowman, Spinks, Barr), sevenfold structure (Lohmeyer, Farrer, A. Y. Collins, Ford), liturgical patterns (O'Rourke, Carnegie, Pokorny, Prigent, Thompson), recapitulation scheme (Bornkamm, Giblin, Hendrickson, Hoekema), and a text-linguistic approach (Waechter).

> The combination of elements [progression and repetition] can best be pictured as a forward-moving spiral, which repeatedly leads readers through scenes of threat and back to the presence of God, even as the broad storyline moves forward to the new creation. Vision cycles both overlap and progress, with individual sections tracing the movement from conflict to victory that shapes the book as a whole.[47]

On the whole, the structure of Revelation is understandable enough for us to proceed with some clarity, but mysterious enough not to bore us or leave us with no loose ends whatsoever.

47. Koester, *Revelation*, 115.

Chapter 10

INTERPRETING REVELATION

BIBLIOGRAPHY

Bandy, Alan S. "The Hermeneutics of Symbolism: How to Interpret the Symbols of John's Apocalypse." *SBJT* 14.1 (2010): 46–58. **Barry Beitzel,** ed. *Lexham Geographic Commentary on Acts through Revelation*. Bellingham, WA: Lexham, 2019. **Bateman, Herbert W., IV,** ed. *Three Central Issues in Contemporary Dispensationalism: A Comparison of Traditional and Progressive Views*. Grand Rapids: Kregel, 1999. **Beale, G. K., and Sean M. McDonough.** "Revelation." Pages 1081–1158 in *Commentary on the New Testament Use of the Old Testament*. Edited by G. K. Beale and D. A. Carson. Grand Rapids: Baker Academic, 2007. **Blackwell, Ben C., John K. Goodrich, and Jason Maston,** eds. *Reading Revelation in Context: John's Apocalypse and Second Temple Judaism*. Grand Rapids: Zondervan, 2019. **Blaising, Craig A., and Darrell L. Bock.** *Progressive Dispensationalism*. Grand Rapids: Baker Books, 1993. **Blomberg, Craig L., and Sung Wook Chung,** eds. *A Case for Historic Premillennialism: An Alternative to 'Left Behind' Eschatology*. Grand Rapids: Baker Academic, 2009. **Boxall, Ian.** "Reception History and the Interpretation of Revelation." *OBHR*, 377–93. **Caird, G. B.** *The Language and Imagery of the Bible*. Grand Rapids: Eerdmans, 1980, 1997. **Chilton, David.** *Days of Vengeance: An Exposition of the Book of Revelation*. Tyler, TX: Dominion, 1987. **Chung, Sung Wook, and David Mathewson,** *Models of Premillennialism*. Eugene, OR: Cascade, 2018. **Duvall, J. Scott, and J. Daniel Hays.** *Grasping God's Word: A Hands-On Approach to Reading, Interpreting and Applying the Bible*. 4th ed. Grand Rapids: Zondervan Academic, 2020. **Fee, Gordon D., and Douglas Stuart.** *How to Read the Bible for All Its Worth*. 4th ed. Grand Rapids: Zondervan, 2014. **Hays, J. Daniel, J. Scott Duvall, and C. Marvin Pate.** *An A-to-Z Guide to Biblical Prophecy and End Times*. Grand Rapids: Zondervan, 2007. **Hemer, Colin J.** *The Letters to the Seven Churches of Asia in Their Local Setting*. Grand Rapids: Eerdmans, 2001. **Hill, Charles E.** "The Interpretation of the Book of Revelation in Early Christianity." *OBHR*, 395–411. **Keener, Craig S.** *The IVP Bible Background Commentary: New Testament*. 2nd ed. Downers Grove, IL: IVP Academic, 2014. **Koester, Craig R.** "On the Verge of the Millennium: A History of the Interpretation of Revelation." *Word and World* 15.2 (1995): 128–36. **LaHaye, Tim.** *Revelation Unveiled*. Grand Rapids: Zondervan, 1999. **Mathewson, David L.** *A Companion to the Book of Revelation*. Eugene, OR: Cascade, 2020. **Milligan, W.** *The Revelation of St. John*. 2nd ed. London: Macmillan, 1887. **Pate, C. Marvin,**

ed. *Four Views on the Book of Revelation*. Grand Rapids: Zondervan, 1998. **Paul, Ian.** "The Book of Revelation: Image, Symbol and Metaphor." Pages 131–47 in *Studies in the Book of Revelation*. Edited by Steve Moyise. Edinburgh: T&T Clark, 2001. **Poythress, Vern S.** "Genre and Hermeneutics in Rev 20:1–6." *JETS* 36.1 (1993): 41–54. **Saucy, Robert L.** *The Case for Progressive Dispensationalism*. Grand Rapids: Zondervan, 1993. **Thomas, Robert L.** *Revelation 1–7: An Exegetical Commentary*. Chicago: Moody, 1992. **Walvoord, John F.** *The Revelation of Jesus Christ: A Commentary*. Chicago: Moody, 1966. **Weima, Jeffrey A. D.** *The Sermons to the Seven Churches of Revelation: A Commentary and Guide*. Grand Rapids: Baker Academic, 2021. **Wilson, Mark.** *Biblical Turkey: A Guide to the Jewish and Christian Sites of Asia Minor*. 4th ed. Istanbul: Ege Yayinlari, 2020. ———. *Charts on the Book of Revelation: Literary, Historical, and Theological Perspectives*. Grand Rapids: Kregel Academic, 2007. ———. "Revelation." Pages 244–377 in vol. 4 of *Hebrews to Revelation*. ZIBBC. Edited by Clinton E. Arnold. Grand Rapids: Zondervan, 2002. **Wright, N. T.** *The New Testament and the People of God*. Minneapolis: Fortress, 1992.

10.1 INTRODUCTION

G. K. Chesterton once wrote, "Though St. John the Evangelist saw many strange monsters in his vision, he saw no creature so wild as one of his own commentators."[1] Ways of reading Revelation do indeed vary wildly, and John's "many strange monsters" present the interpretive challenge that has resulted in the standard traditional approaches. We survey those major lines of thought in the first part of this chapter but then move beyond those somewhat weathered categories to more reliable interpretive principles for reading Revelation well. The balance of the chapter provides a holistic interpretive focus on how to read Revelation, especially its metaphorical language. In the end, reading Revelation well involves the foundational work of good exegesis, an awareness of the literary and historical contexts, and a reliable method for grasping John's symbols as they were intended.[2]

10.2 TRADITIONAL APPROACHES TO INTERPRETING REVELATION

The traditional ways of interpreting Revelation center around how John's message relates to world events, especially the time frame in question. Is he speaking exclusively about events in his day or is he describing what will happen throughout all of church history or perhaps reflecting on events that will occur at the end of the age? There are

1. G. K. Chesterton, *Orthodoxy* (New York: John Lane Company, 1909), 29.

2. For a history of interpretation and influence of Revelation, see Koester, *Revelation*, 29–65.

four basic schools of thought for interpreting Revelation and one final approach that draws together several of the others.[3]

10.2.1 Preterist

For the most part, the preterist view (from the Latin *praeteritus* for "passed by") sees Revelation as a prophecy that was fulfilled in the first century. Some preterists focus on Revelation's depiction of the fall of Jerusalem in AD 70 as God's judgment on apostate Israel ("Babylon the Great") for rejecting Christ as Messiah. The church is portrayed as the true Israel and Christians are reminded that God will judge their persecutors.[4] Other preterists believe John was referring to the Roman Empire as the main antagonist for first-century Christians so that Rome, rather than apostate Israel, is Babylon. Revelation anticipates the fall of Rome in the fifth century AD and encourages Christians to endure persecution faithfully rather than compromise with the idolatrous and immoral imperial system. This version of the preterist view is popular among mainline scholars.[5]

The preterist view has some obvious strengths, especially the version that sees Rome as Babylon. Foremost among them is that it takes Revelation's message to the original recipients seriously. By honoring the book's historical context, preterist interpreters do not skip over them to get to us but stress how John's message addressed the situation and needs of the original audience. Such an emphasis is a much-needed corrective to hyper-futurist readings:

> No other book in the NT is as frequently divorced from its historical setting as is Revelation. But to neglect the relationship of Revelation to its first-century audience is hermeneutically fallacious in that such an approach wrongly assumes that the original recipients were not the seven churches, but Christians living today.[6]

As Fee and Stuart have rightly emphasized over and over, "a text cannot mean what it could never have meant for its original readers/hearers."[7] The preterist reading reminds us to do our exegetical homework in locating John's meaning as something his original readers could have understood.

That said, the weakness of the preterist view (as with most of the others) lies in its strengths taken too far. In this case, the primary flaw is that it restricts the prophetic

3. See the survey of options by C. Marvin Pate, ed., *Four Views on the Book of Revelation* (Grand Rapids: Zondervan, 1998), who discusses the preterist, idealist, and two forms of dispensationalism (a futurist approach).

4. See K. L. Gentry, "A Preterist View of Revelation," in Pate, *Four Views* 37–92. See also David Chilton, *Days of Vengeance: An Exposition of the Book of Revelation* (Tyler, TX: Dominion, 1987).

5. See, e.g., R. H. Charles, A. Yarbro Collins, L. L. Thompson, G. Krodel, D. Barr, E. Schüssler Fiorenza, N. Kraybill.

6. Köstenberger, Kellum, and Quarles, *Cradle, Cross and Crown*, 967.

7. Gordon D. Fee and Douglas Stuart, *How to Read the Bible for All Its Worth*, 4th ed. (Grand Rapids: Zondervan, 2014), 34.

statements of Revelation (e.g., final judgment, final consummation of God's kingdom) to the ancient world, excluding all subsequent readers. The future seems to have been swallowed up by the past according to this reading. Mounce rightly recognizes the problem:

> The major problem with the preterist position is that the decisive victory portrayed in the latter chapters of the Apocalypse was never achieved. It is difficult to believe that John envisioned anything less than the complete overthrow of Satan, the final destruction of evil, and the eternal reign of God. If this is not to be, then either the Seer was essentially wrong in the major thrust of his message or his work was so hopelessly ambiguous that its first recipients were all led astray.[8]

The challenge, then, is how to take seriously the preterist findings without restricting Revelation's message to the first audience.

10.2.2 Historicist

The historicist approach typically views Revelation as a map of major events throughout Western Church history. It was especially popular from the twelfth to the eighteenth centuries as interpreters tried to find in Revelation answers to events occurring during their lifetime (e.g., the invasions by the Goths or Ottoman Turks or the Reformers battle with the papacy or the rise of various militant leaders). The historicist position has, for the most part, been abandoned today, but one can still find lingering examples of viewing Revelation as a road map of current world events (e.g., when classic dispensationalism sees the letters to the seven churches as prophecies of seven periods of the church age or in the theology of Jehovah's Witnesses and some Seventh-Day Adventists).[9] Any attempt to find in Revelation a prediction of today's newsfeed utilizes this approach.

The chief problem here is that while Revelation certainly has relevance for world events, it does not function as a chronological map of these events for only a certain segment of church history. The approach is asking too much of the book by identifying historical movements too specifically and even then, by forcing many of those connections. It also limits the book's prophecies to the Western church, ignoring the worldwide church.[10] And it ignores the value of the book for the original audience, one of the golden rules of exegesis.

10.2.3 Idealist

The idealist approach views Revelation as a symbolic depiction of God's relationship with his creation with a focus on the struggle between good and evil. Revelation features

8. Mounce, *Revelation*, 27.
9. Osborne, *Revelation*, 18; Fanning, *Revelation*, 39.
10. Beale, *Revelation*, 46.

timeless spiritual principles to help God's people relate to him and live faithfully in this context of spiritual struggle. The book was never intended to provide a roadmap of contemporary world events, however, so the focus is on God's redemptive plan between Christ's first and second coming. Milligan summarizes the interpretive goal of idealism: "We are not to look in the Apocalypse for special events, but for an exhibition of the principles which govern the history both of the world and the Church."[11] Some well-known advocates of the idealist approach include Origen and Augustine from early church history, and W. Hendricksen, A. A. Hoekema, P. E. Hughes, and S. Hamstra Jr. more recently. In general, the idealist reading is most closely associated with amillennialism.

The primary strength of the idealist approach is that it appreciates the symbolic nature of Revelation and its potential application to all Christians of all ages. But the weaknesses overshadow the strengths. In short, it fails to connect theology to history. When the book's symbols and figures are disconnected from any sort of historical fulfillment, even the seven churches are robbed of its message. Bauckham concurs:

> Thus it would be a serious mistake to understand the images of Revelation as timeless symbols. Their character conforms to the contextuality of Revelation as a letter to the seven churches of Asia. Their resonances in the specific social, political, cultural and religious world of their first readers need to be understood if their meaning is to be appropriated today. They do not create a purely self-contained aesthetic world with no reference outside itself, but intend to relate to the world in which the readers live in order to reform and to redirect the readers' response to that world.[12]

Even more, idealists fail to deal adequately with prophecies of the final consummation of history. They have made a choice between two options that are not mutually exclusive—timeless truths and specific historical referents.[13]

10.2.4 Futurist

Many of the early church fathers embraced a futurist reading of Revelation. They favored *chiliasm* or the view that Christ would reign on the earth for a thousand years (χίλιοι is the Greek term for one thousand).[14] Over time their more literal reading of Revelation gave way to the allegorical method of Origen and the idealism of

11. W. Milligan, *The Revelation of St. John*, 2nd ed. (London: Macmillan, 1887), 154–55.

12. Bauckham, *Theology*, 19–20.

13. Fanning, *Revelation*, 40.

14. Köstenberger, Kellum, and Quarles, *Cradle, Cross and Crown*, 968. For an overview of the various forms of premillennialism, see Sung Wook Chung and David Mathewson, *Models of Premillennialism* (Eugene, OR: Wipf & Stock, 2018).

Augustine. Not until the late sixteenth century with the contribution of the Spanish Jesuit Franciscus Ribeira did interpreters consider the futurist option afresh.[15] The futurist approach takes two primary forms—"dispensational futurism" and "modified futurism"—but both stress that the events of Rev 4–22 are primarily fulfilled just prior to the end of history.[16]

10.2.4.1 Classical Dispensationalism

Classical dispensational futurism began with John Nelson Darby, a nineteenth century Anglican minister and leader of the Plymouth Brethren movement in England. It was popularized in America by Dwight L. Moody, C. I. Scofield, Lewis Sperry Chafer, and others. More recent advocates of classic or traditional dispensationalism include John Walvoord, Charles Ryrie, Dwight Pentecost, Robert Thomas, and Norman Geisler. The movement became extremely influential through the Scofield and Ryrie study Bibles with their dispensational study notes and through the popular writings of Hal Lindsay, Tim LaHaye, and Jerry Jenkins.[17] This system promotes hermeneutical literalism and maps out salvation history chronologically according to a series of dispensations or ages that highlight God's special relationship with his people, Israel. It makes a clear distinction between Israel and the church. The church age is a parenthesis of sorts as God turns to the gentiles until a final return of national Israel to the Lord (Rom 11:25–32). Since the term "church" (ἐκκλησία) does not occur after Rev 3:22 until 22:15, they conclude that the church will be raptured from the earth, beginning a period of seven years of tribulation. This pre-tribulation rapture view is held most widely by dispensationalists. The antichrist will appear during the tribulation and gather wicked nations to fight against God's people, thus initiating the time of "great tribulation." At the end of this time Christ will return, defeat the evil nations, begin a literal millennium, defeat Satan in the final rebellion, bring final judgment, and usher in the eternal state.[18] Dispensationalists often see Rev 1:19 as the interpretive key to the entire book: "write what you have seen" represents the past (Rev 1), "what is" represents the present (Rev 2–3), and "what will take place after this" represents the future (Rev 4–22).[19]

10.2.4.2 Progressive Dispensationalism

Before moving on to describe the "modified" futurist position, we should note a second variety of dispensationalism: progressive dispensationalism, a view well represented

15. Mounce, *Revelation*, 26. See Franciscus Ribeira, *In sacram Beati Ioannis Apostoli*, Evangelistae Apocalypsin Commentarij (Ludguni: Ex Officina Iuntarum, 1593).

16. Beale, *Revelation*, 47, uses the term "modified futurism."

17. See J. Daniel Hays, J. Scott Duvall, and C. Marvin Pate, *An A-to-Z Guide to Biblical Prophecy and End Times* (Grand Rapids: Zondervan, 2007), 117–20.

18. Osborne, *Revelation*, 21; Beale, *Revelation*, 47.

19. E.g., Robert L. Thomas, *Revelation 1–7: An Exegetical Commentary* (Chicago: Moody, 1992), 115–16; Walvoord, *Revelation*, 47–49. See Beale, *Revelation*, 152–170, for his critique of this reading of Rev 1:19.

by D. L. Bock, C. Blaising, Robert Saucy, and Buist M. Fanning.[20] This approach represents a substantial departure from classic dispensationalism in several ways: (1) the central theological concept is the "already-not-yet" framework rather than the extremely literal hermeneutic of the classic approach, (2) there is no sharp distinction between Israel and the church, although they still see a future restoration for national Israel, (3) they use a more nuanced, genre-sensitive approach to interpreting Revelation, and (4) they move more toward the eclectic approach (see below) rather than a strictly futurist reading. While most progressive dispensationalists are still pretribulational and premillennial, they have departed significantly from the views of their classical dispensationalist forefathers.[21]

10.2.4.3 Modified Futurism (Historic Premillennialism)

Modified futurism is typically associated with historic premillennialism. The name "historic" comes from its connection to early church leaders such as Justin Martyr, Irenaeus, Tertullian, Hippolytus, and others who were futurist but not dispensationalist. Recent historic premillennial scholars include George E. Ladd, G. R. Beasley-Murray, Robert H. Mounce, Millard J. Erickson, Wayne Grudem, Robert Gundry, Leon Morris, D. A. Carson, Douglas J. Moo, Grant R. Osborne, Craig S. Keener, and Craig L. Blomberg.[22] They emphasize that a substantial portion of Revelation will find a future fulfillment but shy away from a strict chronological reading of the text. They employ a holistic hermeneutic, taking into account historical, literary, linguistic, and theological factors. They embrace the already-not-yet theological framework, see the church as the "true Israel," tend to be posttribulational, understand the great Christian hope as Christ's one personal, visible, public return rather than a secret rapture, and view the millennium as a period of Christ's reign on earth prior to (or inaugurating) the eternal state.

The primary strength of the futurist position is that it takes seriously the text of Revelation, much of which seems directed toward a future fulfillment (e.g., Christ's return, the rapture, the millennium, final judgment, and the new creation). But futurists have been charged with being "so heavenly minded, they are no earthly good," so to speak. In other words, they are often accused of neglecting the relevance of the message for first-century readers. Pretribulational futurists will have a harder time countering this criticism since, on a practical level, this theological stance can encourage

20. For a more thorough and nuanced discussion of the dispensational position, see Herbert W. Bateman IV, ed., *Three Central Issues in Contemporary Dispensationalism: A Comparison of Traditional and Progressive Views* (Grand Rapids: Kregel, 1999). For more on "progressive dispensationalism," see Craig A. Blaising and Darrell L. Bock, *Progressive Dispensationalism* (Grand Rapids: Baker Books, 1993); Robert L. Saucy, *The Case for Progressive Dispensationalism* (Grand Rapids: Zondervan, 1993).

21. Hays, Duvall, and Pate, *A-to-Z Guide to Biblical Prophecy*, 120–21.

22. See Blomberg and Chung, eds., *Case for Historic Premillennialism*.

an escapist mentality where believers set their hope not on Christ's return but on a secret rapture delivering them from any tribulation. Perhaps even more subtle for historic premillennialists is the temptation to fixate on coming events and lose the symbolic/theological power of the book.[23]

10.2.5 Eclectic

Many contemporary evangelical scholars are not willing to subscribe to just one of the previous viewpoints since most have some exegetical/theological value worth preserving. Also, there are other frameworks through which to rcad Revelation besides the question of when these events have occurred or will occur. For instance, faithful scholarship is also interested in Revelation's rhetorical, narrative, and theological impact as much as the time of fulfillment. As a result, the eclectic view has become a strong option. This approach draws on the strengths of the various views while trying to avoid their weaknesses.

The eclectic position recognizes with futurists that some portions of Revelation await final fulfillment, especially chapters 19–22. With the idealists, the eclectic view shares the belief that Revelation has a relevant spiritual message for Christians of every age. Truthfully, many of the named representatives of the idealist and especially futurist positions might identify more with the eclectic view (e.g., Craig Keener, Robert Mounce, Stephen Smalley). Some embracing the eclectic view do so with a particular slant in one direction or another. Greg Beale labels his approach as "eclecticism, or a redemptive-historical form of modified idealism," and Grant Osborne adopts the eclectic position with a futurist emphasis.[24]

The first four approaches can lead to misreading Revelation when taken to the extreme. That is why the eclectic view holds the most promise in providing a balanced approach to the book.[25] Here the historical, literary, and theological contexts are taken seriously, and the parts are read in light of the whole. The weaknesses of each approach are tempered by the strengths of the others. All that said, interpreting Revelation responsibly moves far beyond these traditional interpretive schools with their focus on the time framework. We now turn our attention to other interpretive principles for reading Revelation.

10.3 General Interpretive Principles for Reading Revelation Responsibly

Reading Revelation well calls for responsible interpretation at a number of levels. The Apocalypse is a tour de force and not one that is easy to interpret. This begins with the interpreter's attitude and expectations, moves to the hard work of exegesis and

23. Osborne, *Revelation*, 22.
24. Beale, *Revelation*, 48; Osborne, *Revelation*, 22.
25. Smalley, *Thunder and Love*, 146–47, notes the unbalanced nature of the individual approaches by themselves and the need for all the approaches to uncover the richness and complexity of Revelation.

contextual study, includes understanding how symbolic language works, and stresses the overall theological message of the book.[26]

10.3.1 Adopt an Attitude of Hermeneutical Humility

N. T. Wright once said, "There is no such thing as a point of view which is no-one's point of view"—that is, there is no such thing as a "god's-eye" view available to humans.[27] All readings of Revelation come from the interpreter's own grid of "expectations, memories, stories, psychological states, and so on."[28] This involves not only the reader's location but also their worldview, and both are greatly affected by their interpretive communities.[29] In other words, all interpretations of Revelation are filtered through the interpreter's relationship with reality.[30]

This interpretive "given" does not mean there can be no interpretive certainty or that there can never be better (or even a best) readings. But it does mean that we need a heavy dose of humility for the journey. Prideful, self-centered stances lead to skipping over "them" to get to "us" or to reading Revelation with a Bible in one hand and a newsfeed in the other to make sure we do not miss out on what will surely occur during our lifetime. Gorman identifies six common mistakes made when reading Revelation:[31]

1. Failing to recognize Revelation's apocalyptic character and the character and function of apocalyptic literature
2. Failing to take Revelation seriously as a product of, and message to, its own time
3. Postulating arbitrary and detailed contemporary fulfillment of apocalyptic symbols and visions, based on the dubious assumption that prophecy and history must be culminating in the present
4. Treating the Bible like a puzzle with pieces to be fitted together—a text from this book here, another from that book there, and so on—in order to figure out alleged events to come
5. Becoming preoccupied with (sometimes misguided) questions about the meaning of certain unknowable or less significant aspects of the book, such as the identity of the beast, Armageddon, the length and date of the millennium, and so on, including allowing a particular view of the millennium to control one's reading of the entire book
6. Failing to hear Revelation in light of the larger Christian tradition and contemporary scholarship

26. In what follows we propose interpretive wisdom for properly attending to Revelation's message. We are sympathetic to and draw upon the more comprehensive hermeneutical approaches of rhetorical criticism and narrative criticism. See the rhetorical contributions of deSilva, *Seeing Things John's Way*, Witherington, *Revelation*, and the narrative critical work of Resseguie, *Revelation*.

27. N. T. Wright, *The New Testament and the People of God* (Minneapolis: Fortress, 1992), 85, 36, respectively.

28. Wright, *New Testament and the People of God*, 36.

29. Wright, *New Testament and the People of God*, 36.

30. Bandy, "Hermeneutics of Symbolism," 47.

31. Gorman, *Reading Revelation Responsibly*, 69–70.

Every one of these interpretive missteps flows from a lack of interpretive humility, from believing that we absolutely must be at the very center of God's end-time plan. In truth, we need to return over and over to the biblical text, to its literary and historical contexts, and to the wisdom of faithful interpreters to maintain what Osborne calls a "hermeneutics of humility."[32]

10.3.2 Discover the Message to the Original Readers

Sound biblical exegesis constitutes the foundation of responsible interpretation of the Apocalypse. And responsible exegesis, at least from an evangelical point of view, centers on discovering the author's intended meaning reflected in the text. Longtime New Testament exegete Gordon Fee puts it like this:

> The interpreter's first task is to seek John's—and therewith the Holy Spirit's—*original intent* as much as that is possible. The primary meaning of any text, including apocalyptic texts, is that which John himself intended, which in turn must be something the original readers would have been capable of understanding.[33]

This simple step means we take seriously the message to the original readers. The message would have made sense to believers living in Smyrna or Pergamum or Ephesus or any other late first-century Asia Minor church. God does not skip over them to get to us. And who knows, Jesus may not return until AD 4000, which would leave us in the group being skipped over if we adopt that mindset. As Mathewson puts it, "Any interpretation that John could never have intended and his first readers could never have understood is probably incorrect."[34] Caird concurs and offers some simple tests to determine the author's intention to use non-literal language: (1) the use of an explicit statement (e.g., the use of a descriptive term as in Rev 11:8, the addition of a defining noun as in "sword of the Spirit," or a qualifying adjective as in "heavenly Father"); (2) the impossibility of a literal understanding; (3) the imaginative exploration of the imagery by the author (as in development of the New Jerusalem image in Revelation); (4) the piling up of images to describe the referent rather than a single image; and (5) the originality of the metaphor (i.e., the less familiar the metaphors are, the more likely they are to be non-literal).[35]

It remains to explore what a responsible exegesis of John's metaphorical language entails.

32. Osborne, *Revelation*, 16.

33. Fee, *Revelation*, xx–xxi, emphasis original.

34. David L. Mathewson, *A Companion to the Book of Revelation* (Eugene, OR: Cascade, 2020), 15. Most of the hermeneutical and theological problems with the "Left Behind" approach identified by Gorman stem from a failure to take the first audience seriously or, in other words, to do basic exegesis. See Gorman, *Reading Revelation Responsibly*, 69–73.

35. G. B. Caird, *The Language and Imagery of the Bible* (Grand Rapids: Eerdmans, 1980, 1997), 183–92.

10.3.3 Interpret Metaphorical Language Appropriately[36]

Revelation is a book filled with symbolic language that communicates by comparing realities in our world to realities in John's vision. Comparative or metaphorical language is necessary because John is saying something about God and his plan that transcends normal language boundaries. When we are using what we know to describe what we do not know and have not experienced, metaphor is appropriate and necessary. In this section, we will give more definition to the terms "literal" and "symbolic" (sometimes cast as two exclusive and competing hermeneutical approaches) as we explore the nature of metaphorical language, both what these terms mean and what they do not mean. Then, we will discuss interpreting Revelation's metaphorical language responsibly.

10.3.3.1 Literal Language

There is a great deal of imprecision about how the terms "literal" and "symbolic" are used in everyday talk about Revelation. Most scholars would say that words used "literally" are words used in their "primary, matter-of-fact sense"[37]—that is, when words are not used figuratively or metaphorically. We must remember that "*literal* does not automatically equal 'real, actual,' or 'true, accurate,' and *symbolic* does not always equal 'imaginary, existing in someone's mind but not existing in the real world' or 'untrue, deceptive.'"[38] In his classic work on imagery in the Bible, Caird notes that "the type of language we use has very little to do with the truth or falsity of what we say and with the existence or non-existence of the things we refer to."[39] When we admit that John is using a metaphor we do not deny in the least the reality of what he is signifying. To say John uses figurative language does not make the realities to which he alludes any less real. Caird concludes, "For us it is enough to note that if we call an expression 'literal' or 'metaphorical' we are talking about the nature of the language employed, whereas if we call it 'ontological' we are talking about the reality of its referent. Linguistic statements must not be confused with metaphysical ones."[40]

Yet some argue that Revelation should always be interpreted "literally" unless it is impossible to do so. For example, Tim LaHaye contends that we must "take every word at its primary, ordinary, usual, literal meaning unless the facts of the immediate text, studied in light of related passages and axiomatic and fundamental truths, clearly indicate otherwise."[41] One gets the sense here that "literal" refers to both the language and the referent. And when John clearly does use symbolic language, this approach would say he is trying to describe an object or event in the future (our day?) that ancient authors and readers had no way of understanding. Bandy correctly identifies the

---

36. See Ch. 7 for more on the nature of symbolic language.
37. Caird, *Language and Imagery of the Bible*, 133.
38. Fanning, *Revelation*, 33–34.
39. Caird, *Language and Imagery of the Bible*, 131.
40. Caird, *Language and Imagery of the Bible*, 132–33, 193–94.
41. Tim LaHaye, *Revelation Unveiled* (Grand Rapids: Zondervan, 1999), 17. Often this hermeneutical approach is featured in classic dispensationalism.

end-game of such a literalistic hermeneutic: "The goal for interpreting these symbols, then, is to identify the one-to-one correspondence between his [John's] image and a modern parallel (e.g., the locusts are Apache attack helicopters, the mark of the beast is an implanted micro-chip, and the European Union is the revived Roman Empire)."[42] This approach often produces a host of inconsistent and even contradictory interpretations. For example, the fall of Babylon occurs repeatedly in Revelation and on a purely literal level this presents numerous problems, while on a theological level the repetition offers complementary perspectives on a momentous event.[43] Besides trampling over the prophetic-apocalyptic genre and ignoring the author's intended meaning, this approach confuses symbolic language with its referent. If the language is metaphorical then the danger, they suppose, is that we will deny the reality of the referent. As a result, we must stick with a literal interpretation, so the thinking goes, in order to maintain the reality of the referent. Ironically, such literalistic reading distorts the true meaning of the text, which is probably the last thing intended.

In contrast, some scholars push against the literalistic interpretive approach so hard that they deny that symbolic language describes any kind of external reality. This seems to be an overreaction where the referential baby is thrown out with the symbolic bathwater. Language is almost never, if ever, purely literal or symbolic. For Fanning, "language that is literal or symbolic can refer to a range of entities of different character and scope. Those entities can be concrete or abstract, and in either case they can be quite specific or very general."[44] For Fanning, there is an irreducible earthiness to biblical eschatology that "resists complete spiritualization."[45]

10.3.3.2 Metaphorical Language

At the heart of John's figurative language is comparison.[46] In essence, metaphorical language occurs when the author uses words in ways that extend beyond their normal boundaries of meaning. What they are saying is meaningful but cannot be interpreted literally without destroying the intended meaning (e.g., Jesus is the Lamb of God).[47]

---

42. Bandy, "Hermeneutics of Symbolism," 47. One problem among many for this approach is that the referent identified quickly becomes dated.

43. Bauckham, *Theology*, 20–21.

44. Fanning, *Revelation*, 34.

45. Fanning, *Revelation*, 35.

46. I find the terminology of "vehicle, subject and tenor" to be very confusing for most readers since it has not always been defined consistently by scholars. Typically, "vehicle" is a visual or linguistic sign about something known, "tenor" is the subject as depicted by the metaphor, and "subject" is the referent, the known object. But I prefer the levels of communication explained in Chapter 7 to be more helpful and clear, although there is certainly overlap.

47. Beale, *Revelation*, 57, identifies six signs that an author intends to transgress word boundaries. I have reduced these to five and paraphrased them here: (1) connecting two words with totally different meanings (1:20: "the seven lampstands are the seven churches"), (2) alerting the reader to the comparison (11:8: "the great city—which is *figuratively* called Sodom and Egypt"), (3) the impossibility of a literal reading or a literal reading that is blatantly false or contradictory (11:3–4: "my two witnesses . . . are the two olive trees and the two lampstands"), (4) the context argues against a literal reading (3:17: "But you do not realize that you are wretched, pitiful, poor, blind and naked"), (5) repeated use of the figurative use of the same expression elsewhere in the book (12:9: "The great dragon was hurled down—that ancient serpent called the devil, or Satan").

The metaphor is a lens through which the reader can see something about the referent that could never have been understood without it.[48] There are comparisons of sight (e.g., John's vision of one like a son of man in Rev 1:12–20), of sound (e.g., rushing waters, loud voices, and roars of thunder), and of taste and smell (e.g., John's experience of eating a sweet and sour scroll in Rev 10), among others.[49] It is essential from the beginning to recognize the abundant imagery in Revelation.

10.3.3.2.1 Pay Attention When John Identifies an Image

Sometimes John himself identifies the image explicitly. Fee suggests holding fast "to the images when he [John] himself interprets, since these must serve as starting points for all others."[50] The following chart identifies many of the images that John interprets for his readers.[51]

Text	Symbol	Signal	Symbol Identification
1:20	Seven stars	"are"	The seven angels of the seven churches
1:20	Seven lampstands	"are"	The seven churches
2:9; 3:9	Synagogue of Satan	"are"	Those who say they are Jews but are not
4:5	Seven lamps before the throne	"which are"	The seven spirits or sevenfold Spirit of God
5:6	Seven horns and seven eyes of the Lamb	"which are"	The seven spirits of God sent into all the earth
5:8; 8:3–4	Golden bowls of incense	"which are"	The prayers of the saints
7:9, 13–14	Great multitude in white robes	"these are"	The saints coming out of the great tribulation
8:10–11	Great star like a torch	"is called"	Named Wormwood, meaning bitterness
9:11	Angel of the Abyss	"whose name is"	Named Abaddon (Hebrew) and Apollyon (Greek), both meaning Destroyer
11:3–4	Two Witnesses	"these are"	The two olive trees and two lampstands standing before the Lord
11:8	Great city	"which is called"	Sodom and Egypt, where also the Lord was crucified
12:9; 20:2	Great Dragon	"who is"	Ancient serpent, devil, Satan
12:17	Woman's offspring	"those who"	Those who obey God's commandments and hold to the testimony of Jesus

(continued)

48. Caird, *Language and Imagery of the Bible*, 152.

49. Resseguie, *Revelation*, 18–23. On the metaphors of sound, Resseguie labels Revelation the "noisiest book" in the New Testament.

50. Fee, *Revelation*, xxi.

51. The following chart is drawn from Mark Wilson, *Charts on the Book of Revelation*, 46, and Bandy, "Hermeneutics of Symbolism," 50.

Text	Symbol	Signal	Symbol Identification
13:18	666	"it is"	Number of the beast and a man's number
14:1, 3–4	144,000	"these are"	Those who did not defile themselves but followed the Lamb
16:13–14	Three evil spirits	"they are"	Demonic spirits that perform miraculous signs and gather the kings for battle
16:16	Harmagedon (Armageddon)	"the one called"	The Hebrew name for the place where kings are gathered for the great battle
17:1, 15	Many waters	"which you saw are"	Peoples, multitudes, nations, and languages
17:3, 5	Woman sitting on a scarlet beast	"a mystery"	Mother of prostitutes and of the abominations of the earth
17:3, 5, 18	Woman sitting on a scarlet beast	"she is"	Great city Babylon that rules over the kings of the earth
17:3, 7, 9	Seven heads of the scarlet beast	"they are"	The seven hills on which the woman sits and seven kings
17:3, 7, 12	Ten horns of the scarlet beast	"they are"	Ten kings who have not yet received a kingdom but will rule for one hour
19:8	White robes of fine linen	"for . . . is"	Righteous acts of the saints
19:11, 16	Rider on a white horse	"a name"	King of kings and Lord of lords
20:8	Gog and Magog	—	Nations in the four corners of the earth
20:14; 21:8	Lake of fire	"which is"	Second death
21:2, 9–10	Holy City, New Jerusalem	"I saw . . . I heard . . . he showed me"	Bride, wife of the Lamb

John's identification often does help narrow the range for understanding the referent, but it does not always clarify the interpretation completely. Sometimes we are not sure what the stated referent actually refers to. For instance, to say that the "seven stars are the angels of the seven churches" does not solve the interpretive dilemma of whether the "seven angels" are human messengers or leaders, angels as corporate representatives, or personified spirits of the churches (1:20). At other times, the symbol itself is interpreted using another symbol. For example, in 11:3–4 we read the that two witnesses are "the two olive trees and the two lampstands" that "stand before the Lord of the earth." But this identification does not answer the interpretive question about the identity of these witnesses. Are they two historic individuals or do they represent the witnessing people of God or perhaps both? Nevertheless, recognizing John's own identification of an image remains a good starting point. And when John does identify an image early in the book, we should assume that any later reference probably refers to the same thing (e.g., lampstands identified as the churches in chs. 1; 2–3; and 11).[52]

10.3.3.2.2 Be Aware of John's Fluid Use of Images

John also uses images fluidly and is not shy about using the same image to refer to different things. For example, the image of a "star" can refer to the angels of the seven churches (1:16, 20; 2:1; 3:1) but can also refer to God's agents of judgment (8:10–12) or even Jesus himself (22:16). The image of a woman can refer to a false prophetess (2:20), the messianic community (ch. 12), the prostitute city or empire (ch. 17), and the bride of Christ (19:7; 21:9). This fluidity of usage should be kept in mind when trying to make sense of the image. Context is normally the key for discerning the meaning John intends in a specific text.

10.3.3.2.3 Note the Primary Point of Comparison

It is also important to pin down whenever possible the main point of comparison intended by the metaphor and not get bogged down in the details of the symbol.[53] The main point of comparison will often provide the primary theological message John intends to communicate. Details are added for rhetorical effect, as in 6:12–14:

> 12I watched as he opened the sixth seal. There was a great earthquake. The sun
> turned black like sackcloth made of goat hair, the whole moon turned blood red,
> 13and the stars in the sky fell to earth, as figs drop from a fig tree when shaken by a
> strong wind. 14The heavens receded like a scroll being rolled up, and every mountain
> and island was removed from its place.

With the opening of the sixth seal, God provides an answer to the martyrs' prayer in 6:10. The primary point is to compare the coming apart of the entire cosmos with the final judgment, a dramatic portrayal we see in both Testaments (e.g., Isa 13:10–13; 24:1–6; Ezek 32:6–8; Joel 3:15–16; Mark 13:24–27). Details such as sackcloth made of goat hair or figs dropping from a tree in a strong wind or the heavens being rolled up like a scroll only add dramatic power to the comparison. Or, take the detailed description of the heavenly city in Rev 21:9–21. We are not meant to replicate or even visualize every minute detail of the city, especially since the city is also called a "bride"

52. Beale, *Revelation*, 55–56.

53. Beale is correct, however, to note that John sometimes intends multiple points of comparison. He rightly concludes, "To identify more than one point of comparison in a single metaphor is not to be guilty of allegorical interpretation. It is, rather, to discover the original intention of an author's metaphorical usage" (*Revelation*, 56).

(21:2, 9; 22:17) and a "wife" (19:7; 21:9) of the Lamb. The cube shape and jewels and brilliance and gates all overwhelm readers with one unmistakable reality: God's people will one day live in his glorious presence.

10.3.3.2.4 Once Again, Context Is Key

When John does not explicitly identify an image, the reader should look to context to discern its meaning. Three contexts stand out as most significant, and a fourth merits consideration. First, although it perhaps goes without saying, each passage should be read in light of the literary context of Revelation itself—the surrounding words, sentences, paragraphs, and especially the vision in which the image occurs.

Second, John draws heavily on the Old Testament, using its words, images, themes, and theology to shape his message. Bandy provides reliable steps for the interpreter here: (1) determine if the text alludes to an Old Testament passage, (2) grasp the meaning of the Old Testament passage in its context, (3) compare the similarities and differences between the Old Testament and the allusion in Revelation, and (4) discern John's intended message through his use of the Old Testament language and imagery.[54] For example, when John is instructed to eat the little scroll in 10:9, we are reminded of Ezekiel's experience of eating a scroll (Ezek 2:7–3:3). Both prophets get involved in their prophetic vision through a culinary experience. Both taste the sweetness of the scroll at first, but a sweetness followed by the difficult prophetic task of proclaiming God's coming judgment and salvation. Knowing the Old Testament context sheds light on the meaning of John's experience and the message of Revelation 10.[55]

Third, the cultural-historical context also offers valuable insights into John's meaning. John often pulls from the historical setting of the seven churches and the larger Greco-Roman world to communicate his vision. In Part Three of this volume, the reader will see multiple examples of how the local context offers insight for interpreting John's metaphorical language responsibly.[56]

Fourth, the reader should be aware of parallels with extracanonical literature, especially Jewish apocalyptic writings, and how they might affect John's meaning. He lived and moved among many well-known traditions. In his chapter "The Use of Apocalyptic Traditions," Bauckham examines four images in Revelation in light of these traditions: the blood and horses of 14:20b, the completing of the number of the martyrs in 6:9–11, the giving up of the dead in 20:13, and the silence in heaven in 8:1.[57] Other examples

54. Bandy, "Hermeneutics of Symbolism," 51.

55. An indispensable resource for understanding John's use of the Old Testament is Beale and McDonough, "Revelation."

56. For more on the importance of the historical-cultural context for reading Revelation, see Weima, *Sermons to the Seven Churches*; Hemer, *Letters to the Seven Churches*; Mark Wilson, *Biblical Turkey: A Guide to the Jewish and Christian Sites of Asia Minor*, 4th ed. (Istanbul: Ege Yayinlari, 2020). Mark Wilson, "Revelation," in *Hebrews to Revelation*, ZIBBC, ed. Clinton E. Arnold (Grand Rapids: Zondervan, 2002), 4:244–377; and Craig S. Keener, *The IVP Bible Background Commentary: New Testament*, 2nd ed. (Downers Grove, IL: IVP Academic, 2014).

57. See Bauckham, *Climax of Prophecy*, 38–91.

abound in the fine volume edited by Blackwell, Goodrich, and Maston on reading Revelation in light of Jewish apocalyptic traditions.[58]

Of these four contexts, we see the first three as the primary contexts used by John to describe his vision.[59] Perhaps the main thing to keep in mind is that John does not write in a vacuum. He draws on multiple contexts to articulate what he has seen using words that would have connected well with his first readers.

10.3.4 Focus on the Overall Purpose of Worship and Discipleship

In order to interpret Revelation responsibly, we must include a step that is commonly overlooked. We must pay close attention to what lies at the heart and soul of Revelation, its main goal in fact: worship and discipleship. Mathewson says it clearly:

> The main goal of Revelation is to transform the lives of its hearers/readers, not to predict a future sequence of events. Its main function is pastoral and hortatory. . . . It is intended to get Christians to follow and obey God and the Lamb in true discipleship, no matter what the consequences. . . . Any interpretation of Revelation that does not start with this is off on the wrong foot. Revelation calls for perseverance in discipleship and godly living, worked out in the midst of pagan Imperial Roman rule.[60]

Similarly, Gorman proposes a "Lamb-centered, cruciform interpretive strategy, or hermeneutic" for reading Revelation with five pillars:[61]

1. The central, guiding image is the slaughtered Lamb.
2. The book was written by a first-century Christian for first-century Christians using first-century literary devices and images.
3. We favor a hermeneutic of analogy rather than of correlation, which means abandoning literal, linear approaches.
4. Revelation is a call to worship and discipleship.
5. Images of death and destruction should be placed within the larger framework of hope offered in Christ.

Gorman stresses that the theological, political, pastoral, and worshipful aspects of Revelation be given a strong voice in the interpretative process.

---

58. See Blackwell, Goodrich, and Maston, eds., *Reading Revelation in Context*.

59. Mathewson, *Companion to the Book of Revelation*, 16, 32–33; Beale, *Revelation*, 56.

60. Mathewson, *Companion to the Book of Revelation*, 17.

61. Gorman, *Reading Revelation Responsibly*, 77–80. I would make the following adjustments. First, the guiding image seems to be the Triune God. Second, everything is grounded in the first century, but the message does not remain there. This as a starting point, however, is crucial. Third, the analogy vs. correlation tension does not seem to be totally either/or since analogies often have elements of correlation.

All this is to say that symbols overwhelm the imagination and, as a result, transform the mind and heart for making godly choices and maintaining godly loyalties. They exhort and encourage the hearers as they portray "a transforming vision, empowering those who embrace its heavenly perspective to live faithfully in a fallen world until their Lord returns."[62]

As we go about our exegetical work, looking carefully at the historical-cultural context, mapping out the language of the text, reading the narrative closely, and so on, we cannot afford to lose sight of the primary purposes of the book: worship and discipleship. At a minimum this should include asking questions in the interpretive process about how this text affects our worship of the Triune God and discipleship to the risen Lamb—that is, how we live out our faith within the community of the saints and in the midst of a broken world.

10.4 CONCLUSION

We began this chapter with a survey of traditional interpretive approaches to Revelation—preterist, historicist, idealist, and futurist. Most of these approaches focus on the issue of when the events recorded by John have happened or will happen in our world. Under the futurist category, we discussed further the primary forms of futurism—classical and progressive dispensationalism, as well as historic premillennialism (modified futurism). We concluded with a look at the eclectic approach, which draws on the strengths of the other four but tends to avoid their weaknesses. This approach pays close attention to the historical, literary, and theological message of Revelation and takes into consideration the time of fulfillment.

Revelation presents any interpreter with multiple challenges at several different levels. It is not an easy book to understand, and perhaps this explains the diversity of contrasting interpretive conclusions. Playing into this also is the interpreter's pre-understanding, political-cultural agenda, and theological bent. In the second half of the chapter, we suggested a number of interpretive principles for reading Revelation responsibly. We focused on the issue of literal and metaphorical language since that is perhaps the most challenging aspect of reading Revelation well. These principles will not solve all the interpretive problems related to this wonderfully complex book, but they will point the reader in the right direction.

62. Duvall, "Transforming Vision," 255.

Chapter 11

A LITERARY-THEOLOGICAL READING OF REVELATION

AN OUTLINE OF REVELATION

11.1 Prologue (1:1–8)
- 11.1.1 Opening (1:1–3)
- 11.1.2 Greeting and Doxology (1:4–6)
- 11.1.3 Prophetic Confession (1:7–8)

11.2 John's Introductory Vision: The Risen and Glorified Christ (1:9–20)
- 11.2.1 The Setting of John's Vision and His Commission (1:9–11)
- 11.2.2 John's Vision of Jesus (1:12–16)
- 11.2.3 Jesus Confronts John (1:17–20)

11.3 The Messages to the Seven Churches (2:1–3:22)
- 11.3.1 Introduction
- 11.3.2 A Common Structure
- 11.3.3 The Importance of the Local Context
- 11.3.4 Descriptions of Jesus
- 11.3.5 Condition of the Churches—Commendation/Complaint
- 11.3.6 Exhortation/Warning
- 11.3.7 Promises to the Overcomers
- 11.3.8 Admonition to Listen to the Spirit
- 11.3.9 Conclusion

11.4 The Heavenly Throne Room Vision and Resulting Judgments (4:1–16:21)
- 11.4.1 Introduction

11.1 PROLOGUE (1:1–8)

11.1.1 Opening (1:1–3)

The prologue to the book begins with the title in 1:1a: "the revelation from Jesus Christ." Ancient writers often supplied the book's title and a summary of its contents early on as a forecast of what was to come.[1] The opening lines of Revelation also introduce many of the main themes of the book: the centrality of God and Christ, the imminent fulfillment of God's plans, angelic mediation, John's role as witness, the nature of the prophecy as proclamation of God's truth and the appropriate response of obedience, and the blessing on those who respond faithfully. The term ἀποκάλυψις ("revelation") means "to make fully known," as in a revelation or a disclosure.[2] As elsewhere in the New Testament, the term carries associations with prophetic visions and the last days.[3]

The phrase "of/from Jesus Christ" could be understood as an objective genitive (about Jesus), subjective genitive (from Jesus), or a plenary genitive (both from and about Jesus). Many favor the subjective genitive since the context affirms that God gives the revelation to Jesus to pass on to John and other servants (also 22:16), yet the plenary genitive plays well with the larger context of the book where Jesus stands as the central figure.[4] With Jesus as both the source and object of revelation, Resseguie is right to see the Apocalypse as "the last of our gospels that tells the story in vivid pictures of Jesus and his testimony."[5]

The chain of revelation proceeds as follows: God → Jesus → his angel → his servant John → other servants (cf. Rev 22:6, 8, 16). The vision from God through Christ and his angel concerns God's plans for consummating human history, a message that will bring blessing for those who hear and obey. Angelic mediation is common in apocalyptic literature (e.g., Rev 17:1, 7; 21:9; Dan 7–12; Ezek 40–48; Zech 1–6; 1 En. 1:2; 72:1; Jub. 32:21; 3 Bar. 1:8; 6:1).[6] And while John is a respected early Christian leader, he is designated here merely as a "servant" (δοῦλος). The term "servants," a prominent term for Christians throughout the book, sends the subtle message that honor comes through faithful service and suffering (Rev 1:1; 2:20; 7:3; 10:7; 11:18; 15:3; 19:2, 5; 22:3, 6).

The revelation deals with "what must soon take place." John substitutes "soon" (ἐν

1. Aune, *Revelation 1–5*, 9–10.

2. "ἀποκάλυψις," BDAG 112, §1.

3. The same noun is used for the revelation of truth generally (e.g., Luke 2:32; Eph 1:17), for revelation in a prophetic vision (1 Cor 14:6, 26; 2 Cor 12:1, 7; Gal 1:12; 2:2), for revealing the gospel (Rom 16:25; Eph 3:3), and for end-time disclosures related to God (Rom 2:5; 8:19; 1 Cor 1:7; 2 Thess 1:7; 1 Pet 1:7, 13; 4:13).

4. See Wallace, *Greek Grammar Beyond the Basics*, 119–21.

5. Resseguie, *Revelation*, 62.

6. See the excursus "Angels in Revelation" in Smalley, *Revelation*, 28–30.

τάχει) for Daniel's "in the last days" (ἐπ ἐσχάτων τῶν ἡμερῶν in Dan 2:28–29) to show that the Old Testament prophecy is beginning to be fulfilled in his own day.[7] The term "soon" likely stresses that "the end is always imminent," not that it will happen quickly once it begins.[8] Like John and the Christians in Asia Minor, we too live in the last days (cf. Rev 12:6, 10–17). We are fighting many of the same battles and receiving the same comfort as those first-century believers.

This opening section also speaks to how the revelation is communicated, again drawing on Dan 2, where Greek terms found in Rev 1 are used repeatedly (ἀποκαλύπτω, σημαίνω).[9] God communicates to both Daniel and John using symbolic language (cf. Dan 2:23, 45). In addition, we are told that Christ "shows" (δείκνυμι) the vision to his servants through an angel (see the term elsewhere in Rev 1:1; 4:1; 17:1; 21:9, 10; 22:1, 6; cf. 22:8). This cluster of terms—"revelation," "show," "made known"—indicates that the visions were communicated through symbolic language and that, as a general rule, the book should be interpreted accordingly.

John testifies to what he saw—"the word of God and the testimony of Jesus Christ" (1:2). Jesus's "testimony" (μαρτυρία) here refers specifically to his spoken and embodied word, especially through his faithful witness unto death. This thread of "testify" and "testimony" (1:2, 9; 6:9; 11:7; 12:11, 17; 19:10; 20:4; 22:16, 18, 20) anchors Revelation's message in God's truth over against the lies and deception of the forces of evil.

To close this opening section, we have the first of seven beatitudes, this one pronounced on those who read aloud and obey the words of the prophecy (cf. 1:3; 14:13; 16:15; 19:9; 20:6; 22:7, 14). The admonition to obey the prophecy positions the book first and foremost as a proclamation of God's truth with social and ethical implications rather than a prediction of future events.

"What must soon take place" in verse 1 forms an *inclusio* with "the time is near" in verse 3 to provide the temporal point of view, a perspective that pairs with the spatial point of view already established (revelation from above to those living below). Resseguie captures the reader's experience in all this: "Just as readers/hearers live with the tension of not being able to see everything from an above point of view, so they live with the tension of not having a clear picture of what is 'soon' or what is 'not yet.'"[10] Only God who speaks and acts in Jesus Christ provides a safe place from which to navigate the tension. This "already/not fully" understanding of Christian eschatology serves as the foundation to the entire New Testament. In Revelation, however, the final fulfillment receives additional attention for at least two reasons: (1) the book serves as

7. Beale, *Revelation*, 181–82.

8. Mounce, *Revelation*, 41. Compare the use of similar terms of imminence in 1:3, 19.

9. These connections are developed extensively in Beale, *Revelation*, 152–54, 181–83.

10. Resseguie, *Revelation*, 63.

the concluding chapter to the great story of the Bible where the final fulfillment is in view, and (2) the churches, who were first hearing this transforming vision, were in crisis and desperately needed the sustaining hope that a picture of God's final future could provide. As a result, the language of imminent fulfillment runs through Revelation, beginning with the opening paragraph.

11.1.2 Greeting and Doxology (1:4–6)

As a letter, Revelation begins with a greeting and a doxology. The greeting is typical except John provides a fuller description of its source: the Triune God. This section packs a rhetorical punch largely because of the use of the number seven and three throughout. Both numbers represent completeness and fullness. The greeting comes from John to the seven churches of Asia Minor with the number seven representing not just these seven congregations in the first century but the wider Christian community in John's day and beyond.

"Grace and peace," or unconditional favor and well-being, come from the Triune God.[11] God the Father is identified as "him who is, and who was, and who is to come," echoing the "I AM WHO I AM" of Exod 3:14 (cf. Rev 1:8, 17; 2:23; 21:6; 22:1).[12] Mangina observes that "this act of divine *self*-naming brings God dangerously close."[13] John intentionally refers to Yahweh in this way and stresses God's eternal presence with his people, his sovereign faithfulness in history, and his coming intervention. Grace and peace come from the God who is in control and the God who is with us, the Lord of the present, past, and future. The Spirit is identified as "the seven spirits before his throne," an identification made explicit in 4:5 (seven lamps); 5:6 (seven eyes; cf. Rev 3:1; Zech 4:2–10). The background is Zech 4:2–10, where God's mighty work is accomplished by his Spirit.

Jesus Christ is described as faithful witness, firstborn from the dead, and ruler of the kings of the earth. Jesus was a faithful witness to the Father and his plan, living and speaking the truth and exposing the lies of Satan (e.g., John 8:12–59). His supreme expression of faithfulness was his obedience unto death on a cross (Phil 2:5–8; Rev 3:14; cf. Rev 2:13). He is also the firstborn from among the dead and by his resurrection he now stands victorious over death (Rom 8:29; Col 1:18) and reigns over all earthly rulers and kingdoms (Ps 89:27; 1 Tim 6:15).

11. "Grace" is a Christian variation of the typical Greek greeting χαῖρε, with χαίρειν being typical in letters, and it is combined with the Hebrew greeting of "peace" (שָׁלוֹם, *shālôm*). See Smalley, *Revelation*, 32.

12. For an extensive treatment of Rev 1:4 in its historical setting, see Sean McDonough, *YHWH at Patmos: Rev. 1:4 in Its Hellenistic and Early Jewish Setting*, WUNT 2.107 (Tübingen: Mohr Siebeck, 1999; repr., Eugene, OR: Wipf & Stock, 2011).

13. Mangina, *Revelation*, 47, emphasis original.

The doxology in Rev 1:5b–6 celebrates Christ's past and present work: he "loves us . . . freed us . . . made us." His ongoing love for his followers was demonstrated supremely at the cross—his liberating death that freed us from slavery to sin and Satan and formed us into a kingdom of priests prepared to serve God. We see similar emphases in the song of Rev 5. The promise of Exod 19:3–6 that Israel would be a kingdom of priests and a holy nation is now fulfilled in the church (Rev 5:9–10; 20:6; cf. 1 Pet 2:9). Smalley draws the appropriate conclusion:

> This is the first of several occasions when John uses Old Testament images of Israel to describe the Christian Church. The first believers saw themselves as members of the new and true Israel: the inheritors in full of the spiritual blessings which were foreshadowed in the life of God's people following the Exodus from Egypt.[14]

They are citizens of this kingdom now but will one day reign in the new creation (Rev 2:26–27; 20:4, 6; Matt 19:28; 1 Cor 6:2; 2 Tim 2:12; Dan 7:17, 22, 27). As priests, they enjoy special access to God now and will one day live in his presence (Rev 21). The doxology proper ascribes glory and power forever and ever to the Triune God for who he is and all that he has done (1:6).

11.1.3 Prophetic Confession (1:7–8)

In this confession John combines Dan 7:13 and Zech 12:10–12 to announce the second coming of Christ (cf. Matt 24:30; Mark 13:26; John 19:37). Jesus's coming encloses the entire book (Rev 1:7; 22:7, 12, 20), reminding readers that he will bring "God's *shalom*-justice" for all.[15] The clouds are symbols of God's glorious presence. Jesus's coming brings both salvation and judgment, both rejoicing and mourning. The response to God's promised action carries weight: "Yes! Amen!" (1:7, NLT).

God only speaks twice in Revelation, at the beginning (1:8) and the end (21:5–8). As Bauckham puts it, God "has the first word, in creation, and the last word, in new creation."[16] This assurance of God's sovereignty begins with the "I AM" of Exod 3:14 and John's Gospel (e.g., John 6:35; 8:12; 11:25; 14:6; 15:5) and features three aspects. First, the Lord God says, "I am the Alpha and the Omega," the first and last letters of the Greek alphabet. Second, he is identified as the one "who is, and who was, and who is to come." Revelation also consistently connects Jesus Christ with God. Various titles that are used of God are also used of Christ to stress Jesus's deity as well as the unity of the Father and the Son.[17]

14. Smalley, *Revelation*, 36.
15. Resseguie, *Revelation*, 68.
16. Bauckham, *Theology*, 27.
17. See Duvall, *Revelation*, 26. This connection is developed more extensively in Bauckham, *Theology*, ch. 3.

Title/Description	God the Father	Jesus Christ
"I am"	1:8; 21:6	1:17–18; 22:16
Was, Is, Is to Come	1:4, 8; 4:8 (partial in 11:17; 16:5)	Coming soon–1:7; 22:7, 12, 20
Alpha and Omega	1:8; 21:6	22:13
First and Last		1:17; 22:13
Beginning and End	21:6	22:13
Connection to Life	21:5–6	1:18

Third, he is "the Almighty," John's favorite title for God (see also Rev 4:8; 11:17; 15:3; 16:7, 14; 19:6, 15; 21:22; cf. 2 Cor 6:18). The original readers would have heard the Roman emperor revered as the αὐτοκράτωρ, meaning ruler over a limited area. But God is worshiped here as "the Almighty" or παντοκράτωρ, meaning ruler over all. He is firmly in control of human history, and he will work out his plans in both truth and love.

In this prologue to the Apocalypse, John introduces many of the book's main theological themes: the Triune God, revelation, the church, the work of Christ, Christ's return, salvation, judgment, God's sovereignty, witness, presence, resurrection, redemption, priesthood, glory, power, and so on.[18] In these few verses he touches on a multitude of theological categories: theology, Christology, pneumatology, soteriology, ecclesiology, anthropology, hamartiology, and eschatology.

11.2 John's Introductory Vision: The Risen and Glorified Christ (1:9–20)

11.2.1 The Setting of John's Vision and His Commission (1:9–11)

John immediately identifies with his readers on the basis of their common faith experience rather than on the basis of his positional authority (i.e., as an apostle). Both John and his readers are followers of Jesus (ἀδελφός, Rev 1:9) and fellow partners (συγκοινωνός, 1:9) in three important realities. First, they share in "the tribulation" (τῇ θλίψει, 1:9, ESV), a term that conveys suffering, persecution, and duress characteristic of Christians living faithfully in this fallen world. John's theology is a "persevere through tribulation" rather than a "be removed from tribulation" theology (cf. John 16:33). Second, they are fellow citizens of God's kingdom, meaning they participate in God's sovereign rule over the world. And finally, they join in "patient endurance" or perseverance (ὑπομονή), a noun that is used seven times in the book as a key Christian

18. Smalley, *Revelation*, 38–39, notes how John does much the same in the introduction to his Gospel.

virtue (Rev 1:9; 2:2, 3, 19; 3:10; 13:10; 14:12). Endurance is not an apathetic or passive response but "an active resistance to the battle lines drawn by the beast and Babylon, who require assimilation to their values, norms, and beliefs."[19]

John's spatial setting locates him on the island of Patmos "because of the word of God and the testimony of Jesus" (1:9), suggesting he was there because of his faithfulness to live and proclaim the good news of Jesus.[20] It remains plausible that John had been banished by the Roman authorities who viewed him as a political threat and hoped to hinder the church's influence in the region.[21] The temporal setting of John's vision is "on the Lord's Day" (1:10). Early Christians designated Sunday, the first day of the week, as "the Lord's Day," a day of worship chosen because of Jesus's resurrection (cf. Did. 14.1; Pliny, *Ep.* 10.96; Ign. *Magn.*, 9.1). Both the spatial and temporal settings honor John's faithfulness as a disciple to Jesus.

John's theological setting is that of being "in the Spirit." He is said to be "in the Spirit" four times in Revelation, and each time he receives a heavenly vision (1:10; 4:2; 17:3; 21:10). His Spirit-inspired vision is reminiscent of prophetic visions in the Old Testament (e.g., Ezek 3:12; 8:3; 11:1, 24; 37:1; 1 Kgs 18:12; cf. Joel 2:28). At the end of the book we are told that "it is the Spirit of [the] prophecy that bears testimony to Jesus" (Rev 19:10), suggesting God's Spirit as the source of the prophetic message from/about Jesus that John receives during worship. John hears Jesus's "loud voice like a trumpet," reminding us that "the Apocalypse is a profoundly acoustical work, full of sounds and voices . . . , tongues human and angelic, even natural phenomena such as thunder, waterfalls, and the wings of insects. Above all, it is a book of divine voices."[22] John is then instructed to write down this prophetic vision and send it to the seven churches, with these seven particular congregations representing the universal church.

11.2.2 John's Vision of Jesus (1:12–16)

John hears a voice like a trumpet, an image that appears regularly in eschatological contexts (e.g., Matt 24:31; 1 Cor 15:52; 1 Thess 4:16). When he turns to the source of the sound, he sees a glorious figure. This pairing of the prophetic activities of seeing and hearing often accompanies John's being "in the Spirit" (e.g., Rev 1:10–12; 4:2; 5:1–2, 11; 17:3, 6; 18:4; 21:1–3, 10; 22:8).[23]

John is overwhelmed by "someone like a son of man" standing among seven golden

19. Resseguie, *Revelation*, 73.

20. The preposition "because of" or "on account of" (διά plus the accusative) is taken by most to indicate result rather than purpose in Revelation, while Sarah S. U. Dixon, *The Testimony of the Exalted Jesus in the Book of Revelation*, LNTS 570 (New York: Bloomsbury T&T Clark, 2017), 79–85, favors διά as pointing forward to the real reason John was on the island—to receive the vision. Her contribution merits fresh consideration.

21. Hemer, *Letters to the Seven Churches*, 28–29.

22. Mangina, *Revelation*, 49. The embodied voice is reminiscent of John 1 and the Word becoming flesh.

23. Smalley, *Revelation*, 53.

"lampstands" (λυχνία).[24] The lampstands are later explicitly identified as the seven churches (1:20). This image comes from Zechariah's vision of faithful Israel as a lampstand or menorah reflecting the light of God's presence in the temple (Zech 4:2–11; cf. Rev 11 where the two witnesses are referred to as "the two lampstands"). Here John portrays the church's task of reflecting God's presence in a hostile world, a role made possible by the empowering work of the Spirit (cf. Zech 4:6).

The context suggests the voice belongs to Jesus, who instructs John to write his vision on a scroll and send it to the seven churches. Jesus is identified as "someone like a son of man," linking him with the "Ancient of Days" (God) from Dan 7 and 10.[25] Resseguie sees this as one of three major depictions of Christ in Revelation, the other two being the slain/risen Lamb of chapter 5 and the Divine Warrior of chapter 19.[26] What is not to be missed is the emphasis on the risen Christ "among the lampstands," conveying his ongoing presence among his people even between his ascension and parousia.[27]

DESCRIPTIONS OF JESUS IN REVELATION 1 AND REVELATION 2–3[28]

Revelation 1	Old Testament	Revelation 2–3	Possible Symbolism
Rev 1:13—"someone like a son of man"	Dan 7:9–14; 10:5–19; Ps 2:7	2:18 (Son of God)	Deity
Rev 1:13—robe and sash	Dan 10:5		Rank, dignity, exalted status
Rev 1:14—white head/hair	Dan 7:9 (of Ancient of Days)	(indirect connection to Laodicea)	Dignity, wisdom, purity
Rev 1:14—blazing eyes	Dan 10:6	2:18	Penetrating insight
Rev 1:15—glowing feet	Dan 10:6; Ezek 1:7, 27	2:18	Strength, stability, purity
Rev 1:15—voice like rushing water	Ezek 1:24; 43:2		Majesty and power
Rev 1:16—seven stars in right hand		2:1; 3:1	Sovereignty, safety, power, and authority
Rev 1:16—sword coming out of his mouth	Isa 49:2; 11:4	2:12, 16	Truth and judgment
Rev 1:16—face like the sun			Glory

24. Oecumenius writes, "He did not call them 'lamps' but 'lampstands,' for a lampstand itself does not possess the capacity to shine, but it bears that which is capable of illumination" (*Commentary on the Apocalypse* 1:12–16); Weinrich, *Revelation*, 11.

25. For more on the "son of man" as a divine figure to be identified with the "Ancient of Days," see Aune, *Revelation 1–5*, 90–92. Several of the descriptions of Jesus here also appear in the seven letters in Rev 2–3.

26. Resseguie, *Revelation*, 74. These and other depictions of Christ will be explored in more detail in Part Four.

27. Caird, *Revelation of St John*, 25, who concludes that Jesus is "no absentee . . . exercising his authority over the churches by remote control through heavenly representatives, the angels. The first characteristic of Christ revealed by John . . . is that he is present among the earthly congregations of his people, and whatever John has later to say about the coming of Christ must be interpreted in light of this salient fact." The one who is coming soon is already present.

28. Duvall, *Revelation*, 36.

The overpowering description of Christ in 1:13b–16 is intended as a single vision of the glorious power and authority of Christ. Caird has it right when he encourages us to read the vision as a whole: "To compile such a catalogue is to unweave the rainbow. John uses his allusions not as a code in which each symbol requires separate and exact translation, but rather for their evocative and emotive power."[29] Yet, while taking the description as a whole, the multiple parts still suggest characteristics of Christ that transform the imagination, as the chart below depicts:

11.2.3 Jesus Confronts John (1:17–20)

In this section we see John's reaction, Jesus's reassurance, a renewal of John's commission, and the interpretation for the reader of key images. What happens next follows the pattern in Dan 8 and 10: heavenly vision, falling down in fear, strengthening by a heavenly being, and additional instruction.[30] John responds similarly to other biblical prophets who receive a glorious vision (e.g., Isa 6:5; Ezek 1:28; Dan 8:17; 10:9–11). The glory of Christ overwhelms John, and he collapses as though dead.[31]

Jesus reassures John by first placing his right hand of power and protection on him, the same hand that holds the seven stars (Rev 1:16, 20). Jesus first tells his prophet to stop being afraid (cf. Dan 10:12, 19), before reminding him of who stands before him. He begins with a divine declaration, "I am," used of God the Father in Rev 1:8; 21:6 and of Jesus here and in 22:16. The Christology can get no higher. Jesus assures John that he is "the First and the Last" and "the Living One." The life/death contrast stands out: "Living One; I was dead, now . . . alive forever and ever. . . . I hold the keys of death and Hades."[32] The resurrected Life Giver himself sustains the church during her tribulation.

John's commission is renewed in 1:19: "Write, therefore, what you have seen, what is now and what will take place later." This clause is notoriously difficult to interpret and Beale outlines six major options.[33] Although a popular view is to see verse 19 as a chronological outline of the entire book—"what you have seen" = John's vision (Rev 1), "what is now" = the church age (Rev 2–3), and "what will take place later" = the future tribulation period (Rev 4–22)—this remains doubtful. We find future references in Rev 2–3, and past, present, and future aspects throughout Rev 4–22. It seems preferable to take all three clauses as emphasizing how past, present, and future elements intermingle

29. Caird, *Revelation of St John*, 25.

30. Beale and Carson, *New Testament Use of the Old Testament*, 1092.

31. John will again collapse in reverent fear in 19:10; 22:8–9 but is rebuked there for bowing before an angel. God alone is worthy of worship!

32. The terms "death" and "Hades" are paired here, with "Hades" likely referring to the realm of the dead (1:18; 6:8; 20:13, 14) rather than to the place of final punishment or "hell." Both seem to be "temporary abodes that hold the dead until the resurrection." Fanning, *Revelation*, 104.

33. See Beale, *Revelation*, 216; for detail, see 152–70.

to convey the eschatological outlook of the entire book containing a relevant message for every age.[34]

The introductory vision section concludes with Christ's insight into the "mystery" (μυστήριον) or deeper meaning of two key symbols: the seven stars and seven lampstands. The stars are the angels of the seven churches. While the meaning of "angel" here is debated, the usage throughout Revelation to refer to heavenly beings rather than human beings (whether messengers or leaders) probably holds true here as well. They likely serve either as guardian angels or as heavenly counterparts or representatives of the congregations.[35] In some capacity, then, the angels identify with the seven churches, serve them, and represent them before God (cf. Rev 8:3–4; 19:10; 22:9). The seven lampstands are the seven churches of Asia Minor and the recipients of John's vision.

11.3 The Messages to the Seven Churches (2:1–3:22)

11.3.1 Introduction

We first hear of "the seven churches in the province of Asia" (1:4) before they are actually listed in 1:11 and more fully addressed in chapters 2–3. The number seven suggests fullness or completeness, implying that these seven prophetic messages are intended for the entire church.[36] In fact, the entire book of Revelation is best seen as a circular letter to all seven churches, with seven symbolizing the wider church. Every congregation is charged to "hear what the Spirit says to the *churches*," implying that each church is to focus on its own specific message but also to hear what Christ is saying to the other congregations. As the church father Victorinus says in about AD 260 in his commentary on Revelation, "He [John] does this not because they are the only churches, or even the most important of the churches, but because what he says to one, he says to all."[37] The order of the seven—Ephesus, Smyrna, Pergamum, Thyatira, Sardis, Philadelphia, Laodicea—likely corresponds to the order a messenger would visit beginning from Patmos and landing at Ephesus, a leading city in the region. Since they are being addressed together, they are being held "mutually accountable, giving each an interest in the lives of the others."[38]

But not all these churches were alike, just as all contemporary churches are not

34. The middle phrase "what is now" (ἃ εἰσίν) could also be translated "what they are" (i.e., what these things mean) and could refer to v. 20, where Jesus explains key images used in the previous vision. This translation suggests that John is to write down what he has just seen (i.e., the vision of the risen Christ and the interpretive key being given in v. 20) as well as the vision that he is about to see (i.e., Rev 4–22).

35. Osborne, *Revelation*, 98–99.

36. Gorman, *Reading Revelation Responsibly*, 84–86, rightly debunks the notion popular among classic dispensationalists that the seven churches depict seven eras of church history.

37. Victorinus et al., *Latin Commentaries*, 3.

38. Mangina, *Revelation*, 55.

alike. Each church (and reader) comes from a particular spiritual context that plays an important role in what Christ wants to emphasize to that particular congregation. That is the essential nature of New Testament letters. Again, though Christ speaks individually to each church, he does not speak privately to each one since each congregation would have been able to read the others' mail (cf. Col 4:16). This sevenfold introduction to the entire book of Revelation allows for seven different perspectives but within a broader situation shared by all the churches.[39] As a result, we can appreciate the shared situation of responding to pressure from the surrounding culture and suffering persecution or struggling with compromise, but also respect the specific challenge faced by each church. As Bauckham says, Revelation addresses "a representative variety of contexts" since these seven churches are in some way representative of all churches.[40]

Rather than proceed message by message in this section as we see in most commentaries, we will reflect on the theological message conveyed through the larger structure of Rev 2–3. This more integrative approach is not intended to diminish the uniqueness of each message but to facilitate insight into the overall theological message.

11.3.2 A Common Structure

The messages follow a common pattern: address, descriptions of Christ, commendation, complaint, exhortation and/or warning, admonition to listen, and a promise to the overcomers. The following chart helps reveal the similarities and differences among the churches.[41]

Along with the number seven, this common structure suggests that all seven were meant to be read together. It underscores their unity but also displays their uniqueness, whether good or bad.

Weima sees a chiastic structure in the order of presentation:[42]

- A Ephesus: unhealthy church
  - B Smyrna: healthy church
    - C Pergamum: unhealthy church
      - D Thyatira: unhealthy church
    - C′ Sardis: unhealthy church
  - B′ Philadelphia: healthy church
- A′ Laodicea: unhealthy church

39. Bauckham, *Theology*, 14–15.
40. Bauckham, *Theology*, 16.
41. See Duvall, *Revelation*, 36–39, with slight modifications.
42. Weima, *Sermons to the Seven Churches*, 10–11.

Command to write to an angel of a church	**Description of Jesus**	**Commendation**
2:1a"To the angel of the church in <u>*Ephesus*</u> write:	2:1bThese are the words of him who holds the seven stars in his right hand and walks among the seven golden lampstands:	2:2I know your deeds, your hard work and your perseverance. I know that you cannot tolerate wicked people, that you have tested those who claim to be apostles but are not, and have found them false. 2:3 You have persevered and have endured hardships for my name, and have not grown weary. . . . 2:6But you have this in your favor: You hate the practices of the Nicolaitans, which I also hate.
2:8a"To the angel of the church in <u>*Smyrna*</u> write:	2:8bThese are the words of him who is the First and the Last, who died and came to life again.	2:9I know your afflictions and your poverty—yet you are rich! I know the slander of those who say they are Jews and are not, but are a synagogue of Satan.
2:12a"To the angel of the church in <u>*Pergamum*</u> write:	2:12bThese are the words of him who has the sharp, double-edged sword.	2:13I know where you live—where Satan has his throne. Yet you remain true to my name. You did not renounce your faith in me, not even in the days of Antipas, my faithful witness, who was put to death in your city—where Satan lives.
2:18a"To the angel of the church in <u>*Thyatira*</u> write:	2:18bThese are the words of the Son of God, whose eyes are like blazing fire and whose feet are like burnished bronze. . . . 2:23bThen all the churches will know that I am he who searches hearts and minds, and I will repay each of you according to your deeds.	2:19I know your deeds, your love and faith, your service and perseverance, and that you are now doing more than you did at first.

Accusation	Exhortation and/or Warning	Admonition to listen	Promise to Overcomers
2:4Yet I hold this against you: You have forsaken the love you had at first.	2:5Consider how far you have fallen! Repent and do the things you did at first. If you do not repent, I will come to you and remove your lampstand from its place.	2:7aWhoever has ears, let them hear what the Spirit says to the churches.	2:7bTo the one who is victorious, I will give the right to eat from the tree of life, which is in the paradise of God.
	2:10Do not be afraid of what you are about to suffer. I tell you, the devil will put some of you in prison to test you, and you will suffer persecution for ten days. Be faithful, even to the point of death, . . .	2:10band I will give you life as your victor's crown. 2:11aWhoever has ears, let them hear what the Spirit says to the churches.	2:11bThe one who is victorious will not be hurt at all by the second death.
2:14Nevertheless, I have a few things against you: There are some among you who hold to the teaching of Balaam, who taught Balak to entice the Israelites to sin so that they ate food sacrificed to idols and by committing sexual immorality. 2:15Likewise you also have those who hold to the teaching of the Nicolaitans.	2:16Repent therefore! Otherwise, I will soon come to you and will fight against them with the sword of my mouth.	2:17aWhoever has ears, let them hear what the Spirit says to the churches.	2:17bTo the one who is victorious, I will give some of the hidden manna. I will also give that person a white stone with a new name written on it, known only to the one who receives it.
2:20Nevertheless, I have this against you: You tolerate that woman Jezebel, who calls herself a prophet. By her teaching she misleads my servants into sexual immorality and the eating of food sacrificed to idols. 2:21I have given her time to repent of her immorality, but she is unwilling. 2:22So I will cast her on a bed of suffering, and I will make those who commit adultery with her suffer intensely, unless they repent of her ways. 2:23I will strike her children dead. Then all the churches will know that I am he who searches hearts and minds, and I will repay each of you according to your deeds.	2:24Now I say to the rest of you in Thyatira, to you who do not hold to her teaching and have not learned Satan's so-called deep secrets, 'I will not impose any other burden on you, 2:25except to hold on to what you have until I come.	2:29Whoever has ears, let them hear what the Spirit says to the churches.	2:26To the one who is victorious and does my will to the end, I will give authority over the nations— 2:27that one 'will rule them with an iron scepter and will dash them to pieces like pottery'—just as I have received authority from my Father. 2:28I will also give that one the morning star.

(continued)

Command to write to an angel of a church	Description of Jesus	Commendation
3:1a"To the angel of the church in *Sardis* write:	3:1bThese are the words of him who holds the seven spirits of God and the seven stars.	3:1cI know your deeds; you have a reputation of being alive, . . . 3:4Yet you have a few people in Sardis who have not soiled their clothes. They will walk with me, dressed in white, for they are worthy.
3:7a"And to the angel of the church in *Philadelphia* write:	3:7bThese are the words of him who is holy and true, who holds the key of David. What he opens no one can shut, and what he shuts no one can open.	3:8I know your deeds. See, I have placed before you an open door that no one can shut. I know that you have little strength, yet you have kept my word and have not denied my name. 3:9I will make those who are of the synagogue of Satan, who claim to be Jews though they are not, but are liars—I will make them come and fall down at your feet and acknowledge that I have loved you. 3:10Since you have kept my command to endure patiently, I will also keep you from the hour of trial that is going to come upon the whole world to test the inhabitants of the earth. 3:11I am coming soon. Hold on to what you have, so that no one will take your crown.
3:14a"To the angel of the church in *Laocicea* write:	3:14bThese are the words of the Amen, the faithful and true witness, the ruler of God's creation.	

Accusation	Exhortation and/or Warning	Admonition to listen	Promise to Overcomers
3:1d . . . but you are dead.	3:2 Wake up! Strengthen what remains and is about to die, for I have found your deeds unfinished in the sight of my God. 3:3 Remember, therefore, what you have received and heard; hold it fast, and repent. But if you do not wake up, I will come like a thief, and you will not know at what time I will come to you.	3:6 Whoever has ears, let them hear what the Spirit says to the churches.	3:5 The one who is victorious will, like them, be dressed in white. I will never blot out the name of that person from the book of life, but will acknowledge that name before my Father and his angels.
		3:13 Whoever has ears, let them hear what the Spirit says to the churches.	3:12 The one who is victorious I will make a pillar in the temple of my God. Never again will they leave it. I will write on them the name of my God and the name of the city of my God, the new Jerusalem, which is coming down out of heaven from my God; and I will also write on them my new name.
3:15 I know your deeds, that you are neither cold nor hot. I wish you were either one or the other! 3:16 So, because you are lukewarm—neither hot nor cold—I am about to spit you out of my mouth. 3:17 You say, 'I am rich; I have acquired wealth and do not need a thing.' But you do not realize that you are wretched, pitiful, poor, blind and naked.	3:18 I counsel you to buy from me gold refined in the fire, so you can become rich; and white clothes to wear, so you can cover your shameful nakedness; and salve to put on your eyes, so you can see. 3:19 Those whom I love I rebuke and discipline. So be earnest and repent. 3:20 Here I am! I stand at the door and knock. If anyone hears my voice and opens the door, I will come in and eat with that person, and they with me.	3:22 Whoever has ears, let them hear what the Spirit says to the churches."	3:21 To the one who is victorious, I will give the right to sit with me on my throne, just as I was victorious and sat down with my Father on his throne.

The most persuasive evidence that this may have been intentional is the reference in the very center of the central sermon to "church*es*": "Then all the churches will know . . ." (2:23). This is the only use of the plural "churches" outside of the closing admonition to listen in all seven messages. In addition, the letter to Thyatira is the only one to use the double condition—"To the one who is victorious and does my will to the end" (2:26)—rather than the single, "to the one who is victorious" in its various forms. The minority of two healthy congregations are surrounded (beginning, middle and end) by unhealthy churches. Assimilation to the surrounding culture or spiritual complacency were far bigger problems than surviving intense persecution.

Christians were a small minority in these large urban centers—Ephesus (200,000–250,000), Smyrna (75,000–100,000), Pergamum (120,000–180,000), and Sardis (100,000).[43] Accommodation to culture typically centered around the imperial cult and whether Christians should participate in its accompanying paganism when opting out brought serious social, economic, and political consequences. Sometimes, as with Ephesus, dealing with civil religion seems to have indirectly caused the problems (e.g., lack of mutual love). Those being pressured or persecuted were harassed for being Christians, deprived socially or financially, and threatened with arrest or death.

Resseguie shows how the plot of each letter in some ways parallels the plot of the entire book.[44] The "U-shaped plot," as he calls it, includes a stable beginning ("I know . . .") before descending toward disaster ("but" or "nevertheless" in all but two cases). Disaster is then averted when a reversal occurs (a call to repentance or remembrance or endurance) that turns the plot upward to a new stable condition ("listen to what the Spirit says"). One overarching question confronts all seven churches: Will you compromise or will you overcome? Gorman is surely right when he concludes that the primary call in Revelation is not "to death but to discipleship" and "faithful discipleship has both costs and rewards."[45]

11.3.3 The Importance of the Local Context

There are four areas related to the local context that surface repeatedly in these seven messages: the Roman imperial cult, the trade guild system, the worship of pagan deities, and Jewish opposition to Christianity. See Chapter 4 for a discussion of these four factors and how they relate to Revelation's message to the seven churches.

11.3.4 Descriptions of Jesus

The descriptions of Jesus in the seven messages are anticipated in the portrait of the exalted Christ in 1:12–20. The emphasis throughout is on his presence, power, and

43. Gorman, *Reading Revelation Responsibly*, 91.

44. Resseguie, *Revelation*, 84–85.

45. Gorman, *Reading Revelation Responsibly*, 97.

sovereignty. To the church in Ephesus Jesus "holds the seven stars in his right hand and walks among the seven golden lampstands" (2:1; 3:1; cf. 1:16, 13). Holding the stars stresses his sovereign control, likely in contrast to the emperor, while walking among the lampstands highlights his ongoing personal presence.[46]

To the church at Smyrna, Jesus is identified as "the First and the Last, the one who died and came to life again" (2:8; cf. 1:17–18). This first expression, used of both God and Christ, conveys deity as well as eternal sovereignty (1:17; 22:13; Isa 41:4; 44:6; 48:12), and certainly would be meaningful to believers being pressured by those who rejected Christ's deity. Other titles function similarly: "the Alpha and the Omega" (1:8; 21:6) and "the Beginning and the End" (21:6; 22:13). As the resurrected one, Jesus will award "life as [the] victor's crown" to those who are "faithful, even to the point of death" (2:10), thus emphasizing Christ's power over the last enemy.

To the church in Pergamum, Jesus carries "the sharp, double-edged sword" (2:12), a sword that comes out of his mouth in 1:16; 2:16. This instrument symbolizes Jesus's power and authority to judge by his word. Later in this message Jesus promises to judge those who embrace false teaching and refuse to repent of idolatry and sexual immorality (2:16).

To the church at Thyatira Jesus is portrayed as "the Son of God" with eyes of "a blazing fire" and feet of "burnished bronze" (2:18; cf. 1:14–15). The fiery eyes represent penetrating insight and power to judge, while the bronze feet stress his strength and stability (cf. Dan 10:6), perhaps also offering a subtle connection with the powerful metalworkers' guild. The emphasis falls on the title "the Son of God" and surely alludes to Ps 2:7, where God says to his anointed, "You are my son" (cf. Ps 2:9 quoted in Rev 2:27). Both passages emphasize the son's role as judge. This too provides a fitting contrast to Apollo, the son of Zeus and the patron god of Thyatira.[47] The theme of judgment is reinforced in the central section of this letter where Jesus promises to judge Jezebel and her followers and to examine the hearts and minds of all the churches, giving to each according to their deeds (2:20–23).

To the church in Sardis Jesus is described as the one "who holds the seven spirits of God and the seven stars" (3:1; cf. the "seven stars" in 1:16, 20; 2:1). Holding the stars conveys Christ's power and sovereignty over the congregations, a reality closely connected with the work of the Holy Spirit. The "seven spirits of God" refers to the sevenfold Holy Spirit, made clear by the inclusion with the Father and Son in the

46. Mark Wilson, "Revelation," 259, observes that such images suggest deity and were used by Emperor Domitian in AD 83 to celebrate the deification of his infant son following his death. Coins were even issued showing the child seated on a globe surrounded by seven stars.

47. Beale, *Revelation*, 259, notes the connection between "son of man" in Rev 1:13 and "Son of God" in 2:18 as an echo of one "like a son of the gods" in Dan 3:25 and the son of man having flaming eyes and burnished bronze legs in Dan 7 and 10. The one who protected Daniel's three friends would also protect the genuine Christians in Thyatira from spiritual assault.

opening greeting (1:4–5). In 4:5 the seven spirits are seven lamps blazing in front of the throne and in 5:6 they are the seven eyes of the Lamb sent out into all the earth. John is likely drawing on Zech 4:2–10 to show that God's work is done not by human might or power, but by God's Spirit (Zech 4:6).

To the church in Philadelphia Jesus is the "holy and true" one who "holds the key of David" (Rev 3:7). "Holy and true" are both attributes of "the Sovereign Lord" in 6:10 and here stress Christ's deity. Frequently in the Old Testament the phrase "the Holy One" describes Yahweh (e.g., 2 Kgs 19:22; Job 6:10; Pss 78:41; 89:18; Isa 1:4; 37:23; Jer 50:29; 51:5; Hab 3:3). As the "true one" Jesus is the authentic Messiah who is always found faithful by his followers. The image of holding the key alludes to Isa 22:22 where Eliakim replaces Shebna as the steward of Hezekiah's household and the one who shoulders "the key to the house of David." The connection to Rev 1:18 and perhaps also to Matt 16:18–19 strongly portrays Jesus as the sovereign ruler of all.[48] For believers who have been expelled from the local synagogue, the knowledge that Christ alone holds sovereign power to grant entrance into God's kingdom is deeply reassuring.

To the church in Laodicea Jesus is introduced as the "the Amen, the faithful and true witness, the ruler of God's creation" (Rev 3:14). Here Jesus identifies himself using language from Rev 1:6–7. Christ as "the Amen" probably also alludes to Isa 65:16, where the term "amen" (אָמֵן) is used twice in the Hebrew text (i.e., the "God of amen" or "faithful God"), meaning that he himself confirms and guarantees the message (cf. note the repeated "Amen" in Rev 1:6–7).[49] Christ is affirmed here as the true and faithful God, since "the faithful and true witness" stands in apposition to "the Amen" (cf. 1:5 where Jesus is "the faithful witness, the firstborn from the dead, and the ruler of the kings of the earth"). The third Christ title in 3:14 declares Jesus as the "ruler (ἡ ἀρχὴ) of God's creation." Again, the connection to 1:5 supports the interpretation of Christ as "ruler" rather than other meanings of ἀρχή: "beginning" (temporal) or "origin" (source).

Overall, the descriptions of Christ accomplish several goals at the outset of the book. They convey a high Christology by clearly affirming Jesus as divine. They repeatedly stress his presence (both as comforter and judge), as well as his power and sovereignty. These descriptions make meaningful connections to the local church contexts and reinforce Jesus's ability and commitment to make good on his eschatological promises.

48. Osborne, *Revelation*, 187–88, also sees this typological connection.

49. Weima, *Sermons to the Seven Churches*, 232, reinforces this connection to Isaiah: "Out of all the occurrences of this word in the NT [127x], however, there is only one instance where it functions as a name: here in the Christ title. . . . The fact that Isa 65:16 is the only place in the whole OT where the word 'Amen' functions similarly as a name provides the strongest evidence that the first Christ title echoes this Isaiah passage."

11.3.5 Condition of the Churches—Commendation/Complaint

As the present and powerful One, Christ evaluates his church by offering commendation and/or complaint. What is striking is that the commendation (for all but the Laodicean church) is not reversed or erased by the accusation that often follows. The risen Christ is at work among his people who are struggling to stay faithful in a broken world. In other words, the church is a mixed bag. Yet growth in discipleship is presented not only as a possibility but as an expectation from the risen Lord, and the particular areas of growth are addressed through his complaint.

Christ commends every church but the Laodicean church, although the commendation in the Sardis letter is more of a concession to the faithful few. He commends those standing strong in the face of the difficult circumstances, often involving pressure to compromise with or accommodate to the surrounding culture. The commendations highlight ethical conduct, emphasizing that Christ knows their deeds and evaluates accordingly (cf. knowing "deeds" in 2:2, 19; 3:1, 8, 15). Likewise, their faithfulness has been tested and demonstrated over a period of time. In addition, their faithfulness is relational at its core, since they are often commended for faithfulness to Christ's name (2:3, 13; 3:8) and Christ's word or command (3:8, 10).

The Ephesian church is commended for a persistent defense of orthodoxy. Their "deeds" consist of "hard work" and "perseverance," which in the context relates to their unwillingness to tolerate ungodliness and willingness to reject false teachers (with 2:3 being sandwiched between the repetition in 2:2, 4). Further, they "hate the practices of the Nicolaitans," which Christ also hates (2:6).[50] They have prioritized doctrinal purity and have persisted in defending the truth of the gospel.

Those in Smyrna are commended for their spiritual wealth in spite of adversity. They are enduring "afflictions" (θλῖψις), "poverty" (πτωχεία) and "slander" (βλασφημία) from those who claim to be Jews but are actually a "synagogue of Satan" (2:9).[51] These believers are experiencing hardship because of their faithfulness to Christ (e.g., loss of income, confiscation of property, legal trouble, prison time, or even death). Yet Christ declares them rich! The contrast with the material wealth and spiritual poverty of Laodicea is striking (cf. 3:17).[52]

50. Duvall, *Revelation*, 43: "The Nicolaitans (lit. 'victorious over the people' or 'victory people') are a group of false teachers closely connected to the cults of Balaam (2:14) and Jezebel (2:20–23). They are trying to redefine the faith to allow Christians to fit in with (and perhaps profit from) the surrounding culture with its idolatry, immorality, deceit, and false worship." See also Hemer, *Letters to the Seven Churches*, 87–94, for more background on these false teachers.

51. The term "slander" likely refers to Jewish "accusers" who would inform the Roman authorities about Christians, thereby opening them up to persecution. See Beale, *Revelation*, 240; Weima, *Sermons to the Seven Churches*, 68–73, who describes "slander" as (1) verbal slander as typically understood, and (2) denunciation or the bringing of an official charge against Christians before a city's political leaders.

52. Laodicea's wealth is literally being uncovered in recent excavations of the site, showing unusual indications of wealth for a comparatively small city—e.g., secondary streets with columns, four agoras, two theaters.

Believers in Pergamum have remained true to Jesus and have not renounced their faith despite living in a very difficult environment (i.e., "where Satan has his throne" in 2:13).[53] This message features the only named martyr in the book (Antipas in 2:13), who is described like Jesus as a "faithful witness" (3:14; cf. 1:5).

Those in Thyatira are commended for their deeds—consisting of four qualities: love, faith, service, and perseverance—as well as for making progress spiritually (cf. 2:19). This stands in contrast to the Ephesian church where their last works fall short of their first works (2:4–5). Here we have the only mention of the noun "love" (ἀγάπη) in Revelation besides the contrast again with Ephesus forsaking their first love in 2:4. The use of four virtues suggests a healthy congregation generally pleasing to Christ.[54]

Although it is common to read that Sardis lacks any commendation, the faithful few are commended as those "who have not soiled their clothes" and "will walk with [Christ], dressed in white, for they are worthy" (3:4). Christ commends them for resisting moral and spiritual compromise with the pagan culture, portrayed here as staining one's clothing. White garments symbolize positive virtues in Revelation, such as purity, holiness, victory, and glory (e.g., 3:4–5, 18; 4:4; 6:11; 7:9, 13–14; 19:14).

One unusual feature of this final commendation to the Philadelphian church is that Christ mixes his praise with interjections of blessing.[55] The commendation proper is as follows: "I know your deeds. . . . I know that you have little strength, yet you have kept my word and have not denied my name. . . . Since you have kept my command to endure patiently" (3:8, 10). The intermingled blessings include entrance into God's kingdom even when the local synagogue excommunicates them (3:8–9), vindication by Christ before their enemies (3:9), and spiritual protection through trials and tribulation (3:10).

With regard to Christ's complaint against the churches, two churches receive none: Smyrna and Philadelphia. The remaining five are confronted by Christ, and this often takes the form of "yet/nevertheless, I have this against you . . ." formula immediately following the commendation (2:4, 14, 20; cf. 3:3, 17b).

Ephesus is chastised for abandoning the love they had at first (2:4), a reference to either their love for God/Christ or their love for one another. Over time the church in Ephesus has become a church of "loveless orthodoxy."[56] Some of the believers in Pergamum hold to false teachings that promote both the sin of idolatry and the sin of sexual immorality (i.e., the teachings of Balaam and the Nicolaitans, respectively; cf. 2:14–15). The church at Thyatira is tolerating similar problems within their fellowship, led by a prominent prophetess who promotes idolatry and sexual immorality in a

53. For a survey of possible interpretations of "Satan's throne," see Hemer, *Letters to the Seven Churches*, 84–85; Aune, *Revelation 1–5*, 182–84. Our preference is for a reference either to the Roman imperial cult or to Roman opposition to Christianity in general.

54. Weima, *Sermons to the Seven Churches*, 134.

55. See the helpful explanation in Weima, *Sermons to the Seven Churches*, 199–210.

56. Weima, *Sermons to the Seven Churches*, 41. He offers (pp. 39–40) five persuasive reasons for seeing their lack of love for one another as the primary referent.

manner reminiscent of the Old Testament figure Jezebel (2:20). The problem for the church is deception (πλανάω in 2:20—cf. the deceiving actions of the false prophet in 13:14; 19:20, the harlot Babylon in 18:23, and Satan himself in 12:9; 20:3, 8, 10). The setting in Thyatira is rightly linked to trade guilds, although the link is never made explicit.[57] Jezebel seems to be arguing that Christians can participate in the idolatrous and immoral activities associated with the pagan guilds without harming their faith. Jesus strongly disagrees.

At Sardis the current reality of the church's spiritual condition does not match its longstanding civic reputation: "you have a reputation of being alive, but you are dead" (3:1). What is alive is also about to die and their deeds remain "unfinished in the sight of my God" (3:2). Since only a few have not "soiled their clothes" (3:4), the problem in Sardis seems similar to that of Pergamum and Thyatira.[58]

The church at Laodicea receives an especially harsh indictment. Drawing on the local context's poor water supply, black wool industry, banking center, and medical school, Jesus describes the Laodicean church as neither hot nor cold but lukewarm (3:15–16) and accuses them of failing to realize that they are "wretched, pitiful, poor, blind and naked" (3:17). Laodicea's spiritual self-sufficiency is completely unwarranted.

11.3.6 Exhortation/Warning

Following the commendation or complaint we find the exhortation, and this is sometimes followed by a warning linked to Christ's future coming to the church. There are three areas of exhortation in the seven messages. First, both Ephesus and Sardis are called to awaken to their spiritual condition: "Consider how far you have fallen" (2:5) and "Wake up! Strengthen what remains and is about to die" (3:2). Second, the central exhortation used for the five unhealthy or problematic churches is "repent" (μετανοέω)—2:5 (2x), 16, 21 (2x), 22; 3:3, 19. Sometimes the command to repent is coupled with a charge to return to their initial faith commitment as one might expect: "Repent and do the things you did at first" (2:5), "Remember, therefore, what you have received and heard; hold it fast, and repent" (3:3), and "so be earnest and repent" (3:19). In the case of Laodicea, repentance is described using colorful language tied to the local situation: "I counsel you to buy from me gold refined in the fire, so you can become rich; and white clothes to wear, so you can cover your shameful nakedness; and salve to put on your eyes, so you can see" (3:18). The phrase "buy from me" sits near the center of the letter to the Laodiceans and gets at the heart of their idolatrous materialism. Perhaps this specific and extended admonition is the reason why Christ then adds, "Those whom I love I rebuke and discipline" (3:19).

57. As Osborne, *Revelation*, 156, concludes: "The problem in Thyatira centered on the guilds."

58. The other two uses of the verb "soil" (μολύνω) occur in 1 Cor 8:7 and Rev 14:4, where the issue is idolatry and possibly also immorality.

The third area of exhortation constitutes a call to faithful endurance for those churches who are remaining faithful. To Smyrna he says, "Do not be afraid of what you are about to suffer" (2:10). Rather than fearing possible persecution, they are called to "be faithful, even to the point of death" (2:10). To the faithful minority in Thyatira who are resisting the false teachers and their persuasive appeal to participate in the pagan guild feasts, Jesus promises not to impose ("throw"–βάλλω; cf. 2:22) "any other burden on you, except to hold on to what you have until I come" (2:24–25). Many believe Jesus's command here and the letter sent from the Jewish leaders at the Jerusalem Council of AD 49 (see Acts 15:28) reflect similar concerns.[59] The exhortation to Philadelphia is similar: "I am coming soon. Hold on to what you have, so that no one will take your crown" (Rev 3:11). As with Thyatira, the context determines what the Philadelphian Christians are to "hold on to." Here the previous commendation in 3:8–10 supplies the content: an open door into God's kingdom (3:8), Christ's future vindication of their suffering (3:9), and Christ's protection through the trials/tribulation associated with divine judgments (3:10).[60]

Jesus's exhortations are sometimes coupled with warnings that center around his discipline or judgment on faithless churches or on those who oppose faithful believers. Often the idea of Christ's coming appears in the warning section (2:5, 16; 3:3, 16; cf. 2:25; 3:11). The natural question is whether this coming refers to his second coming at the end of the age or to a preliminary coming in judgment on the specific church. Although difficult to say for certain in every case, Weima's conclusion seems wise: "A sharp distinction between these two options should be avoided since a preliminary judgment, though more likely in view here [related to 2:16], functions also as an important harbinger of the final judgment to take place at Christ's parousia."[61]

Jesus warns the Ephesian church that he will come and remove their lampstand from its place (2:5), a likely reference to the church completely losing their identity as a church due to Christ's judgment. He warns Pergamum that he will soon come to them and fight against the disobedient with the sword of his mouth (2:16), an image stressing Christ's judgment on those who encourage assimilation and compromise with the pagan culture. The church in Sardis is warned that unless they wake up, Christ will "come like a thief, and you will not know at what time I will come to you" (3:3). The echo of Jesus's clear teachings elsewhere is hard to miss (cf. Rev 16:15; Matt 24:43; Luke 12:39; also 1 Thess 5:2–4; 2 Pet 3:10). In like manner, Jesus warns the complacent, hedonistic church in Laodicea that their lukewarmness makes him want to vomit them out of his mouth (Rev 3:16).

At times the warning is for those who are hindering faithful believers in their

59. E.g., Charles, *Revelation of St John*, 1:74; Hemer, *Letters to the Seven Churches*, 123; Smalley, *Revelation*, 77; Beale, *Revelation*, 266; Fanning, *Revelation*, 155n41; Koester, *Revelation*, 301.

60. Duvall, *Revelation*, 71–73.

61. Weima, *Sermons to the Seven Churches*, 111.

discipleship. In Thyatira, Jesus will not only punish Jezebel but also "those who commit adultery with her" with intense suffering or "great tribulation" (ESV, θλῖψιν μεγάλην), unless they repent of her ways (2:22).[62] For those believers in Philadelphia who have experienced affliction, poverty, and slander from "those who claim to be Jews though they are not, but are liars," Jesus offers vindication. The pretenders will be forced to bow in submission to the genuine Christ followers, the true Israel of God (3:9; cf. Isa 45:14; 49:23; 60:14; Rom 2:28–29; Gal 6:16). Jesus is referring to the future vindication of the persecuted church rather than a large-scale conversion of Jews.[63]

11.3.7 Promises to the Overcomers

The overcoming formula featuring the verb νικάω appears at the end of each letter. The specific nature of the reward is often tailored to the local context. For instance, believers in Smyrna threatened with death are promised life as a victor's crown and assured that the second death will not harm them (2:11). Those in Pergamum struggling with attraction to the pagan feasts are promised participation in the messianic wedding banquet (2:17). Those in Sardis whose names have been erased from the membership in the local synagogue register because of their commitment to Christ are given the security of having their names registered in the book of life, never to be erased (3:5).

All the promises to the victors are eschatological promises: the right to eat from the tree of life in the paradise of God (2:7), the crown of life and immunity from the second death (2:11), hidden manna and a white stone with a new name (2:17), authority over the nations and the gift of the morning star (2:26–28), dressed in white and inclusion in the book of life with acknowledgment before the Father (3:5), a permanent place in God's temple and inscription with the name of God, the name of God's city, and Jesus's new name (3:12), the privilege of table fellowship with Jesus (3:20), and the right to sit with Jesus on his throne (3:21). If they heed Christ's warning and obey his exhortation, they will receive an eternal reward for their perseverance in faith. This reward, described in a variety of ways, consists of the experience and enjoyment of God's eschatological presence.[64]

11.3.8 Admonition to Listen to the Spirit

In the conclusion of each message, we find a hearing formula tied to the role of the Holy Spirit: "Whoever has ears, let them hear what the Spirit says to the churches" (2:7, 11, 17, 29; 3:6, 13, 22; cf. 13:9 with no mention of the Spirit).[65] The formula

62. Because of the context and the lack of the definite article as in 7:14, this likely refers not to the period of trials just prior to Jesus's return but to suffering in general. Nevertheless, the use of the phrase θλῖψιν μεγάλην marks Jesus's seriousness.

63. Duvall, *Revelation*, 72.

64. Duvall and Hays, *God's Relational Presence*, 307.

65. Anne Marit Enroth, "The Hearing Formula in the Book of Revelation," *NTS* 36 (1990): 598–608.

precedes the conquering formula in the first three messages and follows in the final four messages. The first part of the formula echoes the words of Jesus in the Synoptic Gospels (e.g., Matt 11:15; 13:9, 43; Mark 4:9, 23; Luke 8:8; 14:35), where it draws on the Old Testament prophetic tradition (e.g., Isa 6:9–10; Ezek 3:27; 12:2; Jer 5:21).[66] Revelation adds the connection to the work of the Holy Spirit. What the Spirit says to the churches is equated here with the words of the exalted Christ, who lives among his people through the Spirit.[67] The Spirit plays a pivotal role in Revelation of "mediating prophetic visions and messages (1:10; 4:2; 14:13; 17:2; 19:10; 21:10; 22:6)."[68] The formula reminds the audience that what they have just heard is extremely important and demands their immediate attention. It also points forward (logically but not always textually) to the exhortation to be victorious.

11.3.9 Conclusion

As we step back and look at the seven messages as a whole, which Gorman labels the "pastoral-prophetic messages," we make several observations.[69] First, the risen Christ loves his people. Christ's compassion appears in his continued perseverance with them through exhortation/warning and promises to the overcomers. There is more commendation than one might expect, even as he calls them to repentance, a stance summarized by the line in the letter to the Laodiceans: "Those whom I love I rebuke and discipline" (3:19). Second, Christ clearly understands their context of journeying through trials and temptations common to all churches, chiefly the temptation to accommodate to the beast and Babylon. But third, like a loving parent, Christ calls his people to life, which means repentance and perseverance in faith. His care for them includes his unwillingness to leave them in a sad spiritual state. There is a promised land at the end of this journey. As a result, fourth, the rewards are ultimately eschatological and center around experiencing God's relational presence. Drawing on the Anglican writer Elizabeth Charles, Mangina makes an interesting observation here: "all seven messages are addressed to the church corporately through its angel, while the rewards/promises are held out to the individual victor."[70] This is not to pit community against individual but to emphasize that "the same Lord who is passionately concerned for the welfare of the churches also addresses the individual disciple."[71] It also sends the clear message that "Christ desires a church characterized by fullness of orthodoxy and orthopraxy."[72]

66. Beale, *Revelation*, 234.
67. Bauckham, *Climax of Prophecy*, 160–61.
68. Fanning, *Revelation*, 121n45.
69. Gorman, *Reading Revelation Responsibly*, 88.
70. Elizabeth Rundle Charles, *The Book of Unveiling: Studies in the Revelation of S. John the Divine* (London: SPCK, 1892), 54; Mangina, *Revelation*, 68.
71. Mangina, *Revelation*, 69.
72. Gorman, *Reading Revelation Responsibly*, 100.

11.4 The Heavenly Throne Room Vision and Resulting Judgments (4:1–16:21)

11.4.1 Introduction

The central section of Revelation features the grounding vision—God on his throne as the sovereign Creator, the slain but resurrected Redeemer Lamb found worthy to open the heavenly scroll, and God and the Lamb receiving worship. This centering vision leads to God's response of judging evil through the seal, trumpet, and bowl judgments of chapters 6–16. The third and most extensive interlude in chapters 12–14 again details the challenges faced by God's people in the last days by explaining the war between God and the forces of evil, personified by the dragon and the two beasts. Believers are engaged in spiritual warfare of cosmic proportions, but they fight *from* rather than *toward* victory because of the death and resurrection of Christ.

11.4.2 The Grounding Vision: The Heavenly Throne Room (4:1–5:14)

Following John's introductory vision of the risen and glorified Christ and his messages to the seven churches in Rev 1–3, the scene shifts from earth to heaven in 4:1. The heavenly throne room vision serves as the grounding vision for the remainder of the book. This vision consists of three tightly connected sections. First, we see God seated on his throne as the sovereign Creator of the universe being worshiped by the elders and the living creatures (4:1–11). Next, we learn of the search for someone worthy to open the scroll in God's right hand, and only the Lion-Lamb is found worthy (5:1–7). Finally, God and the Lamb are worshiped by all of creation (5:8–14).

While the Triune God (God on the throne, Lamb of God, and sevenfold Spirit) is the central subject of the grounding vision, God's throne (θρόνος; 4:2 [2x; second rendered "it" in NIV], 3, 4, 5 [2x], 6 [3x], 9, 10 [2x]; 5:1, 7, 11, 13), worthiness (ἄξιος; 4:11; 5:2, 4, 9, 12), and worship (4:8–11; 5:6, 8–14) unite the entire section. The church's earthly struggles of Rev 2–3 now give way to the heavenly reality of Rev 4–5, where the sovereign God and his redemptive plan take center stage. All of creation responds with enthusiastic worship.

The "throne" stands as a foundational image of the entire book since it represents the center of ultimate reality—God's glorious presence and majestic sovereignty.[73] Everything revolves around the throne and all subsequent visions originate from the throne. God now shares his throne with Jesus Christ, the slain yet triumphant Lamb of God (3:21; 5:6; 7:17). In addition, the sevenfold Spirit blazes forth from the throne (4:5; cf. 5:6). At the conclusion of the entire apocalyptic drama, the "throne of God

73. The term "throne" (θρόνος) is used almost fifty times in Revelation, mostly with reference to God.

and of the Lamb" form the centerpiece of the new creation as God's people enjoy his glorious presence forever (22:1, 3).

11.4.2.1 God on His Throne as Sovereign Creator (4:1–11)

After receiving the vision of 1:10–3:22, John sees a door standing open in heaven and hears a voice summoning him heavenward for a prophetic vision (4:1).[74] While some dispensational commentators see this as a reference to the rapture of the church,[75] most scholars reject (rightly, in my view) this conclusion and view this instead as John's personal prophetic vision.[76] John receives a similar prophetic call in 11:12; 17:1; and 21:9. And while the word "church" is not used in Revelation with reference to specific local churches, we do find references to believers using a host of other names and designations (e.g., saints, brothers, those who keep God's commands).[77] In many cases these believers are still located on earth after Rev 4. John is told that he will be shown "what must take place after this," referring to what God will reveal after the throne room vision of chapters 4–5, though not necessarily in strict chronological order.[78]

In 4:2–3 John finds himself "in the Spirit" (cf. 1:10; 17:3; 21:10) and he sees a heavenly vision of God enthroned in glory (cf. Ezek 8:3–4). John is now confronted with the center of all reality: God seated on his throne (cf. Isa 6:1–4). Rather than describing God by name or by human characteristics, John portrays his splendor and brilliance: the appearance of jasper and carnelian with an emerald rainbow encircling the throne (cf. 1 Tim 6:16; 1 John 1:5).

Around the throne are twenty-four other thrones on which are seated twenty-four elders (Rev 4:4). These elders have been identified in a variety of ways.[79] Their function leads us to believe they are an exalted order of angels who serve on the royal council. They play some role in representing the people of God (cf. twelve tribes and twelve apostles) but are clearly distinct from God's people (e.g., 5:5, 8; 7:13; 11:16–18; 19:4). Their adornment in white with golden crowns symbolizes their holiness, exalted status,

74. On "show" (δείκνυμι), see 1:1; 4:1; 17:1; 21:9, 10; 22:1, 6; cf. 22:8. Duvall, *Revelation*, 82–83: "Whereas 'heaven' usually occurs in the plural in the New Testament, reflecting the Jewish idea of multiple heavens (cf. 2 Cor 12:2), in Revelation the term always occurs in the singular as John focuses on heaven as the dwelling place of God (the lone exception being 12:12, which is probably influenced by Isa. 44:23)."

75. LaHaye, *Revelation Unveiled*, 99–100; Walvoord, *Revelation*, 103.

76. Michael J. Svigel, "The Apocalypse of John and the Rapture of the Church: A Reevaluation," *TrinJ* 22 (2001): 28–30; Fanning, *Revelation*, 197; Keener, *Revelation*, 177–79; Koester, *Revelation*, 351; and Mounce, *Revelation*, 119, who writes, "The very discussion of a 'rapture of the church' lies outside John's frame of reference. He knows nothing of such a 'rapture.'"

77. Mark Wilson, *Charts on the Book of Revelation*, 35, identifies over thirty such names for believers in Revelation.

78. On "after this" (μετὰ ταῦτα), see 1:19; 4:1; 7:9; 9:12; 15:5; 18:1; 19:1; 20:3. Beale, *Revelation*, 317, reminds us that this phrase is synonymous with Daniel's phrase "in the last days" (Dan 2:28–29, 45) and indicates that Rev 4–22 is "generally eschatological in scope." On δείκνυμι, see comments on Rev 1:1.

79. For a clear summary of the scholarly options, see Smalley, *Revelation*, 116–18; cf. also Aune, *Revelation 1–5*, 287–92. The elders appear twelve times in the book: 4:4, 10; 5:5, 6, 8, 11, 14; 7:11, 13; 11:16; 14:3; 19:4.

and honor. Their primary role relates to worship since they are usually portrayed as prostrating themselves in worship (e.g., 4:10–11; 5:8–14; 7:11; 11:16; 19:4).

In 4:5–6a we see manifestations of God's holy presence. From the throne come lightning, rumblings, and thunder, symbolizing God's power and glory (cf. the theophany in Exod 19:16–25). Each series of seven judgments concludes with the same phenomena (Rev 8:1–5; 11:15–19; 16:17–18), connecting God directly to the judgments. In front of the throne the "seven lamps" (or torches) blaze, representing the "seven spirits of God" or the sevenfold Holy Spirit. The Spirit in all his fullness and completeness is God's personal presence carrying out his actions in this world (cf. 1:4; 3:1; 5:6; Zech 3:9; 4:6, 10; Ezek 1:12–13).[80] The "sea of glass, clear as crystal" represents God's holiness and transcendent majesty and also symbolizes his separation from creation (cf. Gen 1:7; Ezek 1:22).[81]

As John's throne room vision continues in Rev 4:6b–9, he describes the appearance and activity of the "four living creatures," an exalted order of angels that forms the innermost circle around the throne.

Their appearance resembles both the cherubim of Ezek 1 and 10 and the seraphim of Isa 6, although John adapts and transforms the Old Testament images. They have a dual role: leading the heavenly court in worship (Rev 4:8–9; 5:8, 14; 7:11; 14:3; 19:4) and playing some part in executing judgment (6:1–7; 15:7). Day and night they cry out in worship, praising God for his holiness, power, and eternity.[82] Like the trisagion of the seraphim of Isa 6, they offer a threefold praise to God for his holiness. In terms of power, John changes κύριος σαβαωθ ("Lord of hosts") in Isa 6:3 (LXX) to κύριος ὁ θεὸς ὁ παντοκράτωρ ("Lord God Almighty"). As we saw in Rev 1:8, the term παντοκράτωρ ("ruler over all") surpasses the emperor's title (αὐτοκράτωρ, meaning "one who rules by himself"). God is also eternal: "who was, and is, and is to come" (4:8; cf. 1:4, 8), likely an expansion of the "I AM WHO I AM" of Exod 3:14. This is reinforced in Rev 4:9–10 as the living creatures "give glory, honor and thanks to him who sits on the throne and who lives for ever and ever."

In 4:10–11 the twenty-four elders respond in worship by falling down, laying their crowns before the throne, and praising God as worthy to receive glory, honor, and power because he is the universal Creator. The phrase "you are worthy" was often used to welcome the Roman emperor into a city and the title "our lord and god" (Latin: *dominus et deus noster*) was demanded by Emperor Domitian.[83] In striking contrast

80. The Spirit's vital work among the churches was established in Rev 2–3. See Ch. 14 on the Spirit.

81. The image of a sea appears twice more in the book. In 15:1–4 the sea of glass is mixed with fire and likely represents God's holiness in judgment. In 21:1, the sea has totally disappeared since God has completely judged evil and there is nothing that distances him from his people.

82. Mounce, *Revelation*, 125. Mark Wilson, *Charts on the Book of Revelation*, 74–75, identifies almost twenty hymns in Revelation. See Duvall, *Revelation*, 120.

83. Suetonius, *Lives of Caesar: Domitian*, 13.

with the imperial cult, John now rightfully applies these titles to the one true God who alone is worthy.

For the seven churches undergoing temptation and suffering, John anchors their faith in the throne room vision of the majestic, sovereign, eternal and glorious ruler of the universe, who alone as the Creator is worthy of praise and worship. God is deeply concerned about his world and is at work to fulfill his purposes in creation in opposition to the temporary, counterfeit powers of earthly pagan rulers. God's sovereignty as Creator established in 4:1–11 serves as the basis for his work as Redeemer and Judge in all that follows.[84]

11.4.2.2 Worthy is the Lamb Who Was Slain (5:1–7)

The throne-room vision begun in 4:1 continues throughout chapter 5 as the scene shifts from God the Creator to the Lamb as Redeemer. The chapter opens with John seeing a sealed scroll in God's right hand (5:1), an Old Testament anthropomorphism depicting God's power and authority over its contents (cf. 1:16–17, 20; 2:1; Exod 15:6, 12; Job 40:14; Pss 17:7; 18:3; 21:8; Isa 41:10). The scroll with writing on both sides is reminiscent of Ezek 2:9–10, where Ezekiel is given a scroll with words of "lament and mourning and woe" written on both sides. The fullness of the writing and the seven seals likely point to the full and comprehensive nature of God's redemptive plan.

Revelation actually mentions two scrolls: the "scroll" (βιβλίον) here in chapter 5 and the "little scroll" (βιβλαρίδιον) in chapter 10. While the two scrolls are not identical, they are strongly connected. Most scholars and the context favor seeing the scroll as God's plan of salvation to defeat evil, rescue his people, and transform his creation through the victory achieved by Jesus Christ, the Lamb of God.[85] The general plan of chapter 5 is narrowed with the "little scroll" of Rev 10 to feature the church's role in that larger plan, with a special emphasis on the likelihood of suffering. Both chapters stress the certain success of God's sovereign purposes.

In 5:2–4 we read of the search for one worthy to break the seals and open the scroll. The mighty angel's question is met with universal silence—"No one in heaven or on earth or under the earth could open the scroll or even look inside it" (5:3). When John hears that no created being is found worthy to open the scroll, he weeps uncontrollably (cf. the use of κλαίω when mourning the death of a loved one as in John 11:33; 20:11–15 or when grieving a broken relationship as in Matt 26:75; Luke 19:41). John despairs over the thought of God's plan of victory, redemption, and restoration going unrealized. In one sense, John represents helpless humanity apart from a Savior.

John's despair is finally overcome by the good news of a messianic conqueror

84. Smalley, *Revelation*, 141.

85. Duvall, *Revelation*, 88.

presented in Rev 5:5–6. One of the twenty-four elders (cf. 4:4) commands John to "stop weeping"[86] and shifts his focus to Jesus, the only one found worthy and capable of opening the scroll. The elder identifies Jesus as the one who has triumphed (νικάω), using two well-known messianic titles.[87] The "Lion of the tribe of Judah" is taken from Gen 49:9–10 where it serves as a symbol of the power and sovereignty of the Davidic Messiah. The "Root of David" derives from the promise that an ideal ruler would come from the "Root of Jesse," King David's father (Isa 11:1, 10; 2 Sam 7:1–17; Rom 15:12; Rev 22:16). The combination of these two classic messianic texts "strongly and deliberately evokes the image of the Messiah as a new David who wins a military victory over the enemies of Israel."[88] But this nationalistic understanding is transformed and expanded in 5:6, where we see that victory has come through sacrifice: "Then I saw a Lamb, looking as if it had been slain, standing at the center of the throne" (on "slain" [σφάζω], see 5:6, 9, 12; 6:4, 9; 13:3, 8; 18:24). Bauckham concludes: "By placing the image of a sacrificial victim alongside those of the military conqueror, John forges a new symbol of *conquest* by sacrificial death," so that the hopes and expectations of the true Israel are transformed.[89]

John sees a slain but very much alive Lamb standing at the center of God's throne, encircled by the living creatures and elders (5:6). The term for "lamb" (ἀρνίον) is used twenty-eight times in Revelation with reference to Christ and integrates the Passover lamb image of Exod 11–12 with the Suffering Servant lamb image of Isa 52:13–53:12.[90] The victory of the Lamb over all the forces of evil comes through his life, death, resurrection, and exaltation. His positioning at the "center of the throne" depicts his unique relationship to God since Revelation has only one throne, and it is shared by God and the Lamb (3:21; 5:6; 7:17; 22:1, 3).

The Lamb has seven horns, symbolic of his power and strength (cf. Dan 7:7, 20; 1 En. 90:9) and seven eyes, which are explicitly identified as the "seven spirits of God sent out into all the earth" (cf. Zech 3:9; 4:6, 10). In Zechariah's vision the eyes of God himself "range throughout the earth" (Zech 4:10), while in Revelation the "seven spirits of God" refer to the Holy Spirit (see 1:4; 4:5). Jesus is both one with God on his throne and one with the Holy Spirit in executing God's mission in this world. As we see elsewhere, the Spirit's "location" is "before God's throne" (1:4) or "in front of the throne" (4:5), indicating that "the Spirit's primary role is to make God's powerful presence known in the world, including empowering the church to bear witness to Jesus" (cf. John 14:26; 15:26; 16:7).[91]

This unit closes as the Lamb takes the scroll from the right hand of God on the

86. Mathewson, *Handbook on the Greek Text*, 72; cf. NIV: "Do not weep!"

87. See Duvall, *Revelation*, 42.

88. Bauckham, *Climax of Prophecy*, 215.

89. Bauckham, *Climax of Prophecy*, 215, emphasis original.

90. Osborne, *Revelation*, 255–56.

91. Duvall and Hays, *God's Relational Presence*, 313.

throne (5:7).[92] The grammar of this verse stresses the highpoint of the vision: "He went (aorist ἦλθεν) and took (perfect εἴληφεν) the scroll." As Mathewson discusses, since John uses the aorist of λαμβάνω elsewhere in Revelation, even in the immediate context (5:8, 9, 12), his selection of the perfect is intentional and "should be given its full stative force."[93] The perfect tense here highlights Christ's action as central to the narrative since at this very point the salvation project moves forward as the one worthy to carry out the divine plan embraces the challenge. John may now weep from joy rather than despair.

11.4.2.3 God and the Lamb Are Worthy of Worship (5:8–14)

After the Lamb takes the scroll from the hand of God in 5:7, the focus shifts to heavenly worship with the actions of the living creatures and the elders bracketing the unit (5:8, 14). Worship of the worthy Lamb begins with the living creatures and the elders (5:8–10), progresses to all angelic creatures (5:11–12), and culminates with all of creation offering praise to the Lamb (5:13–14).

In 5:8–10 the living creatures and elders worship the Lamb. The elders, as priestly representatives of God's people, hold harps and golden bowls full of incense.[94] The symbolism is what matters here since it would be extremely difficult if not impossible to play a harp and hold a bowl at the same time. Harps (κιθάρα) are stringed instruments that often accompany praise songs (Rev 14:2; 15:2; cf. 1 Chr 25:1–8; 2 Chr 5:11–13; Pss 33:2; 147:7). And the term "bowl" (φιάλη) appears twelve times in the Apocalypse, eleven of those in connection with God's wrath (Rev 5:8; 15:7; 16:1, 2, 3, 4, 8, 10, 12, 17; 17:1; 21:9). Here, however, these shallow bowls are filled with incense symbolizing the prayers of God's people (cf. Rev 6:9–11; 8:3–4; Ps 141:2).[95] Christ is to be praised for his work of redemption already accomplished, but God's judgments to come are in some way a response to the prayers of God's people to finish this work of eliminating evil and restoring all creation.

The heavenly court that previously worshiped God as Creator (Rev 4:10–11) now worships the Lamb as Redeemer (5:9–10). They sing a new song, a common practice of God's people to worship God for his mighty and awesome acts (e.g., Pss 33:3; 98:1; 144:9). The adjective "new" expresses an eschatological newness (cf. new song in

92. On the apparent discrepancy between the Lamb being at the center of the throne in verse 6 and approaching the throne in verse 7, see Laszlo Gallusz, *The Throne Motif in the Book of Revelation: Profiles from the History of Interpretation*, LNTS 487 (London: Bloomsbury T&T Clark, 2014), 157–58, who suggests that the Lamb is identified and described in 5:5–6 before his activities are narrated in 5:7. In other words, there is chronological discontinuity between vv. 6 and 7.

93. Mathewson, *Revelation*, 75–76.

94. The Greek suggests that the elders alone hold the harps and bowls with the masculine participle "having" (ἔχοντες) referring to the masculine antecedent "elders" (πρεσβύτεροι) rather than the neuter "creatures" (ζῷα).

95. The term ἅγιοι, "the holy ones, saints," is used here and twelve additional times in Revelation to describe people in relationship to God, or "God's people," rather than people who are especially spiritually mature (Rev 8:3, 4; 11:18; 13:7, 10; 14:12; 16:6; 17:6; 18:20, 24; 19:8; 20:9). See Aune, *Revelation 1–5*, 359.

Rev 5:9; 14:3; new name in 2:17; 3:12; new Jerusalem in 3:12; 21:2; new heaven and new earth in 21:1, 1; and a new creation in 21:5).

This new song celebrates the new things God is doing in Christ, things promised by the prophets (Isa 42:1–10). God's people will sing similar songs in celebration of God's mighty acts (cf. Rev 14:3; 15:3–4).

Here the new song praises the Lamb as worthy to carry out God's plan because of his three saving actions. First, he was "slain" (σφάζω), a term describing Christ's sacrificial death on the cross (cf. Isa 53:7 LXX; Rev 5:6, 9, 12; 13:8; see also 6:9; 18:24 where it describes the martyrdom of believers). Second, he "purchased" (ἀγοράζω) people for God. Using the language of the marketplace (ἀγορά), Jesus redeemed a multicultural people for God through his willing sacrifice (cf. 1 Cor 6:19–20; 1 Pet 1:18–19; Rev 14:3–4). The redeemed people come from "every tribe and language and people and nation." This multicultural formula occurs seven times in Revelation, each time varying the order of the terms, to indicate universality (5:9; 7:9; 10:11; 11:9; 13:7; 14:6; 17:15). God has provided salvation in Christ for *all* peoples. (See the following chart.)

EVERY TRIBE, LANGUAGE, PEOPLE AND NATION[96]					
5:9	Tribe	Language	People	Nation	People from this group purchased for God by Christ
7:9	Nation	Tribe	People	Language	Great multitude in heaven drawn from this group
10:11	Peoples	Nations	Languages	Kings	John is to prophesy about (or perhaps "against") this group
11:9	People	Tribe	Language	Nation	These unbelievers will refuse burial to the two witnesses
13:7	Tribe	People	Language	Nation	The beast is given authority over these unbelievers
14:6	Nation	Tribe	Language	People	The gospel is proclaimed to everyone who lives on the earth
17:15	Peoples	Multitudes	Nations	Languages	The prostitute sits on many waters, defined as this group

While this prophecy (10:11) and the gospel (14:6) are intended for all people, some follow the Lamb (5:9; 7:9) yet others refuse to believe (11:9; 13:7; 17:15). In Gen 10, the descendants of Noah are scattered into various groups (Gen 10:5, 20,

96. Duvall, *Revelation*, 96. For a more extensive study of this theme, see J. Daniel Hays, *From Every People and Nation: A Biblical Theology of Race*, NSBT 14 (Downers Grove, IL: IVP Academic, 2003).

31). Exodus 19:5 refers to God calling his treasured possession "out of all nations" (notice the use of Exod 19:6 in Rev 5:10). The most likely background is Daniel's vision of "one like a son of man" coming into the presence of the Ancient of Days where he is given an everlasting kingdom and worshiped by all nations (Dan 7:13–14). This phrase reminds us that God has provided salvation in Christ for all people. He desires a multicultural people.

Third, he "made" (ποιέω) this people into "a kingdom and priests to serve our God, and they will reign on the earth" (Rev 5:10). God promised Israel in Exod 19:5–6 that they would be a kingdom of priests and a holy nation, a promise now fulfilled in Jewish and gentile followers of Christ—the church (Rev 1:6; 20:6; 1 Pet 2:9). As a "kingdom" or royal house, they enjoy full citizenship now. As priests, they enjoy special access to God along with the privileges and responsibilities of serving him (cf. Rom 12:1; 1 Pet 2:5). As a royal priesthood, God's people will one day reign with Christ on the earth (Rev 2:26–27; 20:4, 6; 22:5; cf. Dan 7:18, 22, 27; Matt 19:28; 1 Cor 6:2; 2 Tim 2:12). As Smalley emphasizes, "God's salvific plan will be expressed in his whole creation, and not just (so Rev 4–5) in heaven."[97]

John looks and hears the voice of a countless multitude of angels encircling the throne, the living creatures, and the elders as they join in worshiping the Lamb (5:11–12). Daniel 7:9–10 comes immediately to mind, where an incalculable multitude of heavenly beings surround the Ancient of Days. Worship normally reserved for God alone is now offered to Christ (cf. Rev 4:11; 7:12). In addition, the sevenfold angelic praise—power, wealth, wisdom, strength, honor, glory, and praise—sounds much like the hymn to God in Rev 7:12. Here the first four items highlight qualities of the Lamb while the final three describe the response of the worshipers.[98] The Lamb's qualities are closely tied to his work of conquering evil through his sacrificial death and offering life to his followers.

Angelic worship now flows from all of creation to God the Creator who sits on the throne and to the Lamb, God's agent of redemption. In Revelation, powerful angels refuse worship (19:10; 22:8–9), while Jesus is worshiped alongside God by all of creation. Bauckham rightly concludes that "the worship of Jesus must be understood as indicating the inclusion of Jesus in the being of the one God defined by monotheistic worship."[99] The unity of God and the Lamb continues throughout the rest of the book (e.g., 6:16; 7:9–10; 14:4; 21:22–23; 22:1, 3).

In 5:13 the second of four doxologies in Rev (1:5–6; 5:13; 7:12; 19:1–2) closes the great throne-room vision of chapters 4–5 in a fitting manner. The four living creatures respond with a rousing "Amen" (5:14; cf. 1:6–7; 7:12; 19:4; 22:20), and once again the

97. Smalley, *Revelation*, 138.
98. Mounce, *Revelation*, 137.
99. Bauckham, *Theology*, 60.

elders fall down in worship. Revelation 5:8–14 concludes the throne-room vision of Rev 4–5 and prepares the reader for God's response of salvation in judgment to come. Between the situation of the churches described in Rev 2–3 and the beginning of God's consummative work in Rev 6 stands the grounding vision of chapters 4–5. God is on his throne. The slain but resurrected Lamb is found worthy to open the scroll, which will lead to the final outworking of God's eschatological plan. All creation responds with worship.

11.4.3 The Seal Judgments (6:1–7:17)

The messages to the seven churches in Rev 2–3 and the great throne-room vision in chapters 4–5 prepare for God's righteous judgments to follow. The seal judgments initiate three series of judgments (seal, trumpet, and bowl) detailed in Rev 6–16, with each using a four-plus-three pattern. Jesus, the worthy one, now opens the sealed scroll. Between the sixth and seventh seal stand the two interludes of Rev 7. Finally, with all seven seals unsealed, the scroll unfolds into the trumpet judgments (8:1).

11.4.3.1 The First Six Seal Judgments (6:1–17)[100]

The four-plus-three pattern begins with the famous "four horsemen of the Apocalypse" in 6:1–8. These are "preliminary judgments representing forces operative throughout history" that serve God's sovereign purposes and usher in the events of the end of the age.[101] Beale reminds us that these particular disasters run simultaneously throughout this age rather than consecutively in a severe trial right before Christ returns.[102] Yet when we come to the end of each series (6:12–17; 11:15–19; 16:17–21), we have certainly arrived at the end of history. These events sometimes result in the suffering of God's people, and as a result, John sees the souls of martyred believers in heaven with the opening of the fifth seal (6:9–11). Their cries for justice are heard and God responds without delay as unbelievers face the wrath of God and the Lamb with the opening of the sixth seal (6:12–17).

John often relies upon the Old Testament prophets to articulate his visions. The specific background here is Zech 1:7–11 and 6:1–8, where riders on various colored horses are sent as instruments of God's judgment on his enemies.[103] We also see a reflection in the "birth pains" mentioned by Jesus in his Olivet Discourse: wars, nations rising against nations, earthquakes, famines, pestilence (see Matt 24; Mark 13; Luke 21). In both contexts and here in Rev 6, the larger point centers on God's sovereign plan of judgment and salvation.

100. See Duvall, *Revelation*, 133, for a helpful discussion of the interpretive options for reading the seal, trumpet, and bowl judgments: literal only, primarily spiritual, unknown referent, or theological value.

101. Mounce, *Revelation*, 139.

102. Beale, *Revelation*, 370–71.

103. On the symbolism of colors in Revelation, see Duvall, *Revelation*, 102.

In 6:1–8 the Lamb opens the first four seals. The four living creatures participate by calling out in a loud voice, "Come!" (6:1, 3, 5, 7). As the living creatures summon the four horsemen, John sees a horse of a particular color carrying a rider who executes the judgment. Alongside the actions of the Lamb and the four living creatures, the divine passives (i.e., "was given" in 6:2, 4 [2x], 8, 11) sharpen our focus on the outworking of God's sovereign purposes in human history. The first four seal judgments center on human depravity, showing that "God simply allows human sin to come full circle, turn in upon itself, and self-destruct."[104] Revelation reinforces the truth that often God's judgment consists of allowing evil to run its course.

The rider on the white horse has a bow and a crown to ride out as a conqueror bent on conquest (6:1–2). Because of the immediate context with the four horsemen as destructive forces, this white horse is not to be confused with the white horse ridden by the returning Christ in 19:11.[105] The judgment here represents military conquest or war, and many would have seen a reference to the first-century Parthians, Rome's powerful enemies to the east. Those mounted archers had a reputation as fierce warriors and conveyed a powerful image of a destructive military force.[106] Beyond the first century, the general impact of this image communicates the human lust for power and conquest.

The second horse, a fiery red one, supports a rider given the power to remove peace from the earth, thus paving the way for violence and warfare resulting in bloodshed (6:3–4). His large sword likely symbolizes the judgment of violent death, and John's readers might have thought of persecutions occurring under the reign of Nero or Domitian. At the opening of the third seal we see a rider on the black horse holding a pair of scales and a voice crying out about the inflated prices of wheat and barley (6:5–6). War and bloodshed eventually lead to economic hardship such as famine. The limitation on damaging the oil and the wine may reflect a measure of God's mercy in the process of judgment (cf. 7:3). When the Lamb opens the fourth seal, the fourth living creature summons a corpse-colored horse whose rider is named "Death" with "Hades" following close behind (6:7–8). This pair of destructive agents kills a fourth of humankind in four specific ways: sword, famine, plague or disease, and wild beasts (cf. Ezek 14:12–23). Although God allows human wickedness to bring its own judgment through warfare, bloodshed, famine, disease, and death, we still see a modicum of mercy in that only one-fourth are affected.

At the opening of the fifth seal, John sees the souls of martyrs under the altar being sheltered in God's presence (Rev 6:9).[107] These people have died as martyrs and now

104. Osborne, *Revelation*, 272.

105. Koester, *Revelation*, 394.

106. Fanning, *Revelation*, 241.

107. Stevenson argues for the practice of Greek altar asylum as the background, where a supplicant would gain asylum by coming into physical contact with an altar. The altar offered the protection of the deity and justice for the oppressed, and this justice also included the deity's wrath against the guilty. See Gregory Stevenson, *A Slaughtered Lamb: Revelation and the Apocalyptic Response to Evil and Suffering* (Abilene, TX: Abilene Christian University Press, 2013), 143–49.

wait under God's protective care for their coming resurrection. Unlike the earthly tabernacle and temple, Revelation envisions only one heavenly altar that unites the themes of sacrifice and prayer.[108] These martyrs met their fate because of the "word of God and the testimony" of Jesus.[109] They have imitated the slain Lamb by being faithful to God's Word even unto death (see 5:6, 9, 12; 6:4; 13:3, 8; 18:24). While literal martyrs are no doubt commended, Revelation also celebrates the martyr church—those followers of Jesus who have suffered for their faith but whose suffering does not directly result in physical death (e.g., John himself).

In 6:10 the martyrs cry out for divine justice and vindication. They address God as "Sovereign Lord" (δεσπότης), an unusual term in the New Testament that emphasizes his absolute authority and power (cf. Luke 2:29; Acts 4:24; 2 Pet 2:1; Jude 4). The martyrs affirm God's holiness and truth, essential qualities for executing justice (cf. Rev 3:7; 16:7; 19:2), but have concerns about his timing: How long until you judge? This has been an age-old question posed by God's people as a means of pleading for God's justice (e.g., Pss 79:5–10; 89:46; 119:84; Isa 6:11; Hab 1:2; Zech 1:12; Dan 12:6). They ask God to judge the "inhabitants of the earth," an expression used consistently in Revelation to describe unbelievers who rebel against God and suffer his condemnation (3:10; 6:10; 8:13; 11:10; 13:8, 12, 14 [2x]; 17:2, 8; cf. 14:6).[110] They are deceived by the beast and commit adultery with the great prostitute. They mock and persecute God's people. As a result of their rebellion, their names are not written in the book of life, and they suffer God's wrath.

In 6:11 God responds to this cry for justice and vindication. First, they are given a white robe, a symbol of honor and purity and victory (cf. 3:4–5, 18; 7:9, 13–14; 22:14). Second, they are told to "wait" or "rest" (ἀναπαύω) until God's plan has been fulfilled. This is God's answer to the "until" question. The completion of a number appears in Jewish tradition, but this number does not always refer to martyrs but can also refer to the righteous or even to people who have lived (see 1 En. 47:1–4; 4 Ezra 4:35–37; 2 Bar. 23:4–5).[111] While Rev 6:11 may be interpreted to refer to a certain number of Christians that must be killed before God will bring final justice, it does not necessarily demand such a reading. A more natural interpretation says that the martyrs must wait or rest until the people of God have finished their witness.[112] When the witness of the faithful is complete, God will bring justice and vindication. In other words, just as

108. Mounce, *Revelation*, 146–47; Koester, *Revelation*, 398. In Revelation, heaven is often portrayed as a temple, complete with an altar (e.g., 8:3–5; 9:13; 11:1; 14:17–18; 15:5; 16:7; cf. Ezek 40–48). Interestingly, sacrificial blood was poured out on the golden altar of incense on the Day of Atonement (see Exod 30:1–10; Heb 9:4).

109. *Word* and *testimony* are often connected in Revelation (e.g., 1:9; 12:11; 20:4).

110. On "The 'Inhabitants of the Earth,'" see Duvall, *Revelation*, 73.

111. Bauckham, *Climax of Prophecy*, 48–56.

112. See esp. Koester, *Revelation*, 400–401, who discusses the active vs. passive forms of "finished" (πληρόω) and the implications of each.

the martyrs under the altar rest, their fellow servants on earth must continue to bear faithful witness, unto death if necessary. Then, in God's sovereign timing, he will bring justice.

We come to the sixth seal in 6:12–17. At the end of the seal, trumpet, and bowl judgments, we arrive at the end of history. This section begins with a series of cosmic disturbances (6:12–14) that are often used to portray the coming apart of the cosmos at the final judgment, both in the Old Testament (e.g., Isa 13:10–13; 24:1–6, 17–23; 34:4; Ezek 32:6–8; Joel 2:10, 30–31; 3:15–16; Hab 3:6–11) and in the teachings of Jesus (e.g., Mark 13:24–27 and par. in Matt 24:29–31; Luke 21:25–28; cf. Acts 2:19–20; 2 Pet 3:10). As Jesus returns in power and glory to redeem his people and judge the wicked, the universe gives way (i.e., earthquakes, sun turning dark, moon turning red, stars falling, sky receding, mountains and islands being removed). The Day of the Lord has arrived! Whether these events are literal or metaphorical, the effect on the readers and hearers would have been terrifying.[113]

Divine justice reaches all, even those in places of power (Rev 6:15–16). The sevenfold classification of earth dwellers symbolizes the exhaustive nature of God's judgment (cf. a similar list in 19:18). Osborne writes, "Terror is a great equalizer, and all social distinctions drop away in light of the shaking of the heavens and the arrival of the terrible judgment of God."[114] They first attempt to hide, then plead for a quick death also, as means of hiding from the face of God and the wrath of the Lamb (cf. Isa 2:10, 19–21; Hos 10:8; Luke 23:30).[115] In contrast, believers are comforted by the promise of one day seeing God's face (Rev 22:4).

Revelation 6 closes with a rhetorical question of utmost importance: "Who can withstand [the great day of the wrath of God and the Lamb]?" (6:17). This question recalls day of the Lord passages from the Old Testament (e.g., Joel 2:10–11, 31; Zeph 1:14–18; Mal 4:1, 5; cf. also 1 Thess 5:2; 2 Pet 3:10) and serves as a reminder that no one can withstand or endure the wrath of God and the Lamb unless they have been sealed or protected by God himself—the topic of the interlude in Revelation 7. The opening of the seventh seal must wait until 8:1 and provides a transition to the next series of judgments.

11.4.3.2 The First Interlude (7:1–17)

Revelation features a series of interludes that shed light on the situation faced by God's people, their present responsibilities, and their future hope. These intercalations slow down the narrative pace and draw the reader's attention to what is most important. The interludes of Revelation 7 stand between the sixth and seventh seal judgments

113. Beale and Carson, *New Testament Use of the Old Testament*, 1105. Their suggestion that this is a "figurative scene of the beginning of the literal final judgment" merits consideration.

114. Osborne, *Revelation*, 294.

115. Mangina, *Revelation*, 106, observes: "The earth-dwellers' terror before their Creator is such that they would rather *un*make the life he has made and given them. Better to die, it would seem, than to fall into the hands of the living God."

and consist of two visions: the protective sealing of the 144,000 on earth (7:1–8) and the celebration of the great multitude in heaven (7:9–17). These two visions depict the people of God from two different vantage points. In 7:1–8 we see the saints on earth prepared to do spiritual battle and protected from divine judgments to come. In 7:9–17 we see the same group in heaven celebrating God's faithfulness.

11.4.3.2.1 God's People Protected on Earth (7:1–8)

Chapter 6 concludes with a question: Who can withstand the wrath of God and the Lamb? Answer? Only those who have been sealed or protected by God (6:17). The first interlude of 7:1–8 portrays the people of God sealed before the outpouring of God's judgments. They are protected from God's wrath but are not exempted from the wrath of the beast and his followers. This explains why God's people will never experience the condemning judgment or wrath of God (Rom 8:1) but may encounter opposition, persecution, and even martyrdom as a result of living faithfully in this world.

In Revelation 7:1 we see four angels standing at the four corners of the earth restraining the four winds.[116] The winds are best viewed as destructive forces now held back by God's sovereign command (cf. Dan 7:2–3; Jer 49:36). The servants of God must first be sealed or protected before these winds of judgment blow across the earth. In 7:2–3 another angel comes from the east carrying "the seal (σφραγίς) of the living God" and warning the four angels not to harm anything until a seal has been placed on the foreheads of the servants of God.[117] The seal stands in contrast to the "mark of the beast," and both marks indicate loyalty and ownership since both are placed on a person's forehead (e.g., Rev 7:3; 9:4 with 13:16; 14:9; 20:4) and are tied to the names of God and the Lamb or to the beast (Rev 7:3; 22:4 with 13:17; 14:11; 15:2).[118] The seal here indicates spiritual protection and only those who have been sealed by God may withstand his coming wrath (6:17–7:4; 9:3–4; cf. Ezek 9:4–6). Those not sealed will be deceived by the forces of evil and suffer God's wrath (Rev 13:7–8; 14:9–11). God's seal assures believers that he will protect them spiritually even though they may suffer persecution, even martyrdom. It also distinguishes them from the inhabitants of the earth.

John then hears the number of those sealed as "144,000 from all the tribes of Israel" (7:4).

The number 144,000 appears only in Rev 7:4 and in 14:1, 3, where both interludes stress God's protection of the righteous. Some take the 144,000 in chapter 7 to refer to

116. In apocalyptic literature angels are sometimes put in charge of nature (cf. Rev 14:18; 16:5; Zech 6:5) and here the phrase "four corners of the earth" indicates every part of the world, and perhaps entrances to the underworld are also in view (cf. Ezek 7:2; Isa 11:12; Matt 24:31; Rev 20:8).

117. For more on the "seal of the living God," see Beale, *Revelation*, 409–15, who rightly concludes that "in the light of the broader theology of the NT, the 'seal' may best be identified with the Holy Spirit, since the seal primarily connotes a guarantee of spiritual protection (cf. a similar function of 'seal' as the Holy Spirit in 2 Cor 1:22, Eph. 1:13 and 4:30). However, John never explicitly states this" (p. 415).

118. Duvall, *Revelation*, 114. Also, see "Seal of the Living God" in Hays, Duvall, and Pate, *A-to-Z Guide to Biblical Prophecy*, 403–4.

literal Israel or to a Jewish remnant,[119] but it is more likely that the group represents the true people of God, the whole company of the redeemed, in both chapters 7 and 14.[120]

The number itself results from multiplying the square of twelve by one thousand, emphasizing the people of God in its totality and fullness. Numbers in Revelation normally represent reality figuratively.[121] In addition, the expression "servants [δοῦλος] of . . . God" (7:3) portrays all believers throughout the book (e.g., 1:1; 2:20; 6:11; 10:7; 11:18; 19:2, 5, 10; 22:3, 6, 9; cf. 1 Cor 7:22; Col 4:12; 1 Pet 2:16; Jude 1), and the seal of God is applied to all believers throughout Revelation (7:3–5; 9:4; 14:1; cf. also 3:12; 22:4). There are a number of problems with a literal reading (e.g., does 14:4 really mean that only 144,000 male virgins from twelve tribes of Israel will be protected?).[122] Bauckham, Keener, and others are surely correct in viewing this text as a form of census used to assess military preparation (Num 1:3, 18, 20; 26:2, 4; 1 Chr 27:23). That explains the mention of adult males in Rev 14:4 and why a certain number would be drafted from each tribe (cf. Num 1:20–47). Here we see the people of God arrayed as a messianic army prepared for spiritual battle.[123]

11.4.3.2.2 God's People Celebrating in Heaven (7:9–17)

The single vision portraying the people of God from two different perspectives continues. Here we have another example of John *hearing* about one reality (7:4) while *seeing* another (7:9; cf. 5:5–6). Eugene Boring sums it up this way: "As 7:1–8 presents the church militant on earth, sealed and drawn up in battle formation before the coming struggle, 7:9–17 presents the church after the battle, triumphant in heaven."[124] This unit consists of three sections: the great multitude and company of angels worshiping God and the Lamb in 7:9–12, the identification of the great multitude in 7:13–14, and the great multitude being comforted and sheltered in God's presence in 7:15–17.

In 7:9 John's vision shifts to the heavenly throne room where he sees an innumerable multitude drawn from "every nation, tribe, people and language" (also 5:9; 10:11; 11:9;

119. See, e.g., Walvoord, *Revelation*, 140–41; Thomas, *Revelation 1–7*, 473–82; Fanning, *Revelation*, 262–64, who concludes: "John affirms the widespread ancient Jewish expectation of the regathering in the end-times of all the tribes of ethnic Israel from their exile among the nations" (p. 263).

120. So Mayo, *"Those Who Call Themselves Jews,"* 77–106; Beale, *Revelation*, 416–23; Smalley, *Revelation*, 184–88, and most commentators.

121. See Mark Wilson, *Charts on the Book of Revelation*, 47–49, for the symbolism of numbers in Revelation.

122. For a summary of such difficulties, see Eckhard Schnabel, *40 Questions about the End Times* (Grand Rapids: Kregel, 2011), 86–89. See Mark Wilson, *Charts on the Book of Revelation*, 79, for a comparison of the Old Testament lists of tribes with the list in Revelation. The list in Revelation does not agree with any Old Testament list of tribes, and even those lists do not agree. Also, by John's time most tribes were unidentifiable. More positively, the list of tribes in verses 5–8 hints at a symbolic interpretation (Duvall, *Revelation*, 115): "Judah heads the list because this is the tribe to which Jesus belonged. The tribe of Dan is missing, likely due to its association with idolatry and apostasy, as is Ephraim, perhaps due to its opposition to Judah. Levi is included, maybe because the people of God are portrayed in Revelation as priests. Finally, the term 'tribe' (*phylē*) is used throughout Revelation in a universal sense (e.g., 1:7; 5:9; 14:6; 21:12)."

123. Bauckham, *Climax of Prophecy*, 216 M. Eugene–18; Keener, *Revelation*, 230; Smalley, *Revelation*, 186–88.

124. M. Eugene Boring, *Revelation*, Interpretation (Louisville: John Knox, 1989), 131.

13:7; 14:6; 17:15). This multicultural community stands before the throne and the Lamb, once again showing the unity of the Father and the Son (cf. 7:10, 17). The redeemed are dressed in white robes, symbolizing purity and victory (cf. 3:4–5; 6:11), and holding palm branches, also indicating victory.[125] They cry out in praise to God and the Lamb for providing "salvation" (σωτηρία), a term that emphasizes the victory or deliverance from evil and deliverance into God's presence (cf. Rev 12:10; 19:1). God has been faithful to provide salvation through the Lamb and to protect his people spiritually through tribulation. Now the great multitude around the throne is joined by throngs of angels, along with the elders and the four living creatures (7:11). As Smalley observes, "the air is thick with angels in Revelation."[126] The heavenly beings prostrate themselves before the throne and offer worship bracketed by two exclamations of "Amen!" (7:12). Their sevenfold doxology ascribes full praise to God for rescuing a people and bringing them into his presence (cf. Rev 5:12 where many of these qualities are directed toward the Lamb). Worship is indeed the fitting response to God's provision of salvation through Jesus.

The great multitude is identified in 7:13–14. One of the elders/angels asks John a twofold rhetorical question about the identity and origin of those dressed in white, John pleads ignorance, and the elder supplies the explanation. The elder identifies the great multitude as those "who have come out of the great tribulation; they have washed their robes and made them white in the blood of the Lamb" (7:14). We understand "great tribulation" to refer to a period of trial (e.g., persecution, imprisonment, poverty, and even death) that God's people endure in the last days, which extend from the first to the second coming of Christ (Rev 1:9; 2:9, 22; 7:14; John 16:33).[127] The trial may intensify at the end of the age but will be a continuation of what has already begun. The tribulation is both a past and present reality as well as a future certainty. The present participle (ἐρχόμενοι) is translated "have come" because of its relationship with the aorist verbs in the context ("have washed" and "made white") and points to a past experience—these people have come through this tribulation (perhaps through martyrdom) and arrived victoriously in heaven.

Paradoxically, these victors have their robes made white by washing them in red blood (1:5; 12:11). These robes also link them to the martyrs of 6:11 and the suffering but protected saints of 7:1–8. Their faith in the sacrificial death (blood) of Christ has resulted in their redemption and purification (cf. 22:14; Heb 9:23; 1 John 1:7; Exod 19:10, 14; Isa 1:18).[128]

In Rev 7:15–17 we see the multitude comforted and protected in God's presence. These who have persevered through tribulation by faith in the redemptive work of

125. See David E. Aune, *Revelation 6–16*, WBC 52B (Dallas: Word, 1998), 448–50, 468–70, for a possible connection to the Feast of Booths.

126. Smalley, *Revelation*, 193.

127. Duvall, *Revelation*, 48; Hays, Duvall, and Pate, *A-to-Z Guide to Biblical Prophecy*, 191–94, 451–53; Smalley, *Revelation*, 196; Beale, *Revelation*, 433–35.

128. Duvall, *Revelation*, 120.

Christ now experience the blessings of God's eternal presence. They are "before the throne of God," indicating they live in his presence. They "serve" (λατρεύω) him continuously, a term that shows a connection between service and worship. The celebration of service/worship also reminds the readers that present sufferings are not worth comparing to life in God's glorious presence to come (cf. Rom 8:18; 2 Cor 4:17–5:1; Jude 24–25; Rev 21:1–4). The end of Revelation stresses the heavenly temple as the presence of God (21:3–4, 22; 22:3; cf. Ezek 37:26–28) and here God will "shelter" or "tabernacle over" (σκηνόω) the multitude. Tabernacle language also recalls God's protection and guidance of his people during their wilderness journey as he covered them with his glorious presence (e.g., Exod 13:21–22; 33:7–11; 40:34–38).[129]

Revelation 7:16–17 spells out some of what this divine sheltering includes by alluding to promises originally made to exiles returning from Babylon in Isa 49:10. The "never again" language brings comfort to Christians who have come out of exile in a different Babylon. The comfort is rooted in a person—the Lamb at the center of the throne (another example of Revelation's high Christology) will shepherd them and lead them to springs of living water (the Spirit?). The powerful irony of a Lamb serving as a shepherd picks up the biblical motif of the Lord as the shepherd of his people (Gen 49:24; Ps 23; Isa 40:11; Ezek 34:23; John 10; 1 Pet 2:25; Heb 13:20). The scene concludes as God himself wipes away every tear of suffering with the tender hand of a loving Father (cf. Rev 21:4; Isa 25:8; 65:19).

11.4.4 The Trumpet Judgments (8:1–11:19)

In 8:1–6 the seventh seal is broken and silence in heaven creates the proper setting for the prayers of the saints. This in turn leads to the trumpet judgments of 8:7–9:21, which are in part God's response to the cries of his people for deliverance and justice. Following the trumpet judgments, we encounter the second set of interludes in 10:1–11:14, also featuring two visions: the mighty angel and the little scroll in 10:1–11 and the two witnesses in 11:1–14. The theme of witness unites these two visions that tell us more about God's people and their role in God's plan. The seventh trumpet in 11:15–19 brings us to the consummation of God's kingdom, a topic detailed more fully in chapters 19–22.

11.4.4.1 Transition: The Seventh Seal and Preparation for the Seven Trumpets (8:1–6)

In the seal and trumpet judgments we see a 4 + 2 + 1 pattern with an interlude coming before the seventh element. Following the interludes of chapter 7, the opening of the seventh seal in 8:1 leads to silence in heaven for about half an hour (8:1). A "half

129. Revelation has a total of seven occurrences of the terms "tabernacle over" (σκηνόω—7:15; 12:12; 13:6; 21:3) and "tabernacle" (σκηνή—13:6; 15:5; 21:3).

hour" represents an interruption or delay in the movement toward a climactic event.[130] But the delay has purpose that reaches back to the martyrs' prayer for justice in 6:10. Bauckham examines other apocalyptic texts where silence in heaven allows the prayers of God's people to be heard and concludes, "At the climax of history, heaven is silent so that the prayers of the saints can be heard, and the final judgment occurs in response to them (v. 5)."[131] The silence creates the setting for prayers (8:2–6) that lead into the trumpet judgments (8:7–9:21).

In 8:2 the seven angels who stand before God are given seven trumpets. The seven angels are perhaps a reference to the seven archangels of Jewish tradition: Uriel, Raphael, Raguel, Michael, Saraqa'el, Gabriel, and Ramiel (1 En. 20:1–8). God is the ultimate source of the seven trumpets as the divine passive indicates ("were given").[132] Trumpets are used in various Old Testament settings (e.g., to warn of an attack or to signal retreat in war, to sound the alarm, to celebrate victory or good news, to enthrone a king) and in the New Testament are often associated with Christ's second coming (e.g., Matt 24:31; 1 Cor 15:52; 1 Thess 4:16). In this context, the trumpets announce the coming judgments of God.

Another angel, separate from the seven angels, approaches God's presence carrying a golden censer or firepan (Rev 8:3). The "altar" and the "golden altar" refer to the one heavenly altar (cf. 6:9). The angel is given much incense to offer with the prayers of the saints (not just the martyrs), ensuring the prayers will be heard (8:3). The coals of prayer being sprinkled with incense now ascend to God as a fragrant aroma (cf. Exod 29:18; Lev 1:9; Num 18:17; Ps 141:2; 2 Cor 2:14–17; Eph 5:2; Phil 4:18).[133]

In 8:5 the prayers are answered with plagues. God hears the cries of his people for justice and deliverance and responds with judgment fires (cf. Exod 19:16, 18; Ezek 10:2–7). God's answer is accompanied by the shaking of the cosmos (cf. Rev 4:5; 6:12–14; 11:19; 16:18–21), culminating in an eschatological earthquake signaling the coming of God in judgment.[134]

In 8:6 the seven angels prepare to sound their trumpets.

11.4.4.2 The First Six Trumpets (8:7–9:21)

There are clear parallels between the first four trumpet judgments and the plagues of Egypt (see the chart Seal, Trumpet, and Bowl Judgments below). This exodus typology

130. Resseguie, *Revelation*, 142, observes that the "importance lies not in being half of an *hour* but in being a *half*" (i.e., a broken hour).

131. Bauckham, *Climax of Prophecy*, 71. See the excurses on the silence in 8:1 in *Climax of Prophecy*, 70–81, and Beale, *Revelation*, 446–54, who observes that divine judgment is often associated with silence in the Old Testament. Also, Smalley's survey of interpretive options is helpful (*Revelation*, 211–12).

132. For other divine passives in the context, see 8:3; 9:1, 3–4, 15.

133. Osborne, *Revelation*, 345, notes the contrast between the smoke of the prayers and the smoke of 9:2; 14:11; and 19:3 (i.e., the smoke of torment of evildoers)—the smoke of worship contrasted with the smoke of judgment.

134. See "The Eschatological Earthquake" in Bauckham, *Climax of Prophecy*, 199–209.

highlights God's power over creation and human history, including the competing gods and idols of every age. God responds to the cries of his people by judging evil, but he does so with a degree of mercy at this point, allowing for unbelievers to repent (e.g., 9:20–21). These plagues also serve as a prelude to God's final deliverance of his people from evil and into the new promised land.

SEAL, TRUMPET, AND BOWL JUDGMENTS[135]

	Seals (6:1–17; 8:1)	**Trumpets (8:6–9:21; 11:14–19)**	**Interlude: 12:1–14:20**	**Bowls (16:1–21)**
1	White horse—military conquest	Hail and fire, mixed with blood, burn up ⅓ of earth		Sores on those with beast's mark
2	Red horse—violent bloodshed	Burning mountain causes ⅓ of sea to turn to blood and destroys ⅓ of creatures and ships		Sea turns to blood and everything in it dies
3	Black horse—famine	Blazing star (Wormwood) turns ⅓ of fresh water bitter, killing many people		Rivers and springs turned to blood
4	Pale horse—Death and Hades bring death to 1/4 of earth	⅓ of sun, moon, and stars turned dark		Sun scorches people with fire and they curse God
5	Martyrs cry out to God for vindication and are told to wait	Fallen star opens Abyss, releasing locust-scorpions to harm those without seal of God for five months		Throne of beast cursed with darkness and people in agony curse God
6	Shaking of entire cosmos, followed by the wicked attempting to hide from wrath of God and Lamb	Release of four angels bound at Euphrates, who then raise an army of serpent-lions to kill ⅓ of people on earth		River Euphrates dries up as demonic forces gather kings of earth for Armageddon
	Interlude: 7:1–17	Interlude: 10:1–11:14		No Interlude
7	Silence + seven trumpets	Christ's kingdom arrives as elders thank God for his judgment, rewarding of saints, and vindication of his people	**Interlude: 12:1–14:20**	Voice from temple says, "It is done," followed by storm-quake and destruction of Babylon by God; islands and mountains disappear and huge hailstones fall on people who respond by cursing God
	Storm-earthquake at 8:3 – 5	Storm-earthquake at 11:19		Storm-earthquake at 16:18

135. Duvall, *Revelation*, 127.

11.4.4.2.1 The First Four Trumpets (8:7–12)

The first trumpet brings hail and fire mixed with blood so that a third of the earth, a third of the trees, and all the green grass are burned up (8:7). This recalls the seventh plague on the Egyptians, where God sends lightning, thunder, and a huge hailstorm that devastates the land. The addition of fire and blood in Revelation adds to the judgment motif (e.g., Joel 2:30–31; Ezek 21:32; 38:22). This trumpet depicts a "natural" disaster of epic proportions. Yet the figure of "a third" that is repeated throughout shows how God's judgment ramps up from the "one-fourth" of the seal judgments but is yet to arrive at the fullness of the bowl judgments where no fractions are used.

The second trumpet produces a fiery mountain being thrown into the sea, which causes a third of the sea to turn to blood, a third of the sea creatures to die, and the destruction of a third of the ships (Rev 8:8–9). Here we see an allusion to the first Egyptian plague where God turns the Nile River into blood. Beale argues for Jer 51 as the primary background, where Babylon is described as a blazing mountain; thus, the blazing mountain represents the judgment of a wicked kingdom (cf. Rev 18).[136] The destruction of a third of sea life and shipping would have brought devastating economic consequences to Roman society so dependent on sea trade.

At the sounding of the third trumpet, a blazing star falls from the sky and a third of the rivers and freshwater springs turn bitter, causing many to die from the contaminated water. The name of the star is Wormwood (ἀψίνθιον), perhaps deriving its name from the plant, which produced a dark green bitter oil used to kill intestinal worms. The context does not support a reference to a fallen angel here but instead symbolizes bitterness and affliction resulting from God's judgment (e.g., the first plague in Exod 7:14–24; cf. Jer 9:15; 23:15; Deut 29:17–18).

The fourth trumpet brings darkness to a third of the sun, moon, and stars and to a third of the day and night. This draws on the ninth Egyptian plague when thick darkness covered the land (Exod 10:21–23). Darkness is used throughout Scripture to symbolize divine judgment (e.g., Isa 13:10–11; Joel 2:1–2; Amos 5:18, 20; 8:9; Matt 8:12; Mark 13:24–25; John 3:18–21; 2 Cor 6:14–15). God partially reverses creation as his judgment brings total darkness (cf. Gen 1:14–19).

11.4.4.2.2 The Fifth Trumpet (First Woe) (8:13–9:11)

The eagle's flight in 8:13 provides a short transition from the first four trumpets to the last three.

In the first four, God pours out his judgment primarily on creation and this indirectly

136. Beale, *Revelation*, 476. Interestingly, "ships" are mentioned only here and in 18:19 in Revelation.

affects humanity, but the last three fall directly on unbelievers—the "inhabitants of the earth," a phrase used ten times in Revelation to designate the rebellious (see 6:10). As with other midair announcements in Revelation (see 14:6; 19:17), this one points to a coming judgment (cf. Jer 4:13; 48:40; Ezek 17:3; Hos 8:1; Hab 1:8). The eagle (or perhaps vulture) announces triple "woes" to come, and these correspond to the remaining three trumpets. This threefold "woe" is similar to the "woe oracles" used often in the Prophets to proclaim a coming judgment on the rebellious.

The fifth angel sounds his trumpet and John sees a fallen star that is likely an angelic agent of judgment sent from God (Rev 9:1). The parallel in 20:1–3 clearly marks the figure as an angel sent from heaven to earth on a mission, and such is also the case here. The term "fallen" is not used in a theological sense of spiritually fallen, as with Satan or the demonic (e.g., Jude 13; Luke 10:18; Rev 12:9), but in the physical sense of movement from heaven to earth to carry out its divine mission.[137] The angel/star is given the key to the shaft of the "Abyss," a term used seven times in Revelation to denote the abode or prison for various evil creatures: demonic locusts (9:1, 2; cf. Luke 8:31; also 2 Pet 2:4; Jude 6); Apollyon, the king of the locusts (Rev 9:11); the beast (11:7; 17:8); and Satan (20:1, 3). That God remains in sovereign control over the entire universe, the underworld included, is implied by the divine passives ("was/were given") in 9:1, 3, 4, 5, 15. When the shaft is opened, smoke rises from this demonic furnace to darken the sun and the sky (9:2).

The fifth trumpet recalls the eighth Egyptian plague of locusts that blacken the ground (Exod 10:1–20) and especially the army of invading locusts mentioned in Joel 1–2. These demonic locusts with scorpion-like power are determined to torture anyone not bearing the seal of God (Rev 9:3–4; cf. 7:1–8). They are warned specifically not to harm creation but only the unsealed. They are not allowed to kill them but only torture them for five months, perhaps alluding to the five-month life cycle of a locust or to the dry season when locusts would invade.[138] Whatever the background, this would have been an unbearable time of being "tortured" (βασανίζω in 9:5; 11:10; 12:2; 14:10; 20:10) and enduring "agony" (βασανισμός in 9:5 [2x]; 14:11; 18:7, 10, 15). The unbelievers will wish they were dead to escape the demonic assault, but death will elude them (9:6). Ironically, they are unwilling to repent in order to find life (9:20–21). Smalley correctly concludes that "the fifth trumpet-call is designed to challenge the persecutors of the saints, and those who are tempted to compromise with them, to realize that idolatry and syncretism are without hope, and to bring the rebels back to faith."[139] This provides another example of God allowing evil (demonic locusts) to

137. Mathewson also notes that the perfect participle πεπτωκότα "draws attention to the state of the star (falling) in preparation for the act that is to follow: the loosing of the locusts" (*Revelation*, 116).

138. Mounce, *Revelation*, 497.

139. Smalley, *Revelation*, 230.

judge evil (the inhabitants of the earth). It also serves as part of God's answer to the cry for justice in 6:10.

The origin of these attackers in the Abyss (9:2–3), their hideous appearance (9:7–10), and the demonic nature of their leader (9:11) reinforce their demonic identity. In 9:7–10 John draws on the background imagery of Joel 1–2 to describe these diabolical monsters, making extensive use of simile (using the Greek terms ὅμοιος and ὡς). These other-worldly creatures are "like" things in our world, but their traits are combined in awful ways (e.g., a woman's hair and lion's teeth). The particulars are not as important as the overall chilling impact on the hearer. Evil destroys evil as these cruel creatures are permitted to attack and torment those who oppose God and persecute his people. Caird pinpoints the theological importance of a central aspect of their appearance—their human faces in Rev 9:7: "Evil may take many sinister forms and ramify far beyond the immediate implications of individual sin; but in the last analysis it has a human face, for it is caused by the rebellion of human wills against the will of God."[140] This demonic hoard is permitted to bring judgment for a limited time upon those who oppose God and persecute his people.[141] Their king is "the angel of the Abyss," whose name is Abaddon or Apollyon, meaning "the Destroyer" (9:11). This could refer to Satan himself, the prince of demons (Mark 3:22 par.; Matt 9:34; John 12:31; 14:30; 16:11) or, more likely, to one of Satan's chief leaders since Satan is named elsewhere in Revelation (2:9, 13, 24; 3:9; 12:9; 20:2, 7). This devil-like figure leads his demonic army to bring judgment on the unrighteousness.

11.4.4.2.3 The Sixth Trumpet (Second Woe) (9:12–21)

The sixth trumpet (second woe) continues the outpouring of God's wrath on rebellious humanity in response to the cries of his people for justice. Judgment intensifies with the sixth trumpet as the demonic army moves beyond torturing to killing. The final result, however, is discouraging as rebellious humanity still refuses to repent, preferring idolatry and immorality to change (9:20–21). Prior to the seventh and final trumpet in 11:15–19 we find an extensive interlude in 10:1–11:13.

Following the announcement of the coming second woe (9:12), a voice from the four horns of the one heavenly altar provides instructions (9:13; cf. 6:9). Much like 14:18 where an angel comes from the altar and 16:7 where the altar speaks, here the altar represents the presence of God. The voice commands the sixth angel to release the four angels bound at the great river Euphrates (9:14). Their binding points to their demonic character in contrast to the four angels in 7:1 who hold back the four

140. Caird, *Revelation of Saint John*, 120.

141. The term for "torment" in verse 10 (ἀδικέω) is different from similar terms used in 9:5 and carries the sense of hurt, harm, damage, injure, or torment in Rev 2:11; 6:6; 7:2, 3; 9:4, 10, 19; 11:5 [2x].

winds. They are better compared to the four destructive winds themselves (cf. Dan 7:2; Zech 6:5–8; 2 Bar. 6:4–5; 7:1; 8:1). Much like the angel from the Abyss leads the demonic army of locusts in the fifth trumpet, the four angels here seem to lead or at least set in motion the demonic horsemen of Rev 9:16–19. The river Euphrates has historically been a barrier between Israel and its enemies (e.g., Assyria, Babylonia) and later between Rome and the Parthians. As a result, "the great river Euphrates" becomes part of John's symbolic geography representing a threat from an invading army (cf. 12:15–16; 16:12).[142] Suffering in trumpet judgment five now leads to death in judgment six (9:15). The death to a fourth of the earth in seal four (6:8) is elevated to the death of a third of humanity in trumpet six. The context continues to suggest that only unbelievers are vulnerable to judgment while believers have been sealed (cf. 3:10; 6:10; 7:1–8; 8:13; 9:4). In addition, another divine passive ("had been kept ready") plus the hour-day-month-year allusion reminds the reader of God's sovereign control over the timing of the coming judgment.

In 9:16–19 we come to one of the more colorful texts in the Apocalypse. There is an abrupt shift from the four destructive angels in the previous section to a large number of mounted troops in 9:16. Most commentators see the angels as leaders or at least instigators of this army. As with other numbers in Revelation, one should look first to its figurative significance, and here two hundred million symbolizes "an indefinite number of incalculable immensity."[143] With a standing Roman army of around 125,000 and an auxiliary army about the same size, the demonic army would be roughly eight hundred times more powerful than the world's most powerful army at the time.[144] This would have been overwhelming and shocking to John's first audience. In contrast, God's end-time army of 144,000 seems extremely small, thus focusing attention on God's power and strength in the battle.

In 9:17 John describes this hideous demonic army in manner reminiscent of the Greco-Roman mythological Chimera, a fire-breathing monster with a lion's head, a goat's body, and a snake's tail.[145] More specifically, the background is likely tied to the Parthian cavalry whose horses and riders wore bright armor,[146] and even more so to various Old Testament contexts of fire, sulfur, and smoke judgments (e.g., Gen 19:24, 28; Deut 29:23; 2 Sam 22:9; Job 41:19–21; Isa 34:9–10; Ezek 38:22).[147] Aune observes a chiastic *inclusio* in Rev 9:17b–18 that centers on the plagues of fire, smoke, and sulfur spewing from the mouth of the demonic horses that kill a third of

142. Resseguie, *Revelation*, 148.

143. "δισμυριάς," BDAG 252. This is double the number of worshiping angels in 5:11; cf. Dan 7:10.

144. David Kennedy, "Roman Army," *ABD* 5:791–92. Osborne, *Revelation*, 381, wisely reminds modern readers that "those who point to the size of modern armies like that of China, which is sometimes reported at 200 million, are missing the point. To get a similar effect, one would have to posit an army of *six billion* demonic cavalry today [2002]."

145. Homer, *Il.* 6.181–82. Koester, *Revelation*, 467.

146. Osborne, *Revelation*, 382.

147. Beale, *Revelation*, 511; Fanning, *Revelation*, 304.

humanity.[148] The spoken nature of these plagues may point to deceptive false teaching that promotes idolatry and immorality. The horses' serpent-like tails also inflict injury and would remind readers of the Satanic nature of their deadly attacks (9:19).[149]

Revelation 9:20–21 recaps the disastrous reaction of rebellious humanity to the first six trumpet judgments. Those not killed still refuse to repent. As Mounce writes, "Once the heart is set in its hostility toward God not even the scourge of death will lead people to repentance."[150] Ironically and tragically, those who survive the demonic plagues continue to worship the forces trying to kill them. Here we meet the first of three vice lists in Revelation (see also 21:8 and 22:15). They refuse to repent of their idolatry and immorality—the worship of various idols defined here as demon worship—along with murders, magic arts, sexual immorality, and thieving.[151] God's judgments are not capricious. Rather, they are handed out on those who repeatedly and stubbornly refuse to repent. The inhabitants of the earth have repeatedly rejected God's gracious advances and have chosen idols of their own making. The message of the first six trumpets affirms the depths and fatality of human sin. Idolatry means giving oneself to self-destructive demon worship. Sinful humanity refuses to repent and remains hostile to God, whose judgments are just.[152]

11.4.4.3 The Second Interlude (10:1–11:14)

Between the sixth and seventh seal judgments we encountered two visions: the 144,000 in 7:1–8 and the great multitude in 7:9–17. Likewise, between the sixth and seventh trumpet judgments we see an interlude with two visions: the mighty angel and the little scroll in 10:1–11 with the renewal of John's prophetic commission, and the vision of the two witnesses in 11:1–14, featuring the role and destiny of the witnessing church. Later with the bowl judgments we find no such interlude between the sixth and seventh elements. Things are simply moving too fast at that point.

The interludes in Revelation typically serve to clarify the role of God's people and to offer heavenly perspective that spurs them on to faithful endurance. In 10:1–11:14 the theme of prophecy stands strong: John's role as prophet and the church's role as witness.[153] The first vision in this interlude (10:1–11) features John being commanded to participate in his own vision by eating a little scroll in Ezekiel-like fashion.

148. Aune, *Revelation 6–16*, 540.

149. See Beale's excursus on "The Metaphorical Associations of Serpents and Scorpions in Judaism," in *Revelation*, 515–16.

150. Mounce, *Revelation*, 198.

151. The addition of "magic arts" relates especially to the local context of the churches in Asia, where believers faced enormous challenges from the practice of magic (e.g., Acts 19:19; Gal 5:19–20; Rev 18:23; 21:8; 22:15). See Clinton E. Arnold, "Magic and Astrology," *DLNT* 701–5.

152. See "Repent in Revelation" in Duvall, *Revelation*, 139.

153. Note the use of prophetic language: "to prophesy" in 10:11; 11:3; "prophet" in 10:7; 11:10; and "prophecy" ("prophesying" in NIV) in 11:6. Smalley, *Revelation*, 253–54, provides literary and theological reasons for linking the two visions of this interlude. Osborne, *Revelation*, 390, notes how the entire first half of Revelation is framed by the motif of prophetic witness (i.e., 1:9–20 and 10:1–11:13).

11.4.4.3.1 John Recommissioned to Prophesy (10:1–11)

John sees "another mighty angel" descending from heaven (10:1), the second of three mighty angels in Revelation (cf. 5:2; 18:21). The first two are associated with the scroll of God's redemptive plan. John's description of this second angel sounds a lot like his description of Christ in 1:12–16 with attributes given only to God in the Old Testament or to God and Christ in Revelation, leading Beale to conclude that this heavenly being is "either the divine Christ or the divine angel of Yahweh."[154] While the exalted portrayal of this second mighty angel is lofty indeed, the fact that Christ never appears elsewhere in Revelation as an angel, that this angel mediates between John and the Godhead, and that it seems out of place for Christ to take an oath (10:6), leads us to conclude with Smalley that this angel is a "heavenly representative of Jesus, who possesses characteristics of Christ," but is not Christ himself.[155]

The mighty angel holds a "little scroll" (βιβλαρίδιον, referred to as βιβλίον in v. 8) open in his hand. There is debate about whether the "scroll" (βιβλίον) of Rev 5 is identical to the little scroll here in chapter 10.[156] There are differences between the two scrolls to be sure (e.g., scroll vs. little scroll, sealed vs. open, heavenly scene vs. earthly scene), but the similarities point to a single scroll. Both are held by a mighty angel, both allude to Ezekiel's prophetic calling (Ezek 2:9–3:3), and both focus on God's redemptive purpose for the world. The differences likely highlight that God's plan is being viewed from different vantage points. The scroll of Rev 5 centers on the redemptive work of the Lamb who opens the scroll's seven seals in chapter 6, while the little scroll lies open in the angel's hand. The focus now shifts to how the witnessing church, including John, will carry out God's plan.[157] This scroll reveals more about how God will defeat evil once and for all, rescue his people, and transform creation, and how this relates to God's people on earth.

The mighty angel shouts and the seven thunders speak (10:3b–4). John is prepared to write down what the thunders have said but a heavenly voice commands him instead to seal up (keep secret or not disclose) their message (note a parallel command in Dan 8:26; 12:4, 9, and a contrasting command in Rev 1:19; 22:10). Thunder is usually connected to judgment in Revelation, suggesting that the seven thunders are yet another series of judgments (cf. 4:5; 6:1; 8:5; 11:19; 16:18). Many have speculated about why John is told to seal up the thunders. The most convincing explanation relates to the angel's proclamation in verse 6 that "there will be no more delay," which yet another series of judgments would have prolonged. The thunders then will

154. Beale, *Revelation*, 522.

155. Smalley, *Revelation*, 258. He speculates that this angel could be Michael, who represents Christ in 12:7–9, or Gabriel, whose name means "strong man of God" and is linked to the Hebrew term for "strong."

156. Mark Wilson, "Revelation," 308–9, suggests that perhaps the designation "little scroll" says more about the large size of the mighty angel than the small size of the book.

157. Resseguie, *Revelation*, 153.

stay sealed, but the scroll lies open, both images suggesting no further delay in the fulfillment of God's purposes.

In 10:5–7 the mighty angel swears an oath, the only oath in Revelation. The threefold repetition of the angel standing on the sea and the land points to God's sovereign control over his world (10:2, 5, 8). The mighty angel raises his right hand to heaven and swears to the God who is both eternal ("who lives for ever and ever") and Creator ("who created the heavens, . . . the earth . . . and the sea"). God is the eternal Maker of all the actors in this cosmic drama and therefore has power over them. But why an oath? The background is Dan 12, where Daniel asks about the end of time: "How long will it be before these astonishing things are fulfilled?" (Dan 12:6). Daniel learns of a delay from "the man clothed in linen," who lifts his hands toward heaven and swears by "him who lives forever" (Dan 12:7–9). What is delayed in Daniel is about to be fulfilled: "There will be no more delay!" (10:6).[158]

God has not forgotten the martyrs' prayer of 6:10. When the seventh angel sounds his trumpet, "the mystery of God will be accomplished" (10:7).[159] The "mystery" (μυστήριον) surely refers to God's redemptive plan to defeat the powers of evil, rescue his people, and restore his creation. The sounding of the seventh trumpet points to the climactic events recorded in Rev 19–22 (i.e., the coming of the kingdom proclaimed in 11:15). God "announces" this good news (εὐαγγελίζω) to his servants the prophets, including both Old and New Testament prophets (cf. Ezek 38:17; Amos 3:7; 1 Pet 1:10–12).

In Rev 10:8–11 the heavenly voice calls John to participate in his dramatic vision by taking and eating the little scroll. Ezekiel too is commanded to eat a scroll to represent ingesting God's prophetic message, and that scroll also tasted as sweet as honey (Ezek 2:7–3:3). John follows instructions and asks for the scroll from the mighty angel, who tells John to eat it, an act that symbolizes consuming the scroll's message. The angel also warns John about the bittersweet experience to come. The scroll tastes like honey in his mouth but gives him a terrible stomachache. Most interpretations of the bittersweetness of the scroll relate to the positive and negative aspects of the outworking of God's plan. The sweetness ties to the fulfillment of God's scheme of salvation—his vanquishing of evil, vindication of his people, and restoration of creation. The belated bitterness refers either to the coming judgment or, more likely, to the suffering and persecution God's people will encounter as God's purposes are finalized (Rev 6:9–11;

158. Resseguie, *Revelation*, 155, observes the complexity of narrative time: "This pattern of 'soon but not yet' or 'delay canceled yet story continues' characterizes narrative time in Revelation. 'A little longer' is counterbalanced by 'no more delay' heightening the reader's anticipation of fulfillment and frustration at delay. In the process the reader becomes attuned to the rhythm of God's time and ways." See also Koester, *Revelation*, 479–80, for the interpretive options for the phrase "there will be no more time" (χρόνος οὐκέτι ἔσται).

159. The phrase in verse 7 that the NIV translates "when the seventh angel is about to sound" is better translated "when the seventh angel will sound," since μέλλη with the infinitive is likely used as a future indicative in this instance. See Beale, *Revelation*, 540–41; Mathewson, *Revelation*, 135.

7:14). The temptation to escape the bitterness by abandoning his prophetic witness is countered by the closing admonition to John: "you must prophesy again about (or perhaps 'against') many peoples, nations, languages and kings" (10:11; cf. 5:9; 7:9; 11:9; 13:7; 14:6; 17:15). The divine calling ("must" or δεῖ) to be a faithful witness, no matter how difficult, must be fulfilled.

11.4.4.3.2 The Church's Role as Witness (11:1–14)

The interlude of 10:1–11:14 addresses the situation and mission of God's people in this fallen world. The first vision (10:1–11) centers on John's recommissioning to his prophetic task while the second vision extends that ministry to the prophetic people of God, symbolized here by the two witnesses (11:1–14). This second vision has three parts: (1) John's charge to measure the temple but exclude the outer court in 11:1–2, (2) the account of the two witnesses in 11:3–13, and (3) the announcement of the coming third woe in 11:14.[160]

In 11:1–2 John is told to "measure the temple of God and the altar, with its worshipers" but to exclude the outer court (leave it unmeasured) since it has been given over to the gentiles who will trample on the Holy City for forty-two months.[161] The background is Ezekiel's measuring of the temple in Ezek 40–42, but unlike Ezekiel, John is told not to measure the outer court (see also Dan 8:11–14). As in the rest of Revelation where the temple is always figurative, such is the case here too (3:12; 7:15; 11:19; 14:15, 17; 15:5–6, 8; 16:1, 17; 21:22; and the use of temple as a metaphor for the church in 1 Cor 3:16–17; 2 Cor 6:16; Eph 2:19–22; Heb 3:6; 1 Pet 2:5). I take the entire temple complex to represent the church but from two different vantage points (cf. the two different perspectives on the same reality with the 144,000 and the great multitude in Rev 7).[162]

The temple, the altar, and its worshipers represent the church as protected spiritually by God. This is the equivalent of the sealing of God's people against demonic attack and immoral/idolatrous powers in chapter 7. The outer court or that section of the temple complex not measured also represents the church, but the church vulnerable to persecution and martyrdom. The description of the outer court as "the holy city" also supports this reading and portrays the "not yet" aspect of the future heavenly city (see 3:12; 21:2, 10; 22:19). Bauckham summarizes: "He [John] is distinguishing the inner, hidden reality of the church as a kingdom of priests (cf. 5:10) who worship God in his presence from the outward experience of the church as it is exposed to persecution by

160. Revelation 11 may be the most difficult section in the entire book to interpret. My approach favors the more figurative view over the more literal, but, as Mounce reminds us, "symbolism is not a denial of historicity but a figurative method of communicating reality" (*Revelation*, 212).

161. On the significance of the period of forty-two months, see Duvall, *Revelation*, 149. In sum, it represents a "limited period of time in which evil is allowed to triumph over God's people (cf. Dan. 7:25; 9:27; 12:7, 11–12)." This time of persecution and even martyrdom corresponds to their time of witness, as the next section indicates.

162. So Bauckham, *Climax of Prophecy*, 266–73; Smalley, *Revelation*, 269–72; Koester, *Revelation*, 484–86; Mounce, *Revelation*, 213–15, and others.

the kingdom of the nations. The church will be kept safe in its hidden spiritual reality, while suffering persecution and martyrdom."[163]

In the second part of the vision (11:3–13), we read of the ministry, death, and resurrection of the two witnesses. While this passage could refer to two historical individuals, the number "two" likely results from the need for two witnesses to constitute a valid testimony (e.g., Num 35:30; Deut 17:6; 19:15; Matt 18:16; John 8:17; Heb 10:28). The image best represents the witnessing church, fulfilling their prophetic ministry of proclaiming God's truth in a fallen world.[164]

Their attire of black goat's hair sackcloth indicates the nature of their message as one calling for mourning and repentance (see Isa 3:24; Jer 4:8; 6:26; Ezek 7:18; Dan 9:3; Rev 6:12) and stands in contrast to the white clothing worn by God's people in heaven (7:9, 14).[165] They are to prophesy for 1,260 days (= forty-two months, or three-and-a-half years), the equivalent of the time of persecution by the powers of evil (11:3).

The two witnesses are further described as "the two olives trees" and "the two lampstands" that stand before the Lord of the earth (11:4). These images are drawn from Zech 4, where the two olives trees (Zerubbabel and Joshua representing Israel's kingship and priesthood) are anointed by God's Spirit to lead the people. The olive trees supply oil to fuel the fire for the two lampstands or menorahs, an image representing the church in 1:12–13, 20. The witnessing church is the Lord's ambassador in this world, bearing faithful and true witness to the world.

The powerful ministries of God's people are patterned after the prophetic activity of Moses and Elijah (Mal 4:4–5; Matt 17:3–4; Luke 1:17). Elijah called down fire from heaven that consumed his enemies (1 Kgs 18:38; 2 Kgs 1:2–17; cf. Luke 9:54) and shut up the heavens, preventing it from raining (1 Kgs 17:1; 18:41–42). In the first of the ten plagues on Egypt, Moses was empowered to turn the Nile River into blood (Exod 7:14–24). These are images of spiritual weapons bringing judgment on those who are hostile to God (cf. Rev 11:10; also 1:16; 2:12, 16; 19:15, 21). Like Moses and Elijah, the witnessing church is empowered by God and given authority to fulfill its mission.

At the conclusion of their time of witness, the beast ascends from the haunt of demons (the Abyss) overpowers, and kills the witnesses (11:7). Introduced here, this beast will receive full description in chapters 13 and 17 (cf. Dan 7:7–22). His origin is demonic, as is his mission—to destroy the witnesses (cf. the spiritual conflict described in Rev 12:7–9, 11–12, 17; 17:14; 19:19–20; 20:9). Resseguie notes the historical pattern

163. Bauckham, *Climax of Prophecy*, 272.

164. For persuasive reasons for interpreting the two witnesses as the entire community of faith, see Beale, *Revelation*, 572–75, and Keener, *Revelation*, 291–92. For an outstanding study of Rev 11, see Dalrymple, *Revelation and the Two Witnesses.*

165. Mark Wilson, "Revelation," 312.

for God's people: "Where the gospel is preached, opposition follows. Christ's ministry is the paradigm for the church."[166]

The world then celebrates their demise (11:8–10). After the death of the two witnesses, their "bodies" (singular in Greek) are refused a proper burial, a symbol of shame and humiliation in the ancient world (cf. 11:8–9; Pss 79:3–4; Jer 22:18–19). In Revelation "the great city" is mentioned eight times (Rev 11:8; 16:19; 17:18; 18:10, 16, 18, 19, 21), always representing "Babylon," the center of pagan power that opposes God and his people (i.e., Rome in the first century). The "great city" is "figuratively" [or "spiritually"—πνευματικῶς] called Sodom and Egypt, the place "where also their Lord was crucified" (11:8), meaning the ungodly world compares to those power centers set against "the holy city," the church (the New Jerusalem).[167] "The center of wickedness can be symbolized as a place of moral depravity (Sodom), a place of oppression and slavery (Egypt), or a place responsible for the unjust death of Jesus Christ (Jerusalem)."[168] For "three and a half days"—a limited period of defeat contrasting with the much longer three-and-a-half years of witness (11:3)—the inhabitants of the earth gloat over them and celebrate their death because they had been tormented by the truth of their witness (11:10).

We see in 11:11–13 the resurrection and ascension of the two witnesses and the consequences of God's reversal of the world's judgment. Two references to terror bracket this (11:11, 13). After a short-lived celebration by the nations of three and a half days, God breathes the breath of life into the witnesses (cf. Ezek 37) and they stand resurrected, leaving the wicked nations terrified. They are then called to heaven while their enemies look on.[169] Resurrection is God's reversal of the curse of death, and it defeats evil's greatest and last weapon (cf. 1 Cor 15:26, 51–57). This resurrection and ascension of believers could refer to their resurrection at the end of the age or it could symbolize in a general way their vindication by God.[170]

The consequences of God's life-giving actions are spelled out in Rev 11:13, a verse whose interpretation has divided scholars. A severe earthquake destroyed a tenth of the city and seven thousand people were killed, while the survivors were terrified and "gave glory to the God of heaven."[171] Does "gave glory to . . . God" indicate the genuine repentance and conversion of nine tenths of the world (i.e., the rest of

---

166. Resseguie, *Revelation*, 163.

167. Beale, *Revelation*, 592, notes that the use of ὅπου ("where") elsewhere in the Apocalypse always introduces symbolic, spiritual—rather than literal—geography (e.g., spiritual realms of protection in 12:6, 14; 14:4; the dwelling of Satan and his allies in 2:13; 20:10; cf. 17:3 with 17:9 (NIV "on which"), wilderness in 12:6, 14; heads and mountains in 17:9; lake of fire and brimstone in 20:20).

168. Duvall, *Revelation*, 151.

169. We see elsewhere the pattern of God's enemies being paralyzed with fear after God reverses their curse (e.g., the Egyptians following the exodus in Exod 15:16 and the Roman guards following Jesus's resurrection in Matt 28:4).

170. As Mark Wilson, "Revelation," 315, rightly observes, this event symbolizes "the resurrection of the dead saints, not the rapture of the living ones."

171. For more on the eschatological role of earthquakes, see "Earthquakes" in Hays, Duvall, and Pate, *A-to-Z Guide to Biblical Prophecy*, 126–28.

humanity)?[172] Or, does it indicate a forced acknowledgment of God's sovereignty and glory by his defeated enemies?[173] While such good news of a massive conversion would certainly be worth celebrating, and "give glory to" can refer to genuine conversion elsewhere in Rev (e.g., 14:6–7; 15:4; 16:9; 19:7; cf. Dan 4:34–37), we are hesitant to fully embrace such a large-scale turning of the nations to the Lord at the very end of history, an idea that is not supported in the rest of Revelation (see 6:15–17; 9:20–21; 13:3–4; cf. Matt 28:1–4; Phil 2:10–11).[174] The terror *inclusio* with Rev 11:11, the coming last judgment mentioned in 11:18, the whole world following the beast in 13:3–4, and the responses of "terror" and "glory" arising not from prophetic witness but from God's intervening resurrection of the saints and the subsequent earthquake of judgment give us pause. All we can say at this point is that this passage *may* teach a large-scale conversion at the end of the age, but doubts remain, and the passage should not be used as a proof text for Revelation's full-scale support of such a view.

To conclude this section, we hear an announcement about the second woe being past and the third woe coming (11:14; cf. 9:12). The eagle in 8:13 had announced the coming of three "woes" prepared for the inhabitants of the earth. These have been tied to the final three trumpet judgments. The second woe concludes here after the interlude of 10:1–11:13 to give insight into how God's judgments vindicate his people. Since John never formally indicates the beginning of the third woe, some have tied it to 12:12 where the term "woe" is used or to a larger section such as chapters 12–15, the seven bowl judgments in chapter 16, or the fall of Babylon in chapter 18 (cf. 18:10, 16, 19, which use the term "woe"), but the immediate connection to the seventh trumpet in 11:15–19 makes the most sense (cf. 8:13; 10:7).

11.4.4.4 Transition: The Seventh Trumpet (11:15–19)

We were told in 10:7 that when the seventh angel sounds his trumpet, "the mystery of God will be accomplished"; thus, 11:15–19 brings us to the consummation of God's kingdom. Following the interlude of 10:1–11:14, the seventh trumpet also constitutes the third "woe."[175] But unlike the previous two woes, this one leads us not to another series of plagues but to a heavenly celebration of God taking his great power and judging the ungodly nations while rewarding his servants (11:18). This third woe also presents

172. See, e.g., Bauckham, *Theology*, 86–87; Resseguie, *Revelation*, 165–66; Smalley, *Revelation*, 286; Aune, *Revelation 6–16*, 628; Witherington, *Revelation*, 160; Osborne, *Revelation*, 133–34; Koester, *Revelation*, 504; John Sweet, *Revelation*, TPI New Testament (Philadelphia: Trinity Press International, 1990), 189; Caird, *Revelation of St John*, 140; Keener, *Revelation*, 297; Fanning, *Revelation*, 338; Mathewson, *Companion to the Book of Revelation*, 126; Alexander E. Stewart, *Reading the Book of Revelation: Five Principles for Interpretation* (Bellingham, WA: Lexham, 2021), 123–24.

173. See, e.g., Beale, *Revelation*, 603–4; Mounce, *Revelation*, 224; Mark Wilson, "Revelation," 316; Fee, *Revelation*, 155; Schnabel, *40 Questions about End Times*, 218.

174. Beale, *Revelation*, 607.

175. See Beale's helpful excursus on the topic of the seventh trumpet and third woe in *Revelation*, 609–10.

the positive side of judgment by celebrating God's victory over evil. Since Revelation spirals forward rather than unfolding in a neat, linear sequence, there is much more to come for a full reporting on the consummated kingdom in chapters 19–22, but readers will certainly welcome this prelude.

In 11:15 the heavenly voices sing out a chorus of praise made famous by Handel's *Messiah*: "The kingdom of the world has become the kingdom of our Lord and of his Messiah, and he will reign for ever and ever."[176] The eternal reign of God has arrived, Jesus's long-awaited messianic kingdom has come, and the Triune God is now King of all creation (cf. Isa 9:7; 52:7; Dan 2:44; Zech 14:9). The singular references here highlight the trinitarian nature of John's theology, a theme stressed throughout Revelation (e.g., 5:1, 6; 7:10; 14:4; 20:6; 21:1, 22; cf. Ps 2:2).

The mention of the twenty-four elders in Rev 11:16–18 reconnects us to chapter 4 by revisiting many of the themes found in that larger unit.[177] As an exalted order of angels, the elders represent God's people and lead out in worship, always prostrating themselves in the act of worship (see comments at 4:1–11; cf. 5:5–14; 7:11–13; 11:16; 14:3; 19:4). They give thanks to the "Lord God Almighty," the primary description of God in Revelation (see comments at 1:7–8; cf. 4:8; 11:17; 15:3; 16:7, 14; 19:6, 15; 21:22). God is further portrayed in terms of his eternal self-existence and sovereignty over history: "the One who is and who was." The final element ("is to come"), added in 1:8 and 4:8, is now omitted because the future has invaded the present, that is, the "is to come" has arrived. God has exercised his mighty power and has begun to reign (11:17).

Verse 18 features a battle of wraths: the "anger" (verb ὀργίζω) of the nations versus the "wrath" (noun ὀργή) of God. Throughout Revelation, the term "nations" can be used positively or negatively.[178] The term can designate God's people drawn from every people group (e.g., 5:9; 7:9; 15:4; 21:24, 26; 22:2). But negatively, the "nations" can designate those who oppose God and his people (e.g., 11:2, 9, 18) or those who are taken in by evil powers (e.g., 13:7; 14:8; 16:19; 17:15; 18:3, 23; 20:3, 8). In these instances, as is the case here in chapter 11, "nations" is equivalent to "inhabitants of the earth" and refers to unbelievers. The nations' anger at God and his people is no match for God's wrath to come (see further comments at 14:14–20 on God's wrath). God's wrath refers to his deliberate and intentional response to sin and evil based on his holy and righteous character.[179] The seventh trumpet is certainly a "woe" of destruction for the wicked or "those who destroy the earth," likely referring to the persecution of God's people by the unbelieving nations (11:18; cf. 19:2; 2 Thess 1:6–7).

176. As Mathewson, *Revelation*, 152, rightly notes about the extensive use of the aorist tense in 11:15–19, "the absolute certainty of the events yet to take place comes from the context and the one speaking, not from any specific tense usage."

177. Osborne, *Revelation*, 438.

178. For more on "the nations," see Duvall, *Revelation*, 157.

179. For more on "God's Wrath," see Hays, Duvall, and Pate, *A-to-Z Guide to Biblical Prophecy*, 474–76.

The coming of God's kingdom is wonderful news for God's people since "judgment" also includes the rewarding of the righteous (Rev 11:18). The list in verse 18 describes God's people: your servants the prophets, the saints (people), and those who revere your name—both small and great. The list stresses that God will reward every last believer regardless of their status in this world. There is no favoritism with the Lord, the righteous Judge (Rev 19:5; 20:12; Jas 2:1–11). The seventh trumpet provides a glimpse of God defeating his enemies, rewarding people, and establishing his kingdom, realities receiving a more extensive description in Rev 19–22.

The elders' hymn of praise receives a response from heaven in 11:19. God's temple is opened and inside the ark of the covenant is visible, symbolizing God's covenant faithfulness and relational presence (21:2–7, 22–27; cf. Heb 8:1–9:28).[180] Every child of God, and not just the high priest, has access to God's presence. The storm theophany that occurs at the end of the seal, trumpet, and bowl judgments closes this section with an emphasis on the holiness and coming judgment of God (8:5; 11:19; 16:18; cf. 4:5), yet another reminder that he has not forgotten about his suffering people (6:10).

11.4.5 The Third Interlude: The Cosmic War between God and the Forces of Evil (12:1–14:20)

Revelation 12:1–14:20 constitutes the final of three interludes and like the other two (7:1–17; 10:1–11:14) specifies the church's role in the last days (from incarnation to parousia). This section details the cosmic conflict between God and the forces of evil, as well as God's vindication of his people and judgment of the wicked. Revelation 12 marks not only a new section but stands as the theological heart of the book, showing why the people of God face hostility in this world and how God provides the victory. Revelation 12:1–6 reveals the basic story, followed by the war in heaven (12:7–12), the war on earth (12:13–17), and the part played in the battle by the two beasts (13:1–10, 11–18). Chapter 14 portrays both the victory and vindication of the saints (14:1–5) as well as the judgment of the unrighteous in two paired visions (14:6–13, 14–20). As a result, the hearers understand more about the spiritual war they are fighting, and this larger perspective fosters faithful endurance. They can expect persecution as participants in the ongoing conflict between God and Satan (e.g., John 15:20), but the enemy is already a defeated foe through the death and resurrection of Jesus. Much like earlier units (Rev 8:1–6; 11:15–19), 15:1–8 serves as a transition, concluding what precedes and preparing for the seven bowl judgments to come.

180. For more on the temple in Revelation, see the summary in Duvall, *Revelation*, 295, and the full-scale treatment in G. K. Beale, *The Temple in the Church's Mission: A Biblical Theology of the Dwelling Place of God*, NSBT 17 (Downers Grove, IL: InterVarsity Press, 2004).

11.4.5.1 The False Trinity Versus God and His People (12:1–13:18)

In 12:1–13:18 we encounter the battle between the false trinity (Satan, sea beast, and earth beast) and the Triune God and his followers. More specifically, chapter 12 consists of three scenes: the conflict between the dragon and the woman and her son (12:1–6), the war in heaven between Michael and his angels and the dragon and his angels (12:7–12), and the resumption of the conflict between the dragon and the woman with the announcement of the dragon's pursuit of the rest of the woman's offspring (12:13–18).

11.4.5.1.1 The Woman, the Son, and the Dragon (12:1–6)

In one sense Rev 12 stands as the theological center of the book because it summarizes why the church suffers persecution in this world and how God brings victory over evil.[181] Having learned from 10:1–11:13 in a general way that "everyone who wants to live a godly life in Christ Jesus will be persecuted" (2 Tim 3:12), readers now discover behind-the-scenes details about the spiritual battle they are waging. This unit offers a wide-angle perspective on the cosmic war in hopes of encouraging faithful endurance. In Revelation 12:1–6 we meet one of the leading characters in the drama, the pregnant woman, and her formidable adversary, the dragon.

The action moves forward as if John is seeing it in real time. A "great sign" appears in heaven in 12:1 (the pregnant woman) that stands superior to the other "sign" in 12:3 (the enormous red dragon). The term "sign" (σημεῖον) simply means a "symbol that has a deeper significance" but also reminds readers that they are looking at picture language.[182] The woman's heavenly adornment with sun, moon, and stars stands in stark contrast to "the whore's earthbound, royal clothing" (17:4; 18:16).[183]

The woman who cries out in the pains associated with childbirth (12:2) is obviously not the Virgin Mary because of the reference in 12:17 to "the rest of her offspring." This unnamed woman represents the community of faith that brings forth the Messiah, that is, the faithful remnant within Israel. She is one of the noble women of Revelation (cf. the bride of the New Jerusalem in 21:2) in contrast to the unfaithful women (Jezebel in 2:20–23; the scarlet woman who rides the beast in 17:1–18). As Kiddle puts it, the woman is "the true Israel in her pre-messianic agony of expectation."[184]

The other sign of an enormous red dragon with seven heads and ten horns with seven crowns on its heads appears in 12:3. The Old Testament portrays serpents and sea

181. For a thorough discussion of the possible backgrounds for the combat story in Rev 12, see the excursus in Aune, *Revelation 6–16*, 667–74.

182. Aune, *Revelation 6–16*, 679. Smalley, *Revelation*, 313, notes "the meaning of signs in Revelation is close to the significance of the signs in the Fourth Gospel . . . , where the miracles of Jesus point beyond themselves to reveal him as the Son through whom God acts in a decisively salvific way." The noun σημεῖον appears seven times in Revelation: 12:1, 3; 13:13, 14; 15:1; 16:14; 19:20.

183. Resseguie, *Revelation*, 170.

184. Martin Kiddle, *The Revelation of St. John* (London: Hodder & Stoughton, 1940), 220. See also Tabb, *All Things New*, 105–8.

monsters as evil forces set against God and his people, a fitting image of the archenemy of God—Satan (e.g., Gen 3:1–24; Ezek 29:3; Isa 27:1; Jer 51:34).[185] His identity is made explicit in Rev 12:9—"that ancient serpent called the devil, or Satan, who leads the whole world astray" (cf. 20:2). The fiery red symbolizes violence, war, and bloodshed in Revelation (cf. 6:4; 16:6; 17:6; 18:24). The "seven heads" and "ten horns" give readers a sober reminder of the widespread nature of the dragon's evil influence (cf. the beast in 13:1; 17:3, 7; and the Lamb's seven horns in 5:6). The image of the "ten horns" is reminiscent of the ten-horned fourth beast of Dan 7:7–8, 20, 24. The "crowns" (διάδημα) signify real power, but a power that only parodies the absolute power of the King of kings and Lord of lords (cf. Rev 19:12, 16; John 12:31; 14:30).[186]

In Rev 12:4 the dragon goes to war and prepares to devour the child the moment he is born. This echoes Dan 8:10 where the little horn throws some of the starry host to earth and tramples on them, referring historically to the persecution of the Jewish people by Antiochus Epiphanes. For this reason, Beale takes the stars in Rev 12:4 to represent God's people and the casting down to refer to persecution.[187] But more likely, "stars" should be understood here to carry the normal meaning of angels rather than human beings, supported by the explicit reference to angels in 12:9.[188] In Revelation, when stars (ἀστήρ) refer to beings, they normally refer to angels rather than people (1:16, 20; 2:1; 3:1; 9:1; 22:16 [Jesus]).[189] This could be pointing to an initial rebellion of Satan that resulted in the fall of many angels (cf. 1 Pet 3:19–22; 2 Pet 2:4).[190] With his army in tow, the dragon turns his wrath against the woman and her Messiah child (Gen 3:15). Throughout the New Testament we read of Satan's many attempts to kill Jesus.[191]

In Rev 12:5–6 we learn that God protects both the woman and her son. The male child is described, using the language of Ps 2, as one who "will rule all the nations," placing emphasis on Jesus as the defender and protector of his persecuted people (also Rev 2:27; 19:15). The child is then "snatched up to God and to his throne," referring

185. See "Dragon" in Hays, Duvall, and Pate, *A-to-Z Guide to Biblical Prophecy*, 124–25.

186. Duvall, *Revelation*, 317: "Revelation features two types of 'crowns'": (1) the victor's wreath (στέφανος) worn by victorious believers in 2:10; 3:11; by the twenty-four elders in 4:4, 10; by the rider on the white horse in 6:2; by the locusts in 9:7; by the woman in 12:1; and by Christ in 14:14; and (2) the ruler's crown (διάδημα) worn by the dragon in 12:3; by the beast in 13:1; and by Christ in 19:12."

187. Beale, *Revelation*, 635–36; cf. Fanning, *Revelation*, 351.

188. E.g., John E. Goldingay, *Daniel*, WBC 30 (Dallas: Word, 1989), 209–10; Ernest C. Lucas, *Daniel*, AOTC 20 (Downers Grove, IL: InterVarsity Press, 2002), 215.

189. Osborne, *Revelation*, 461, who concludes: "There is no instance when the people of God are called 'stars.'" A possible exception is 12:1 where the "sun, moon, and stars" might symbolize Israel or its faithful remnant, alluding to Gen 37:9 (see Keener, *Revelation*, 314). Osborne views this as the primordial fall of Satan where he led the rebellion of one-third of the heavenly host, certainly one possible interpretation.

190. Also in Jewish literature: 1 En. 6:7; 8:3; 18:14–16; 20:4; 21:3, 6; 80:6–8; 86:1–4; 88:3; 2 En. 7:3; 29:4–5; 2 Bar. 51:10; T. Sol. 20:16–17; cf. Gen 6:1–4; Isa 14:12–15.

191. Verlyn D. Verbrugge, *A Not-So-Silent Night: The Unheard Story of Christmas and Why It Matters* (Grand Rapids: Kregel, 2009), 22–26, identifies at least seven Satan-inspired attempts on Jesus's life in the New Testament. At the crucifixion, the emphasis falls on Jesus dying or giving his own life rather than just being killed.

to Jesus's ascension and assuming his life, ministry, crucifixion, and resurrection. Beale notes that this "apocalyptic abbreviation," or telescoping, is common in the New Testament (e.g., John 3:13; 8:14; 13:3; 16:5, 28; Rom 1:3–4; 1 Tim 3:16; Rev 1:5; 2:8; 17:8) and here highlights God's protection and enthronement of the Son (Phil 2:5–11; Acts 13:33; Heb 1:2–6; 5:5).[192]

The woman then flees into a God-prepared place in the wilderness where she is "taken care of" (τρέφω, "feed," "nourish") for 1,260 days. Satan now turns his attention to terrorizing the people of God on earth. The wilderness is not only a place of trial, but also a refuge of protection and provision.[193] This image echoes God's protective care of his people during their wilderness journeys (Exod 13:17–22; 16:4–35; Deut 1:31; 8:2–18; Hos 2:14; Acts 7:36), of his prophets in their desert distress (e.g., Elijah and others in 1 Kgs 17–19), and of Jesus during his wilderness temptations (Mark 1:12–13). For the people of God, the time of wilderness provision corresponds to the time of witness (Rev 11:2–3) and trials (13:5–7)—to the entire period between the advent and parousia of Christ (cf. the sequencing in 12:10–17). Also, in New Testament theology the period of tribulation follows immediately upon the death/resurrection/ascension of Christ. Thus, Christians between the first and second comings of Christ are said to be living in "the last days," a period of trial, witness, and spiritual protection (Acts 2:17; 2 Tim 3:1–5; 2 Pet 3:3).[194]

11.4.5.1.2 The War in Heaven (12:7–12)

The interlude of 12:1–14:20 continues with a heavenly war between Michael and the dragon (12:7–9), followed by a hymn proclaiming God's victory (12:10–12). God delegates the fight to his archangel Michael (12:7), a battle-tested warrior on behalf of the saints (Dan 10:13, 21; 12:1; cf. Jude 9). The warfare atmosphere of Rev 12:7–17 emerges through the use of military terms ("war," "fought," "triumphed," "wage war"), in addition to the multiple references to Satan being "hurled down" from heaven to earth (12:9 [2x], 10, 13). There is no actual chronicling of the battle, simply the results: the strong man was "not strong enough" to retain his place in heaven (12:8; cf. Mark 3:23–27). Ironically, Satan and his demonic angels lost their "place" (τόπος) in heaven even as God had to prepare a "place" (τόπος) of refuge for his persecuted people. Whatever access Satan had formerly to God's presence after his initial fall has now been revoked (cf. Job 1:6–9; 2:1–6; Zech 3:1–2).

The primordial battle of Rev 12:4 is now conflated with the decisive downfall of Satan at the cross/resurrection/exaltation of Jesus Christ. Osborne observes, "The

192. Beale, *Revelation*, 639.

193. See Beale's excursus, "The Desert as a Place of Both Trial and Protection," in *Revelation*, 645–46.

194. See Duvall, *Revelation*, 162; also see Keener, *Revelation*, 319–20, for additional arguments supporting this view. Resseguie, *Revelation*, 171, writes, "The messianic community is a wilderness community . . . victorious with a home in heaven, yet it lives in the wilderness during the significant three and a half years that designates the in-between times of the messianic age."

telescoping of time in chapters 11–12 continues here, and all three 'bindings' of Satan (in the primordial past, at the ministry and death of Jesus, and at the eschaton) are intertwined in chapter 12."[195] Michael's battle in heaven reflects Jesus's decisive victory on earth (cf. Rev 3:21; Luke 10:18–19). In Rev 12:9 John identifies the dragon in more detail as "that ancient serpent called the devil, or Satan, who leads the whole world astray"[196] (cf. 20:2). He is the ancient snake of Gen 3 who tempted Adam and Eve (2 Cor 11:3, 14), the leading liar or "father of lies" (John 8:44; 1 John 3:8). He is the "devil" (διάβολος) or "Satan," meaning "adversary" or "accuser" (1 Chr 21:1; Job 1:6–12; Zech 3:1–2). He is also the deceiver who leads astray (πλανάω) the whole world (cf. Rev 20:2–3, 7–8, 10; 13:14; 18:23), a character quality in stark contrast to Jesus and his followers as faithful and true witnesses (1:5; 2:13; 3:14; 11:1–13; 14:5). The great dragon is tempter, accuser, and deceiver, but he is also now a defeated and desperate foe who has lost his heavenly influence. He turns his fury toward God's people on earth, but God continues to provide for and protect his children.

A loud heavenly voice announces the significance of what John has just seen (12:10–12). This hymn-like proclamation of praise celebrates God's victory and its implications for believers. In 12:10 the "now" points to the arrival of God's salvation, power, and kingdom, which coincides with the life, death, resurrection, and exaltation of Jesus the Messiah. Jesus, the advocate for God's people (John 14:16; 1 John 2:1), has silenced the lies and accusations of the diabolical prosecutor (1 John 3:4–10; Rom 8:33–34; Heb 2:14; Eph 6:16).

Revelation 12:11 stands as a theological summation of the entire book. Because of Jesus's decisive victory, his followers also now conquer the devil. They have triumphed (νικάω) over him first and foremost through (basis and means) the finished work of the Lamb, who shed his blood on the cross for the sins of the world (1:5; 5:6, 9; 7:14; 19:13).[197] Believers implement this secured victory by means of their word, which is their testimony, meaning their faithful witness to Christ even unto death (1:9; 6:9; 11:3–7; 12:17; 20:4). Throughout Revelation the martyrs represent the faithful. Bauckham rightly observes, however, that "it is not a literal prediction that every faithful Christian will in fact be put to death. But it does require that every faithful Christian must be prepared to die."[198] It remains, however, a holistic testimony reflecting both lifestyle and speech.

In the already/not yet of God's kingdom prior to the consummation, the decisive

195. Osborne, *Revelation*, 469. Many scholars are hesitant to acknowledge a primordial fall and place all the emphasis on Jesus's victory at the cross and resurrection.

196. See Duvall, *Revelation*, 169; Clinton E. Arnold, "Satan, Devil," *DLNT* 1077–82.

197. For more on "overcome" or "victory," see the summary in Duvall, *Revelation*, 42, and the works by Mark Wilson: *The Victor Sayings in the Book of Revelation* (Eugene, OR: Wipf & Stock, 2007) and *Victory through the Lamb: A Guide to Revelation in Plain Language*, 2nd ed. (Bellingham, WA: Lexham, 2014).

198. Bauckham, *Theology*, 93.

victory has been achieved but it is not yet the final eschatological victory to come. As a result, the devil knows his space is limited and his time is short, so he vents his "great wrath" (θυμὸν μέγαν) against God's people on earth. This is the ongoing "woe" for the saints prior to Jesus's second coming. In the chapters ahead we will see the devil's chief weapons of war—the seduction of idolatry and immorality combined with the pressure of persecution. This calls for faithful endurance (13:10).

11.4.5.1.3 The Earthly War between the Dragon and the Woman and Her Children (12:13–17)

The cosmic war continues in 12:13–17. Since the dragon failed to devour the male child or defeat the archangel Michael, as a wounded serpent he now vents his rage against the woman, the faithful remnant, and her other children. John describes the dragon's attacks using a variety of Old Testament allusions, drawn especially from Israel's exodus and wilderness experiences. Throughout the ordeal God protects his people, Jewish and gentile followers of Jesus, from these demonic assaults. This unit reveals much about the true source of the church's persecution, with chapter 13 disclosing more details about the dragon's war strategy.

The dragon now hunts down the woman who had given birth to the male child. Satan is the ultimate source of persecution of God's people, hating both Jesus the Messiah and his messianic community (John 15:18–21). This pursuit is reminiscent of Pharaoh's rage against the Israelites following the exodus (Exod 14:5–12; cf. Isa 51:9–10; Pss 74:13–14). But the woman "was given" (another divine passive) a protective flight on eagle's wings to a place of spiritual refuge, just as God had provided physical safety for Israel in the exodus experience (Exod 19:4).

The image of an eagle is often used throughout the story of Israel to represent God's protective care (e.g., Exod 19:4; Deut 32:10–14; Isa 40:31). Just as Israel was nourished with manna, quail, and water during their wilderness pilgrimage, so here "wilderness" symbolizes a place of God's protection and provision for his people (τρέφω, "taken care of," in Rev 12:6, 14).

The time of God's sustenance lasts for "a time, times and half a time," representing the limited period of the church's tribulation extending from the first to the second coming of Christ (cf. 11:2–3, 9, 11; 12:6, 14; 13:5–7; cf. Dan 7:25; 12:7).[199] Resseguie wisely notes that this figure in all its forms represents more than a divinely limited time. It also signifies an interruption to the cadence, a "broken seven" that raises expectations about a full and uninterrupted time of completion and abundance to come.[200] God's protection does not spare believers from physical persecution, as the context of

199. Beale, *Revelation*, 669; Keener, *Revelation*, 319–20.

200. Resseguie, *Revelation*, 176.

Revelation makes clear, but from Satan's deceptive lies, condemning indictments, false teaching, and demonic attacks (e.g., Matt 6:13; John 17:15; 2 Thess 3:3).

In Rev 12:15–16 we see the nature of the dragon's attacks on the woman and God's method of rescue.

The serpent spews from his mouth a torrent of water, hoping to sweep away the woman. This river of venom depicts the lies, deceit, false teaching, slander, accusations, persecution, and bogus signs and wonders directed toward God's people by Satan in hopes of destroying them (cf. Matt 24:24; 2 Cor 2:11; 11:3, 13–15; 2 Thess 2:9–10; 1 Tim 4:1; 5:15; 2 Tim 2:23–26; Rev 13:13–15; 16:14). Again, drawing on powerful Old Testament stories, John drives home the point that this wounded dragon remains powerful and dangerous for God's people. The image of floodwaters provides a general picture of persecution by God's enemies (e.g., Pss 18:4, 16; 144:7–8, 11; Isa 43:2). Two stories in particular from Israel's exodus experience resonate with this threat/deliverance experience. God rescues his people from the pursuing Egyptians through the waters of the Red Sea, the same waters that subsequently swallow their enemies (Exod 15:12). Later, in the wilderness, the earth swallows up the families of Korah, Dathan, and Abiram for rebelling against God's leader, Moses (Num 16:23–33; Deut 11:5–6; Ps 106:17). While the dragon plotted to destroy the woman, the earth rescued her by opening its mouth (στόμα) and swallowing the torrential river spewed out of the dragon's mouth (στόμα). The personified earth signifies the Creator's intervention to rescue his people. The earth does not destroy the dragon but does swallow up his venomous river.

Enraged even further, the dragon now wages war against the rest of the woman's offspring, defined here as "those who keep God's commands and hold fast their testimony about Jesus" (Rev 12:17).[201] If the woman represents the messianic community that gives birth to the Messiah, the "rest of her offspring" refers to the members of the church besides the male child of 12:5, 13 (i.e., Jesus). The "rest of her offspring," then, represents the "members of the true Israel in its totality" (Rom 2:28–29; 4:16; Gal 3:29; 6:15–16; Heb 8:8–10).[202] The woman's children are distinguished by their obedience and loyalty to Jesus and are protected spiritually, even as they are subject to physical harm (cf. the sealing of Rev 7:4–8 and the measuring of 11:1–2).

11.4.5.1.4 The Beast from the Sea (13:1–10)

The statement "The dragon stood on the shore of the sea" concludes chapter 12 in the Greek text but has been moved to 13:1a by some translations (e.g., NIV, NASB20). The point is that chapters 12 and 13 should be read together. Having failed in his

201. On this phrase, "the testimony of Jesus," and variations, see Duvall, *Revelation*, 174.

202. Smalley, *Revelation*, 333–34.

pursuit of the woman and her other offspring, the dragon now calls forth two evil agents to continue his diabolical mission of blaspheming God, persecuting believers, and deceiving the inhabitants of the earth: the beast from the sea (13:1–10) and the beast from the earth (13:11–18). The dragon, the beast from the sea (antichrist?), and the beast from the earth (false prophet) constitute an "unholy trinity." In this section we learn of the beast's origin, his relationship to the dragon, his actions toward God and his people, and his widespread influence in the world. Through it all, however, we are reminded that God is still sovereign since there are still divine limits on the beast's evil schemes ("was given" five times in 13:5–7, 14–15). The section closes with a prophetic warning to believers, challenging them to endure faithfully.

In 13:1–2 the hideous beast emerges from the sea and is empowered by the dragon. In Scripture, the sea often symbolizes the chaos and evil that threatens God's people, featuring sea monsters such as Leviathan or Rahab (e.g., Job 40–41; Pss 74:13–14; 89:10; Isa 27:1; 51:9; Dan 7). As a result, it naturally follows that the dragon stands on the seashore and calls for the beast from the sea.[203]

Imitating the dragon, this sea beast has ten horns and seven heads, with the crowns in this case appearing on its horns rather than its heads (Rev 12:3). The "crowns" (διάδημα) represent strength and power, as the repeated use of "authority" suggests (13:2, 4, 5, 7, 12). The beast having characteristics of a leopard, bear, and lion draws on Dan 7, where four similar beasts come up from the sea and represent kingdoms opposed to God's people. John also probably has in view nations and rulers who attack God's people. The blasphemous names on its heads serve as a reminder of the divine names accepted by Roman emperors (e.g., "Lord," "Savior," "Our Lord and God"). This beast symbolizes the "perpetual deification of secular authority"[204] or "the powers of evil which lie behind the kingdoms of this world."[205] In other words, it represents political, military, social, and economic power used in the service of the dragon to oppose God and his people. Usually, such secular power is personified by a single evil leader (e.g., Nero and Domitian in first-century Rome, or Hitler in Nazi Germany; cf. the many "antichrists" of 1 John 2:18, 22; 4:3; 2 John 7).[206]

John reports that one of the heads of the beast received a death wound but the wound had been healed (Rev 13:3; cf. 5:6). This healing imitates Christ's resurrection as part of a larger parody of Christ. Historically, this would remind readers of Nero's suicide in AD 68 followed by rumors that he had not actually died (or had died and come back to life—the *Nero redivivus* myth) but rather escaped to the east where he

203. Leland Ryken et al., eds., "Sea," *DBI* 765–66.

204. Mounce, *Revelation*, 246. Keener, *Revelation*, 335, notes that Jewish tradition viewed the fourth beast of Dan 7 as Rome (4 Ezra 12:10–11; 2 Bar. 39:7).

205. Smalley, *Revelation*, 336.

206. See "Antichrist," in Hays, Duvall, and Pate, *A-to-Z Guide to Biblical Prophecy*, 31–32; "Antichrist," in Duvall, *Revelation*, 180; and "Who Is the Beast in John's Prophecy?" and "Who Is the Antichrist?" in Schnabel, *40 Questions about End Times*, 163–83.

was preparing an army to one day return and take power. Beyond the first century, the most plausible takes are (1) the repeated rise of secular powers that oppose God and his people, and/or (2) the death and apparent resuscitation of a final antichrist figure at the end of the age.

Understandably, such a display of power would gain a following and many now worship both the dragon and the beast he empowers (13:3–4). Mounce writes, "Deification of secular power is in fact the worship of Satan."[207] The rhetorical question, "Who is like the beast?" imitates the praise that Yahweh alone deserves (cf. Exod 15:11; Pss 71:19; 89:8; Mic 7:18). Although God has already won the decisive battle against the dragon (Rev 12:7–9, 11), people worship the dragon and the beast because of their godlike power. Blasphemy (or slander, 13:1, 5, 6 [2x]) becomes a "defining trait of evil."[208]

In 13:5–7 we see that God, whose power far surpasses that of the unholy trinity, permits the beast to fulfill its role.[209] The beast is allowed to blaspheme God and to slander both God and his people for a limited period of time (cf. Dan 7:8, 11, 25; 2 Thess 2:4). Blasphemy is a principal characteristic of evil throughout Revelation, indicating a "self-deifying intention to displace God as the ruling authority of the world."[210] God's "dwelling place" (σκηνή) refers to people with heavenly citizenship, whether presently located on earth or in heaven (cf. Rev 21:3; Dan 8:10–13). The beast is also given power to "wage war against God's holy people and conquer (νικάω) them" (Rev 13:7; cf. Dan 7:21). One of the great reversals in Revelation is that though the beast conquers the saints through persecution and martyrdom, they actually conquer the beast (Rev 12:11; 15:2).

Yet the beast's deceptive authority seduces unbelievers from among the nations as "inhabitants of the earth" worship the beast (13:8). The future tense ("will worship") may point to widespread worship of a final beast at the end of the age. These earth dwellers are defined as "all whose names have not been written in the Lamb's book of life, the Lamb who was slain from the creation of the world." The "book of life" is the heavenly register of all true believers, meaning those with citizenship in God's kingdom.[211] But a syntactical choice presents itself here. The phrase "from the creation of the world" could modify "written," following the parallel in 17:8, indicating the time when names are written in the book.[212] Or, the phrase could modify its natural antecedent, "slain," referring to when God determined his redemptive plan would

207. Mounce, *Revelation*, 249.

208. Resseguie, *Revelation*, 182.

209. Note the divine passive "was given" occurring in 13:5 [2x], 7 [2x] in the Greek text; cf. also 6:2, 4 [2x], 8, 11; 7:2; 8:3; 9:1, 3, 5; 11:1, 2; 13:14, 15; 16:8; 19:8; 20:4.

210. Resseguie, *Revelation*, 182. Terms for "blasphemy" occur in 2:9 (of unbelievers), in 13:1, 5, 6 [2x]; 17:3 (of the beast), and in 16:9, 11, 21 (of those who refuse to repent after the bowl judgments).

211. Duvall, *Revelation*, 67.

212. So CSB, NET, ESV, NRSVue translations and Smalley, *Revelation*, 343; Aune, *Revelation 6–16*, 746–47; Beale, *Revelation*, 702.

center on the cross.[213] The second option is preferable because it is the most natural syntactically, with the first option placing twelve words between the antecedent and the modifying temporal clause. This interpretive decision does not diminish God's sovereignty but directs it, in this case, toward the timing of his redemptive plan (cf. Heb 4:3; 9:26; 1 Pet 1:20).

This section closes with a direct appeal to the church, calling for "patient endurance and faithfulness on the part of God's people," using an allusion to Jer 15:2 and 43:11 to warn believers about what to expect (Rev 13:9–10). While God's people are protected from God's wrath and the spiritual assaults of the unholy trinity, they are susceptible to persecution and even martyrdom (cf. Matt 24:9; Rev 2:10, 13; 6:9–11; 7:14; 11:2, 7; 13:7; 14:13; 16:6; 17:6; 18:24; 20:4). The phrase "whoever has ears to hear" points back to the initial calls to the seven churches to stay faithful (e.g., 2:7, 11, 17, 29; 3:6, 13, 22), calls that will continue throughout the book (e.g., 14:12; 17:14; cf. 6:9; 11:7; 12:11; 20:4). As secular power comes against the church, believers are to imitate Jesus in trusting the Father and refusing to retaliate. Osborne concludes, "The message is clear: do not make war against the beast; that is the work of God. Live faithfully and persevere in witness, but leave the battle to the Lord."[214]

11.4.5.1.5 The Beast from the Earth (13:11–18)

This section introduces the final member of the unholy trinity, the beast from the earth. Elsewhere in Revelation this beast is designated "the false prophet," highlighting its religious task of using deception and falsehood to draw people into false worship (16:13; 19:20; 20:10). Once again, evil parodies good: "As Christ received authority from the Father (Matt 11:27), so Antichrist receives authority from the dragon (Rev 13:4); and as the Holy Spirit glorifies Christ (John 16:14), so the false prophet glorifies the Antichrist (Rev 13:12)."[215]

John describes this second beast as looking like a lamb but speaking like a dragon (13:11–12; cf. Matt 7:15–20). Since he is allied with Satan and promotes the worship of the first beast, many take this beast to represent pagan religious power or ideology that supports wicked political/ military/social/economic power structures and/or leaders (i.e., the first beast). In the first century, this beast would surely have been identified in some way with the Roman imperial cult, whether wealthy supporters, the priesthood, a provincial council, or Greco-Roman religion in general—that is, some religious individual or structure that compelled emperor worship.[216] Since by the end of the first century all seven cities of Rev 2–3 contained temples dedicated to the worship of

213. So NIV, NLT translations and Caird, *Revelation of Saint John*, 168; Mounce, *Revelation*, 256; Osborne, *Revelation*, 503; Mathewson, *Revelation*, 174–75.

214. Osborne, *Revelation*, 506.

215. Mounce, *Revelation*, 255.

216. Koester, *Revelation*, 589–90. Also, see "False Prophet" in Hays, Duvall, and Pate, *A-to-Z Guide to Biblical Prophecy*, 152–53. See also Smalley, *Revelation*, 345.

the Roman emperor, the challenge of pagan religious power was indeed formidable. Throughout the rest of history, this beast has taken many forms, but its religious function remains a trademark.

The earth beast's primary weapon is that of signs—powerful but false and deceptive works (13:13–15). This fits with the general expectation that end-time eschatological figures would use signs to mislead people.[217] The reference to fire coming from heaven echoes the true prophet Elijah, who called down fire from heaven (1 Kgs 18:36–39; 2 Kgs 1:10–14). Such public displays of power constitute a massive propaganda campaign to draw people into worshiping the first beast. God's people have been repeatedly warned not to allow powerful signs and wonders to direct them away from their loyalty and allegiance to the one true God (e.g., Exod 7:11; Deut 13:1–4; Ezek 13:1–23; Matt 7:15; Mark 13:5–6, 21–23 par.; 2 Thess 2:9; 1 John 4:1–3). But unbelievers are vulnerable to deception.

This beast orders the earth dwellers to set up an image (εἰκών) in honor of the wounded-but-resuscitated first beast. He then breathes life into the image, causing it to speak. This "inspirational" work is yet another example of evil imitating good, in this case the Holy Spirit's work of inspiration and empowerment to speak. Such a counterfeit miracle calls to mind the ultimatum issued by King Nebuchadnezzar to worship or die (Dan 3:1–17). Statues and images of Roman emperors were commonplace throughout Asia, including a twenty-five-foot statue of Domitian (or perhaps Titus) in Ephesus.[218] Pagan religious leaders attempted to use sorcery and magic to animate images and idols.[219] The result here is that the demonic idol demands worship on pain of death (Rev 13:14; cf. 16:14; 19:20). Christians face the choice of giving allegiance to false gods to gain "life" or staying faithful to Christ with the real possibility of physical death.

In 13:16–18 the earth beast forces all people to receive a mark (χάραγμα) on their right hands or foreheads in order to buy and sell.[220] The penalty of economic persecution alludes to the power of trade guilds in the first century—organizations that promoted the worship of local deities and the Roman emperor in connection with social and economic activities. Most importantly, the beast's "mark" stands in contrast to the "seal" of the living God (7:3–4; 22:4), as both invisible stamps represent ownership, loyalty, and commitment. Every person bears one of these two imprints, but it is impossible to receive both. Every time the "mark" is mentioned, it is connected to idolatrous worship (13:16, 17; 14:9, 11; 16:2; 19:20; 20:4)

This "mark" is the "name of the [first] beast or the number of its name (i.e., "the

217. Deuteronomy 13:1–2; Did. 16.4; Ascen. Isa. 4.6–11; Sib. Or. 2.165–68; 3.63–67; Apoc. Dan. 13.1–13; Gk. Apoc. Ezra 4.26–27.

218. See "Images of the Roman Emperor," in Mark Wilson, "Revelation," 329.

219. See Steven J. Scherrer, "Signs and Wonders in the Imperial Cult: A New Look at a Roman Religious Institution in the Light of Rev 13:13–15," *JBL* 103 (1984): 599–610; Aune, *Revelation 6–16*, 762–64; Keener, *Revelation*, 351–52.

220. See "The Mark of the Beast," in Duvall, *Revelation*, 187.

number of a man . . . 666"). More ink has been spilled in trying to identify this "mark" than just about anything else in Revelation. Most scholars appeal to gematria, the Jewish practice of representing words or names by calculating their numerical equivalent. Using this method, the leading option for the beast is "Nero(n) Caesar," whose name equals 666 when the final "n" is added (i.e., Neron) and the name is converted to Hebrew: *N R O N Q S R* (N = 50, R = 200, O = 6, N = 50, Q = 100, S = 60, R = 200).[221] The use of gematria, however, can also present problems, like the needed extra step of converting to Hebrew to make the numbers work out. In addition, to see a historical reference to Nero does not exclude the likelihood of future beastly persons and structures or even a final eschatological beast. But the symbolism may run deeper than solving a mathematical problem.

Since numbers are consistently used in Revelation to symbolize spiritual realities, the primary significance of 666 is that it represents fallen humanity in rebellion against the Creator (i.e., "the number of a man" in 13:18) or, as Resseguie puts it, "humanity in collusion with the underworld striving for divinity."[222] While this does not rule out an allusion to Nero in the first century, neither does it demand that we always identify a particular figure as the beast. Fallen humanity in rebellion against the Triune God is often personified by evil rulers and structures, but the ultimate significance of the image is not to give us a puzzle to solve but to remind us that the trinity of imperfection (666) falls short of the trinity of perfection (777) and pales in comparison to the number of "Jesus"—888 (I = 10, H = 8, S = 200, O = 70, U = 400, S = 200).

11.4.5.2 The Lamb and the 144,000 (14:1–5)

In 14:1–20 we come to the last section of the extended interlude of 12:1–14:20. Whereas chapter 13 opens with the dragon standing on the seashore gathering his minions, chapter 14 portrays the Lamb standing victorious on Mount Zion with his faithful followers. The battle of chapter 13 gives way to the victory of chapter 14. Chapter 14 falls into three sections, each beginning with a reference to some form of seeing to provide the vision, followed by hearing to explain it (14:1–2, 6–7, 14–15). What John sees and hears—the glorious outcome of the battle between God and evil—provides abundant encouragement to persevere.

In his vision John sees before him the Lamb standing on Mount Zion (14:1). Geographically, Mount Zion was a common reference to the Temple Mount in Jerusalem or even to the entire city or its inhabitants (Pss 2:5–6; 9:11; Isa 40:9; 52:1–2). In the Old Testament, the term symbolized God's reign or the people following him,

221. See the extensive discussion on "Nero and the Beast" in Bauckham, *Climax of Prophecy*, 384–452, who also notes that 666 is a rare "doubly triangular" number, the eighth such number, perhaps suggesting Nero's relationship to the seven heads as an eighth (17:11). Cf. also Aune, *Revelation 6–16*, 771–73, on the practice of gematria.

222. Resseguie, *Revelation*, 190.

meaning God's true city (e.g., 2 Kgs 19:31; Pss 2:6; 48:2, 9–14; Isa 4:2–5; 37:30–32; Joel 2:17; Obad 17, 21; Mic 4:5–8).[223] Eschatologically, the Messiah will reign as King on Mount Zion, judging the wicked and bringing justice for his people (e.g., Pss 2:6–12; 4 Ezra 13:25–52; 2 Bar. 40). In 14:1, the only time the term is used in Revelation, "Zion" represents God's dwelling place and the center of his eternal kingdom—the new Jerusalem, the Holy City (cf. 21:1–2; Heb 12:22–23; Zech 2:10; 8:3). Revelation is assuming the prophetic restoration of Zion (e.g., Isa 1:27; 4:5; 46:13; 51:3; 62:11; Mic 4:2, 7). Standing with the Lamb on Mount Zion are the 144,000, a number depicting the people of God, the whole company of the redeemed.[224] These people carry the name of the Lamb and the Father written on their foreheads in contrast to unbelievers who are branded on their foreheads with the mark of the beast (13:16; 14:9; 20:4). The name on the forehead (7:3; 9:4; 14:1; 22:4; cf. 2:17; 3:12) reinforces that God's people belong to him, sealed with spiritual protection.

In 14:2–5 John sees the true character of God's people on display. First, they are people overflowing in praise to God (14:2–3). John hears a resounding heavenly anthem, booming forth like the roar of a rushing river or a deafening clap of thunder or a company of "harpists harping their harps" (alliteration in the Greek text). Although these realities can represent God's voice (e.g., 1:15; cf. Job 37:5; Ps 29:3; Ezek 43:2), here they represent the loud voices of praise from the heavenly multitude (Rev 19:6). Harps are also used in Revelation to accompany the praise of God's people and angelic beings (5:8–9; 15:2–4). Their praise continues with the singing of a "new song." They have overcome the world and now celebrate God's mighty victory (cf. 5:6–14; 7:9–12; 15:2–4; see also the Israelites praise to God for defeating their enemies in Exod 15:1–21). Only the 144,000 have endured as faithful followers of Jesus and grasp what this song signifies—participating in the victory of the Redeemer, the conquering Lamb.[225]

Second, they "did not defile themselves with women, for they remained virgins" (Rev 14:4). There are two reasonable interpretations of this difficult expression. Some turn to the cultural context for an explanation. Only men fought in the armies of ancient Israel and in preparation for a holy war they were required to maintain ceremonial purity (Deut 23:10; 1 Sam 21:5; 2 Sam 11:8–11). This reading sees God's people arrayed in battle formation, spiritually prepared for the war against God's enemies. Thus, the metaphor has nothing to do with being a woman or being a virgin but focuses on the common biblical image of God's people as a virgin betrothed to the Lord (e.g., 2 Kgs 19:21; Isa 37:22; Jer 31:4, 21; Amos 5:2). Being "defiled with women" in context functions as a symbol of spiritual adultery (Rev 14:4; cf. 14:8; 17:1–5; 18:3, 9; cf. Jer 3:1–10; 13:27; Ezek 16:15–58; 23:1–49; Hos 5:4). The other

223. Beale, *Revelation*, 731–32.

224. For more on the "144,000," see Duvall, *Revelation*, 193.

225. Koester, *Revelation*, 609. Bauckham, *Climax of Prophecy*, 230, observes that the "new song" celebrates a victory in a holy war in 2 Chr 20:28; Pss 98:1–3; 144:9; Isa 42:10–13; Jdt 16:2–3.

viable interpretation understands "virgins" (παρθένος) in the Greek text with what follows rather than what precedes—"The ones who follow the Lamb wherever he goes are virgins," with "virgins" functioning as a predicate nominative in relation to "are" (εἰσιν).[226] Most translations go with the first option but the point is similar either way: "Just as biblical prophets often portrayed Israel as either an unfaithful prostitute or as a pure virgin or bride for God, so Revelation portrays unrepentant humanity as a prostitute (Rev 17:1–5) and those faithful to Christ as his pure spouse (19:7; 21:2, 9)."[227] John is not condemning women or marriage but is calling for spiritual faithfulness and purity among God's people.[228]

Third, they are devoted disciples—"They follow the Lamb wherever he goes" (14:4). This expression provides a foundational definition of biblical discipleship (cf. Mark 8:34).[229] Discipleship may be many things, but chief among them is its Christocentricity—the people of the Messiah following Jesus, the Lamb of God. In exploring this theme of discipleship in Revelation in more detail, I have identified several important patterns of spiritual formation: the impact of righteous deeds, the necessity of rejecting evil, the value of repentance, and the significance of witness, obedience, perseverance, and worship (see 18.5).[230]

Fourth, they were purchased from among mankind and offered as firstfruits to God and the Lamb (Rev 14:4). Those who could not buy or sell (13:17) have been bought or redeemed (ἀγοράζω) by the precious blood of the Lamb (5:9; 14:3; cf. 1 Cor 6:20; 7:23). They are then offered to God and the Lamb as "firstfruits," a term used elsewhere of both Jewish and gentile disciples of Jesus (e.g., Rom 8:23; 11:16; 16:5; 1 Cor 15:23; 16:15; 2 Thess 2:13; Jas 1:18). The firstfruits of the harvest, whether grain, grapes, or other crops, were often brought to the temple ahead of the rest of the harvest and presented as a sacrifice to the Lord (e.g., Exod 23:19; 34:22; Num 18:12–13; Deut 26:1–11). The emphasis here is on the 144,000 representing *all* those who are purchased by the Lamb rather than on the first of many to follow.[231]

Fifth, "no lie was found in their mouths; they are blameless" (Rev 14:5; cf. Isa 53:9; Zeph 3:13). Lying usually ties to immorality, idolatry, falsehood, and deceit

226. Koester, *Revelation*, 611.

227. Keener, *Revelation*, 371.

228. Given our symbolic reading of the 144,000, the contrast in the book between godly women and evil women (e.g., the great prostitute Babylon/Rome vs. the bride of Christ), and the massive problems with a literal reading, the term "virgins" should be understood as a metaphor for all genuine believers who have refused to compromise with the world (cf. Rev 3:4; 19:7–9; 21:2; 2 Cor 11:2). For a lengthy discussion of the problems associated with interpreting 14:4 literally and why the figurative reading is much preferred, see Beale, *Revelation*, 737–41.

229. See David E. Aune, "Following the Lamb: Discipleship in the Apocalypse," in *Apocalypticism, Prophecy and Magic in Early Christianity* (Grand Rapids: Baker Academic, 2006), 66–78. Also Douglas D. Webster, *Follow the Lamb: A Pastoral Approach to The Revelation* (Eugene, OR: Cascade, 2014).

230. See J. Scott Duvall, "Following the Lamb: Spiritual Formation in the Book of Revelation" (paper presented at ETS, San Francisco, CA, November 2011).

231. Smalley, *Revelation to John*, 358; Beale, *Revelation*, 742. Resseguie, *Revelation*, 196–97, notes a similar "qualitative" usage in Jer 2:3 where all Israel is redeemed and Jas 1:18 where "firstfruits" probably refers to the whole people of God. Used in this way, the image complements the concept of virginity.

(e.g., Rev 2:2; 3:9; 16:13; 21:8, 27; 22:15). While the beast utters blasphemies (13:5), the redeemed speak without lies or deceit. They are ambassadors of truth, and for this reason they are "blameless," a term emphasizing ethical integrity (e.g., Eph 1:4; 5:27; Phil 2:15; Col 1:22; Jude 24).

11.4.5.3 Proclamations of Judgment and Reward (14:6–13)

Following the vision of the Lamb standing with his people on Mount Zion celebrating their victory, we encounter three angelic proclamations of judgment (14:6–13), followed by two visions of judgment (14:14–20). In this first section, the three proclamations (14:6–11) precede a call for the saints to endure (14:12) and the second of seven beatitudes (14:13).

The first angel proclaims the "eternal gospel" to people from every nation (14:6–7; cf. 5:9; 7:9; 21:24, 26; Mark 13:10). This is the only use of the noun "gospel" (εὐαγγέλιον) in the book (cf. the verb εὐαγγελίζω, "to proclaim," in Rev 10:7; 14:6). The list "nation, tribe, language and people" here is not equivalent to the "inhabitants of the earth," so hope for their conversion remains—that they will "fear God and give him glory" and "worship him" (14:7; cf. 11:13; 15:4; 19:5, 7; Ps 96:2–3). The context of judgment, however, does not offer encouragement. The motivation to turn to God, the Creator of the heavens, earth, sea, and springs, presents itself as urgent since "the hour of his judgment (κρίσις) has come" (Rev 14:7; cf. 16:7; 18:10; 19:2). People are confronted with the most basic of all spiritual decisions: Who or what is the true object of worship?

The second angel announces the future fall of Babylon the Great as though it has already occurred. Mathewson notes, "It refers to the *verdict of judgment* by the angel given in advance of the *execution* of the verdict in the actual fall of Babylon in 16:19; 18:2" (cf. Isa 21:9; Jer 51:8).[232] The ancient city of Babylon was the capital of an empire that destroyed Jerusalem in 587/586 BC and came to symbolize the enemies of God's people. Revelation refers to "Babylon the Great" six times (14:8; 16:19; 17:5; 18:2, 10, 21; cf. Dan 4:30), an image that represents any great center of pagan power (cf. the early Christian reference to Rome as Babylon in 1 Pet 5:13).

Forcing the nations to drink the wine of her adulteries refers to the great prostitute influencing the nations to join in her idolatry and immorality (Rev 17:2, 4; 18:3, 9; cf. Jer 51:7).

With the third angel's announcement in Rev 14:9–11, God's judgment falls on the beast's followers. The *inclusio* in verses 9 and 11 that highlights the worship of the beast and the reception of the beast's mark joins together this unit. Consequently, judgment

232. Mathewson, *Revelation*, 192. See also 10:7 (cf. John 13:31) for this use of the futuristic or proleptic aorist (ἐτελέσθη—"will be accomplished").

comes on those who willfully and continuously rebel against their Creator.[233] There is nothing random or arbitrary about the dispensing of God's wrath. Those judged are forced to "drink the wine of God's fury, which has been poured full strength into the cup of his wrath" (14:10), indicating the wine of God's judgment will not be diluted as was customary with wine in the ancient world. The wicked will encounter God's undiluted wrath—his "holy and righteous condemnation of sin and evil" (cf. Jer 25:15; Isa 51:17; Pss 11:6; 75:8).[234]

The recipients of God's wrath will be "tormented" in the presence of the holy angels and the Lamb and the smoke of their torment "will rise for ever and ever" (14:10–11). This judgment is verified by the heavenly court consisting of the holy angels and the Lamb, affirming the justice of God's judgments. Despite attempts to dilute the severity or duration of this judgment, the evidence points toward eternal conscious suffering. Throughout Revelation the verb "torment" (βασανίζω) refers to conscious suffering rather than annihilation of personal existence (9:5; 11:10; 12:2; 18:7, 10, 15; 20:10).[235] Burning sulfur is often associated with punishment (19:20; 20:10; 21:8), and the use of the phrase "for ever and ever" supports this reading.[236] In contrast to the saints who "rest from their labor" (14:13), the wicked experience an eternal restlessness, indicating spiritual and psychological suffering apart from God's life-giving presence (cf. 1 En. 102:3). The beast worshipers are rewarded with the object of their worship, revealing the chaotic and self-destructive nature of evil, a deathly restlessness that closes them off from God's presence. Mangina notes the progressive nature of these three angelic announcements showing God's merciful hesitation to judge—beginning with the proclamation of an eternal gospel, moving to the pronouncement of judgment on the pagan center of power, and finally narrowing down to those who pledge loyalty to the beast even after hearing of Babylon's sure and certain fall.[237]

In Rev 14:12 God's people once again are called to perseverance or "patient endurance" (ὑπομονή), a term appearing seven times in Revelation to spell out the commitment required of Jesus's followers (1:9; 2:2, 3, 19; 3:10; 13:10; 14:12). Here God's persevering people are defined as those "who keep his commands and remain faithful

233. See Terence Nichols, *Death and the Afterlife: A Theological Introduction* (Grand Rapids: Brazos, 2010), 176–81. Nichols observes: "They are in hell by their own choice and would not want to be in heaven, because heaven would mean choosing God over themselves or their ego" (176). Also, see C. S. Lewis, *The Great Divorce* (1945; reprint, New York: HarperSanFrancisco, 1973).

234. For more on "God's Wrath," see Duvall, *Revelation*, 205.

235. See Beale, *Revelation*, 762; Osborne, *Revelation*, 541–42; Fanning, *Revelation*, 395; Keener, *Revelation*, 374–75; Stewart, *Reading the Book of Revelation*, 140. Mounce, *Revelation*, 274–75, concludes: "The teaching of the NT on the eternal consequences of willfully rejecting the love of God as manifested in the death of Christ for our sins does not allow us to put the doctrine aside as sub-Christian or reinterpret it in such a way as to remove the abrasive truth of eternal punishment."

236. Duvall, *Revelation*, 198: "It also applies to God and Christ receiving eternal praise and glory (1:6; 5:13; 7:12), to God and Christ's eternal nature (1:18; 4:9–10; 10:6; 15:7), to Christ's reign as Messiah (11:15), to the believer's future reign (22:5), and to the eternal suffering of the unholy trinity—the devil, the beast, and the false prophet—and their wicked followers (19:3; 20:10; cf. 20:13–15)."

237. Mangina, *Revelation*, 175–76.

to Jesus." Such endurance involves allegiance to the Lord and active resistance to the idolatry and immorality promoted by a pagan empire.

This section closes with the second of seven beatitudes in Revelation announcing what God has in store for his faithful people (1:3; 14:13; 16:15; 19:9; 20:6; 22:7, 14). The call to faithful endurance in verse 12 may result in physical martyrdom but always calls for dying as a faithful disciple (cf. 1 Thess 4:16) and applies to believers of every age (i.e., "from now on"). The Holy Spirit joins in with a resounding "Yes," followed by a promise/blessing that those who die in Christ will "rest from their labor, for their deeds with follow them." Eternal rest is a reward to the righteous for staying faithful through hardship (Rev 14:13; cf. 2 Thess 1:7; Heb 4:1–11; Rev 7:14–17; 21:5–7). Such faithfulness is demonstrated by actions, which reflect the true character of a person.[238]

11.4.5.4 The Harvest of the Earth (14:14–20)

The judgment theme of 14:6–13 continues in 14:14–20, a unit that consists of two visions: the grain harvest (14:14–16) and the grape harvest (14:17–20). The main debate is whether the first vision shows the gathering of the righteous at Christ's return[239] or whether both visions depict God's judgment of the wicked.[240] Revelation affirms both truths elsewhere, but the meaning of the grain harvest remains difficult to discern. For several reasons (see below) we take both visions as symbolic portraits of judgment on the unrighteous, the first more general and the second more specific.

John now sees a white cloud and seated on it "one like a son of man" with a gold crown on his head and a sharp sickle in his hand (14:14). The phrase "one like a son of man" is no doubt drawn from Dan 7:13 and refers to the risen Christ (cf. Rev 1:7, 13). He comes with the "clouds of heaven" in Daniel, and here is seated on a cloud (14:14, 15, 16), signifying his power and glory as both Savior and Judge (cf. Matt 24:30–31; 26:62–65). The gold crown represents his sovereign kingship (Rev 14:14; cf. 19:12), and the sharp sickle (δρέπανον) serves as an instrument of judgment (14:14, 15, 16, 17, 18 [2x], 19).

Another angel comes out of the temple with a message from God for the Son of Man: "take your sickle and reap" since the harvest is ripe for reaping (14:15–16; cf. 1 Thess 4:16). While some see here a harvest of the righteous by Jesus (cf. Matt 9:37–38; John 4:34–38), the context weighs in favor of a judgment of the wicked.[241] First, Jesus will return to judge as well as to redeem (e.g., Rev 1:7, 13–20; 19:11–21; Dan 7:13–14).

238. See "Judgment according to Deeds" in Duvall, *Revelation*, 61.

239. See, e.g., Bauckham, *Climax of Prophecy*, 289–96; Bauckham, *Theology*, 94–98; Osborne, *Revelation*, 549–53; Smalley, *Revelation*, 372–74.

240. See e.g., Mounce, *Revelation*, 278; Beale, *Revelation*, 772–79; Fanning, *Revelation*, 398; Keener, *Revelation*, 377; Aune, *Revelation 6–16*, 801–3; Witherington, *Revelation*, 196.

241. See Eckhard J. Schnabel, "John and the Future of the Nations," *BBR* 12.2 (2002): 243–71, esp. 257–62; Beale, *Revelation*, 776–79.

Second, the harvest metaphor may be used of the gathering of the righteous or the wicked (e.g., Matt 13:30, 40–42; cf. Jer 51:33; Hos 6:11). Third, the term "firstfruits" in Rev 14:4 denotes the redemption of all God's people (5:9) and does not require a greater harvest later in the chapter. Fourth, the "time" (ὥρα) of reaping occurs ten times in Revelation, usually referring to the judgment of the wicked (3:3, 10; 9:15; 11:13; 14:7, 15; 17:12; 18:10, 17, 19). Fifth, both visions are joined by verbal threads (e.g., angels, sickle, temple area, loud voice, the earth). Sixth, and most importantly, both visions in 14:14–20 are patterned after Joel 3:9–15, especially verse 13, which features both a grain and grape harvest: "Swing the sickle, for the harvest is ripe. Come, trample the grapes, for the winepress is full and the vats overflow—so great is their wickedness!" Beale adds that the Joel passage is "the only OT passage where harvesting with a 'sickle' is spoken of figuratively."[242] Revelation 14:14-20 presents another case where the second vision adds detail to or interprets the first (e.g., Rev 7:1–17). The doubling highlights the severity of judgment—the fate of the wicked in the two visions (14:6–20) standing in sharp contrast to the fate of the righteous (14:1–5).

As the second vision begins, God sends forth another angel of judgment with a sharp sickle (14:17). Then, still another angel, the one in charge of the fire, comes from the heavenly altar to instruct the first angel, perhaps suggesting that God's judgments are in response to the prayers of his people for vindication (14:18; cf. 6:9–11; 8:3–5). Throughout Scripture, fire often symbolizes judgment (e.g., Isa 66:15; Jer 15:14; Ezek 21:31; Zeph 3:8; 2 Thess 1:7; Heb 10:27; 2 Pet 3:7). The first angel swings his sickle to harvest the clusters of grapes and throws them into the great winepress of God's wrath (Rev 14:19). In biblical times, the winepress was a small pit where the harvested grapes were trampled to squeeze out the juice. Figuratively, the winepress commonly represents God's judgment on his enemies (e.g., Isa 18:5; 63:3; Joel 3:13; Lam 1:15). In Rev 19:15 Jesus himself "treads the winepress of the fury of the wrath of God Almighty." There, the trampling occurs "outside the city," signifying separation from God's people (e.g., Rev 22:14–15; Heb 13:12). Here the trampling of the winepress outside the city produces the gruesome image of blood rising to the height of a horse's bridle and flowing for 1,600 stadia (cf. 1 En. 100:1–3).[243] As Fanning and others note, at this point the vehicle and tenor of the metaphor are intermingled.[244] But the intent of the image is clear—to shock the readers back into spiritual reality by awakening them to Babylon's deadly influence and to God's serious commitment to judge sin thoroughly and completely. As Resseguie concludes, "Revelation 14 sharpens the choice

242. Beale, *Revelation*, 774.

243. The distance of "1,600 stadia" likely represents the universal scope of God's judgment. The number four represents the earth or creation and ten represents completeness, so that $4^2 \times 10^2 = 1{,}600$, signifying the totality of God's judgment.

244. Fanning, *Revelation*, 399–400. Caird, *Imagery of the Bible*, 152, defines "vehicle" as "the thing to which the word normally and naturally applies," and "tenor" as "the thing to which it is transferred." See also Resseguie, *Revelation*, 18–22, for a helpful discussion of metaphor and simile in Revelation.

that all must make: one cannot bear the name of God and the Lamb *and* the imprint of the beast."[245]

11.4.6 The Bowl Judgments (15:1–16:21)

An *inclusio* of seven angels with seven plagues (15:1, 8) sets off 15:1–8 as a unit. The expression "And I saw/looked" (καὶ εἶδον) divides the passage into three sections: the introduction (15:1), the celebration of God's people (15:2–4), and the seven angels receiving the bowls of God's wrath (15:5–8). The sandwiching of the victory song in 15:2–4 shows a connection between the prayers/praises of God's people and the outpouring of God's justice (cf. 5:8; 8:3–5; Rom 12:14–21).[246] Revelation 15 then introduces the bowl judgments of chapter 16, the third and final series of seven judgments (cf. seals in 6:1–8:1, trumpets in 8:2–9:21; 11:14–19). As the action intensifies, there is no interlude between the sixth and seventh elements in this series.

11.4.6.1 Transition: Seven Angels with Seven Last Plagues (15:1–8)

John sees "another great and marvelous sign" in heaven (15:1; cf. 12:1, 3) consisting of seven angels with seven last plagues. They are the "last" (ἐσχάτας) plagues *because* (ὅτι) God's wrath is completed (the divine passive ἐτελέσθη) with them, meaning this third and final set of seven plagues displays God's full commitment to judge evil (cf. the "it is done" of the seventh bowl judgment in 16:17). John is not so much interested in delineating a chronological timeline, however, as he is in stressing the eschatological certainty of God's wrath against evil. Caird also notes the use of Exodus imagery throughout and in keeping with this new exodus theme, people respond much like the rebellious Pharaoh: they refuse to repent and instead curse God (16:9, 11, 21).[247] Similarly, Beale suggests that the seven last plagues correspond generally to the ten plagues that precede the deliverance of God's people from slavery in Egypt.[248]

The crystal-clear sea of glass in 4:6 symbolized God's holiness and transcendent majesty, while the context here suggests that the sea mingled with fire relates in some way to God's judgment.[249] More importantly, victorious Christians are portrayed as standing beside ("on," ἐπί, perhaps symbolizing triumph) the sea holding harps given them by God. They have overcome or conquered (νικάω) a multitude of evil enemies: the beast, its image, and the number of its name (13:1–2, 14, 17–18).[250] They have

245. Resseguie, *Revelation*, 202.

246. Keener, *Revelation*, 384.

247. Caird, *Revelation*, 197, notes "a more complete and systematic Exodus typology than in any other part of John's book: the plagues, the crossing of the sea, the engulfing of the pursuers, the song of Moses, the giving of the law amid the smoke of Sinai, and the erection of the Tent of Testimony."

248. Beale, *Revelation*, 383.

249. Resseguie, *Revelation*, 205, notes that the "plagues of fire (8:7, 8–9; 9:17–18; 16:8) are God's judgment on earth, and the lake of fire is God's judgment on evil (19:20; 20:10, 14–15; 21:8)."

250. See "'Overcome' in Revelation," in Duvall, *Revelation*, 42.

persevered through the trials and tribulations common to the seven churches, chiefly the pressure to conform to the immoral and idolatrous pattern of this world, and have remained faithful to Jesus.

The song of Moses originally celebrated God's deliverance of his people through the flood in victory over Pharaoh and his army (Exod 15:1–18; Deut 32:1–43). This song now becomes the song of the Lamb who through the eschatological exodus delivers his people from the dragon and his demonic army. This repeats the scene of the 144,000 singing triumphantly the new song in Revelation 14:1–3.

The song itself in 15:3b–4 emphasizes God's character and mighty works followed by the worshipful response of his people. In addition, there is the subtle thread of God's righteous rule over the nations (15:3, 4). Various Old Testament texts are woven together to form the hymn. The first half of the song uses synonymous parallelism to highlight God's actions and ways, complete with titles reflecting his attributes:

> Great and marvelous are your deeds, [Exod 34:10; Pss 86:10; 111:2; 139:14]
> Lord God Almighty. [e.g., Rev 4:8; 11:17; 16:7; 19:6; 21:22; cf. 1:8; 16:14; 19:15]
> Just and true are your ways, [Deut 32:4; Ps 145:17; cf. Rev 16:5, 7; 19:2]
> King of the nations. [Jer 10:7]

God's mighty acts here relate primarily to God's ability to judge his enemies and save his people (note the "great and marvelous sign" of the seven last plagues in 15:1). These awesome deeds of judgment and salvation are administered in a way that is righteous and true. In contrast, we see the dragon's use of power in ways that are deceitful and manipulative. God's actions flow from his character: sovereign, all-powerful, faithful, holy, and righteous.

The second half of the song (Rev 15:4) joins two rhetorical questions into one, followed by three explanatory clauses (all begin with "for," ὅτι):

> Who will not fear you, Lord,
> and bring glory to your name? [Jer 10:7; Ps 86:9; in contrast to Rev 13:4]
> For you alone are holy.
> [For] all nations will come
> and worship before you,
> for your righteous acts have been revealed. [On all three clauses, see Exod 15:11; Ps 86:8–10; Jer 10:6–7.]

This section of the hymn rejoices that God alone is the glorious, holy, worthy-to-be-worshiped God. Because he is uniquely worthy of praise and devotion, people from all nations will join in the worship (Rev 7:9; 14:6).

The scene now shifts from the heavenly worship back to the great and marvelous sign of 15:1. John sees the heavenly temple, namely, the tabernacle of the covenant law, opened (15:5; cf. 11:19). This recalls the tabernacle that accompanied Israel on its wilderness journey and the tablets of stone bearing the Ten Commandments placed in the ark of the covenant (Exod 16:34; 25:16, 21; Num 17:7; 18:2). The sign of God's presence now stands behind his faithfulness to judge evil and save his people from their enemies, hence the symbolism of the seven angels with seven plagues coming from the temple (Rev 15:6). The clean, shining linen and golden sashes worn by the angels reflect their priestly (Lev 16:4, 23) and royal (Rev 1:13) roles as Christ's agents in administering these judgments (cf. Ezek 9:2; Dan 10:5; 12:6–7).

One of the living creatures gives the seven angels the seven golden bowls filled with God's wrath, but these judgments come ultimately from God, the eternal One.[251] The "bowls" (φιάλη), mentioned twelve times in the New Testament, all in Revelation (5:8; 15:7; 16:1, 2, 3, 4, 8, 10, 12, 17; 17:1; 21:9), are likely the wide, shallow vessels used by the priests to carry offerings and libations (e.g., Exod 25:29; 27:3). The strong link with Revelation 5:8 ("bowls" are only described as "golden" in 5:8 and 15:7) makes it more likely that the prayers of God's people play a major role in bringing forth God's justice to make things right in the world (also 8:3–5).

At the giving of the bowls of wrath to the seven angels, the temple is filled with smoke or cloud, an expression of God's glorious and powerful presence (cf. Exod 24:15–16; 40:34–38; 1 Kgs 8:10–12; 2 Chr 5:13–14; Isa 6:1–6; Ezek 44:4; 1 Tim 6:15–16; 1 John 1:5). Our God is a "consuming fire," says the writer of Hebrews (12:29), full of glory and power (cf. Exod 24:17; Deut 4:24; 9:3; Ps 97:3; Isa 33:14). No one can enter his presence until judgment has been completed (Rev 15:8). There are several primary interpretations of this reference to the completion of God's plagues,[252] the most likely being that "the true worship of God—the very purpose of the tabernacle—cannot be resumed until the world is actually remade, renewed, and purged of every evil."[253] Hence, the holy Triune God is the temple of the new creation (21:22).

11.4.6.2 The Bowl Judgments (16:1–21)

Revelation 16 supplies details about the bowl judgments introduced in chapter 15. Both the trumpet and bowl judgments are patterned after the plagues against Egypt reported in Exodus, so there are many similarities between these last two series of plagues.[254] All three series describe events that occur in the last days—the time between

251. The living creatures are an exalted order of angels who surround God's throne (4:6; 5:6, 8, 11; 7:11; 14:3), lead in heavenly worship (4:8–9; 5:8, 14; 7:11; 14:3; 19:4), and serve to execute God's judgment (6:1–7; 15:7). See comments in 4:1–11.

252. Smalley, *Revelation*, 392–93.

253. Mangina, *Revelation*, 185.

254. See chart at 11.4.4.2; Mark Wilson, *Charts on the Book of Revelation*, 80, with some modifications, and also Beale, *Revelation*, 809–10.

the first and second comings of Christ.[255] Even with the recapitulation of events over the same time period, there is some intensification from seals to trumpets to bowls, and each series concludes at the end of history and the final judgment. We see God's sovereign hand at work throughout—the temple voice of God initiating the plagues (16:1), the declaration that God's judgments are just (16:5–7), his control over the judgments (16:9), the cursing of God as the one responsible (16:9, 11, 21), the voice from the throne declaring, "It is done!" (16:17), and God giving Babylon the cup of his wrath (16:19). The repeated use of the term "great" (μέγας) occurs eleven times in chapter 16 to emphasize the cosmic magnitude of the battle between God and the forces of evil.[256] There is a hymn praising God for his justice in 16:5–7 that briefly interrupts the outpouring of the seven bowls. And with the seventh bowl, God gives Babylon the Great the cup of his wrath (16:18–19), with more details about Babylon's downfall to come in chapters 17–18.

With the pouring out of the first bowl those who have pledged allegiance to the beast by receiving his mark are now marked by God with festering sores (16:1–2). The second and third bowls bring a bloody death both to the sea and inland waters (16:3–4), as God gives those who have shed the blood of his people blood to drink (16:6). God's judgment of the prostitute Babylon is often described using "blood for blood" imagery (e.g., 17:6; 18:24; 19:2). But unlike the partial trumpet plagues, the bowl judgments affect the entire earth. Between the third and fourth bowls we find an angelic doxology (affirmed by the heavenly altar, perhaps including the martyrs of 6:9–11) that applauds the integrity and validity of God's justice (16:5, 7). The Holy One has judged justly; the judgments of the Lord God Almighty are true and right. Many commentators see hear a clear expression of the principle of *lex talionis* (the law of retribution).[257]

The fourth bowl intensifies the sun's heat but even when scorched by fire, the wicked refuse to repent and glorify God (16:8–9). The fifth bowl is poured out on the throne of the beast so that searing light is now replaced by darkness (16:10–11). Whether suffering judgment by light or darkness, three times we are told that the ungodly stubbornly refuse to repent (16:9, 11, 21; cf. 2:20–22; 9:20–21; 21:8; 22:15). They gnaw their tongues in agony, perhaps symbolic of their severe spiritual torment (cf. 9:5–6). Despite their agony, they cling to demon worship, idolatry, murder, magic arts, sexual immorality, deception, and falsehood. Rather than owning up to their sinful ways, they stubbornly harden their hearts like Pharaoh and curse (βλασφημέω) God, following the example of their beastly master (16:9; cf. 13:1, 5, 6 [2x]; 17:3).

255. See Schnabel, *40 Questions about End Times*, 67–74, and Beale, *Revelation*, 810.

256. Resseguie, *Revelation*, 212.

257. E.g., Osborne, *Revelation*, 601, who says that "the *lex talionis* of divine judgment reaches its high point in 16:5–7."

The sixth bowl judgment prepares for the epic battle first by drying up the barrier between God's people and their enemies, symbolized by "the great river Euphrates" (16:12; cf. 9:14; Gen 15:18; Deut 1:7; Josh 1:4).[258] The "kings from the East" (Rev 16:12) and the "kings of the whole world" (16:14) depict wicked political powers loyal to the beast and willing to follow him into battle. In Ezekiel 38–39 Gog and Magog represent enemies who battle God's people—the likely background here (cf. Rev 19:17; 20:7–8).

In 16:13–14 demonic spirits, like a plague of frogs, come out the mouth of the false trinity: the dragon, the beast, and the false prophet. The repetition of "mouth" (στόμα) shows that their primary weapon is not military but demonic false teaching and deceptive propaganda (cf. 13:3, 12–14). Diabolical signs lure the wicked powers to a place called "Armageddon" for the "battle on the great day of God Almighty" (16:15–16).[259] This "mountain of Megiddo" was the site of significant ancient battles between Israel and her enemies (e.g., Judg 5:19–21; 2 Kgs 23:29–30; 2 Chr 35:20–25), and the term "Armageddon" came to signify not so much a specific geographical location but an eschatological battle between God and the forces of evil (see Rev 17:14; 19:11–21; 20:7–10 for more details on the one-sided victory).

Revelation 16:15 serves as an important parenthesis and the third beatitude in the book. With this abrupt interjection Jesus offers an important message for the readers: considering the state of warfare, Christians should stay faithful and resist compromise. In his eschatological discourse in the Gospels, Jesus repeatedly warns his followers to stay alert because his return will occur suddenly and (for some) unexpectedly, like a thief in the middle of the night (e.g., Matt 24:43; Luke 12:39; Rev 3:3; cf. 1 Thess 5:2, 4; 2 Pet 3:10). Nakedness here represents shame, guilt, and liability to judgment (cf. Rev 3:4–5, 17–18; 19:8–9). As Resseguie observes, "The great eschatological battle turns out to be an individual spiritual battle."[260]

The seventh and final bowl judgment brings history to a close (16:17–21). God's voice from the throne declares the achievement of salvation through judgment: "It is done!" (cf. 10:7; 21:6; John 19:30). A storm theophany concludes not only the seals and trumpets but the bowls as well (cf. Rev 6:12–14; 8:3–5; 11:19; Exod 19:16–18), except the earthquake here is the most severe of all time, heralding the finality of God's justice (Rev 16:18). The "great city" or "Babylon the Great" represents any great secular center of cultural, political, economic, social, and military power, and Rome in the first century certainly fit the bill (14:8; 17:5; 18:2, 10, 21; Dan 4:30; 1 Pet 5:13).[261]

258. Resseguie, *Revelation*, 213, observes how the Euphrates is "the antithesis of the 'river of the water of life' (22:1) . . . [that] flows through the new Jerusalem and sustains the inhabitants of the eternal city."

259. See "Armageddon," in Duvall, *Revelation*, 217; Jon Paulien, "Armageddon (Place)," *ABD* 1:394–95; Fanning, *Revelation*, 423–25. Although the etymology of the term is debated, the symbolism seems clear.

260. Resseguie, *Revelation*, 215.

261. Beale, *Revelation*, 843.

Personified as a wicked prostitute, she is "remembered before God"[262] and made to drink "the wine of the fury of his wrath" (16:19). God's splitting of the city into thirds and the resulting collapse of the nations demonstrates the complete destruction of the system (14:8–10). The disintegration of the cosmos is also noted in 6:14 and 20:11 (cf. Exod 9:13–35; Ezek 38:19–22) and, as in much of Scripture, the plague of huge hailstones here denotes divine judgment (e.g., Josh 10:11; Job 38:22–23; Isa 28:17; Ezek 38:22; Hag 2:17). Sadly, the response of the wicked is not submissive repentance but rage-filled curses aimed at God (Rev 16:21).

11.5 THE DESTRUCTION OF BABYLON THE GREAT (17:1–19:5)

11.5.1 Introduction

Following the bowl judgments, one of the angels with the seven bowls invites John to witness in greater detail God's judgment of the prostitute. Consequently, the judgment of Babylon the Great in 17:1–19:5 should be viewed as extending the final bowl judgments of chapter 16. In 17:1–6 John receives a vision of the great prostitute riding the scarlet beast, followed by the revealing angel's interpretation of the vision in 17:7–18. Most commentators note the numerous parallels between Revelation 13 and 17, illustrating again the cyclical presentation of truth in the book.

As this section progresses, believers are called to come out of Babylon in order not to share in her sins or receive her punishment (18:1–8). At Babylon's fall, we hear the lament of the kings, merchants, and mariners in 18:9–19. This unit closes with celebration that God has brought justice and vindication for his people (18:20–19:5). Babylon's destruction is complete and all of heaven rejoices!

11.5.2 The Vision of the Great Prostitute and the Scarlet Beast (17:1–6a)

One of the seven angels with the seven bowls invites John to join him on a visionary tour of God's judgment on Babylon (17:1–2). The vision of the harlot and the vision of the bride begin similarly: "Come, I will show you . . ." (17:1; 21:9–10; cf. 1:1; 4:1; 22:1, 6, 8), stressing the contrast between the two. Two different cities, two different women, two different peoples, two different Gods/gods, two different destinies. John is about to witness firsthand God's judgment of the harlot, but the vision begins with her influence and affluence. She "sits on many waters," meaning she has widespread influence and rule over humanity (cf. 17:15 where the expression

262. See the insightful comments on God "remembering" in Mangina, *Revelation*, 191–92.

is defined as "peoples, multitudes, nations, and languages"). The "great prostitute" is equivalent to Babylon the Great and represents any influential center of ungodly power (e.g., first-century Rome). She peddles immorality and idolatry, summed up here as "adulteries."[263]

John is carried away "in the Spirit" to a wilderness, where he sees a woman sitting on a scarlet beast (17:3). Four times in Revelation we find John "in the Spirit" or "carried away by/in the Spirit" (1:10; 4:2; 17:3; 21:10), indicating that his prophetic visionary experience/message comes from God (cf. Ezekiel's experience in Ezek 3:12; 8:3; 11:1; 37:1; 43:5). Although the "wilderness" serves as a positive symbol of protection in Revelation 12, here it depicts a desolate venue for judgment (cf. Isa 21:1–10). While the prostitute sits on "many waters" in Revelation 17:1, she sits on "a scarlet beast" here in 17:3, and both images symbolize the beast's evil partnerships and influence. Revelation's symbols are often polyvalent, a flexibility that usually reinforces the primary message. The beast first rose from the sea in 13:1 and represents secular power allied with Satan to oppose God and the saints. Here the beast is scarlet or red, tying it to the red dragon (12:3), is covered with blasphemous names or claims to deity (13:1), and has seven heads and ten horns, indicating its extensive power and authority (17:9–14; cf. 12:3).

The woman's attire of purple and scarlet and her flashing gold adornments (cf. 18:16) spotlight her luxurious royalty and contrast sharply with the "fine linen, bright and clean" worn by God's people (19:8; cf. 21:9–21). She is holding a golden cup full of "abominable things," further described as "the filth of her adulteries," revealing her idolatrous and immoral character, especially her self-centered lust for power. The name written on her forehead is most revealing of her true allegiance: *BABYLON THE GREAT THE MOTHER OF PROSTITUTES AND OF THE ABOMINATIONS OF THE EARTH* (13:16; 14:9; 17:5; 20:4). This "mystery" name shows that end-time events once hidden are now not only being revealed but, as Beale points out, are being revealed in an unexpected or ironic manner.[264] As the "mother of prostitutes" Babylon the Great aggressively reproduces her corruption of idolatry and immorality throughout the world.

As we have come to expect, at pivotal moments in his recounting of his vision John speaks forthrightly about the circumstances and responsibilities of God's people (e.g., 12:11; 13:9–10; 14:4, 13; 16:6–7, 15), and such is the case here. The woman, John sees, is intoxicated with the blood of believers, described here as "God's holy people, . . . those who bore testimony to Jesus" (17:6; see 1:2, 9; 6:9; 11:7; 12:11, 17; 19:10; 20:4). The image of shedding blood, according to Beale, embraces multiple forms of persecution, including economic ostracism, exile, imprisonment, and martyrdom.[265] John

263. Duvall, *Revelation*, 221: "Her adulterous influence is highlighted by the sevenfold occurrence of Greek words with the *porn*-root throughout this chapter ('prostitute' in 17:1, 5, 15, 16; 'adulteries' or 'commit adultery' in 17:2 [2x], 4)."

264. Beale, *Revelation*, 858. He notes that this is also the case in 17:8–18, where the kingdom of evil will be defeated in an unexpected way (i.e., it will self-destruct).

265. Beale, *Revelation*, 860.

probably had in view sufferings under Emperor Nero and/or the increasing pressure under Domitian. The angel's interpretation of the vision follows in 17:6b–18.

11.5.3 The Interpretation of the Vision (17:6b–18)

The angel begins the interpretation of the vision by describing the beast ridden by the woman, along with its widespread influence in the world (17:7–8). Next, the angel details the beast's seven heads (17:9–11) and ten horns (17:12–14), along with the destruction of the prostitute (17:15–18). Through it all, we hear again about Jesus's triumph, the difficult task ahead for his followers, and God's sure and certain plan to destroy evil.

John was "greatly astonished" when he saw the woman (17:6b), likely a mixture of fear, surprise, and confusion, since he was summoned to observe her punishment (κρίμα in 17:1) but now sees her living blasphemously and murdering God's people (cf. Dan 4:19; 7:15). The angel then explains the "mystery" of the woman and the beast she rides. The beast, with its seven heads and ten horns is described similarly to God and Christ: "once was, now is not, and yet will come up" (Rev 17:7, 8; cf. 1:4, 8, 18; 2:8; 4:8; 11:17; 16:5). Throughout Revelation, evil continually attempts to imitate good, and the beast's dying and rising also parodies Christ's death and resurrection (cf. 1:18; 2:8). Ultimately, the beast has both a demonic origin (the Abyss; cf. 11:7; 13:1) and a destiny of an eternal destruction (cf. 20:10). John may be alluding to the *Nero redivivus* legend as he points to the repeated risings of antichrists throughout history and the appearance of the final antichrist at the end of the age (cf. the healing of the beast's fatal wound in 13:3, 12, 14).

The "inhabitants of the earth" (unbelievers throughout) are captivated ("astonished" in 17:7, 8) by this counterfeit resurrection (cf. 13:3). They are described here as those "whose names have not been written in the book of life from the creation of the world" (17:8). Whereas the Lamb was slain "from the creation of the world" in 13:8, here the names of unbelievers were never recorded in the heavenly register—symbolic of the assurance and preservation of believers (3:5; 20:12; 21:27). Mounce wisely reminds us that "John is not teaching a form of determinism (according to 3:5 names may be blotted out of the book of life) but emphasizing the great distinction that exists between the followers of the Lamb and those who give their allegiance to the beast."[266]

The call for wisdom is repeated (17:9; cf. 13:18) and both instances stress the need for God's wisdom to understand the apocalyptic imagery. God's plan to save his people includes issuing such warnings and exhortations to which they can respond.[267] The beast's heads are identified as seven hills, perhaps an allusion to the seven hills of ancient Rome. Yet the term translated "hill" here (ὄρος) is translated "mountain" the other seven times it appears in the book (6:14, 15, 16; 8:8; 14:1; 16:20; 21:10) and suggests

266. Mounce, *Revelation*, 314.

267. Beale, *Revelation*, 867.

strength and authority.[268] This connection to powers is made explicit in verse 10 where the heads/mountains are also said to be seven kings or rulers. An apocalyptic riddle follows: 5 (fallen) + 1 (is now) + 1 (has not yet come but will only remain for a little while) + 1 (the beast = the 8th king). Many commentators turn to the line of Roman emperors to solve the riddle, but interpretive problems remain (e.g., whether to begin counting with Julius Caesar or Augustus and whether to count Galba, Otho, and Vitellius, who each reigned only a short time).[269]

A better option is to consider the symbolic significance of the numbers. Seven represents the fullness of Roman imperial power (cf. 12:3; 13:1–2). The final manifestation of these wicked kingdoms, personified in an evil leader, is portrayed as an "eighth king" (17:11). In addition, since the number of Jesus is 888 (in contrast to 666) and since he was raised on the eighth day (the eighth day extends beyond the seven days of creation), the beast is characterized as a counterfeit christ or messiah, complete with a fake resurrection (13:3, 12, 14; 17:8). Whether taking the more historical or the more literary approach, one ends up at a similar place: the beast remains a messianic pretender and, like all the other false messiahs, is doomed to destruction. Mangina captures the essential theology well: "Just as Jesus is the *summum bonum* ("the highest good"), so we may say that the beast is a *summum malum* ("the highest evil"), a bodily recapitulation of all the powers of hell."[270]

The ten horns are ten kings who are given authority along with the beast (17:12). Historically, the background is likely Rome's practice of using client kings to reign over its provinces (e.g., Herod the Great and his sons). Yet these kings represent what kings mentioned elsewhere in Revelation represent: pagan political and economic powers allied with the beast against the Lamb in the epic eschatological battle (16:12, 14; 17:2, 18; 18:3, 9; 19:19). Their reign will be short-lived (i.e., "one hour"), but their purpose is clear—to give the beast their resources and influence for an all-out war against the Lamb and his followers (17:13).

They war against the Lamb but have no hope of victory (17:14). Rather, the Lamb will "triumph over" (νικάω) them because he is "Lord of lords and King of kings," well-known titles used by God elsewhere (e.g., Deut 10:17; Ps 136:2; Dan 2:47; 4:37; 1 Tim 6:15; cf. 1 En. 9:4). The Lamb is joined by his people, described as "called, chosen and faithful followers." Here we have one of the more holistic descriptions of God's people in Revelation. "Called" and "chosen" stress God's sovereign hand at work in their discipleship, while "faithful followers" emphasizes the human response. Believers participate in the great victory of the Lamb by following him faithfully (cf. Rev 2:10, 13; 6:9–11; 12:11; 13:10; 14:4; 19:14; cf. Dan 7:21–22).

268. Beale, *Revelation*, 868.

269. See the helpful chart of options using Roman emperors in Beale, *Revelation*, 874. Osborne, *Revelation*, 618–20, provides the most helpful explanation, but trying to solve the riddle by looking at Roman emperors alone raises more questions than it answers.

270. Mangina, *Revelation*, 199.

In 17:15–18 we see war not between the forces of good and evil but within the evil camp, fulfilling God's promise to punish the prostitute (17:1). The beast and the ten horns will hate the prostitute who sits on many waters (i.e., the "many waters" of peoples, multitudes, nations, and languages). They will bring her to ruin and strip her naked (symbolizing shame; cf. 3:18; 16:15), eating her flesh (anticipating the feast of 19:17–18, 21, where the wicked are devoured) and burning her with fire (a common image of judgment throughout Revelation)—graphic imagery that illustrates the self-destructive power of evil (cf. Ezek 16:37–41; 23:11–35). Mounce observes that "the wicked are not a happy band of brothers, but precisely because they are wicked they give way to jealousy and hatred" that result in mutual destruction.[271] Smalley captures the message of Revelation 17:17: "in the end, the powers of evil serve the purposes of the sovereign God, in addition to being condemned by him."[272]

11.5.4 The Coming Judgment Calls for the Saints to Leave Babylon (18:1–8)

The angel's promise in 17:1 to reveal the destruction of the prostitute continues into chapter 18 (cf. earlier allusions in 14:8; 16:19; 17:16). Here the focus turns to her economic downfall. For those loyal to Babylon, the mood is that of a funeral dirge. This passage stresses Babylon's fate and heightens the drama using repetition (the triplets of 18:3, 6, 8) and other literary features such as rhythm and alliteration (18:2, 4, 6). Underlying it all we hear echoes of the words and imagery of the Prophets, especially Jeremiah and Isaiah.

Another powerful and glorious angel comes from heaven and announces with a mighty voice: "Fallen! Fallen is Babylon the Great!" (18:1–2; cf. 14:8; 16:19; Isa 21:9; Jer 51:8).[273] The devastation of Babylon leaves her a fitting dwelling place or home for demons, impure spirits, unclean birds, and detestable animals (cf. Isa 13:21–22; 34:11–14; Jer 50:39; 51:37; Rev 19:17–18, 21). Of the descriptions applied to what the New Jerusalem will be—a glorious, beautiful garden city—we find the opposite applied to Babylon: a desolate, demonic wasteland, devoid of God, God's people, and God's life.

Babylon's demonic character and influence surfaces most clearly in her adulterous seduction of the nations, kings, and merchants (18:2b–3, 9–19). In the first century, the patronage system pulled nations and ruling powers surrounding the Roman Empire into reliance upon her prosperity. Yet the lure of economic security led to a willing

271. Mounce, *Revelation*, 320.

272. Smalley, *Revelation*, 441.

273. This is an example of a futuristic or proleptic aorist that stresses the certainty of Babylon's coming destruction. Fanning, *Revelation*, 457, notes that in the literary sequence Babylon's fall does not occur until chapter 19 and the actual fulfillment in history awaits the future return of Christ.

participation in Rome's idolatry and immorality in order to maintain that relationship (cf. 14:8; 17:2).[274]

In 18:4 God's people are commanded by another heavenly voice to "come out of" Babylon (cf. Jer 51:45: "Come out of her, my people! Run for your lives! Run from the fierce anger of the Lord"; cf. Isa 48:20; Jer 50:8; Jer 51:6; 2 Cor 6:14, 17).[275] Although obedience to this command may involve geographical relocation, it is primarily a call to spiritual separation, to allegiance to Christ's kingdom rather than the kingdom of this world. Resseguie captures the idea well: "The trek to the new promised land is a continuous journey of dissociation from the city of this world; a spiritual, political, and socioeconomic rebellion against the city's unjust and corrupt values."[276] God's people are to separate for two reasons: (1) so they will not share in Babylon's sins and (2) so they will not receive any of her plagues. This clarion call to holiness would both warn complacent believers about their idolatrous compromise and encourage loyal believers to stay the course by reminding both groups of the impossibility of serving two opposing masters (cf. Matt 6:24; Luke 16:13).[277]

In Revelation 18:5–8 God's judgment of Babylon is demanded and explained. Babylon's sins, in the words of Jeremiah, have reached up to the heavens (Jer 51:9), and God is now remembering her crimes (Rev 16:19; cf. Jer 14:10; Hos 8:13; 9:9). The angel instructs three unidentified agents of judgment to repay Babylon (cf. Rev 14:15, 18; Ezek 9:1–11). The principle of *lex talionis* holds here—just as Babylon has forced the nations to drink her wicked potion (Rev 14:8; 17:2, 4), so now she will be made to drink the cup of the wrath of God. The expressions "pay her back double" and "pour her a double portion" in 18:6 are likely calling for full and just recompense rather than literally twice the amount.[278] In any case, the imagery highlights the seriousness of Babylon's offenses.

While she boasts of her own self-proclaimed power and authority ("glory and luxury"), she will be given judgment ("torment and grief") by God. Though she feels untouchable ("I sit enthroned as queen" incapable of experiencing death), she is in fact destined for destruction. These words echo Babylon's boast in Isaiah 47:7–8: "I am forever—the eternal queen! . . . I am, and there is none besides me. I will never be a widow or suffer the loss of children." Her crimes consist of self-deification, idolatrous luxury, and prideful arrogance, the very opposite of virtues characteristic of the heavenly city. Her judgment will come suddenly—"In one day her plagues will overtake her:

274. Beale, *Revelation*, 895–96. See also Kraybill, *Apocalypse and Allegiance*, ch. 9, on the "Economics of Worship," where he discusses the patronage system that underlies much of what John is describing.

275. Why must believers separate in order not to receive judgment when they have already been assured of divine protection? Beale, *Revelation*, 867–68, suggests it is because God often protects his people specifically *through* his exhortations and warnings.

276. Resseguie, *Revelation*, 229. See also Barbara R. Rossing, *The Choice between Two Cities: Whore, Bride, and Empire in the Apocalypse* (Harrisburg, PA: Trinity Press International, 1999).

277. Smalley, *Revelation*, 446.

278. Beale, *Revelation*, 901.

death, mourning and famine" (Rev 18:8; cf. Isa 47:9). The "mighty" queen is no match for the Almighty God, who will condemn the earthly city with fiery judgment (e.g., Isa 47:14; Jer 51:25–28; Rev 9:17–18; 14:10; 16:8; 17:16).

11.5.5 Three Funeral Laments over Babylon the Great (18:9–19)

In this section we hear funeral laments from three groups: kings (18:9–10), merchants (18:11–17a), and mariners (18:17b–19). But they grieve selfishly, not out of genuine sorrow for Babylon's demise, but because Babylon's fall brings economic disaster for them. The language is drawn from Ezekiel 27, with its lengthy lament by the same groups over Tyre, the commercial power of the day. Smalley notices that each lament involves four literary and formulaic elements: (1) each group stands at a distance, showing the selfish nature of evil (18:10, 15, 17), (2) each weeps and mourns over Babylon (18:9, 11, 15), (3) each begins their lament with a double "woe" (18:10, 16, 19), and (4) each ends their lament with the expression "in one hour," stressing how rapidly Babylon falls (18:10, 17, 19).[279] The list of goods and services in the center of the section reflects the prosperity and opulence of the empire. The entire unit calls the reader to an awareness of the economic consequences and effects of evil, even on those who simply partner with such corruption. This section leads into the final scene of 18:20–19:5, where Babylon's judgment is finalized, and God's people rejoice in God's justice and salvation.

First, we hear of the lament of the "kings of the earth" who have participated in Babylon's adultery as well as her prosperity and power (18:9–10; cf. 17:2, 4; 18:3; Ezek 27:33; Isa 23:8). These are local rulers who are loyal to Satan and his followers and whose fate is tied to Babylon's through their economic and political partnership. They mourn with a selfish sorrow because Babylon's downfall spells financial disaster for them. In fact, her demise terrifies them, and they distance themselves to exclaim, "Woe! Woe!" and watch her burn.[280] They are utterly dismayed that she has collapsed so suddenly ("in one hour" in 18:10, 17, 19; "in one day" in 18:8).

Similarly, the merchants lament in 18:11–17a, primarily because they have lost their major market to sell their goods (18:15). As Keener notes, this is "ironic retribution for those who worshiped the beast that they might buy and sell (13:17)!"[281] John's list resembles Ezekiel's list regarding Tyre (Ezek 27:4–24), although John updates it for the Roman context with its far-reaching international trading network. The twenty-eight items are grouped into six categories: (1) precious stones and metals, (2) expensive fabrics, (3) costly woods and building materials, (4) spices and perfumes, (5) foods, and

279. Smalley, *Revelation*, 425.

280. As in 8:13; 12:12; and here (18:10, 16, 19), "woe" serves as an "expression of pain or lament over what is or is to come" (Fanning, *Revelation*, 288). It can also denote "a state of intense hardship or distress" (e.g., Rev 9:12; 11:14; 1 Cor 9:16). See "οὐαί," BDAG 734.

281. Keener, *Revelation*, 427.

(6) animals and human slaves.[282] The list is overwhelmingly luxurious and opulent. Most indicative of Babylon's wickedness is the final item on the list: "bodies, even the souls of human beings" (literal translation), referring to human slaves (Ezek 27:13; 1 Tim 1:10). Rome imported huge numbers of slaves to service its extravagance, with estimates ranging from 10 to 30 percent of the total population of the empire. With God's destruction of Babylon, the luxury and splendor has also disappeared, never to be recovered (Rev 18:11, 14, 21–23).

The funeral dirge of the merchants resumes after the listing of goods and services (18:15–17a). As with the kings before and mariners to follow, the merchants' mourning is less genuine sympathy and more worldly sorrow mixed with fear about their own impending judgment. The city is personified here as a wealthy woman adorned with luxurious clothing and glittering jewelry, signaling that she has played the harlot by using her wealth idolatrously (cf. 17:4–6). In contrast, the heavenly Jerusalem will also display items such as gold, precious stones, and pearls (21:18–21), but "these items become building blocks for the new city; they are not worshiped, nor are they the center of people's lives."[283] Their repeated lament, "Woe! Woe to you, great city!" (18:10, 16, 19) expresses shock and panic about Babylon's dramatic downfall and its disastrous implications (cf. 17:16).

The mariners and sea traders lament in 18:17b–19. They react similarly to the kings and merchants by standing at a distance and lamenting aloud. The sight of Babylon going up in flames—a vivid image for those who were familiar with the great fire of Rome under Emperor Nero—brings forth the obvious question, "Who is like this great city?" (13:4; cf. Ezek 27:32). Babylon and the beast saw themselves as unrivaled and invincible, but their human "greatness" could not prevent the sudden and complete judgment of God for their systemic wickedness. Throwing dust on one's head was a traditional sign of mourning (e.g., Ezek 27:30; Josh 7:6; 1 Sam 4:12; Job 2:12).

11.5.6 God's Judgment of Babylon Calls for Rejoicing and Praise (18:20–19:5)

This section details the final stage of Babylon's destruction, begun in chapter 17. In contrast to the laments of Babylon's business clients in 18:9–19, stands the rejoicing of the righteous in 18:20–19:5. The people of God are commanded to celebrate God judging the world powers that have falsely judged the saints (18:20). The declaration of Babylon's certain destruction (18:21) follows this command and focuses on what is now

282. See Osborne, *Revelation*, 648–50, and Bauckham, *Climax of Prophecy*, 350–71, for more details on each category of goods. Bauckham observes that seven (symbolizing completeness) multiplied by four (symbolizing the world) equals twenty-eight, showing that the list represents "*all* the products of the whole *world*" (p. 31). Cf. also the luxuries enjoyed by King Solomon in 1 Kgs 4:26–28; 10:26–29.

283. Resseguie, *Revelation*, 230.

missing from the wicked city (i.e., the sixfold repetition of "never again" in 18:21–23). Chiefly, Babylon is guilty of self-glorification, deceiving the nations, and murdering the saints (18:23–24). The rejoicing that began in 18:20 now extends to heaven as the great multitude praises God for condemning the prostitute and avenging on her the blood of his people (19:1–5). The theme of worship binds together 19:1–10. Yet, although worship is the common theme, it moves in separate directions, with 19:1–5 focused on praising God for his judgment of Babylon and 19:6–10 centered on praising God for the arrival of the Lamb's wedding.

The heavens, the people of God, and the apostles and prophets are called to celebrate God's judgment of Babylon the great (18:20). Earlier in 11:10 the earth dwellers rejoiced over the death of the two witnesses, an image representing the witnessing church. But now this same church has the final word. To clarify, God's people are not commanded to delight in the suffering of the wicked or to quench a thirst for revenge, but to celebrate God's defeat of evil and his deliverance of justice. God has judged her judgment of you—a clear demonstration of his faithfulness. This is an answer to the martyr's question in 6:9–11: "How long, Sovereign Lord, holy and true, until you judge the inhabitants of the earth and avenge our blood?" (cf. 11:18; 15:4; 16:5–6; Jer 51:48–49). In God's courtroom, the people condemned by Babylon in her clown courtroom of injustice are the victors while Babylon is brought to justice.[284]

For the third time in the book we encounter a "mighty angel" (cf. 5:2; 10:1) and here the angel throws a huge boulder into the sea, symbolizing God's judgment of Babylon (18:21; cf. Jer 51:63–64; Ezek 26:12, 21). Most readers would have pictured a heavy millstone that weighed several tons and was turned by a work animal (e.g., Mark 9:42). The certainty of Babylon's judgment ("never to be found again") also brings a loss of the city's vibrancy and life. Six times the phrase "never . . . again" occurs in Revelation 18:21–23 to depict what the city now lacks: music, commerce, food, light, marriage, etc. Resseguie observes how the "never again" language describing Babylon's demise contrasts sharply with the "no more" language showing what is missing from the new creation: no more sea, tears, death, mourning, crying, or pain (21:1, 4).[285] In the end, sin unmakes creation.

In 18:23–24 we see three reasons for God's condemnation of Babylon. First, her powerful leaders promoted themselves as "the world's most important people," a status that entailed glorifying themselves rather than God as the source of life and doing so with an attitude of pride and arrogance. This complete lack of humility or acknowledgment of God played a role in their experiencing God's wrath. Second, she deceived the nations through her magic spells or sorcery, likely a figurative allusion to Babylon's idolatrous materialism that enslaved the dependent nations (cf. 9:21; 21:8;

284. Osborne, *Revelation*, 655, notes the theme of *lex talionis* elsewhere in Revelation: 2:23; 6:9–11; 11:5, 18; 14:8, 10; 16:5–7; 18:6; 19:2; 20:12–13.

285. Resseguie, *Revelation*, 232. Duvall, *Revelation*, 245–46: "The absence of all good in the wicked city stands in contrast to the absence of all evil from the heavenly city."

22:15).[286] Third, she murdered God's people (cf. 6:9–11; 7:14; 11:7; 13:7, 15; 14:13; 16:6; 17:6; 19:2). Believers are listed in a variety of ways in this section: "my people" (18:4), "people of God," "apostles and prophets" (18:20), "prophets" (18:24), "God's holy people" (18:24; 19:8), "his servants" (19:2, 5), and, in the next section, "brothers and sisters who hold to the testimony of Jesus" (19:10). Babylon is "never to be found again" (18:21) because "in her was found the blood" of God's people (18:24), a fitting *inclusio* summarizing the reason for Babylon's condemnation.

The great multitude in heaven, representing the church triumphant (cf. 7:9), now roars forth praise to God for delivering justice. The command to rejoice in 18:20 becomes a hallelujah chorus in 19:1–6 with its four "hallelujahs" to God for judging the wicked city (i.e., "praise Yahweh" in 19:1, 3, 4, 6). God's attributes of "salvation, glory and power" portray him as the Guardian not just of personal salvation but also of the entire redemptive program (cf. 7:10–12; 15:3–4).[287] God's judgments are not capricious or arbitrary, however, since they flow out of his true and just character (19:2; cf. 3:7; 15:3; 16:7). The corrupter of the earth has now been condemned as God avenges on her the blood of his people. In the heavenly courtroom, God's people stand vindicated! His judgments are true, just, and eternal as "the smoke from her goes up for ever and ever" (19:3), signaling the completeness and finality of her condemnation (cf. Isa 34:9–10; 14:11; 18:9, 18).

Now the angelic worship leaders—the twenty-four elders and four living creatures—make their final appearance in the book and echo a response of praise (cf. Rev 4:8–10; 5:8–14; 7:11–17; 11:16; 14:3; 19:4). Three groups now join in worshiping God for executing justice: the great multitude in heaven (19:1), the elders and living creatures (19:4), and all of God's people on earth (19:5). As the book spirals forward, it also circles back and here we return to the glorious worship scene of Revelation 4–5 where adoration is directed to God on his throne. The term "Amen" (ἀμήν), meaning "let it be so," confirms the praise of 19:1–3 (cf. 1:6–7; 3:14; 5:14; 7:12; 19:4; 22:20). To conclude this section, a voice from the throne calls all of God's servants to praise him (19:5; cf. 16:17; 21:3). Believers are often sometimes designated as "servants" in Revelation (1:1; 2:20; 7:3; 11:18; 19:2, 5; 22:3, 6), and here every category of Christian is summoned to worship—"all you his servants, you who fear him, both great and small!" (19:5; cf. 11:17–18).

11.6 THE FINAL VICTORY (19:6–20:15)

11.6.1 Introduction

Following Babylon's destruction (17:1–19:5), we come to God's full and final victory over the forces of evil (19:6–20:15). Again, 19:1–10 is transitional, united by the common theme of worship, with 19:1–5 emphasizing worship of God for his judgment

286. Mounce, *Revelation*, 339.

287. Mounce, *Revelation*, 342; Smalley, *Revelation*, 477.

of the great prostitute and 19:6–10 stressing celebration for the upcoming wedding of the Lamb. The announcement of 19:6–10 is immediately followed in the literary presentation by the return of the Warrior Messiah who comes for his bride and conquers the two beasts and their followers in 19:11–21. This is followed by the temporary imprisonment of Satan (20:1–3), the millennial reign and Satan's judgment (20:4–10), and the final judgment (20:11–15). The way is now prepared for the renewal of all creation detailed in chapters 21–22.

11.6.2 Transition: The Announcement of the Wedding of the Lamb (19:6–10)

The roar of the great multitude in 19:1 praising Yahweh ("Hallelujah") for judging the wicked city now reaches a crescendo in 19:6–10 as the multitude praises God for beginning his universal reign (cf. 1:15; 7:9–17; 14:2–3; cf. Ezek 1:24; 43:2; Dan 10:6).[288] The celebration continues with the announcement of the wedding of the Lamb and the readiness of his bride, the fourth beatitude, and a word about the true nature of worship.

In Revelation 19:6–8 the great multitude sings the hallelujah chorus in praise of "our Lord God Almighty," who has begun to reign (cf. 1:8; 4:8; 11:17; 15:3; 16:7, 14; 19:6, 15; 21:22). The personal ("our") and powerful ("Lord God Almighty") nature of God contrasts sharply with temporary tyrannical rulers such as Nero and Domitian, who demanded the title "Our Lord and God."[289] The worship becomes even more specific due to the coming wedding of the Lamb, a centerpiece of the universal reign of God. The Gospel writers and Paul both use wedding imagery featuring Jesus as the groom and his people as the bride to describe his future return (e.g., Matt 22:1–14; 25:1–10; 2 Cor 11:2; Gal 4:26; Eph 5:30–32). Jewish wedding customs prescribed a time of betrothal, followed by the wedding proper. On her wedding day the bride would make herself ready with bathing, anointing, and adornment with special clothing (cf. Ezek 16:9–13).[290] According to custom, the bridegroom and his entourage would then proceed to the bride's home and escort her back to his home for the consummation of the marriage and the wedding feast (John 14:1–3).

The "bride" of Christ is explicitly identified here as "God's holy people" or the saints (Rev 14:4; 21:2, 9; 22:17; Ezek 16:8–14). From the larger context, we see that she has made herself ready by faithfully persevering in allegiance to Jesus. In other words, she has held fast to the testimony about Jesus (Rev 19:10) and followed the Lamb in faithful discipleship (14:4). The "bride," then, is "a corporate image for God's redeemed people

288. The aorist of the verb βασιλεύω in verse 6 is an ingressive or inceptive aorist, referring to the beginning of God's universal reign (cf. the aorist form of the verb in 11:17; 20:4).

289. Suetonius, *Dom.* 13.

290. Interestingly, the verb "made herself ready" (ἑτοιμάζω) is used seven times in Revelation to emphasize how God is working out his sovereign plan: 8:6; 9:7, 15; 12:6; 16:12; 19:7; 21:2.

in their eschatological purity and joy, representing not the church's *present* reality but its *future* identity from the perspective of Christ's return."[291]

God has graciously given her (another divine passive: "was given") special clothing: "fine linen, bright and clean," which is then defined as "the righteous acts of God's holy people" (19:8).[292] These brilliantly white clothes (cf. 3:4; 6:11; 7:9, 13–14; 19:14; Isa 61:10) stand in contrast to the purple and scarlet garments worn by the prostitute (Rev 17:4; 18:12, 16). The fine linen (or "righteous acts of the saints") likely represents both their righteous responses to God (subjective genitive) and God's righteous acts presented to them (objective genitive), specifically God's gift of vindicating them by judging their oppressors (cf. 7:13–14; 15:4; 19:14; Ps 58:10–11).[293]

In Revelation 19:9 the angel commands John to write the fourth of seven beatitudes in the book: "Blessed are those who are invited to the wedding supper of the Lamb!" (cf. 1:3; 14:13; 16:15; 20:6; 22:7, 14). The angel then certifies the command with the statement that "these are the true words of God." The image of the messianic wedding banquet or the eschatological wedding feast celebrates the union of God with his people for eternity (cf. Isa 25:6–9; Matt 8:11; 22:1–14; 25:1–13; 26:29; Luke 13:29; 14:16–24).[294] In Revelation 19:7 God's people are portrayed as a bride while in 19:9 the image shifts to guests invited to a wedding banquet. In prophetic-apocalyptic literature images are somewhat flexible, and here the fluidity adds a layer of depth to the reader's understanding of the church. Corporate church as the bride and individual believers as banquet guests—both are true and important.[295] John reacts by falling at the angel's feet in reverence but is quickly reprimanded by the messenger and told the angel is but a "fellow servant" with those who hold to the testimony of Jesus (19:10). The angel quickly adds, "Worship God!" and follows the command with an explanation: "for the testimony of Jesus is the Spirit of this prophecy" (author's translation).[296] God alone deserves worship because the message about (or perhaps from) Jesus is the same message spoken by the Holy Spirit in this prophecy, that is, in the book of Revelation.[297] In addition, this statement reminds us that all true Spirit-inspired prophecy exalts Jesus.[298] We see a parallel of sorts in 22:8–11, which also implies that God alone deserves worship because he is the author of the prophetic message communicated in this book (cf. Acts 2:17–18; 1 Cor 12:3; 1 Pet 1:10–11; 2 Pet 1:21).

291. Tabb, *All Things New*, 84; Bauckham, *Climax of Prophecy*, 167.

292. Revelation rarely provides an interpretation of the imagery; cf. 1:20; 4:5; 5:8; 17:9, 12, 15, 18.

293. Beale, *Revelation*, 941. See pp. 934–44 for his excursus "The Wedding Clothes."

294. See "The Wedding Supper of the Lamb" in Duvall, *Revelation*, 253.

295. Smalley, *Revelation*, 485. Resseguie, *Revelation*, 236, notes how the "metaphors capture the paradox of gift and responsibility. The bride prepares herself with righteous deeds, yet the guests attend the feast at the invitation of the host."

296. See Mark Wilson, "The Spirit in Revelation: Explorations in Imagery and Metaphor," *CTR* 17 (2019): 83–96, esp. 87–89.

297. See Fanning, *Revelation*, 484–85, for a discussion of the subjective/objective genitive options for the phrase "the testimony of Jesus."

298. Keener, *Revelation*, 452.

11.6.3 The Warrior Messiah Conquers the Two Beasts and Their Followers (19:11–21)

God's full and final victory over evil continues to unfold through 20:15. Following the announcement of the marriage supper of the Lamb in 19:6–10, we hear of the return of Christ—the Warrior, Judge, and King—as he comes to defeat his enemies and establish his universal reign (19:11–21). This section begins with the attributes and actions of Jesus, the conquering Christ (19:11–16). The second part features an invitation to the great supper of God and an account of Christ's defeat of his enemies (19:17–21). The much-anticipated great eschatological battle turns out to be a nonevent as Christ wins merely by appearing and speaking. The passage closes with an ironic twist as God's enemies become banquet food for the birds of prey, a gruesome image that contrasts sharply with the messianic wedding banquet of the Lamb.

John now sees heaven standing open, signaling a new phase of the vision: the return of Christ to earth (cf. 4:1; 11:19; 15:5; Ezek 1:1).[299] The heavenly vision highlights eight attributes of the conquering Christ (Rev 19:11–16), drawing on divine warrior imagery from Isaiah 63:1–6 as well as the custom of Roman triumphal procession familiar to the first readers. Images such as the white horse, diadems, titles, and other military images stress Jesus's decisive victory.[300] First, Christ rides a white horse, symbolizing his victorious return as the conquering king (cf. Rev 14:14; 20:11). Second, he is called "Faithful and True," confirming his qualifications as a reliable witness (cf. 1:5; 3:14) and the faithful executor of God's just judgments (16:7; 19:2). Third, his "eyes are like blazing fire," betraying wisdom and insight to judge (cf. 1:14; 2:18; Dan 10:6). Fourth, his "many crowns" (diadems or rulers' crowns) show him to be creation's legitimate ruler in contrast to the dragon and the beast with their limited number of crowns (Rev 12:3; 13:1). Fifth, he has a secret name, certainly a divine name and perhaps the sacred name for God himself: Yahweh.[301] Sixth, he wears a robe dipped in blood. The immediate context of spiritual battle suggests the blood on the robe belongs to God's enemies (cf. Isa 63:1–3; Rev 14:20; 19:15), although the presence of the blood before the battle might link the blood to Christ's sacrificial death. Seventh, his name is "the Word of God," depicting Jesus as God's powerful presence (cf. John 1:1, the Word). Mounce reminds us that "in Hebrew thought a word is not a lifeless sound but an active agent that achieves the intention of the one who speaks" (e.g., Gen 1; Heb 4:12).[302] Finally, in Rev 19:16 we see Jesus wearing a title on part of his robe that falls across his thigh: "KING OF KINGS AND LORD OF LORDS." This Old Testament title for God himself now

299. See "Key Greek Terms for Jesus's Return" in Duvall, *Revelation*, 259.

300. Aune, *Revelation 17–22*, 1050–51.

301. Smalley, *Revelation*, 490–91; Beale, *Revelation*, 954–55. Like other images in this list of attributes, the hidden name likely represents Christ's character rather than serving as a literal secret identification.

302. Mounce, *Revelation*, 354.

describes Christ in his sovereign rule over all competing powers, Caesar included (Deut 10:17; Dan 2:47; Zech 14:9; 1 Tim 6:15; Rev 1:5; 17:14).

The note in 19:14 adds that "armies of heaven" are following the conquering Christ, themselves dressed in "fine linen, white and clean" and riding white horses. This group likely includes both angels and saints. Angels wearing bright linen war against the beast and his followers in 15:6. Jewish tradition features angels forming an army (e.g., Ps 68:17; Zech 14:5; Dan 7:10; 1 En. 1:9; T. Levi 3:3), and the New Testament supports this idea that Christ will be accompanied by angels at his return (e.g., Matt 13:40–42; 16:27; 24:30–31; 25:31–32; Mark 8:38; Luke 9:26; 1 Thess 3:13; 2 Thess 1:6–8; Jude 14–15; cf. Joel 2:2; Zech 14:5; Rev 12:7). Believers also seem to be included in this group as the parallels in 17:14 and 19:8 indicate (believers wearing white robes in 3:5; 6:11). Interestingly, this heavenly army does very little when it comes to actual fighting. They merely follow the Lamb (14:4).

The actions of the Warrior Messiah are depicted in 19:11, 15. First, he wages war by judging justly (19:11; cf. 16:7; 19:2) and his work as Judge is grounded in his righteous character.[303] The second and third actions are complementary. Christ conquers the nations with the sharp sword from his mouth and he rules them with an iron scepter (19:15; cf. 1:16; 2:12, 16; 19:21; Isa 11:4; 49:2; 2 Thess 2:8). Jesus conquers by appearing and speaking. Just as his word creates and heals and calls to discipleship, so his word sets the captives free and defeats the powers of darkness. The iron scepter or staff serves as an instrument of judgment on those who attack his flock (Rev 2:26–27; 12:5; Ps 2:9; Isa 11:4). Fourth, he treads the winepress of God's furious wrath (Rev 14:19–20; 16:19; 19:13; Isa 63:1–6). As we have seen previously, the title "Almighty" (παντοκράτωρ) stresses God sovereign authority, including his power over evil (Rev 1:8; 4:8; 11:17; 15:3; 16:7, 14; 19:6, 15; 21:22).[304] This picture of the Warrior Messiah leaves no room for a domesticated, sentimental view of Christ.

Revelation 19:17–21 portrays Christ's defeat of his enemies as a battle. This account draws on Ezekiel's prophesy against Gog where God's enemies become a feast (Ezek 39:17–20). Everyone participates in one of two contrasting eschatological feasts: the righteous enjoying the wedding supper of the Lamb or else the unrighteous becoming the meal at the "great supper of God." Such gruesome imagery reveals God's final judgment of the wicked from every social rank, from the mighty to the slave, great and small (cf. Rev 6:15; 13:16). Worldly status will not rescue the wicked from God's wrath.

The battle begins with a report of the participants: "the beast and the kings of the earth and their armies" vs. "the rider on the horse and his army" (v. 19). This

303. Osborne, *Revelation*, 680, writes: "If there has ever been a 'just' or 'holy war,' this is the one! The whole theme of *lex talionis* (law of retribution) that has been so prevalent in the book culminates in this passage."

304. Smalley, *Revelation*, 495, notes that the nouns *thymos* ("anger," "fury") and *orgē* ("wrath") occur thirteen times in Rev 6–19 and show God's reaction to human injustice and rebellion.

epic eschatological battle, mentioned elsewhere in 16:12–16 and 17:14, is sometimes designated "Armageddon."[305] While not a literal military battle, it does symbolize God's victory over the forces of evil. The "day of the Lord" prophesied throughout the Old Testament has finally arrived![306] Although the evil forces have amassed to wage war (19:19; cf. 16:14, 16), the much-anticipated never occurs. The "battle" is completely one-sided. Jesus conquers simply by appearing and speaking judgment over his enemies (cf. the sharp sword in 19:15). In addition, Messiah's army does not appear to participate in the battle. "But the beast was captured" in verse 20 provides the only combat details. After judging the two wicked leaders, the "rest"—19:19: "the kings of the earth and their armies"—are judged by Christ's word (v. 21).[307]

In Revelation 19–20, four groups are thrown into the fiery lake: the beast and false prophet (19:20), the dragon or Satan (20:10), the wicked (20:15), and death and Hades (20:14). Here the beast and false prophet are again identified by their deception, leading people to pledge allegiance to the beast and worship its image (19:20; cf. 13:13–17). While Hades refers to the grave or the realm of the dead, the lake of fire refers to Gehenna, or what is traditionally understood as "hell" (i.e., the place of final punishment).[308] Another result of the eschatological war in verse 21 is that "the rest" (most likely the evil armies) were killed with Jesus's words (i.e., the sword coming out of his mouth) and eaten by birds—the ultimate humiliation (cf. the treatment of the two witnesses in 11:7–9).

11.6.4 The Temporary Imprisonment of Satan (20:1–3)

After Christ returns in victory (19:11–21), Satan is seized and imprisoned (20:1–3) in preparation for the millennial reign of the saints (20:4–6). Satan appears throughout Revelation not as a "figure of power . . . but a figure of deception, and his only triumph is to deceive the ungodly masses into opposing God and worshiping the beast and himself."[309] Satan is judged in two stages: his temporary imprisonment in the Abyss (20:1–3), followed by his eternal punishment in the fiery lake (20:10). The visions of Revelation 20 reaffirm God's power and sovereignty, Satan's coming destruction, and the hope available to God's people.

John now witnesses an angel coming from heaven with the key to the Abyss and a

---

305. Schnabel, *40 Questions about the End Times*, 231–37. The return of Christ is also connected with the great battle in 16:15.

306. Osborne, *Revelation*, 688–89, references Isa 31:4; 42:13; 59:17–20; 63:1–5; Ezek 38–39; Dan 12:1–3; Joel 1:15; 3:9–16; Mic 4:11–12; Zech 12:3–9; 14:2–9.

307. Mathewson, *Companion to the Book of Revelation*, 109, notes that the lack of actual fighting and the presence of the sword shows that the battle symbolizes a judgment scene.

308. John likely draws on several biblical sources for the lake of fire image: the fiery rain on Sodom (Gen 19:24), the "river of fire" and the "blazing fire" of Dan 7:9–11 in which the beast's body was thrown, multiple Jewish apocalyptic references (e.g., 1 En. 54:1–5; 90:24–27), and Jesus's own teachings about hell as a place of fiery punishment (e.g., Mark 9:42–48; Matt 13:40–42). See Duvall, *Revelation*, 259.

309. Osborne, *Revelation*, 697.

great chain. John often uses the expression "and I saw" (καὶ εἶδον) to move from one vision to another without necessarily signaling chronological sequence (e.g., in the surrounding context, see 19:11, 17, 19; 20:1, 4, 11, 12; 21:1). To indicate chronological sequence, John often uses terms such as "until" (20:3, 5), "after that" (20:3), and "when" (20:7). Here God delegates the imprisonment of Satan to an anonymous angel, a move that again shows how Satan may be God's opponent, but he is not God's opposite. The "Abyss" (lit. "without depth") appears seven times in the book and refers to the prison house of demonic spirits (9:1, 2, 11; 11:7; 17:8; 20:1, 3; cf. Luke 8:31; 2 Pet 2:4; Jude 6). Revelation mentions four "keys": the "keys of death and Hades" (Rev 1:18), the "key of David" (3:7), the "key to the shaft of the Abyss" (9:1), and "the key to the Abyss" (20:1). Apart from the more positive use in 3:7, the other three occurrences describe God's sovereign control over Satan and his demonic followers. The great chain or manacle emphasizes the certainty of Satan's confinement in his subterranean prison.

The angel seizes the dragon who is named "that ancient serpent, . . . the devil, or Satan" (20:2; cf. the naming in 12:9). In the ancient world, naming someone in this manner indicated having power over them, a reality emphasized here as well. Satan's names relate to his various roles as God's archenemy.[310] The dragon is God's primeval enemy, the serpent is the tempter and deceiver from Genesis 3, and the devil or Satan is the accuser and adversary of God's people (cf. Rev 12:15). Satan is imprisoned for a "thousand years" (χίλια ἔτη), an expression used six times in the immediate context (20:2, 3, 4, 5, 6, 7). As with most numbers in Revelation, this should be understood to symbolize a full and complete but indefinite period of time (i.e., the cube of 10, which represents completeness). The Latin translation combines *mille* ("thousand") and *annus* ("year") to give us the English word "millennium," a term over which there has been extensive discussion and debate.[311]

The angel arrests Satan in a decisive manner.[312] Notice the series of forceful verbs used to indicate Satan's imprisonment: seized, bound, threw, locked, sealed. The text naturally points to a complete and total lockdown of Satan at the end of the age (premillennialism) rather than a mere curbing of his actions during the present age (amillennialism).[313] This conclusion gains support from the absence of deception noted in 20:3b, an evil activity consistently linked to the devil in Revelation. The first coming of Christ certainly dealt a death blow to Satan and his empire (e.g., John 12:31; Col

310. Beasley-Murray, *Revelation*, 284–85.

311. See Schnabel, *40 Questions about the End Times*, 267–71. See also Robert G. Clouse, ed., *The Meaning of the Millennium* (Downers Grove, IL: InterVarsity Press, 1977); Darrell L. Bock, *Three Views on the Millennium and Beyond* (Grand Rapids: Zondervan, 1999).

312. Aune, *Revelation 17–22*, 1082, observes that the metaphor of "binding" or imprisoning Satan or demons occurs frequently in Judaism (e.g., 1 En. 10:4, 11–12; 13:1; 14:5; 18:16; 21:3–6; Jub. 5:6; 10:7–11; 2 En. [Rec. J and A] 7:2; 2 Bar. 56:13; see Jude 6).

313. See Osborne, *Revelation*, 702–3; Fanning, *Revelation*, 499–500, for reasons why premillennialism is a more probable reading of this text than amillennialism. Cf. also Chung and Mathewson, *Models of Premillennialism*; Blomberg and Chung, eds., *Case for Historic Premillennialism.*

2:15), but the New Testament also makes it clear that he continues to do damage during the present age (e.g., 2 Cor 4:3–4; Eph 2:2; 2 Tim 2:26; 1 Pet 5:8). This passage, however, seems to depict Satan on total lockdown.

Revelation 20:3b reveals the purpose and duration of Satan's imprisonment. The stated purpose of his confinement is to "keep him from deceiving the nations anymore until the thousand years were ended." Deception serves as a primary weapon of the forces of evil throughout the book (e.g., 2:20; 12:9; 13:14; 18:23; 19:20; 20:8, 10). An imprisoned Satan can no longer deceive the nations (i.e., the people not part of evil armies destroyed in 19:19, 21). Yet even after a full and complete time of being exempt from Satan's deceptive schemes, upon his release they fall for his lies and rebel against their Creator. Fanning identifies six purposes of the millennium—it provides the context for God's vindication and reward of the faithful, confirms the goodness of creation and God as Creator, shows the importance of human history in God's plan of redemption, demonstrates God's faithfulness to keep his promises to his Old Testament people, demonstrates God's righteousness in judging human sin, and motivates and directs our actions now.[314]

11.6.5 The Millennial Reign and Satan's Judgment (20:4–10)

Following Satan's imprisonment (20:1–3), believers will join Christ in his millennial reign (20:4–6). In 20:7–10 we read of Satan's release and his gathering of the nations for a final battle, where his followers are destroyed and he is thrown into the fiery lake forever. Once again, we see that the millennium validates God's justice in destroying evil: "The release of the satan, though unexpected and unwelcome to us, seems to be part of the strange divine plan to ensure that all evil, every trace, is rooted out of the world. . . . The point, yet again, is that evil must be allowed, under certain controls, to do its worst, so that it can be at last defeated."[315]

John's millennial vision begins with thrones and those seated on them being given authority to judge (20:4a). Those seated on thrones could refer to (a) the twenty-four elders (4:4, 9–10; 11:16–17), (b) only those physically martyred (6:9–11; 20:4b), or (c) all believers, including the martyrs (2:26–27; 3:11, 21; 5:10; 20:4a, 9; cf. Matt 19:28; Luke 22:30; 1 Cor 6:2). Since "elders" are not mentioned and because this group is later described as "the camp of God's people, the city he loves" (Rev 20:9), it seems that all believers, including the martyrs, are in view. In addition, all believers must be included in the group that experiences the first resurrection in order to be exempted from the second death (20:4b–6). Consequently, all believers—Christian martyrs and

314. Fanning, *Revelation*, 508–14. See also Judith L. Kovacs, "The Purpose of the Millennium: Perspectives Ancient and Modern on Revelation 20:1–6," in *New Perspectives on the Book of Revelation*, ed. Adela Yarbro Collins (Leuven: Peeters, 2017), 367–75.

315. N. T. Wright, *Revelation for Everyone* (Louisville: Westminster John Knox, 2011), 182–83.

other faithful Christians—will be present during the millennium. Christ's martyr church will be given authority to judge, further defined in verses 4 and 6 as fulfilling their function of ruling or reigning as kings and priests with Christ over the nations (cf. 2:26–28). They have held fast to their testimony about Jesus and stayed true to the word of God, have refused to worship the beast or its image, and have refused its mark. While not exclusively referring to martyrs (i.e., "the souls of those who had been beheaded"), this group does receive special honor and attention here as those who have paid the ultimate price.

Believers come to life and reign with Christ for a full and complete period of time ("a thousand years"). This is deemed "the first resurrection" (20:4–5). The term translated "came to life" (the aorist of ζάω) in verses 4 and 5 certainly can refer to someone who is alive but most naturally refers to bodily resurrection (e.g., Matt 9:18; Luke 24:5, 23; John 4:50; 5:25; 11:25; Acts 1:3; 9:41; 20:12; 25:19; Rom 14:9; 2 Cor 13:4; Rev 1:18; 2:8; 13:14; 20:4–5). The immediate context must decide for sure, and physical (rather than spiritual) resurrection appears more likely in both 20:4 and 20:5.[316] Those raised with Christ now reign or rule with him over the remaining nations and all of creation.

In the parenthetical expression of verse 5, John notes that the "rest of the dead did not come to life until the thousand years had been completed." If 20:4 refers only to martyrs, then "the rest of the dead" would be other Christians who have died plus unbelievers. But if, as we suggest, 20:4 refers to all believers, then "the rest" refers only to unbelievers. As Osborne points out, "the mention of the 'first resurrection' in 20:5b would hardly exclude the saints who had not been martyred, and the 'second death' in 20:6 would hardly include them."[317] At the end of the millennium, unbelievers are brought back to face God's great white throne judgment (20:11–15).[318]

In 20:5b–6 John provides another reason for seeing all believers, rather than just martyrs, as taking part in the first resurrection at Christ's parousia that inaugurates his millennial reign. He begins with a beatitude, the fifth in the book: "Blessed and holy are those who share in the first resurrection." The addition of "holy" strongly hints at the inclusion of all God's people since "saints/holy ones" is a common description of Christians throughout the book. This blessedness is characterized in three ways. First, the "second death" (eternal death) has no power over them (cf., 2:11; 20:14; 21:8; cf. Luke 20:35). Eternal condemnation has absolutely no sway over those raised to new life by Christ. Second, they will be priests of God and Christ, fulfilling God's promise

316. This is the crux of the debate between premillennialists and amillennialists. See Beale, *Revelation*, 1004–17, for a defense of the amillennial position. We concur with Mounce, *Revelation*, 366, who notes that "if 'they came to life' in verse 4 means a spiritual resurrection to new life in Christ, then we are faced with the problem of discovering within the context some persuasive reason to interpret the same verb differently within one concise unit. No such reason can be found." For an overview of this complicated issue, see Matthew Waymeyer, "The First Resurrection in Revelation 20," *MSJ* 27 (2016): 3–32.

317. Osborne, *Revelation*, 707–8.

318. The context suggests that ζάω in verse 5 represents a resuscitation of unbelievers for judgment rather than a resurrection (i.e., a new body prepared for life in the new creation).

that his people would be a kingdom of priests (Rev 1:6; 5:10; 7:15; 22:3; 1 Pet 2:5, 9; Exod 19:6). Third, they will reign with him for a thousand years, fulfilling their royal or kingly calling as well.

Now in Revelation 20:7–10 we read of Satan's release, final rebellion, defeat, and eternal punishment. At the conclusion of the thousand years, Satan is released from his prison and resumes his chief activity of deceiving the nations—those unbelievers not part of the antichrist's army that was destroyed in 19:17–21. One thing the millennium makes clear is that, again in Mounce's words, "neither the designs of Satan nor the waywardness of the human heart will be altered by the mere passing of time."[319] They are incalculably numerous, like sand on a seashore (20:9; 12:18–13:1), and dispersed across the world (indicated by the expression "four corners of the earth" in 20:8). John likens them to Gog and Magog, reminiscent of the incident in Ezekiel 38–39 and symbolic of the final eschatological battle between wicked nations and the people of God in apocalyptic Judaism.[320]

These ungodly nations, now marching under the evil spell of Satan, surround the people of God. John describes the saints as "the camp of God's people" as well as "the city he loves" (Rev 20:9). Walker perceptively observes that the twin images of the "camp" and the "city" depict God's people as "'on the move' and yet 'having arrived'; they are simultaneously vulnerable, but ultimately secure."[321] In addition, we see the focused obligation of the saints not to take the battle into their own hands but to encamp before the Lord, awaiting his deliverance.[322]

God's judgment fire descends from heaven and devours his enemies (20:9b). Again, this is not a fair fight. As with Armageddon (16:13–16; 19:11–21), the evil forces gather to fight but there is no battle. God Almighty wins simply by acting or speaking. As the enemy ascends or gathers (ἀναβαίνω) to war against the saints (20:9a), fire from heaven descends (καταβαίνω) to consume the unrepentant (cf. Gen 19:24–25; Ezek 39:6). Throughout Scripture, "fire from heaven" represents divine judgment (cf. Rev 11:5; 2 Kgs 1:9–12; Ezek 38:22; 39:6; Luke 9:51–54). Finally, after having wreaked so much horrendous havoc on the world, the deceiving devil is finally thrown into the lake of burning sulfur, where the other two members of the unholy trinity had been thrown (Rev 20:10; cf. 19:20; 21:8). There they will be eternally tormented.

319. Mounce, *Revelation*, 371; cf. Osborne, *Revelation*, 711.

320. Cf. 1QM 15.2–3; 4 Ezra 13:34–35; 1 En. 90:13–19; Sib. Or. 3.663–68. Osborne, *Revelation*, 711–12, notes how the battle here parallels the order in Ezekiel: a coalition of nations comes to destroy Israel after the nation is resurrected and reconstituted before being destroyed themselves. The victorious people of God then enjoy the eschatological temple. John has previously referred to Old Testament figures and places to highlight theological significance (e.g., Balaam in 2:14; Jezebel in 2:20; Sodom and Egypt in 11:8). Cf. also Mounce, *Revelation*, 273; Smalley, *Revelation*, 512. See Keener, *Revelation*, 465–66, for parallels between Ezek 36–48 and Rev 19–22.

321. P. W. L. Walker, *Jesus and the Holy City: New Testament Perspectives on Jerusalem* (Grand Rapids: Eerdmans, 1996), 260. He also notes how this parallels the temple's inner and outer courts in Rev 11.

322. Osborne, *Revelation*, 714.

11.6.6 The Final Judgment (20:11–15)

Prior to the renewal of all creation in chapters 21–22, John records his vision of the final judgment of the ungodly who fell for Satan's deceit and followed him in his final rebellion. John has already referenced the final judgment of the wicked but provides more detail here (cf. 14:9–11; 19:11–21; 20:7–10).[323] While some take 20:11–15 as a general judgment of both believers and unbelievers, the context favors seeing those standing before God's great white throne as unbelievers only.[324] This is a "second resurrection" (or better "resuscitation") of the ungodly dead to face divine judgment. Believers will share in the first resurrection, coming to life at Christ's return prior to the millennium (see 20:5). On this reading, Christ returns and raises his people from the dead, giving them resurrection bodies ready for life in the new creation. This is the final judgment for Christians! God judges the eternal destiny of his people by resurrecting them at Christ's parousia. This reading is supported by the rest of the New Testament (e.g., Matt 24–25; 1 Thess 4–5; 2 Thess 1; 2 Pet 3) and explains the apostle Paul's humble hope that he might somehow attain to the resurrection of the dead (Phil 3:11, 20–21).

The phrase "then I saw" (καὶ εἶδον) in Revelation 20:11 is better translated "and I saw," indicating a move to the next vision rather than a specific chronological marker. Also, verse 11 is best translated: "And I saw a great white throne and sitting on it was he from whose presence the earth and the heavens fled, and there was no place for them."[325] The relative clause is not emphasizing *when* the earth and heavens fled so much as *from whom* they fled—Almighty God, majestic in holiness (cf. a similar description in 6:12–17; cf. 4:2–3; 5:7, 13; 7:10; 1 Kgs 10:18; Dan 7:9–10). John portrays the theophany in language consistent with ancient cosmology—the earth and the sky above are removed so that the ungodly dead now come face to face with their Creator.

In Revelation 20:12–13 the ungodly dead are judged, and this judgment is reported in parallel in the chart below.

20:11b–12a—The earth and the heavens fled from his presence, and there was no place for them. And I saw the dead . . . standing before the throne.	20:13a—The sea . . . and death and Hades gave up the dead that were in them.
20:12b—The dead were judged according to what they had done.	20:13b—Each person was judged according to what they had done.

323. Schnabel, *40 Questions about End Times*, 290, observes multiple connections between 20:4–10 and 20:11–15.

324. Some interpreters see verse 12 as applying to believers and verses 13–15 applying to unbelievers, which remains a possible reading (e.g., Osborne, *Revelation*, 721–22). This reading would see the judgment seat of Christ where believers give an account of how they have lived (Rom 14:10; 2 Cor 5:10; Gal 5:6; Eph 2:10; Phil 2:12–13; 1 Thess 1:3; cf. Dan 12:1–2) as equivalent to the great white throne judgment. Also, this reading likely sees the two visions of judgment in Rev 14:14–20 as applying to both believers (grain harvest) and unbelievers (grape harvest). For the present reading, see Jan Lambrecht, "Final Judgments and Ultimate Blessings: The Climactic Visions of Revelation 20,11–21,8," *Bib* 81.3 (2000): 369; Fanning, *Revelation*, 518–19; Schnabel, *40 Questions about End Times*, 274, 294–95; Wilson, *Victory through the Lamb*, 195–96; Mathewson, *Companion to the Book of Revelation*, 113–15.

325. Mealy, *After the Thousand Years*, 164–65.

None of the wicked dead can escape God's judgment—"great and small" (20:12). There is no hiding place, whether in the sea (often symbolic of evil) or in death/Hades, images that together depict "the demonic realm of death."[326] Those not experiencing the first resurrection cannot escape divine condemnation.

Two kinds of books are opened. First, "the books" record a person's deeds. The righteous (at the judgment seat of Christ mentioned by Paul in 2 Cor 5:10 but not described in Revelation) and the unrighteous (described here) are judged according to works.[327] In this context the ungodly are called to account for their unrighteous actions. Second, their wicked lifestyle is confirmed by their names not being written in the book of life (Rev 20:12, 15; cf. 3:5; 13:8; 17:8; 21:27).[328] In Revelation, the "book of life" image is used either to assure Christians that eternal life awaits them (3:5; 21:27) or to stress why the ungodly are being denied such life (13:8; 17:8).

In verse 14 we see the death of death! The last enemy, death, is now thrown into hell (1 Cor 15:26; Rev 21:4). Verse 15 makes it clear that anyone whose name is not found in the book of life will be thrown into the "lake of fire." The burning lake is what is traditionally called "hell" and represents the place of final punishment, though the exact term (γέεννα) is not used outside of the Gospels and James. The image represents eternal separation from the presence of God and all that is good. More specifically John identifies the lake of fire as the "second death" or eternal death. At this point we see all of God's enemies suffering the same fiery fate—the beast and the false prophet (19:20), Satan (20:10), death (20:14), and wicked humans (20:15; 21:8).

11.7 THE NEW CREATION: GOD'S PRESENCE AMONG HIS PEOPLE (21:1–22:5)

11.7.1 Introduction

In Revelation 21:1–22:5 John presents the primary goal and theme of the entire book, and indeed all of Scripture: God's relational presence among his people in the new creation.[329] Sin's intrusion upon God's good creation has now been repelled as God lives among his people in the new garden city. This final vision of Revelation

326. Smalley, *Revelation*, 518.

327. See "Judgment according to Deeds" in Duvall, *Revelation*, 61, and Hays, Duvall, and Pate, *A-to-Z Guide to Biblical Prophecy*, 235–37. The focus on the judgment seat of Christ for believers is on reward or loss of reward rather than on the determination of one's eternal destiny.

328. See "The 'Book of Life'" in Duvall, *Revelation*, 67. For a survey of how the image of a heavenly register was used in the Old Testament, ancient Judaism, and early Christianity, see Leslie Baynes, *The Heavenly Book Motif in Judeo-Christian Apocalypses, 200 B.C.E.–200 C.E.*, *JSJSup* 152 (Leiden: Brill, 2012).

329. For a brief overview of the significance of God's relational presence, see J. Scott Duvall and J. Daniel Hays, *Living God's Word: Discovering Our Place in the Great Story of Scripture*, 2nd ed. (Grand Rapids: Zondervan Academic, 2021), 309–16. For a comprehensive study of God's presence among his people, see Duvall and Hays, *God's Relational Presence*; G. K. Beale, *The Temple and the Church's Mission: A Biblical Theology of the Dwelling Place of God* (Downers Grove, IL: InterVarsity Press, 2004); J. Ryan Lister, *The Presence of God: Its Place in the Storyline of Scripture and the Story of Our Lives* (Wheaton, IL: Crossway, 2015). For a thorough study of Rev 21:1–22:5, see Mathewson, *New Heaven and a New Earth.*

fulfills the promises to the victors (Rev 2–3), the realization of the throne-room worship (Rev 4–5), the long-awaited answer to the martyrs' prayer (6:9–11), the intended outcome of the judgments (Rev 6–10), and the final overthrow of evil (Rev 17–19).

In 21:1–8 we have a transition between God's final victory (19:6–20:15) and the new creation (21:1–22:5). We also find another doublet with 21:1–8 and 21:9–22:5, both visions of the eternal state. More specifically, 21:1–8 summarizes what will be expanded upon in more glorious detail in 21:9–22:5: the new creation as Holy City (21:9–21), temple city (21:22–27), and garden city (22:1–5).

11.7.2 Transition: The New Heaven and New Earth (21:1–8)

This summary section transitions the reader to the more detailed account that follows and includes a vision of the descent of the new heaven and new earth (21:1–2), a voice from the throne explaining what John sees in the arrival of God's promised presence (21:3–4), and God's sevenfold speech confirming his finished work (21:5–8).

The final "and I saw" (καὶ εἶδον) occurs here in John's vision of the new creation (cf. 19:11, 17, 19; 20:1, 4, 11, 12; 21:1). It is not just "heaven" John sees but a "new heaven and a new earth," echoing the language of Isaiah (Isa 65:17–19; 66:22). The first heaven (or sky) and first earth (or land) with its death and decay is no more, in contrast to the new heaven and earth which will remain for eternity. Within Judaism one can find the idea of a total replacement of the old creation (e.g., 1 En. 72:1; 83:3–4; 91:14, 16; 2 Bar. 44:12; Sib. Or. 3:75–90), as well as the transformation of the old into the new (e.g., Jub. 1:29; 4:26; 23:18; 1 En. 45:4–5; 2 Bar. 32:2–6; 57:1–3). Revelation hints at a radically new creation as seen elsewhere in the New Testament (e.g., Mark 13:31; 2 Pet 3:10–13; 1 Cor 7:31; Heb 12:27; 1 John 2:17), but also suggests a transformation that fulfills the original pattern (e.g., the new Eden; cf. Rom 8:19–22). As Koester notes, the emphasis in Revelation is on "the destruction of the earth's destroyers (11:18), not on the destruction of the earth itself."[330] Altogether, there is both continuity and discontinuity. In addition, John observes that the new creation does not include any sea, a common symbol of evil and chaos in the Scriptures (cf. 13:1).[331]

In verse two John describes this transformed creation as both a place and a people (cf. 3:12). Whereas human cities of power have attempted to ascend to heaven (Gen 11:4), the Holy City or new Jerusalem, descends from heaven as a gift from God (cf. Rev 3:12; 21:10; Gal 4:26; Heb 11:10; 12:22; 13:14). The heavenly city constitutes a

330. Koester, *Revelation*, 795.

331. Beale, *Revelation*, 1042, notes five uses of "sea" in Revelation: (1) origin of cosmic evil, (2) rebellious nations who persecute God's people, (3) place of the dead, (4) location of world's idolatrous trade activity, and (5) a literal body of water. He thinks the use in 21:1 encompasses all five meanings. Koester, *Revelation*, 795–96, notes five common interpretations of the sea being no more, with the most viable including the removal of the sea as a sign of a new order (vs. the reign of Babylon and her reliance on the sea; cf. 18:17, 19), and the end of death as the sea gives up its dead (20:13).

temple city—a permanent dwelling place for God among his people. But the city as a place metaphor takes on a personal, relational feature when John describes the city as people, specifically as Christ's bride. This recalls Zion, the bride of Yahweh (cf. Isa 61:10),[332] and draws attention to God's people as a "bride beautifully dressed for her husband" (Rev 21:2; cf. 19:7–8; 21:9–27; 2 Cor 11:2; Eph 5:23; Isa 61:10; 62:5). The wedding was announced in Revelation 19:7–9 but now with the city's descent, the bride appears.[333] The wedding imagery reflects the steadfast love and intimacy of God's relational presence among his people.

In 21:3–4 we hear a loud voice from the throne explaining John's vision of the arrival of God's promised presence. God fulfills his long-standing three-part covenant promise to live with/among his people (e.g., Lev 26:11–12; Ezek 37:26–28; Zech 2:10–11; 8:8; 2 Cor 6:16; Rev 21:22). God's people become his permanent "dwelling place" or tabernacle (σκηνή), a term used in its verbal form later in the verse and also in John 1:14 to describe Jesus's incarnation (cf. Rev 7:15; 13:6). God lives with his people, and the textual variant "peoples" (λαοί) is most likely original and stresses yet again the multiethnic character of God's redeemed people.[334] Those coming into God's glorious presence will find an abundance of divine comfort and protection (22:4). Echoing Isaiah 25:8, God is said to "wipe away every tear." His presence means the absence of all that disrupts shalom, including death, mourning, wailing, and pain. These are eliminated because the "old order of things has passed away" (cf. Rev 7:17; Isa 65:16–17).

Not since Revelation 1:8 has God spoken directly (cf. the heavenly voice in 10:4; 14:13; 16:1, 17; 18:4; 19:5), and here his speech serves as a rhetorical high point.[335] This seven-part speech joins with 1:8 to frame the entire book and remind hearers of God's eternal character and sovereign plan. First, God asserts that he is making everything new, fulfilling new creation prophecies of Isaiah by pointing to a future time when he will make all creation new (e.g., Isa 43:18–19; 65:17; 66:22; cf. 2 Cor 5:17).[336] Second, John is instructed to write down these words, likely referring to the entire book (cf. Rev 1:11, 19), because God's words are trustworthy and true (cf. 19:9; 22:6). God's faithful and true character provides the basis for his true, reliable, faithful revelation. Third, in the new creation we see the climactic fulfillment of God's proclaimed salvation—"It is done" (γέγοναν). We see similar exclamations in God's speaking forth the first creation (ἐγένετο, Gen 1:3, 6, 9, 11; John 1:3), when Jesus cries "It is finished" on the

332. Mathewson, *New Heaven and a New Earth*, 44–49.

333. Koester, *Revelation*, 804.

334. Bruce M. Metzger, *A Textual Commentary on the Greek New Testament*, 2nd ed. (New York: United Bible Societies, 1994), 688. Beale, *Revelation*, 1048, notes that while both readings have strong manuscript support, the plural is preferred on the basis of context and external evidence, while the singular arises from the desire to conform to the typical Old Testament use of the singular (e.g., Lev 26:12; Ezek 11:20; 37:37; Zech 2:11; 8:8). The context emphasizes the redemption of many peoples or nations (e.g., Rev 21:24, 26; 22:2; cf. also the use alongside other plural terms in 5:9; 7:9; 10:11; 11:9; 13:7; 14:6; 17:15).

335. Koester, *Revelation*, 806.

336. Beale, *Revelation*, 1052–53, who rightly notes that this refers to the future consummation of all creation rather than to universal salvation.

cross (τετέλεσται, John 19:30), and at the completion of the seven bowl judgments (γέγονεν, Rev 16:17). As Bauckham says, "He is the origin and goal of all history. He has the first word, in creation, and the last word, in new creation."[337] Fourth, God the great "I AM" stands as the personal end goal of all history, the sovereign ruler of the universe—"The Alpha and the Omega, the Beginning and the End" (21:6; cf. 1:8, 17; 22:13; Exod 3:14; Isa 44:6; 48:12). Fifth, God will satisfy the thirsty with the water of life, a symbol of the Spirit and the resurrection life he gives (Rev 21:6; cf. 7:17; 22:1, 17; John 4:10; 7:37–38; Isa 44:3; 55:1). Sixth, the victorious (ὁ νικῶν) will inherit the blessings of the new creation, chiefly life as God's children in his presence (Rev 21:7). Their share or inheritance for persevering faithfully will include the blessings promised to the overcomers in the seven messages (e.g., 2:7, 11, 17, 26; 3:5, 12, 21). Koester notes how the traditional covenant language that earlier had marital overtones (21:2–3) is here paired with adoption language—"They will be my children" (21:7).[338] God's presence in Revelation is relational to the core. Seventh, in contrast to the heirs of blessings stand the heirs of punishment. They have compromised with the immoral, idolatrous world system summarized by the vice list, the second in Revelation (cf. 9:20–21; 21:8; 22:15).[339] Their punishment is to be excluded from God's presence for eternity. Instead of God's presence with all its attendant blessings, they will inherit the fiery lake, which is the second death. In the present list eight categories of people face God's judgment. Perhaps cowardice and faithlessness lead the way because they reflect the issues that present the most temptation to compromise. The list functions to highlight and clarify contrasting outcomes, to encourage readers to respond faithfully since God wins in the end, and to encourage the resistance to the evil forces seeking to lure them away from the Lord.

11.7.3 A Vision of the New Jerusalem (21:9–22:5)

The introductory description of God's dwelling among his people in 21:1–8 expands in 21:9–22:5.[340] The glorious new creation has characteristics of a city (21:9–21), a temple (21:22–27), and a garden (22:1–5). Throughout this section John draws on Ezekiel 40–48. The initial passage (Rev 21:9–21) features one of the seven angels who had poured out the bowl judgments giving John a tour of the celestial city. In contrast to the worldly city the celestial city radiates the glory of God's presence and offers beauty, healing, life, unity, protection, and hope. This is the place where God will be united with his people forever, as the abundance of wedding imagery suggests.

337. Bauckham, *Theology*, 27.

338. Koester, *Revelation*, 800, 808.

339. Mark Wilson, *Charts on the Book of Revelation*, 81, correlates the vice lists in Revelation with the Ten Commandments. Five forms of evil and wickedness surface repeatedly throughout the book: false worship, idolatry, sexual immorality, deception, and murder. All five are expressly prohibited in the Ten Commandments.

340. Gerhard A. Krodel, *Revelation*, ACNT (Minneapolis: Fortress, 1990), 352–54, maps out the contrasts between the earthly city Babylon and the heavenly city of God that run through 17:1–22:5.

11.7.3.1 A Description of the Heavenly City (21:9–21)

John's tour guide for his vision of the heavenly city is one of the angels responsible for the seven bowl judgments. The parallel in 17:1 highlights the contrast between Babylon, the great prostitute, and the new Jerusalem, the wife of the Lamb.[341] Koester notes the various ways in which the bridal imagery functions: (1) to depict Jesus's followers as betrothed maidens devoted to him, (2) to contrast the Lamb's wife with the whore Babylon, and, less directly, (3) to continue the story of the woman in Revelation 12 who gave birth to the Messiah.[342]

The bridal imagery echoes the Old Testament theme of God's people as his wife (see comments on 19:6–10). Osborne writes, "This means that now the sacred marriage has taken place, and Christ and the church (Eph 5:25–27) will now spend eternity together as husband and wife."[343] The image of Christ as the bridegroom is used seven times in this final section (Rev 21:9, 14, 22, 23, 27; 22:1, 3), perhaps drawing attention to his sacrificial gift of life that makes the eternal marriage possible.

John is then carried away in the Spirit to a great and high mountain to witness the Holy City, Jerusalem, descending out of heaven from God (21:10; cf. being carried into the wilderness in 17:3 to see Babylon). Mountains play an important theological role in the history of God's people.[344] Keener notes that the mountain here may represent the end-time Mount Zion (14:1; cf. Isa 2:2–3) and stand in contrast to the seven mountains on which Babylon sits (Rev 17:9).[345]

The Holy City reflects God's glorious and holy presence using terms such as "shine," "glory," "brilliance," "pure," and "clear" (cf. "glory of God" in 15:8; 21:11, 23). The "glory" word group occurs nineteen times in Revelation, with a semantic range that includes praise (1:6; 4:9, 11; 5:12, 13; 7:12; 14:7; 15:4; 18:7; 19:1, 7), recognition or acknowledgment (11:13; 16:9), splendor (21:24, 26), and presence (15:8; 18:1; 21:11, 23).[346] God's people will now experience his Shekinah presence permanently (cf. Exod 24:15–16; 1 Kgs 8:1–13; Isa 6:1–4; Ezek 43:2–5). The mention of jasper continues the emphasis on God's presence. The city walls are made of jasper (Rev 21:18) and it is the first of the twelve foundation stones (21:19). In 4:3 God is seated on his throne which has the appearance of jasper. This translucent stone, perhaps opal or even diamond, is specifically associated with the light and glory of God (21:11).[347] The whole of the new creation shines with God's splendid presence.

341. Note that the term "wife" (γυνή) in 21:9 is also used repeatedly in ch. 12 to refer to the messianic community and contrasts with the term "woman" (γυνή) referring to Babylon in 17:3, 4, 6, 7, 9, 18. The "wife" in this context, however, is also the νύμφη ("bride"), reinforcing the contrast.

342. Koester, *Revelation*, 811–12.

343. Osborne, *Revelation*, 748.

344. E.g., Moses on Mount Sinai in Exod 19, Ezekiel's vision in 40:1–2, Isaiah's prophecy of the coming Jerusalem in Isa 25:6–26:2, Jesus's transfiguration in Mark 9:2–13, and Jesus's apocalyptic discourse on the Mount of Olives in Mark 13.

345. Keener, *Revelation*, 492.

346. Duvall and Hays, *God's Relational Presence*, 321.

347. "ἴασπις," BDAG 465; Beale, *Revelation*, 321. On the basis of the connection between 4:3 and 21:11, Mealy concludes that the new Jerusalem is the great white throne of God, the epicenter of reality, God's glorious presence among his people (*After the Thousand Years*, 175).

The heavenly city has "a great, high wall with twelve gates, and with twelve angels at the gates" (21:12). With no enemies and given the wall is made of jasper (21:11, 18), its primary purpose is to reflect God's glory. The twelve gates are reminiscent of Ezekiel 48:30–35, where the new temple also has twelve gates.[348] The twelve angels are stationed as supernatural gatekeepers (cf. Isa 62:6), but since there are no threats, their presence symbolizes "the perpetual security of God's people in the city, much the same way that the 'healing leaves' in [Rev] 22:2 symbolize the perpetual well-being of the people without entailing that they will ever suffer the ills of the first heaven and earth."[349] The numerical symbolism throughout—three (sufficiency), four (creation), and twelve (completeness, number of God's people)—portrays a perfect city, abounding in security and safety for all nations (Rev 21:13). The names of the twelve tribes on the gates and the twelve apostles on the foundations suggests that "the city integrates the totality of God's people from both the old and new covenants."[350] Entrance into the heavenly city comes through membership in the people of God (21:12, 14; cf. Eph 2:20).

Whereas in Revelation 11 only the inner sanctuary of the temple is measured or protected (equivalent to sealing in 7:1–8), here the entire temple is measured, emphasizing God's full and complete protection of his people for eternity (21:15–17). With no more enemies or threats of any kind, we see that "in making everything new, God has also made it safe."[351] The city does not need a temple (21:22) simply because the entire city is the temple of God, laid out as a cube like the holy of holies in the ancient temple (1 Kgs 6:20; 2 Chr 3:8–9). The measurements are multiples of twelve, again stressing completeness. The tremendous height of the city (12,000 stadia equaling about 1,500 miles) stresses that "what humanity could not accomplish in Babel—a city to the heavens (Gen 11:4)—God grants as an overwhelming gift."[352] The wall measures 144 cubits (about 216 feet or 66 meters), a number that likely refers to its width rather than its height. Rather than a literal description of the wall, 144 again signifies the people of God (cf. Rev 7:4–8; 14:1–5). In all, the "symmetrical proportions of the new Jerusalem replicate the place where God's presence was localized among his people, where his glory was to be found on earth, a typological pattern here fulfilled on a grand scale in God's presence with his people in the renewed creation."[353]

In 21:18–21 we see the material makeup of the city, relying on Isaiah 54:11–12. References to gold as clear as transparent glass frame the unit (Rev 21:18, 21) and use temple imagery to describe the city in to contrast to the gaudy golden wardrobe of the

348. Keener, *Revelation*, 495, suggests that city gates presented an opportunity to flaunt the power and beauty of the Roman Empire. Revelation takes advantage of this image to apply biblical meaning to a cultural symbol in a Christocentric way.

349. Mathewson, *New Heaven and a New Earth*, 111.

350. Mathewson, *New Heaven and a New Earth*, 111.

351. Duvall, *Revelation*, 289.

352. Keener, *Revelation*, 494.

353. Fanning, *Revelation*, 541.

harlot city (17:4; 18:16; cf. Ezek 28:13).[354] As in Revelation 21:11, the wall of jasper connotes God's glorious presence. Precious jewels represent the majesty and splendor of the heavenly city.[355] The twelve stones correspond generally to the jewels on the high priest's breastplate (Exod 28:17–20), perhaps emphasizing the priestly nature of God's people who now have full and unhindered access to his presence and function as kings and priests (cf. Rev 1:6; 5:10; 20:6; 22:3–5; Exod 19:6).[356] Pearls signify value, beauty and affluence (e.g., 1 Tim 2:9; Matt 13:45–46). Ironically, the witnesses once unburied in the street (or public square) of Babylon will one day walk the great street of the heavenly city and bask in God's glorious presence.

11.7.3.2 The Internal Features of the Temple City (21:22–27)

The description of the heavenly city initiated in 21:1–8 continues in 21:22–27, where the focus shifts to the conditions inside the city as God's people live in his presence. Certain things typically present in an ancient city are missing (e.g., temple, sun, moon, closed gates) since God's presence meets the need. Only true citizens with their names in the heavenly registry are allowed to enter, including the redeemed nations who will bring their glory and honor into the city. The emphasis on God's mission to the nations throughout Revelation and John's reliance on Isaiah 60 in this context perhaps explain why this theme is repeated here.

John seems shocked that the celestial city includes no temple, since the expectation was that a glorified Jerusalem would have a magnificent temple (e.g., Ezek 40–48; Zech 14:16–21; Tob 14:5; 1 En. 91:13; 2 Bar. 32:4; Sib. Or. 5:422). Yet the city contains no physical temple, because "the Lord God Almighty and the Lamb are its temple" (Rev 21:22). Ezekiel's vision of a restored temple (Ezek 41–48), although fulfilled in an unexpected way, concludes by naming the city: "THE LORD IS THERE" (Ezek 48:35). The immediate, personal presence of God and the Lamb permeates the Holy City and replaces the need for any kind of a mediating temple. The new creation has become the holy of holies where God is fully and finally present among his people. The final use of the title "Almighty" (παντοκράτωρ) occurs here to stress God's sovereign power (Rev 1:8; 4:8; 11:17; 15:3; 16:7, 14; 19:6, 15; 21:22), and the inclusion of "the Lamb" once again stresses the unity of the Father and the Son.

There is no need for earthly sources of light such as the sun or moon since God's glorious presence illuminates the new creation (21:23). The source of light alludes to Isaiah 60:19: "The sun will no more be your light by day, nor will the brightness of

354. Mathewson, *New Heaven and a New Earth*, 129–30.

355. On the possible background of the precious stones, see Beale, *Revelation*, 1080–88; Mathewson, *New Heaven and a New Earth*, 130–49.

356. Osborne, *Revelation*, 756–58; and Mathewson, *New Heaven and a New Earth*, 139. Interestingly, Resseguie (*Revelation*, 255) notes, "Each stone is listed one after the other, establishing a rhythmic syncopation that amplifies the harmonious symmetry of this beautiful city. The euphony consists of nine *s* sounds and three *n* sounds that create rhythmic sets of threes.

the moon shine on you, for the LORD will be your everlasting light, and your God will be your glory." John adds "and the Lamb is its lamp" to underscore yet again Jesus's oneness with God. In addition, there are multiple subtle allusions in the surrounding context to the Holy Spirit, who plays a less visible but equally important role in mediating God's presence to his people: temple, light, empowerment for the mission to the nations, purity or holiness, water, and, most of all, presence, and glory (cf. the living water flowing out of Jerusalem in Zech 14:8). Also, the presence of God's glory and light in the eschatological city stands in contrast to Babylon, where "the light of a lamp will never shine in you again" (Rev 18:23).

Unlike what was typical for an ancient city where the gates were open during the day for transportation and trade and closed at night for protection, the gates of the temple city will never close since there will be no darkness or enemies (21:25; 22:5; cf. Isa 60:11). The open gates and continual light illustrate how God's people will experience his perfect protection from their enemies. In addition, the continually open gates symbolize the full and unhindered access the redeemed have to God's presence.

Not only will the redeemed nations and kings be admitted into the eternal city, but they will also contribute their "splendor," "glory and honor" (Rev 21:24, 26). In contrast to the wicked nations who once brought their wealth into Babylon (18:12–16), the redeemed nations will "devote their gifts and energies to worship the one true God" (cf. 4:9, 11; 5:12–13; 7:12).[357] The arrival of redeemed gentiles into the Holy City fulfills Old Testament passages such as Isaiah 60; 61:6; Jeremiah 3:17; Zechariah 2:11; 8:22–23. Throughout Revelation, God has invited the nations to receive his offer of salvation. Although many reject the offer and face divine judgment (e.g., 11:2, 9, 18; 13:7; 14:8; 16:19; 17:15; 18:3, 23; 20:3, 8; 21:27), some among the nations respond positively and enter the glorious city as citizens of God's eternal kingdom (5:9; 7:9; 15:4; 21:24–26; 22:2).[358] Revelation simply does not support a universalist reading regarding the fate of the nations.[359] The warnings in 21:8, 27; 22:15 and elsewhere make it clear that only the redeemed will enter the city, and the nations/kings who rebel against God will experience his judgment (19:18–21; 20:8–10, 13–15). Yet the multicultural formula used seven times in the book (5:9; 7:9; 10:11; 11:9; 13:7; 14:6; 17:15) shows that redeemed from among the nations will be part of the heavenly citizenry.

John concludes his description of the internal features of the temple city with a reminder that nothing impure or shameful or deceitful will ever enter the city. Only

357. Beale and Carson, *New Testament Use of the Old Testament*, 1153. Beale, *Revelation*, 1095, observes that "glory and honor" only appear together elsewhere in Revelation in 4:9, 11; 5:12, 13, where the expression refers without exception to praise of God and the Lamb.

358. Mathewson, *New Heaven and a New Earth*, 170–75, offers a helpful survey of options and observations about the presence of nations and kings in the new Jerusalem.

359. Contra Mathias Rissi, *The Future of the World: An Exegetical Study of Rev. 19:11–22:15*, SBT 23 (London: SCM, 1972).

true citizens or those "whose names are written in the Lamb's book of life" may enter (21:27; cf. 3:5; 13:8; 17:8; 20:12, 15). Specifically, three groups are denied entrance: (1) the impure or unclean, alluding to the idolatrous and immoral (e.g., 9:20–21; 21:8; 22:15); (2) those who do what is shameful or detestable to God (e.g., the "abominable" [βδέλυγμα] things associated with Babylon in 17:4–5), and (3) anyone who practices deceit or falsehood, emphasizing how truly evil deception really is.[360] Bauckham observes, "The most important contrast between the forces of evil and the army of the Lamb is the contrast between deceit and truth."[361] God in his pure and perfect holiness will not allow anything unholy to enter his city.

11.7.3.3 The Garden City as Paradise Transformed (22:1–5)

The temple city of 21:22–27 gives way to the garden imagery of 22:1–5. In this climactic vision of the new creation, the world has been transformed into a perfect eternal paradise. John draws on Ezekiel 47:1–12, where the prophet pictures a river flowing from a renewed temple and trees growing along both sides of the river (cf. Zech 14:8). The background also likely reflects the garden of Eden in Genesis so that the entire Bible is bracketed by a garden (Gen 2–3; Rev 22). God's plan to live among his people in eternal fellowship is realized at last. The vision of 22:1–5 includes a river of life, tree(s) of life, the lack of any curse, the throne of God and the Lamb, and the servants of God.

John first sees the river of the water of life, clear as crystal, flowing from the throne of God and the Lamb down the middle of the main city street (22:1–2a). In the original garden the river flows from Eden (Gen 2:10), and in Ezekiel it flows from the temple (Ezek 47:1–2), while here it flows directly from the throne of God and the Lamb.[362] The "throne" represents God's "life-giving and life-sustaining" presence among his creation and stands in stark contrast to the throne of the beast which is marked by "oppression and domination that denies life to those who fail to recognize its supremacy ([Rev] 13:15)."[363] The water is "clear as crystal" (λαμπρὸν ὡς κρύσταλλον), a phrase highlighting the purity and glory of God's presence. In John's Gospel Jesus identifies himself (4:10–14) and the Holy Spirit (7:37–39) as the "living water." The Spirit as the one who makes God's personal presence known to believers fits well with the river of life imagery (7:17; 21:6; 22:17) and completes the picture of the Triune God giving life to his creation.

The river of life flowing through the heart of the city is surrounded by the tree(s) of life (22:2b). While the term "tree" (ξύλον) is singular, it is likely a collective singular picturing both the many trees lining both banks of the river as portrayed in Ezekiel

360. See "Deception" in Duvall, *Revelation*, 235.

361. Bauckham, *Theology*, 91.

362. Osborne, *Revelation*, 769–70, observes how God and the Lamb are once again juxtaposed, continuing the theme of Jesus's oneness with God (see 3:21; 4:9–11; 5:9–12, 13; 6:16; 7:10; 11:15; 14:4; 20:6; 21:22). See also Bauckham, *Theology*, 54–65, for an excellent study of the worship of Jesus as God in Revelation.

363. Resseguie, *Revelation*, 257.

47:12 as well as the one tree of life in the garden of Eden described in Genesis 2:9–10; 3:22. John is much more concerned with theological symbolism than geographical precision. The tree represents God's life that surrounds and sustains his people. Unlike the seasonal trees of Ezekiel and the inaccessible tree of Genesis, this tree never stops providing full and complete nourishment, yet another sign that restored Eden will surpass the original Eden.[364] Jesus's promise to the overcomers of food from the tree of life in the paradise of God is now fulfilled (Rev 2:7). There will be never-ending provision in God's presence and his people will never hunger or thirst again (cf. 7:16–17; 21:6; 22:17), a comfort to those suffering financially under the pressures of empire.

In addition to God's abundant provision, the leaves of the tree are for "the healing of the nations" (22:2c). All disease will be totally abolished from the new creation. Ezekiel had observed that the leaves of these trees are for healing (47:12), and John notes that this divine healing will also apply to redeemed gentiles (cf. Rev 7:9; 21:24–25; cf. 4 Ezra 7:123). Such healing involves the total absence of any "curse" (κατάθεμα), as Rev 22:3a specifies, a likely allusion to Zechariah 14:11:

> "And people shall dwell in it, and there shall be no more an anathema" (DRA). In the new creation God's people need never fear the curse of destruction that God brought on wicked nations (cf. 21:27; Josh 6:17–18; Mal 4:6).[365]

The description of the heavenly paradise is bracketed by the mention of the throne of God and the Lamb (Rev 22:3b). This highlights how the glorious presence of the Triune God stands as the center of all reality, around which everything else revolves. Since God is the source of life for all creation, his people will experience this life in significant ways. First, they are servant-priests who "serve" or "worship" (λατρεύω) him (22:3c), a term implying priestly service or worship in what is now the heavenly temple (also in 7:15).[366] All God's people are now priests (e.g., 1:6; 5:10; 20:6). Second, in the heavenly holy of holies, the entire community of priests will see the very face of God (22:4a), meaning they will experience his unmediated presence.[367] Not even Moses could see God's face (Exod 33:20, 23), but all the saints will now see his face at last, fulfilling a long-standing hope (e.g., Pss 11:7; 17:15; 27:4; Matt 5:8; 1 Cor 13:12; 1 John 3:2; Heb 12:14). In contrast, the wicked cry out to be hidden from God's face (Rev 6:16; cf. 20:11). Third, believers will also bear God's name on their foreheads (22:4b;

364. Tremper Longman III, *Revelation through Old Testament Eyes* (Grand Rapids: Kregel Academic, 2022), 307.

365. Mathewson, *New Heaven and a New Earth*, 202.

366. Elsewhere in the New Testament the term is translated "serve" or "minister" (Matt 4:10; Luke 1:74; 4:8; Acts 26:7; 27:23; Rom 1:9, 25; Phil 3:3; 2 Tim 1:3; Heb 8:5; 9:14; 13:10; Rev 7:15; 22:3) or "worship" (Luke 2:37; Acts 7:7, 42; 24:14; Heb 9:9; 10:2; 12:28).

367. Aune, *Revelation 17–22*, 1179, notes that "the phrase 'seeing the face of God' is a metaphor in Judaism and early Christianity for a full awareness of the presence and power of God."

cf. 2:17; 3:12; 7:3; 9:4; 14:1), a mark of relational allegiance that stands in contrast to evil marks of loyalty (cf. 13:16, 17; 14:9, 11; 17:5). Fourth, the Lord God will supply all light, surpassing the glory of the sun or any lamp and forever eliminating the night (22:5a–b). The glorious presence of the Creator God and the Covenant Lord will shine on his people (21:23; cf. Isa 60:19–20; Zech 14:6–7).[368] Fifth, God's priestly people will also reign as kings forever and ever (Rev 22:5c), a theme echoed throughout Revelation (e.g., 2:26–27; 3:21; 20:4; cf. Dan 7:18, 27; 2 Tim 2:12). Just as Adam and Eve were supposed to rule over the original creation (Gen 1:28), so God's people will now serve as his "image-bearers and dominion-keepers, ruling over and tending God's good creation as vice-regents for God and the Lamb (Gen 1:26–28; 2:15–17; Ps 8:3–8; cf. 1 Cor 15:20–28; Eph 1:20–23; Heb. 2:5–10)."[369]

11.8 Epilogue (22:6–21)

11.8.1 Introduction

The epilogue has the sense that John is trying to accomplish many things in a short amount of space. There are various speakers (John, an angel, Jesus, the Spirit and the bride, the hearers), significant parallels with the prologue in 1:1–8,[370] and three key themes that reinforce the overall message of the book: (1) the book is an authentic prophecy from God (22:6–8, 10, 16, 18–19), (2) Jesus Christ's return is imminent (22:6–7, 10, 12, 20), and (3) those who obey the prophecy will be blessed (22:7, 9, 11, 12, 14, 17, 18–19).[371] The introductory section (22:6–7) highlights the three themes and features a beatitude for the faithful. The epilogue continues with the angel's commands (22:8–11), the words of Christ (22:12–16), and a final assurance of Christ's return (22:20), before concluding with a benediction (22:21).

11.8.2 Blessings for Those Who Obey the Authentic Revelation from God (22:6–7)

An anonymous angel, perhaps the same one who spoke in 21:9, proclaims this book to be "trustworthy and true" (cf. 19:9; 21:5), consistent with the faithful and true Christ

368. The expression "Lord God" is used in Rev 1:8; 4:8, 11; 11:17; 15:3; 16:7; 18:8; 19:6; 21:22; 22:5, 6. Kenneth A. Matthews, *Genesis 1–11:26*, NAC (Nashville: B&H, 1996), 192, notes that this combination makes an important theological point: "Yahweh, the Lord of his people, is in fact that all-wise and powerful Elohim-Creator. Hence, the antecedents of Israel's precious communion with its Creator and Covenant Lord had their inception in the garden when man first knew that fellowship. The personal presence of Yahweh-Elohim among his people Israel was not an anomaly but the pattern God inaugurated from the beginning."

369. Fanning, *Revelation*, 556.

370. Osborne, *Revelation*, 777–78, notes the following parallels between the prologue (1:1–8) and the epilogue (22:6–21): the revelation is shown to his servants (1:1 = 22:6), authentication of the prophecy from God (1:1 = 22:6), the content of "what must soon take place" (1:1 = 22:6), the beatitude (1:3 = 22:7), the "words of the prophecy" (1:3 = 22:7, 10), obeying the words of the book (1:3 = 22:7), the imminent return of Christ (1:3, 7 = 22:7, 12, 20), the call to faithfulness (1:3, 6 = 22:7, 9, 11, 14, 17), and the Alpha and Omega (1:8 = 22:13).

371. Duvall, *Revelation*, 304. On the outline of this section, I have relied upon on Osborne, *Revelation*, 778–79, with some modification.

(cf. 1:5; 3:7, 14; 19:11). In other words, these words from "the Lord, the God of the spirits of the prophets" (CSB) constitute an authentic proclamation from heaven. God through his prophetic Spirit has spoken through his prophets to reveal his plan to his people. This redemptive plan centers on Jesus Christ, whose return is always imminent (22:6–7, 10, 12, 20).

Christ's imminent return calls the church to obedient holiness, a repeated emphasis throughout the epilogue. Like the first beatitude in 1:3, the sixth blessing in 22:7 falls upon those who obey the prophecy. The emphasis on obedience also reminds us to see Revelation primarily as proclamation rather than prediction. Instead of focusing on the times and dates of Christ's parousia, we are enjoined with living faithfully in light of the imminence of his certain coming (cf. Rom 13:11; 1 Pet 4:7).

11.8.3 The Angel's Commands (22:8–11)

In a manner similar to 19:10, John initially responds to the angel's revelation by falling down to worship the messenger (22:8). As earlier, the angel quickly rebukes John, reminding him that he is a fellow servant with him and his fellow prophets and with all true believers (i.e., "all who keep the words of this scroll" in 22:9). Instead, John should "Worship God!" (cf. 19:10). In light of all that John has seen, heard, and experienced, no wonder he reacts by falling in worship. But the angelic rebuke brings him back to his senses with a clear reminder of the role that angels play—"ministering spirits sent to serve those who will inherit salvation" (Heb 1:14). God alone deserves worship!

John is then told not to "seal up the words of the prophecy of this scroll, because the time is near" (Rev 22:10). At the end of Daniel's prophecy, he is told to "seal the words of the scroll until the time of the end" (Dan 12:4). Since John's readers are living in the last days, the time between the first and second comings of Christ (e.g., Acts 2:16–18; 1 Tim 4:1; 2 Tim 3:1–5; Heb 1:2; 9:26; 1 Pet 1:20; 2 Pet 3:3–4), Revelation is to remain an unsealed book, a revelation (ἀποκάλυψις) to be heard and obeyed. The nearness of the end supplies the motivation for the book to remain open. In the last days, the time of fulfillment has already begun in the work of Christ and his parousia is constantly imminent.

The angel concludes his message with two commands for the unrighteous and two for the righteous (Rev 22:11; cf. Dan 12:10), with both bracketed by references to Christ's second coming (Rev 22:10b, 12a). These exhortations warn the "wicked" and "vile" that a life of habitual sin and rebellion leads to certain judgment (21:8; 22:15; cf. Isa 6:9–10; Ezek 3:27; Matt 13:13–15; John 9:39–41). They also encourage the righteous and holy to continue walking in faithful obedience.

11.8.4 Christ Speaks (22:12–16)

Christ speaks in 22:12a, repeating his announcement in 22:7a: "Look, I am coming soon!" Both the prologue (1:1, 7) and the epilogue (22:7, 10, 12, 20) stress Jesus's return.

And Christ returns with his reward, his eternal recompense for believers' faithful actions (22:12b; see also 11:18 where it speaks of "judging the dead" and "rewarding your servants the prophets"; cf. Isa 40:10; 62:11; Prov 24:12).[372]

Just as Jesus assumes the role of Yahweh as Judge, so he closely identifies with Yahweh in Revelation 22:13 through his use of Yahweh titles: "I am the Alpha and the Omega, the First and the Last, the Beginning and the End" (cf. 1:4–5, 8; 5:13; 6:16–17; 21:6; cf. Isa 41:4; 44:6; 48:12). Jesus is the Sovereign Lord of history who will accomplish God's purposes for his creation.[373] In the final "I am" saying in Revelation related to God the Father or Jesus occurs in Revelation 22:16 (1:8, 17–18; 21:6; 22:13, 16; cf. 2:23), Jesus says more about his divine identity and mission. He is the Messiah from the line of David, the ideal ruler and shepherd of his people (cf. 5:5; 2 Sam 7:12–16; Isa 9:6–7; 11:1; Jer 23:5–6; Matt 1:1; Luke 1:32, 69). He is also the "bright Morning Star," a messianic fulfillment of Numbers 24:17: "A star will come out of Jacob; a scepter will rise out of Israel." The celestial image points to a new day dawning beginning with Jesus's eternal reign, bringing an end to the long night of tribulation.[374]

The final beatitude in the book (Rev 22:14–15) continues the emphasis on a person's actions, and specifically, contrasts the righteous and the wicked. The faithful wash their robes (cf. 3:5, 18; 7:14; 16:15) rather than defile their garments (3:4; 14:4), meaning they persevere in allegiance to Christ and refuse to compromise with the world system, even when faced with persecution. They will be blessed with eternal life in God's presence.

In contrast, the unrighteous are denied access to God's eternal presence, represented here by the eternal city (cf. 21:8, 27). Living outside the city or outside the camp signifies living under God's curse, separated from his people (e.g., Lev 24:14; Num 15:36; Heb 13:12–13). The pejorative term "dogs" represents wicked, impure people and sometimes carries sexual connotations (e.g., a euphemism for a male prostitute in Deut 23:17–18).[375] The vice list, the third in Revelation (cf. 9:20–21; 22:15), includes magic arts, sexual immorality, murder, idolatry, and falsehood. The final group may allude more specifically to anyone who follows the false prophet's lies or the beast's deception (cf. 13:11–17; 16:13).[376]

The section closes with Jesus's statement that he has sent his angel to give "you"

---

372. Osborne, *Revelation*, 788, observes that the idea of "judged according to works" occurs throughout Revelation (e.g., 2:23; 11:18; 14:13; 18:6; 20:12–13; 22:12), as well as the Old Testament (e.g., 2 Chr 6:23; Job 34:11; Pss 28:4; 62:12; Prov 24:12; Jer 17:10) and the rest of the New Testament (e.g., Matt 16:27; Rom 2:6; 14:12; 1 Cor 3:12–15; 2 Cor 5:10; 11:15; 2 Tim 4:14; 1 Pet 1:17). The link is between "ethical responsibility and its eschatological consequences." It is not justification by works but is salvation by grace through faith that leads to a faithful life. As Osborne puts it, "we are saved by grace and judged by works."

373. Bauckham, *Theology*, 23–30, 54–65.

374. See the comments by Mounce, *Revelation*, 408–9, and Beale, *Revelation*, 1147.

375. Mounce, *Revelation*, 408. See Mark Wilson, "Revelation," 373–75, for more insight into the emphasis on sexual sins.

376. Fanning, *Revelation*, 562.

(plural) this testimony "for the churches" (22:16a) just prior to identifying himself (22:16b discussed earlier).[377] This "revelation of/from Jesus Christ" (1:1) has been communicated by angelic messengers (1:1) by means of "testimony" (1:2; 22:18, 20) to the seven churches and beyond to the whole people of God. The larger point is that it is a reliable, trustworthy, heaven-sent message authenticated by Jesus himself.

11.8.5 Exhortations to Come to Christ (22:17)

While on the surface it appears we have a series of calls for Christ to return, a closer look makes it more natural to take at least three (and possibly all four) of the imperatives of 22:17 ("come" and "take") as invitations to respond positively to Jesus. The second imperative, "and let the one who hears say, 'Come!'" may be directed to Jesus, asking him to return. But if John is relying upon Isaiah 55:1 (cf. John 6:35; 7:37) both here and in Rev 21:6, then this too may be a summons to allegiance to Christ. The surrounding context certainly stresses the return of Christ, and these twin theological themes go hand in hand: in light of Jesus's imminent return, the Spirit and the church call urgently to the nations (and also to the compromising church) to come to faithful discipleship in Jesus and experience the presence of God's Spirit. It is he alone who can quench the human thirst for life through his free gift of the water of life.

11.8.6 A Warning against Adding to or Subtracting from the Book (22:18–19)

The closing warning draws on Deuteronomy 4:2: "Do not add to what I command you and do not subtract from it, but keep the commands of the LORD your God that I give you" (cf. Deut 12:32). This is a warning against a willful distortion or misrepresentation of the book's message through idolatrous and deceitful false teaching (e.g., the Nicolaitans and the Jezebel group).[378] The punishment for intentionally twisting and falsifying God's word has eternal consequences. In essence those who take this road, even though they may claim to be part of Christ's church, indicate by their actions that they are moving in a different direction. They will suffer the fate of unbelievers described throughout the book. God cannot be deceived.

11.8.7 A Final Promise and Prayer for Christ's Return (22:20)

The book closes with a final promise from Jesus and prayer for his return (22:20) followed by a closing benediction (22:21). The promise from Christ that he will certainly return runs like a thread throughout the epilogue: 22:7, 12, (17), and 20.[379] The

377. Beale, *Revelation*, 1143–46, has a thorough discussion of the interpretive options for understanding the expressions "you" and "for the churches."

378. Mounce, *Revelation*, 410, observes that once again the book is described as a prophecy: "Apocalyptic imagery is pressed into the service of NT prophecy."

379. On the theme of Christ's return, see the insightful comments by Schnabel, *40 Questions about End Times*, 247–63.

affirmation of Christ's return anchors "the blessed hope" (Titus 2:13) and is met with a prayer of longing echoed by the church through the ages, "Come, Lord Jesus" (cf. 1 Cor 16:22–23; Did. 10.6).

11.8.8 Concluding Benediction (22:21)

Revelation begins as a letter and closes with a benediction typical of Pauline letters, calling for grace to empower believers to persevere in faithfulness to Jesus (see Rom 16:20; 1 Cor 16:23; 2 Cor 13:13; 1 Thess 5:28; 2 Thess 3:18; Gal 6:18; Phil 4:23; Phlm 25; cf. Eph 6:24; Col 4:18; 1 Tim 6:21; 2 Tim 4:22; Titus 3:15).[380] Although the book comes to a close, its message that the Triune God is in control and will defeat the powers of evil, rescue his people, and restore creation lives on.

We turn our attention now to the nine primary themes of this grand book as anchored in the story itself. We begin with the Triune God—Father, Son, and Spirit—before turning our attention to the people of God, those who choose to follow the Lamb. Such worship leads them to persevere in the mission despite opposition and persecution at the hands of God's enemies (i.e., the unholy trinity and their followers). In the end, God wins! He will condemn all evil and usher in the new creation where he will live with his people forevermore. The book is titled a "revelation" for a reason. It unveils both God's message and the hearts of those who hear it. As the refrain in the seven messages goes, "Whoever has ears, let them hear what the Spirit says to the churches." And all God's people said, "Amen. Come, Lord Jesus."

380. Mark Wilson, "Revelation," 377, writes: "The final word 'Amen' in the NIV is not found in some manuscripts of Revelation and may be a scribal addition. If original, it would also be the last word in the New Testament and in the Bible, and stand like a divine punctuation mark underscoring the extraordinary revelation that precedes it."

Part 4

Major Theological Themes in Revelation

Chapter 12

"THE ONE WHO IS, AND WHO WAS, AND WHO IS COMING": GOD

BIBLIOGRAPHY

Allen, Michael. *Grounded in Heaven: Recentering Christian Hope and Life on God.* Grand Rapids: Eerdmans, 2018. **Aune, David E.** *Apocalypticism, Prophecy and Magic in Early Christianity.* Grand Rapids: Baker, 2006. **Beale, G. K.** *John's Use of the Old Testament.* JSNTSup 166. London: Bloomsbury T&T Clark, 1998. **Boring, M. Eugene.** "The Theology of Revelation: 'The Lord Our God the Almighty Reigns.'" *Int* 40.3 (1986): 257–69. **Forsyth, P. T.** *The Work of Christ.* London: Hodder & Stoughton, 1910. **Gallusz, Laszlo.** *The Throne Motif in the Book of Revelation.* LNTS 487. London: Bloomsbury T&T Clark, 2014. **Gentry, Peter J.** "The Meaning of 'Holy' in the Old Testament." *BSac* 170 (2013): 400–417. **Karrer, Martin.** "God in the Book of Revelation." *OHBR* 205–22. **Köstenberger, Andreas J.** *A Theology of John's Gospel and Letters: The Word, the Christ, the Son of God.* BTNT. Grand Rapids: Zondervan Academic, 2009. **Lane, Tony.** "The Wrath of God as an Aspect of the Love of God." Pages 138–67 in *Nothing Greater, Nothing Better: Theological Essays on the Love of God.* Edited by Kevin J. Vanhoozer. Grand Rapids: Eerdmans, 2001. **McDonough, Sean.** *YHWH at Patmos: Rev. 1:4 in Its Hellenistic and Early Jewish Setting.* WUNT 2.107. Tübingen: Mohr Siebeck, 1999. Reprint, Eugene, OR: Wipf & Stock, 2011. **McIlraith, Donal A.** *The Reciprocal Love Between Christ and the Church in the Apocalypse.* Rome: Columban Fathers, 1989. **Middleton, J. Richard.** *A New Heaven and a New Earth: Reclaiming Biblical Eschatology.* Grand Rapids: Baker Academic, 2014. **Osborne, Grant R.** "Theodicy in the Apocalypse." *TrinJ* 14 (1993): 63–77. **Paul, Ian.** "The Trinitarian Dynamic in the Book of Revelation." Pages 85–108 in *Trinity Without Hierarchy: Reclaiming Nicene Orthodoxy in Evangelical Theology.* Edited by Michael F. Bird and Scott Harrower. Grand Rapids: Kregel, 2019. **Smith, Brandon D.** *The Trinity in the Book of Revelation: Seeing Father, Son, and Holy Spirit in John's Apocalypse.* SCDS. Downers Grove, IL: IVP Academic, 2022. **Stephens, Mark B.** "Creation and New Creation in the Book of Revelation." *OBHR* 257–73. **Wright, Christopher J. H.** *Salvation Belongs to Our God: Celebrating the Bible's Central Story.* Downers Grove, IL: IVP Academic, 2007.

12.1 INTRODUCTION

Richard Bauckham perceptively notes that the "theology of Revelation is highly theocentric," a characteristic he labels the book's "greatest contribution to New Testament theology."[1] Tabb concurs, positing that "God is utterly supreme and central in the Apocalypse." Revelation is without a doubt God-centered, an emphasis that surfaces repeatedly and in a variety of fascinating ways. In this chapter we will explore Revelation's focus on the nature and work of God.

We begin with the God who speaks and explore how God discloses his message to his people and his world. God's character as trustworthy and true is the ultimate source of his prophetic word, a word aimed at informing as well as transforming his people. Revelation also stresses God as the Sovereign Creator and sustainer of the world, a reality that provides the basis of our eschatological hope. God's name and his many titles, along with captivating images such as God's throne, reaffirm his sovereign lordship. God is King over the universe and as such he alone is worthy of worship.

The Sovereign Creator is also the God who loves as the perfect Father, caring for and comforting his children, answering their pleas for justice, and carrying out his plan to judge evil and live eternally with his people. As a result, we see God's love as holy love. His wrath flows out of his love and does so in a manner consistent with his holy and righteous character. God is patient in his judgment but will, in time, vindicate his people and rid the universe of evil. God is coming to judge and to save, and to dwell among his people in fulfillment of his longstanding promise. Seeing God as the God who speaks, the sovereign Creator and sustainer, the One worthy of worship, the loving Judge, and the One who is coming provides the necessary theological foundation for grasping and applying the overall message of the Apocalypse.

12.2 THE GOD WHO SPEAKS

We would be amiss if we did not begin with the obvious but often understated—Revelation's emphasis on God as the God who speaks. John's Gospel opens by highlighting the God who speaks: "In the beginning was the Word, and the Word was with God, and the Word was God. . . . The Word became flesh and made his dwelling among us. We have seen his glory, the glory of the one and only Son, who came from the Father, full of grace and truth" (John 1:1, 14). The Apocalypse begins similarly: "The revelation [of/]from Jesus Christ, which God gave him to show his servants what must soon take place. He made it known by sending his angel to his servant John, who

1. Bauckham, *Theology*, 23. In addition to Bauckham, see esp. deSilva, *Seeing Things John's Way*, 158–74; Tabb, *All Things New*, 29–45; Flemming, *Foretaste of the Future*, 35–54.

testifies to everything he saw—that is, the word of God and the testimony of Jesus Christ" (1:1–2). God is the ultimate source of the revelation. Such a beginning not only brings attention to God himself but also demonstrates his devotion to disclose truth to his people and his world, truth that transforms. The chain of revelation runs from God to Christ to an angel to John to God's servants. Ultimately this is a "revelation from above that makes sense of things here on earth."[2] The theme of God speaking runs throughout the book in a number of ways.

John refers to his visions as "the word of God and the testimony of Jesus Christ" (1:2). The expression "the word of God" (τὸν λόγον τοῦ θεοῦ or οἱ λόγοι τοῦ θεοῦ) is used seven times and refers to prophetic statements (1:2; 17:17; 19:9), to the apostolic message (1:9; 6:9; 20:4), and even to Jesus's name (19:13). Every use highlights God's revelation to human beings. The term "word" can also refer to Jesus's instructions and commands (3:8, 10) in addition to depicting the victor's witness or testimony (12:11). On two occasions God's "commands" (ἐντολή) are specified (12:17; 14:12). Koester writes that "word of God" is a "biblical expression for what God had conveyed through the prophets (Jer 1:2; Hos 1:1; Joel 1:1; Mic 1:1; Zeph 1:1; cf. Rev 10:7), including his commandments (1:9; 12:17; 14:12). When bearing witness, John uses the familiar biblical expression to show the continuity between his words (19:9; 22:6) and earlier prophetic words from God."[3]

The God who speaks repeatedly instructs John to write down the revelation (1:11, 19; 2:1, 8, 12, 18; 3:1, 7, 14; 21:5; cf. 1:3; 5:1; 14:13; 19:9). The words of this revealed message (15:4) are deemed "trustworthy and true" (21:5; 22:6), the "true words of God" (19:9). As many have observed, God only speaks directly twice in the book, and the second time is 21:5: "He who was seated on the throne said, 'I am making everything new!' Then he said, 'Write this down, for these words are trustworthy and true.'" The background, noted by Beale, is Isa 65:16–17, where it is the "one true God" or God of truth who creates a new heaven and new earth.[4] This prophecy that is Revelation is both reliable and true and "fits the character of the true God (6:10; 15:3) and Christ his faithful and true witness (3:14; 19:11)."[5]

The terms "prophecy/prophet" (προφητεία, προφήτης) and "scroll" (βιβλίον) are also used to stress God's revelation. The noun "prophecy" (προφητεία) is used seven times and in all but one instance refers to the words of the/this prophecy that is the book of Revelation (1:3; 19:10; 22:7, 10, 18, 19). The outlier is 11:6, where the term describes the message of the two witnesses. The noun "prophet" (προφήτης) is used eight times to refer to the prophets (22:6, 9), God's servants the prophets (10:7; 11:18), the saints and prophets (16:6; 18:20, 24), and the two prophets (11:10). Whether explicit or implied, God is the ultimate source of the prophetic message in each case.

2. Resseguie, *Revelation*, 63.
3. Koester, *Revelation*, 213.
4. Beale, *Revelation*, 1053.
5. Koester, *Revelation*, 799.

God announces his message to his prophets (10:7). They are his witnesses or prophets (11:10; 16:6). God rewards his prophets (11:18) and verifies their message of salvation and judgment (18:20, 24). God inspires the prophets (22:6) and his prophets obey him (22:9). In contrast, we hear of Jezebel the "prophetess" (προφῆτις—2:20, NIV "prophet") and the false prophet (ψευδοπροφήτης—16:13; 19:20; 20:10) as sources of revelation other than God.

In addition, the term "scroll" (βιβλίον) reinforces the idea that God speaks.[6] John is told to write on a scroll what he sees in his God-given vision and send it to the churches (1:11). In Rev 5 and 10, the scroll (or little scroll) likely represents God's plan to judge evil, redeem his people, and transform creation, a plan anchored in the life and work of Christ. Consequently, Jesus alone is worthy to open the scroll and work out the plan of God. Near the end of the book, the penultimate beatitude pronounces a blessing on those who obey the proclamation or "prophecy written in this scroll" (22:7). The revealing angel in that same context identifies himself as a fellow servant with "all who keep the words of this scroll" (22:9; cf. 19:10). And since the time is near, the "words of the prophecy of this scroll" are to remain unsealed or available to all (22:10). God has spoken, and his words will be accepted and obeyed or else rejected. We find the final two occurrences of the prophecy/scroll combination in 22:18–19, where those who hear the words of the prophecy of this scroll are warned against adding to or subtracting from them. In fact, God's word is so inextricably tied to his person and will that rejecting his prophetic word results in receiving his judgment (i.e., the plagues described in the scroll and loss of any share in the tree of life and citizenship in the Holy City).

We also learn a lot about the God who speaks from his self-designation in 1:8 and 21:6: "the Alpha and the Omega" and "the Beginning and the End."[7] Bauckham notes that these designations convey that God is "the origin and the goal of history," the one having "the first word, in creation, and the last word, in new creation."[8] The first and last letters of the Greek alphabet in this context certainly depict God as the sovereign Lord of history but also present him as the God who speaks, since the first and last letters imply the inclusion of everything in between.[9] The "I am" introduction in both cases also connects with the divine name in Exod 3:14, "I AM WHO I AM," and the context of his self-revelation to Moses. Karrer concludes that "since the letters were used to form words and numerals, his [the writer's] implication is that every human

6. Certain uses of "scroll" move in a different, though not in some cases in a totally unrelated, direction: the heavens receding like a scroll (6:14), the book or scroll of life (13:8; 17:8; 20:12; 21:27) and the book or scroll of deeds (20:12, 12).

7. We will discuss the self-designation of Christ in 1:17 as "the First and the Last" and in 22:13 as "the Alpha and the Omega, the First and the Last, the Beginning and the End" in 13.2.

8. Bauckham, *Theology*, 27.

9. Fanning, *Revelation*, 87. Aune, *Apocalypticism, Prophecy, and Magic*, 266–67, also observes a connection to the seven Greek vowels, αεηιουω (*aeēiouō*), thought to represent the "unutterable divine name."

thought, every communication, every reflection, and every numeric calculation involves God's presence."[10]

This takes us back to the opening paragraph of the book. God is the ultimate source of the revelation, and those who read this prophecy and take it to heart will be blessed (1:1–3). Here we have yet another reminder that the emphasis falls on proclamation rather than prediction. Gorman concludes that Revelation is "a call to conversion and discipleship *in light of* past, present, and future realities, . . . an alternative way of being grounded in the vision of God."[11]

To miss this point, he says, is to miss the whole point of Revelation. The God who speaks does not simply desire to inform us but to form and transform us.[12]

12.3 THE SOVEREIGN CREATOR AND RULER

12.3.1 God the Creator and Sustainer

God's sovereignty rests upon him being the Creator and sustainer of the world.[13] Revelation affirms God as both. After the introductory picture of the risen and glorified Christ and his words to the seven churches in 1:9–3:22, the scene shifts from earth to heaven for the great throne-room episode of chapters 4–5, the anchoring and centering vision of the entire book. Tabb observes that Rev 4 emphasizes God as the supreme Creator in at least three ways: (1) the rainbow around the throne in 4:3 (cf. Ezek 1:28) recalls the sign of God's covenant in Gen 9:13–16 to convey God's faithfulness to his creation through judgment (Rev 11:18) and the new creation to come, (2) the four living creatures in 4:6 represent creation and indicate that all creation glorifies the Creator, and (3) the worship song in 4:11 declares that all things have God to thank for their very existence.[14] The chapter culminates in the praise of 4:11 that declares God to be worthy of glory, honor, and power "for" or "because" (ὅτι) he "created all things" and by his will "they were created and have their being" (ἦσαν καὶ ἐκτίσθησαν). The combination of the imperfect and aorist tenses here has been interpreted variously, but most likely the imperfect points to the ongoing preservation of creation and the aorist to the initial act of creation.[15]

Throughout Revelation God is seen and worshiped as the Creator and sustainer of all things. In fact, he is worshiped precisely because he is the Sovereign Creator. Because

10. Martin Karrer, "God in the Book of Revelation," *OHBR* 213.

11. Gorman, *Reading Revelation Responsibly*, 82, emphasis original.

12. Gorman, *Reading Revelation Responsibly*, 82.

13. Flemming, *Foretaste of the Future*, 37.

14. Tabb, *All Things New*, 41.

15. Beale, *Revelation*, 335, notes that the meanings of the verbs themselves and not only the tenses point in this direction. Smalley, *Revelation*, 125, observes that "everything existed first in the eternal mind and will of God (imperfect), and then at an appointed time, through his will, came into being (aorist)"; cf. also Mounce, *Revelation*, 127. Mathewson, *Revelation*, 41, 68, cites this as an example of hysteron-proteron, where the author foregrounds the most important element (cf. 3:3).

"he alone has ultimate power over everything, . . . he alone is to be worshipped."[16] "Every creature in heaven and on earth and under the earth and on the sea" owes its existence to the Creator (5:13). It is "God's creation" (3:14). The mighty angel in chapter 10 affirms the universal scope of God as Creator when he swears by "him who lives for ever and ever, who created the heavens, . . . the earth, . . . the sea," and all that is in them (10:6). Therefore, every creature is summoned to worship. An anonymous angel calls out to every nation, tribe, language, and people: "Fear God and give him glory. . . . Worship him who made the heavens, the earth, the sea and the springs of water" (14:7).

The final reference to God as Creator points forward. In 21:5, the second time God speaks directly, we see the Creator as the Recreator or the "Everything-new Maker": "He who was seated on the throne said, 'I am making everything new!'"[17] The creation of Gen 1–2 and the new creation of Rev 21–22 bookend the entire story of Scripture, affirming God as source and sovereign over everything, creation and new creation included. God as Creator becomes the basis of eschatological hope. Bauckham concludes, "If God was the transcendent source of all things, he could also be the source of quite new possibilities for his creation in the future."[18] On the other hand, if God is not in control, then the ground of hope is lost: "Where faith in God the Creator wanes, so inevitably does hope for resurrection, let alone the new creation of all things. It is the God who is Alpha who will also be Omega."[19] Bauckham and others have observed the disappearance of the sea in the new creation since the sea symbolizes evil and chaos (21:1).[20] This also points to God as the Sovereign Creator: "In new creation God makes his creation eternally secure from any threat of destructive evil."[21] He is indeed making all things new!

12.3.2 A Name and a Title: Sovereign Lord

Throughout Revelation God is identified in ways that reaffirm his sovereign lordship. We see this first with the name of God—Yahweh. When Jewish Christians wrote (or spoke) Greek they used Κύριος ("Lord") as a Greek equivalent for the divine name.[22] John uses this term repeatedly in Revelation with reference to God (1:8; 4:8, 11; 11:4, 15, 17; 15:3, 4; 16:7; 18:8; 19:6; 21:22; 22:5, 6) and, interestingly, also when referring to Jesus (11:8; 14:13; 17;14; 19:16; 22:20, 21).

God is identified as "the Lord God, . . . the Almighty" in 1:8 (κύριος ὁ θεός . . . ὁ

16. Bauckham, *Theology*, 48.

17. Flemming, *Foretaste of the Future*, 39.

18. Bauckham, *Theology*, 48.

19. Bauckham, *Theology*, 51.

20. Bauckham, *Theology*, 53. Cf., e.g., Tabb, *All Things New*, 42; J. Richard Middleton, *A New Heaven and a New Earth: Reclaiming Biblical Eschatology* (Grand Rapids: Baker Academic, 2014), 169; Smalley, *Revelation*, 524–25.

21. Bauckham, *Theology*, 53.

22. Karrer, "God in the Book of Revelation," 207–8; McDonough, *YWHW at Patmos*, 58–62, 97–98, who notes that Jewish Christians could possibly have used the name YHWH when they wrote and spoke Hebrew but when they wrote and spoke Greek, they used κύριος (p. 98).

παντοκράτωρ); as "Lord God Almighty" (κύριος ὁ θεὸς ὁ παντοκράτωρ) with slight variation in 4:8; 11:17; 15:3; 16:7; 19:6; 21:22; as "God Almighty" (τοῦ θεοῦ τοῦ παντοκράτορος) in 16:14; 19:15; as "the Lord God" or "the Lord, the God" (κύριος ὁ θεός) in 18:8; 22:5, 6; as "Lord and God" (ὁ κύριος καὶ ὁ θεός) in 4:11; and as "Lord" (κύριος) in 11:4, 15; 15:4.[23] These expressions draw on similar uses in the LXX prophetic books (e.g., Amos 3:13; 4:13; 5:8, 14–16; 9:5–6, 15; Nah 3:5; Zech 10:3; Mal 2:16). In addition, John's readers would have noticed the not-so-subtle contrast between God and Roman emperors, who were often acclaimed using the term "Lord."[24] In all, the name "Lord" clearly signals God's power and sovereignty over history, especially when combined with titles or designations such as "Alpha and Omega" or "who is, and who was, and who is to come." And while it may be true that God has one name and many titles, certain titles, such as "Almighty," were so closely tied to the name that they became part of John's "definition" of God.[25]

The title "Almighty" (παντοκράτωρ) occurs nine times in Revelation: "Lord God Almighty" (4:8; 11:17; 15:3; 16:7; 19:6; 21:22), "Lord God . . . Almighty" (1:8), and "God Almighty" (16:14; 19:15). It was a common title in the LXX, especially the prophetic books, where it renders the Hebrew phrase יהוה אֱלֹהֵי צְבָאוֹת (*yhwh 'elohe tseva'ot*) translated "The Lord, the God of hosts" (e.g., Jer 5:14; Hos 12:5[Heb. and LXX 6]; Amos 3:13; 4:13).[26] Boring argues that the use of "Almighty" exclusively for God illustrates Revelation's "theocentric character."[27] In contrast, we find a different term used of Caesar: "Whereas Caesar (*autokratōr*, or emperor) rules over a limited area and could have threatened them with persecution, the Lord God 'Almighty' (*pantokratōr*) rules over the entire universe and promises to come to their rescue."[28] Overall, the title "Almighty" points to God's universal sovereignty: highlighting "Yahweh's unrivalled power over all things and therefore his supremacy over the course of historical events . . . not so much God's abstract omnipotence as his actual control over all things."[29]

12.3.3 The Throne: Sovereign Ruler

John uses another implicitly political image to portray God as the sovereign ruler of the universe—the throne. The term "throne" (θρόνος) is used sixty-one times in the New Testament, of which almost fifty occur in Revelation with nearly twenty of those coming in Rev 4–5. In Revelation the term "throne" is used in various ways, with some overlap between categories:

23. Jesus is identified as "Lord" (κύριος) in 11:8; 14:13; 17:14; 19:16; 22:21. See Ch. 13 for more on Jesus sharing God's name.

24. See the examples in Karrer, "God in the Book of Revelation," 209.

25. Karrer, "God in the Book of Revelation," 210.

26. Bauckham, *Theology*, 30. The vowels of יהוה vary.

27. M. Eugene Boring, "The Theology of Revelation: 'The Lord Our God the Almighty Reigns,'" *Int* 40.3 (1986): 259.

28. Keener, *Revelation*, 74.

29. Bauckham, *Theology*, 30; also Boring, "Theology of Revelation," 260; Resseguie, *Revelation*, 69; Tabb, *All Things New*, 36.

- God on his throne: 4:2 [2x], 3, 4, 5, 6 [2x], 9, 10 [2x]; 5:1, 7, 11, 13; 6:16; 7:9, 10, 11, 11, 15 [2x]; 12:5; 19:4; 20:11 (great white throne); 21:5
- The Father on his throne: 3:21
- The throne (presumably God's throne): 8:3; 14:3; 20:12
- Voice from the throne: 16:17; 19:5; 21:3
- The throne of God and the Lamb: 22:1, 3
- Jesus sits on the throne: 3:21; 5:6 (standing at center); 7:17 (at center)
- Seven spirits (or sevenfold Holy Spirit) before the throne: 1:4; 4:5
- Twenty-four thrones: 4:4, 4; 11:16
- Those seated on thrones given authority to judge: 20:4
- Lightning, rumblings, peals of thunder from the throne: 4:5
- Demonic thrones: 2:13; 13:2; 16:10

In the anchoring vision of Rev 4–5, the central image is God's throne.[30] The "throne" is a foundational image in the book, with everything revolving around the throne and subsequent visions originating from the throne. This scene echoes the prophets' depiction of God on his throne surrounded by heavenly beings (e.g., Isa 6:1–6; Ezek 1:4–28; Dan 7:9–10; cf. 1 Kgs 22:19) as a means of stressing God's sovereignty.[31]

In addition to the throne image to which we will return shortly, Revelation also stresses God's kingly rule or reign. To begin with, both God and Christ are identified as "king" (βασιλεύς)—God as "king of the nations" (15:3), Jesus as ruler (ἄρχων) of the kings of the earth (1:5) and "King of kings and Lord of lords" (19:16). In 11:15 when the seventh angel blows his trumpet, loud voices in heaven announce, "The kingdom of the world has become the kingdom of our Lord and of his Messiah, and he will reign for ever and ever." We then hear of the twenty-four elders falling on their faces before God and worshiping him saying, "We give thanks to you, Lord God Almighty, the One who is and who was, because you have taken your great power and have begun to reign" (11:17). When Satan is hurled down, God is praised: "Now have come the salvation and the power and the kingdom of our God, and the authority of his Messiah" (12:10). In 19:6 the great multitude shouts praises to God as the reigning King: "Hallelujah! For our Lord God Almighty reigns." Ultimately, God's people are called to share in his kingdom and kingly reign (1:6, 9; 5:10; 20:4, 6; 22:5).

What theological message does the throne image and God as King send to the original hearers of Revelation? For starters, Revelation positions God seated on his throne at the center of the universe, the "transcendent Mission Control of the universe"

30. For an in-depth analysis of the throne motif in Revelation, see Gallusz, *Throne Motif.*

31. Tabb, *All Things New*, 37–38; deSilva, *Seeing Things John's Way*, 165–69.

as Boring puts it.[32] The "theocentric" nature of all reality again points to God's sovereignty over all things.[33] By focusing attention on the throne, Revelation emphasizes God's transcendence as well as sovereignty.[34] In addition, Flemming observes several profound missional implications of God seated on his cosmic throne.[35] First, no other powers can hinder or frustrate God's purposes for his creation. The throne surrounded by worshiping subordinates presents an unmistakable counter image to Roman imperial imagery.[36] Second, God's mission is to all people, as Christopher Wright observes: "The missional task of God's people flows directly from the universal offer of salvation. And that in turn flows from the universal sovereignty of God—that is, from the very throne of God to the world."[37] Third, only God can save the world. Salvation belongs to God and the Lamb (7:10). Fourth, as in heaven so also on earth. John calls his readers to "live within their specific settings as a present embodiment of the sovereign reign of God in Christ."[38]

God now shares his throne with Jesus Christ (3:21; 5:6; 7:17) and the sevenfold Spirit blazes forth from the throne (1:4; 4:5; cf. 5:6). At the conclusion of the entire apocalyptic drama, the "throne of God and of the Lamb" constitutes the centerpiece of the new creation as God's people enjoy his glorious presence forever (22:1, 3).

12.4 THE ONE WORTHY OF WORSHIP

Because God is the Creator and sovereign ruler of the universe, he alone is worthy of worship. We explore the topic of worship in greater detail in chapter 17. Here we will highlight what worship tells us about God and our relationship to God. First, God is indeed worthy of worship. He is seated on the throne as the eternal Sovereign of the universe (4:2–3, 9; 11:15, 17; 19:6). Throughout the hymnic sections we hear of God as the only true and appropriate recipient of worship. The living creatures and elders and 144,000 and great multitude and all of creation recognize God's worthiness as the proper recipient of praise and adoration. What is dramatically significant in Revelation is that the Lamb is also found worthy as a corecipient of worship (see Ch. 13). Second, as we have seen in the previous section, God is praised initially because he is the Creator and sustainer of all things. Third, we repeatedly hear the worshipers rehearsing attributes of the God: holy, Almighty, eternal, glorious, honorable, powerful, praiseworthy, wise, just, true, righteous, as well as many others. Fourth, God, the rightful King, has

32. Eugene Boring, *Hearing John's Voice: Insights for Teaching and Preaching* (Grand Rapids: Eerdmans, 1999), 97.

33. Bauckham, *Theology*, 31–33; Flemming *Foretaste of the Future*, 44.

34. Bauckham, *Theology*, 32.

35. Flemming, *Foretaste of the Future*, 46–49.

36. Brandon D. Smith, *The Trinity in the Book of Revelation: Seeing Father, Son, and Holy Spirit in John's Apocalypse*, SCDS (Downers Grove, IL: IVP Academic, 2022), 61; Bauckham, *Theology*, 33–35.

37. Christopher J. H. Wright, *Salvation Belongs to Our God: Celebrating the Bible's Central Story* (Downers Grove, IL: IVP Academic, 2007), 145.

38. Flemming *Foretaste of the Future*, 49.

begun his eternal reign (11:15, 17; 19:6). Fifth, this reign includes both judgment and salvation. He pours out his wrath on the powers of darkness and rescues his people (e.g., 11:18; 12:10; 16:5–7; 19:1–8). His judgments are true and just, and his salvation is gracious and glorious.

As a result, God's worthiness forces a choice on all humanity. Gallusz explains: "God's legitimate authority as the First Cause of the universe (4:11) whose character provides the basis for moral order is either acknowledged by expressing loyalty or denied by refusing to give him glory (14:6)."[39] The choices are the worship of God who receives crowns (e.g., by the living creatures in 4:10) or the worship of the dragon who retains his crowns (12:3; cf. also the beast's crowns in 13:1).[40] Revelation confronts listeners with a prophetic word that proclaims God alone as God and calls for the proper response of loving God with all our being (cf. the Shema in Deut 6:4–6), hence John's emphasis on keeping God's commands and giving him glory (e.g., Rev 12:17; 14:6–7, 12; 15:3–4).[41]

To expand upon this final point, Revelation insists that any object of worship other than God constitutes idolatry, whether angels or the emperor or any other created being. In 19:10 and 22:8–9 at the conclusion of major visions, John reacts by falling down before the revealing angel to worship and is immediately rebuked: "Don't do that! I am a fellow servant with you and with your brothers and sisters who hold to the testimony of Jesus. Worship God!" (19:10) and "Don't do that! I am a fellow servant with you and with your fellow prophets and with all who keep the words of this scroll. Worship God!" (22:9). Bauckham provides a detailed history of angels rejecting worship and concludes that both scenes come at the end of two major visions (17:1–19:10 and 21:9–22:9) and serve to contrast the judgment of Babylon the harlot with the establishment of Jerusalem the bride.[42]

John also counters the pressures and temptation directed at his readers to worship the emperor. Scholars have often observed that the title "lord" is used for Roman emperors and that people praised emperors as "worthy."[43] John's emphasis on worshiping God alone would be viewed by many as "an act of political displacement," elevating God above all competing powers.[44] Aune concludes, "The result is that the sovereignty of God and the lamb have been elevated so far above all pretensions and claims of earthly rulers that the latter, upon comparison, become only pale, even diabolical imitations of the transcendent majesty of the King of kings and Lord of lords."[45]

39. Gallusz, *Throne Motif*, 295.

40. Gallusz, *Throne Motif*, 295.

41. DeSilva, *Seeing Things John's Way*, 159–60.

42. Bauckham, *Climax of Prophecy*, 120–40. Contrast the positive affirmation in 1:17 when John falls at Jesus's feet in worship and the elders repeatedly falling down before God and the Lamb.

43. E.g., Karrer, "God in the Book of Revelation," 209.

44. Ian Paul, "The Trinitarian Dynamic in the Book of Revelation," in *Trinity Without Hierarchy: Reclaiming Nicene Orthodoxy in Evangelical Theology*, ed. Michael F. Bird and Scott Harrower (Grand Rapids: Kregel, 2019), 97. For more detail, see "The Influence of Roman Imperial Court Ceremonial on the Apocalypse of John" in Aune, *Apocalypticism, Prophecy, and Magic*, 99–119.

45. Aune, *Apocalypticism, Prophecy, and Magic*, 118.

12.5 THE GOD WHO LOVES

Although Revelation only makes one direct reference to the love of God (20:9; cf. 1:5; 3:9, 19), the book conveys God's love in various other, quite powerful, ways. He is not just the Almighty ruler or the holy Judge, he is also the Father, the caregiver and comforter, the provider and protector. On second look, God's love abounds for his creation and drives his pursuit of the repentance of the wicked and the healing of the nations. God's mission, centered in Christ, flows from his love.[46] The God who sits on the throne is also the God revealed in the slain Lamb.

The image of God as Father is an important image of his love.[47] Jesus refers to God as "my Father," from whom he receives authority (2:27), before whom he confesses the names of his followers (3:5), and with whom he shares the throne (3:21). Jesus makes his people to be "a kingdom and priests to serve his God and Father" (1:6). It is God the Father of our Lord Jesus Christ who writes his name on the foreheads of the 144,000, signifying God's protective presence with his people (14:1). God the Father also secures the relationship with his people through tribulation and into the new creation:

> He who was seated on the throne said, "I am making everything new!" Then he said, "Write this down, for these words are trustworthy and true." He said to me: "It is done. I am the Alpha and the Omega, the Beginning and the End. To the thirsty I will give water without cost from the spring of the water of life. Those who are victorious will inherit all this, and *I will be their God and they will be my children*" (21:5–7, italics mine).

Only God the Father is perfectly good, the one who cares for and comforts his people. He hears their prayers (5:8; 8:3–4) and answers their pleas for justice with judgment fire from the heavenly altar (8:5). In Rev 7, the great multitude—those who have come through the great tribulation—are comforted with the assurance of God's presence: "they are before the throne of God and serve him day and night in his temple; and he who sits on the throne will shelter them with his presence" (7:15). The verb "shelter" (σκηνόω) recalls God's comforting presence with Israel through the wilderness by means of his tabernacle, the pillar of cloud and fire, and God's Shekinah glory (cf. John 1:14; Exod 13:21–22; 33:7–11; 40:34–38). The promise of eternal comfort appears clearly in the image of God as a loving parent wiping away tears from the eyes of his children: "God's dwelling place is now among the people, and he will dwell with them.

46. Flemming, *Foretaste of the Future*, 53.

47. Interestingly, Jesus calls God "Father" especially in John's Gospel. There are 136 instances of God as πατήρ in John with 120 having God as a referent, compared with forty-five in Matthew, the only NT writer who even comes close. See Köstenberger, *Theology of John's Gospel and Letters*, 370–71.

They will be his people, and God himself will be with them and be their God. 'He will wipe every tear from their eyes. There will be no more death' or mourning or crying or pain, for the old order of things has passed away" (21:3–4; cf. 7:15).

Revelation also emphasizes God as provider. As a typical New Testament letter, the book opens and closes with the provision of grace and peace from the Lord (1:4; 22:21). In chapter 11, after the beast overpowers and kills the two witnesses, it is "the breath of life from God" that provides resurrection life (11:11). In the new heaven and new earth, God's eternal light replaces the light from any earthly source such as a lamp or the sun (22:5). God's primary provision is life. His people are promised life in God's paradise (2:7), illustrated using the image of the river or the spring of the water of life, water that flows from the throne of God and the Lamb (21:5–7; 22:1). God's most significant provision is life through the cross and resurrection of Jesus, as Flemming observes: "Above all, . . . God's love is embodied in the slaughtered Lamb."[48] It is the Lamb who "loves us and freed us from our sins" (1:5), the Lamb who rebukes and disciplines his people out of his love for them (3:19), and the Lamb who will make their enemies acknowledge that he has loved them (3:9).[49]

God's love is a holy love rather than sentimentality or indulgence or manipulation.[50] It cannot allow evil to defeat and destroy his people. As a result, God also manifests his love through his judgment of evil (see 12.6 below) and through his divine protection. God responds to the martyrs' cry for justice (6:10) by pouring out his wrath against evil (6:16–17 and the series of judgments that follow). After the third angel pours out his bowl on the rivers and springs, turning them into blood, the angel in charge of the waters says, "You are just in these judgments, O Holy One, you who are and who were; for they have shed the blood of your holy people and your prophets, and you have given them blood to drink as they deserve" (16:5–6). At the end of the millennium, Satan is released to deceive the nations—Gog and Magog—and gather them for war against the saints. We read that they "marched across the breadth of the earth and surrounded the camp of God's people, the city he loves. But fire came down from heaven and devoured them" (20:9). God's love is the ultimate source of his justice and wrath. McIlraith writes, "It is precisely the reciprocity of love that ensures the survival of this camp/city and offers it a future."[51]

48. Flemming, *Foretaste of the Future*, 53.

49. Both φιλέω (3:19) and ἀγαπάω (1:5; 3:9) are used for Jesus's love for his people. See Ch. 13 for more on the Lamb's sacrificial love for his people.

50. See Tony Lane, "The Wrath of God as an Aspect of the Love of God," in *Nothing Greater, Nothing Better: Theological Essays on the Love of God*, ed. Kevin J. Vanhoozer (Grand Rapids: Eerdmans, 2001), 138–67. Thomas and Macchia, *Revelation*, 431, write: "God's love is . . . not one that is morally neutral. It does not seek to avoid conflict so as to let evil have its way. It does not cower in fear of evil, nor is it subject to being seduced by evil. Divine love is an almighty and a holy love that does not compromise with evil but rather overcomes evil in merciful and righteous judgments."

51. Donal McIlraith, *The Reciprocal Love Between Christ and the Church in the Apocalypse* (Rome: Columban Fathers, 1989), 121.

We also observe God's protection in the sealing of the saints and guarding them with his name. The "seal of the living God" (7:2; 9:4) is his stamp of ownership and spiritual protection that safeguards God's people against demonic defeat and exempts them from the wrath of God.[52] The seal does not free the saints from physical persecution or trials in this world but protects them from being deceived by the forces of evil and suffering divine judgment. God's seal is linked to God's name, in contrast to those who bear the mark and name of the beast (13:17; 14:11; 15:2). To the victors Jesus guarantees a new name (2:17) and the promise that he will write on them "the name of my God and the name of the city of my God, . . . and I will also write on them my new name" (3:12), all indicating a secure, permanent place in God's presence in the new creation. Similarly, we are told that the 144,000 will stand with the Lamb on Mount Zion having "his name and his Father's name written on their foreheads" (14:1). In the end, God's people "will see his face, and his name will be on their foreheads" (22:4), a sure sign that his loving protection has shepherded them to their eschatological home.

We also hear of God's protection of his people historically through caring for the woman and her child. In Rev 12 the woman gives birth to a son who is quickly "snatched up to God and to his throne" (12:5), while the woman flees "into the wilderness to a place prepared for her by God, where she might be taken care of" (12:6; cf. 12:14). Like many, we take the son to represent Jesus and the woman to symbolize the covenant community that gives birth to the Messiah. God's people are said to be "taken care of" (τρέφω), a verb meaning to "feed, nourish or support."[53] Another sure sign of God's love in Revelation is his protection of his people in a manner in line with Jesus's prayer in John 17:15: "My prayer is not that you take them out of the world but that you protect them from the evil one."

12.6 THE GOD WHO JUDGES[54]

P. T. Forsyth and others refer to "God's holy love," indicating that God's love leads to his holy justice and wrath against evil.[55] As we will see, Revelation will not allow us to separate God's love and holiness into two completely independent categories. The two are perfectly united in God. As Lane puts it, "There is no love of God that is not holy and no holiness of God that is not loving. There is nowhere that God is love but not

52. Duvall, *Revelation*, 313. John may have in mind the Holy Spirit as the seal (cf. 2 Cor 1:22; Eph 1:13).

53. "τρέφω," BDAG 1014. God's pattern of protecting his covenant community can be seen during Israel's wilderness wanderings (Exod 16:4–35; Deut 1:31; Hos 2:14; Acts 7:36). See also Beale's excursus "The Desert as a Place of Both Trial and Protection" in *Revelation*, 645–46.

54. For more on God's judgment of evil, see Ch. 19. In this section we will focus on what God's judgment of evil tells us about him.

55. P. T. Forsyth, *The Work of Christ* (London: Hodder & Stoughton, 1910), 78–80.

light, and nowhere he is light but not love. . . . It is mistaken to divide the attributes."[56] God is both a warrior and a savior, as Karrer puts it.[57]

In fact, we contend that God's wrath, rather than being arbitrary or reactive, is God's sustained and determined opposition to all that is unholy. In the end, his wrath flows out of his love. The absence of wrath and opposition to Satan and sin would actually indicate a lack of love. Thomas and Macchia are on target when they conclude, "Divine love in Revelation is not weak sentiment but an all-powerful redemptive force that casts a dark shadow of judgment over those who continue to oppose its liberating work in the world."[58] They continue,

> God is holy *love*; divine holiness is pure love. In this sense, it is important to note that God hates evil or responds in wrath against it because God loves creation so much and knows what evil does to it. Evil separates creation from God and destroys the creation. God thus strikes out against those destroying the creation in order to bring an end to it (Rev 11:18). God's holy love is an all-consuming fire ultimately for the sake of creation and not against it.[59]

The God who is love promises to destroy evil, avenge his people, and renew his creation, doing so with enormous patience in hopes that the wicked will repent. The certainty of God's commitment to destroy evil appears throughout the book. From Jesus's warnings to those who fail to repent in the seven messages (e.g., 2:6, 16, 21–23), to the three sets of seven judgments (seals, trumpets, and bowls), to the judgment of Babylon the Great (18:1–8, 10, 17, 19–20, 21–24), to his judgment of the beast, kings of the earth and their armies (19:19–21), Satan (20:7–10; cf. 12:10), and wicked humanity (20:9, 11–15), the certainty of God's wrath stands strong and clear.[60]

The two key terms used for God's wrath (**ὀργή** [**wrath**] and θυμός [wrath, fury]) also affirm the certainty of God's commitment to judge evil. With the opening of the sixth seal the inhabitants of the earth cry out in fear in light of the coming wrath of God and the Lamb: "for the great day of their **wrath** has come, and who can withstand it?" (6:16–17). At the seventh trumpet God's **wrath** has come (11:18). The seven bowls are "filled with the wrath of God" (15:7; cf. 16:1), and with these seven last plagues "God's wrath is completed" (15:1). The judgment of Babylon is also portrayed as a pouring out of God's wrath: "God remembered Babylon the Great and gave her the cup filled with the wine of the fury of his **wrath**" (16:19; cf. 18:5). When the third angel announces

56. Lane, "Wrath of God as an Aspect of the Love of God," 162–63. On p. 167 Lane writes, "The love of God and the wrath of God are not ultimately in contradiction, but there is a tension between them."

57. Karrer, "God in the Book of Revelation," 215.

58. Thomas and Macchia, *Revelation*, 411.

59. Thomas and Macchia, *Revelation*, 432.

60. We comment on the "divine passives" used throughout in Ch. 19.

judgment on those who worship the beast, we are told they will "drink the wine of God's fury, which has been poured full strength into the cup of his **wrath**" (14:10). In chapters 14 and 19 the image of a winepress is used to convey the awful certainty of God's coming judgment: "He [Christ] treads the winepress of the fury of the **wrath** of God Almighty" (cf. 14:19).[61] God's certain judgment also surfaces in the word group for "judge" and "judgment."[62] The time or hour of God's judgment will certainly arrive in the future (11:18; 14:7). Babylon will meet her doom (18:10). Her condemnation is sure (17:1; 19:2). The mighty Lord God is her Judge (18:8).

God's wrathful response to evil flows out of his righteous character. The universal Judge is perfectly just. In chapter 15, prior to the pouring out of the bowl judgments, those who had been victorious over the beast and its image and number sing the song of Moses and the Lamb, crying out in praise: "Great and marvelous are your deeds, Lord God Almighty. *Just and true* are your ways, King of the nations. Who will not fear you, Lord, and bring glory to your name? For you alone are holy. All nations will come and worship before you, for your *righteous* acts have been revealed" (15:3–4). The bowl judgments that follow are not haphazard or biased, but instead are born out of God's righteous character. Between the third and fourth bowl judgments we find a hymn of praise for God's justice, complete with a heavenly response: "'You are *just* in these judgments, O Holy One, you who are and who were; for they have shed the blood of your holy people and your prophets, and you have given them blood to drink as they deserve.' And I heard the altar respond: 'Yes, Lord God Almighty, *true and just* are your judgments'" (16:5–7). As chapter 19 opens, the great multitude roars shouts of praise to God "for his *true and just*" judgments, for condemning (ἔκρινεν) the great prostitute who has corrupted the earth (19:1–2). Later in the chapter Jesus, the rider on the white horse, is called "Faithful and True" as he judges and wages war "*with justice*" (19:11). God's righteous judgment is according to deeds as recorded in the heavenly books (20:12–13) and stands in contrast to the injustice experienced by God's people throughout.

Closely related to God's righteousness or justice is his holiness, which also forms the basis of his judgments. The term "holy" (ἅγιος) occurs twenty-five times and is applied to God (4:8; 6:10), to Jesus (3:7), to the holy angels (14:10), to the Holy City (11:2; 21:2, 10; 22:19), and to God's holy people (or the saints) (5:8; 8:3, 4; 11:18; 13:7,

61. Most take τοῦ θυμοῦ as a genitive of apposition and τῆς ὀργῆς as attributive or adjectival genitive. Even more important is the perceptive insight by Mathewson, *Revelation*, 267, regarding the string of five genitives, the longest in the book: "This piling up of genitives functions to lend prominence to the display of God's wrath. This is more important than the individual labels given to each individual genitive."

62. The following terms related to judgment appear throughout Revelation: κρίνω (6:10; 11:18; 16:5; 18:8, 20; 19:2, 11; 20:12, 13), κρίσις (14:7; 16:7; 18:10; 19:2), and κρίμα (17:1; 18:20; 20:4). In this section we will highlight selected passages.

10; 14:12; 16:6; 17:6; 18:20, 24; 19:8; 20:6, 9; 22:11). In the two uses applied to God, we again see God's judgment flowing from his holiness.

It is the "Sovereign Lord, holy and true" who will in time judge the inhabitants of the earth (6:10), the Almighty God who is "holy, holy, holy." While traditionally holiness has been understood as the equivalent to moral purity and/or transcendence, Gentry shows that in the Old Testament the fundamental meaning of "holiness" is rooted in being consecrated or devoted and, when applied to God, it describes his complete devotion and consecration to his character and purposes. God is totally committed to his plan related to his people and his creation and therefore will certainly judge all that seek to derail those purposes.[63] The "saints" or "holy ones" are those people who are rightly related to God and firmly devoted to his presence and purposes. John also uses the term "holy" (ὅσιος) to emphasize God's holiness that grounds his judgment: "You are just, the Holy One, who is and who was, because you have passed judgment on these things" (16:5, CSB). All nations should fear and glorify the Lord because he alone is holy (15:4). Thomas and Macchia conclude, "God's holiness in Revelation undergirds the righteousness of divine judgments in response to cries for justice. The God who reigns is not seduced by evil or manipulated by it; rather, God overcomes evil through redemptive self-giving and righteous acts of judgment."[64]

God judges also for the purpose of avenging his people.[65] The martyrs in chapter 6 ask God "How long?" not only with regard to his judgment but also with respect to his avenging their blood (6:10). In 19:2 we read that God has "avenged on her [the great prostitute] the blood of his servants." The term "avenge" (ἐκδικέω) used in both passages refers to inflicting an "appropriate penalty for wrong done . . . to punish or take vengeance for," thus placing the emphasis on the just punishment for the wrongdoer.[66] We see a similar message elsewhere apart from specific terms. In 16:6 at the pouring out of the third bowl judgment, God is acclaimed for giving those who shed the blood of his holy people and prophets "blood to drink as they deserve." In a similar vein, God has remembered (μιμνῄσκομαι, μνημονεύω) Babylon's crimes (16:19; 18:5) and judged her accordingly (cf. Ps 109:14; Jer 14:10; Hos 8:13; 9:9). In 18:20 the heavens and the saints are called to rejoice at Babylon's judgment, "for God has judged her with the judgment she imposed on you." The martyrs' cry is finally answered. Their cries for justice are not forgotten or filed away. They are heard as God responds with his holy, righteous judgment. As Osborne puts it, "God does not punish out of vindictive bitterness but out of the need to vindicate his people."[67]

63. Peter J. Gentry, "The Meaning of 'Holy' in the Old Testament," *BSac* 170 (2013): 400–417.

64. Thomas and Macchia, *Revelation*, 431.

65. See Smalley's helpful excursus on "Vengeance in the Apocalypse," in *Revelation*, 160–64. See also Grant R. Osborne, "Theodicy in the Apocalypse," *TrinJ* 14 (1993): 63–77.

66. "ἐκδικέω," BDAG 300–301.

67. Osborne, "Theodicy in the Apocalypse," 76. Osborne, *Revelation*, 601, notes that the principle of *lex talionis* of divine judgment reaches its high point in the book in 16:5–7. See Ch. 19 on divine judgment.

Yet while God as Judge is unmistakable from reading Revelation, we also need to pay attention to his patience in judgment. The martyrs seem frustrated that God will not judge and vindicate their cause *now*, and that they must "wait [or rest] a little longer" (6:11). Thus, they cry, "How long, Sovereign Lord, . . . until . . ." (6:10). The full number of martyrs implies an extension of the mission of God in hopes that more will repent. Peter's words come to mind here: "The Lord is not slow in keeping his promise, as some understand slowness. Instead, he is patient with you, not wanting anyone to perish, but everyone to come to repentance" (2 Pet 3:9). And God's patience is further illustrated by the recurring emphasis on the rebellious repeatedly refusing to repent (Rev 9:20–21; 16:9–11). In addition, we see God's patience in the slow ramping up of judgment in the three series of seven judgments and the call to repentance in the proclamation of the eternal gospel to those who live on earth (14:6–7). As Flemming observes, "Judgment in Revelation, then, represents not the revenge of an angry God against sinners but the passionate pursuit of a just God who seeks repentance, worship, and wholeness for people from every nation."[68]

12.7 The God Who Is Coming

The opening greeting of grace and peace comes from "him who is, and who was, and who is to come" and from the seven spirits and from Jesus Christ (1:4). As is commonly observed, in this phrase describing God, where one would expect the future (was, is, *will be*), instead we find the present participle: "is coming" (ὁ ὢν καὶ ὁ ἦν καὶ ὁ ἐρχόμενος). This designation of God occurs five times (translations mine):

1:4	the One who is, and who was, and who is coming
1:8	the One who is, and who was, and who is coming
4:8	the One who was, and is, and is coming
11:17	the One who is and who was
16:5	the One who is and who was

John's move from the expected "will be" to "is coming" stresses that God is more than the One who lives forever; he is the One who is coming to rescue his people and transform creation.[69]

This expression is found nowhere elsewhere in the Old Testament or early Jewish or Christian literature prior to the third century AD.[70] As a result, most scholars conclude that it is John's interpretation of the divine name mentioned in Exod 3:14 LXX (Ἐγώ

68. Flemming, *Foretaste of the Future*, 135–36.
69. McDonough, *YHWH at Patmos*, 216.
70. Aune, *Apocalypticism, Prophecy, and Magic*, 263; McDonough, *YHWH at Patmos*, 214.

εἰμι ὁ ὤν).[71] As Revelation is something of a "New Exodus," McDonough notes, "it would be most fitting to introduce such a work with a reference to YHWH, the personal name of God of the Exodus."[72]

John is making the point that God is coming into this world to judge and to save. Again, this is more than a statement about God's future existence; it serves as an announcement of his mission—"his coming to the world to consummate his kingdom."[73] Karrer notes that the grammatical present also highlights another aspect of God and his plans: "It presupposes that 'the one who is coming' has departed. He is already on the way. In Revelation God is now coming to John and the Asian churches (1:4) and to the entire world (1:8; 4:8)."[74]

In the list of five passages above, we immediately notice that 11:17 and 16:5 are missing the final portion ("is coming"). This is because in these contexts God's eschatological coming has arrived. God's coming becomes a present reality when the seventh angel sounds his trumpet: "The kingdom of the world has become the kingdom of our Lord and of his Messiah, and he will reign for ever and ever" (11:15). The "Lord God Almighty, the One who is and who was," has now taken his great power and begun to reign (11:17). Likewise, in the pouring out of the seven bowls of God's wrath, "the final act of God has been inaugurated, and the future is here" (cf. 16:5).[75]

It should be noted here that Jesus says seven times that he is coming, twice in a local sense (2:5, 16) and five in an eschatological sense (3:11; 16:15; 22:7, 12, 20).[76] Revelation sends the message that God's coming is Christ's coming![77] God's coming to judge and to save is manifested in the second coming of Christ to consummate the kingdom.[78] He will in the end eliminate all evil powers and collapse heaven and earth in the great transformation. His sovereign rule will extend Eden to the entire creation so that the whole city is now a garden and a temple.[79]

Part of God's coming is that he is coming to dwell among his people.[80] The promises to the victors in chapters 2–3 are not only eschatological promises but also relational ones (e.g., 3:12: "I will write on them the name of my God and the name of the city of

71. See, e.g., Aune, *Apocalypticism, Prophecy, and Magic*, 263; Bauckham, *Theology*, 28; McDonough, *YHWH at Patmos*, 199–202; Beale, *Revelation*, 187–89. For a discussion of this famous solecism, see Beale, *John's Use of the Old Testament in Revelation*, 327–29, who affirms John's intentionality. Smith, *Trinity in the Book of Revelation*, 51–52, concludes, "John's 'poor' grammar is in fact a vehicle for his theology. Put simply: John appears to choose the title and grammatical construction intentionally; he knows the rules, and he knows how to break them." And he appears to do so since it better suits his eschatology. See Smalley, *Revelation*, 32.

72. McDonough, *YHWH at Patmos*, 200.

73. McDonough, *YHWH at Patmos*, 214.

74. Karrer, "God in the Book of Revelation," 212. He elaborates (p. 212): "This understanding of God touches the apocalyptic horizon of Revelation. The new heaven and new earth are nearby in space and time (21:1–22:5). The coming break in time is so close that we can almost speak of a present eschatology in Revelation."

75. Osborne, *Revelation*, 582.

76. Paul, "The Trinitarian Dynamic," 88–89.

77. McDonough, *YHWH at Patmos*, 216–17.

78. God's coming in Christ will be explored in more detail in Ch. 13.

79. See Mark B. Stephens, "Creation and New Creation in the Book of Revelation," *OHBR* 266–70.

80. See Duvall and Hays, *God's Relational Presence*, 318–22, as well as Ch. 20 below on the new creation.

my God, . . . and I will also write on them my new name"). God's people form God's city, the Holy City, the new Jerusalem, the bride of Christ (21:2). The Holy City shines with God's glorious presence (21:10–11, 23). Although John does not see a temple in the heavenly city (21:22), the full and unmediated presence of God and the Lamb eliminate the need for a physical temple as Ezekiel had envisioned (Ezek 40–48).[81] The city's cube shape signifies that the entire city is the holy of holies in God's celestial temple. The people of God live eternally in the holy of holies. They are permanent fixtures in the new creation temple (Rev 3:12).

The relational aspect of God coming to his people appears in several significant ways. In 21:3 we see the fulfillment of God's longstanding tripartite covenant promise to live among his people eternally: "God's dwelling place is now among the people, and he will dwell with them. They will be his people, and God himself will be with them and be their God" (21:3; cf. Lev 26:11–12; Ezek 37:26–28; Zech 2:10–11). In Revelation, however, the typical order is reversed to emphasize that the fulfillment of God's promised coming has arrived at last. God lives among his people as a loving Father lives with his children: "Those who are victorious will inherit all this, and I will be their God and they will be my children" (21:7). God's people will bear his name and see his face (22:3–4).[82] As a loving Father, God will "wipe away every tear from their eyes" as he simultaneously eliminates all that would cause his people to cry in the first place (7:17; 21:4).

12.8 CONCLUSION

Our consideration of Revelation's glorious and awe-inspiring portrait of God shows that theology in the Apocalypse touches virtually every other aspect of the book. And this depiction of God profoundly forms the faith and practice and destiny of God's people. To begin with, God does not leave his people confused or uninformed about his plans. He is the God who speaks. His revelation discloses and reminds his people that he will defeat evil, rescue the saints, and renew creation. His word is trustworthy and true. God means what he says.

The grounding vision of the entire book—God on his throne in chapter four—reveals God as the Sovereign Creator and sustainer of the world. He is the "I am" of the exodus, the God who has delivered, and he will continue to deliver. He is the Almighty, the One over and above any earthly ruler. God's throne is the epicenter of the universe, and he is the sovereign ruler of all. God's throne is shared with Jesus Christ who is King of kings and Lord of lords (19:16). As such, God and the Lamb deserve undivided worship and wholehearted praise. God as worthy of worship counters the temptation for readers to bow to Caesar, angels, or any other unworthy object.

81. DeSilva, *Seeing Things John's Way*, 171.

82. Duvall and Hays, *God's Relational Presence*, 322.

In subtle but strong ways, Revelation highlights God as the God who loves. The perfectly good Father cares for, comforts, provides for, and protects his people. And his love is a holy love that generates his wrathful response to evil. God's judgment will fully and finally rid creation of every ounce of evil, vindicating his people and leading the way for God to live among his people in the new creation. God's original purposes previewed in the garden of Eden are ultimately realized in the new heaven and new earth, the heavenly garden, the Holy City. And it all goes back to God himself.

Chapter 13

"THE LION AND THE LAMB": JESUS CHRIST

BIBLIOGRAPHY

Allen, Garrick V. "The Son of God in the Book of Revelation and Apocalyptic Literature." Pages 53–71 in *Son of God: Divine Sonship in Jewish and Christian Antiquity*. Edited by Allen, Garrick V., et al. Winona Lake, IN: Eisenbrauns; University Park, PA: Pennsylvania State University, 2019. **Aune, David E.** "Following the Lamb: Discipleship in the Apocalypse." Pages 66–78 in *Apocalypticism, Prophecy and Magic in Early Christianity*. Grand Rapids: Baker Academic, 2006. **Barr, David L.** "The Lamb Who Looks Like a Dragon? Characterizing Jesus in John's Apocalypse." Pages 205–20 in *The Reality of the Apocalypse: Rhetoric and Politics in the Book of Revelation*. Edited by David L. Barr. SBLSymS 39. Atlanta: Society of Biblical Literature, 2006. **Blount, Brian K.** *Revelation: A Commentary*, NTL. Louisville: Westminster John Knox, 2009. **Boring, M. Eugene.** "Narrative Christology in the Apocalypse." *CBQ* 54 (1992): 702–23. **Brighton, Louis A.** "Christological Trinitarian Theology in the Book of Revelation." *ConJ* 34 (2008): 292–97. **Carnegie, David R.** "Worthy is the Lamb: The Hymns in Revelation." Pages 243–56 in *Christ the Lord: Studies in Christology Presented to Donald Guthrie*. Edited by Harold H. Rowdon. Downers Grove, IL: InterVarsity Press, 1982. **Dixon, Sarah S. U.** *The Testimony of the Exalted Jesus in the Book of Revelation*. LNTS 570. London: Bloomsbury T&T Clark, 2017. **Forsyth, P. T.** *The Work of Christ*. London: Hodder & Stoughton, 1910. **Gallusz, Laszlo.** *The Throne Motif in the Book of Revelation*. LNTS 487. London: Bloomsbury T&T Clark, 2014. **Goldsworthy, Graeme.** *The Son of God and the New Creation*. Wheaton, IL: Crossway, 2015. **Guthrie, Donald.** "The Christology of Revelation." Pages 297–409 in *Jesus of Nazareth: Lord and Christ: Essays on the Historical Jesus and New Testament Christology*. Edited by Joel B. Green and Max Turner. Grand Rapids: Eerdmans, 1994. ———. "The Lamb in the Structure of the Book of Revelation." *VE* 12 (1987): 64–71. **Hays, Richard B.** "Faithful Witness, Alpha and Omega: The Identity of Jesus in the Apocalypse of John." Pages 69–83 in *Revelation and the Politics of Apocalyptic Interpretation*. Edited by Richard B. Hays and Stefan Alkier. Waco, TX: Baylor University Press, 2012. **Hieke, Thomas.** "The Reception of Daniel 7 in the Revelation of John." Pages

47–67 in *Revelation and the Politics of Apocalyptic Interpretation*. Edited by Richard B. Hays and Stefan Alkier. Waco, TX: Baylor University Press, 2012. **Holtz, Traugott.** *Die Christologie der Apokalypse des Johannes*. 2nd. ed. Berlin: Akademie-Verlag, 1971. **Huber, K.** "Jesus Christus—der Erste und der Letzte: Zur Christologie der Johannesapokalypse." Pages 435–72 in *Die Johannesapokalypse: Kontexte–Konzepte–Rezeption*. Edited by J. Frey, J. Kelhoffer, and F. Toth. WUNT 287. Tübingen: Mohr Siebeck, 2012. **Johns, Loren L.** "Jesus in the Book of Revelation." *OBHR* 223–39. ———. *The Lamb Christology of the Apocalypse of John: An Investigation into Its Origins and Rhetorical Force*. WUNT 2.167. Tübingen: Mohr Siebeck, 2003. Repr., Eugene, OR: Wipf & Stock, 2015. **Laws, Sophie.** *In the Light of the Lamb: Imagery, Parody, and Theology in the Apocalypse of John*. Wilmington, DE: Glazier, 1988. **McDonough, Sean.** *YHWH at Patmos: Rev. 1:4 in Its Hellenistic and Early Jewish Setting*. WUNT 2.107. Tübingen: Mohr Siebeck, 1999. Reprint, Eugene, OR: Wipf & Stock, 2011. **McGrath, James F.** *The Only True God: Early Christian Monotheism in Its Jewish Context*. Urbana, IL: University of Illinois Press, 2009. **McIlraith, Donal A.** *The Reciprocal Love Between Christ and the Church in the Apocalypse*. Rome: Columban Fathers, 1989. **McKnight, Scot, with Cody Matchett.** *Revelation for the Rest of Us: A Prophetic Call to Follow Jesus as a Dissident Disciple*. Grand Rapids: Zondervan Reflective, 2023. **Middleton, Paul.** *The Violence of the Lamb: Martyrs as Agents of Divine Judgement in the Book of Revelation*. LNTS 586. New York: Bloomsbury T&T Clark, 2018. **Moyise, Steve.** "Does the Lion Lie Down with the Lamb?" Pages 181–94 in *Studies in the Book of Revelation*. Edited by Steve Moyise. Edinburgh: T&T Clark, 2001. **Neville, David J.** *A Peaceable Hope: Contesting Violent Eschatology in New Testament Narratives*. Grand Rapids: Baker Academic, 2013. **Paul, Ian.** "The Trinitarian Dynamic in the Book of Revelation." Pages 85–108 in *Trinity Without Hierarchy: Reclaiming Nicene Orthodoxy in Evangelical Theology*. Edited by Michael F. Bird and Scott Harrower. Grand Rapids: Kregel, 2019. **Skaggs, Rebecca, and Thomas Doyle.** "Lion/Lamb in Revelation." *CurBR* 7 (2009): 363–75. **Smith, Brandon D.** "The Identification of Jesus with YHWH in the Book of Revelation: A Brief Sketch." *CTR* 14.1 (2016): 67–84. ———. *The Trinity in the Book of Revelation: Seeing Father, Son, and Holy Spirit in John's Apocalypse*. SCDS. Downers Grove, IL: IVP Academic, 2022. **Stevenson, Gregory.** *A Slaughtered Lamb: Revelation and the Apocalyptic Response to Evil and Suffering*. Abilene, TX: Abilene Christian University, 2013. **Stuckenbruck, Loren T.** *Angel Veneration and Christology: A Study in Early Judaism and in the Christology of the Apocalypse of John*. WUNT 2.70. Tübingen: Mohr Siebeck, 1995. **Talbot, Charles H.** *The Development of Christology During the First Hundred Years: And Other Essays on Early Christian Christology*. Leiden: Brill, 2011.

1. Loren L. Johns, "Jesus in the Book of Revelation," *OHBR* 228.

13.1 INTRODUCTION

More than a book about antichrist, Armageddon, or other end-time details, Revelation is a book about Jesus. The "revelation [of/]from Jesus Christ" (1:1: ἀποκάλυψις Ἰησοῦ Χριστοῦ) is "the central unveiling in the book."[1] And the Apocalypse does not disappoint. Hays notes that "this visionary book deploys a kaleidoscopic profusion of imagery to depict its chief protagonist."[2] Revelation offers a multifaceted portrayal of Jesus, but one that is unified in its complexity. There are three extended visions of Jesus—the Ancient of Days and Son of Man (1:12–20), the Lion-Lamb (5:1–12), and the conquering Christ (19:11–16). But there is much more to Jesus in Revelation than we find in these three visions, as the following discussion will demonstrate.

We begin with Jesus's identity. Revelation's Christology is sky high as it clearly establishes Jesus's divine identity and oneness with God. Using key Old Testament connections, divine titles, repeated allusions to his deity, visions of the heavenly throne, worship scenes, Jesus's divine roles, his place in the new creation, and much more, Revelation leaves no doubt that Jesus Christ is one with God. From his identity we turn to his role in redemption. Jesus is the faithful witness who lives and speaks the truth even at the cost of his life. He models a life of persevering faithfulness, which he also calls his followers to live. Although God's plan cost Jesus his life, Jesus is the firstborn from among the dead. He is sovereign as the crucified and resurrected Lord! Next, we turn to Jesus as the Lion-Lamb, and we find in "Lamb" Revelation's most prominent Christological title. The slain but resurrected Lamb conquers like the Lion he is but does so through his sacrifice and word. He is Conqueror and Judge, who will defeat evil and rescue his people. He is indeed King of kings and Lord of lords. A major theme that runs through the entire book is Jesus's relationship with his people—his personal presence with them, his atoning death on their behalf, his call to discipleship, and his future presence with them in the new creation. The entire incarnation project comes full circle in Revelation—he with them and finally they with him.

13.2 ONE WITH GOD

Jesus's divine identity and oneness with God could be a chapter all its own. Bauckham describes Revelation's "extraordinarily high Christology" as "What Christ does, God does."[3] Hays notes that "from Jesus's first appearance on the stage of the drama of Revelation, he is *intertextually* marked as bearing the visible signs of divine identity" (emphasis original).[4]

2. Richard B. Hays, "Faithful Witness, Alpha and Omega: The Identity of Jesus in the Apocalypse of John," in *Revelation and the Politics of Apocalyptic Interpretation*, ed. Richard B. Hays and Stefan Alkier (Waco, TX: Baylor University Press, 2012), 69.

3. Bauckham, *Theology*, 63.

4. Hays, "Faithful Witness, Alpha and Omega," 72.

This richly layered topic showcases Revelation's high Christology and appears in almost every major section of the book, as the following overview will illustrate. The opening greeting in 1:4–5 finds "grace and peace" coming from God ("him who is, and who was, and who is to come"), the Spirit ("the seven spirits before his throne"), and from "Jesus Christ, who is the faithful witness, the firstborn from the dead, and the ruler of the kings of the earth." As Smith notes, the divine persons are "joined together grammatically (using ἀπὸ and καὶ ἀπὸ) and theologically," a construction Bauckham labels "deliberately trinitarian."[5] What is more, the doxology of 1:5b–6 is the first early Christian doxology where Christ receives glory rather than God, although the worship of God seems implied.[6]

In the opening confession of 1:7 and John's vision of Christ in 1:9–20 we find numerous affirmations of the Son's oneness with God. In 1:7a John alludes to the Apocalypse's most quoted chapter in the Old Testament—Dan 7, where "one like a son of man" approaches the "Ancient of Days" and is given "authority, glory and sovereign power," is worshiped by all nations, and receives an everlasting kingdom that will never be destroyed (Dan 7:13–14; cf. Mark 14:62).[7] As Smith notes with reference to Dan 7:13–14, "YHWH is not simply giving some underling a piece of his kingdom—he is giving this divine Son, Jesus, the keys to the whole thing."[8] Perhaps most surprisingly is that Jesus, the Son of Man, is the one who comes with the clouds, whereas riding the clouds in the Old Testament is a divine privilege (e.g., Pss 68:4; 104:3–4; Isa 19:1; Jer 4:13).[9] In Rev 1:7b John recalls Zech 12:10 where God is the one pierced as Israel wounds him with their disobedience. Now John points to Jesus as the one pierced. Fanning observes that John 19:37 applies the Zech 12 passage specifically to the spear wound suffered by Jesus during his crucifixion.[10] As Middleton concludes, "Clearly, John is here using the 'Son of Man' beyond its Jewish Messianic function."[11]

In Rev 1:10 John hears a voice behind him like a trumpet and then turns to see "someone like a son of man" among the seven golden lampstands (1:13). The images of 1:13–16 featuring his royal clothing, presence among the lampstands, blazing eyes and feet, sword out of his mouth, glorious countenance, and white hair recall Dan 7:9–14

5. Brandon D. Smith, "The Identification of Jesus with YHWH in the Book of Revelation: A Brief Sketch," *CTR* 14.1 (2016): 72; Bauckham, *Theology*, 24.

6. Paul Middleton, *The Violence of the Lamb: Martyrs as Agents of Divine Judgement in the Book of Revelation*, LNTS 586 (New York: Bloomsbury T&T Clark, 2018), 112 and esp. fn. 38.

7. See Hieke, "Reception of Daniel 7," 47, 55–59. See the helpful chart on p. 51 showing the uses of Daniel in Revelation. In the NT the "son of man" figure plays several roles, even when the specific title is not present: (1) a heavenly figure (Dan 7:13; Matt 25:31; Mark 14:62; Rev 1:13; 14:14), (2) a ruler given eternal dominion and authority (Dan 7:14; Matt 16:27; Rev 1:5; 3:21; 17:14), (3) a judge who executes final judgment (Matt 13:41–43; 19:28; 25:31–46; Rev 1:18; 14:14; 19:11), and (4) a warrior victorious over evil (John 14:30; 16:8–11; Rev 2:16; 3:21; 17:17; 19:11). All four uses appear in Revelation. See Hays, Duvall, and Pate, *An A-to-Z Guide to Biblical Prophecy*, 432–33.

8. Smith, "Identification of Jesus with YHWH," 75.

9. Fanning, *Revelation*, 84–85.

10. Fanning, *Revelation*, 86.

11. Middleton, *Violence of the Lamb*, 117; cf. 1 En. 46:1–6; 48:2; 69:27–29; 70:1; 74:14, 17.

and 10:5–6 and highlight attributes of the Ancient of Days (cf. Exod 34). John puts the Son of Man figure in close relationship to the Ancient of Days as qualities of God are attributed to Jesus.[12]

We also see Jesus's oneness with God in the pattern of certain titles applied to both God and Christ, beginning in Rev 1:8 and extending to the end of the book:

1:8	God:	I am the Alpha and the Omega
1:17	Jesus:	I am the First and the Last
21:6	God:	I am the Alpha and the Omega, the Beginning and the End
22:13	Jesus:	I am the Alpha and the Omega, the First and the Last, the Beginning and the End

Bauckham notes "the remarkable extent to which Revelation identifies Jesus Christ with God."[13] The placement of "the First and the Last" between the other two titles when applied to Christ in 22:13 reinforces this conclusion. Just as God is the Creator of all things and the eschatological fulfillment of all things, so is Christ, as the use of the title "the First and the Last" for God's self-declarations in Isa 44:6; 48:12 (cf. 41:4) indicates.[14] With regard to the interweaving of titles, Hays concludes, "The only possible implication, within the symbolic world of Revelation, is that Jesus and God are one. . . . Otherwise, the claims made here by and for Jesus are simply blasphemous profanations of the name of God."[15]

We also find other allusions to Jesus's divine identity and oneness with God within the seven messages of chapters 2–3.[16] The only place in Revelation where the title "Son of God" occurs is in the message to Thyatira, which emphasizes Jesus's penetrating knowledge of the church. Throughout the seven messages Jesus is depicted as the one who "knows" his people completely (2:2, 9, 13, 19; 3:1, 8, 15), and here he is additionally identified as the one "who searches hearts and minds" and repays according to deeds (2:23). Jesus's power to know hearts and reward or punish deeds is a power that "Israel's Scripture ascribed to God *alone*."[17] In 3:1 Jesus "holds the seven spirits of God and the seven stars," implying a close relationship with the Holy Spirit (see 14.2 The "Seven Spirits"). In 3:7 Jesus is "holy and true," the one "who holds the key of David," identifying Jesus as "equivalent with the eternal sovereignty of God over the Kingdom of all kingdoms."[18] Finally, in 3:14 Jesus's oneness with God is highlighted by the expression "the Amen, the faithful and true witness, the ruler of God's creation."

12. Hieke, "Reception of Daniel 7," 66.
13. Bauckham, *Theology*, 55.
14. Bauckham, *Theology*, 55, 58; Tabb, *All Things New*, 62.
15. Hays, "Faithful Witness, Alpha and Omega," 75.
16. See the helpful survey in Smith, "Identification of Jesus with YHWH," 78–81.
17. Hays, "Faithful Witness, Alpha and Omega," 71.
18. Smith, "Identification of Jesus with YHWH," 79.

According to Beale, Jesus as the risen Lord is "the inaugurator of the new creation" (cf. 1:5; Col 1:15–20; Isa 65:17).[19]

We also see the Lamb's divine identity and oneness with God in the vision of the heavenly throne in Rev 4–5. To begin with, the Lamb is located at the center of God's throne, thereby sharing God's throne (5:6; 7:17). In addition, the throne itself is sometimes designated "the throne of God and of the Lamb" (22:1, 3). In 22:3 when it says, "his servants will worship him" (ESV), we find a singular antecedent (αὐτῷ) where we would expect the plural. Hays concludes, "The seemingly ungrammatical singular αὐτῷ makes a deeper point of theological/christological grammar: God and the Lamb are one."[20] In fact, as Tabb notes, 22:3–4 refers to the joint occupants of the throne four times using the singular pronoun: "The throne of God and of the Lamb will be in the city, and *his* servants will serve *him*. They will see *his* face, and *his* name will be on their foreheads," with the singular referring not only to God or the Lamb but recognizing "their profound unity."[21] At other times God and the Lamb are mentioned in parallel statements, both receiving worship (5:13; 7:9–10; cf. 12:10), both being feared in judgment (6:16–17), and both sharing in the arrival of the everlasting kingdom (11:15; cf. Ps 2:2; Dan 2:44; 4:34; 6:26; 7:14, 27; Zech 14:9).

Revelation stresses the Lamb's inclusion in worship addressed to God.[22] In Rev 4:9–11 the living creatures and the elders praise God as the Creator and sustainer of all things. Then in the next chapter the same group (living creatures and elders) uses similar language (worthy, glory, honor, power) in worship of the Lamb (5:8–12). This is followed in 5:13 by all of creation praising both God and the Lamb using similar terms: praise, honor, glory, and power. Jesus is one with God the Father![23] This is even more meaningful in light of the "refusal tradition," where an angel rejects human worship intended for God alone (Rev 19:9–10; 22:8–9; cf. Tob 12:16–22; Apoc. Zeph. 6:11–15; Ascen. Isa. 7:18–23; 8:1–10, 15; 2 En. 1:4–8; 3 En. 1:7; 16:1–5).[24] Against the backdrop of Jewish monotheism, where God alone is to be worshiped, it becomes clear that Jesus belongs on the God side of the ledger rather than the creature side. As Bauckham puts it, "If it is in worship that monotheism is tested in religious practice, the devotional attitude to Jesus in worship is the critical test of Christology," and in that setting Jesus "is not classed with the servants who may not be worshipped but with God to whom

19. See Beale, *Revelation*, 301, and his excursus on pp. 297–301: "The Old Testament Background of Christ's Titles in 3:14."

20. Hays, "Faithful Witness, Alpha and Omega," 76.

21. Tabb, *All Things New*, 197 (emphasis added); also Beale, *Revelation*, 1113.

22. Bauckham, *Climax of Prophecy*, 118–49.

23. Hays, "Faithful Witness, Alpha and Omega," 76. Contra James F. McGrath, *The Only True God: Early Christian Monotheism in Its Jewish Context* (Urbana, IL: University of Illinois Press, 2009).

24. Hays, "Faithful Witness, Alpha and Omega," 76. The phrase "refusal tradition" seems to originate with Loren T. Stuckenbruck, *Angel Veneration and Christology: A Study in Early Judaism and in the Christology of the Apocalypse of John*, WUNT 2.70 (Tübingen: Mohr Siebeck, 1995). See also Bauckham, *Climax of Prophecy*, 120–32.

worship is due."[25] Worship in Revelation reveals that we should understand Jesus as one with the eternal God, an "extraordinarily high Christology."[26]

Jesus's oneness with God also appears in the motif of Jesus as the divine Judge. In Rev 14:14 John says, "I looked, and there before me was a white cloud, and seated on the cloud was one like a son of man with a crown of gold on his head and a sharp sickle in his hand." The "son of man" image is drawn from Dan 7:13 and refers to the risen Christ (cf. Rev 1:7, 13).[27] Jesus is "seated on the cloud" (14:14, 15, 16), demonstrating his power and glory as Redeemer and Judge (cf. Matt 25:31; Mark 13:27; 14:62).[28] This comports well with Rev 14:1 where we see the Lamb standing on Mount Zion with the 144,000 who had his name and his Father's name written on their foreheads, as well as the reference in 14:4 to those who had been purchased being offered as "firstfruits to God and the Lamb." Jesus's role as judge of the world affirms his divine identity and oneness with God (cf. 2:5, 16, 22–28; 3:2–5, 16, 21; 19:11–16). It is after all "the Lamb's book of life" (3:5; 13:8; 17:8; 20:12, 15; 21:27).

To conclude this section on Jesus's oneness with God, we recall John's observation that he did not see a temple in the heavenly city "because the Lord God Almighty and the Lamb are its temple. The city does not need the sun or the moon to shine on it, for the glory of God gives it light, and the Lamb is its lamp" (21:22–23). The Son takes his place alongside the Father (and the Spirit) as the divine Presence that illuminates the eternal temple city.

13.3 FAITHFUL WITNESS

Jesus is designated "the faithful witness" twice in Revelation (cf. Ps 89:37). In Rev 1:5b–6 the phrase occurs in the first of three titles correlating to Jesus's death, resurrection, and glorification: "the faithful witness (ὁ μάρτυς, ὁ πιστός), the firstborn from the dead, and the ruler of the kings of the earth." The term "witness" likely had not yet taken on its more technical meaning of one who dies for the faith (i.e., a martyr) but here points to the verbal witness of Jesus and his faithfulness to bear that witness even unto death.[29] We also see the term "witness" (μάρτυς) used in the message to Pergamum with reference to "Antipas, my faithful witness, who was put to death in

25. Bauckham, *Climax of Prophecy*, 148, 137, respectively. He observes that John "never makes them [God and Christ] the subjects of a plural verb or uses a plural pronoun to refer to them both. The reason is surely clear: he places Christ on the divine side of the distinction between God and creation, but he wishes to avoid ways of speaking which sound to him polytheistic" (pp. 139–40).

26. Bauckham, *Theology*, 60, 63.

27. Hieke, "Reception of Daniel 7," notes that Dan 7 centers on God's intervention to conquer his enemies.

28. Duvall, *Revelation*, 202; Hays, "Faithful Witness, Alpha and Omega," 73.

29. Bauckham, *Theology*, 72. As Middleton, *Violence of the Lamb*, 110, reminds us, the term even at this stage could have had martyrdom as one of its meanings. Hays, "Faithful Witness, Alpha and Omega," 79, observes that "the Passion Narrative is the christological subtext that undergirds all of the Apocalypse's references to Jesus as Faithful Witness/Martyr."

your city" (2:13), in 11:3 with reference to the two witnesses who bore witness, were crucified, then resurrected and taken to heaven (11:7, 11–12), and in 17:6 with the scene of the woman "drunk with the blood of God's holy people, the blood of those who bore testimony to Jesus." All these subsequent witnesses are patterned after Jesus in his willingness to live and speak the truth even at the cost of his own life.[30]

The second mention of "faithful witness" referring to Jesus occurs in the message to Laodicea in 3:14, where Jesus is identified as "the Amen, the faithful and true witness (ὁ μάρτυς ὁ πιστὸς καὶ ἀληθινός), the ruler of God's creation." Here we see a more forward-looking understanding of the term drawing our attention to Christ's parousia where, as Bauckham puts it, "the witness becomes the judge."[31] Interestingly, the identification "Faithful and True" also applies to the rider on the white horse who comes to accomplish God's final victory, although the term "witness" is not used (19:11).

The two uses of 1:5b–6 and 3:14 are not unrelated. It seems that the death of Christ as the faithful witness does not take away from the book's high Christology but rather lays the foundation for Jesus's authority as the "ruler" (or perhaps "beginning") of God's creation.[32] Jesus's victory over evil through his death stands as fundamentally crucial to God's plan (see esp. 13.4–5 below). He is the Lamb who was slain (5:6, 9, 12; 13:8; cf. 11:8), who shed his blood to liberate and redeem his people and make them to be a kingdom and priests (1:5b–6; 5:9–10; 7:14; 12:11; cf. 19:13). He is qualified to carry out God's plan to redeem and restore because of his obedience unto death. We see this emphasis on the Lamb's mission to carry out God's redemptive plan repeated throughout. For example, in chapter 5 the slain Lamb takes the scroll from God on his throne (5:7) and is alone found worthy to open its seals (5:9–10 and each seal) precisely because of his faithfulness unto death. Later in Rev 12 the woman gives birth to the male child who "will rule all the nations with an iron scepter," who was later snatched up to God (12:5), but not before shedding his redemptive blood (12:11).

The related expression "testimony of Jesus" (τὴν μαρτυρίαν Ἰησοῦ) occurs with slight variation in 1:2, 9; 12:17; 19:10 [2x]; 20:4 and parallels the term "witness." Depending on the context, this expression may reflect either our testimony about Jesus or the testimony given by Jesus or both.[33] The same term appears with reference to the testimony given by the souls now under the altar (6:9), by the two witnesses (11:7), and by all those who triumph over the devil (12:11). We also see the verb "bear witness"

30. On God's people as prophetic witnesses, see 16.2.6.

31. Bauckham, *Theology*, 73, also observes that the "world is a kind of court-room in which the issue of who is the true God is being decided. In this judicial contest Jesus and his followers bear witness to the truth." This leads to the witness becoming Judge in the final phase of Christ's work. Tabb, *All Things New*, 54, notes that the key terms "*martys* (witness), *martyria* (testimony) and *martyreô* (testify) are all drawn from the law court."

32. Middleton, *Violence of the Lamb*, 111–12.

33. On this phrase functioning as an objective-subjective genitive on several occasions, see most commentators (e.g., Beale, *Revelation* 184; Osborne, *Revelation*, 57). See also Hays, "Faithful Witness, Alpha and Omega," 77–78; Dixon, *Testimony of the Exalted Jesus*, 135–37, although her inclination to relate "testimony of Jesus" primarily to the book of Revelation seems too restrictive.

or "offer testimony" at the conclusion of the book when Jesus speaks directly about sending his angel to give the readers "this testimony for the churches" (22:16), "warns" everyone who hears the prophecy about how to receive it (22:18–19), and "testifies" to these things with the promise that he is coming soon (22:20). Jesus and his followers are those who testify to the truth, and this testimony in word, based on the testimony of the Word, is what conquers the evil one (12:11).

13.4 FIRSTBORN FROM THE DEAD

While Christian readers assume Jesus's resurrection, Revelation makes this theological foundation explicit, beginning in 1:5 where Jesus is identified as the "firstborn from the dead" (cf. Rom 8:29; Col 1:15, 18; Ps 89:27). Jesus is "firstborn" not in the sense that he was created first but "in the sense that he is the inaugurator of the *new* creation by means of his resurrection."[34] All that is said about Jesus's atoning sacrifice as the Lamb of God is meaningless apart from his bodily resurrection. Two things stand out here. First, the phrase stresses Jesus's sovereignty as the crucified and resurrected Lord, as the entire title in 1:5 indicates—faithful witness, firstborn from the dead, ruler of the kings of the earth. This risen, sovereign Lord will come again as eschatological Judge (see 13.6). Whereas "ruler (ἀρχὴ) of God's creation" in 3:14 could instead refer to Jesus as the source of creation,[35] it likely carries the sense of "the beginning of God's new creation through his resurrection from the dead" (cf. 21:6; 22:13).[36] Second, the term "firstborn" also implies that Jesus is the first of many who will experience resurrection (Acts 26:23; 1 Cor 15:20–23; Heb 12:23). In fact, his resurrection provides the basis and assurance for the future resurrection of the faithful (e.g., Rev 2:11; 20:6; cf. Rom 8:29; Col 1:18; and the idea of "firstfruits" in 1 Cor 15:20, 23).

In response to his vision of the risen "son of man" in Rev 1:12–16, John falls at Jesus's feet as though dead. Jesus then puts his right hand on John and reassures him that he has conquered death. Jesus's title "the Living One" is explained as resurrection and exaltation—"I was dead, and now look, I am alive for ever and ever! And I hold the keys of death and Hades" (1:17–18).[37] Bauckham observes, "His eternal livingness was interrupted by the experience of a human death, and he shares the eternal life of God through triumph over death."[38] Likewise, Jesus identifies himself to the church at Smyrna as "the First and the Last, who died and came to life again" (2:8). Jesus urges this suffering church to stay faithful "even to the point of death," and he as the resurrected Lord will give them life as their victor's crown (2:10). The implication is

34. Beale, *Revelation*, 191.

35. Bauckham, *Theology*, 56.

36. Tabb, *All Things New*, 63; Beale, *Revelation*, 297–301.

37. This is a prime example of what Hays, "Faithful Witness, Alpha and Omega," 81, calls Revelation's "proto-Chalcedonian Christology"—a fully divine yet human figure who suffers a martyr's death.

38. *Theology*, 56. On "the First and the Last," see 11.3.4 above.

that as the resurrected and Living One, Jesus is now the life giver. In addition to life as their victor's crown (2:10), he offers the right to eat from the tree of life (2:7), assuring them that they will never have their names removed from the book of life (3:5) but will be registered in the Lamb's book of life (13:8; 21:27; cf. 17:8; 20:12, 15) and the gift of drinking the water of life (21:6; 22:17; cf. 22:1).

Jesus's position as the resurrected Lord is also implied throughout the book in a variety of ways. He is the male child who was "snatched up to God and to his throne," referring to his resurrection and exaltation (12:5). Jesus promises the victors among the Laodicean church the right to sit with him on his throne, just as he was victorious and sat down with his Father on his throne (3:21). We see repeated references to Jesus as the slain Lamb who is now very much alive. One of the elders comforts John in 5:5–6 telling him not to weep since "the Lion of the tribe of Judah, the Root of David, has triumphed" and John sees "a Lamb looking as if it had been slain, standing at the center of the throne." The Lamb's victory is grounded in his death and resurrection. In Rev 5:9 the elders sing a new song of praise to the Lamb who was slain but now lives, and in 5:12 a multitude of angels shouts praise to "the Lamb, who was slain" but now lives to receive worship. The Lamb who shed his blood (7:14) is now positioned at the center of God's throne (7:17). And the book of life is described as "the Lamb's book of life, the Lamb who was slain from the creation of the world" (13:8). The slain but resurrected Lamb provides a central image of Jesus in the Apocalypse.

13.5 LION AND THE LAMB

When John realizes that no creature is found worthy to break the seals and open the scroll (5:2–3), he weeps and weeps at the prospects of a permanently sealed scroll and no answer for evil (5:4). An elder then calls John's attention to God's victory in Christ: "See, the Lion of the tribe of Judah, the Root of David, has triumphed" (5:5). The term "lion" (λέων) is used nine times in the New Testament, with six occurring in Revelation (4:7; 5:5; 9:8, 17; 10:3; 13:2). The image can be used negatively to describe the locusts' lion-like teeth (9:8), the lion-like heads of the demonic horses (9:17), and the beast's lion-like mouth (13:2), or positively with the first living creature resembling a lion (4:7), the mighty angel shouting like a lion (10:3), and as a messianic title describing Jesus (5:5).

The title "the Lion of the tribe of Judah" is drawn from Gen 49:8–10 (cf. 4 Ezra 11–12) and, along with the description "the root of David" (Isa 11:1, 10), portrays Jesus as the messianic warrior and king who will defeat his enemies through judgment.[39] By

39. Beale, *Revelation*, 349. Bauckham, *Climax of Prophecy*, 180–81, notes that both these OT texts were "*loci classici* of Jewish Messianic hopes in John's time."

itself the lion image communicates "ferocity, destructiveness and irresistible strength."[40] The one use of the term in Revelation connected to Jesus (5:5) stresses that he "has triumphed" (ἐνίκησεν). As a result, the Lion of Judah is found worthy to open the scroll and unfold its judgments against evil. But the nature of his triumph awaits a second explanatory image, one that brings a surprising theological twist—John *hears* about the Lion but turns to *see* a Lamb.[41] The Conqueror is the one who has been conquered, yet lives. Bauckham notes the importance of this shift: "Precisely by juxtaposing these contrasting images, John forges a symbol of conquest by sacrificial death, which is essentially a new symbol."[42] What is more, as Thomas and Macchia contend, "The vulnerable Lamb does not simply qualify our understanding of the ferocious Lion but is rather the lens through which the Lion's acts are to be understood. The God who is victorious over the dragon and the beast has won through the exercise of wounded love."[43] In other words, "Christ is worthy also because he conquers in a completely different way from the powers of this world."[44]

John uses "Lamb" as the most prominent and significant of Revelation's Christological titles.[45] The term "lamb" (ἀρνίον) occurs twenty-nine times, but only in 13:11 does the image not refer to Jesus, as the beast is said to be "like a lamb," stressing the contrast between the second member of the Holy Trinity and the corresponding member of the unholy trinity (i.e., Father, Son, Spirit in contrast to Satan, beast from the sea, beast from the earth). Bauckham picks up on the symbolic significance of the number 28 (7 × 4), since "it is through the Lamb's conquest that God's rule over his creation comes about, the 7 × 4 occurrences of 'Lamb' appropriately indicate the worldwide scope of his complete victory."[46] In the rest of this section we will unpack the significance of John's multifaceted use of the image of Lamb to represent Jesus. As we will see, this is a sustained and profound metaphor, mentioned in half the chapters of the book, rather than just a passing comparison.[47]

As we have already noted, the Lamb is one with God and is worshiped alongside God. More than half of the references to Jesus as Lamb are also connected in some way

40. Bauckham, *Climax of Prophecy*, 182.

41. On the relationship between seeing and hearing, see Sweet, *Revelation*, 125; Resseguie, *Revelation*, 118, who notes that John hears the inner reality while seeing the outward reality. Rebecca Skaggs and Thomas Doyle, "Lion/Lamb in Revelation," *CurBR* 7 (2009): 362–75, identify the main options for understanding the lion's relationship to the lamb.

42. Bauckham, *Climax of Prophecy*, 183. John sometimes combines two complementary images to send a single message, often using the hearing/seeing formula: the 144,000 and the great multitude (7:1–17), seeing a beast coming from the sea with two horns like a lamb but hearing the voice of the dragon (13:11), seeing a woman sitting on seven hills (17:1–6) but hearing the mystery concerning the woman (17:7–18), the mighty angel and little scroll alongside the vision of the two witnesses (10:1–11:14), and seeing a new heaven and a new earth (21:1–2) before hearing more about the meaning of this image (21:3–8).

43. Thomas and Macchia, *Revelation*, 442.

44. Resseguie, *Revelation*, 118.

45. The synonym ἀμνός occurs only four times in the NT (John 1:29, 36; Acts 8:32; 1 Pet 1:19) and always denotes Jesus as the Lamb of God. For more on Lamb symbolism in the OT and Revelation, along with an insightful discussion of the significance of the imagery, see chaps. 5–6 in Loren L. Johns, *The Lamb Christology of the Apocalypse of John: An Investigation into Its Origins and Rhetorical Force* (Eugene, OR: Wipf & Stock, 2015).

46. Bauckham, *Climax of Prophecy*, 34.

47. Johns, "Jesus in the Book of Revelation," 227.

to the throne of God. The Lamb stands at the center of the throne (5:6; 7:17), takes the scroll from him who sits on the throne (5:8), is praised by angels encircling the throne (5:9–12), is praised by all creation alongside him who sits on the throne (5:13; 7:10; cf. 15:3), judges with him who sits on the throne (6:16), is worshiped by the great multitude who stands before the throne and the Lamb (7:9), and is worshiped with a new song by the 144,000 who stand on Mount Zion with the Lamb before the throne (14:1, 3). Those who have come out of the great tribulation have washed their robes and made them white in the Lamb's blood (7:14), and they are before the throne serving God day and night (7:15). The throne belongs to both God and the Lamb (22:1, 3; cf. also 19:4–7, 9; 21:3, 5, 14). In addition, the Lord God Almighty and the Lamb are the temple in the New Jerusalem (21:22), and the city receives its light from both God and the Lamb (21:23). Clearly, the Lamb is one with God.

Paradoxically, the Lamb who is standing, receiving worship, judging evil, and working among his people is the "slain" Lamb. The term for "slain" (σφάζω) is used ten times in the New Testament and only twice outside of Revelation, both in 1 John 3:12 recounting Cain's murder of Abel. In Revelation the Lamb is slain (5:6, 9, 12; 13:8), people are killed (6:4, 9; 18:24), and the beast has a fatal wound that has been healed (13:3). In the LXX the term carries the idea of the violent killing of human beings (e.g., Isa 57:5; Jer 52:10; Ezek 23:39) or the slaughter of sacrificial animals (e.g., Exod 12:6; 34:25; Ezek 34:3; 40:39, 42). "Lamb" and "slain" seem appropriate terms to describe Jesus's sacrificial death as the Passover Lamb, while also emphasizing the warfare context and Jesus's martyrdom or death in battle that is reversed by his resurrection.[48] This certainly highlights not only the theological implications of Christ's death but also the political ramifications. Yet the repeated mention of Jesus's blood retains the theological importance and keeps the image from becoming purely political (e.g., Rev 1:5; 5:9; 7:14; 12:11; cf. 19:13).[49] The blood of the Lamb who was slain from the creation of the world (13:8) "purchased for God persons from every tribe and language and people and nation" (5:9). Here we have an echo of the redemptive death of the Lamb in 1:5b. As Middleton notes, "In the Apocalypse, the blood of the Lamb has expiatory force."[50] In addition, the Lamb standing as though slain keeps Jesus's death and resurrection together as one image and "treats the significance of Jesus's death as inseparable from the significance of his resurrection."[51]

Jesus as the Lamb of God has a profound effect on his people (see 13.7 below). They

48. See Middleton, *Violence of the Lamb*, 79–83, for a defense of the link to the paschal lamb tradition.

49. Perhaps a more balanced reading than that of Johns, "Jesus in the Book of Revelation," 229–31, who stresses the political. Cf. also Brian K. Blount, *Revelation: A Commentary*, NTL (Louisville: Westminster John Knox, 2009), 115. Beale, *Revelation*, 351, also notes that the term "lamb" (ἀρνίον) is "a most suitable word to combine the Passover lamb with the servant lamb of Isaiah 53."

50. Middleton, *Violence of the Lamb*, 71.

51. Johns, "Jesus in the Book of Revelation," 229.

are a redeemed people from every nation (5:9), who have been purified by the work of Christ on the cross (7:14). This purification is linked with their perseverance and their ongoing victory over the dragon (7:14; 12:11). They have been formed into a kingdom and priests to serve God with the promise of a future reign in the new creation (5:10). Ironically, Jesus the Lamb shepherds his people and leads them to springs of living water (7:17).

Jesus the Lamb also plays a significant role as messianic Conqueror and Judge (see 13.6 below). As Flemming reminds us, "*The Lamb is still the Lion.* The Lamb does not *replace* the powerful messianic Lion of Judah; he *redefines* that role. The wounded Lamb is also the triumphant, victorious Lord."[52] To the church in Laodicea Jesus the Victor makes promises to the victors (3:21). John portrays Jesus's sacrificial death as "the fulfillment of Jewish hopes of the messianic conqueror."[53] He takes the scroll from the right hand of God on the throne (5:7) and opens the seals of judgment (5:9; 6:1–17; 8:1). The Lamb triumphs over the evil empire because he is Lord of lords and King of kings (17:14).

We also see the Lamb depicted as eschatological Judge (see 13.6; 19.6). The slain Lamb standing at the center of the throne is described as having "seven horns and seven eyes, which are the seven spirits of God sent out into all the earth" (5:6). Horns often symbolize strength and power (Dan 7–8; Zech 1:18; 1 En. 90:6–16) and eyes depict perception and wisdom (Zech 4:10; Isa 11:2; Rev 1:14; 2:18; 19:12) in prophetic and apocalyptic literature.[54] Along with God, the Lamb is said to be the source of divine wrath against evil—it is the "great day of *their* wrath" (6:16–17), emphasis added. The divine register of all true believers, the "book of life," is deemed "the Lamb's book of life" (13:8; 21:27), implying the Lamb's role in judgment. In addition, those who experience God's wrath do so "in the presence of the holy angels and of the Lamb" (14:10), depicting the Lamb as the supervisor or verifier of divine judgment.

Yet another aspect of the Lamb's ministry is his presence with his people in victory (see 13.7 below). Even in the book of Revelation, Jesus is "Immanuel, God with us" (cf. Matt 1:23). We see his "with-ness" especially in the seven messages of chapters 2–3. He walks among the seven lampstands (2:1) and knows their deeds (2:2–3, 9, 19; 3:1, 8, 15). He knows their local context (2:13), calls them to renewed fellowship (3:20), and promises them his presence in victory (2:7, 10, 17, 28; 3:4–5, 12, 21). He will shepherd his people and lead them to springs of living water (7:17). His people stand before him in 7:9, and he stands with them on Mount Zion in 14:1. They are described as those who "follow the Lamb wherever he goes" (14:4). And in 17:14 we read that with the Lamb in his victory will be his "called, chosen and faithful followers."

52. Flemming, *Foretaste of the Future*, 60, emphasis original.

53. Bauckham, *Climax of Prophecy*, 184.

54. Michael Kuykendall, *Lions, Locusts, and the Lamb: Interpreting Key Images in the Book of Revelation* (Eugene, OR: Wipf & Stock, 2019), 197–98, 218–19; Tabb, *All Things New*, 60.

The Lamb plays a major role in the coming new creation (see Ch. 20). Jesus is portrayed as the bridegroom and the church as his bride in the anticipated wedding of the Lamb. The bride has prepared herself (19:7) and those invited to the wedding feast are blessed (19:9). The Holy City, the new Jerusalem descends from God "as a bride beautifully dressed for her husband" (21:2), and John is given a tour of the heavenly city—"the bride, the wife of the Lamb" (21:9–21).

The wall of the celestial city has twelve foundations stones on which are written the names of the twelve apostles of the Lamb (21:14). The temple city does not have an actual temple because its temple is "the Lord God Almighty and the Lamb" (21:22). The city does not need the sun or moon "for the glory of God gives it light, and the Lamb is its lamp" (21:23). Only those whose names are written in the Lamb's book of life may enter the heavenly city (21:27). And the river of the water of life flows from the throne of God and of the Lamb (22:1). The city is built around the throne of God and the Lamb and God's people will worship him (22:3).

Jesus is chiefly identified as the Lion-Lamb in Revelation. This unique symbol communicates Jesus's mission to conquer evil through his sacrificial death and resurrection. It also reinforces multiple aspects of Revelation's high Christology—his oneness with God, his redemptive death and its effects, his role as messianic Conqueror and eschatological Judge, his shepherding presence among his people, and his glorious presence in the new creation.

13.6 RETURN AS CONQUEROR AND JUDGE

Revelation focuses not just on what Jesus has accomplished in his incarnate life and ministry but also, perhaps more than any other New Testament book, on what he will do in the future.[55] Although the term *parousia* does not appear, Revelation stresses Jesus's return. Seven times he declares, "I am coming" (ἔρχομαι in 2:5, 16; 3:11; 16:15; 22:7, 12, 20; cf. 3:3, 20). The book opens with the promise of his coming, an allusion to Dan 7:13 and Zech 12:10, 12, in Rev 1:7: "'Look, he is coming with the clouds,' and 'every eye will see him, even those who pierced him'; and all peoples on earth 'will mourn because of him.' So shall it be! Amen." And it closes with a triple assurance of his return: "I am coming soon" (22:7, 12, 20). He prefaces the third beatitude with a reminder that he will come like a thief, unexpectedly and suddenly (16:15). Jesus references his "coming" multiple times in the seven messages (ἔρχομαι in 2:5, 16; 3:11 and ἥκω in 2:25; 3:3, 3) and also alludes to his coming judgment apart from specific terms for coming (e.g., 2:10, 17, 22–23, 26–28; 3:5, 9, 12, 16, 20–21). As we will see, his coming includes both the judgment of the unrighteous and rewarding of the righteous.

55. Flemming, *Foretaste of the Future*, 64.

In addition, the return of Christ appears in the description of God as "the One who is and who was and who is to come" (1:4, 8; 4:8). As Bauckham says, "This 'coming' of God to bring his purposes for his creation to fulfillment is the coming of Christ."[56] This is confirmed by the omission of "is to come" in the description in 11:16 when the seventh trumpet is sounded. God's coming has occurred in the return of Christ (cf. 11:15).

Jesus comes as the Conqueror/Ruler and Judge (see 19.6). The Jews expected a Davidic Messiah who would defeat God's (and Israel's) enemies and establish God's rule on earth.[57] Revelation both affirms and transforms this expectation. Jesus stands as the "ruler (ἄρχων) of the kings of the earth" (1:5; cf. 3:14 where ἀρχή could refer to the "ruler" of God's creation). This is an allusion to Ps 88:28 (LXX; EVV 89:27, MT 89:28), where the context portrays David as the anointed king who reigns over his enemies and whose descendent will sit on his throne forever. Jesus is thus viewed as "the ideal Davidic king" whose eternal kingship and reign have been established through his death and resurrection.[58]

In chapter 5 Jesus, the slain Lamb, stands at the center of God's throne (5:6, 13), meaning he shares God's nature and authority. He is described as "the Lion of the tribe of Judah, the Root of David" (5:5). We have already noted that "Lion" is not replaced by but defined by "Lamb" imagery—victory through sacrifice. Drawing on both Gen 49:9–10 and Isa 11:1, 10, Revelation highlights Jesus's victory at the cross/resurrection, a past victory that will be worked out in the future through the judgment of his enemies and deliverance of his people.

Revelation identifies the Conqueror/Ruler Jesus as the Davidic Messiah. The term Χριστός ("Messiah" or "Christ") is used seven times in Revelation (1:1, 2, 5; 11:15; 12:10; 20:4, 6) and reinforces the truth that Jesus as the Lord and Messiah will defeat the rulers or kings of the earth and usher in God's kingdom (cf. Ps 2:2). At the sounding of the seventh trumpet, loud voices in heaven proclaim: "The kingdom of the world has become the kingdom of our Lord and of his Messiah, and he will reign for ever and ever" (Rev 11:15). Likewise, at the defeat of Satan, a loud voice in heaven announces, "Now have come the salvation and the power and the kingdom of our God, and the authority of his Messiah. For the accuser of our brothers and sisters, who accuses them before our God day and night, has been hurled down" (12:10). He is the male child who will "rule all the nations with an iron scepter" (12:5; cf. 2:27; Ps 2:9).

The messianic war theme continues in Rev 17, where we read that the ten kings wage war against the Lamb, but the Lamb triumphs over them because he is "Lord of lords and King of kings" (17:14). The language of battle is mentioned throughout Revelation

56. Bauckham, *Theology*, 63. Cf. also Middleton, *Violence of the Lamb*, 114–16.

57. For more detail on this Jewish eschatological expectation, see ch. 8, "The Apocalypse as a Christian War Scroll," in Bauckham, *Climax of Prophecy*, 210–37.

58. Beale and McDonough, "Revelation," 1089.

(e.g., 11:7; 12:7–8, 17; 13:7; 16:14; 17:14; 19:11, 19), as is the Messiah's victory over the wicked nations (e.g., 2:18, 26–28; 11:1–5, 18; 12:5, 10; 14:1; 16:14, 16; 19:15).[59] The title "King of kings and Lord of lords" (17:14; 19:16; cf. 1 En. 9:4; Dan 4:37 LXX, EVV [MT 4:34]; 1 Tim 6:15) identifies Jesus as the supreme ruler and conqueror who will defeat the earthly powers fully and finally at the last battle.

Although the decisive victory was won at the cross and resurrection, Jesus will also conquer at the parousia, and the final battle scene occurs in 19:11–21. Jesus, the rider on the white horse, "judges and wages war" with justice (19:11). Accompanied by the "armies of heaven," Jesus, the "Faithful and True" One, the "Word of God," wears a robe dipped in blood and has eyes like blazing fire and many crowns (19:11–13).[60] He judges the nations with the sharp sword of his word and "will rule them with an iron scepter" (19:15; cf. 2:27; 12:5; Ps 2:8–9). The last battle is narrated in Rev 19:19–21:

> Then I saw the beast and the kings of the earth and their armies gathered together to wage war against the rider on the horse and his army. But the beast was captured, and with it the false prophet who had performed the signs on its behalf. With these signs he had deluded those who had received the mark of the beast and worshiped its image. The two of them were thrown alive into the fiery lake of burning sulfur. The rest were killed with the sword coming out of the mouth of the rider on the horse, and all the birds gorged themselves on their flesh.

The final battle is never described in detail. The account simply reads, "But the beast was captured, and with it the false prophet" (19:20). Christ returns as the victorious Lord of lords and King of kings.

Closely related to Jesus returning as the Conqueror/Ruler is his role as Judge. God's judgment of evil appears throughout the Apocalypse (see Ch. 19).[61] Here we focus on Jesus's role. As noted above, in the seven letters we see numerous allusions to his coming to judge the wicked and reward the victors. He warns the unrepentant in Ephesus that he will come to them in judgment (2:5) and those enticed by the false teaching in Pergamum that he will come and fight against them (2:16). He reminds Thyatira that "all the churches will know that I am he who searches hearts and minds, and I will repay each of you according to your deeds" (2:23). He warns the church in Sardis that should they not wake up they will experience his coming like a stealthy thief (3:3; cf. 16:15). Even the image of Jesus patiently knocking at the door portrayed in the letter

59. Both the battles and the victories are noted in Bauckham, *Theology*, 69.

60. Interpreters differ on whose blood covers Jesus's robe, with some suggesting it is his own blood (e.g. Mangina, *Revelation*, 221–22; Koester, *Revelation*, 756) and others opting for the blood of his enemies (e.g., Smalley, *Revelation*, 491; Osborne, *Revelation*, 682–83).

61. For a thorough review, see "The Lamb as Divine Judge" in Middleton, *Violence of the Lamb*, 132–87.

to Laodicea speaks of his hesitancy to judge but his commitment to do so if they fail to respond (3:20).

Throughout the rest of the book, Jesus's role as Judge stands clear. At the opening of the sixth seal, we are taken to the end of history. The response of unbelievers from across the social spectrum is to cry out to the mountains and rocks, "Fall on us and hide us from the face of him who sits on the throne and from the wrath of the Lamb! For the great day of their wrath has come, and who can withstand it?" (6:16–17). Final judgment is in view here. In 14:9–11 those who worship the beast and receive its mark "will drink the wine of God's fury, which has been poured full strength into the cup of his wrath. They will be tormented with burning sulfur in the presence of the holy angels and of the Lamb" (14:10). Whether the grain harvest of 14:14–16 is a gathering of the righteous at Christ's return or a judgment of the wicked is a matter of debate (see 11.4.5.4). Most likely this scene refers to Christ's judgment of the wicked as the "one like a son of man" swings his sickle and harvests the earth (14:14; cf. Joel 3:9–15).

The emphasis on Jesus as Judge culminates in the vision of the rider on the white horse in Rev 19:11–21. His rule includes his judgment of evil. The sharp sword from his mouth and the image of treading the winepress of God's wrath both point to Jesus's pivotal role in final judgment (19:11, 15, 20–21). Even in the final judgment scene of 20:11–15, it is the "Lamb's book of life" (13:8; cf. 20:12, 15), that register of all true believers, that is used to determine the terrible destiny of those facing the wrath of the Lamb.

Jesus plays a central role in judging evil in Revelation. And while Lamb does redefine Lion by emphasizing the crucial role of Jesus's atoning sacrifice, the Lamb nevertheless has "seven horns and seven eyes," images of omnipotence and omniscience respectively, and is deemed worthy to take the scroll and open its seals, a scroll that features God's judgment of the wicked (5:6–9).[62] The martyrs cry out for justice (6:9–10) and justice God will bring through the person and work of the Lion-Lamb. We cannot expect justice apart from the judgment of evil by the Triune God. "Give us justice!" and "Judge not!"—two popular cries of contemporary society—simply do not go together in God's kingdom when we are talking about God and his Messiah. Human misjudgments, of course, are another matter.

Christ returns not only to judge the wicked but also to reward his people. Judgment does have a positive dimension. The concept of rewarding the righteous surfaces in the promises to the victors in the seven messages (2:7, 10–11, 17, 26–28; 3:4–5, 11–12, 22). The bridegroom will come for his bride (19:7–9; 21:2, 9). He will come to shepherd and comfort his people (7:17). He will be their temple (21:22), their eternal light (21:23), their security (21:27), and their source of eternal life (22:1). Jesus's return

62. Osborne, *Revelation*, 257.

is the embodiment of God's coming to his people and will fulfill all that God has promised.[63] He is coming to give life, comfort, and rewards to his people (22:12).[64] The proleptic judgment scene of 11:15–19 summarizes both aspects of Jesus's coming as Judge. Positively, the "kingdom of the world has become the kingdom of our Lord and of his Messiah, and he will reign for ever and ever" (11:15). The full reign of God has come, resulting in the "rewarding your servants the prophets and your people who revere your name, both great and small" (11:18). Negatively, the rebellious nations will face God's wrath as the dead are judged and those who destroy the earth are destroyed (11:18).

13.7 JESUS AND HIS CHURCH

Jesus's relationship with his church involves his personal presence with his people, his redemptive work on their behalf, his call to discipleship and faithful endurance, and his future presence with them in the new creation. All of this is wrapped in an *inclusio* of grace for his people (1:4; 22:21). To begin with, Revelation emphasizes Christ's personal presence among the churches. This presence includes his revelation to his people. While on Patmos and in the Spirit on the Lord's Day, John receives his commissioning: "Write on a scroll what you see and send it to the seven churches" (1:11). John turns to see the voice speaking to him and sees "one like a son of man" dressed in all his glory among the seven lampstands or seven churches (1:12–20). The words of the risen Christ (2:1, 8, 12, 18; 3:1, 7, 14) are mediated to and through John to the seven churches by the Spirit (2:7, 11, 17, 29; 3:6, 13, 22; see 14.4). Jesus is present among his people as one who speaks words of comfort and/or rebuke, words calling them away from the idolatry and immorality of this world system and drawing toward faithful discipleship.[65]

Jesus's presence among his people is a living, engaged presence. He says to the Ephesian church that he "holds the seven stars in his right hand and walks among the seven golden lampstands" (2:1). "All the churches will know," he tells the church at Thyatira, "that I am he who searches hearts and minds, and I will repay each of you according to your deeds" (2:23). He reminds the church at Sardis, "I know your deeds; you have a reputation of being alive, but you are dead" (3:1). He tells the Laodicean church that he stands at the door knocking, eager for his followers to hear his voice and open the door to renewed fellowship, the intimate fellowship of a shared meal. At the close of the book, Jesus says, "I, Jesus, have sent my angel to give you this testimony for the churches" (22:16).

63. Flemming, *Foretaste of the Future*, 64–65; Fanning, *Revelation*, 84.

64. Hays, "Faithful Witness, Alpha and Omega," 74; Bauckham, *Theology*, 64.

65. For an excellent, up-to-date study of the sermons to the seven churches, see Weima, *Sermons to the Seven Churches*.

A second primary aspect of Christ's relationship with his people is his redemptive work on their behalf and its resulting effects. The opening greeting portrays Jesus as "the faithful witness, the firstborn from the dead, and the ruler of the kings of the earth" (1:5a). The doxology that follows celebrates Christ's work and the benefits for his followers: "To him who loves us and has freed us from our sins by his blood, and has made us to be a kingdom and priests to serve his God and Father—to him be glory and power for ever and ever! Amen" (1:5b–6). His love leads to his sacrificial death (cf. 5:6, 9, 12; 7:14; 12:11; 13:8), and the outcome of his atoning death is to liberate God's people from their sins and make them into a kingdom and priests to serve God (cf. 1 Pet 2:5, 9–10 and the central covenant promise in Exod 19:6). Later, with a new song the living creatures and elders celebrate the Lamb's redemptive work on behalf of his people: "You are worthy . . . because you were slain, and with your blood you purchased for God persons. . . . You have made them to be a kingdom and priests to serve our God, and they will reign on the earth" (5:9–10). Likewise, we are told in chapter 14 that only the 144,000, those who "had been redeemed from the earth" (14:3), can learn the new song of praise to the Lamb and that these Lamb-followers have been "purchased from among mankind and offered as firstfruits to God and the Lamb" (14:4). The goal of Christ's redemptive work includes freedom from past sins as well as their installation as kings and priests in the new creation (20:4–6).

Christ's relationship to his people also includes his call to discipleship and faithful endurance (see Ch. 17). This theme runs strong and clear through the seven messages. Here Christ's call typically includes both commendation and correction, though not each component is included in every sermon. He "knows" their situation and their works (οἶδα in 2:2, 9, 13, 19; 3:1, 8, 15) and commends them for what they are doing right. He then offers a correction accompanied by the imperatives "repent" (μετανοέω in 2:5 [2x], 16; 3:3, 19; cf. 2:21 [2x]) and "remember" (μνημονεύω in 2:5; 3:3) and various others along the way (2:5, 10 [2x], 25; 3:2 [2x], 3, 11, 19) to drive home his point.

Throughout the rest of the book, God's people are often identified as those who demonstrate allegiance to the Lamb. At the beginning of the book when John details his vision and commissioning, he describes himself as the readers' "brother and companion in the suffering and kingdom and patient endurance that are ours in Jesus" and reminds them that he is on Patmos "because of the word of God and the testimony of Jesus" (1:9). In the major interlude of chapters 12–14, which gives insight into the cosmic war between God and the forces of evil, God's people are again identified as those who follow the Lamb. They triumph "by the blood of the Lamb and by the word of their testimony; they did not love their lives so much as to shrink from death" (12:11). They are those who "keep God's commands and hold fast their testimony about Jesus" (12:17).

Near the close of this interlude, when John sees the Lamb standing on Mount Zion with the 144,000, he describes them as those who "follow the Lamb wherever he goes," as opposed to those who commit spiritual adultery (14:4; cf. 19:14). God's people—those who "keep his commands and remain faithful to Jesus"—are called to "patient endurance" (14:12). God's holy people, his martyr people, are those who bear the testimony of Jesus and hold to the word of God rather than worshiping the beast (17:6; 20:4; cf. 19:10). As McKnight and Matchett put it, "Disciples follow Jesus by waging a battle with evil by the Word of God, even if it means suffering in nonviolent witness. Such disciples are dissident, allegiant witnesses, and they form part of Team Lamb."[66]

Finally, Jesus will be eternally present with his people in the new creation. Throughout Revelation we have previews of this life with Christ in the eternal city. Many of the promises to the victors in chapters 2–3 move in this direction. Jesus promises "the right to eat from the tree of life, which is in the paradise of God" (2:7). This assumes resurrection as the promise to Smyrna indicates: "the one who is victorious will not be hurt at all by the second death" (2:11). The victors will walk with Jesus, dressed in white, and their names will never be blotted from the Lamb's book of life (3:4–5; cf. 13:8; 20:12; 21:27). The victors have a permanent place in the temple of Jesus's God and will be inscribed with the name of Jesus's God, the name of the city of Jesus's God—the new Jerusalem coming down out of heaven from Jesus's God—and Jesus's new name (3:11–12). They will sit with Jesus on his throne in the new creation (3:21).

Throughout the rest of the book, the saints are promised bodily resurrection and the privilege of reigning with Christ (20:4–6; cf. 22:5). These "called, chosen and faithful" are with the Lamb and participate in his triumph (17:14; cf. 19:14, 19). The Lamb stands on Mount Zion with the 144,000 who have Jesus's name and his Father's name written on their foreheads (14:1). Another image for the church, the great multitude, stands triumphantly before the throne and before the Lamb, celebrating God's victory (7:9). These faithful people who died in the Lord (14:13) are resurrected and now celebrate God's victory in the new creation with their Lord. They are comforted and shepherded by God and the Lamb at the center of the throne (7:17). The climactic image of Christ's people with him in the new creation is that of a wedding. The marriage of the Lamb arrives and his bride—God's holy people—has made herself ready (19:7–9; 21:2, 9; cf. 22:17). The metaphor of Christ's presence with his people in the new creation offers the most captivating picture possible of the loving, intimate relationship the Lord will have with his people.

66. Scot McKnight with Cody Matchett, *Revelation for the Rest of Us: A Prophetic Call to Follow Jesus as a Dissident Disciple* (Grand Rapids: Zondervan Reflective, 2023), 83.

13.8 CONCLUSION

Revelation's Lamb-Lion Christology offers the primary window through which we can view the entire narrative. Jesus's divine identity and oneness with God permeates the entire vision (e.g., the Lamb at the center of the throne, the Lamb receiving worship alongside God, the Lamb as divine Judge, the Lord God Almighty and the Lamb as the new creation temple). Jesus's incarnational mission centers in his role as "the faithful witness" unto death. His cruciform life is paradigmatic for his followers (e.g., 6:9; 18:24). The Lamb's sacrifice qualifies him to take the scroll and open its seals, thus unfolding the plan of God. Jesus, the Lion of the tribe of Judah, the Root of David, has triumphed. The Lion is the Lamb. His sacrificial, atoning death wins the victory over Satan and sin and death. Yet the Lamb is now very much alive. Jesus's resurrection remains foundational to Revelation's Christology. He is the "firstborn from the dead" and, as a result, the sovereign Lord. Jesus's resurrection serves as the basis for and assurance of the future resurrection of believers. He holds the keys of death and Hades (1:17–18).

And the Lamb is still the Lion and will come as the eschatological Judge. Revelation emphasizes Jesus's return: "I am coming soon." He will come to save and to judge. The final battle is won simply by his appearing and stresses that Jesus is the coming Judge. He will bring God's justice and right wrongs. He will reward his faithful followers who have persevered. Through Jesus, God wins!

Revelation also brings heaven down to earth by reminding readers of every generation that Jesus is not only crucified and risen but present by his Spirit with his people (see Ch. 14). Jesus walks among the churches, strengthening, encouraging, confronting, and warning. His work benefits his people. All that he has done demonstrates his love and builds his people into kings and priests, equipped to reign and serve in the new creation. The church is identified as those who follow the Lamb, who calls them to faithful perseverance. He promises them his presence not only during their wilderness pilgrimage but also eternally in the promised land that is the new heaven and new earth.

Chapter 14

"WHAT THE SPIRIT SAYS TO THE CHURCHES": HOLY SPIRIT

BIBLIOGRAPHY

Allison, Gregg R., and Andreas J. Köstenberger. *The Holy Spirit.* ThPG. Nashville: B&H Academic, 2020. **Archer, Melissa L.** *"I Was in the Spirit on the Lord's Day": A Pentecostal Engagement with Worship in the Apocalypse.* Cleveland, TN: CPT, 2015. **Archer, Melissa, and Robby Waddell.** "The Spirit in John's Apocalypse: Vision, Prophecy, Discernment." *Pneuma* 43 (2021): 553–66. **Barr, David L.** *Tales of the End: A Narrative Commentary on the Book of Revelation.* 2nd ed. Salem, OR: Polebridge, 2012. **Bauckham, Richard J.** "The Role of the Spirit in the Apocalypse." *EvQ* 52.2 (1980): 66–83. **Bloesch, Donald G.** *The Holy Spirit: Works and Gifts.* ChrF. Downers Grove, IL: InterVarsity Press, 2000. **Briggs, Robert A.** *Jewish Temple Imagery in the Book of Revelation.* StBL 10. New York: Peter Lang, 1999. **Bruce, F. F.** "The Spirit in the Apocalypse." Pages 333–44 in *Christ and the Spirit in the New Testament: In Honour of Charles Francis Digby Moule.* Edited by Barnabas Lindars and Stephen S. Smalley. Cambridge: Cambridge University Press, 1973. **Bruner, Frederick Dale, and William Hordern.** *The Holy Spirit: Shy Member of the Trinity.* Eugene, OR: Wipf & Stock, 2001. **Burge, Gary M.** *The Anointed Community: The Holy Spirit in the Johannine Tradition.* Grand Rapids: Eerdmans, 1987. **Cole, Graham A.** *He Who Gives Life: The Doctrine of the Holy Spirit.* FET. Wheaton, IL: Crossway, 2007. **De Smidt, J. C.** "The Holy Spirit in the Book of Revelation—Nomenclature." *Neot* 28 (1994): 229–44. **De Smidt, Kobus.** "Hermeneutical Perspectives on the Spirit in the Book of Revelation." *JPT* 14 (1999): 27–47. **Dixon, Sarah S. U.** *The Testimony of the Exalted Jesus in the Book of Revelation.* LNTS 570. London: Bloomsbury T&T Clark, 2017. **Ferguson, Sinclair B.** *The Holy Spirit.* CCT. Downers Grove, IL: InterVarsity Press, 1996. **Herms, Ronald.** "πνευματικῶς and Antagonists in Revelation 11 Reconsidered." Pages 135–46 in *The Book of Revelation: Currents in British Research on the Apocalypse.* Edited by Garrick V. Allen, Ian Paul, and Simon P. Woodman. WUNT 2.411. Tübingen: Mohr Siebeck. **Jeske, R. L.** "Spirit and Community in the Johannine Apocalypse." *NTS* 31 (1985): 452–66. **Johnson, David R.** *Pneumatic Discernment in the Apocalypse: An Intertextual and Pentecostal Exploration* 18. Cleveland, TN: CPT, 2018. **Kuykendall, Michael.** "An Expanded Role for the Spirit in the Book of Revelation." *JETS* 64.3 (2021): 527–44. ———. *Lions, Locusts, and* *the Lamb: Interpreting Key Images in the Book of Revelation*. Eugene, OR: Wipf & Stock, 2019. **Lee, Hee Youl.** *A Dynamic Reading of the Holy Spirit in Revelation: A Theological Reflection on the Functional Role of the Holy Spirit in the Narrative*. Eugene, OR: Wipf & Stock, 2014. **Moltmann, Jürgen.** *The Spirit of Life: A Universal Affirmation. Systematic Contributions to Theology*. Minneapolis: Fortress, 2001. **Montague, George T.** *The Holy Spirit: Growth of a Biblical Tradition*. New York: Paulist, 1976. **Moule, C. F. D.** *The Holy Spirit*. Grand Rapids: Eerdmans, 1978. **Smalley, Stephen S.** "The Paraclete: Pneumatology in the Johannine Gospel and Apocalypse." Pages 289–300 in *Exploring the Gospel of John*. Edited by R. Alan Culpepper and C. Clifton Black. Louisville: Westminster John Knox, 1996. **Smith, Brandon D.** *The Trinity in the Book of Revelation: Seeing Father, Son, and Holy Spirit in John's Apocalypse*. SCDS. Downers Grove, IL: InterVarsity Press, 2022. **Song, Seung-In.** *Water as an Image of the Spirit in the Johannine Literature*. StBL 171. New York: Peter Lang, 2019. **Tabb, Brian J.** *All Things New: Revelation as Canonical Capstone*. NSBT 48. Downers Grove, IL: IVP Academic, 2019. **Thiselton, Anthony C.** *The Holy Spirit—In Biblical Teaching, through the Centuries, and Today*. Grand Rapids: Eerdmans, 2013. **Thomas, John Christopher.** "New Jerusalem and the Conversion of the Nations: An Exercise in Pneumatic Discernment (Rev 21:1–22:5)." Pages 228–45 in *The Spirit and Christ in the New Testament and Christian Theology: Essays in Honor of Max Turner*. Edited by I. Howard Marshall, Volker Rabens, and Cornelis Bennema. Grand Rapid: Eerdmans, 2012. ———. "Revelation." Pages 257–66 in *A Biblical Theology of the Holy Spirit*. Edited by Trevor J. Burke and Keith Warrington. Eugene, OR: Cascade, 2014. ———. "The Spirit in the Book of Revelation." *OHBR* 241–55. **Thompson, Marianne Meye.** "The Breath of Life: John 20:22–23 Once More." Pages 69–78 in *The Holy Spirit and Christian Origins: Essays in Honor of James D. G. Dunn*. Edited by Graham N. Stanton, Bruce W. Longenecker, and Stephen C. Barton. Grand Rapids: Eerdmans, 2004. **Waddell, Robby.** *The Spirit of the Book of Revelation*. JPTSS 30. Dorset: Deo, 2006. **Wilson, Mark W.** Review of *The Spirit of the Book of Revelation*, by Robby Waddell. *JEPTA* 27.2 (2007): 153–160. ———. "The Spirit in Revelation: Explorations in Imagery and Metaphor." *CTR* 17.1 (2019): 83–96. ———. "The Water of Life: Three Explorations into Water Imagery in Revelation and the Fourth Gospel." *Scriptura* 118 (2019:1): 1–17. **Yarnell, Malcolm B., III.** *God the Trinity*. Nashville: B&H Academic, 2016.

14.1 INTRODUCTION

Throughout Revelation references abound to God Almighty and Jesus, the Lamb of God, while references to the Spirit seem few and far between. But first appearances can be deceiving. Yes, the Spirit has been rightly labeled the "shy member of the Trinity,"[1]

1. Frederick Dale Bruner and William Hordern, *The Holy Spirit: Shy Member of the Trinity* (Eugene, OR: Wipf & Stock, 2001).

but we should not mistake "shyness" for relegation to second-class status. Rather, this is a shyness of humility, as the Spirit fulfills his mission of pointing people to the Father and the Son (cf. John 14:26; 15:26; 16:13–14). No, the phrases "Holy Spirit" and "the Spirit of God" are never mentioned in John's Apocalypse, but a closer look reveals that the Spirit plays a surprisingly significant role in this book.[2] In spite of fewer mentions, the Spirit remains a fully involved member of the Triune Godhead, and figures prominently in the theology of Revelation.[3] Bauckham warns that "it would be a mistake to conclude that in the theology of Revelation the Spirit is unimportant." Rather, "the Spirit plays an essential role in the divine activity of establishing God's kingdom in this world."[4]

We come to know the Spirit's role first by examining the uses of πνεῦμα throughout, and these form many of the key chapter headings: "seven spirits" (1:4; 3:1; 4:5; 5:6), "in the Spirit" (1:10; 4:2; 17:3; 21:10), the Spirit speaking to the seven churches (2:7, 11, 17, 29; 3:6, 13, 22), the Spirit of prophecy (19:10), the Spirit speaking (14:13; 22:17), the "breath" of life (11:11), the spirits of the prophets (22:6), and the adverb πνευματικῶς (11:8).[5] In this way, we build our theology of the Spirit in Revelation on a solid exegetical base. But such a theology cannot be limited to the uses of this important term. We must also examine images that depict the Spirit to get a holistic understanding on the Spirit's role in the book (e.g., blazing lamps, smoke, glory, light, water of life, numerical symbolism, the location of the Spirit, and the seal of the living God). Such imagery reinforces the theology drawn from the uses of πνεῦμα.

The theology of the Spirit in Revelation is surprisingly robust and extensive. He is present in power and fullness to accomplish God's work in the world. The Spirit's partnership with Christ shines brightly as the Spirit speaks prophetically to the churches the words of Christ. He confronts the church and the world with God's truth, encourages the saints to endure tribulation, and empowers the church in its calling to be witnesses. The Spirit is God's relational presence sent out to indwell, comfort, empower, protect, and sustain God's people until they arrive at the heavenly city, a city filled with the glory of the Triune God, the Spirit included.

14.2 THE "SEVEN SPIRITS"

The important phrase "the seven spirits" (τῶν ἑπτὰ πνευμάτων) occurs four times in Revelation: 1:4; 3:1; 4:5; 5:6. To unravel its meaning, we begin with the significance

2. For a comprehensive and insightful examination of the Holy Spirit from both a biblical-theological and systematic-theological perspective, see Gregg R. Allison and Andreas J. Köstenberger, *The Holy Spirit*, ThPG (Nashville: B&H Academic, 2020). The "Biblical-Theological Synthesis of the Holy Spirit in Scripture" on pp. 201–15 is especially helpful.

3. Kobus De Smidt, "Hermeneutical Perspectives on the Spirit in the Book of Revelation," *JPT* 14 (1999): 27, observes, "Quantitatively the Spirit is not prominent in Revelation, but he is qualitatively active throughout."

4. Bauckham, *Theology*, 109.

5. This study does not include uses of πνεῦμα to represent evil, such as impure spirits (16:13, 14; 18:2) or the "breath" of the beast (13:15).

of numbers. Since four represents the whole world or cosmic completeness, the four occurrences imply an influence throughout the world when coupled with 5:6: "the seven spirits of God sent out into all the earth." Interestingly, Bauckham notes how the "four references to the sevenfold Spirit correspond to the seven occurrences of the fourfold phrase which designates all the peoples of the earth (5:9; 7:9; 10:11; 11:9; 13:7; 14:6; 17:15)."[6] The number seven also plays a crucial role, symbolizing fullness, completeness, perfection, and, as Lee notes, usually representing divine qualities in apocalyptic literature.[7] Regarding the number seven here, Barr concludes: "The quality of the number seven is a divine quality, signifying fulfillment, perfection, and completion. John signifies with this symbol that the quality of the spirit is seven/perfect not that there is a quantity of spirits."[8] Resseguie also observes John's preference for using metaphors with sevens to describe the Holy Spirit (seven spirits, seven lamps, seven eyes).[9] In 1:4, John's use of "seven spirits" also falls within a threefold reference to God and points to the Holy Spirit as God's personal and powerful presence throughout the world.

Traditionally scholars have interpreted "the seven spirits" in two main ways: (1) as seven angels or (2) as the Holy Spirit.[10] The first view has ancient support in Oecumenius (6th c. AD) who concludes, "The seven spirits are seven angels," but quickly adds, presumably because of the trinitarian positioning of the phrase in verse 4, "However, they are not to be regarded as of equal honor or coeternal with the holy Trinity."[11] In recent scholarship, while admitting that in early Jewish literature the term "spirits" is rarely used of angels, Aune identifies the seven spirits as "the seven principal angels of God," referring to the seven archangels who stand before God in Rev 8:2 (cf. Luke 1:19; Tob 12:15; 1 En 20:1–7).[12] Koester also concludes, though more cautiously, that the spirits are angels since both the seven spirits and seven angels (8:2) are before God's throne, and because Christ holds both the angels and the spirits (1:20; 3:1).[13]

The second view, that the seven spirits represent the Holy Spirit, has even more ancient roots plus substantial support from contemporary scholarship. Victorinus of Pettau (d. AD 304) says John's greeting comes in part from "the sevenfold Spirit" who is identified in Isa 11:2–3 as "a Spirit of wisdom and understanding, of counsel and strength, of knowledge and piety, a Spirit of the fear of the Lord."[14] Other considerations also point toward a reference to the Holy Spirit.

6. Bauckham, *Theology*, 109.
7. Hee Youl Lee, *A Dynamic Reading of the Holy Spirit in Revelation: A Theological Reflection on the Functional Role of the Holy Spirit in the Narrative* (Eugene, OR: Wipf & Stock, 2014), 80; also, Bauckham, *Theology*, 26–27.
8. Barr, *Tales of the End*, 56.
9. Resseguie, *Revelation*, 66.
10. Waddell, *Spirit of the Book of Revelation*, 7–21.
11. Oecumenius and Andrew of Caesarea, *Greek Commentaries*, 4.
12. Aune, *Revelation 1–5*, 34–35. Also, Boxall, *Revelation*, 86; Boring, *Revelation*, 75; Witherington, *Revelation*, 75.
13. Koester, *Revelation*, 216, 226.
14. Victorinus et al., *Latin Commentaries*, 1. The LXX of Isa 11:2–3 does feature seven elements, adding "piety" or godliness (εὐσεβείας) to the six listed in the MT.

In 1:4–5 John offers a greeting of grace and peace from "him who is, and who was, and who is to come, and from the seven spirits before his throne, and from Jesus Christ, who is the faithful witness, the firstborn from the dead, and the ruler of the kings of the earth." First, we note the location of the "seven spirits" between a clear reference to God and to Jesus Christ, undoubtedly sending a trinitarian message to the readers (cf. 1 Pet 1:2; 2 Cor 13:13).[15] The three members of the divine community are the source of grace and peace for believers, qualities that nowhere else in the New Testament are said to proceed from angels.[16] About the mentioning of the Spirit second rather than third, de Smidt concludes, "The Spirit is therefore in the closest interactive working relationships with the Father and the Son."[17]

Second, the location of the seven spirits "before his [God's] throne" hints at divine status (see also 4:5; 5:6). While other entities are located near the throne in Revelation (e.g., twenty-four elders, four living creatures, the angels and the dead in 4:6, 10; 7:9, 11, 15; 8:3; 14:3; 20:12), Wilson rightfully argues that this positioning is different.[18] The overall structure of Revelation links the opening and closing in parallel ways so that the trinitarian references in the epilogue clarify the opening salutation. Here again the Spirit is located between the two other members of the Godhead (Jesus in 22:16, Spirit in 22:17, and God in 22:18–19). Wilson concludes, "The second trinitarian sandwich in chapter 22 with worship directed at all three members sustains the interpretation that the 'seven Spirits' of 1:4 is a Johannine locution for the Holy Spirit."[19] "Before the throne" in this context indicates the place where God's might and power are made known, the place where God connects directly with the world. Third, spirits and angels are two distinct groups. As Bauckham notes, while the term "spirit" (πνεῦμα) could be used of angels (frequently in the DSS), "it very rarely has this meaning in early Christian literature and never in Revelation."[20] As we will see below, the grammar of 3:1 also points toward maintaining this distinction.

In 3:1a John writes, "To the angel of the church in Sardis write: These are the words of him who holds the seven spirits of God and the seven stars." Since Jesus is holding the seven spirits and the seven stars, some have merged the two, but this reading seems unlikely. Once again, we see a close connection to other members of the Trinity: *the Son* holding the seven spirits *of God*. Throughout Revelation there is a distinction between spirits and stars/angels. The grammar of 3:1 lends support. While stars can be tied to angels in Revelation (e.g., 1:16, 20), here spirits and stars both have their own

15. For a recent comprehensive look at the Trinity in Revelation, see Smith, *Trinity in the Book of Revelation*.

16. John Christopher Thomas, "The Spirit in the Book of Revelation," *OHBR* 243–44.

17. De Smidt, "Hermeneutical Perspectives," 42. Smith, *The Trinity in Revelation*, 172, concurs: "The Spirit's continued role in John's vision(s) reveal [*sic*] what was later called inseparable operations—he is of the same divine nature and therefore exercises the same divine power, authority, and will as the Father and Son."

18. Wilson, "Spirit in Revelation," 84–86.

19. Wilson, "Spirit in Revelation," 86.

20. Bauckham, *Theology*, 110. Malcolm Yarnell offers numerous reasons why the seven spirits do not represent angels in *God the Trinity* (Nashville: B&H Academic, 2016), 202–4, 211–17.

definite article and are separated by καί.[21] While the seven stars are said to be "of the seven churches" in 1:20, the seven spirits are said to be "of God" in 3:1; 4:5; 5:6. The link between the Spirit and the Father and Son that began in 1:4 continues. Lee notes that the "of God" phrase implies the unity of the seven spirits with God, conveys a separation between the seven spirits and other heavenly beings such as the seven stars, and denotes a God-like character. The narrator, according to Lee, "attempts to describe the Seven Spirits as the Holy God-like Spirit with the direct expression 'of God.'"[22]

In 4:5 and 5:6, John draws from Zechariah 4 to clarify the connection to the Holy Spirit.[23]

In his throne room vision, John sees the gloriously brilliant God seated on his throne and, in front of the throne, seven blazing lamps (λαμπάς) identified as the seven spirits of God (4:5). In Zechariah's vision, God reassures the prophet that God's plans will be accomplished "'not by might nor by power, but by my Spirit,' says the Lord Almighty" (Zech 4:6). God's power differs markedly from the power of the unholy trinity.[24] As God tells Zechariah, he conquers evil through Spirit-empowered witness, as the seven lamps and two olives trees of Zech 4 symbolize the divine Spirit and the witnessing people of God (cf. Rev 11). In Rev 5:6 the seven eyes (and likely also the seven horns) of the Lamb are "the seven spirits of God sent out into all the earth." The eyes of Yahweh in the Old Testament affirm "not only his ability to see what happens throughout the world, but also his ability to act powerfully wherever he chooses."[25]

Thomas also observes the divine function in 5:6 of being sent into all the earth, a mission that includes divine knowledge.[26] This connects the Lamb with the Holy Spirit in divine partnership (as in 1:4, 3:1, and the seven messages) and reinforces our understanding of "seven spirits" as representing the Holy Spirit—God's empowering presence continuing his prophetic work in this world.

14.3 "In the Spirit"

The phrase "in the Spirit" (ἐν πνεύματι) occurs four times in Revelation:

- 1:10: "On the Lord's Day I was ***in the Spirit***, and I heard behind me a loud voice like a trumpet."

21. Wilson, "Spirit in Revelation," 85, concludes that "Koester's attempt to conflate πνεῦμα and ἄγγελος as a single spiritual entity is highly problematic."

22. Lee, *Dynamic Reading*, 83.

23. See Bauckham, *Theology*, 110–15; Beale, *Revelation*, 189.

24. See Bauckham, *Theology*, 112–15, for a brief but rich discussion of the nature of divine power in contrast to the power of the dragon and his two beasts.

25. Bauckham, *Theology*, 112.

26. Thomas, "Spirit in the Book of Revelation," 244. He adds that the embedded "eyes" of the Lamb imply the Spirit as the recipient of universal worship in 5:8–14.

- 4:1–2: "After this I looked, and there before me was a door standing open in heaven. And the voice I had first heard speaking to me like a trumpet said, 'Come up here, and I will show you what must take place after this.' At once I was ***in the Spirit***, and there before me was a throne in heaven with someone sitting on it."
- 17:3: "Then the angel carried me away ***in the Spirit*** into a wilderness. There I saw a woman sitting on a scarlet beast that was covered with blasphemous names and had seven heads and ten horns."
- 21:10: "And he carried me away ***in the Spirit*** to a mountain great and high, and showed me the Holy City, Jerusalem, coming down out of heaven from God."

There is wide agreement that the expression plays a significant role as a literary/structural marker, resulting in the following narrative units (see Ch. 9):

1:1–8	Prologue
1:9–3:22	John's Introductory Vision and the Messages to the Churches
4:1–16:21	The Heavenly Throne Room Vision and Resulting Judgments
17:1–21:8	The Destruction of Babylon the Great and the Final Victory
21:9–22:5	The New Creation: God's Presence among His People
22:6–21	Epilogue

There is room for minor adjustments even while recognizing these major sections (e.g., 21:1–8 serves as a transition unit, uniting the final victory section with the vision of the new creation). Yet overall, this phrase sheds light on the structure of the book.[27]

There is debate about the actual meaning of the phrase,[28] however, most scholars understand "spirit" as referring to the divine Spirit rather than to John's human spirit.[29] Even those who see a reference to the Holy Spirit have different understandings of John's relationship to the Spirit in this experience. Some see John entering an ecstatic trance (cf. Acts 11:5; 22:17), suggesting that the vision was received as part of an out-of-body experience.[30] In contrast, some deny that the expression has any connection to an ecstatic experience and view it primarily as a literary creation.[31] There are mediating positions between these two extremes.[32]

27. Waddell, *Spirit of the Book of Revelation*, 138–50; Bandy, "Layers of the Apocalypse," 475. Thomas, "Spirit in the Book of Revelation," 244, keenly observes that each occurrence of the phrase locates John in a different place—on Patmos, in heaven, in a wilderness, and on a great mountain, solidifying the importance of place in the book.

28. For a history of interpretation of the phrase, see J. C. De Smidt, "The Holy Spirit in the Book of Revelation—Nomenclature," *Neot* 28 (1994): 233–38.

29. On the latter, see, e.g., Thomas, *Revelation 1–7*, 90, who sees a reference to John's spirit entering into a trance-like experience.

30. Aune, *Revelation 1–5*, 82.

31. Schüssler Fiorenza, *Revelation: Vision of a Just World*, Proclamation Commentaries (Minneapolis: Fortress, 1991), 51.

32. See the insightful excursus "Did John Really See Things?" in deSilva, *Seeing Things John's Way*, 121–24, who rightly argues against this kind of either/or approach.

Jeske takes the phrase as "symbolic code for participation in the community of the Spirit" and emphasizes the Spirit's work in relationship to John's community.[33] This reading stresses an important aspect of John's experience but does not go far enough since John's personal, prophetic relationship to the Spirit is in view here. Others point out the strong connection between the phrase and John's worship context: "I was in the Spirit on the Lord's Day," referring to Sunday, the day of worship (1:10). This highlights John's reception of the apocalypse in a state of worship.[34] While rightly stressing the worship setting, the phrase points beyond John's present activity to an unusual experience with the Spirit that better fits all four occurrences of the phrase.

Most commentators rightly move beyond community participation or liturgical activity to John's personal visionary experience that features a profound involvement with the Spirit, leading to a later conscious shaping of the visionary experience into the literary-theological masterpiece that is the book of Revelation. John's experience of being under the Spirit's control was chiefly a prophetic visionary experience. Being under the Spirit's control on the day of worship was an ecstatic experience, but not strictly trance-like in the sense that John lost all control of his faculties. He was "in the Spirit" as a true prophet, experiencing and later articulating an authentic prophetic visionary message from God (cf. 2 Cor 12:2–3; Acts 16:9). The language is similar to certain Old Testament prophets, chiefly Ezekiel (e.g., Ezek 11:24; 37:1; 43:5; cf. Mic 3:8), and highlights John's equally authoritative prophetic experience.[35] As de Smidt notes, the Spirit lifts the thin veil between this physical world and the unseen spiritual world and displays to John, "in a unique state of personal visionary consciousness, the spiritual world from his place in the physical world."[36] Even then, the focus is not on John's psychological experience so much as his prophetic experience. John has a Spirit-inspired vision followed by a time of personal reflection and literary shaping, drawing on his extensive knowledge of the Old Testament Scriptures (especially the Prophets) to pen the book of Revelation.[37] All this suggests that the Holy Spirit is the prophetic Spirit, speaking to and showing John otherworldly visions to communicate God's truth to his people.

The four occurrences of the phrase "in the Spirit" and the resulting heavenly visions also provide a theological summary of the overall message of Revelation: worship, the Triune God as the center of reality, judgment of Babylon, and the new creation. The Spirit speaks to John first in worship, an anchoring experience introduced in 1:10. After

33. R. L. Jeske, "Spirit and Community in the Johannine Apocalypse," *NTS* 31 (1985): 462–64.

34. Melissa L. Archer, *"I Was in the Spirit on the Lord's Day": A Pentecostal Engagement with Worship in the Apocalypse* (Cleveland, TN: CPT, 2015), 130–31. On the Spirit's role in worship, see Michael Kuykendall, "An Expanded Role for the Spirit in the Book of Revelation," *JETS* 64.3 (2021): 543; Thomas, "Spirit in the Book of Revelation," 246–47; De Smidt, "Hermeneutical Perspectives," 35–37. See also Ch. 17.

35. Bauckham, *Climax of Prophecy*, 154–59; Beale, *Revelation*, 203; Tabb, *All Things New*, 72.

36. De Smidt, "Holy Spirit in the Book of Revelation," 239.

37. deSilva, *Seeing Things John's Way*, 124; Witherington, *Revelation*, 36–38; Bauckham, *Theology*, 116–17.

John hears about the struggling churches in chapters 2–3, he is lifted up to heaven in a second vision to see the center of all reality in chapters 4–5: God seated on his throne and the worthy Lamb who will carry out the divine plan to judge evil, save his people, and restore creation. In chapter 17, the Spirit continues the vision by showing John how God will judge the great prostitute, Babylon. Finally, in 21:10, the Spirit shows John a very different woman/city—the bride of Christ or New Jerusalem, an image that announces the victorious vision of God's plan accomplished.

14.4 What the Spirit Says to the Churches

At or near the end of each of the seven messages in Rev 2–3, the risen Christ says, "Whoever has ears, let them hear (ἀκουσάτω) what the Spirit says (λέγει) to the churches" (2:7, 11, 17, 29; 3:6, 13, 22). Almost half of the references to πνεῦμα in Revelation occur in these seven sayings. In this context, the third person imperative should be taken as a full command rather than as conveying mere permission or toleration, and can be translated "he/she must hear" or "I command him/her to hear."[38] Many scholars see the background as Jesus's exhortation in the Gospels, "Whoever has ears to hear, let them hear" (Matt 11:15; 13:9, 43; Mark 4:9, 23; Luke 8:8; 14:35), a saying that draws on Isa 6:9–10 (cf. Jer 5:21; Ezek 3:27; 12:2) and other prophetic texts where the Lord is warning his people to embrace faithfulness and reject idolatry (e.g., Ezek 3:24–27; 12:2; cf. Jer 5:21)—a context similar to that of the seven churches.[39]

What is most striking is that the seven messages are introduced by the τάδε λέγει formula ("these are the words of him who"), referring to the words of the risen Christ (Rev 2:1, 8, 12, 18; 3:1, 7, 14). Yet, at the end of each message we find the Spirit speaking to the churches. The connection between Christ (Christology) and the Spirit (pneumatology) remains strong throughout the book. Bauckham concludes, "What the Spirit says is what the exalted Christ says. He inspires the prophetic oracles in which the prophet John speaks Christ's words to the churches."[40] Near the center of the seven messages we see Christ holding "the seven spirits of God" or the Holy Spirit (3:1). In 5:6 the seven spirits are identified with the eyes of the Lamb. Also, in 19:10 we see the connection between the testimony of Jesus and the Spirit of the prophecy. Thus, the words of Christ are also the words of the Spirit, and it is through the Spirit that Christ indwells the churches.[41] In many ways, this relationship fulfills Jesus's promise in John 16:12–15 to join with the Spirit in speaking to his people. Yet while the two are inseparable, the exalted Christ and the Spirit are not identical, and their unity maintains

38. Wallace, *Greek Grammar Beyond the Basics*, 486; Mathewson, *Revelation*, 22.

39. Beale and McDonough, "Revelation," 1093.

40. Bauckham, *Theology*, 117.

41. Beale, *Revelation*, 234; Thomas, "Spirit in the Book of Revelation," 253–54, who notes the connection in 1:4–5; 3:1; 5:6; 19:10. Thomas and Macchia, *Revelation*, 92, conclude that "Jesus and the Spirit speak with one voice."

a clear distinction. Throughout Revelation, the Spirit is differentiated from Jesus in a number of ways, and the two should never be conflated (e.g., 11:3–13; 14:13; 22:17).

The Spirit of God speaking the words of Christ to the churches also reinforces the Spirit's prophetic role (cf. 14.5 below). Aune says that this phrase serves as a kind of "prophetic signature" calling the hearer or reader "to hear and obey what has (or will) be proclaimed."[42] The churches now know God's will without question and face the challenge of remaining faithful as the bride and resisting the prostitute's enticements. For the third time the term "hear" appears in the book (cf. 1:3, 10), again stressing the idea of discerning obedience to the words of this prophecy (cf. 3:3).[43]

The prophetic word of comfort or rebuke matches the mixed audience—churches that display faithfulness in some contexts and idolatrous compromise in others. Those churches forsaking their love of Christ while pursuing false teaching, idolatry, immorality, and spiritual self-sufficiency receive the Spirit's prophetic message as warning. In contrast, those who are suffering hardship and persecution due to their faithful discipleship to Jesus hear the Spirit's words of comfort and encouragement. The prophetic hearing formula calls the churches to recognize their true spiritual condition and respond appropriately.

In addition, it is important to note that this prophetic word goes out to the universal church. The number seven suggests a message not limited to seven particular churches in Asia Minor but meant for the whole church. Messages tailored for each church also carry a timeless message for the corporate church of all ages. The Spirit's prophetic word is far reaching indeed, and its aim is to encourage the churches to stay faithful to Christ even during times of tribulation.[44]

14.5 THE PROPHETIC SPIRIT

Here we come to the heart of the Spirit's role in the Apocalypse, that of speaking the words of Jesus to God's people and empowering them to be faithful witnesses. More specifically, the Spirit of prophecy entrusts Christ's words to Christian prophets and through them to the prophetic church who speaks to the world (cf. John 15:26–27). Bauckham observes that the special vocation of the Christian prophets is widened to the general vocation of all believers so that "the Spirit speaks through the prophets to the churches and through the churches to the world."[45] As we have seen already and will see again in a closer look at key passages below, the Spirit plays a crucial role in the prophecy that becomes the book of Revelation. The Spirit who spoke to and through Old Testament prophets (e.g., Isa 61:1; 1 Pet 1:11–12) now speaks to and through John: "John was writing what he understood

42. Aune, *Revelation 1–5*, 150.

43. Thomas and Macchia, *Revelation*, 93.

44. Smalley, *Revelation*, 63–64.

45. Bauckham, *Climax of Prophecy*, 162.

to be a work of prophetic scripture, the climax of prophetic revelation, which gathered up the prophetic meaning of the Old Testament scriptures and disclosed the way in which it was being and was to be fulfilled in the last days."[46] In this section we will focus our attention on three key texts in Revelation: 11:3–10; 19:10; and 22:6.

In chapter 11 the Spirit works his prophetic ministry in and through the two witnesses. To begin with, we are taking the image of the lampstands or menorahs to represent a corporate entity—the whole people of God in their Spirit-empowered prophetic mission.[47] The witnesses are described as "'the two olive trees' and the two lampstands" that "'stand before the Lord of the earth'" (11:4). Here we have an allusion to Zech 4, where the prophet sees a gold lampstand with seven lamps and two olive trees, whom the angel connects with the Spirit of the Lord God Almighty (Zech 4:6). Zechariah is later told of "seven eyes of the Lord that range throughout the earth" (4:10). John links the seven lamps with the seven eyes of the Lord, which are the Spirit (cf. Rev 5:6). Bauckham notes that Zech 4 "lies behind not only the four references to the seven Spirits but also the description of the two witnesses in 11:4" and serves as "the key Old Testament passage for John's understanding of the role of the Spirit in the divine activity in the world."[48]

Overall, John adapts Zech 4 to emphasize the Spirit's central role in the prophetic ministry of the church. The witnesses stand "before the Lord" (Rev 11:4), the same location as the Spirit himself (1:4; 4:5; cf. 22:1). Jesus walks among and speaks prophetically to the seven churches, yet it is the prophetic words of the Spirit that go out to the churches (chs. 2–3). We also see the authority and power granted by the Spirit to the two witnesses, echoing the power-packed ministries of Elijah and Moses (cf. 11:6). We find a subtle allusion to the Spirit in the description of the place where the witnesses are martyred in 11:7–8: "Now when they have finished their testimony, the beast that comes up from the Abyss will attack them and overpower and kill them. Their bodies will lie in the public square of the great city—which is figuratively [πνευματικῶς] called Sodom and Egypt—where also their Lord was crucified." While the adverb is often translated "figuratively" or "symbolically," John seems to be making the point that it is the Spirit who provides discernment for the church to see the antichristian powers for what they are: Sodom, a place of moral corruption, and Egypt, the location of slavery and oppression.[49] Waddell sees the prophetic perspective alluded to in 11:8 as crucial

46. Bauckham, *Climax of Prophecy*, xi.

47. See Dalrymple, *Revelation and the Two Witnesses*, 34–46; Bauckham, *Climax of Prophecy*, 273–74; Aune, *Revelation 6–16*, 602–3; Beale, *Revelation*, 572–75; Keener, *Revelation*, 291–92; Smalley, *Revelation*, 275, and many others.

48. Bauckham, *Theology*, 110.

49. John Christopher Thomas, "Revelation," in *A Biblical Theology of the Holy Spirit* ed. Trevor J. Burke and Keith Warrington (Eugene, OR: Cascade, 2014), 262; Melissa Archer and Robby Waddell, "The Spirit in John's Apocalypse: Vision, Prophecy, Discernment," *Pneuma* 43 (2021): 565; David R. Johnson, *Pneumatic Discernment in the Apocalypse: An Intertextual and Pentecostal Exploration* 18 (Cleveland, TN: CPT, 2018), 348–92; Bauckham, *Climax of Prophecy*, 169; "πνευματικῶς," BDAG 837, §1: "pert. to transcendent influence, *spiritually, in a spiritual manner, in a manner caused by or filled with the Spirit*" (italics original).

to the entire book: "In the center of the Apocalypse, John places the story of the two witnesses, and in the center of this brief narrative, John describes the spiritual insight of the church discerning the reality of the great city" with the help of the Spirit.[50] As we will see below, the Spirit is also responsible for resurrecting the witnesses following their martyrdom (11:11—"the Spirit of life from God" [πνεῦμα ζωῆς ἐκ τοῦ θεοῦ]). Lastly, the faithful witness of God's people is set in contrast to the deadly deception of the false prophet in Rev 13.

As a result, Rev 11 should be seen as a story of paradigmatic prophetic witness anchored in the Old Testament. It reminds God's people that true witness cannot be separated from the teachings of Jesus and is empowered by the Spirit in the face of difficult circumstances where false prophets abound. The story calls the witnesses to faithfulness even unto death with the promise of vindication and life through resurrection.[51]

Revelation 19:10 also powerfully highlights the prophetic Spirit. After receiving visions in the Spirit, John falls down to worship the revealing angel but is quickly rebuked: "Don't do that! I am a fellow servant with you and with your brothers and sisters who hold to the testimony of Jesus. Worship God! For it is the Spirit of prophecy who bears testimony to Jesus (ἡ γὰρ μαρτυρία Ἰησοῦ ἐστιν τὸ πνεῦμα τῆς προφητείας)." There is disagreement about whether "testimony of Jesus" should be taken as an objective (about Jesus) or subjective (from Jesus) genitive. An objective genitive makes sense because (1) on several occasions "the testimony of Jesus" parallels "the Word of God" as the content of the prophetic witness (1:2, 9; 20:4; cf. 1:1; 12:17)[52] and (2) the saints are often portrayed as having the testimony or testifying about Jesus (6:9; 11:7; 12:11; 17:6).[53] Yet, a subjective genitive cannot be ruled out since Jesus himself is "the faithful witness" (1:5; 3:14; 22:20) and "the witness Jesus bore [subjective genitive] is the content of Spirit-inspired prophecy" and "therefore also the content of John's own prophecy, the Apocalypse itself."[54] Since both the objective and subjective genitives have strong support and since they do not contradict but rather complement one another, a plenary genitive is likely in view here.[55]

Mark Wilson makes a good case for translating 19:10 as follows: "For the testimony of Jesus is the Spirit of the prophecy."[56] The expression "of prophecy" is used seven times in Revelation (1:3; 11:6; 19:10; 22:7, 10, 18, 19).[57] On five occasions it modifies "word"

50. Waddell, *Spirit of the Book of Revelation*, 182.

51. Bauckham, *Climax of Prophecy*, 168–73.

52. See Dixon, *Testimony of the Exalted Jesus*, 163, who takes ἡ μαρτυρία Ἰησοῦ to refer to the prophetic message of the book of Revelation.

53. Mathewson, *Revelation*, 263.

54. Bauckham, *Climax of Prophecy*, 161; Tabb, *All Things New*, 76.

55. John Christopher Thomas, "Revelation," 249; Wallace, *Greek Grammar Beyond the Basics*, 120; Cf. "the revelation of Jesus Christ" in Rev 1:1).

56. Mark Wilson, "Revelation," 355. Also, many other commentators, including Koester, *Revelation*, 732; Keener, *Revelation*, 452; Smalley, *Revelation*, 487; Tabb, *All Things New*, 77–79.

57. The term "prophet" (προφήτης) is used in 10:7; 11:10, 18; 16:6; 18:20, 24; 22:6, 9.

or "book," with the remaining two modifying "day" or "time" (11:6) and "Spirit" (19:10). This supports Wilson's translation, especially because of the emphasis on the "true words of God" in the immediate context (19:9; cf. 1:2, 9; 6:9; 20:4).[58] The idea is that "the testimony that Jesus is speaking to the churches is the same message that the Holy Spirit is speaking through the rest of the prophecy in Revelation."[59] Rather than 19:10 referring to prophecy in general, the verse likely reaffirms the Holy Spirit's inspiration of the prophecy (i.e., the Apocalypse).[60] And this Spirit-inspired prophecy takes us back to the angel's words: "Worship God!" (cf. 22:9), what Bauckham calls "the central theme of all prophecy." He continues, "To distinguish the one true God and his righteousness from idolatry and its evils is the theme of true prophecy."[61] Thus, the Spirit is saying through the testimony of Jesus and the Word of God to John that all true, God-given prophecy leads us to authentic God-centered worship.

The final key text is 22:6, where we find a reference to "the Lord, the God who inspires the prophets" or, more literally, "the Lord, the God of the S/spirits (πνευμάτων) of the prophets" (cf. 1:1). If πνευμάτων refers to human spirits, it could include all Christians as a prophetic people or be limited to only those holding prophetic office. Beale argues that the bracketing of this phrase by allusions to Dan 2 makes a reference to a special circle of prophets more likely.[62] Yet even if a circle of prophets is in view in the use of "prophets," the term "servants" later in the verse surely points to the whole people of God due to its use elsewhere in the book (e.g., 2:20; 7:3; 11:18; 19:5; 22:3).[63]

On the other hand, some understand πνευμάτων to refer to the Holy Spirit rather than to human spirits. Leithart concludes that 22:6 "refers not to the human spirits of the prophets, over which God is indeed the Lord, but to the Spirit-Breath of God whose expirations inspire prophets (cf. Num. 11:29; 1 Sam. 10:10; Neh. 9:30; 1 Cor. 14:32)."[64] The use of the plural is not a hindrance to this view since the plural does occur for the Spirit several times earlier (1:4; 4:5; 5:6). The parallel with the trinitarian statement in Rev 1 leads Leithart to suggest that "22:6 is another subtle Trinitarian allusion."[65]

Yet even if we conclude that the referent is human spirits as do most commentators,

58. Lee, *Dynamic Reading*, 84.

59. Wilson, "Spirit in Revelation," 89.

60. Some Pentecostal scholars would see this as evidence for the "prophethood of all believers," the view that each member of the community is anointed by the Spirit in the same way that John was anointed. See Waddell, *Spirit of the Book of Revelation*, 193–94; John Christopher Thomas, "Revelation," 250. Other scholars take the expression to refer to the Spirit giving the gift of prophecy (i.e., proclamation or bearing witness), while they stop short of saying that believers today can speak words having the same authority as inspired Scripture. See, e.g., Boring, *Revelation*, 142; Kuykendall, "Expanded Role for the Spirit," 543; likely Keener, *Revelation*, 452, who writes: "The prophetic Spirit empowers those who speak the message about Christ (19:10; cf. Acts 1:8; 2:17–18; 1 Cor 12:3); all believers are thus potential prophets, anointed with God's Spirit to speak his message in his place."

61. Bauckham, *Theology*, 121; also Koester, *Revelation*, 740; Tabb, *All Things New*, 78–80.

62. Beale, *Revelation*, 1125.

63. Bauckham, *Climax of Prophecy*, 85–86.

64. Leithart, *Revelation*, 416.

65. Leithart, *Revelation*, 416.

Revelation has already demonstrated a "tight connection between the seven Spirits of God (Rev 1:4; 4:5; 5:6) and the prophetic activity of the Spirit-anointed community in the world."[66] There seems to be a partnership between the Holy Spirit and the human spirits of the prophets and indeed all the saints in the prophetic task. Koester notes that "the prophet's spirit is understood to be the vehicle for God's Spirit, which inspires prophecy (Joel 2:28; Luke 1:67; Acts 11:27–28)."[67] Fanning concurs: "As often true in biblical usage, reference to the human 'spirit' or 'spirits' reflects the work of God's 'Spirit' in the background (BDAG 833; e.g., Mark 8:12; John 4:23; Acts 17:16; 1 Cor 4:21; Gal 6:1)."[68] The primary theological point in 22:6 is that the Spirit remains integrally involved in advancing the prophetic witness of the Triune God in the world.

14.6 The Spirit Speaks

On two occasions the Spirit "speaks" briefly but directly, both times affirming a heavenly promise and longing for either Christ to return or for people to follow Christ—14:13; 22:17. In the first instance, a blessing—the second of seven beatitudes in the book—is pronounced by a heavenly voice on believers who remain faithful even unto death, and the blessing is joined by the Spirit's affirmative "Yes." The Spirit explains, "They will rest from their labor, for their deeds will follow them" (14:13). Following the call for God's people to endure faithfully (14:12) and in contrast to the restlessness of those who worship the beast (14:11), Christ-followers are assured they will one day experience eternal rest in God's presence (cf. 6:9–11; Dan 12:13). The faithful demonstrate their inward faith through their outward deeds (cf. Rev 2:23; 22:12). The Spirit speaks to encourage God's people to persevere and endure and to remind them of the heavenly reward that awaits them.

In the second instance, both the Spirit and the bride say, "Come!" (22:17)—to be understood either as the first of four invitations to respond positively to Jesus or as a plea urging Christ to return.[69] The exhortation to respond positively could be an evangelistic plea to unbelievers or an exhortation calling believers to respond to the revelation. Both the exhortation to respond in faith and the call for Christ to return are theological truths found throughout the book; but if John is echoing Isa 55:1 here (cf. John 6:35; 7:37) and in Rev 21:6, then 22:17 probably reflects a call to loyalty

66. Thomas and Macchia, *Revelation*, 391.

67. Koester, *Revelation*, 838. The phrase "God of the spirits" is likely a genitive of subordination meaning the God who rules over or influences the spirits of the prophets by means of his own Spirit (cf. Num 27:16). See Mathewson, *Revelation*, 303; cf. F. F. Bruce, "The Spirit in the Apocalypse," in *Christ and the Spirit in the New Testament: In Honour of Charles Francis Digby Moule*, ed. Barnabas Lindars and Stephen S. Smalley (Cambridge: Cambridge University Press, 1973), 339; Smalley, *Revelation*, 567.

68. Fanning, *Revelation*, 557n18.

69. On the former reading, see, e.g., see Mounce, *Revelation*, 409; Lee, *Dynamic Reading*, 90. On the latter, see Bauckham, *Climax of Prophecy*, 160; Smalley, *Revelation*, 577; Koester, *Revelation*, 844.

to Christ. The bride as the eschatological people of God joins the Spirit's call for the church in its present circumstance to persevere in faith.[70] Beale connects the dots here:

> Not all in the visible church can say "come," but only those who "have ears to hear" the Spirit's exhortation. The command to "come" thus includes a paraphrase of the repeated formulaic exhortations in the seven letters (likewise 13:9). The Spirit's admonitions do not penetrate the spiritual ears of false church members, but such admonitions do serve to shock genuine members out of the stupor from which the entire visible church suffers.[71]

The Spirit speaks, then, as the eschatological Spirit, uniting the much-anticipated parousia with the urgent call for the church to become the bride she is intended to be. The Spirit is at work now forming the church into the age-to-come people of God.

14.7 The Spirit of Life

John's vision of the two witnesses in Rev 11 includes a subtle reference to the Holy Spirit in verse 11—the "breath of life from God" (πνεῦμα ζωῆς ἐκ τοῦ θεοῦ).[72] As the vision unfolds, the beast kills the two witnesses, identified in 11:4 as the "lampstands" (symbolizing the church in 1:20),[73] but death is not their ultimate fate. God manifests his powerful presence through resurrection as God's Spirit raises the witnesses to life and calls them to heaven. God reverses the death verdict of the beast through resurrection life from the Spirit. Osborne is probably correct here when noting that πνεῦμα ζωῆς carries a double meaning—the life-giving Holy Spirit who gives resurrection life.[74] The use of πνεῦμα, the qualifiers "of life" and "from God," and the Old Testament connections support taking the "breath of life from God" as a reference to the life-giving Holy Spirit. We also see other examples in John's writings where the Spirit serves as "the agent through whom God imparts life to others" (e.g., John 3:3, 5; 6:63; 20:23).[75]

The reference to the Spirit here recalls the creation story where God breathes the "breath of life" (πνοὴν ζωῆς) into the man of dust so that the man becomes a living

70. Tabb, *All Things New*, 84; Bauckham, *Climax of Prophecy*, 167.

71. Beale, *Revelation*, 1148.

72. The phrase "of life" is used seventeen times in Revelation: tree of life (2:7; 22:2, 14, 19), water of life (7:17; 21:6; 22:1, 17), book of life (3:5; 13:8; 17:8; 20:12, 15; 21:27), crown of life (2:10), living things in the sea (16:3), and breath of life (11:11).

73. On a corporate interpretation of the two witnesses, see Tabb, *All Things New*, 95–97.

74. Osborne, *Revelation*, 430. See also Keener, *Revelation*, 296; Lee, *Dynamic Reading*, 72; Fee, *Revelation*, 154; Kuykendall, "Expanded Role for the Spirit," 536. The parallel phrase τοῦ πνεύματος τῆς ζωῆς in Rom 8:2 should be translated "the Spirit who gives life" or "the Spirit of life" or "the life-giving Spirit" (NIV, CSB, NET, ESV, NRSVue).

75. Marianne Meye Thompson, "The Breath of Life: John 20:22–23 Once More," in Graham N. Stanton, Bruce W. Longenecker & Stephen C. Barton, eds., *The Holy Spirit and Christian Origins: Essays in Honor of James D. G. Dunn* (Grand Rapids: Eerdmans, 2004), 77.

being (Gen 2:7; cf. Wis 15:11). But we find an even stronger connection to the valley of dry bones episode in Ezek 37, signifying the restoration of Israel after exile: "Behold, I am bringing into you a spirit of life (πνεῦμα ζωῆς). . . . And the breath came into them (καὶ εἰσῆλθεν εἰς αὐτοὺς τὸ πνεῦμα) and they lived and stood upon their feet, a very great gathering" (Ezek 37:5, 10 LXX).[76] Although the death of Israel and the death of the two witnesses do not parallel each other, God's response of resurrection by his Spirit for a whole community of faith certainly does.

This entire episode reminds hearers that the Holy Spirit is the one who brings life. Since the two witnesses represent the church, the Spirit brings new life initially to believers, sustains life through his indwelling presence, empowers the church for witness in this hostile world, and will one day raise them to eternal life.[77] In the Revelation context, the final vindication of believers through resurrection is uppermost in view. The work of the Spirit extends beyond death and guarantees a future resurrection for the people of God.

14.8 Spirit Imagery in Revelation

The theology of the Holy Spirit in Revelation cannot be limited to the uses of the term πνεῦμα. We must also consider imagery denoting the Spirit to get a holistic understanding on the Spirit's role in the book. Briefly we touch on several such images in this section: blazing lamps of fire; smoke, glory, and light; water of life; and other Spirit imagery (numerical symbolism, the phrase "in front of / before the throne," and the "seal of the living God"). These images reinforce rather than replace our theology of the Spirit drawn from the more explicit references above.

14.8.1 Blazing Lamps of Fire

In 4:5 we read about lightning and thunder coming from the throne and about seven lamps or torches blazing (ἑπτὰ λαμπάδες πυρὸς καιόμεναι) in front of the throne. These seven blazing lamps are then identified as the "seven spirits of God." The language itself—seven, lamps of fire, blazing— conveys the reality of divine presence.[78] We previously noted the connection to the Spirit in Zech 4 where it says the Spirit's power will rebuild God's temple (see 14.2 above). We are also reminded of the seven-branched lampstand that stands in God's presence in the most holy place (Exod 25:31–40; 37:17–24).[79] Along with conveying God's presence, the "blazing

76. The translation is that of J. Noel Hubler, trans., "Iezekiel," in *A New English Translation of the Septuagint (Primary Texts)*, eds. Albert Pietersma and Benjamin G. Wright (New York; Oxford: Oxford University Press, 2007), 975.

77. Kuykendall, "Expanded Role for the Spirit," 542; Duvall and Hays, *God's Relational Presence*, 314.

78. See Lee, *Dynamic Reading*, 99–102, for more on the significance of "fire" in Revelation.

79. See the discussion of lampstands in the tabernacle, Solomon's Temple, Zerubbabel's Temple, and Herod's Temple in Robert A. Briggs, *Jewish Temple Imagery in the Book of Revelation*, StBL 10 (New York: Peter Lang, 1999), 55–66.

lamps are symbols of divine power and majesty and of judgment."[80] The Spirit in Revelation is imaged as God's holy, personal presence who mightily carries out God's purposes in this world.

14.8.2 Smoke, Glory, and Light

The image of "smoke" (καπνός) is normally used in Revelation to symbolize divine judgment (8:4; 9:2 [2x], 3, 17, 18; 14:11; 18:9, 18; 19:3). The lone exception is 15:8 where is it used positively: "the temple was filled with smoke from the glory of God and from his power" (cf. Isa 6:4). This latter instance recalls Israel's tabernacle and temple experience of the glorious presence of God encountered through smoke or, frequently, a cloud.[81] Osborne notes that "often in the OT smoke that signified the Shekinah glory of God made the temple too sacred to enter (Exod 40:35; 1 Kgs 8:11; 2 Chr 7:2)."[82] The visible evidence of God's glorious presence (i.e., smoke or cloud) in Rev 15:8 is most likely a manifestation of the Holy Spirit.[83]

We also see the Spirit represented in Revelation through the combination of glory and light. The "glory" word group occurs nineteen times in Revelation, with a semantic range of "praise" (1:6; 4:9, 11; 5:12, 13; 7:12; 14:7; 15:4; 18:7; 19:1, 7), "recognition" or "acknowledgment" (11:13; 16:9), "splendor" or "honor" (21:24, 26), and "glorious presence" (15:8; 18:1; 21:11, 23). Along with 15:8 being a possible allusion to the Spirit, the images of glory and light appear in the description of the new Jerusalem in Rev 21–22. Mounce concludes, "In apocalyptic literature the glory of God is a designation for his presence (Ezek 43:5)."[84] The reader frequently encounters terms such as "shine," "glory," "brilliance," "pure," and "clear," terms that reflect God's glorious presence (21:11). John says he did not see a temple in the heavenly city "because the Lord God Almighty and the Lamb are its temple" (21:22). The city does not need the sun or moon for "the glory of God gives it light, and the Lamb is its lamp" (21:23). New creation light comes from the Triune God: the glory of God provides light and the Lamb serves as the lamp, with glory and light imagery again reflecting the Spirit's presence. After describing the "river of the water of life," another likely symbol for the Spirit in 22:1–2 (see below), John again mentions light:

80. Kuykendall, "Expanded Role for the Spirit," 537.

81. Wilson, "Spirit in Revelation," 92–95, explores this rich Old Testament background of cloud, smoke, and glory. He also argues (pp. 89–92) that the image of the cloud in Rev 14:14–16 represents the Holy Spirit, but this seems unlikely. More probably the "cloud" image in this context represents Christ's power and majesty.

82. Osborne, *Revelation*, 574.

83. Wilson, "Spirit in Revelation," 94. Smalley, *Revelation*, 392, says that smoke is a "theophanic image, associated with the self-disclosure of God in several Old Testament accounts" (e.g., Exod 19:16–18; 40:34–35; Lev 16:12–13; 2 Chr 5:13–14; 7:1–2; Isa 6:1–4; Ezek 10:1–5). He also writes that "the phrase 'the glory of God (the Lord)' is often an Old Testament circumlocution for the presence of God" (e.g., Exod 24:16–18; Num 14:10; Ezek 11:23).

84. Mounce, *The Book of Revelation*, 390.

"There will be no more night. They will not need the light of a lamp or the light of the sun, for the Lord God will give them light" (22:5).[85]

14.8.3 Water of Life[86]

John often uses water as a symbol of the Spirit in his writings (e.g., John 4:4–26; 7:37–39). In Revelation, while he does use water imagery negatively (e.g., 8:10–11; 11:6; 12:15; 16:4–5, 12), he sometimes uses it positively to connote the Spirit. Four key passages deserve a closer look. First, we read in 7:17 that "the Lamb at the center of the throne will be their shepherd; 'he will lead them to springs of living water.' 'And God will wipe away every tear from their eyes.'" This comes at the end of the vision portraying God's people celebrating in heaven following the tribulation. Those who come through the great tribulation will be sheltered and comforted in God's presence (7:14–15). The combination of Lamb, God, and springs of living water seems like another subtle trinitarian reference. John often uses the theme of water and "living water" in his Gospel as a symbol of the life and revelation that comes through the Spirit (e.g., John 4:10–11, 13–14; 7:37–39; cf. Isa 49:10).[87] That also seems to be the case here.

Second, in the opening vision of the new creation of Rev 21:1–8, we find another indirect trinitarian reference: "Alpha and Omega" and "Beginning and the End" depict both the Father and the Son (1:8; 21:6; 22:13), both are associated with the throne (3:21; 22:1, 3), and the Spirit is represented through the image of the water of life (21:6). Again, Seung-In Song says the phrases "living water" and "water of life" function as "technical terms for referring to the Spirit throughout the Johannine literature."[88]

In 22:17, our third key text, we have a close parallel to the two previous passages, especially 21:6. Here the water of life constitutes the gift of eternal life that comes by means of the Holy Spirit: "The Spirit and the bride say, 'Come!' And let the one who hears say, 'Come!' Let the one who is thirsty come; and let the one who wishes take the free gift of the water of life." God's glorious presence, the Holy Spirit himself and the life he gives, is the gift of the water of life (cf. John 4:10–24; 7:37–39).[89]

In the final passage of Rev 22:1–5, the climactic vision of the new creation utilizes garden imagery, beginning with "the river of the water of life, as clear as crystal, flowing

85. There are also "subtle clues that the Holy Spirit joins the Father and Son in showering God's people with his triune presence, clues such as God, the Lamb, and light in 21:23; God, the Lamb, and the water of life in 22:1; and God, the Lamb, and his name in 22:3–4. If this is indeed the case, then references to the Triune God desiring to be present with his people bookend the entire Apocalypse (see 1:4–5)" (Duvall and Hays, *God's Relational Presence*, 321).

86. For more on water as an image of the Spirit in Revelation and John's Gospel, see Seung-In Song, *Water as an Image of the Spirit in the Johannine Literature*, StBL 171 (New York: Peter Lang, 2019); Mark Wilson, "The Water of Life: Three Explorations into Water Imagery in Revelation and the Fourth Gospel," *Scriptura* 118 (2019:1), 1–17; Wai-yee Ng, *Water Symbolism in John: An Eschatological Interpretation*, SBL 15 (New York: Peter Lang, 2001); and Craig R. Koester, *Symbolism in the Fourth Gospel: Meaning, Mystery, Community* (Minneapolis: Fortress, 1995).

87. Osborne, *Revelation*, 332; Koester, *Revelation*, 423; Thomas and Macchia, *Revelation*, 174.

88. Song, *Water as an Image of the Spirit*, 146–47.

89. Thomas and Macchia, *Revelation*, 498.

from the throne of God and of the Lamb" (22:1). The imagery draws on Ezek 47 as well as the water of life symbolism already noted in John's Gospel. With these connections in mind, Bruce concludes that "the water to be had without price in Rev. 21:6b and 22:17b may be identified with the Spirit—but if so, it is now the Spirit of life, not the Spirit of prophecy that is in view."[90]

Although Revelation is not focused on inner-trinitarian relations, 22:1 does offer an "early picture of the later Christian confession that the Spirit proceeds from the Father and the Son."[91] These four texts and their intertextual relationship to John's Gospel supply a predominantly eschatological metaphor in Revelation, as Wilson observes, featuring the Spirit as "the eternal life-source" in the new creation.[92]

14.8.4 Other Possible Spirit Imagery

Revelation points to the Spirit in several more subtle ways. These images are not enough to sustain a robust theology of the Spirit on their own, but added to the more explicit imagery, they reaffirm the Spirit's dynamic role in the book. To begin with, we note the importance of numerical symbolism in connection with the Spirit's role.[93] The number "two" signifies "completeness and is often connected to a valid testimony and effectual witness (Num 35:30; Deut 17:6; 19:15; Matt 18:16; Heb 10:28)."[94] As we have already seen (see 14.5), the Spirit plays a crucial role in empowering God's people for witness (Rev 11). The number "four" is connected to the created world, especially highlighting universality. Already noted, in Revelation the Spirit (including its person and work) is sometimes linked to the number four: four references to "the seven spirits" (1:4; 3:1; 4:5; 5:6), four occurrences of the phrase "in the Spirit" (1:10; 4:2; 17:3; 21:10), and four invitations to respond positively to the Spirit's invitation (22:17). Of course, the number seven is the number most directly related to the Spirit, with seven symbolizing fullness and sometimes perfection, imagery fitting for the Spirit.[95] At times, these numbers are also combined to highlight the Spirit—the phrase "the Spirit" occurring fourteen (7 × 2) times (1:10; 2:7, 11, 17, 29; 3:6, 13, 22; 4:2; 14:13; 17:3; 19:10; 21:10; 22:17),[96] and four references to "the seven spirits" (7 × 4). Numerical symbolism illuminates the Spirit who empowers faithful witness throughout the world.

The Spirit's location "before the throne" or "in front of the throne" also reinforces

90. Bruce, "Spirit in the Apocalypse," 343. Yet both life and prophetic revelation flow from the same Spirit.

91. Smith, *Trinity in Revelation*, 155; Beale, *Revelation*, 1104; George T. Montague, *Holy Spirit: Growth of a Biblical Tradition* (Peabody, MA: Hendrickson, 1976), 331; Mangina, *Revelation*, 246, who notes that "the verb for 'flowing' in 22:1 is *ekporeuomenon*, the same word used in the Nicene-Constantinopolitan Creed to denote the Spirit's procession 'from the Father.'"

92. Wilson, "Water of Life," 7.

93. See Kuykendall, "Expanded Role for the Spirit," 528–30. On the use of numbers and colors in Revelation, see Kuykendall, *Lions, Locusts, and the Lamb*, 273–99.

94. Kuykendall, "Expanded Role for the Spirit," 528.

95. Kuykendall, "Expanded Role for the Spirit," 528–29, observes that "seven" (ἑπτά) occurs fifty-five times in Revelation (63% of its uses in the NT) and thirty different words occur seven times.

96. Although there are more than twenty references to the Spirit using πνεῦμα (1:4; 3:1; 4:5; 5:6; 11:11; 22:6; cf. 11:8), only the fourteen are translated "the Spirit."

his sustaining presence on behalf of God's people. God himself is seated on the throne (e.g., 4:2; 19:4) and Jesus, the Lamb, shares God's throne at times but also is seen to take the scroll from him who sits on the throne (e.g., 5:6–7; 22:1, 3). But the Spirit's "location" is "before the throne" or "in front of the throne" (ἐνώπιον τοῦ θρόνου), an expression used ten times in Revelation: two references to things (the golden altar [8:3] and the sea of glass [4:6]), two references to angels (4:10; 7:11), three references to God's people (7:9, 15; 14:3), one to the dead preparing for judgment (20:12) and two allusions to the Holy Spirit:

- 1:4: "John, To the seven churches in the province of Asia: Grace and peace to you from him who is, and who was, and who is to come, and from the seven spirits before his throne."
- 4:5: "From the throne came flashes of lightning, rumblings and peals of thunder. In front of the throne, seven lamps were blazing. These are the seven spirits of God."

The repetition of the Spirit's location before the throne indicates his primary role of making God's presence known in the world especially by empowering the church to bear witness to Jesus.[97] In 5:6 the Lamb has seven horns and seven eyes, which are the seven spirits (or sevenfold Spirit) of God "sent out into all the earth." In the Old Testament, the eyes of Yahweh often represent God's ability to see and act mightily throughout the world (cf. 2 Chr 16:7–9; Zech 4:10). Jesus had already told his followers that the Holy Spirit would be sent by the Father and the Son to carry out their mission in the world (see John 14:26; 15:26; 16:7). Interestingly, the great multitude (Rev 7:9, 15) and the 144,000 (14:3) are also located before the throne, supporting the idea that the Spirit's main role is to work in and through God's people in the world. God on his throne shelters them in his presence (7:15), the Lamb at the center of the throne shepherds them (7:17) and leads them to springs of living water (7:17; see 14.8.3).

In 14:1–5 we read of the 144,000 (a number representing all true followers of Jesus) standing with Jesus on Mount Zion with his name and his Father's name on their foreheads (14:1). They sing a new song before the throne and are described as faithful, devoted, truthful, and blameless, along with being portrayed as those "purchased from among mankind and offered as firstfruits to God and the Lamb," key concepts that are used elsewhere in the New Testament in connection with the Spirit (financial language similar to the deposit or down payment idea in 2 Cor 1:22; 5:5; Eph 1:14, and firstfruits as in Rom 8:23; 2 Thess 2:13). Interestingly, we also find another water image in this context (14:2: "the roar of rushing waters"). In all, "the Spirit is God's

97. Lee, *Dynamic Reading*, 112–13.

'before-the-throne' Shekinah presence" empowering God's people for witness and sheltering them in their pilgrimage to the new creation.[98]

Another possible way the Holy Spirit appears in Revelation relates to the "seal of the living God" (7:2, 3, 4, 5, 8; 9:4).[99] God's seal (σφραγίς) stands in contrast to the "mark of the beast." Both marks indicate ownership since they are placed on a person's forehead (cf. 7:3; 9:4 with 13:16; 14:9; 20:4) and are linked to the names of either God and the Lamb or the beast (cf. 7:3; 22:4 with 13:17; 14:11; 15:2). In addition to ownership, the seal signifies spiritual protection (see Ezek 9 where God marks the faithful for protection from divine judgment). Similarly, in Revelation only those who are marked with the seal of the living God can withstand God's coming wrath (e.g., Rev 6:17–7:4; 9:3–4). The seal does not exempt believers from physical persecution or suffering but does protect them from spiritual defeat and enables them to remain loyal to Christ. Those who are not sealed, on the other hand, will be deceived by evil forces and will suffer God's wrath (13:7–8; 14:9–11).

The only explicit identification of the seal comes in 14:1: "Then I looked, and there before me was the Lamb, standing on Mount Zion, and with him 144,000 who had his name and his Father's name written on their foreheads." More specifically, the apostle Paul equates God's seal with the Holy Spirit, and this may be what John has in mind here also (2 Cor 1:22; Eph 1:13; 4:30).[100] Beale draws a similar conclusion:

> In the light of the broader theology of the NT, the "seal" may best be identified with the Holy Spirit, since the seal primarily connotes a guarantee of spiritual protection (cf. a similar function of "seal" as the Holy Spirit in 2 Cor. 1:22, Eph. 1:13 and 4:30). However, John never explicitly states this.[101]

God's seal indicates an authentic relationship to God and brings assurance that God will protect his people spiritually even though they will suffer persecution.

14.9 CONCLUSION

Our investigation of the Spirit's role has demonstrated that while the term "Holy Spirit" does not occur in Revelation, the Spirit appears throughout in a variety of ways and plays an absolutely crucial role in the book. To begin with, the Spirit is viewed as the third member of the Trinity in the closest possible relationship with the Father and the

98. Duvall, *Heart of Revelation*, 80.

99. See Duvall, *Revelation*, 114; Beale, *Revelation*, 409–12.

100. If the term "seal" is closely tied to the term "name" and name is equivalent to person, then it is hard to draw a strong distinction between God and the Lamb's name/person inscribed on the believer and the Spirit's protective indwelling of the believer. You come to much the same reality using complementary language. Both the seal and the name are placed on a person's forehead (7:3; 9:4; 14:1; 22:4).

101. Beale, *Revelation*, 415. Also, Smalley, *Revelation*, 355.

Son, rather than simply being an extended attribute or even an exalted angel. We see this perhaps most clearly in several subtle Trinitarian references (1:4; 7:15–17; 21:1–8; 22:6, 16–19) and in the Spirit's partnership with the Lamb in speaking to the seven churches (Rev 2–3).

The Spirit is directly involved in the world, evidenced by his position "before the throne," a phrase that points to the place where God's might and power are made known. God accomplishes his will in this world through the Spirit, present in all his fullness (Zech 4:6). This pneumatic work also takes place in partnership with Christ, as the work of the Spirit and the work of the Lamb are inseparably connected. What the Spirit says, Christ says, and through the Spirit Christ indwells believers. The Spirit inspires the prophecy that is the book of Revelation.

The Spirit's prophetic role has three emphases: (1) to confront the church and the world with the Word of God and the testimony of Jesus and force a choice between the Lamb and the beast,[102] (2) to encourage the saints to stay faithful to Christ during times of tribulation, and (3) to empower God's people to share in the prophetic task of bearing witness to Jesus. The Spirit of prophecy entrusts Christ's words to Christian prophets and through them to the prophetic church who speaks to the world (cf. John 15:26–27). Ultimately, all true, God-given prophecy leads us to authentic, God-centered worship.[103]

Finally, the eschatological Spirit not only encourages and empowers God's people to bear witness and endure, but also reminds them of the heavenly rewards that await them. As the Spirit of life (Rev 11:11), his work extends beyond death to make resurrection life in the new creation a reality for God's people. He is the "responsive Spirit," calling the hearers to come drink of the water of eternal life (22:17; cf. 21:6), knowing that many will do so and find their thirst quenched by Christ, while others will refuse to drink and thus incur judgment.[104] For those who come to Christ, they find in the Spirit God's glorious, comforting, protective presence to indwell them and guide them to the heavenly city.

102. Bauckham, *Theology*, 123–25; Tabb, *All Things New*, 84–85.

103. Bauckham, *Theology*, 121, who says that worship of the one, true God is "the central theme of all prophecy."

104. Bruce, "Spirit in the Apocalypse," 342–44.

Chapter 15

"SALVATION BELONGS TO OUR GOD": SALVATION

BIBLIOGRAPHY

Decock, Paul. "The Works of God, of Christ, and of the Faithful in the Apocalypse of John." *Neot* 41 (2007): 37–66. **Du Rand, Jan A.** "The New Jerusalem as Pinnacle of Salvation: Text (Rev 21:1–22:5) and Intertext." *Neot* 38 (2004): 275–302. ———. "Soteriology in the Apocalypse of John." Pages 492–95 in *Salvation in the New Testament: Perspectives on Soteriology.* Edited by Jan G. van der Watt. Leiden: Brill, 2005. **Duvall, J. Scott.** "A Synchronic Analysis of the Indicative-Imperative Structure of Pauline Exhortation." Ph.D. diss., Southwestern Baptist Theological Seminary, 1991. **Flemming, Dean.** "Revelation and the *Missio Dei*: Toward a Missional Reading of the Apocalypse." *JTI* 6 (2012): 161–78. **Franke, John R.** *Missional Theology: An Introduction.* Grand Rapids: Baker Academic, 2020. **Gundry, Robert H.** "The New Jerusalem: People as Place, Not Place for People." *NovT* 29 (1987): 254–64. **Guthrie, Donald.** "The Lamb in the Structure of the Book of Revelation." *VE* 12 (1981): 64–71. **Johnson, Andy.** *Holiness and the* Missio Dei. Eugene, OR: Cascade, 2016. **Lane, Tony.** "The Wrath of God as an Aspect of the Love of God." Pages 138–67 in *Nothing Greater, Nothing Better: Theological Essays on the Love of God.* Edited by Kevin J. Vanhoozer. Grand Rapids: Eerdmans, 2001. **Lee, Pilchan.** *The New Jerusalem in the Book of Revelation: A Study of Revelation 21–22 in Light of Its Background in Jewish Tradition.* WUNT 129. Tübingen: Mohr Siebeck, 2001. **Mathewson, David L.** "A Re-examination of the Millennium in Rev 20:1–6: Consummation and Recapitulation." *JETS* 44.2 (2001): 237–51. **Middleton, J. Richard, and Michael J. Gorman.** "Salvation," *NIDB* 5:45–61. **Miller, Kevin E.** "The Nuptial Eschatology of Revelation 19–22." *CBQ* 60 (1998): 301–18. **Morales, Jon.** *Christ, Shepherd of the Nations: The Nations as Narrative Character and Audience in John's Apocalypse.* LNTS 577. London: T&T Clark, 2018. **Rowland, Christopher.** "The Lamb and the Beast, the Sheep and the Goats: 'The Mystery of Salvation' in Revelation." Pages 181–92 in *A Vision for the Church: Studies in Early Christian Ecclesiology in Honor of J. P. M. Sweet.* Edited by Markus Bockmuehl and Michael B. Thompson. Edinburgh: T&T Clark, 1997. **Schüssler Fiorenza, Elizabeth.** "Redemption as Liberation: Apoc 1:5f. and 5:9f." *CBQ* 36 (1974): 220–32. **Stewart, Alexander E.** *Soteriology as Motivation in the Apocalypse of John.* Gorgias Biblical Studies 61. Piscataway, NJ: Gorgias,

2015. **Talbert, Charles H.** "Divine Assistance and Enablement of Human Faithfulness in the Revelation of John Viewed within Its Apocalyptic Context." Pages 265–82 in *Getting 'Saved': The Whole Story of Salvation in the New Testament*. Edited by Charles H. Talbert and Jason A. Whitlark. Grand Rapids: Eerdmans, 2011. **Wright, Christopher J. H.** *The Mission of God: Unlocking the Bible's Grand Narrative*. Downers Grove, IL: IVP Academic, 2006. **Wright, N. T.** *Surprised by Hope: Rethinking Heaven, the Resurrection, and the Mission of the Church*. New York: HarperOne, 2008.

15.1 INTRODUCTION

God's salvation is one of the more comprehensive theological themes in Revelation.[1] At a minimum it features the person and work of the Triune God, the people of God and their discipleship to the Lamb, the fate of the nations, God's judgment of evil, and the new creation. But it would not do simply to assume the theme of salvation among the others and leave it unexamined on its own. We understand God's salvation to center on his commitment to rescue his people, judge evil, and restore creation. God's rescue mission is more specifically how God works out his salvation plan in history. God's salvation and mission are integrally related as complementary aspects of the same reality.

Revelation paints a holistic picture of salvation rather than merely focusing on the beginning of a right relationship with God (conversion-initiation) or the end goal (a heavenly home). Middleton concurs: "Salvation is much wider than that; it cannot be limited to forgiveness of sins or escaping judgment. In the Bible [and in Revelation particularly], salvation is a comprehensive reality, both future and present, and affects every aspect of existence."[2] Salvation is God's deliverance from all that destroys shalom, a deliverance that leads to restoration of relational wholeness.[3] Salvation includes both deliverance and restoration, all within the framework of a "now and not yet" eschatology.[4]

We look first at terms for salvation. Du Rand identifies the key soteriological terms in Revelation: "salvation" (σωτηρία), "purchase" (ἀγοράζω), and "free" (λύω).[5] We can draw several significant conclusions from the use of these terms in their contexts:[6]

1. Alexander E. Stewart, *Soteriology as Motivation in the Apocalypse of John* (Piscataway, NJ: Gorgias, 2015), 205, successfully argues that "John primarily employs soteriology as motivation in the Apocalypse; that is, John presents full and final salvation as a future event that would not decisively culminate until Christ's return in order to motivate his hearers to overcome in the present through complete faithfulness to Jesus unto death."

2. Middleton, *New Heaven and a New Earth*, 79.

3. Middleton, *New Heaven and a New Earth*, 79. Cf. also J. Richard Middleton and Michael J. Gorman, "Salvation," *NIDT* 5:45–61.

4. Stewart, *Soteriology as Motivation*, 177–203, rightly speaks of an "inaugurated soteriology" as well.

5. See Jan A. Du Rand, "Soteriology in the Apocalypse of John," in Jan G. van der Watt, ed., *Salvation in the New Testament: Perspectives on Soteriology* (Leiden: Brill, 2005), 465–504. The terms appear in the following locations: σωτηρία (7:10; 12:10; 19:1), ἀγοράζω in the sense of "purchase" or "redeem" (5:9; 14:3, 4), and λύω in the sense of "free" or "liberate" (1:5).

6. See Du Rand, "Soteriology in the Apocalypse," 468–71, for similar conclusions.

- The ultimate source of salvation is the Triune God, with a focus on the work of God and the Lamb (1:4–7; 5:6–9; 7:10, 12, 15, 17; 12:10, 11; 14:1, 4; 19:1, 3, 5).
- Salvation is intended for the great multitude of nations, but Revelation does not advocate universalism (1:5–6; 5:9; 7:9; 14:1, 3, 4; 19:1, 5, 6).
- Salvation includes the judgment of and victory over evil (1:5, 7; 7:16; 12:7–10, 12; 19:2).
- God's salvation provides the reason for the response of praise from God's people (5:9–10; 7:10, 12; 12:10–12; 14:3; 19:1, 3, 4).
- Salvation requires a response of faithfulness on the part of God's people to be effective (7:14, 16; 12:11; 19:2, 5, 7–8).
- Salvation includes a future restoration (1:7; 5:10; 7:15–17; 12:10; 14:1; 19:7–8).

A survey of the specific terms for salvation certainly does not exhaust Revelation's robust soteriology, but it does provide a helpful framework for further exploration. In this chapter we turn our attention to God, the ultimate source of salvation, and his mission to save the nations; to the work of Jesus, the Lamb of God; to God's commitment to judge evil; to the response of praise and faithfulness on the part of God's people; and to the future restoration that culminates in the new heaven and new earth.

15.2 The God of Salvation and His Mission to Save the Nations

Salvation begins with God (e.g., 7:10; 19:1). As Flemming observes, "Revelation, above all, tells the story of a sovereign and loving God who is on a mission to save people of all nations and to bring the whole creation to its intended goal. And God accomplishes this magnificent purpose in and through Jesus Christ, the slaughtered Lamb."[7] Revelation clearly reveals the *missio dei* (mission of God) and presents the final chapter in God's heart to save the nations and restore creation.[8] It all begins with God as Sovereign Creator (see 12.3).

God as Creator and Sustainer anchors the mission of salvation. Along with the living creatures, the elders worship God precisely for this reason: "you created all things, and by your will they were created and have their being" (4:11; cf. 3:14; 10:6; 14:7). Why would the perfect Triune God create in the first place if not to commune forever with his creation (Gen 1–2)? The intrusion of sin and evil in Genesis 3 provides the necessary

7. Flemming, *Foretaste of the Future*, 35.

8. Dean Flemming, "Revelation and the *Missio Dei*: Toward a Missional Reading of the Apocalypse," *JTI* 6 (2012): 161–78; Christopher J. H. Wright, *The Mission of God: Unlocking the Bible's Grand Narrative* (Downers Grove, IL: IVP Academic, 2006); John R. Franke, *Missional Theology: An Introduction* (Grand Rapids: Baker Academic, 2020); Andy Johnson, *Holiness and the* Missio Dei (Eugene, OR: Cascade, 2016).

occasion for the mission of salvation, a mission already grounded in the nature of God as loving Creator. In other words, the salvation mission truly begins with God's decision to create rather than originating with his response to the fall beginning in Genesis 12.

In addition, Revelation reminds us that God's mission embraces the entire creation and anticipates its accomplishment in the new creation (Rev 21–22). The centering image of the book—God on this throne—assures readers that God's salvific mission will succeed in the end (see 12.3.3). Flemming notes several important implications of God on his throne as Sovereign Creator: (1) no competing powers can thwart God's mission, (2) God's mission is universal in scope, (3) only God can redeem the world, and (4) what is true in heaven must become true on earth.[9]

God's love for the nations motivates him to pursue their salvation (see 12.5).[10] As Creator, God loves his creation and longs for its restoration. The fourfold formula depicting the peoples of the world is used seven times throughout the book, each time in a different order (cf. Gen 10:5, 20, 31; Dan 7:14):[11]

5:9	Tribe	Language	People	Nation
7:9	Nation	Tribe	People	Language
10:11	Peoples	Nations	Languages	Kings
11:9	People	Tribe	Language	Nation
13:7	Tribe	People	Language	Nation
14:6	Nation	Tribe	Language	People
17:15	Peoples	Multitudes	Nations	Languages

This formula indicates universality and reminds us that God desires an international, multicultural people and has made his salvation through Christ available to all people. The eternal gospel (14:6) reflected in "this prophecy" (10:11; cf. 1:3; 11:6; 19:10; 22:7, 10, 18, 19) goes out to the nations. Many respond in faith and follow the Lamb (5:9; 7:9), while others refuse to believe (11:9; 13:7; 17:15).[12] In 5:9–10 the angelic leaders praise the Lamb who was slain for purchasing "*for God*" people from all nations, making them "to be a kingdom, and priests to serve *our God*" (emphasis added) and enabling them to reign on God's created earth. As we will see below, the exodus theme plays an important role in Revelation, and we hear an echo in 5:9–10 of Exod 19:5–6,

9. Flemming, *Foretaste of the Future*, 44–49; see n7.

10. For a comprehensive treatment of the nations in Revelation, see Jon Morales, *Christ, Shepherd of the Nations: The Nations as Narrative Character and Audience in John's Apocalypse*, LNTS 577 (London: T&T Clark, 2018).

11. The terms used include "tribe" (φυλή), "language" (γλῶσσα), people (λαός), and nation (ἔθνος), with "kings" (βασιλεύς) and "multitudes" (ὄχλος). Most terms are used in both singular and plural, depending on the context, but without a distinction in meaning.

12. More specifically, Morales, *Christ, Shepherd of the Nations*, 5–25, identifies five positions regarding the nations in Revelation: (1) the church becomes the nations, (2) thoroughgoing universalism, (3) large-scale conversion of the nations, (4) the text is inconsistent on the nations, and (5) the language about the nations is rhetorical.

which refers to God's people (initially Israel and now the church drawn from all nations) as his "treasured possession . . . a kingdom of priests and a holy nation." God is surely pleased when a great multitude from every nation stands before the throne and the Lamb (Rev 7:9). God is their true and just King who will gladly receive the worship of the nations (15:3–4). In 20:9 we read of "the camp of God's people, the city he loves," an expression that portrays the saints as a "wandering people of God who have now found a home and are protected by God even from a vast invading army" (cf. Ezek 38:9, 18–23).[13] Finally, God delights when the healed (i.e., redeemed) nations bring their glory and honor into the new creation and walk in God's light (Rev 21:24, 26; 22:2). All this points to Franke's conclusion: "there is mission because God loves."[14]

The greatest saving act of God in the Old Testament is the exodus.[15] As a paradigm of God's salvation, the exodus offers insight into what God's rescue involves for his people, initially for Israel and ultimately for the nations who follow the Lamb. Middleton identifies eight elements of salvation seen through the lens of the exodus motif:[16]

1. We begin with a barrier to wholeness and well-being and flourishing. The Pharaoh of Egypt has enslaved and is oppressing God's people, but sin and death constitute the most challenging impediment. The bad actors in Revelation include the dragon, the two beasts, and wicked humanity.
2. People in need cry out for help. The Israelites groan in their bondage and cry out to God. Suffering is the context of Revelation (e.g., 1:9; 6:9–11; 7:14; see 18.2).
3. God comes from his heavenly throne and enters the earthly situation of those in need. He "comes down to deliver" (Exod 3:8). God's involvement or immanence is made possible by his transcendence. God has decided to get involved and help. The incarnation of Christ, the Lamb of God, provides the supreme example of God's involvement.
4. God, the divine King, fights for his people. He intervenes with power and sends plagues of judgment against the kings of the earth who enslave his people. He removes the barrier to flourishing and well-being. This appears throughout Revelation, especially in the seal, trumpet, and bowl judgments and in God's judgment of Babylon and the evil trinity.
5. God often uses human agents to assist in bringing salvation. God is the ultimate agent of salvation, but judges, kings, prophets, and others are the human agents.

13. Osborne, *Revelation*, 714.

14. Franke, *Missional Theology*, 8.

15. See ch. 8 in Wright, *Mission of God*, 265–88, where he explains how the exodus provides "the primary model of God's idea of redemption" (p. 265).

16. See J. Richard Middleton, *New Heaven and a New Earth*, 77–93; Cf. also Middleton and Gorman, "Salvation"; Du Rand, "Soteriology in the Apocalypse," 499–500. I have added general comments about the relevance to Revelation with more detail below.

Jesus, the unique divine-human agent of salvation, stands as the One through whom God delivers his people ultimately. In Revelation, the people of God participate as prophetic witnesses (see 18.6).

6. God delivers and restores. Salvation is never just deliverance *from* something but also restoration *to* flourishing and wholeness. For Israel this included the promised land. This speaks of the concrete earthly nature of God's salvation and culminates in the coming of the new heaven and new earth in Revelation.
7. A response of obedient faith is necessary to appropriate God's salvation. The laws and commandments given to Israel are grounded in her deliverance from slavery. The gift precedes the obligation or call to obedience (e.g., Exod 19:4–5). In Revelation God's people are consistently called to follow the Lamb faithfully.
8. God comes to live among those who have been rescued. The purpose of the exodus is ultimately that God may dwell among his people (Exod 29:45–46). His longstanding promise to live among his people is ultimately fulfilled in the temple that is the new creation (e.g., Lev 26:11–12; Ezek 34:30; 37:37; 2 Cor 6:16; Rev 21:3).

How does this relate to God's love for the nations? In every way. Repeatedly in Revelation God's covenant people are broadened beyond ethnic Israel to include all believing nations (see 16.2.4 and 16.2.5). This whole complex of God's salvation, often using exodus imagery, demonstrates God's deep and persevering love for the nations. It also illustrates God's plan to save people from every tribe, language, people, and nation.

God's mission to save humanity surfaces in a number of ways in Revelation, many echoing the exodus paradigm. First, we see God's firm commitment to judge sin and evil and remove the barrier to wholeness and flourishing (see Chs. 12.6; 15.4; 19). Second, God hears the cries of his people and responds. He is the God who speaks to his people (see 12.2; 14.4; cf. Rev 1:1, 2, 9; 6:9; 10:11; 12:17; 14:12; 19:9, 13; 20:4; 22:6). We regularly see expressions such as "revelation," "prophecy," "scroll," "mystery of God," and "eternal gospel," all reminding us that God hears and responds to his people. Third, God gets involved in saving his people through the coming of Jesus, the Lamb of God, through his death and resurrection, and through the continuing witness of Jesus's followers to the nations. Along the way God hears prayers (8:4), protects his people on their wilderness journey (e.g., 7:2, 3; 9:4; 11:1; 12:6), and judges their enemies. Fourth, God promises ultimate restoration in the new heaven and new earth to come, where God will live among his people. The resurrection of the witnesses (11:11), the book of life, the tree of life, God's temple, God's comfort and protection and presence, all point to final restoration (see Ch. 20 below). Finally, this salvation calls for praise and a response of faithful obedience from his people, a calling we see the churches wrestling with in chapters 2–3 and beyond (e.g., the new song of praise in 5:9–10; 14:3; 15:3–4; cf. Exod 15:1–19; Isa 42:10). In the end, God hopes and works for the healing of the nations (Rev 22:2; see 16.2.5).[17]

15.3 The Work of Jesus, the Lamb of God

Revelation stresses that Jesus the Lamb of God plays a crucial role in bringing salvation: "Salvation belongs to our God, who sits on the throne, and to the Lamb" (7:10; see Ch. 13). The coming of salvation results in the kingdom of the world becoming "the kingdom of our Lord and of his Messiah" (11:15). It is the ultimate fulfillment of the exodus paradigm of rescue and restoration, hence the song of both Moses and the Lamb (15:2–4). Du Rand correctly notes that the Lamb plays a pivotal role in the soteriology of the Apocalypse.[18] Mounce concludes that the "redemptive work of the Son is central to the eschatological drama."[19] This dominant theme appears right out of the gate (1:4–7):

> John, To the seven churches in the province of Asia: Grace and peace to you from him [i.e., God] . . . and from Jesus Christ, who is the faithful witness, the firstborn from the dead, and the ruler of the kings of the earth. To him who loves us and has freed us from our sins by his blood, and has made us to be a kingdom and priests to serve his God and Father—to him be glory and power for ever and ever! Amen. "Look, he is coming with the clouds," and "every eye will see him, even those who pierced him"; and all peoples on earth "will mourn because of him." So shall it be! Amen.

In this opening passage we find a summary of Christ's salvific contribution. The "faithful witness" motif speaks to his faithful life and sacrificial death on behalf of his people (1:5a). The expression "firstborn from the dead" points to his resurrection (1:5b). As the "ruler of the kings of the earth" he will return in glory (1:5c, 7). Finally, we see the effects of his work on behalf of his people (1:5d, 6)—his love, liberating sacrifice, and commissioning or appointment of his people as kings and priests. Each aspect deserves further comment.[20]

First, Jesus is the "faithful witness" (1:5; 3:14; cf. 22:16–20; John 18:37) who has freed his people from their sins by his blood (see 13.3). The theme of Christ's sacrificial

17. See 16.2.5 below on the question of the final conversion of the nations.

18. Du Rand, "Soteriology in the Apocalypse," 473, 480–81, 492–95. Whereas "God is the initiating *origin* of salvation, Christ the Lamb's sacrificial death is the *means* through which the identity of the followers is constituted and that the believers are freed *from sin*" (p. 471). Emphases original.

19. Mounce, *Revelation*, 49.

20. Beale, *Revelation*, 190–91, rightly sees the connection to Ps 88:27, 37 LXX (MT 89:27, 37; EVV 89:26, 36), where the immediate context refers to David as "the 'anointed' king who will reign over all his enemies and whose seed will be established on his throne forever."

death runs deep in Revelation. Du Rand rightly observes that "soteriology in the Apocalypse is predominantly focused on the Lamb-event, the crucifixion of Jesus Christ."[21] We see allusions to the blood of Christ, a symbol of his sacrificial death, in the description of the slain but now victorious Lamb (5:6, 9, 12).[22] Not surprisingly, believers are described as those who have washed their robes white in the red blood of the Lamb (7:14) and triumphed over the accuser by the Lamb's blood and their faithful testimony (12:11). Bauckham concludes, "The continuing and ultimate victory of God over evil which the rest of Revelation describes is no more than the working-out of the decisive victory of the Lamb on the cross."[23]

Second, Jesus is the resurrected Lord, the "firstborn" from among the dead ones (see 13.4). Salvation for the many has begun with the resurrection of the One. Jesus was dead but is now alive for ever and ever (1:18). He died and came to life again (2:8). God's people now share in the first resurrection and will be exempt from the second death because of Jesus's resurrection (20:6), the event that altered the course of human history.

Third, Jesus's work includes his return in glory as the "ruler of the kings of the earth" (1:5c, 7; see 13.6). He comes riding the clouds as King of kings and Lord of lords (Dan 7:13; Rev 17:14; 19:16; cf. 11:15; 12:10; 15:3; 1 Tim 6:15), and "every eye will see him, even those who pierced him, and all peoples on earth will mourn because of him," indicating either repentance or judgment (Rev 1:7; cf. Zech 12:10–12; 14:16). It is the Lamb who opens the first six seals (Rev 6). In other words, the Lamb never stops being the Lion. Jesus as ruler is also related to Jesus as Shepherd, a theme that seems to include both the idea of judging his enemies (2:27; 12:5; 19;15) and shepherding (leading, guiding, protecting, nurturing, healing) his people (7:17).[24]

Fourth, we notice the fruit of Jesus's soteriological work on behalf of his people (1:5d, 6). The main participles/verbs in this passage summarize the results of his work: "loves" (ἀγαπῶντι), "freed us from our sins" (λύσαντι ἡμᾶς ἐκ τῶν ἁμαρτιῶν), and "made us to be a kingdom and priests to serve his God and Father" (ἐποίησεν ἡμᾶς βασιλείαν, ἱερεῖς τῷ θεῷ καὶ πατρὶ αὐτοῦ).

Christ's ongoing, sustaining love provides the foundation for his liberating sacrifice. Jesus "purchased" or "redeemed" (ἀγοράζω) for God people from every nation (5:9; 14:3, 4). This suggests a satisfying of the justice of God (rather than a ransom payment to the devil) and a liberation of his people from slavery (cf. 1 Cor 6:20; 7:23; 2 Pet 2:1).[25]

21. Du Rand, "Soteriology in the Apocalypse," 492.

22. Bauckham, *Theology*, 74, notes that John forges a "new symbol of conquest by sacrificial death" when he combines Lamb with Lion in Rev 5. Donald Guthrie rightly observes that Jesus as the Lamb is not a symbol of weakness but "of strength through suffering." See Donald Guthrie, "The Lamb in the Structure of the Book of Revelation," *Vox Evangelica* 12 (1981): 65.

23. Bauckham, *Theology*, 75.

24. Beale, *Revelation*, 267. Cf. Morales, *Christ, Shepherd of the Nations*, who admits that the final outcome related to the nations in Revelation is binary: judgment or salvation (see pp. 160–63) but urges readers to honor and appreciate the book's developing storyline.

25. Du Rand, "Soteriology in the Apocalypse," 470; Elizabeth Schüssler Fiorenza, "Redemption as Liberation: Apoc 1:5f. and 5:9f.," *CBQ* 36 (1974): 220–32.

Jesus not only did something for his people; he also made them into something—the commissioning or appointment of his people as kings and priests (see 13.7; 16.2.4; cf. Mark 3:14).

15.4 God's Commitment to Judge Evil

God is repeatedly worshiped and honored as holy in Revelation (4:8; 6:10; 15:4; 16:5; cf. Isa 6:3 and Jesus as holy in Rev 1:12–16; 3:7; see Ch. 12.4), and his perfect holiness ("holy, holy, holy") guarantees the success of his mission, which includes the destruction of evil.[26] Things are not as they should be with his creation, and God will, in the end, make things right. His creation cannot flourish and experience well-being and wholeness in his presence without the full and final removal of evil (see Chs. 12.6 and 19). Thus, God's mission to save involves his commitment to judge. Du Rand notes that "judgment and salvation are seen as the two sides of the same soteriological coin."[27]

Chapters 4 and 5 are foundational to all that follows: God and the Lamb receiving universal worship and God entrusting to the Lamb the scroll of salvation that involves judgment. In the rest of the book we see the Lord's Prayer fully and finally answered: your name be hallowed, your kingdom come, your will be done on earth as it is in heaven (Matt 5:9–10).[28] The judgment aspect of this answer takes numerous forms, including the three major series of judgments: seals (Rev 6:1–17; 8:1), trumpets (8:2–9:21; 11:14–19), and bowls (15:1–16:21). These three series increase in severity and all end with final judgment and salvation, where evil is destroyed and God's kingdom comes fully and finally. God's judgment continues with the destruction of Babylon the Great, that center of rebellion and opposition to God (17:1–19:5), and the final judgment of Satan, the two beasts, and their followers (19:11–21; 20:1–15). God's judgment even includes the participation of God's people as human agents of judgment (e.g., 11:3–6, 11–14). There are repeated references to God's "wrath" (θυμός: 14:10, 19; 15:1, 7; 16:1), "anger" (ὀργή: 6:16, 17; 11:18; 14:10; 16:19; 19:15), and "judgment" (κρίσις: 14:7; 16:7; 18:10; 19:2), as well as general references to a final judgment (e.g., 16:14; 18:5, 8, 20; 19:17; 22:18–19). His judgment will certainly come and will come with truth and justice (16:7).

Ultimately God's judgment flows out of his love for his creation, a topic we will explore in more detail later (see 12.6; 19).[29] His just judgments make possible his salvation. As Flemming observes, "God's love for his people and all creation means that *nothing, absolutely nothing* will be allowed to derail God's missional purpose to make

26. Duvall, *Heart of Revelation*, 141–44; Flemming, *Foretaste of the Future*, 50–51.

27. Du Rand, "Soteriology in the Apocalypse," 472.

28. Bauckham, *Theology*, 40.

29. Lane, "Wrath of God as an Aspect of the Love of God," 138–67.

everything new."[30] Gorman concurs: "Nothing can or will thwart the purposes of God to liberate, save, and redeem the world."[31] As a result, we see judgment as a means to the ultimate end of salvation.

15.5 GOD'S PEOPLE PARTICIPATE IN HIS SALVATION

From a human perspective, God's salvation must be embraced to be effective, and that brings us to consider the response of God's people (see Chs. 16 and 18.5).[32] Without a doubt, Revelation emphasizes actions on the part of God's people, actions such as repentance, worship, witness, and obedience. This emphasis alongside the warnings throughout the book often leads to the common question, "Can Christians lose their salvation?" Stewart contends that this question (1) fails to recognize that salvation belongs to the Triune God and (2) restricts salvation to the conversion-initiation or the "now" of salvation. Revelation affirms, he says, the need for Christians to overcome to be saved in the final day in keeping with a "full-bodied New Testament soteriology" that includes "past, present, and future dimensions."[33] According to Stewart, the real danger for John's readers (and for all who claim to be Christians)

> consists in being excluded from membership and participation in the people of God who will be saved in that day. Soteriology is thus closely linked to ecclesiology in the Apocalypse; not an ecclesiology based on denominational affiliation, sacraments, or outward appearances, but based upon allegiance, worship, and witness to the true God and his Christ—in a word—overcoming. The danger of exclusion from God's people can only be overcome through faithfulness unto death, or as Jesus put it, 'the one who endures to the end, this one will be saved' (Matt. 10:22).[34]

The expectation of the Apocalypse is that God's people will respond faithfully. In fact, faith is "the unstated assumption behind John's conception of the human response and reception of God's salvation."[35] Works are stressed throughout but remain actions that flow from a genuine relational faith. Works are "an integral component of a holistic believing human response to God's saving initiative. Gift and obligation are brought

30. Flemming, *Foretaste of the Future*, 138–39; emphases original.

31. Gorman, *Reading Revelation Responsibly*, 154.

32. Peters, *Mandate of the Church*, 40–41. See esp. Stewart, *Soteriology as Motivation*, 197–202.

33. Stewart, *Soteriology as Motivation*, 197–98. We might say that our experience of salvation consists of salvation inaugurated, salvation sustained, and salvation consummated. See also the insightful discussion by Talbert, "Divine Assistance," 265–82, and Decock, "Works of God," 37–66.

34. Stewart, *Soteriology as Motivation*, 200.

35. Stewart, *Soteriology as Motivation*, 201.

seamlessly together in Rev 19:8: "Fine linen, bright and clean, was given her to wear"; fine linen stands for the righteous acts of God's holy people.[36]

We see Revelation's focus on deeds from the outset. The book opens and closes with blessings on those who obey the prophecy (1:3; 22:7, 18–19). The seven churches are repeatedly admonished to listen to the voice of the Spirit (2:7, 11, 17, 29; 3:6, 13, 22), the voice that calls them to repentance and faith (e.g., 2:5, 16, 25; 3:2–3, 10, 18–20). In Revelation the true people of God respond in multiple ways: they follow, bear witness, reign and serve, persevere, worship, and enjoy the full and final salvation God has secured.

God's people respond faithfully in discipleship to the Lamb. They are "the called, chosen and faithful followers" of the Lamb who accompany him into spiritual warfare (17:14). They are the 144,000 who have been redeemed from the earth, those who resist evil and "follow the Lamb wherever he goes" (14:3–4). They are committed to "the word of God and the testimony of Jesus Christ," even at the greatest cost (6:9; 12:17; 14:12; 20:4; cf. 1:2, 9; 12:11; 19:10). To be sure, this response of faithfulness is not automatic or without threat as the seven messages demonstrate, yet through all the chaos of spiritual battle, God's people keep the faith. They say "no" to evil empires and the demonic rulers that empower them (e.g., false teaching, false worship, ungodly behavior, relational unfaithfulness) and "yes" to Jesus and his kingdom of righteousness (e.g., loving obedience to the truth, patient endurance to the end).[37] Make no mistake: the struggle to remain faithful is real and fraught with setbacks, yet those who are genuinely faithful continue to open the door and allow the renewal of fellowship with their gracious Lord (3:19–20).

God's people bear witness faithfully to Christ and his kingdom and to God's great salvation story (see 16.2.6). Faithful witnesses live and speak God's truth clearly and boldly. They go public with their faith commitments. They pledge allegiance to the Lamb and his kingdom in the face of pressure from worldly empires. As "faithful witnesses" (e.g., 2:13) they imitate "the faithful witness" (1:5; 3:14). As noted above, this includes their devotion to the "word of God and the testimony of Jesus." Often, at least as portrayed in the Apocalypse, living as a faithful witness involves suffering (e.g., 2:13; 6:9; 12:11; 17:6; 20:4). The account of the two witnesses in Rev 11, with these two representing the whole witnessing church, illustrates this reality vividly (see 16.2.6; 18.6).

God's people also participate in salvation by assuming their God-given responsibilities to reign and to serve (i.e., as a kingdom and priests or a "priestly kingdom"—cf.

36. Stewart, *Soteriology as Motivation*, 202. On the relationship between faith and works in Paul, see Jeffrey S. Duvall, "A Synchronic Analysis of the Indicative-Imperative Structure of Pauline Exhortation" (Ph.D. diss., Southwestern Baptist Theological Seminary, 1991).

37. Duvall, *Heart of Revelation*, 187–93.

1:6; 5:10; 20:6; Exod 19:5–6). In this world, the saints mediate God's salvation to the surrounding nations in hopes that they will become followers of the Lamb, a mission originally rooted in the charge to Abraham in Gen 12:1–3 and later conferred on Israel (see 16.2.4).[38] Building on Jesus's teachings and ministry, Revelation portrays the church as the true Israel, comprised of both Jewish and Gentile followers of Jesus. Jesus's commission to "make disciples of all nations" (Matt 28:19) thus depicts a central aspect of the church's missional role. They participate with God in bringing salvation to the world. In addition, God's salvation includes restoring his people to their kingly and priestly function on earth, a responsibility that certainly stretches into the new creation.[39]

Without a doubt God's people embrace salvation by persevering (see 16.2.7). The seven churches are exhorted to overcome and promised eschatological rewards for doing so (2:7, 11, 17, 26; 3:5, 12, 21). They win the victory (νικάω) by refusing (or ceasing) to compromise with sin and evil and by remaining faithful to Christ and his word. The chief categories of temptation include idolatry and immorality (see 18.3–18.5). This calls for patient endurance as God's people persevere, stand firm, and endure in the face of ongoing pressure from a wicked world system (ὑπομονή—1:9; 2:2, 3, 19; 3:10; 13:10; 14:12).[40]

One of the most powerful resources for persevering and the most obvious indicators of faithfully appropriating God's salvation is worship (see Ch. 17). Throughout Revelation we see the power and importance of worship—of responding to who God is and what he has done with thanksgiving, praise, and obedience. Revelation features numerous hymns of praise but also highlights liturgical expressions, songs, doxologies, prayers, bodily devotion, service, following the Spirit, and the glorification of God. Only those who genuinely participate in God's salvation will respond in a worshipful manner. And no one other than the Triune God deserves such allegiance and devotion (e.g., 19:10; 22:9). Likewise, true believers will not be deceived but will refuse to worship the dragon or the beast or its image or any other earthly power or object (13:15; 14:7; 20:4 versus repeated references to those who worship false gods or powers). Revelation very clearly contrasts true worship with false worship. In one way or the other, ultimately loyalties are announced through our worship.

On a related note, God's people appropriate God's salvation by listening to the voice of the Spirit now and by enjoying God's presence in the new creation. The churches are repeatedly admonished to "hear what the Spirit says to the churches" (2:7, 11, 17, 29; 3:6, 13, 22; cf. 13:9; see 14.4), even as the Spirit draws attention to the words of Christ (the τάδε λέγει formula in 2:1, 8, 12, 18; 3:1, 7, 14). The faithful will heed the Spirit's voice by submitting to Christ's words—it is the Spirit of *the* prophecy [that is

38. Wright, *Mission of God*, 329–33.
39. Wright, *Mission of God*, 415.
40. Duvall, *Heart of Revelation*, 185–86.

the book of Revelation] who bears witness to Jesus (19:10), and faithful disciples listen to and obey his voice. The Spirit says "amen" to the blessing on believers who remain faithful unto death (14:13). Those who embrace God's salvation join the Spirit in calling the whole people of God to persevere in faith (22:17). Just as the two witnesses were resurrected by the "breath of life from God" (11:11: πνεῦμα ζωῆς ἐκ τοῦ θεοῦ), so all faithful disciples are ultimately and totally dependent on the Spirit for life (see Ch. 14).

The new life given now by the Spirit guarantees future bodily resurrection and citizenship in God's new creation to come. Believers will enjoy God's personal presence in the new heaven and new earth.[41] Revelation has a lot to say about the future of God's people (see 16.2.9; 20). And that future will be a heightened and perfectly fulfilled experience of God's presence that begins now for genuine disciples with their experience of the Spirit and the body of Christ. God's tabernacling presence in the new creation is Eden restored, and the whole of this new world is the new temple. Even better, the holy of holies extends to the whole of the new creation as God's people live in his personal presence for eternity (see 20.7).[42]

In addition to the various responses of God's people, Revelation offer glimpses of God's salvation through a series of images and metaphors. These would have been most reassuring to the original readers, as they are to us. As noted above (see 15.3), God's people have been "purchased" and "freed," liberated from slavery to Satan and sin to enjoy fellowship with God. They have been "sealed" (7:3–4) and "measured" (11:1), both suggesting spiritual protection from evil forces. They have been "nourished" and cared for during this time of distress and tribulation (12:6, 14).

15.6 THE FUTURE RESTORATION

Revelation emphasizes not only past and present aspects of salvation but especially the future culmination of salvation. The coming new creation is the "ultimate fulfillment of the whole salvation story."[43] Middleton and Gorman rightly claim that "soteriology (theology of salvation) is eschatology realized."[44] God's salvation properly understood certainly includes the "now" but must move on to the "not yet" so that the kingdom of this world will become the kingdom of our Lord and his Messiah (11:15). We treat the topic of God's consummated kingdom more fully later (see Ch. 20). Here we survey key restoration passages throughout Revelation and consider the implications.

Any future at all for creation rests with God himself, the Creator and Redeemer. The

41. For a fuller treatment of the presence of God in the Apocalypse, see Duvall and Hays, *God's Relational Presence*, 303–23.

42. Duvall, *Heart of Revelation*, 78–82.

43. Jan A. Du Rand, "The New Jerusalem as Pinnacle of Salvation: Text (Rev 21:1–22:5) and Intertext," *Neot* 38 (2004): 298. Cf. Middleton, *New Heaven and a New Earth*, 38–39, 57–73; Duvall, *Heart of Revelation*, 162–63, comparing the beginning of Genesis and the end of Revelation. In ch. 9 Duvall describes the new creation in terms of promise, place, people, and presence.

44. Middleton and Gorman, "Salvation," 45.

book opens with a greeting and doxology (1:4–6), followed by a prophetic confession (1:7–8) that locates our future hope in the God who comes to us. In 1:7 John draws on Dan 7:13 and Zech 12:10–12 to announce Christ's return, when he will bring final judgment and salvation. This is followed by God speaking directly in Rev 1:8—the God "who is, and who was, and who is to come, the Almighty" (see 12.7). God, being the faithful God he is, will come to judge evil and to save his creation. This opening reaffirmation of his plan to come and save is a shot across the bow of the powers pretending to be sovereign lords. Their days are numbered.

God's promise to save appears throughout the seven messages, and most references are future oriented: the right to the tree of life (2:7), the crown of life (2:10), deliverance from the second death (2:11), hidden manna and a white stone with a new name (2:17), authority over the nations (2:26), the morning star (2:28), white garments as they walk with Christ (3:4), protection through trials (3:10), a permanent place in God's temple city (3:12), a feast with Christ (3:20), and the right to sit with Christ on his throne (3:21).[45] In various ways these promises, often tied to the local context, reflect God's longstanding tripartite promise to live among his people in perfect community: I will be your God, you will be my people, and I will live among you (e.g., Lev 26:12; Jer 31:33; Ezek 37:37; cf. 2 Cor 6:16). This is the end-goal of the whole salvation project—God with his people.[46]

We also see God's plan of restorative salvation in the image of the two scrolls of Rev 5 and 10. The scroll(s) represent God's design to destroy evil, save his people, and transform creation, a plan centered in the person and work of the Lamb of God. Only Jesus, the Lion-Lamb, can open the scroll and unleash God's plans for salvation through judgment. Yet God also calls his people to participate in the plan through faithful witness even in the face of suffering, a bittersweet experience, as chapter 11 reveals. With the opening of the scroll and the sounding of the seventh trumpet, "the mystery [μυστήριον] of God will be accomplished, just as he announced [εὐαγγελίζω] to his servants the prophets" (10:6–7; cf. Mark 4:11 and par.; Rom 11:25; 16:25; 1 Cor 2:7; 4:1; Eph 1:9; 3:3, 9; 5:32; Col 1:26; 2:2). The seventh trumpet (11:15–19) signals the time when God's kingdom comes in full. God is praised for taking his great power and beginning his eternal reign, for judging his enemies but also for rewarding his people (11:18). God's salvation plan, hidden in ages past, is now revealed in Christ and fully realized with his second advent (cf. 16:15).[47]

As we have noted above, Revelation emphasizes the future role of God's people as a kingdom and priests, a stewardship inaugurated now and continuing throughout

45. Du Rand, "Soteriology in the Apocalypse," 474. Cf. Hemer, *Letters to the Seven Churches*; Weima, *Sermons to the Seven Churches*.

46. See Duvall, *Heart of Revelation*, 161–63; Duvall and Hays, *God's Relational Presence*, 334–36.

47. Osborne, *Revelation*, 401.

eternity (1:6; 5:10). We are told they will "reign on the earth" (5:10; cf. 20:4, 6; 22:5). And what is perhaps most surprising is that the kings and priests are drawn from "every tribe and language and people and nation" (5:9), meaning the redeemed come from all nations. John's vision of the great multitude in 7:9–10 reinforces the idea of God's people coming from every nation as they stand before the throne and the Lamb and cry out in praise to the God of salvation. Meaningful work predates the fall, and future restoration includes the people of God assuming their God-given responsibility to accompany him in superintending the new creation.

Restoration also gets personal as God comforts his people who have been on their dangerous wilderness journey. In 7:14–17 we are reminded that this great multitude has come through the great tribulation and are now before the throne of God serving him continually in his new-creation temple. Even as martyrs, those who "die in the Lord" are blessed (14:13). They will be sheltered (σκηνόω) in God's presence (7:15; cf. 12:12; 13:6; 21:3; John 1:14) and will know his perfect comfort—they will "never again" hunger or thirst or be scorched by the sun's fierce heat. The Lamb at the center of the throne will "shepherd" (ποιμαίνω) them, leading them to springs of living water (7:17). And God will "wipe away every tear from their eyes" (7:17). This section anticipates the more detailed account to follow in Rev 21–22.

The most complete account of God's restorative salvation occurs at the end of the book—the account of final victory (19:6–20:15) and the description of the new creation (21:1–22:5). The final victory scene centers on judgment, but elements of restoration are mixed in (see Chs. 19 and 20).[48] Here we emphasize the restorative elements in God's full and final victory to come. Rev 19:6–20:15 divides into four sections.

First, 19:6–10 emphasizes the great multitude's praise of God for culminating his sovereign reign in the eschatological marriage of the Lamb. The worship is anticipated by the new song of the 144,000 in 14:1–5 and the victors' song of Moses and of the Lamb in 15:2–4. The Lamb's wedding has finally arrived, and his bride has prepared herself.

Du Rand rightly concludes that the marriage of the Lamb is the climax of salvation.[49] The groom has returned. The bride is ready. The invited wedding guests are eternally blessed. Structurally, the honored bride stands in contrast to the judgment of the great prostitute (chs. 17–18). Nuptial imagery occurs throughout Rev 19–22 to stress God's personal intimacy with his people (19:7–9; 21:2, 9; cf. Isa 54:1–8; Hos 1–3).

The second section, 19:11–21, recounts the final battle as the Lamb returns to conquer the two beasts and their followers, a battle anticipated in the sixth bowl (16:12–16;

48. One subtle but powerful way this entire section draws attention to judgment and salvation is through the lens of things present and things absent from the new creation. See Mathewson, *Companion to the Book of Revelation*, 118; Koester, *Revelation and the End of All Things*, 191–94.

49. Du Rand, "Soteriology in the Apocalypse," 495–96.

cf. 17:14), which includes the third beatitude, reminding readers that Jesus will return suddenly and surprisingly (like a thief). Those who stay alert are blessed.

Third, 20:1–10 features Satan's judgment and the millennial reign of the saints. It is important to note the context of the millennium (20:4–6) within the two-stage judgment of Satan (20:1–3 and 20:7–10). The purpose of the millennium is to emphasize "the resurrection and vindication of the saints."[50] The martyr church is resurrected at Christ's return and reigns with him, while the dragon is permanently defeated and destroyed. Quite possibly, 20:1–10 recapitulates the last battle of 19:11–21.[51] The symbolic nature of numbers in the book makes this reading likely and puts the emphasis on comparing Satan's judgment and the church's victory. The point is not a literal thousand years but the thematic and theological value it attaches to the ultimate victory of Christians who have suffered. The complete and total victory of the saints far outweighs their temporary suffering depicted through numbers highlighting limitedness or incompleteness (e.g., "ten days" in 2:10; "a short time" in 12:7–10; and three and one-half years / forty-two months / 1,260 days in 11:2–3; 12:6, 14; 13:5).[52] What is stressed is the resurrection of the saints and their privileged responsibility of serving as priests of God and reigning with Christ (20:4, 6).

Lastly, in 20:11–15 we see the great white throne judgment of unbelievers. Most likely, this is yet another angle on Christ's ultimate victory over evil (cf. 19:11–21; 20:1–10). At Christ's return, believers experience the first resurrection, a bodily resurrection to eternal life. As a result, the second death (i.e., eternal death) has no power over them. Rather, they will live unto God as priests and kings, reigning with him (20:4–6). Those who are not raised to eternal life are brought before God for judgment and sentenced to the second death—eternal separation from God. They join the beasts and the dragon in the lake of fire. Looking back over the account of the final victory in 19:6–20:15, God's restorative salvation includes victory over enemies, justice, resurrection to eternal life, experience of God's intimate presence, responsibility as priests and kings, and the joyful response of celebratory worship. At the end of chapter 20, God has judged all his enemies. The way is paved for the arrival of the new creation in 21:1–22:5.

John presents two visions of the eternal state—21:1–8 serves as a summary and 21:9–22:5 presents the expanded version with a focus on the new creation as a Holy City (21:9–21), a temple city (21:22–27), and a garden city (22:1–5). Again, our purpose here is to highlight the restorative elements in this two-part description of the new creation. Yet we begin in 21:1–8 with the removal of particular threats: the sea (as a symbol of chaos and evil in v. 1), death, mourning, crying and pain (v. 4), the old

50. Mathewson, *Companion to the Book of Revelation*, 112–13; David L. Mathewson, "A Re-examination of the Millennium in Rev 20:1–6: Consummation and Recapitulation," *JETS* 44/2 (2001): 237–51.

51. Mathewson, "Re-examination," 246–47 observes that the same Old Testament text (Ezek 38–39) underlies both Rev 19:11–21 and 20:1–10.

52. Mathewson, "Re-examination," 246–47.

order of things (v. 4), and wicked human beings (v. 8). John sees "a new heaven and a new earth" (v. 1). With all things considered, this is more than a mere renewal and less than a total destruction and replacement of the old order. We would characterize "new" here as representing a radical transformation, with both continuity and discontinuity in relation to the present creation.[53] The "Holy City, the new Jerusalem" comes down from heaven as a divine gift. The celestial city is also portrayed as a beautifully dressed bride, prepared for her marriage to the Triune God (v. 2). The contrast between the bride and prostitute of chapters 17–18 stands clear (cf. John being shown the cities in 17:1 and 21:9–10). God's promise to one day live among his people is now perfectly fulfilled (v. 3; cf. 21:7). The people of God will spend eternity in the glorious presence of God. And he is present as the Comforter wiping away tears (v. 4) and as the Sovereign Creator (seated on the throne, making everything new in v. 5). This Alpha-and-Omega, Beginning-and-End God has accomplished what he set out to accomplish (v. 6). God's resurrection life permeates the new creation (v. 6), and the victors will inherit all this for eternity (v. 7).

The expansion in 21:9–22:5 echoes many of these same themes with more colorful detail. Four particular elements stand out. First, as in 21:1–8, anything opposed to God's full and final salvation must be excluded from the new creation—no threats (21:25; 22:5), no barriers to fellowship with God (21:22), and no sin and evil (21:27; 22:3). The removal of danger paves the way for the reader to embrace God's full and unmediated blessings.

Second, God's people will include the redeemed from all nations—the twelve tribes of Israel and the twelve apostles of the Lamb (21:12) as well as the nations and kings of the earth (21:24–25; 22:2). Yet, these must be redeemed nations since "nothing impure will ever enter it, nor will anyone who does what is shameful or deceitful, but only those whose names are written in the Lamb's book of life" (21:27). God's people are securely his with his name written on their foreheads (22:4).

Third, God's people will "serve" or worship him (22:23) and reign forever as kings (22:5), suggesting they will be engaged, participatory stewards and caretakers of God's new creation.

Lastly, and the element that receives the most attention by far, God's salvation will feature his glorious, sovereign presence among his people. The throne of God and the Lamb stands at the center of the new creation (22:1, 3), and the Spirit, symbolized by the water of life, flows out from the throne (22:1). The entire creation is the temple or dwelling place of the Triune God (21:22) as God's people live in the cube-shaped holy

53. Admittedly, John's emphasis leans here more toward discontinuity as Mathewson observes: "John grounds his articulation of eschatological hope in the Isaianic new creation promises. By employing Isaian creation language here, the author emphasizes the discontinuity between the present order and the decisive new beginning in the face of the harsh realities of the present order" (*New Heaven and a New Earth*, 39).

of holies that expands into a whole new world (21:16–17). God's beautiful presence appears throughout with the city's gates, walls, foundations, and streets composed of precious materials to reflect his glory (21:19–21). God and the Lamb are the temple in the new creation (21:22). God's glorious presence illuminates this new world (21:11, 23; 22:5). God's people will be engulfed in his life and abundant provision (22:1–2), and best of all "they will see his face"—an unmediated, intimate experience of God himself (22:4).

God's presence with his people in the new creation detailed in Rev 21–22 using rich, complex, and inspiring imagery stands as the ultimate goal of God's salvation.[54] This goal has been foreseen by the Old Testament prophets, accomplished by Jesus the Lamb of God, embraced by God's people, and is now described more fully at the end of the biblical story. Here we have the fulfillment of the promises to the victors (chs. 2–3) that includes not only God's judgment of evil but his deliverance of his people to himself and the transformation of creation. The heavenly city is the temple-garden fit for eternal life in God's presence. In the end, "the place is the people. The sacred marriage has occurred, and God and his people will now spend eternity as husband and wife."[55]

15.7 CONCLUSION

God's salvation consists of judging and destroying evil, rescuing his people, and restoring his creation. This moves far beyond the individualistic conceptions of "salvation" often bandied about within evangelical Christianity, as if salvation were strictly "ours" or "mine." What God has revealed about his salvation in John's Apocalypse is much more holistic and all-encompassing than we can imagine. It is much, much more than "going to heaven when you die." It is high and wide and long and deep. It is about God removing all threats to his intimate relationship with his redeemed, multicultural people in a whole new world. It is about the past, present, and future. It is about God's kingdom coming in full. It is about the restoration of the entire cosmos.[56]

We have seen that God is the ultimate source of salvation. As the Sovereign Creator, God is on a mission to redeem the world. Jesus and his redemptive work (life, death, and resurrection) serve as the centerpiece of God's salvation. Jesus is the faithful witness, the firstborn from the dead, the returning King of kings and Lord of lords, and the one who has purchased a people to live in his presence eternally.

54. Duvall and Hays, *God's Relational Presence*, 318–22, 329–36; Mathewson, *Companion to the Book of Revelation*, 121–28.

55. Duvall and Hays, *God's Relational Presence*, 321.

56. See N. T. Wright, *Surprised by Hope: Rethinking Heaven, the Resurrection, and the Mission of the Church* (New York: HarperOne, 2008).

God's salvation is intended for all peoples since it is those whom he created that God desires to rescue. But the experience of God's salvation requires a response of faith. The redeemed must be a people in relationship with God, a people who participate with him through repentance, faith, worship, witness, and obedience. They anticipate their new responsibilities in the new heaven and new earth through serving, worshiping, and reigning. God's almost unbelievably good plan calls for praise and worship from the saints and all creation.

In some ways, the first exodus was but a shadow of the full reality of God's final exodus of salvation. The biblical paradigm of salvation is fulfilled ultimately through the story of consummation told in the book of Revelation. The evil powers and wicked people must be judged and removed so there will be no remaining barriers between God and his people. God's wondrous plan of salvation is to live among his people in the transformed garden city, which itself is the holy of holies in the new cosmic temple. God has a wondrous, glorious restoration planned where his whole creation will find their true home in him.

Chapter 16

"HIS SERVANTS": THE PEOPLE OF GOD

BIBLIOGRAPHY

Alexander, T. Desmond. *The City of God and the Goal of Creation*. SSBT. Wheaton, IL: Crossway, 2018. ———. *From Eden to the New Jerusalem: An Introduction to Biblical Theology*. Grand Rapids: Kregel Academic, 2008. **Bandstra, Andrew J.** "'A Kingship and Priests': Inaugurated Eschatology in the Apocalypse." *CTJ* 27 (1992): 10–25. **Bauckham, Richard J.** "The List of the Tribes in Revelation 7 Again." *JSNT* 42 (1991): 99–115. **Beale, Gregory K.** *The Temple and the Church's Mission: A Biblical Theology of the Dwelling Place of God*. NSBT 17. Downers Grove, IL: InterVarsity Press, 2004. **Dalrymple, Rob.** *Revelation and the Two Witnesses: The Implications for Understanding John's Depiction of the People of God and His Hortatory Intent*. Eugene, OR: Wipf & Stock, 2011. **Daniels, T. Scott.** *Seven Deadly Spirits: The Message of Revelation's Letters for Today's Church*. Grand Rapids: Baker Academic, 2009. **Elgvin, Torleif.** "Priests on Earth as in Heaven: Jewish Light on the Book of Revelation." Pages 257–78 in *Echoes from the Caves: Qumran and the New Testament*. Edited by F. García Martínez. Leiden: Brill, 2009. **Fekkes, J., III.** "'His Bride Has Prepared Herself': Revelation 19–21 and Isaian Nuptial Imagery. *JBL* 109 (1990): 269–87. **Flemming, Dean.** *Foretaste of the Future: Reading Revelation in Light of God's Mission*. Downers Grove, IL: InterVarsity Press, 2022. **Giblin, Charles Homer.** "Revelation 11.1–13: Its Form, Function, and Contextual Integration." *NTS* 30 (1984): 433–59. **Gladd, Benjamin L.** *From Adam and Israel to the Church: A Biblical Theology of the People of God*. ESBT. Downers Grove, IL: IVP Academic, 2019. **Gundry, Robert H.** "The New Jerusalem: People as Place, Not Place for People." *NovT* 29 (1987): 254–64. **Hays, J. Daniel.** *The Temple and the Tabernacle: A Study of God's Dwelling Places from Genesis to Revelation*. Grand Rapids: Baker Academic, 2016. **Hays, Richard B.** "Faithful Witness, Alpha and Omega: The Identity of Jesus in the Apocalypse of John." Pages 69–83 in Richard B. Hays and Stefan Alkier, eds., *Revelation and the Politics of Apocalyptic Interpretation*. Waco, TX: Baylor University Press, 2012. **Hemer, Colin J.** *The Letters to the Seven Churches of Asia in Their Local Setting*. BRS. Grand Rapids: Eerdmans, 2001. **Holwerda, David E.** "The Church and the Little Scroll (Revelation 10, 11)." *CTJ* 34 (1999): 148–61. **Homcy, Stephen L.** "'To Him Who Overcomes': A Fresh Look at What 'Victory' Means for the Believer according to the Book of Revelation." *JETS* 38 (1995): 193–201. **Huber, L. R.** *Like a Bride Adorned: Reading Metaphor in John's Apocalypse.* ESEC 10. New York: T&T Clark, 2007. **Jeske, R. L.** "Spirit and Community in the Johannine Apocalypse." *NTS* 31 (1985): 452–66. **Koester, Craig R.** *The Dwelling of God: The Tabernacle in the Old Testament, Intertestamental Jewish Literature, and the New Testament.* CBQMS 22. Washington, DC: Catholic Biblical Association of America, 1989. **Korner, Ralph J.** *The Origin and Meaning of Ekklēsia in the Early Jesus Movement.* AJEC 98. Leiden: Brill, 2017. **Kuykendall, Michael.** *Lions, Locusts, and the Lamb: Interpreting Key Images in the Book of Revelation.* Eugene, OR: Wipf & Stock, 2019. **Malone, Andrew S.** *God's Mediators: A Biblical Theology of Priesthood.* NSBT 43. Downers Grove, IL: InterVarsity Press, 2017. **Marshall, I. Howard.** "Church and Temple in the New Testament." *TynBul* 40 (1989): 203–22. **Mathewson, David L.** *A Companion to the Book of Revelation.* Eugene, OR: Cascade, 2020. **Mayo, Philip L.** *"Those Who Call Themselves Jews": The Church and Judaism in the Apocalypse of John.* PTMS 60. Eugene, OR: Wipf & Stock, 2006. **McCaulley, Esau.** *Reading While Black: African American Biblical Interpretations as an Exercise in Hope.* Downers Grove, IL: IVP Academic, 2020. **McKelvey, R. J.** *The New Temple: The Church in the New Testament.* OTM. Oxford: Oxford University Press, 1969. **McNicol, Allan.** "Revelation 11:1–14 and the Structure of the Apocalypse." *ResQ* 22 (1979): 193–202. **Metzger, Bruce M.** *A Textual Commentary on the Greek New Testament.* 2nd ed. New York: United Bible Societies, 1994. **Middleton, Paul.** "Male Virgins, Male Martyrs, Male Brides: A Reconsideration of the 144,000 'who have not dirtied themselves with women' (Revelation 14:4)." Pages 193–208 in *The Book of Revelation: Currents in British Research on the Apocalypse.* Edited by Garrick V. Allen, Ian Paul, and Simon P. Woodman. WUNT 2.411. Tübingen: Mohr Siebeck, 2015. **Morton, Russell.** "Revelation 7:9–17: The Innumerable Crowd Before the One Upon the Throne and Lamb." *ATJ* 32 (2000): 1–11. **Pattemore, Stephen.** *The People of God in the Apocalypse: Discourse, Structure and Exegesis.* SNTSMS 128. Cambridge: Cambridge University Press, 2004. **Perry, Peter S.** "The People of God in the Book of Revelation." *OHBR* 325–40. **Peterson, Eugene H.** *Reversed Thunder: The Revelation of John & the Praying Imagination.* New York: HarperSanFrancisco, 1988. **Ramsay, William M.** *The Letters to the Seven Churches.* Updated ed. Edited by Mark W. Wilson. Peabody, MA: Hendrickson, 1994. **Robinson, Andrea L.** *Temple of Presence: The Christological Fulfillment of Ezekiel 40–48 in Revelation 21:1–22:5.* Eugene, OR: Wipf & Stock, 2019. **Rossing, Barbara R.** *The Choice between Two Cities: Whore, Bride, and Empire in the Apocalypse.* Harrisburg, PA: Trinity Press International, 1999. **Russell, D. S.** *The Method and Message of Jewish Apocalyptic.* London: SCM, 1964. **Smith, Christopher R.** "The Portrayal of the Church as the New Israel in the Names and Order of the Tribes in Revelation 7.5–8." *JSNT* 39 (1990): 111–18. **Stewart, Alexander E.** *Reading the Book of Revelation: Five Principles for Interpretation.* Bellingham, WA: Lexham, 2021. **Swete, J. P. M.** "Maintaining the Testimony of Jesus: The Suffering of Christians in the Revelation of John." Pages 101–17 in *Suffering and Martyrdom in the New Testament: Studies Presented to G. M. Styler.* Cambridge: Cambridge University Press, 1981.

Weima, Jeffrey A. D. *The Sermons to the Seven Churches of Revelation: A Commentary and Guide*. Grand Rapids: Baker Academic, 2021. **White, J. R.** "The 144,000 in Revelation 7 and 14: Old Testament and Intratextual Clues to Their Identity." Pages 179–97 in *From Creation to New Creation: Biblical Theology and Exegesis: Essays in Honor of G. K. Beale*. Edited by D. M. Gurtner and B. L. Gladd. Peabody, MA: Hendrickson 2013. **Williams, Jarvis J.** *Redemptive Kingdom Diversity: A Biblical Theology of the People of God*. Grand Rapids: Baker Academic, 2021. **Wilson, Mark.** *The Victor Sayings in the Book of Revelation*. Eugene, OR: Wipf & Stock, 2007. **Wong, Daniel K. K.** "The Two Witnesses in Revelation 11." *BSac* 54 (July 1997): 344–54. **Wright, Christopher J. H.** *The Mission of God's People: A Biblical Theology of the Church's Mission*. BTL. Grand Rapids: Zondervan Academic, 2010. **Zimmermann, Ruben.** "Nuptial Imagery in the Revelation of John." *Bib* 84 (2003): 153–83.

16.1 INTRODUCTION

What many people expect from Revelation regarding the church and what they actually get are very different indeed. Of course, we should not be surprised by this, given the imaginative, creative nature of this prophetic-apocalyptic masterpiece. It never ceases to amaze because it is a visionary reflection of the glorious Triune God. Revelation fails to meet certain popular expectations about the church being raptured prior to the great tribulation. The term or concept of rapture out of tribulation never appears in Revelation. The good news, however, is that when we lay aside expectations and commit to listening carefully to what Revelation itself says in all its apocalyptic wonder, we will certainly not be disappointed. We will be heartened and encouraged!

Revelation presents the people of God by means of a host of images, figures, and symbols.[1] God's people are servants or slaves, assemblies or churches, saints or "holy ones," the true Israel—a kingdom and priests, the redeemed nations, a prophetic, witnessing people, victors or overcomers, family (children, brothers and sisters, bride), and a heavenly temple-city. Each image provides a crucial glimpse of the reality of God's people from a slightly different angle, bringing those who see John's vision of the church to a deeper, richer understanding of who we are and what we are called to do. Revelation showers the reader with such a flurry of aspects of this great reality called "God's people" that at times the images overlap (witnesses are lampstands, the bride is a city). But this repetition is a small price to pay and even a beautiful reminder that God highly values his people.

In this chapter we will focus on the identity of God's people, and in chapter 17 we will turn our attention to the task of God's people. But, of course, there will be overlap . . . because it is Revelation. We should not be surprised.

1. See a summary of the many descriptions given to believers in Wilson, *Victor Sayings*, 88–89.

16.2 Identity of God's People: A Host of Images

16.2.1 Servants

Along with the rest of the New Testament, John regularly uses the image of servants or slaves (δοῦλοι) to refer to God's people (Rev 1:1; 2:20; 7:3; 10:7; 11:18; 19:2, 5; 22:3, 6; cf. Acts 4:29; 16:17; Rom 1:1; 2 Cor 4:5; Gal 1:10; Phil 1:1; Col 4:12; Titus 1:1; Jas 1:1; 2 Pet 1:1; Jude 1:1). Before we highlight several uses of the slave imagery in Revelation, we note that the negative connotation of the slave trade is connected to Babylon (18:13), while "slave/servant" is consistently used as a positive symbol for God's people. Even the typical low-status elements such as being bought or owned are transformed since God's people have been purchased by the blood of Christ (5:9) and now reign as kings and priests (5:10). The Lord's ownership results in true freedom (1:5).[2]

The slave/servant image communicates several important characteristics of God's people. First, they are recipients of God's revelation. We see this chain of communication from the get-go: God—Christ—his angel—John—God's servants (1:1). John is included as one of God's servants but also singled out for a leadership role by being named as the one who "testifies to everything he saw" (1:2). He is also commissioned to write what he sees and send it to the seven churches (1:11, 19; cf. 2:1, 8, 12, 18; 3:1, 7, 14; 14:13; 19:9; 21:5). On several occasions, God's "servants" are identified with the prophets. God has announced to "his servants the prophets" the "mystery," a mystery accomplished when the seventh angel sounds his trumpet (10:7). In 22:6 the revealing angel says to John, "These words are trustworthy and true. The Lord, the God who inspires the prophets, sent his angel to show his servants the things that must soon take place."

Second, servants or slaves are followers of the Lamb and are sealed or protected by God. They are those who fear the Lord (19:5), who hold to the testimony of Jesus (19:10), and who keep the words of the scroll that is the book of Revelation (22:9). As followers of the Lamb, they are portrayed both as the 144,000 engaged in spiritual battle on earth but protected by God (7:3–4) and as the great multitude praising God in heaven following the battle (19:1–2, 6). This sealing or protection stands in contrast to the mark of the beast (cf. 13:16, 17; 14:9, 11; 16:2; 19:20; 20:4). Aune rightly concludes that the brand of the beast is "a parody of the seal of God that is placed on the foreheads of his servants (7:3; 9:4)."[3] Another reason to see both the 144,000 and the great multitude as representing the people of God is that both groups have been purchased as slaves. The 144,000 "were purchased from among mankind and offered as firstfruits to God and the Lamb" (14:4), while the purchase price of the great multitude

2. Koester, *Revelation*, 211.

3. Aune, *Revelation 6–16*, 768.

is none other than "the blood of the Lamb" (7:14).[4] This divine protection enables the people of God to endure faithfully.

Third, although protected, God's servants or slaves are still engaged in spiritual battle. The seal on the foreheads of God's servants, the 144,000, indicates ownership and protection during the battle (7:3–8). As we will see below, the 144,000 from the tribes of Israel is symbolic of God's people arrayed in battle formation. Keener notes that the number suggests a census used to assess military readiness (e.g., Num 1:3, 18, 20; 26:2, 4; 1 Chr 27:23), a reading that also explains the reference to adult males in Rev 14:4.[5] We also see an allusion to spiritual warfare in the reference to Jezebel leading astray some of Jesus's servants in Thyatira (2:20) and in 6:11, where the martyrs are told to wait a little longer, "until the full number of their fellow servants, their brothers and sisters, were killed just as they had been."

Finally, this image reminds readers that God's people will be rewarded at the eschaton. At the sounding of the seventh trumpet, the time arrives "for rewarding your servants the prophets and your people who revere your name" (11:18; cf. 10:7). In the heavenly city, God's servants will worship him, see his face, bear his name, and reign forever (22:3–5). They are before God's throne being sheltered in his presence and worshiping him day and night (7:15).[6]

16.2.2 Churches

A Jewish gathering in Revelation is designated a "synagogue" (συναγωγή: 2:9; 3:9), while a gathering of Jesus's disciples is labeled an "assembly" or "church" (ἐκκλησία).[7] The term ἐκκλησία occurs twenty times in the book and is usually translated "church" (1:4, 11, 20 [2x]; 2:1, 7, 8, 11, 12, 17, 18, 23, 29; 3:1, 6, 7, 13, 14; 22; 22:16). In every case a local congregation is in view, with the seven churches of Rev 2–3 receiving focused attention.[8]

The term ἐκκλησία draws on the cultural understanding of an assembly as compared to a building or an organization. In John's world, it referred to groups in each city with political or religious aspirations (cf. Acts 19:39). This understanding has implications for the use of the term in Revelation since God's "assembly" shares beliefs and makes decisions that carry social, political, and religious ramifications.[9] Although not strictly counter-imperial, the end-result of the church's beliefs and commitments has profound and far-reaching effects in relation to the dominant

4. Peter S. Perry, "The People of God in the Book of Revelation," *OHBR* 332.

5. Keener, *Revelation*, 230; cf. Bauckham, *Climax of Prophecy*, 218–19.

6. The term λατρεύω is used in 7:15 and 22:3 and refers to service of a cultic nature (i.e., worship).

7. Koester, *Revelation*, 215.

8. We will discuss the image of "lampstands" under 16.2.9.

9. Perry, "People of God," 328–30. See also Ralph J. Korner, *The Origin and Meaning of Ekklēsia in the Early Jesus Movement*, AJEC 98 (Leiden: Brill, 2017).

worldly empire. These seven assemblies function as "an alternative society in contrast to the Roman Empire."[10]

Another subtle implication of the use of ἐκκλησία is the emphasis it places on the communal nature of faith. Peterson writes: "The gospel is never [only] for individuals but always for a people. Sin fragments us, separates us, and sentences us to solitary confinement. Gospel restores us, unites us, and sets us in community. . . . A believing community is the context for the life of faith."[11] The seven churches of Revelation illustrate this reality splendidly. In addition, as most commentators observe, the number seven reflects the idea of fullness or completeness and suggests the universality of the church beyond these seven.[12] This universal reality is also supported by the literary structure, where the only plural use of "churches" outside the closing hearing formula occurs at the very center of the central Thyatira sermon. This placement calls each church to hear and obey the messages to the other churches as well.[13]

There have been many excellent studies of the seven messages in Revelation.[14] Our concerns here relate to the overall theology of the church conveyed by the sermons. Their common literary structure provides a framework for our theological understanding of the church: address, descriptions of Christ, commendation, complaint, exhortation and/or warning, admonition to listen, and a promise to the overcomers. To begin with, from the opening descriptions of Christ, we see that the church is rooted and grounded in its relationship to Christ. Each description begins with the τάδε λέγει formula, which alludes to the "thus says the Lord" formula used frequently in the Septuagint. The descriptions are often drawn from the opening vision of the risen Christ (1:9–20) and remind the hearers that the church is not merely a civic assembly but is a kingdom-of-God, Christocentric assembly/community. Revelation's clear message is "No Christ, no church!"

Running through all seven messages is "one overarching issue: whether or not to compromise."[15] Specifically, "Will these churches be faithful witnesses both *to* Jesus and *like* Jesus (and John!) by refraining from participation in the cultural norm of pagan religion, including the imperial cult, even if it carries serious negative consequences: social, economic, and political?"[16] Jesus's commendation and/or complaint about each assembly stems from his intimate knowledge of each situation.

10. Perry, "People of God," 329.

11. Eugene H. Peterson, *Reversed Thunder: The Revelation of John & the Praying Imagination* (New York: HarperSanFrancisco, 1988), 42–43.

12. See, e.g., Weima, *Sermons to the Seven Churches*, 11, who notes that other churches in the area could have been included, such as Troas, Colossae, and Hieropolis.

13. Weima, *Sermons to the Seven Churches*, 10–11.

14. See, e.g., Ramsay, *Letters to the Seven Churches*; Hemer, *Letters to the Seven Churches*; Weima, *Sermons to the Seven Churches*; Barry Beitzel, ed., *Lexham Geographic Commentary on Acts through Revelation* (Bellingham, WA: Lexham, 2019); Stephen Pattemore, *The People of God in the Apocalypse: Discourse, Structure and Exegesis*, SNTSMS 128 (Cambridge: Cambridge University Press, 2004); T. Scott Daniels, *Seven Deadly Spirits: The Message of Revelation's Letters for Today's Church* (Grand Rapids: Baker Academic, 2009).

15. Gorman, *Reading Revelation Responsibly*, 96.

16. Gorman, *Reading Revelation Responsibly*, 96, emphases original.

Most of the seven churches present a mixture of faithfulness and unfaithfulness. Ephesus is commended for its hard work, perseverance, intolerance of false teachers, and the endurance of hardship (2:2–3, 6). Smyrna is applauded for its spiritual health in the midst of afflictions and poverty, in light of slander from the synagogue of Satan, and in anticipation of further persecution and even martyrdom (2:9–10). Pergamum has remained faithful in a difficult environment even to the point of death (2:13). Thyatira is praised for its love, faith, service, perseverance, and spiritual growth (2:19). Sardis has only a few people who have not compromised (3:4), and Philadelphia has remained obedient and endured patiently (3:8, 10). Laodicea receives no commendation.

Equally prevalent are the areas of weakness or vulnerability to compromise.[17] Ephesus had forsaken the love they had at first (2:4). Pergamum is compromised with false teachers (2:14–15), and Thyatira tolerates false teachers who encourage immorality and idolatry (2:20–25). Sardis is spiritually dead even though they maintain a civic reputation of life and maturity (3:1–2). Laodicea is spiritually lukewarm while boasting in human riches and self-sufficiency (3:15–17). At the extremes we find Smyrna and Philadelphia receiving no rebuke and Laodicea hearing no praise. The other four churches receive a mixed assessment report.

Because of Christ's love for his church, his assessment leads to words of correction and/or encouragement. Christ's response also reveals that the church from God's perspective often differs markedly from the church from a human perspective.[18] The past faithfulness of a congregation does not guarantee its future faithfulness. With regard to Ephesus, Gorman concludes, "The situation is better read as a case of *incomplete orthopraxy* requiring repentance and supplementation, rather than *inappropriate orthodoxy* requiring the rejection of allegedly rigid beliefs."[19] Likewise, Jesus is discerning about individuals within each fellowship. Although Sardis is spiritually dead while keeping up appearances of life and maturity (3:8, 10), there remain a few people who "have not soiled their clothes" (3:4), and Jesus's promises are directed toward this minority group. On the other hand, in the most desperate case of Laodicea, we are reminded that a complete lack of faithfulness does not automatically eliminate the possibility of future faithfulness. Ongoing accountability, repentance, and renewed commitment are needed across the board.

At or near the end of each message, the assemblies are called to listen to what the Spirit says.

In the Spirit's messages, two themes consistently stand out. First, the dangers of compromise with Roman imperialism are real, especially as promoted through false teaching. The rival teachers and prophets embracing the teachings of Balaam, the

17. See the summary chart of Metzger, Peterson, and Daniels on the dangers facing the churches in Gorman, *Reading Revelation Responsibly*, 98.

18. Stewart, *Reading the Book of Revelation,* 84–85.

19. Gorman, *Reading Revelation Responsibly*, 92, emphasis original.

Nicolaitans, and Jezebel would have presented a powerful temptation to compromise. Second, Jesus makes it clear that allegiance to him is the primary criterion for a positive assessment. Allegiance even trumps ethnicity. The congregations in Philadelphia and Smyrna, the two who receive no rebuke, are both being opposed by the "synagogue of Satan" (2:9; 3:9). Stewart observes, "In Revelation, the ethnic Jews who rejected Jesus are identified with the gentile nations, and the Christians (both Jews and gentiles) embody the identity of ethnic and national Israel in the restoration."[20]

Our final observation from the seven messages is that the church is a people of promise. Every letter concludes with a victor's promise from the risen Christ. Christ is coming back (2:5b, 16b, 25; 3:3b, 11a, 20), and he will return with judgment or eternal reward. The motivation of eternal life is communicated through a variety of images: eating from the tree of life (Ephesus), life rather than death (Smyrna), a white stone with a new name (Pergamum), authority over the nations and the morning star (Thyatira), white garments and a place in the book of life (Sardis), God's temple and God's name (Philadelphia), and eating and reigning with Christ (Laodicea). God's church is an eschatological church, anticipating God's promises to come.

We find one occurrence of ἐκκλησία outside of Rev 2–3: "I, Jesus, have sent my angel to give you this testimony for the churches" (22:16). This certainly implies that the entire revelation is given to the churches, both the local congregations of chapters 2–3 and the universal church portrayed through a host of images in chapters 4–22. The concrete manifestations of the church in the historical present must be paired with the eschatological people God intends her to become to give a complete picture of Revelation's theology of the church.[21] We now turn to survey several of those important images.

16.2.3 Saints

The church as God's holy people finds its origin in the holiness of God and the Lamb. God's people are holy because they are in relationship with a holy God. In 3:7 Christ is described as "him who is holy and true." In 4:8 the term ἅγιος describes the all-powerful, eternal God by echoing the well-known "Holy, Holy, Holy" of Isa 6:3. In Rev 6:10 the martyrs under the altar address their prayers to the "Sovereign Lord, holy and true," as they ask about the timing of his judgment on the inhabitants of the earth. Those who worship the beast will be judged in "the presence of the holy angels and of the Lamb" (14:10). Even in this small sample, Revelation lays the foundation of holiness in God's identity and character. God is the One who defines *holy*, and holiness stands as a marker of association with God.[22]

20. Stewart, *Reading the Book of Revelation*, 86. For more on the hostility between the synagogue and the church, see deSilva, *Seeing Things John's Way*, 55–62.

21. See Flemming, *Foretaste of the Future*, 81–84.

22. Perry, "People of God," 333.

God's people as his "holy ones" or "saints" (τῶν ἁγίων) are identified by and called to faithful obedience. This theme appears throughout the book.[23] In 11:18 the twenty-four elders praise God for, among other things, "rewarding your servants the prophets and your people who revere your name [τοῖς ἁγίοις καὶ τοῖς φοβουμένοις τὸ ὄνομά σου], both great and small" (11:18).[24] This text reminds us that the saints or holy ones revere God, that they come from every social class, and that they will be rewarded by God. In 13:10, after learning that persecution and even martyrdom are a possibility, the saints are reminded of the call to "patient endurance and faithfulness" (cf. the sevenfold use of ὑπομονή—1:9; 2:2, 3, 19; 3:10; 13:10; 14:12). The phrase "whoever has ears to hear" recalls the initial challenge to the seven churches to stay faithful (e.g., 2:7, 11, 17, 29; 3:6, 13, 22). We see a similar call to obedience in 14:12: "This calls for patient endurance on the part of the people of God who keep his commands and remain faithful to Jesus" (cf. 6:9; 12:11, 17; 17:14; 20:4).

The identity marker of faithful obedience also appears through a variety of images: "virgins" (παρθένοι) in 14:4, which emphasizes the whole-hearted commitment of a holy warrior; the "fine linen" given to the bride in 19:8, which "stands for the righteous acts of God's holy people"; the call to "come out of her [Babylon], my people" in 18:4; and the commands in 22:11 to "let the righteous go on in righteousness; let the holy still be holy" (CSB).

But the faithfulness of the saints does not go unchallenged. Revelation makes it clear that the saints will suffer at the hands of evil powers. The outer court of the temple complex in 11:2 represents the church susceptible to persecution, and we are told that the gentiles will "trample on the holy city" for a limited time. The beast wages war against "God's holy people" and conquers them (13:7; cf. Dan 7:21). All who refuse to worship the image of the beast will be killed (Rev 13:15), and all who refuse the mark of the beast cannot buy or sell (13:16–17). Babylon is said to be "drunk with the blood of God's holy people," further described as "those who bore testimony to Jesus" (17:6). Babylon contains the "blood of prophets and of God's holy people, of all who have been slaughtered on the earth" (18:24). Because of Babylon's corruption and ruthless opposition to God and his people, two responses are called for. First, believers are to "come out of" Babylon so as to not share in her sins or receive her plagues (18:4). This is both a call to spiritual separation from the wicked power center and her values as well as a call to renewed allegiance to Christ and his kingdom.

23. The term ἅγιος ("holy one/s") is used to depict the people of God twelve times in Revelation: 5:8; 8:3, 4; 11:18; 13:7, 10; 14:12; 16:6; 18:20; 19:8; 20:9; 22:11. In addition, the same emphasis comes through in various contexts apart from the term "saints"—e.g., blessed are those who stay awake and remain clothed (16:15), who keep the words of this prophecy (22:7), and who wash their robes for the right to the tree of life (22:14). Similarly, the Lamb's followers are "called, chosen and faithful" (17:14), and the righteous continue to do right and the holy continue to be holy (22:10–11).

24. The καί after the term "saints" describes the "saints" as those who "fear your name" rather than introducing a different group to be rewarded. See Fanning, *Revelation*, 342.

Second, the saints are to acknowledge (and even celebrate) God's judgment of Babylon. Since Babylon has put to death God's people, God is true and just to judge her (16:5–7). Such justice calls for celebration since evil will not win in the end (18:20). God's judgments on the wicked are at least in part a response to the prayers of his people as the judgment fires fall after the prayers rise to God (5:8; 8:3–5). At the conclusion of the millennium, the nations from the four corners of the earth—Gog and Magog—surround "the camp of God's people [τὴν παρεμβολὴν τῶν ἁγίων], the city he loves," but these nations are judged by fire from heaven before they can harm God's people (20:8–9).

The picture of saints is completed by the assurance that they will experience God's resurrection life and restoration in the new creation. The seventh trumpet announces that the saints will be rewarded by God (11:18). At the wedding of the Lamb, the bride has made herself ready and is adorned in bright and clean fine linen, with linen representing "the righteous acts of God's holy people" (19:7–8). In contrast to the purple and scarlet garments worn by the prostitute (17:4; 18:12, 16), the bride's clothing signifies both God's gift of righteousness and her righteous response to God. In 20:4–6 the martyr church who refused to worship the beast comes to life and reigns with Christ (i.e., the first resurrection). The fifth beatitude then proclaims: "Blessed and holy are those who share in the first resurrection" (20:6). The addition of "holy" implies the inclusion of all God's people.

The image of God's people as the Holy City also reinforces that God's people will experience the great eschatological blessing. In 21:2 John sees "the Holy City, the new Jerusalem, coming down out heaven from God, prepared as a bride beautifully dressed for her husband." We are then told that God's dwelling is now among his people in fulfillment of the age-old promise that he will live with them, they will be his people (λαοὶ αὐτοῦ), and God himself will be their God (e.g., Lev 26:11–12; Ezek 37:26–28; Zech 2:10–11; 8:8; 2 Cor 6:16; Rev 21:22).[25] John is then carried away in the Spirit to a great and high mountain to witness the Holy City, Jerusalem, descending out of heaven from God (21:10). The closing warning to any who would willfully and intentionally distort the prophecy is that they will not have a share in the tree of life or the Holy City (22:19). The book closes with a benediction (22:21): "The grace of the Lord Jesus be with God's people." [26]

25. The textual variant "peoples" (λαοί) is most likely original and stresses the multiethnic character of God's redeemed people.

26. The NA28 closes 22:21 with simply, μετὰ πάντων. The "all" certainly refers to the churches who had gathered to hear the words of this prophecy and has produced a host of textual variants, most of which include "the saints" (τῶν ἁγίων). See Metzger, *Textual Commentary*, 690–91. Thus, the translation "God's people" (NIV) or "God's holy people" (NLT) or "all the saints" (NRSVue) seems appropriate.

16.2.4 True Israel

Two primary images are used to show that the people of God are the true Israel.[27] First, God's people are referred to as "a kingdom" and "priests," in contrast to those who claim to be Jews but are not (2:9; 3:9). There are three occasions in Revelation where God's people are described using royal and priestly language (1:6; 5:10; 20:6). Both 1:6 and 5:10 draw on Exod 19:5–6 (cf. also Isa 61:6), a summary of God's desire for his people Israel to be a "kingly and priestly nation mediating Yahweh's light of salvific revelation by witnessing to the gentiles (e.g., Isa. 43:10–13), a purpose that the OT prophets repeatedly observed went unfulfilled by Israel."[28] Osborne notes that these passages in Revelation are "part of the NT tradition that viewed the church as the true Israel" (cf. 1 Pet 2:5, 9).[29]

In Rev 1:5–6 Christ's work includes his ongoing love for his people, his act of liberating them from their sins, and his finished work of making them into a kingdom (or kingship) and priests (the aorist ἐποίησεν in this context suggests a completed action). In 5:9–10 the heavenly praise song celebrates the Lamb's worthiness based on his work: "you purchased" people for God from every nation and "you have made [ἐποίησας] them to be a kingdom and priests . . . and they will reign [βασιλεύσουσιν] on the earth." Bandstra rightly concludes that these promises originally made to Israel are fulfilled in the Christian church.[30] Furthermore, God's people have already been made citizens of the kingdom and have already begun to reign (1:6; 5:10a), although their future reign on the earth is yet to come (5:10b; 20:6; cf. 2:26; 3:21; 20:4; 22:5). Here we see Revelation affirming an inaugurated eschatology, including both "inaugurated priests" and "forthcoming rulers."[31]

Revelation does not go into great detail about what the priestly duties involve but hints at what Keener calls a "spiritual priesthood" featuring worship (4:10–11; 5:8–10; cf. 22:3) and offerings, including both prayer (5:8; 8:4) and giving their lives as living sacrifices (6:9).[32] The priestly promise likely includes both access to God's presence as well as the missional task of mediating his presence to the nations (cf. Rom 12:1).[33]

---

27. Arguably, the woman of Rev 12 is yet another image portraying the people of God as true Israel. We will discuss this below under 16.2.8. See Tabb, *All Things New*, 105–8.

28. Beale and McDonough, "Revelation," 1090. Andrew S. Malone, *God's Mediators: A Biblical Theology of Priesthood*, NSBT 43 (Downers Grove, IL: InterVarsity Press, 2017), 154–60, sees a close connection between the priestly language and ruling language in the NT since political and religious roles are often interrelated in the ancient world.

29. Osborne, *Revelation*, 65. Cf. Smalley, *Revelation*, 36. Here we see, according to Malone, that "God's promises to and expectations of his old-covenant people are extended to Christian believers of all backgrounds" (*God's Mediators*, 154).

30. Andrew J. Bandstra, "'A Kingship and Priests': Inaugurated Eschatology in the Apocalypse," *CTJ* 27 (1992): 16–17.

31. Malone, *God's Mediators*, 160; Tabb, *All Things New*, 91, concludes: "The saints *presently* reign in an inaugurated sense that anticipates their future experience in the consummated kingdom of God and Christ" (emphasis original). And this inaugurated service and rule could be embraced by various millennial views, since it would include both earthly service as well as activities in the new heaven and new earth. See Malone, *God's Mediators*, 161, emphasis original.

32. Keener, *Revelation*, 72.

33. Osborne, *Revelation*, 66; Christopher J. H. Wright, *The Mission of God's People: A Biblical Theology of the Church's Mission* (Grand Rapids: Zondervan, 2010), 120–22.

A second image used to show God's people as the true Israel is that of the 144,000 (Rev 7:3–8; 14:1–5). In chapter 7 an angel comes up from the east holding the "seal of the living God" (7:2). He tells the four angels with power to harm the land and the sea not to do so "until we put a seal on the foreheads of the servants of our God" (7:3). The noun "seal" (σφραγίς) is used thirteen times, with most referring to the seven seals, but two denoting God's seal (7:2; 9:4). The verb "seal" (σφραγίζω) also refers to God's seal several times in 7:3–5. The seal is placed on the "foreheads" (μέτωπον) of God's servants, signifying spiritual security and protection (3:12; 14:1; 22:4; cf. 2 Cor 1:22; Eph 1:13; 4:30), in contrast to those not sealed in Rev 9:4 and those bearing the mark of the beast (13:16; 14:9; 20:4; cf. 17:5). The term "servant" (δοῦλος) elsewhere in Revelation represents all believers (1:1; 2:20; 6:11; 10:7; 11:18; 19:2, 5, 10; 22:3, 6, 9).[34] The number sealed are "144,000 from all the tribes of Israel." This image depicts followers of Jesus as the true Israel, the whole company of the redeemed (see 11.4.5.2).

The number itself represents the square of twelve (twelve tribes and twelve apostles) multiplied by one thousand to symbolize completeness. The same figure is used in Rev 21 in the description of the New Jerusalem—the names of the twelve tribes and twelve apostles on its gates and foundations. The city is laid out as a perfect cube, representing the whole people of God (21:9–10) as God's temple people. Mayo concludes, "This symbolic link between the new Jerusalem, the bride of the Lamb, and the 144,000 sealed proposes conclusively an interpretation of the 144,000 as the universal church composed of both Jews and Gentiles."[35]

The repetition of the 144,000 in 14:1–5 further supports taking this image as a reference to the true Israel. In chapter 14 the Lamb is standing on Mount Zion with the 144,000 who have "his name and the Father's name written on their foreheads" (14:1; cf. 3:12; 22:4). They are people of exuberant praise (14:2–3). They are described as those "who had been redeemed from the earth" (14:3). They are pure and devoted, prepared for spiritual battle and engaged in following the Lamb (14:4a). They represent all those who have been purchased by the Lamb (14:4b; on the image of firstfruits, see Rom 8:23; 11:16; 16:5; 1 Cor 15:23; 16:15; 2 Thess 2:13; Jas 1:18). And they are blameless, devoid of lies and deceit (Rev 14:5). This extended description points toward a wider

34. The parallels in 19:1–8 are especially pertinent since the great multitude is equated with "servants" in 19:5 (cf. 19:2), the people of God praising him for his true and just judgment of the great prostitute, for the wedding of the Lamb, and for God's eternal reign. Keener, *Revelation*, 231–32, comments on how taking 144,000 "servants" literally is problematic: "If 'servants' represents all believers, then the total number of the genuinely saved through history (or, on other readings, through the Tribulation) are limited to 12,000 male Jewish virgins from each tribe (though the passage that specifies 144,000 male virgins does not specify their ethnicity [14:1–5]). If one takes 'servants' here in a narrower sense than it usually appears in Revelation (by identifying 'prophets' with a special group of believers in 10:7; 22:9), then God affords his special protection only to a group within the church based on their ethnicity, gender, and marital status; all gentile, female, and married believers must suffer from the plagues (9:4)."

35. Mayo, *"Those Who Call Themselves Jews,"* 102.

group of God's people, the true Israel, rather than a group restricted to ethnic Israel.[36] This reading of the 144,000 as the whole people of God is reinforced by its pairing with the vision of the great multitude in 7:9–17, to which we now turn.

16.2.5 Redeemed Nations

Yet another reason to interpret the 144,000 as the whole people of God is the pairing of the two visions in 7:1–8 and 7:9–17. This is one of several occasions where John hears about one reality and then sees another so that the two visions or scenes are mutually interpretative (e.g., 1:10–12; 5:5–6). John hears about the 144,000 (7:4) and then sees a countless multitude (7:9). We are looking at a single vision portraying God's people from two vantage points—the church prepared for spiritual battle in the first scene (7:4–8) and the church triumphant, celebrating the victory before the throne in the second (7:9, 15).[37] The second scene makes it clear that God's people, the true Israel, will indeed be a countless multitude of believers from every nation.

There are also several interesting parallels between 7:9–17 and the second 144,000 passage in 14:1–5. First, the location is with/before the Lamb on Mount Zion or before the throne (7:9; 14:1). Second, God's people have the Father's name written on their foreheads, symbolizing security and protection (14:1), realities described even more vividly in 7:15–17—sheltered in his presence, no more hunger or thirst, no more scorching heat, shepherded by the Lamb who provides living water, and God's eternal comfort. Third, they are singing or shouting songs of praise (7:10; 14:2–3). And fourth, both passages emphasize God's people as a holy, committed people—"virgins" and blameless followers of the Lamb without deceit (14:4–5), dressed in robes made white in the blood of the Lamb and holding palm branches, symbols of purity and victory (7:9, 13–14). These parallels reinforce viewing the 144,000 and the countless multitude as the same group, seen from different perspectives—the people of God protected from his wrath yet persecuted by the world, and God's people enjoying their eschatological reward (cf. 15:1–5).

The great multitude comes from "every nation, tribe, people and language" (7:9; cf. 5:9; 10:11; 11:9; 13:7; 14:6; 17:15), a formula indicating universality (cf. Dan 7:13–14).[38] The seven occurrences of this fourfold phrase, arranged differently every time, send a clear message that God's people will be a multitude drawn from all corners of the earth.[39]

36. Mayo, *"Those Who Call Themselves Jews,"* 77–106; Beale, *Revelation*, 416–17; Tabb, *All Things New*, 102–5.

37. Keener, *Revelation*, 231–33, offers a clear and convincing summary of why this is the preferred reading.

38. See the chart below taken from Duvall, *Revelation*, 96. Cf. Hays, *From Every People and Nation*.

39. We do recognize, however, that not all nations will follow the Lord. In Revelation the "nations" fall into two groups: wicked nations who follow the beast in rebellion against God and redeemed nations who follow the Lamb. See Schnabel, "John and the Future of the Nations."

5:9	Tribe	Language	People	Nation	People from this group purchased for God by Christ
7:9	Nation	Tribe	People	Language	Great multitude in heaven drawn from this group
10:11	Peoples	Nations	Languages	Kings	John is to prophesy about (or perhaps "against") this group
11:9	People	Tribe	Language	Nation	These unbelievers will refuse burial to the two witnesses
13:7	Tribe	People	Language	Nation	The beast is given authority over these unbelievers
14:6	Nation	Tribe	Language	People	The gospel is proclaimed to everyone who lives on the earth
17:15	Peoples	Multitudes	Nations	Languages	The prostitute sits on many waters, defined as this group

The intended scope of God's salvation is as wide as his creation.[40] After an extended discussion of the influence of Daniel and Gen 10 on this formula, Bauckham concludes that the fourfold phrase "encapsulates what we have seen to be John's central prophetic conviction about the coming of God's kingdom on earth: that the sacrificial death of the Lamb and the prophetic witness of his followers are God's strategy for winning all the nations of the world from the dominion of the beast to his own kingdom."[41]

God's missional purpose to redeem the nations also appears clearly in the portrait of the new creation in Rev 21–22. Wright concludes that from the perspective of biblical theology "we can draw a great trajectory—from the 'tribes, languages and nations' of Genesis 10, who stood in need of redemptive blessing, to that 'great multitude that no one could count,' . . . the redeemed humanity in the new creation."[42] In Rev 21:24 we see that the nations walk by the light of the glory of God and the Lamb, and the (redeemed) kings of the earth bring their splendor into the city. Likewise, in 21:25–26 the redeemed nations bring their glory and honor into the heavenly city. Whatever else "splendor" and "glory and honor" might mean, they certainly point to the created

40. Resseguie, *Revelation*, 121, notes that "the fourfold listing—the significant number related to the whole world—affirms the universal scope of God's redemption and contrasts with the beast's destructive influence over 'every tribe and people and language and nation' (13:7)."

41. Bauckham, *Climax of Prophecy*, 336–37.

42. Wright, *Mission of God's People*, 71.

goodness and giftedness given to the nations by God and now given back to God as an act of praise and worship.[43] In 22:1–2 we read that the leaves of the tree of life are "for the healing of the nations" (22:2), an expansion of the "leaves for healing" on the trees beside the temple river in Ezekiel (47:12). This stresses again that God's multicultural people are drawn from the nations and the new creation would not be complete without them.

God's people as the redeemed nations fulfill the original promise to Abraham in Gen 12:3: "all the peoples on earth will be blessed through you" (cf. Rom 4:11, 16; 9:8). According to Paul, this is the gospel announced in advance to Abraham (Gal 3:7–9). As Wright notes, "God's promise to Abraham in Genesis 12 is God's answer to the problem of the nations in Genesis 10 and 11."[44] Wright imagines God's conversation with Abraham when all is said and done: "As redeemed humanity, together with all angels and all creatures in creation, joins to celebrate that great achievement, I picture God turning to Abraham and saying, 'There you are. I kept my promise. 'All nations,' I said, and all nations it is. Mission accomplished.'"[45]

16.2.6 Prophetic Witnesses

God accomplishes his missional purposes on earth chiefly through his prophetic people.[46] The theme of prophecy/witness/testimony flows consistently throughout the book and even bookends the entire work as a "prophecy" (προφητεία)—1:3; 22:7, 10, 18, 19. The source of this prophetic message from/about Jesus is "the Spirit of prophecy" (19:10; cf. 22:6). John himself is designated a prophet and grouped with his fellow prophets (22:9; cf. 10:11). He "testifies to everything he saw—that is, the word of God and the testimony of Jesus" (1:2) as Jesus sent his angel to give John "this testimony for the churches" (22:16). Revelation intentionally portrays the whole people of God as a prophetic people (11:18; 16:6; 18:24). And this prophetic community stands in contrast to the many false prophets (e.g., Jezebel in 2:20 and "the false prophet" in 16:13; 19:20; 20:10). Revelation goes into deeper detail about the church's prophetic task using the language of testimony and witness.

The pioneering witness for the people of God is Jesus himself.[47] He is deemed "the faithful witness" (1:5; cf. 3:14: "the faithful and true witness") and indeed serves as

43. Fanning, *Revelation*, 545–46, comments on the earthiness of these multicultural gifts to God: "Verses 24–26 (as well as 22:1–5) reflect lively, productive human life and commerce on a renewed earth. Its redeemed people move in and out of the city that forms the center of God's new creation. They use their creative skills and crafts (21:24, 26), till and tend the fruitful earth (22:2–3a), learn and grow (22:2e), and worship God with direct intimacy and commitment (21:3, 22; 22:3–4)." Cf. Middleton, *New Heaven and a New Earth*, 21–34.

44. Wright, *Mission of God's People*, 70.

45. Wright, *Mission of God's People*, 77.

46. See Hays, "Faithful Witness, Alpha and Omega," 77, asserts, "The concept of witness-bearing (μαρτυρία) is central to the message of Revelation, and to its hortatory purposes." For a great many insights, see also chapter three in Olutola K. Peters, *The Mandate of the Church in the Apocalypse of John* (New York: Peter Lang, 2004), 77–118, on the "terminology and function of witness in John's Apocalypse."

47. See 13.3 on Jesus as the faithful witness.

"the paradigmatic witness."[48] Jesus bears witness through both his word and his life, the embodiment of that testimony.[49] The "sharp double-edged sword" of truth and judgment comes out of his mouth (1:16; 2:12, 16; 19:15, 21). His weapon is his word. What is more, Jesus's witness or testimony comprises the entire book of Revelation. Jesus has given this testimony (μαρτυρέω) to John for the churches (22:16), he testifies (μαρτυρέω) to everyone who hears the prophecy not to distort its message (22:18), and he testifies (μαρτυρέω) to all that is written, saying, "Yes, I am coming soon" (22:20).

Following the example of Jesus, God's people are faithful witnesses. The named martyr/witness Antipas is also described as "my faithful witness" (ὁ μάρτυς μου ὁ πιστός μου) in 2:13, thus mirroring Christ's faithfulness. Antipas and others like him live in difficult circumstances, remain true to Jesus's name, do not renounce their faith under pressure, and often suffer for their witness to Jesus. In short, they "follow the Lamb wherever he goes" (14:4). Besides the named witnesses John and Antipas, there are numerous unnamed witnesses. We find references throughout to the "testimony" (μαρτυρία or μάρτυς) of believers, including:

- those mentioned in 1:9 who share with John in the suffering, kingdom, and patient endurance that belong to those who follow Jesus
- the souls under the altar mentioned in 6:9 who were slain because of God's word and their testimony
- the victors in 12:11 who triumph by "the blood of the Lamb and by the word of their testimony"
- the rest of the woman's offspring in 12:17 who "keep God's commands and hold fast their testimony about Jesus"
- God's holy people who bear witness to Jesus and have been put to death by the prostitute in 17:6
- John's brothers and sisters "who hold to the testimony of Jesus" in 19:10
- the souls of those beheaded "because of their testimony about Jesus and because of the word of God" in 20:4

Before we draw together several important implications from the people of God as witnesses, let us look briefly at the central image of the witnessing church: the story of the two witnesses in Rev 11. Interpreters differ on the nature of these two figures, largely

48. Perry, "People of God," 337. Hays, "Faithful Witness, Alpha and Omega," 77, rightly observes that the prominence of this identification in 1:5 "leads us to expect that the Christology of the Apocalypse will place heavy emphasis on Jesus' role as one who testifies to the truth."

49. Flemming, *Foretaste of the Future*, 99–101.

50. See the list of such scholars in Kuykendall, *Lions, Locusts, and the Lamb*, 171n92, to which we would add the important monograph by Dalrymple, *Revelation and the Two Witnesses*, esp. 34–37.

divided along the lines of a literal versus symbolic interpretive approach. We prefer the figurative reading and follow the majority of scholars in identifying the two witnesses as the witnessing church.[50] Beale offers six reasons why the two witnesses should be taken as a symbol of the whole people of God: (1) they are called "two lampstands" in 11:4, an image identified as churches in 1:20, (2) the beast of verse 7 fights against God's people (cf. the corporate group persecuted in Dan 7:21), (3) the entire world of unbelievers will see in 11:9–13 the defeat and resurrection of the witnesses, meaning they are visible throughout the earth, (4) their time of witness (1,260 days) matches the time of oppression in other metaphors symbolizing the people of God—"the holy city," "the woman," and "those tabernacling in heaven" (11:2; 12:6, 14; 13:6), (5) the entire community of believers is often identified as the source of "testimony" to Jesus (e.g., 6:9; 12:11, 17; 19:10; 20:4), and (6) the two witnesses share powers attributed to both Moses and Elijah rather than those powers being divided between them.[51]

Dalrymple concurs with this reading and details four central themes/implications resulting from viewing the two witnesses as the people of God.[52] In other words, what do we learn about God's people as a result of the two-witness symbolism? First, God's people are protected spiritually even though they may suffer physically. This appears in the measuring of the temple (11:1), the power to defend themselves (11:5–6), and their ability to finish their testimony prior to martyrdom (11:7). Second, they faithfully execute their God-given task of bearing witness (11:3, 7). As we learned in 11:3–4 the two witnesses are the two lampstands, already identified in 1:20 as the seven churches (cf. 1:12, 13; 2:1, 5). The lampstands represent God's people called to be a light to the world. This power to bear witness also provides a powerful weapon in the cosmic war (11:5). In addition, as Hays observes, their testimony "constitutes an act of countercultural resistance through public prophetic proclamation of Jesus as Lord, an act of resistance that leads to persecution and (ultimately) martyrdom."[53] Third, they will in fact be persecuted and perhaps put to death by the world system (11:7). This stands in direct contradiction to popular escapist literature that promises a rapture out of any possible trouble prior to tribulation. The noun "witness" (μάρτυς) is used with reference to the righteous only in 2:13; 11:3; and 17:6, and in every case there is a connection to those who die for their faith. Fourth, God's people will be vindicated. Although attacked and killed by the beast, the witnesses are resurrected and taken up to heaven in a cloud in the presence of their enemies (11:11–12). God wins!

---

51. Beale, *Revelation*, 574–75.

52. Dalrymple, *Revelation and the Two Witnesses*, 47–55. We add observations of our own throughout. Flemming, *Foretaste of the Future*, 110–16, notes three take aways: (1) the church's witness is verbal and embodied, (2) the church's witness is public, and (3) the church's witness is also for the sake of the world.

53. Hays, "Faithful Witness, Alpha and Omega," 78.

16.2.7 Victors

The term νικάω is used seventeen times in Revelation in various contexts. The leading translations of the word include (1) the general term "overcome," stressing persistence and endurance but also carrying modern baggage (e.g., overcoming an addiction), (2) the rendering "conquer," featuring military associations that can be useful in describing the spiritual battle recounted in the book, and (3) "victor" language emphasizing the imagery of ancient games (along with wreaths, palm branches, white robes), a translation that fits the ancient context well.[54] As Koester notes, the term draws on three spheres of meaning: military, games or competition, and the virtue of faithfulness.[55] When we survey the uses of the term, we find the following: a conqueror or a conquest (6:2, 2), evil powers temporarily overpowering God's people (11:7; 13:7), the Lamb triumphing over evil powers (17:14), the victory of the Lamb (3:21; 5:5), believers triumphing over evil powers (12:11; 15:2), and promises made to the one who is victorious (2:7, 11, 17, 26; 3:5, 12, 21; 21:7). We see that νικάω can be used in three primary ways: (1) evil powers temporarily conquering God's people physically and politically, (2) the victory of the Lamb, both at the cross/resurrection and at the eschaton, a victory that is spiritual with ultimate physical and political implications, and (3) the resulting spiritual victory of God's people, also with wider ramifications.[56]

The specific nature of the victory of God's people can be seen in the "exhortation/warning" and "promises to the overcomers" sections of the seven messages.[57] The churches are expected to heed the commands and warnings in the here and now, while the promises are all eschatological, highlighting various aspects of enjoying God's presence in the new creation. The churches are being called to spiritual victory by continuing to stand strong against the world system or by discontinuing their current compromise with the system. We can clearly see the church's already-not-yet situation as well as the earthly/heavenly perspective on this situation. There is a real spiritual battle being fought. Those who "win" actually lose, and those who "lose" from the world's point of view actually win. Tabb rightly concludes, "In the world view of the Apocalypse 'victory' is not a matter of military might, political influence or athletic achievement; rather, it entails enduring faithfulness to Christ and his Word and spiritual conquest against sin and evil."[58] As Koester puts it, "Revelation transforms the images of conquest and victory, which brought high honor in Greco-Roman culture, into a call for Christians to resist aspects of that culture. Faithfulness to Jesus could

54. Wilson, *Victor Sayings*, 85. Wilson comments on two other important symbols of victory used in Revelation: the color white and palm branches (pp. 92–94).

55. Koester, *Revelation*, 265.

56. Cf. the similar conclusions of Kuykendall, *Lions, Locusts, and the Lamb*, 165.

57. See 11.3. For more detail, see Weima, *Sermons to the Seven Churches*, and Wilson, *Victor Sayings*, 103–229.

58. Tabb, *All Things New*, 109.

bring dishonor in society, yet in Christ's eyes the faithful are worthy of the victory wreath (Rev 2:10; 3:11)."[59] Thus, Beale's excursus on νικάω is titled, "The Ironic Notion of 'Overcoming'" (cf. 3:21; 5:5–6).[60]

The church as victors can anticipate eschatological rewards (21:7). Wilson observes that while relationship with God may be the ultimate outcome, the various images relate to how God will provide for his people in the heavenly kingdom. The promises fall into three broad categories: provision (e.g., tree of life, crown of life, shepherd the nations, white garments, book of life, confession of name, divine throne), place (e.g., paradise of God, pillar in the temple, New Jerusalem), and person (e.g., hidden manna, new name, morning star, divine names).[61] Anticipating the glorious blessings of life in God's eternal presence would have provided a personal and powerful incentive to persevere in faithfulness. We sometimes forget that the early church anticipated an imminent return of Christ and thus a near-term experience of reward, compared to those of us living in the twenty-first century.[62]

One lingering question remains—must all the victors be martyrs? Following his comprehensive survey of the people of God in the Apocalypse, Pattemore draws three primary conclusions about Revelation's martyr ecclesiology: (1) the church in Revelation is portrayed as a martyr church, (2) the martyr church is modeled on Christ in every respect, and (3) the readers of the book of Revelation are consistently challenged to identify with the martyr church, primarily involving faithful witness even to the point of death, ethical choices, and obedient lifestyle.[63] The five key martyr passages include 6:9–11; 12:10–12; 16:5–7; 19:1–2; and 20:3–4. While the martyrs receive special attention, the overall message of Revelation focuses on faithfulness to the point of being willing to die. After all, as Peters notes, victory is achieved through faithful witness rather than primarily through death since "death itself is not synonymous with victory."[64] In addition, the promises to the victors are not limited to the martyrs. All true Christians are victors and every disciple of Jesus "must be in principle a martyr and be ready to lay down his life for his faith," even though not all will be required to do so.[65] The victory comes through faithfulness in the face of suffering and opposition of all kinds, not just martyrdom. As Beale notes, "It is not just how people die that proves them to be overcomers, but the whole of their Christian lives are to be characterized by 'overcoming,' which is a process completed at death. . . . Overcoming refers to the victory of one's whole life of faith."[66]

59. Koester, *Revelation*, 265.

60. Beale, *Revelation*, 269–72.

61. Wilson, *Victor Sayings*, 170–71. On pp. 228–29 Wilson shows how the promises to the seven churches are fulfilled in the new creation.

62. See the section on "Perseverance of the Saints" in Osborne, *Revelation*, 42–46.

63. Pattemore, *The People of God*, 113–16.

64. Peters, *Mandate of the Church*, 106.

65. Wilson, *Victor Sayings*, 91.

66. Beale, *Revelation*, 271.

16.2.8 Family

John also uses family imagery to describe the people of God—the woman, her offspring, children, brothers and sisters, and the bride. One of the leading characters in the drama is "the great sign . . . in heaven: a woman clothed with the sun, with the moon under her feet and twelve stars on her head" (12:1). This pregnant woman is attacked by "another sign," an enormous red dragon (12:1–6, 13–17). She cries out in labor until she gives birth to a male child who will rule the nations (12:2, 5; cf. Ps 2:9; Rev 2:27; 19:15). The son is then snatched up to God and his throne (12:5), and the woman flees into the wilderness where she is protected and nourished by God for 1,260 days (12:6). The son is clearly Jesus the Messiah, but the identity of the woman is less clear.

The image of the woman far surpasses an individual such as Mary. She gives birth to Jesus the Messiah and has other "offspring," a term defined in 12:17 as "those who keep God's commands and hold fast their testimony about Jesus" (cf. 14:12). As a result, the woman clearly has a connection to the church but also precedes the church in some way. We take the woman to symbolize the "singular community of faith spanning the Old and New ages," a community that both brings forth and follows the Messiah.[67] While the image of the "crown of twelve stars on her head" could hint at national Israel, the number here more likely signifies the totality of God's people.[68] In addition, we find it likely that the woman and her offspring both represent the whole people of God from two perspectives, as with the 144,000 and the great multitude: "the people of God are kept safe spiritually (the woman), but are subject to physical harm in the form of persecution (her offspring)."[69] The image of the woman also anticipates the people of God portrayed as the bride and stands in contrast to the unrighteous depicted as the prostitute later in the book. This imagery reinforces the reality of unity of God's people—Jewish and gentile followers of Jesus—along with God's protection of his people even though they will be subject to opposition and persecution.

We also find John's vision incorporating the images of "children" and "brothers and sisters" throughout. In the vision of the new heaven and new earth in 21:1–8, Jesus proclaims, "It is done. I am the Alpha and the Omega, the Beginning and the End. To the thirsty I will give water without cost from the spring of the water of life. Those who are victorious will inherit all this, and I will be their God and they will be my children (υἱός)" (21:6–7). We notice two things here. First, the promise to the victors is framed in the language of God's long-standing covenant promise to his people: I will be your God, you will be my people, and I will dwell among you (e.g., Lev 26:11–12; Jer 31:33;

67. Tabb, *All Things New*, 107; cf. Mathewson, *Companion to the Book of Revelation*, 89; Beale, *Revelation*, 624–32; Koester, *Revelation*, 542–44; Osborne, *Revelation*, 456–58.

68. Kuykendall, *Lions, Locusts, and the Lamb*, 175.

69. Mathewson, *Companion to the Book of Revelation*, 89.

Ezek 36:28; 37:27; Zech 2:10–11; 8:8; Hos 2:23; 2 Cor 6:16; Rev 21:22). Second, as Koester notes, here the covenant imagery uses adoption language, and the redeemed are described as "sons" or "children."[70] This picks up on the ancient practice of the son having the right to inherit his father's property (P.Oxy. 1206.6–10; Cicero, *Dom.* 35; Cicero, *Fam.* 13.19; Gal 4:5–7).[71] John uses the image to send the message that God's adopted children have a share in the heavenly city.

The term "brothers" or "brothers and sisters" is used four times in the plural (ἀδελφοί—Rev 6:11; 12:10; 19:10; 22:9) and once in the singular to refer to John himself (1:9).[72] The plural form includes male and female followers of Christ, as the contexts show. The martyrs are told in 6:11 to wait until "the full number of their fellow servants (σύνδουλοι), their brothers and sisters (ἀδελφοί)," are killed just as they have been. Likely this refers to the same group—fellow believers—and emphasizes the family bond between Christians as they fulfill their faithful witness. Revelation 12:10–11 celebrates the coming of God's kingdom and his Messiah along with the defeat of the "accuser of our brothers and sisters" (12:10) and their triumph by the Lamb's blood and their testimony. Here the imagery places all family members together as fellow partakers in God's eschatological victory. In 19:10 an angel declares himself a fellow servant with John and his "brothers and sisters who hold to the testimony of Jesus," again stressing the family unity of all those who share a common confession of Jesus. In 22:9 the term is used in reference to Christian prophets (lit. "and your brothers the prophets") or perhaps as another way of describing the whole people of God as a prophetic family—"and with your fellow prophets (τῶν ἀδελφῶν σου τῶν προφητῶν) and with all who keep the words of this scroll."

A central familial image in Revelation is the portrayal of the church as the bride. The Old Testament often portrays the people of God as the bride or wife of Yahweh (e.g., Isa 49:18; 54:5–8; 61:10–62:5; Jer 2:2; 3:14; 31:32; Ezek 16; Hos 2:14–20). For this reason, spiritual unfaithfulness was also depicted in terms of marital infidelity (e.g., Hos 2:1–23; Ezek 16:15–63). The New Testament continues the marriage metaphor with Christ as the bridegroom and the church as his bride (e.g., Matt 9:14–17; 25:1–13; John 3:22–30; 2 Cor 11:2; Eph 5:25–27, 32).

In Rev 17–21 the bride stands in stark contrast to the prostitute.[73] John intentionally plays one against another using similar phrases, sequences, and patterns.[74] The harlot Babylon seduces people to join an evil system out of allegiance to the dragon and the

70. Koester, *Revelation*, 808–9.

71. Koester, *Revelation*, 808.

72. Kuykendall, *Lions, Locusts, and the Lamb*, 159, raises the possibility that John's four plural references of ἀδελφοί might be a symbolic representation of the "totality and full coverage of the earth by believers."

73. See the helpful chart contrasting Babylon the Great and the New Jerusalem in Tabb, *All Things New*, 183.

74. See Jan Fekkes III, "'His Bride Has Prepared Herself': Revelation 19–21 and Isaian Nuptial Imagery," *JBL* 109 (1990): 269, 283–84.

beasts, while the bride New Jerusalem calls people to worship the true God. Perhaps we find here the context for the characterization of the 144,000 (the full people of God) as spiritual "virgins," undefiled and blameless in 14:4–5. They do indeed "follow the Lamb wherever he goes" (14:4).

Nuptial imagery appears in 18:23; 19:7–9; 21:2, 9–10; 22:17.[75] The usage in 18:23 refers not to the people of God but to literal brides (and bridegrooms) whose celebratory voices will no longer be heard in Babylon after God judges the pagan city. The four remaining passages are especially relevant to our discussion. Following the celebration of the prostitute's judgment in 19:1–4, the bride theme is introduced in 19:7–9. The announcement of the Lamb's wedding is coupled with a proclamation of the bride's readiness. She "has made herself ready" yet has also been given "fine linen, bright and clean," which represents the "righteous acts of God's holy people," thus signifying a life of faith and righteous deeds. This first passage concludes with the fourth beatitude, blessing those who are invited to the wedding supper of the Lamb. The church here is depicted both as the bride and as invited wedding guests, once again illustrating how Revelation sometimes uses imagery fluidly to identify the same referent.[76] This introduction in chapter 19 prepares the reader for the presentation and description of the bride more fully in 21:2 and 21:9–21.[77]

In 21:2 the Holy City, the New Jerusalem, is portrayed coming down out of heaven "as a bride beautifully dressed for her husband." This brings to mind the grand entrance of the bride in the traditional wedding ceremony. In keeping with the ceremony, her entrance is then followed by the restatement of God's longstanding covenant vow that he would live among his people—"They will be his people, and God himself will be with them and be their God" (21:3). The final destination of God's people is an experience of "the caring, relational presence of the Triune God."[78] In 21:9–10 John begins his more comprehensive angelic tour of the bride/wife, the Holy City/New Jerusalem.[79] Once again, the bride-city imagery blends together to convey something of the reality that God's eternal dwelling place is his people. John draws especially on Isaiah as he presents the heavenly city as a bride dressed for her wedding (e.g., Isa 49:18; 54:5, 11–12; 61:10). The subsequent adornment of the city in Rev 21:11–21 is equivalent to the adornment of the bride (21:2). Certainly, the focus in chapter 21 is the eschatological community living in God's presence, but we also catch a glimpse of all that came before—the overcoming in the churches, the righteous deeds of saints, and

75. The term νύμφη ("bride") is used in 18:23; 21:2, 9; 22:17, and γυνή occurs in 19:7; 21:9. The latter can refer to a woman, a married woman, or a newly married woman (i.e., a bride). See "γυνή," BDAG 208–9.

76. Tabb, *All Things New*, 182.

77. Fekkes, "His Bride Has Prepared Herself," 283.

78. Duvall and Hays, *God's Relational Presence*, 304; cf. 310, 315, 320, 335. The image of "dwelling" (σκηνή) recalls God's glorious presence sheltering or tabernacling over his people throughout the story and culminating here.

79. For more detail, see Fekkes, "His Bride Has Prepared Herself."

everything the bride had to do to prepare herself. Fekkes says it well: "When viewed from the perspective of nuptial imagery, the glorious bridal attire and ornaments of the New Jerusalem reach back from the future into the present and serve as a symbolic testimony to the faithfulness of the earthly community."[80]

The final use of bride language occurs in the conclusion to the book and features the Spirit and the bride saying, "Come!" (22:17). As discussed in Part Three, while this could serve as a call for Christ to return, it is more natural in context to view it as an invitation to respond positively to Christ. This would mean *the church plays an important role in calling the nations to faithful discipleship to Jesus.*

16.2.9 New Jerusalem

The book of Revelation was initially written to those who lived in cities, and as Bauckham notes, most readers early on "lived, both geographically and symbolically, between Jerusalem and Rome."[81] Revelation truly is the tale of two cities—Rome/Babylon/the great prostitute/city of man on the one hand, and Jerusalem/New Jerusalem/bride/city of God on the other. John is given tours of both in his grand vision (cf. 17:3; 21:10). Bauckham lists numerous contrasts between these two cities in Revelation (see the chart below).[82]

New Jerusalem, the Bride	Babylon, the Prostitute
Chaste bride, wife of Lamb (21:2, 9)	The harlot with whom the kings of the earth fornicate (17:2)
Her splendor is the glory of God (21:11–21)	Her splendor is from exploiting her empire (17:4; 18:12–12, 16)
Nations walk by her light = glory of God (21:24)	Her corruption and deception of the nations (17:2; 18:3, 23; 19:2)
Kings of the earth bring their glory into her (i.e., their worship and submission to God: 21:24)	She rules over the kings of the earth (17:18)
They bring the glory and honor of the nations into her (i.e., glory to God: 21:26)	Her luxurious wealth extorted from all the world (18:12–17)
Uncleanness, abomination, and falsehood are excluded (21:27)	Her abominations, impurities, and deceptions abound (17:4–5; 18:23)
Water of life and tree of life for healing of the nations (21:6; 22:1–2)	Her wine makes the nations drunk (14:8; 17:2; 18:3)
Life and healing (22:1–2)	Blood of slaughter (17:6; 18:24)
God's people are called to enter the New Jerusalem (22:14)	God's people are called to come out of Babylon (18:4)

80. Fekkes, "His Bride Has Prepared Herself," 286–87.
81. Bauckham, *Theology*, 126.
82. Bauckham, *Theology*, 131–32.

The renewal of 21:1–22:5 shines most brightly against the dark backdrop of the Babylon visions—the signs of life are "no more" in 18:22–23, but in 21:4 death, mourning, crying, and pain are "no more."[83] Going all the way back to Babel in Gen 10:10; 11:9, which really should be called "Babylon," we get a picture of a city "in which all the God-given abilities of humans are deliberately focused on creating a society that has no need of God . . . the symbol of humanity's attempt to govern themselves without reference to and in defiance of God."[84]

The heavenly city stands in contrast to this unholy city/empire. In our brief look at the city of God we will focus on how the imagery informs our understanding of God's people. In Ch. 20 we will explore the wider significance of the new creation.

We begin with tabernacle imagery that Revelation sometimes uses to describe God's people. The great multitude in 7:9–17, likely a symbol of all the redeemed, is sheltered (σκηνόω) in God's tabernacling presence (7:15; cf. Ezek 37:27).[85] Historically, the tabernacle was in some ways a continuation of the garden of Eden as it became the dwelling place of God on earth and reminded God's people that one day God's presence would fill the entire cosmos.[86] In 12:12 and 13:6 God's people are described as those who "dwell" in heaven in contrast to those who dwell on the earth (cf. 13:12). They worship God and Christ, are protected by God, and enjoy his presence as permanent citizens of the heavenly city. The vision of seven angels with seven last plagues (15:1, 5–8), featuring the "temple of the tabernacle of testimony" in 15:5, should be paired with the vision of the faithful standing beside the glassy sea (15:2–4) and suggests that God's faithfulness to his people carries with it his commitment to judge evil. In 21:3 we read of the fulfillment of God's longstanding promise to tabernacle among his people (e.g., Lev 26:11–12; Ezek 37:27; Zech 2:10–11): "God's dwelling is now among the people, and he will dwell with them."

Revelation uses the image of a lampstand, part of the furnishings of the original tabernacle, to signify God's presence with his people and to represent the church (Exod 25:31–40; 37:17–24; Heb 9:2).[87] The noun "lampstand" (λυχνία) occurs seven times in Revelation: 1:12, 13, 20 [2x]; 2:1, 5; 11:4. In the opening vision John sees "someone like a son of man" in all his glory standing among the seven golden lampstands (1:12–13; 2:1). These lampstands are identified explicitly in 1:20 as the "seven churches" (cf. 2:5).

83. Tabb, *All Things New*, 175.

84. T. Desmond Alexander, *The City of God and the Goal of Creation*, SSBT (Wheaton, IL: Crossway, 2018), 26–29.

85. For more on tabernacle imagery in Revelation, see Craig R. Koester, *The Dwelling of God: The Tabernacle in the Old Testament, Intertestamental Jewish Literature, and the New Testament*, CBQMS 22 (Washington, DC: Catholic Biblical Association of America, 1989), 116–51; Andrea L. Robinson, *Temple of Presence: The Christological Fulfillment of Ezekiel 40–48 in Revelation 21:1–22:5* (Eugene, OR: Wipf & Stock, 2019), 131–36. For a look at how the theme of God's dwelling places runs through the whole of Scripture, see J. Daniel Hays, *The Temple and the Tabernacle: A Study of God's Dwelling Places from Genesis to Revelation* (Grand Rapids: Baker Academic, 2016).

86. T. Desmond Alexander, *From Eden to the New Jerusalem: An Introduction to Biblical Theology* (Grand Rapids: Kregel Academic & Professional, 2008), 31–42.

87. Hays, Duvall, and Pate, *A-to-Z Guide to Biblical Prophecy*, 248–50.

John changes the one lampstand in Zech 4 to seven in Revelation to signify Jesus's full presence among all of God's people, rather than being limited to the seven particular congregations of Asia Minor. The number of lampstands changes in Rev 11, where the *two* lampstands "stand before the Lord of the earth."[88] Here they are equated with the two witnesses and the two olive trees (11:3–4), another indication that the lampstands represent God's people. The lampstand image portrays the light and life given by God to his people and potentially, through his people, as witnesses to the world.[89] Ultimately the lamp/lampstand imagery is fulfilled in the new creation where the glory of God and of the Lamb will provide light (21:23; 22:5; cf. also 14.8 where the Holy Spirit symbolizes light).

Revelation moves beyond the image of the tabernacle and its furnishings to portray God's people as his temple.[90] In 3:12 Jesus promises to make the victors "a pillar in the temple of my God" and to "write on them the name of my God and the name of the city of my God, the new Jerusalem." In this way Jesus identifies the heavenly city with those who overcome. The great multitude standing before the throne of God is said to "serve [λατρεύω] him night and day in his temple" (7:15). Both these references to an eschatological temple are consistent with understanding God's eternal temple as his presence among his people in the new creation, so that John can later say that the New Jerusalem does not contain a temple as earthly temples go (21:22: "the Lord God Almighty and the Lamb are its temple").

This eschatological temple is an entire temple city, a heavenly city, a New Jerusalem. God's people have their names written in the heavenly register, the book of life (3:5; 21:27; cf. 13:8; 17:8; 20:12, 15). In 20:9 the "camp of God's people" is equivalent to "the city he loves," another indication that the city itself is people. In 21:2–3 John is shown the "Holy City, the new Jerusalem, coming down out of heaven from God prepared as a bride," and this people-city-bride is "God's dwelling place." God has a people for a temple. This imagery continues in 21:9–10 as John is invited to see "the bride, the wife of the Lamb" and then subsequently sees "the Holy City, Jerusalem, coming down out of heaven from God." In 22:14, 19 the city is once again described as "holy."

Aside from the captivating effects of the imagery itself, what does it tell us about God's people? Several things are worth noting. First, the symbol of the city reminds us of the sheer size of God's people, along with the rich cultural diversity she embodies. The great multitude of chapters 7 and 19, along with the enormous dimensions of the city in chapter 21 speak of the "innumerability of the saints." Gundry notes the

88. Kuykendall, *Lions, Locusts, and the Lamb*, 268, observes that John uses multiple images in his visions that include different numbers: "believers are symbolized as one woman, two witnesses, seven churches, twelve tribes, one hundred and forty-four thousand servants, and an incalculably great multitude."

89. Tabb, *All Things New*, 96–97.

90. See the comprehensive work by Beale, *Temple and the Church's Mission*, and a summary of the uses of "temple" (ναός) in Revelation in Kuykendall, *Lions, Locusts, and the Lamb*, 260–62.

significance: "Sufferers naturally tend to think of themselves as few, often as even alone. John aims to lift the suffering saints out of their sense of isolation by pointing to the immense number of the redeemed."[91] And this not-so-small mass of redeemed humanity brings to the new creation their own cultural uniqueness. The people of God, the church as God intended, will be from every nation, every culture, and every race: "These distinct peoples, cultures, and languages are eschatological, everlasting. At the end, we do not find the elimination of difference. Instead, the very diversity of cultures is a manifestation of God's glory."[92]

Second, the city is repeatedly called "holy" (11:2; 21:2, 10; 22:19), matching the description of God's people as "holy ones" or "saints" (5:8; 8:3–4; 11:18; 13:7, 10; 14:12; 16:6; 17:6; 18:20, 24; 19:8; 20:9). Outside the city are the unholy (21:8, 27; 22:15). God's people come to imitate his very character.

Third, the city is "new" with people having a "new name" (2:17; 3:12), singing a "new song" (5:9; 14:3), living in a "new heaven and new earth," the "new Jerusalem" (21:1–2). They are people belonging to the God who is "making everything new" (21:5). This newness will also include a material newness—a new heaven and a new earth. Most importantly, God's people are destined to live in God's presence for eternity, in God's safe, secure, life-giving presence. As many have observed, the cubical shape of the city depicts God's people as the eternal holy of holies (21:15–21; cf. 1 Kgs 6:20).[93]

16.3 CONCLUSION

Revelation's theology of the people of God uses a variety of images and figures to paint a remarkable portrait of those who follow the Lamb. This depiction includes essential relationships as well as insights into the saints' journey through this world to the next. Four themes stand out.[94] First, God's people belong to him, and he will protect them spiritually through their wilderness journey. They are God's servants, his temple people. They are secure and sealed or protected as they anticipate a new exodus out of Babylon and entry into the new Jerusalem.

Second, they are a Christocentric community who follows the Lamb. They are pledged to Christ as bride, living in faithful obedience. They are holy in relation to their holy God. As a kingdom and priests, their rule and service anticipate their future roles. As the 144,000, they are arranged for spiritual battle. They are the bride preparing

91. Robert H. Gundry, "The New Jerusalem: People as Place, Not Place for People," *NovT* 29 (1987): 260.

92. Esau McCaulley, *Reading While Black: African American Biblical Interpretation as an Exercise in Hope* (Downers Grove, IL: IVP Academic, 2020), 116.

93. Duvall and Hays, *God's Relational Presence*, 318–22.

94. Cf. the concluding reflections in Pattemore, *People of God in the Apocalypse*, 216–19, and Dalrymple, *Revelation and the Two Witnesses*, 47–55.

herself for the wedding day. Their mission of witness to the nations flows out of this fundamental discipleship relationship to Jesus.

Third, because of their faithfulness and allegiance to the kingdom of God, they can expect to face opposition and persecution, even martyrdom. The forces of evil abound and seek to do them harm. They are to respond with spiritual separation from Babylon and by entrusting it all to God's just and righteous judgment to come. They will not all be physical martyrs, but they will all live with a willing-to-die quality of faith.

Lastly, God's people will eventually be vindicated and restored. These victors can anticipate their final reward. They are people of promise and will one day experience resurrection life and restoration in the new creation. They will be sheltered in God's tabernacling presence, living in the holy of holies that is the new Jerusalem. Their response is an eternity of worship.

Chapter 17

"YOU ARE WORTHY!": WORSHIP

BIBLIOGRAPHY

Archer, Melissa L. *"I Was in the Spirit on the Lord's Day": A Pentecostal Engagement with Worship in the Apocalypse*. Cleveland, TN: CPT, 2015. **Aune, David E.** "The Influence of Roman Imperial Court Ceremonial on the Apocalypse of John." *BR* 28 (1983): 5–26. **Barnett, Paul W.** *Apocalypse Then and Now: Reading Revelation Today*. South Sydney: Aquila, 2004. **Bauckham, Richard J.** "The Worship of Jesus in Apocalyptic Christianity." *NTS* 27 (1981): 322–41. **Belcher, Kimberly Hope.** "Early Trinitarian Hymns (East and West)." Pages 95–105 in *An Introduction to the History of Hymns*. Edited by Benjamin K. Forest, Mark A. Lamport, and Vernon M. Whaley. Eugene, OR: Cascade, 2019. **Block, Daniel I.** *For the Glory of God: Recovering a Biblical Theology of Worship*. Grand Rapids: Baker Academic, 2014. **Blount, Brian K.** *Revelation: A Commentary*. NTL. Louisville: Westminster John Knox, 2009. **Boring, M. Eugene.** "The Theology of Revelation: 'The Lord Our God the Almighty Reigns.'" *Int* 40.3 (2001): 257–69. **Carnegie, David R.** "Worthy is the Lamb: The Hymns in Revelation." Pages 243–56 in *Christ the Lord: Studies in Christology Presented to Donald Guthrie*. Edited by Harold H. Rowdon. Downers Grove, IL: InterVarsity Press, 1982. **Du Rand, J.** "'Now the Salvation of Our God Has Come . . .': A Narrative Perspective on the Hymns in Revelation 12–15." *Neot* 27.2 (1993): 313–30. **Ford, Josephine M.** "The Christological Function of the Hymns in the Apocalypse of John." *AUSS* 36 (1998): 207–29. **Friesen, Steven J.** *Imperial Cults and the Apocalypse of John: Reading Revelation in the Ruins*. Oxford: Oxford University Press, 2001. **Gallusz, Laszlo.** *The Throne Motif in the Book of Revelation: Profiles from the History of Interpretation*. LNTS 487. London: Bloomsbury T&T Clark, 2014. **Giblin, Charles.** *The Book of Revelation: The Open Book of Prophecy*. Collegeville, MN: Liturgical Press, 1991. **Gloer, W. H.** "Worship God! Liturgical Elements in the Apocalypse." *RevExp* 98 (2001): 35–57. **Grabiner, Steven.** *Revelation's Hymns: Commentary on the Cosmic Conflict*. LNTS 511. London: Bloomsbury T&T Clark, 2015. **Gruenwald, Ithamar.** *Apocalyptic and Merkavah Mysticism*. AGJU 14. Leiden: Brill, 1980. **Horn, Stephen N.** "Hallelujah, the Lord our God, the Almighty Reigns: The Theology of the Hymns of Revelation." Pages 42–54 in *Essays on Revelation: Appropriating Yesterday's Apocalypse in Today's World*. Edited by Gerald L. Stevens. Eugene, OR: Pickwick, 2010. **Howard-Brook, Wes, and Anthony Gwyther.** *Unveiling Empire: Reading Revelation Then and Now*. Maryknoll, NY: Orbis Books, 1999. **Hurtado, Larry W.** "Revelation

4–5 in the Light of Jewish Apocalyptic Analogies." *JSNT* 25 (1985): 105–24. **Kelly, Balmer H.** "Revelation 7:9–17." *Int* 40.03 (2001): 288–95. **Knight, Jonathan.** "The Enthroned Christ of Revelation 5:6 and the Development of Christian Theology." Pages 43–50 in *Studies in the Book of Revelation*. Edited by Steve Moyise. Edinburgh: T&T Clark, 2001. **Koester, Craig R.** "The Distant Triumph Song: Music and the Book of Revelation." *WW* 12.3 (1992): 243–49. **Kooy, V.** "The Apocalypse and Worship—Some Preliminary Considerations." *RefR* 30 (1976): 198–209. **Kraybill, J. Nelson.** *Apocalypse and Allegiance: Worship, Politics, and Devotion in the Book of Revelation*. Grand Rapids: Brazos, 2010. **Martin, Ralph P.** *Worship in the Early Church*. Grand Rapids: Eerdmans, 1974. **McGowan, Andrew B.** *Ancient Christian Worship: Early Church Practices in Social, Historical, and Theological Perspective*. Grand Rapids: Baker Academic, 2014. **McKinnon, James W.** *Music in Early Christian Literature*. Cambridge: Cambridge University Press, 1987. **Michaels, J. Ramsey.** *Revelation*. IVPNTC. Downers Grove, IL: InterVarsity Press, 1997. **Morton, Russell.** "Glory to God and to the Lamb: John's Use of Jewish and Hellenistic/Roman Themes in Formatting His Theology in Revelation 4–5." *JSNT* 83 (2001): 89–109. ———. *One Upon the Throne and the Lamb: A Tradition Historical/Theological Analysis of Revelation 4–5*. New York: Peter Lang, 2007. **Mowry, L.** "Revelation 4–5 and Early Christian Liturgical Usage." *JBL* 71.2 (1952): 75–84. **O'Rourke, J. J.** "The Hymns of the Apocalypse." *CBQ* 30 (1968): 399–409. **Peters, Olutola K.** *The Mandate of the Church in the Apocalypse of John*. New York: Peter Lang, 2004. **Peterson, David G.** *Engaging with God: A Biblical Theology of Worship*. Downers Grove, IL: InterVarsity Press, 1992. ———. "Worship in the New Testament." Pages 51–91 in *Worship: Adoration and Action*. Edited by D. A. Carson. Grand Rapids: Baker, 1993. ———. "Worship in the Revelation to John." *RTR* 47 (1986): 67–77. **Peterson, Eugene H.** *Reversed Thunder: The Revelation of John & the Praying Imagination*. New York: HarperSanFrancisco, 1991. **Piper, O.** "The Apocalypse of John and the Liturgy of the Ancient Church." *CH* 20.1 (1951): 10–22. **Powery, Luke A.** "Painful Praise: Exploring the Public Proclamation of the Hymns of Revelation." *ThTo* 70 (2013): 69–78. **Ross, Allen P.** *Recalling the Hope of Glory: Biblical Worship from the Garden to the New Creation*. Grand Rapids: Kregel Academic, 2006. **Ruiz, Jean-Pierre.** "Revelation 4:8–11; 5:9–14: Hymns of the Heavenly Liturgy." *SBLSP* 34 (1995): 216–19. **Samra, James.** "Hymns and Credal Worship in the New Testament." Pages 3–15 in *An Introduction to the History of Hymns*. Edited by Benjamin K. Forest, Mark A. Lamport, and Vernon M. Whaley. Eugene, OR: Cascade, 2019. **Saunders, S.** "Revelation and Resistance: Narrative and Worship in John's Apocalypse." Pages 119–22 in *Narrative Reading, Narrative Preaching*. Edited by Joel B. Green and M. Pasquarello III. Grand Rapids: Baker Academic, 2003. **Schedtler, Justin P. Jeffcoat.** *A Heavenly Chorus: The Dramatic Function of Revelation's Hymns*. WUNT 2.381. Tübingen: Mohr Siebeck, 2014. ———. "The Hymns in Revelation." *OHBR* 115–30. **Schimanowski, Gottfried.** "'Connecting Heaven and Earth': The Function of the Hymns in Revelation 4–5." Pages 67–84 in *Heavenly Realms and Earthly Realities in Late Antique Religions*. Edited by Ra'anan S. Boustan and Annette Yoshiko Reed. Cambridge: Cambridge University Press, 2004. **Siew, Antonius King Wai.** *The War* *between the Two Beasts and the Two Witnesses: A Chiastic Reading of Revelation 11:1–14:5*. London: T&T Clark, 2005. **Smith, Robert S.** "Songs of the Seer: The Purpose of Revelation's Hymns." *Them* 43.2 (2018): 193–204. **Stevenson, Gregory M.** "Conceptual Background to Golden Crown Imagery in the Apocalypse of John (4:4, 10; 14:14)." *JBL* 114/2 (1995): 257–72. **Tabb, Brian J.** "Prayer in Apocalyptic Perspective." Pages 191–208 in *For It Stands in Scripture: Essays in Honor of W. Edward Glenny*. Edited by Ardel B. Caneday with Anna Rask and Greg Rosaver. St. Paul, MN: University of Northwestern-St. Paul, 2019. **Thompson, Leonard.** *The Book of Revelation: Apocalypse and Empire*. Oxford: Oxford University Press, 1990. **Thompson, Marianne Meye.** "Worship in the Book of Revelation." *ExAud* 8 (1992): 45–54. **Tonstad, Sigve.** *Saving God's Reputation*. LNTS 337. London: T&T Clark, 2006. **Voorwinde, Stephen.** "Worship, the Key to the Book of Revelation?" *VR* 63 (1998): 3–35. **Westermeyer, Paul.** "The Book of Revelation in Music and Liturgy." *OHBR* 431–46. **Yarbro Collins, Adela.** *The Combat Myth in the Book of Revelation*. Eugene, OR: Wipf & Stock, 2001.

17.1 INTRODUCTION

Revelation is the primary worship book of the New Testament, perhaps of the entire Bible. In this final book of the Christian canon, we have "the last word on worship."[1] Marianne Meye Thompson explains: "There is no book of the New Testament in which worship figures so prominently, provides so much of the language and imagery, and is so fundamental to its purpose and message as the book of Revelation."[2] Worship plays such a significant role in the Apocalypse because it lies at the heart of the central conflict between the Triune God and the forces of evil, a conflict that engages the church at every turn. Worship does not just appear on the side streets or cul-de-sacs of the story, but all along the *cardo maximus* of the entire dramatic narrative.[3] And Revelation moves beyond simply teaching about worship; it shows the reader how to worship by including multiple scenes of worship.[4]

The term "worship" can mean many things, but we are using it to refer to a response of praise and thanksgiving to, acclamation of, and dependence upon God for who he is and for his mighty acts (past, present and future), so that this affirmation of supreme worth leads the worshiper to deeper devotion and loyalty. Ultimately, faithful obedience flows out of worship, and while these two realities are not identical, they can never be completely separated.[5] As Jesus told his disciples on the night before his crucifixion,

1. Peterson, *Reversed Thunder*, 57.

2. Marianne Meye Thompson, "Worship in the Book of Revelation," *ExAud* 8 (1992): 45.

3. Leonard Thompson, *Book of Revelation*, 53.

4. Wes Howard-Brook and Anthony Gwyther, *Unveiling Empire: Reading Revelation Then and Now* (Maryknoll, NY: Orbis Books, 1999), 197.

5. Similar to the relationship between worship and obedience, my work on the relationship between the indicative and the imperative in Paul's letters arrived at the following: the two realities should never be reversed, separated, or totally merged. Paul's expression "the obedience of faith" in Rom 1:5; 16:26 captures the idea well. See Duvall, "Synchronic Analysis," 219–42.

"Whoever has my commands and keeps them is the one who loves me" (John 14:21; cf. 14:15, 23). Worship means loving God with our words in a way that leads to loving God with our lives. In short, "Worship is an act of attention to the living God who rules, speaks, and reveals, creates and redeems, orders and blesses."[6] In this chapter we will look at the multifaceted terminology for worship, the setting of worship, the temptation to false worship, the various aspects of worship (especially the many hymns), and Revelation's theology of worship.

17.2 THE MULTIFACETED TERMINOLOGY OF WORSHIP

Worship takes many forms in Revelation, including blessing, doxology, benediction, acclamation, speaking, singing, hymns, prayers, and prostration. We begin to get a handle on the rich variety of worship language in Revelation by looking first at various terms most directly related to worship:

- **αἰνέω**: verb for "praise" (19:5)
- **εὐλογία**: noun for "praise" or "blessing" (5:12, 13; 7:12)
- **εὐχαριστέω**: verb for "give thanks" (11:17)
- **εὐχαριστία**: noun for "thanksgiving" or "gratitude" (4:9; 7:12)
- **τιμή**: noun for "honor" (4:9, 11; 5:12, 13; 7:12; 21:26)
- **δόξα**: noun for "glory" (1:6; 4:9, 11; 5:12, 13; 7:12; 11:13; 14:7; 15:8; 16:9; 18:1; 19:1, 7; 21:11, 23, 24, 26)
- **δοξάζω**: verb for "glorify" (15:4; 18:7)
- **ἄξιος**: noun for "worthy" (3:14; 4:11; 5:2, 4, 9, 12; 16:6)
- **ᾄδω**: verb for "sing" (5:9; 14:3; 15:3)
- **ᾠδή**: noun for "song" (5:9; 14:3 [2x]; 15:3)
- **κράζω**: verb for "cry out" or "shout" (6:10; 7:2, 10; 12:2; 14:15; 18:2, 18, 19; 19:17)
- **προσευχή**: noun for "prayers" (5:8; 8:3, 4)
- **ἀμήν**: noun for "Amen" (1:6, 7; 3:14; 5:14; 7:12 [2x]; 19:4; 22:20)
- **ἀλληλουϊά**: noun for "Hallelujah" (19:1, 3, 4, 6)
- **χαίρω**: verb for "rejoice" (19:7; negatively "gloat" in 11:10)
- **ἀγαλλιάω**: verb for "exult" or "be glad" (19:7)
- **εὐφραίνω**: verb for "rejoice" (12:12; 18:20; negatively "celebrate" in 11:10)
- **λατρεύω**: verb for "to serve" or "worship" (7:15; 22:3)
- **προσκυνέω**: verb for "worship" or "fall down" (3:9; 4:10; 5:14; 7:11; 9:20; 11:1, 16; 13:4 [2x], 8, 12, 15; 14:7, 9, 11; 15:4; 16:2; 19:4, 10 [2x], 20; 20:4; 22:8, 9)

6. Peterson, *Reversed Thunder*, 59.

Many of these terms occur within one of the eight major hymn sections—4:8–11; 5:8–14; 7:9–12; 11:15–18; 12:10–12; 15:3–4; 16:5–7; 19:1–8 (underlined in the above list). We will discuss those occurrences within the contexts of those hymnic units (see 17.5 below). But the rest deserve brief comment in order to grasp the wider context of worship in Revelation.[7]

First, Revelation is uncompromising in its insistence that God alone is worthy of worship. On two occasions John falls down to worship the revealing angel only to be immediately and sharply rebuked and told to "Worship God!" (19:10; 22:8–9; contrast with 1:17). True believers "serve" God in worshipful service (1:6; 7:15; 22:3) and refuse to worship the beast (13:15; 20:4).

Second, the kingdom of darkness also values worship but worships unworthy objects. Unbelievers refuse to repent and give God glory (16:9). Instead, they revere the dragon and the beast, the demonic (9:20; 13:4 [2x], 8, 12; 14:9, 11; 16:2; 19:20). The wicked rejoice or celebrate the death of the righteous (11:10 [2x]). Little wonder Babylon is described as a self-glorifying power (18:7).

Third, because God's people have faced enormous injustice at the hands of Babylon-like powers, worship proves a fitting response to God's judgment of the kingdom of evil, including Satan (12:12) and Babylon (18:20). The souls under the altar cry out for justice (6:10). God is worshiped as the "Holy One, you who are and who were," who is just in his judgments of those who "shed the blood of your holy people and your prophets" (16:5–6). Jesus even reassures the church in Philadelphia that he will make "those who are of the synagogue of Satan, who claim to be Jews though they are not, but are liars—I will make them come and fall down at your feet and acknowledge that I have loved you" (3:9).

Fourth, worship takes various forms, including singing (14:3), praying (5:8; 8:3–4), responding with an "Amen" (1:7; 22:20; cf. 3:14 where Christ is "the Amen"), and even prostrating oneself (e.g., the elders on every occasion).

Fifth, in some cases worship is equivalent to genuine repentance and conversion (a possible interpretation in 11:13; 14:7; cf. 16:9).

Sixth, we also see a subtle emphasis on worship in the vision of the new creation. "Glory" as an attribute of God's brilliant presence characterizes the New Jerusalem (21:11, 23) and the "glory and honor" of the nations will be brought into the heavenly city (21:24, 26). In the new creation, the great multitude before the throne of God is said to "serve him day and night in his temple" (7:15) and again in 22:3 we are told that God's "servants will serve him" (22:3), both using the verb λατρεύω, a term implying priestly service or worship.

7. Some uses of worship terminology are not relevant to our discussion (e.g., several uses of "cry out" in other contexts as in 7:2; 12:2; 14:15; 18:2, 18, 19; 19:17; the promise to a few in Sardis who have been faithful to one day walk with Jesus dressed in white in 3:4; and the glory/splendor of an angel in 18:1).

Again, these various emphases outside of the more formal hymn sections often complement what we will find in a closer look at those hymns below. Already, we are developing a theology of worship in Revelation that is central to the entire narrative—God-centered, uncompromising, holistic, varied, and at times, a bit surprising (e.g., praising God for his judgments). We now turn our attention to the vision setting of worship in Revelation.

17.3 THE SETTING OF WORSHIP

Before we explore the hymns of Revelation in more detail, we will look briefly at the book's worship setting and then the context of false worship faced by its readers. These two issues play an important role in understanding the overall theology of worship. When it comes to the setting, we begin with the prologue (1:1–8) and epilogue (22:6–21). These bookends intentionally place the entire book in a worship setting. In the opening doxology, Jesus is praised as the one who "loves us and has freed us from our sins by his blood, and has made us to be a kingdom and priests to serve his God and Father—to him be glory and power for ever and ever! Amen" (1:5–6). In verse 7 we read that he is coming again as Judge and this calls for another "Amen." In essence, the entire beginning of Revelation is filled with liturgical elements: blessing (1:3), a confessional greeting/benediction (1:4–6), a doxology (1:6), and acclamations of "Amen" (1:6, 7).[8] The book closes with Jesus's promise to return, which is met with a prayer for Christ to return: "Amen. Come, Lord Jesus" (22:20). The concluding benediction is possibly followed by a final "Amen" depending on the text-critical decision in 22:21. It is hard for readers to miss how worship frames the entire book.

In addition, in 1:10–11 the worship setting is made explicit when John testifies, "On the Lord's Day I was in the Spirit, and I heard behind me a loud voice like a trumpet, which said: 'Write on a scroll what you see and send it to the seven churches.'" The reference to the "Lord's Day" is taken by most to refer to Sunday, the day of worship. By identifying himself as being "in the Spirit," Melissa Archer concludes that "John is making a statement about the significance of worship as the point of contact between heaven and earth."[9] This serves as a clue that the worship scenes to follow are depicting an alternative reality for God's people, a true reality compared to the reality of this world order.[10]

Revelation 2–3 details the struggles and victories of the church on earth, along with attendant warnings and words of encouragement from Christ through the Spirit. It is no accident that the vision of the church is immediately juxtaposed with the visions of heavenly worship in chapters 4–5. What is more, as we shall see, the opening scenes of worship (chiefly Rev 4–5) are balanced by the closing scenes (esp. chs. 17–22).[11]

8. Peters, Mandate of the Church, 47–49.

9. Archer, *'I Was in the Spirit on the Lord's Day'*, 131.

10. Archer, *'I Was in the Spirit on the Lord's Day'*, 299.

11. Marianne Meye Thompson, "Worship in the Book of Revelation," 49.

The point is hard to miss—what is happening in heaven becomes the pattern for what should happen on earth, much like Jesus says in his model prayer: "as in heaven, so also on earth" (Matt 6:10).[12] Heaven does not reflect earth; rather, earth is called to reflect Heaven.[13] Interestingly, none of the major worship scenes in Revelation occur on earth; they are all heavenly worship scenes. Earth is called to reflect heaven as the eschatological provides the foundation for the ethical/relational response of discipleship. And ultimately worship is what grounds eschatology![14]

Another major feature of the worship setting in Revelation is the centrality of the hymns (see 17.5 below)—4:8–11; 5:8–14; 7:9–12; 11:15–18; 12:10–12; 15:3–4; 16:5–7; 19:1–8, with 16:5–7 being the most tentative. Ford rightly surmises that hymns are placed at strategic locations throughout the narrative and "carry the 'story line' of the Apocalypse. . . . [A]ll the major events of the book are accompanied by heavenly hymns."[15] One interesting observation from this arrangement is that in Revelation the hearer/reader is not merely provided instruction in worship, theory or practice, but is engaged in the very act of worship: "Revelation, though, like the work of a good novelist, *shows* rather than *tells* its audience how to offer prayer and worship."[16] Perhaps this is an added reason why the hymns recur throughout. Such catechetical worship is an ongoing and even central aspect to Christian discipleship. Integrally related to the setting of worship in Revelation is the larger context of false worship.

17.4 THE CONTEXT OF COUNTERFEIT WORSHIP

When studying the primary term for "worship" (προσκυνέω) in Revelation, it comes as a surprise to see how often it is used for false worship:

- 9:20–21: worshiping demons and idols
- 13:4 [2x], 8, 12, 15: worshiping the dragon, the beast, or the image that honors the beast
- 14:9, 11: worship the beast and its image
- 16:2: worship the image of beast
- 19:20: worship the image of beast
- 20:4: the martyrs who had *not* worshiped the beast or its image

12. Marianne Meye Thompson, "Worship in the Book of Revelation," 48–49.

13. David Peterson, "Worship in the Revelation to John," *RTR* 47 (1986): 77, who concludes, "John wrote to encourage his readers to reflect the pattern of the heavenly assembly in their life on earth, . . . Christian Worship was intended to be parallel to the Worship of heaven."

14. Leonard Thompson, *Book of Revelation*, 57.

15. Josephine M. Ford, "The Christological Function of the Hymns in the Apocalypse of John," *AUSS* 36 (1998): 208, 211; cf. Leonard Thompson, *Book of Revelation*, 72; Koester, *Revelation*, 127, 129; Osborne, *Revelation*, 47.

16. Howard-Brook and Gwyther, *Unveiling Empire*, 197, emphasis original.

Of the twenty-four uses of this primary term for worship, over half have some connection to counterfeit worship. Even John is guilty on two occasions of misplaced worship, although not on the same level, when he mistakenly falls down to worship an angelic messenger. Peterson notes how this contrast between true and false worshipers reaches its climax in these two visions at the end of the book: the fall of Babylon (17:1–19:10) and the new Jerusalem (21:9–22:9), and the parallel conclusions where an angel reprimands John with the command, "Worship God!" (19:10; 22:8–9).[17] Bauckham rightly argues that the main problem in these two passages is not the temptation to angel worship in the congregations per se, but the larger issue of true vs. false worship: "In a sense the theme of his whole prophecy is the distinction between true worship and idolatry, a distinction for which Christians in the contemporary situation needed prophetic discernment."[18] The attention to counterfeit worship highlights the temptation the readers faced at the ground level.

The conflict that provides the context of worship is both political and spiritual. It is political in the sense that the church is under pressure to conform to the worship of the imperial cult (see Ch. 4 for specifics). The primary question is who is worthy of worship: God and the Lamb or the Roman emperor (or any human ruler)? Kraybill reminds us that all worship demonstrates political allegiance, either to the kingdom of God or to the kingdoms of this world, and this was certainly the case for Revelation's first readers.[19] Even the songs and symbols of worship reflect this conflict. Aune observes similarities between the hymns of Revelation and the imperial hymns composed to honor the emperor, hymns that highlighted attributes of the emperor that John uses of God (e.g., Holy One, glory, salvation, authority, worthy to receive power, righteous are your judgments, our God the Almighty).[20] By appropriating terms and symbols used in emperor worship to encourage worship of God and the Lamb, John was engaging in an act of political rebellion.[21]

But the conflict is also spiritual in the sense that the church is involved in a larger cosmic battle against supernatural forces of evil. This explains why Revelation warns against worship of both the dragon (Satan and the demonic) and the beast (human anti-Christian political powers). These two realms are distinct but interrelated. In his fine work on Revelation's hymns, Grabiner zeroes in on the issue of cosmic conflict and explores the identity and role of Satan in the narrative.[22] The broader theme of a war in heaven fits the story (e.g., Rev 12; 20) and explains what lies behind the battle for

17. David Peterson, *Engaging with God: A Biblical Theology of Worship* (Downers Grove, IL: InterVarsity Press, 1992), 264–65.

18. Bauckham, *Climax of Prophecy*, 135.

19. Kraybill, *Apocalypse and Allegiance*, esp. 13–25, 53–69.

20. Aune, *Revelation 1–5*, 316–17.

21. Justin P. Jeffcoat Schedtler, "The Hymns in Revelation," *OHBR* 121–22; Tabb, *All Things New*, 122–24.

22. See Steven Grabiner, *Revelation's Hymns: Commentary on the Cosmic Conflict*, LNTS 511 (London: Bloomsbury T&T Clark, 2015), 35–68. Cf. also Sigve Tonstad, *Saving God's Reputation*, LNTS 337 (London: T&T Clark, 2006).

the soul of the churches. Grabiner concludes, "The hymnic portions (which are placed in a temple and divine council setting) need to be heard with the dissonant echoes of Satan's rebellion in the background."[23] As a result, worship in Revelation is not simply a matter of adopting correct liturgical practices. It occurs within a charged and tense environment of conflict—conflict with the Roman Empire and conflict with Satan's evil empire. Revelation clearly and consistently calls people to worship God alone as Creator, Redeemer, and Sustainer (e.g., 14:6–7; 15:4).

17.5 Revelation's Hymns

The hymns of Revelation are not simply theological detours or optional accessories; they are central to the book's theology: "hymns are one of the primary vehicles through which the author of the Apocalypse makes theological, Christological, and soteriological claims."[24] Revelation's depiction of God occurs through song more than through prose or narrative.[25] Koester is correct to note that "Music plays a larger role in the book of Revelation than in any other book of the New Testament, and few books in all of Scripture have spawned more hymns sung in Christian worship today."[26] It is certainly true that worship goes beyond music, but in Revelation singing takes center stage as the primary mode of worship. "Worship sings," as Peterson says, and, in this sense, we can view singing as "speech intensified and expanded."[27] These hymns call for participation rather than simple observation; they show rather than merely advise; they engage and unify the community, drown out heretical songs, and above all, draw the singers into a deeper relationship with the Lord.[28]

Each hymn originates from the heavenly throne room and by doing so provides the church on earth with the content and pattern for worship as God intended. These hymns offer an alternative to the ever-present "songs" of the empire. In addition, the hymns provide assurance that God will one day fully and finally judge evil. Peterson concludes that "John wrote to encourage readers to *reflect the pattern of the heavenly assembly in their life on earth.*"[29]

On a literary level, the hymns play a crucial role in moving along the overall storyline. They typically summarize and/or interpret surrounding narratives and visions (e.g., 4:8–11 and 5:9–14 both interpret chs. 2–3 and introduce chs. 6–19; 7:9–17 summarizes and interprets 7:1–8; 11:15–18 summarizes and interprets 8:1–11:14 and

23. Grabiner, *Revelation's Hymns*, 68.

24. Schedtler, "Hymns in Revelation," 115.

25. Marianne Meye Thompson, "Worship in the Book of Revelation," 49.

26. Craig R. Koester, "The Distant Triumph Song: Music and the Book of Revelation," *WW* 12.3 (1992): 243–49.

27. Peterson, *Reversed Thunder*, 66.

28. Howard-Brook and Gwyther, *Unveiling Empire*, 197.

29. David G. Peterson, "Worship in the New Testament," in *Worship: Adoration and Action*, edited by D. A. Carson (Grand Rapids: Baker, 1993), 89–90, emphasis original.

prepares for what is to come).[30] On the whole, the hymns provide a worship framework, and thus a theological framework, for the entire Apocalypse.

The genre of hymns in the ancient world often included certain formal features, such as an invocation of the deity in the second or third person, praise of the deity, and closing prayer. Other features might include introductory formulae such as λέγω, parallelism, *inclusio*, and elements within the text like quotations of praise or lament, petitions for help, prayers, crying out, and loud voices.[31] A close reading of Revelation shows important features shared by the hymns: (1) verbs of saying, speaking, crying out, shouting, or singing—some explicit form of verbal expression near the beginning (4:8, 10; 5:9, 12, 13, 14; 7:10, 12; 11:15, 17; 12:10; 15:3; 16:5; 19:1, 3, 4, 5, 6), (2) the frequency of the topic of worship—worship, thanks, praise, rejoicing, song (4:9, 10; 5:9, 13, 14; 7:11, 12; 11:16, 17; 15:3, 4; 19:4, 5, 7), (3) varied celebrations or affirmations of worship such as "Amen" or "Hallelujah" or "You are worthy" or the trisagion "Holy, Holy, Holy" (4:8, 11; 5:9, 12, 14; 7:12; 19:1, 3, 4, 6), (4) numerous lists of attributes of and praises for God and the Lamb, including several doxologies (4:9, 11; 5:12, 13; 7:10, 12; 12:10; 15:3; 16:7; 19:1–2, 7), and (5) kinesthetic movement, such as falling down or encircling the throne or laying down crowns or wearing robes or holding palm branches or harps (e.g., 4:10; 5:11, 14; 7:9, 11; 11:16; 15:2; 19:4). The features of hymns mentioned above, in addition to their theological function in the context, lead us to classify the following eight passages in Revelation as hymnic units: 4:8–11; 5:9–14; 7:10–12; 11:15–18; 12:10–12; 15:2–4; 16:5–7; 19:1–8.[32] The unit of 16:5–7 has the fewest hymn-like features and is sometimes omitted from the list. Others subdivide these units into smaller sections, raising the hymn count.[33]

Before looking more closely at each of these eight hymns, we have the question of the sources that influenced John's imagery.[34] There are several possibilities. Some would say that John simply recorded the visions as he experienced them in a mechanical fashion, but most scholars agree that the details of the hymns point to some editorial work on John's part. One option is the more mystical stream of Rabbinic Judaism known as *merkabah* mysticism, where mystics sought to reach the throne room of God through visionary experiences.[35] While there are interesting parallels here, other influences seem more dominant. Other scholars have pointed toward hymnic traditions used in the Old

30. Beale, *Revelation*, 657; Russell Morton, "Glory to God and to the Lamb: John's Use of Jewish and Hellenistic/Roman Themes in Formatting his Theology in Revelation 4–5," *JSNT* 83 (2001): 91–93.

31. Schedtler, "Hymns in Revelation," 116; Jan A. Du Rand, "'Now the Salvation of Our God Has Come . . .': A Narrative Perspective on the Hymns in Revelation 12–15," *Neot* 27.2 (1993): 315–16; Stephen N. Horn, "Hallelujah, the Lord our God, the Almighty Reigns: The Theology of the Hymns of Revelation," in *Essays on Revelation: Appropriating Yesterday's Apocalypse in Today's World*, ed. Gerald L. Stevens (Eugene, OR: Pickwick, 2010), 42.

32. Schedtler, "Hymns in Revelation," 116; Du Rand, "'Now the Salvation of Our God Has Come," 316.

33. Aune, *Revelation 1–5*, 315–16.

34. Grabiner, *Revelation's Hymns*, 6–12; Koester, *Revelation*, 127–30.

35. Ithamar Gruenwald, *Apocalyptic and Merkavah Mysticism*, AGJU 14 (Leiden: Brill, 1980).

Testament since the hymns are chock full of Old Testament allusions and echoes.[36] Some consider hymnic material used in Roman imperial court ceremonies as the key influence.[37] The growing consensus opts for a more complex solution. Most likely the hymns in Revelation are John's Spirit-inspired creations in light of Old Testament worship language and practices, the worship challenges within the seven churches, and the larger contextual setting of the Roman imperial cult.[38] In the following overview of the eight hymnic units, I will focus on the position/role of the hymn in the narrative and particular theological emphases within the hymn, since we have already provided a basic exegesis of these passages (see Part Three).

17.5.1 Revelation 4:8–11

Following the messages to the seven churches in Rev 2–3, the scene shifts to heaven in 4:1 for the throne room vision of chapters 4–5, with the final promise to the Laodicean church in 3:21 serving as a thematic bridge: "To the one who is victorious, I will give the right to sit with me on my throne, just as I was victorious and sat down with my Father on his throne." The term "throne" (θρόνος) is mentioned nineteen times in twenty-five verses (4:1–5:14) and serves as the foundational image for all that follows: "God's throne is portrayed in Rev. 4 as the *axis mundi*, the immovable centre of all reality."[39] The hymnic unit of 4:8–11 is located at the end of this initial grounding vision and anchors the reader's faith in God himself. God is mentioned as the recipient of worship in every verse in this hymn, featuring majestic attributes ("Holy, holy, holy," "who was, and is, and is to come," and the double mentions of "him who sits on the throne" and "who lives for ever and ever") and lofty titles ("Lord God Almighty" and "our Lord and God").[40] The hymn uses a variety of worship language to praise God—glory, honor, thanks, worship, worthy, and power. The reason for worship is made explicit in the final verse: "for you created all things, and by your will they were created and have their being." In this way, God is identified as the Sovereign Creator. The worshipers include the four living creatures and the twenty-four elders (4:8–10), and these two angelic groups worship in different ways: they never stop speaking praise, giving honor, falling down in worship, and laying down crowns (4:8–10).

In terms of theology, the hymn is above all theocentric.[41] God is worshiped for his

36. David R. Carnegie, "Worthy is the Lamb: The Hymns in Revelation," in *Christ the Lord: Studies in Christology Presented to Donald Guthrie*, ed. Harold H. Rowdon (Downers Grove, IL: InterVarsity Press, 1982); Koester, *Revelation*, 127; Schedtler, "Hymns in Revelation," 118; Beale, *Revelation*, 31–35; see, e.g., 366–69 for a discussion of the influence of Dan 7 on Rev 4–5.

37. David E. Aune, "The Influence of Roman Imperial Court Ceremonial on the Apocalypse of John," *BR* 28 (1983). See also Kraybill, *Apocalypse and Allegiance*, 82–107.

38. Carnegie, "Worthy is the Lamb," 246–47; Schedtler, "Hymns in Revelation," 117–18.

39. Gallusz, *Throne Motif*, 103.

40. Horn, "Hallelujah," 44, notes that the first unit of the hymn in verse 8 is a triadic series ("Holy, holy, holy," "Lord, God, Almighty," "who was, and is, and is to come") that sets God apart from all creation (cf. Isa 6:3).

41. Robert S. Smith, "Songs of the Seer: The Purpose of Revelation's Hymns," *Them* 43.2 (2018): 200–201.

unique identity and his mighty acts. The hymn opens with a triple tribute to God's holiness drawn from Isa 6:3: "Holy, holy, holy." Next, he is acclaimed as "the Lord God Almighty" or the absolute King and Sovereign Ruler of all (cf. 1:8; 11:17; 15:3; 16:7; 19:6; 21:22). Then, God is worshiped as the eternal one: "who was, and is, and is to come." Lastly, God is praised as the Creator of all things (4:11).[42] Resseguie concludes: "That God is creator serves as a reminder that the disorder within this world will ultimately be ordered by the one on the throne, for the universe belongs to God."[43] In sum, God is worshiped in 4:8–11 as the holy, eternal, sovereign Creator. He is the center; we are the circumference. The rest of the hymn also conveys important aspects of worship.

First, the worship of heaven is meant to guide and motivate the churches on earth, from now until the eschaton. Here the worshipers are restricted to heaven (four living creatures and twenty-four elders) and their enthusiastic praise contrasts sharply with the situation in many of the churches. Worship in the heavenly realm stands as the reality toward which the churches should aspire and grow until the kingdom of heaven comes fully to earth. The hymn hints at this eschatological goal in the final phrase describing God's eternal nature in 4:8 ("is to come") and in 4:9 when the falling down of the elders is conditioned upon the worship of the living creatures—a likely reference to the now and the not yet illustrated throughout the book (e.g., 5:13–14; 7:9; 19:4).[44]

Second, this hymn reminds us that true worship is counter-imperial or, perhaps better, pro-kingdom of God. Howard-Brook and Gwyther observe that "each term used by the cherubim and the elders as an attribute of God gives to God something otherwise offered to the emperor himself or to gods in the Greco-Roman pantheon and celebrated in the local cults."[45] As we have seen, the title "Lord God Almighty" (παντοκράτωρ) overrules the title "Caesar" (cf. 1:8; 11:17; 15:3; 16:7; 19:6, 15; 21:22), the centrality of the throne image overpowers Caesar's throne and the demand for emperor worship (as well as Satan's throne in 2:13; 13:2), and the significance of the elders falling down and laying their crowns before the throne (4:10) points to the cosmic triumph and reign of God over all competing powers.[46]

Third, as we will see throughout, worship has an unmistakable kinesthetic dimension. Again we note that one or both groups of the heavenly beings engaged in worship in this hymn "never stop saying" (4:8), "give glory, honor and thanks" (4:9), "fall down"

42. The awkward Greek phrasing in 4:11, "they were and were created" (ἦσαν καὶ ἐκτίσθησαν), is probably an example of the rhetorical device hysteron-proteron (last-first), which foregrounds the more important element of the pair (cf. also εἴληφας in 3:3). See Mathewson, *Revelation*, 41, 68.

43. Resseguie, *Revelation*, 114.

44. Osborne, *Revelation*, 61, says the "is to come" stresses "that God's decisive intervention in history, namely the eschaton, is imminent." On the meaning of ὅταν in 4:9, see the discussion in Mathewson, *Revelation*, 66; Grabiner, *Revelation's Hymns*, 88–89.

45. Howard-Brook and Gwyther, *Unveiling Empire*, 205; Carnegie, "Worthy is the Lamb," 254.

46. There are additional points of contrast such as the "day and night worship" (4:8) vs. the cessation of music in fallen Babylon (18:22), and the one "who lives for ever and ever" (4:9–10) vs. the beast who "once was, now is not," and will go to his destruction (17:8, 11).

(4:10), "worship" (4:10), "lay their crowns" (4:10) and "say" (4:10). The action of saying or speaking is consistent throughout and familiar to modern readers, but the acts of prostration and laying down crowns are especially telling about the theocentric nature of heavenly worship. Whereas a great star (8:10), cities (11:13; 16:19), kings (17:10), Babylon (14:8; 18:2), and potentially the Ephesian church (2:5) have fallen, the angelic worship leaders willingly prostrate themselves before the holy and sovereign God. Even John on a couple of occasions mistakenly falls down in worship before an angel (19:10; 22:8). Worship once again forces a decision regarding allegiance: "Once one knows that there is a God and that God stands against empire, one must choose whether one falls down in joyous worship or in stubborn resistance to that God."[47] Likewise, the elders cast their crowns before him who sits on the throne (4:10), symbolizing that God is the Sovereign Ruler of all. Stevenson explores the conceptual background of the golden crown imagery in Revelation more extensively and concludes that it was capable of expressing four different concepts: "victory, royalty, divine glory and honor."[48] All these are reflected in the hymns of Revelation.

Finally, this hymn reflects the multifaceted nature of worship using a host of worship terms. God is praised for being "holy" and "Almighty." They "worship" him for being the eternal God. He is acclaimed as "worthy." And there are two triads: "glory, honor and thanks" (4:9) and "glory and honor and power" (4:11). Smalley notes that "glory" and "honor" "acknowledge God's inherent and supreme nature and authority; while 'thankfulness' denotes a human response to God's gifts in creation and redemption."[49] The addition of "power" in the second set reflects his sovereignty and authority, especially celebrated in creation.[50] All this both reassures and challenges the churches then and today. They need not fear the Caesars and empires that claim divine status and demand allegiance. God is indeed on his throne, and he is worthy to be praised. He is the holy, eternal, sovereign Creator. The churches are also called by the strongest of examples to join in the worship of heaven.

17.5.2 Revelation 5:8–14

The throne room vision that began in Rev 4 continues through chapter 5. The tension and uncertainty created when no one is found worthy to break the seals and open the scroll is resolved when the slain Lamb is found worthy, and he takes the scroll from the one seated on the throne (5:1–7). This is reminiscent of "one like a son of man" in Dan 7:13–14 approaching the Ancient of Days to receive authority, glory, and

47. Howard-Brook and Gwyther, *Unveiling Empire*, 207.

48. Gregory M. Stevenson, "Conceptual Background to Golden Crown Imagery in the Apocalypse of John (4:4, 10; 14:14)," *JBL* 114.2 (1995): 258. Stevenson identifies three types of crowns in Revelation: (1) an organic wreath (2:10; 3:11; 6:2; 12:1), (2) the diadem (12:3; 13:1; 19:12), and (3) the golden wreath (4:4, 10; 9:7; 14:4).

49. Smalley, *Revelation*, 124.

50. Smalley, *Revelation*, 125.

sovereign power, along with everlasting dominion and an indestructible kingdom.[51] In Revelation, this messianic figure is worshiped by all nations and peoples. After the Lamb takes the scroll, the scene shifts to heavenly worship in the hymn of 5:8–14, a unit bracketed by the actions of the four living creatures and the twenty-four elders in verses 8 and 14. The hymns of Rev 4–5 have, for good reason, been traditionally read together as the grounding vision of the entire book. But Rev 5 is anything but a restatement of chapter 4. Rather, the two hymns are complementary in their theology, but the chapter 5 hymn advances our understanding of God through its very high Christology. Hurtado notes that while Jewish apocalyptic elevates roles and positions of chief angels and famous leaders (e.g., Enoch or Moses), in all those examples the important figure is always distinguished from God himself. As a result, there is no true parallel with what happens with the Lamb in Rev 5. Hurtado concludes, "However widely shared was the author's exalted view of Christ among other Christians, this does not minimize the fact that it represented a radical mutation of the monotheistic commitment characteristic of most of the ancient Jewish evidence."[52]

In looking at the overall pattern and elements of the hymn, the recipients of worship include the Lamb (5:8, 9, 10, 11, 12, 13, 14) and him who sits on the throne (5:11, 13, 14). While God is identified simply as "God" (5:9) and "him who sits on the throne" (5:13), Jesus is identified as "the Lamb" (5:8, 13) and "the Lamb who was slain" (5:12). The worshipers include the four living creatures (5:8, 11, 14), the twenty-four elders (5:8, 11, 14), a countless multitude of angels (5:11), and every created being (5:13). In terms of their actions, the worshipers fall down (5:8, 14), hold harps and golden bowls (5:8), sing a new song (5:9), speak, sometimes with a loud voice (5:9, 11, 12, 13, 14), encircle the throne (5:11), and worship (5:14). Their worship terminology includes acclaiming the Lamb as worthy (5:9, 12) with a sevenfold ascription to the Lamb: power, wealth, wisdom, strength, honor, glory, and praise (5:12); worshiping both God and the Lamb with the fourfold tribute: praise, honor, glory, and power (5:13); and concluding with an "Amen" from the four living creatures and bowing down in worship by the elders (5:14).

Theologically, what stands out almost immediately is that the Lamb is worshiped alongside God. It is no exaggeration to say that Rev 5 is "the most important Christological chapter in the book of Revelation."[53] The same angelic worshipers who bow in adoration before God on his throne in 4:8–11 now bow before the Lamb in 5:8. The scope then widens as multitudes of angels and finally all creation encircle the throne and worship both God and the Lamb on the throne (5:10–13). This ever-widening scope—including both the worshipers and those being worshiped—is no accident.

51. Beale, *Revelation*, 366–69, explores the model of Dan 7 for Rev 4–5. See also Gallusz, *Throne Motif*, 156.

52. Larry W. Hurtado, "Revelation 4–5 in the Light of Jewish Apocalyptic Analogies," *JSNT* 25 (1985): 116–18; cf. also Smith, "Songs of the Seer," 201–2.

53. Gallusz, *Throne Motif*, 143.

The Lamb is not arbitrarily praised because he is simply in the right place at the right time. Rather, God and the Lamb share the throne (5:6) and both are intentionally worshiped as divine beings of equal status, a divine unity.[54] They are "inextricably joined together as objects of Christian worship. Again and again throughout John's visions they will be seen together as equals sharing the same throne, both as objects of fear or worship, and as the decisive actors in the drama of salvation" (e.g., also Rev 6:16; 7:9, 10; 14:4; 21:22, 23; 22:1, 3).[55] Bauckham notes that the mention of God and Christ together is sometimes followed by a singular verb (11:15) or singular pronouns (6:17; 22:3–4), meaning that John is "reluctant to speak of God and Christ together as a plurality. He never makes them the subjects of a plural verb or uses a plural pronoun to refer to them both. The reason is surely clear: he places Christ on the divine side of the distinction between God and creation."[56] Interestingly, as Bauckham observes, the highest Christology often occurs within worship settings, meaning that it should be taken even more seriously because it has passed the test of religious practice: "the devotional attitude to Jesus in worship is the critical test of Christology."[57] Thus, the theology of 5:8–14 rests solidly upon the "highest possible christological understanding in the whole New Testament," according to Paul.[58]

This hymn also explicitly identifies why the Lamb is found worthy to open the scroll. The titles used in 5:5 hint at his worthiness: "Lion from the tribe of Judah" and "Root of David," two messianic images drawn from Israel's tradition that describe a mighty conqueror (cf. Gen 49:9–10; Isa 11:1, 10). But this conqueror has conquered (ἐνίκησεν) in a completely unexpected way—through his sacrificial death. Expectations of military victory are replaced with expectations of spiritual victory through death (and resurrection implied).[59] These contradictory symbols portray a paradox that is also seen in the two images of Lion and Lamb.[60] In the hymn that follows, the heavenly worshipers proclaim the true nature of divine power. The Lamb is worthy of a new song of worship because he has conquered, but the means of his conquest comes as a surprise: (1) by his death (5:9)—"because you were slain," (2) by ransoming a people (5:9)—"with your blood you purchased for God persons from every tribe and language and people and nation," and (3) by forming them into a kingdom (5:10)—"you have

54. Gallusz, *Throne Motif*, 156. Jonathan Knight, "The Enthroned Christ of Revelation 5:6 and the Development of Christian Theology," in *Studies in the Book of Revelation*, ed. Steve Moyise (Edinburgh: T&T Clark, 2001), 43–50, explores Rev 5:6 in some detail and concludes that one throne of God is in view and that the Lamb shares that throne: "Two beings, one throne means one shared authority and as close a possible union as it is possible to achieve. . . . Revelation as a whole leaves no doubt that Christ is a divine being" (pp. 47–48). What is more, since the horns and eyes of the Lamb are identified with the Holy Spirit, the Spirit too shares God's throne (p. 50).

55. J. Ramsey Michaels, *Revelation*, IVPNTC (Downers Grove, IL: InterVarsity Press, 1997), 97–98.

56. Bauckham, *Climax of Prophecy*, 139–40.

57. Bauckham, *Climax of Prophecy*, 148.

58. Paul, *Revelation*, 138.

59. Bauckham, *Climax of Prophecy*, 215. Grabiner, *Revelation's Hymns*, 99, rightly contends that in Revelation "Lamb" is the key Christological noun while "conquer" is the key Christological verb.

60. Peters, *Mandate of the Church*, 59.

made them to be a kingdom and priests to serve our God, and they will reign on the earth." John is stressing that the Lamb's victory comes not by worldly force or coercion, as Caesar conquers, but through sacrificial love. This holistic salvation achieved by the Lion-Lamb—slain, purchased, made—legitimizes his authority to reign and judge alongside God and thus makes him worthy of worship.

The theological unity of God and the Lamb continues with shared worship. The Lamb is worshiped with sevenfold praise (5:12), and four of those terms are also used in worship of God and the Lamb (5:13):

> Lamb—power, wealth, wisdom, strength, honor, glory, and praise (5:12)
> God and Lamb—praise, honor, glory, and power (5:13)

The terms "glory and honor and thanks" and "glory and honor and power" are also used in the worship of God in 4:9, 11. From here on in Revelation, God and the Lamb "appear together as equals sharing the same throne. They are disclosed as objects of fear or worship and as key players in the drama which is being enacted" (cf. 6:16; 7:9–10; 14:4; 21:22–23; 22:1, 3).[61] And Marianne Meye Thompson reminds us that the worship of Christ arises within an "unrelenting monotheistic framework."[62]

Finally, this hymn displays both a kinesthetic sophistication and a comprehensiveness. As noted earlier, the worshipers fall down, hold harps and golden bowls, sing a new song, speak with a loud voice, and encircle the throne. Yet this embodied worship expands beyond the angelic leaders to an innumerable assembly of angels and even to all of creation. Theologically, this serves as an example of a larger pattern. In Revelation evil continues to shrink, diminish, and dwindle (e.g., Satan loses territory through his multiple falls), while God's kingdom continues to grow, flourish, and expand.

17.5.3 Revelation 7:9–12

As we saw in Part Three, the whole of Rev 7 serves as an interlude between the sixth and seventh seal judgments and consists of two visions: the sealing of the 144,000 on earth (7:1–8) and the celebration of the great multitude in heaven (7:9–17). Both visions depict the people of God but from different vantage points—those protected but engaged in spiritual battle and the same group celebrating God's faithfulness following the eschatological victory.[63] The unit 7:9–17 consists of the hymn in 7:9–12, the identification of the great multitude in 7:13–14, and the multitude receiving comfort and shelter in God's presence in 7:15–17. Within the hymn, the victory song of the

61. Smalley, *Revelation*, 140–41.

62. Marianne Meye Thompson, "Worship in the Book of Revelation," 50–51.

63. Beale, *Revelation*, 424–26.

great multitude in verses 9–10 stirs a doxological response of praise from the angelic host in verses 11–12.

The great multitude comes from every "nation, tribe, people, and language" (7:9), emphasizing the universal scope of worship.[64] They have come through the "great tribulation" (7:14), another sign that this hymn celebrates the eschatological victory secured by God and the Lamb. They have endured that period of trial faced by God's people in "the last days" (John 16:33; 1 Tim 4:1; 2 Tim 3:1; 2 Pet 3:3). John has experienced tribulation (1:9), as have some of the churches (2:9–10), and the tribulation appears to intensify as the parousia nears. Blount rightly identifies what is at stake: "if the dragon cannot rule in heaven, he is determined to destroy God's people on earth."[65] God be praised since the great multitude has endured this final battle.

In terms of the overall pattern and elements within the hymn, the great multitude stands before the throne wearing white robes, holding palm branches, and crying out praise to God who sits on the throne and to the Lamb at the center of the throne (5:6; 7:17). The standing posture of the great multitude is coupled with the multitude of angels prostrating themselves before God and the Lamb. The white clothing promised to the victors (e.g., 3:4–5, 18; cf. 19:8) and given to the martyrs (6:11) likely represents victory over evil. This victory rests upon the faithfulness of Christ since their robes have been "washed . . . and made white in the blood of the Lamb" (7:14). In addition, the robes symbolize purity as they stand in contrast to the purple and scarlet of the immoral harlot Babylon (17:4; 18:16).[66] The palm branches also reinforce the theme of triumph and victory, since this was a common symbol of victory over an enemy (1 Macc 13:51; 2 Macc 10:7). John mentions the crowds waving palm branches as they welcomed Jesus as he entered Jerusalem, the one expected to be their conquering king (John 12:13). There may also be a connection to the Feast of Tabernacles or Booths, which celebrated Yahweh's presence and protection during the wilderness wanderings (cf. Rev 7:15). In addition, this image anticipates the "consummation of the messianic age" (cf. the eschatological allusions in Zech 14:4, 16–19).[67] Throughout Revelation worship has an eschatological orientation. The hymn concludes with a sevenfold doxology in 7:12: "Amen! Praise and glory and wisdom and thanks and honor and power and strength be to our God for ever and ever. Amen!" The first "amen" comes as a response to the victory song of the great multitude in 7:9–10, with the second "amen" concluding the doxology. Six of the seven attributes also occur in the doxology to the Lamb in 5:12, although in a

64. Peters, *Mandate of the Church*, 62; Tabb, *All Things New*, 118, notes that the countless multitude is reminiscent of the ancient promise to the patriarchs (e.g., Gen 15:5; 32:12), and its multiethnic identity echoes God's promise to bless "all the tribes" (Gen 12:3) and "all the nations of the earth" (Gen 22:18).

65. Blount, *Revelation*, 233.

66. Grabiner, *Revelation's Hymns*, 119.

67. Smalley, *Revelation*, 191–92; Aune, *Revelation 6–16*, 448–50; 468–70.

different order ("thanks" in 7:12 replaces "wealth" in 5:12). The Lamb is also an implied recipient of worship in 7:12 (cf. 7:9, 10, 17).

Theologically, this hymn makes two essential points. First, worship is the proper response to the final deliverance of God's people through the great tribulation. Suffering will one day end and the eschatological victory will come. The great multitude cries out, "Salvation belongs to our God, who sits on the throne, and to the Lamb" (7:10). The term "salvation" (σωτηρία) indicates final victory over evil and deliverance into God's presence (cf. the service/worship as well as sheltering in God's presence; the total absence of hunger, thirst, scorching heat; the shepherding care from the Lamb who provides springs of living water; and God himself wiping away every tear; cf. 7:15–17).[68] The salvation in view is an eschatological deliverance through tribulation into God's presence.

Second, this salvation/victory comes from both God and the Lamb. Whereas God alone is named as the recipient of worship in 7:11–12: "before the throne and worshipped God . . . be to our God," other expressions clarify that the Lamb is a co-recipient of worship: "before the throne and before the Lamb" (7:9) and "salvation belongs to our God, who sits on the throne, and to the Lamb" (7:10). In addition, in the remainder of chapter 7, the robes of the great multitude are made white "in the blood of the Lamb" (7:14), and the Lamb is "at the center of the throne" shepherding God's people and leading them to springs of living water (7:17). In Revelation the term "throne" often implies both God and the Lamb, even if only one member is mentioned explicitly in a particular context (7:17). God and the Lamb are united in providing the final victory for their people.

17.5.4 Revelation 11:15–18

The heavenly setting of this hymn stands in contrast to the earthly battle scene of the previous episode (11:1–14), where the witnessing church proclaims God's truth in the face of diabolical opposition.[69] Likely the seventh trumpet constitutes the third woe and stresses the arrival of God's final judgment and final salvation (cf. 10:7). Aune describes this as a "two-part responsory hymn that juxtaposes the celebration of the reign of God with the final judgment in which all the dead are judged; the righteous are rewarded and

68. See Grabiner, *Revelation's Hymns*, 123–25, who rightly contends that "salvation" in this context primarily connotes victory. Also Schedtler, "Hymns in Revelation," 124, who contends that salvation "denotes rescue from a perilous situation in Christian literature, especially situations of eschatological conflict (e.g., 1 Cor 3:15; 5:5; Rom 10:9, 13; 11:11, 26)."

69. Notice the heavenly emphasis with the loud voices in heaven, the elders seated on thrones before God and God's open temple with the ark visible in 11:15–16, 19. Several interpreters have located this hymn in a larger chiastic structure. Charles Giblin, *The Book of Revelation: The Open Book of Prophecy* (Collegeville, MN: Liturgical Press, 1991), 117–19, says that 11:15 through 15:8 forms a chiasm that "underscores the centrality of worship and liturgy to Revelation's message." Antonius King Wai Siew, *The War between the Two Beasts and the Two Witnesses: A Chiastic Reading of Revelation 11:1–14:5* (London: T&T Clark, 2005), identifies the center of this chiasm as the war in heaven in 12:7–12 with the hymn of 11:15–19 about the arrival of God's kingdom paralleling the kingdom of the beast in 13:1–6.

the wicked are punished."[70] The context certainly supports reading the hymn's many aorist verbs as indications that, from the hymn's point of view, God's universal reign has begun.

The theology of this hymn centers on the worship of God but also includes Christ, his Messiah, as a co-recipient. The description "Lord God Almighty" (v. 17) also appears in 1:8 and in other hymns in 4:8; 15:3; 16:7; 19:6, as well as in the description of the New Jerusalem in 21:22 (cf. "Almighty" also in 16:14; 19:15). The title also stands as a direct warning to Caesar and all other earthly sovereigns. The second title, "the One who is and who was" (v. 17) is a shortened form of the triad "who is, and who was, and who is to come" used in 1:4, 8; 4:8 and abbreviated here because God's kingdom has finally arrived. The future is here! Christ also receives worship: "The kingdom of the world has become the kingdom of our Lord and of his Messiah" (v. 15). The term "messiah" (Χριστός) is used sparingly in Revelation—three times in combination with Jesus (1:1, 2, 5), once simply as "Christ" (20:4), and three times in connection with God (12:10; 11:15; 20:6). There is a close connection between God's reign and Christ's work as Messiah (cf. Ps 2:2: "the Lord and his Anointed").[71]

The two groups of worshipers include "loud voices in heaven" (Rev 11:15) and the "twenty-four elders" (vv. 16–17). The loud voices are not identified but could include an anonymous angelic choir or the great multitude or perhaps both groups united in praise. The voices rejoice that "the kingdom of the world has become the kingdom of our Lord and of his Messiah, and he will reign for ever and ever" (v. 15). The "kingdom of this world" refers to competing, adversarial kingdoms and rulers that stand against God's kingdom.[72] False rulers have now been forced to give up their kingdoms and their temporary reign gives ways to God's eternal kingdom. The loud voices worship not only God but "our Lord and his Messiah" (v. 15).

As is their habit, the twenty-four elders worship by prostrating themselves and thanking God for saving his people and judging his enemies (11:16). More specifically, they worship God for exercising his great power in beginning his eschatological reign (11:17), for pouring out his wrath on the raging nations who reject God as king and rebel against his kingdom, and for judging the dead (11:18). A poetic chiasm in verse 18 reinforces the truth that worship is the appropriate response for God's just judgment, both positively for his people and negatively for his enemies:

A The time has come for judging the dead,
  B and for rewarding your servants the prophets
  B′ and your people who revere your name, both great and small—
A′ and for destroying those who destroy the earth.[73]

70. Aune, *Revelation 6–16*, 635.

71. Grabiner, *Revelation's Hymns*, 135.

72. Schedtler, "Hymns in Revelation," 124.

73. Osborne, *Revelation*, 444.

Overall, this hymn stresses that the world is coming under the reign of God and Jesus, the Messiah, and that this coming reign will bring eternal blessings to the righteous and destruction for the rebellious.

17.5.5 Revelation 12:10–12

Revelation 12 occurs in the long interlude of 12–14 that precedes the bowl judgments. While the previous hymn in 11:15–18 centered on earthly opposition to God and his people, the present hymn has cosmic implications.[74] The immediate context of Rev 12 features three primary units unfolding in an A—B—A′ pattern:

12:1–6: the conflict between the dragon and the woman and her son
  12:7–12: the war in heaven
12:13–18: the ongoing conflict between the dragon and the woman and offspring[75]

The hymn in 12:10–12 occurs after the great defeat of the dragon and his angels by Michael and his angels in 12:7–8a, resulting in the loss of his place in heaven: "The great dragon was hurled down—that ancient serpent called the devil, or Satan, who leads the whole world astray. He was hurled to the earth, and his angels with him" (12:8b–9). Most scholars connect the defeat of Satan with the life, death, and resurrection/exaltation of Jesus Christ.[76] The spatial contrast between the male child who was born and snatched up to God and his throne (12:5) and the devil who was defeated and thrown down to earth (12:10) emphasizes the opposing directions, purposes, and outcomes of the kingdom of God versus the chaotic empire of evil.[77] Revelation 12:10–12 is a praise response to what John sees in 12:1–9. The scene shifts from heaven (12:1, 3) to earth (12:5–6) and back to heaven (12:7–12). The heavenly setting is not simply a general heavenly context but, as Grabiner suggests, God's temple and, more specifically, God's throne room (cf. 11:19).[78]

The hymn proper consists of three sections corresponding to the three verses of the hymn. John hears "a loud voice in heaven say"—an introduction that sets this unit off from the normal narrative flow. The anonymous voice likely belongs to an angelic being but could also be understood in a collective sense referring to the entire heavenly council of angels. The hymn begins in verse 10 by highlighting the attributes of God and Christ that make them worthy of worship: "salvation, power, and kingdom" of God

74. Schedtler, "Hymns in Revelation," 125.

75. Cf. Grabiner, *Revelation's Hymns*, 154.

76. Sweet, *Revelation*, 201, refers to the cross as "the turning point in world history . . . the longed-for time when God's 'direct rule' replaces Satan's abuse of his powers, and *authority* passes to God's *Christ*," emphasis original.

77. See Collins, *Combat Myth*.

78. Grabiner, *Revelation's Hymns*, 143.

and the "authority" of his Messiah.[79] The three traits modifying God seem particularly suited for the ruler of the eternal kingdom, in contrast to the dragon as the ruler of the counterfeit kingdom. Christ's "authority" (ἐξουσία) stands in contrast to the authority of the unholy trinity (13:2, 4, 5, 7, 12; 17:12, 13). Such worship is fitting because (ὅτι) the accuser "has been hurled down (ἐβλήθη)" (12:10). The winner of the cosmic conflict deserves praise.

The second section stresses the implications of God's victory for his people who share in that victory. The brothers and sisters "triumphed" (ἐνίκησαν) over the accuser by the Lamb's sacrifice, by the word of their testimony, and by their faithfulness even unto death. The cross and resurrection of Christ are appropriated by faithful confession and obedience. Although this is a hymn of worship directed toward God and Christ, the witness and faithfulness of Christ's followers also becomes part of the reason for worship. In other words, though worship is primarily vertical, it often has significant horizontal implications.

The final section of the hymn calls for rejoicing from the heavens and those who dwell in them along with a sobering caution to those who live on earth (v. 12). Heaven's joy stems from the announcement that Satan has been cast down and that is precisely the reason for the earth's woe. The raging devil has little time before his next punitive descent, so he renews his efforts to wage war against God and his people. The time between the cross/resurrection of Christ and Christ's return features a defeated but still dangerous adversary, filled with fury, and devoted to persecuting the saints.

Theologically, the hymn underscores at least three important truths. First, God has won the cosmic war with Satan, resulting in Satan's fall and anticipating God's full and final victory. Satan's fall at the cross foreshadows his ultimate fall at the eschaton.[80] This is the primary struggle portrayed in Revelation and one that continues between the dragon and the woman's offspring (12:17). The kingdom of God is the victorious kingdom. The outcome is secure. The appropriate response is worship. God's defeat of the evil one provides motivation for worship.

Second, Christ's death/resurrection lies at the center of God's cosmic victory. They key phrase is "the blood of the Lamb" in 12:11. Mangina notes that while "Satan's defeat occurs in some sense before the dawn of time, the *reason* for that fall lies *in* time: the Lamb's victory and his followers' faithful participation in that victory."[81] Revelation makes it clear that God's power is demonstrated through the Lamb's sacrifice and God's reversal of the death sentence in resurrection. This display of divine

79. The introductory adverb followed by the aorist verb (ἄρτι ἐγένετο) emphasizes the beginning of the fulfillment to come. As Beale, *Revelation*, 658, notes, Rev 12:10 "does not merely anticipate the future kingdom, but celebrates the fact that the kingdom has begun immediately following Christ's death and resurrection."

80. Grabiner, *Revelation's Hymns*, 164; Osborne, *Revelation*, 468–69.

81. Mangina, *Revelation*, 153. Emphasis original.

power through sacrificial love stands in sharp contrast to the destructive power of the dragon and the beasts.

Third, believers' faithful witness and perseverance in discipleship proves essential to an individual experience of God's cosmic victory. While the heavens rejoice, the earth and sea mourn because the spiritual struggle is real and the consequences are serious.[82] But in this already/not-yet configuration, believers are citizens of heaven while residing on earth. As such they can participate in worship with the heavens while simultaneously struggling in the earthly war. Recognizing the importance of witness and perseverance is one crucial result of worship. Authentic worship encourages and recalibrates God's people for the ongoing battle.

17.5.6 Revelation 15:3–4

Revelation 15 opens with John seeing another great sign—seven angels with seven last plagues, the third and final set of plagues delivering God's wrath (15:1). John sees those who had been victorious over the beast and its image and number standing on the sea of glass, holding harps given them by God (15:2). The victors sing the hymn of 15:3–4, a song that brings theological perspective to the final outpouring of God's wrath.[83] Following the hymn John sees the opening of the tabernacle of the covenant in the heavenly temple, and out of the temple come the seven angels with the seven plagues (15:5–8). The scene then shifts to earth for the pouring out of the bowl judgments (16:1).

The hymn in 15:3–4 is described as "the song of God's servant Moses and of the Lamb." Although this could be referring to two separate songs, the conjunction καί should probably be translated epexegetically as "that is," referring to one song of deliverance.[84] The victors praise the Lamb for achieving the eschatological victory, a victory preceded by God's mighty act of deliverance through his servant Moses (Exod 15; cf. Deut 31:30–32:43). It is the typological connection rather than a quotation of Moses's song that is in view here. God's victory accomplished through Moses is but a prelude to the final victory over the unholy trinity achieved by the Lamb.[85]

The hymn of Rev 15:3b–4 consists of three strophes as follows:

> Great and marvelous are your deeds,
>   Lord God Almighty.
> Just and true are your ways,
>   King of the nations.

82. Resseguie, *Revelation*, 175, observes that the mention of the earth and the sea likely signals the coming of Satan's two accomplices: the sea beast (13:1–10) and the earth beast (13:11–18).

83. Horn, "Hallelujah," 49.

84. Beale, *Revelation*, 792; Fanning, *Revelation*, 406–7; Grabiner, *Revelation's Hymns*, 186; Tabb, *All Things New*, 159; Peters, *Mandate of the Church*, 69–70; Smalley, *Revelation*, 385–86.

85. Bauckham, *Climax of Prophecy*, 296–307.

Who will not fear you, Lord,
and bring glory to your name?

For you alone are holy.
(For) all nations will come and worship before you,
for your righteous acts have been revealed.

In the first strophe, God is named as "Lord God Almighty" (cf. 4:8; 11:17; 16:7; 19:6; 21:22), paralleled by "King of the nations," a designation used only here in Revelation. These titles reinforce God's sovereignty over both the nations and all other enemies of his people. God is worshiped for his great and marvelous deeds as well as his just and true ways, echoing numerous Old Testament passages that praise God for his righteous and true actions displayed clearly through his mighty works of deliverance.

The second strophe includes a rhetorical question aimed at calling the worshiper to recognize the "incomparability of God" (Exod 15:11; Jer 10:6–7; Ps 86:8–10).[86] The question asks who will fear the Lord and glorify his name or, in other words, Who will worship the Lord? The answer comes in the final strophe with the three ὅτι clauses and packs a theological punch all its own. God is uniquely holy, and his righteousness has been revealed through his actions. As theologians are known to say, we know who God is by what he has done. God's holiness is revealed by his righteous acts, and this revelation stands in contrast to the unholiness of the dragon and the two beasts displayed through their wicked and deceitful ways. All nations will be drawn to worship the one true God. Grabiner notes the tension within Revelation itself concerning the fate of the nations, with some bowing in worship (e.g., 15:4; 21:24–26; 22:2) while others persist in rebellion (e.g., 6:15–17; 19:15, 19–21; 20:8).[87] Revelation leaves it up to the nations to respond to the uniquely holy God who alone is worthy of worship (7:9; 14:6–7).

This hymn makes a substantive theological contribution in a short space. First, the song is sung by the victors, but even in their overcoming they are dependent on God's gracious enabling. They have certainly been involved in the battle, but the Lamb's victory provides the basis for their victory. They are standing on the sea of glass, an image that likely represents God's victory given to the saints, perhaps connoting the idea of resurrection.[88] As Beale observes, "They are victorious only because the Lamb has conquered and granted them a share in the effects of his victory at the sea."[89] In addition, they are holding harps given by God (genitive of source) to play songs of praise to God. And the song itself celebrates God's deliverance of his people from an

86. Bauckham, *Climax of Prophecy*, 305.

87. Grabiner, *Revelation's Hymns*, 190–93.

88. See Beale, *Revelation*, 791; Osborne, *Revelation*, 562–63.

89. Beale, *Revelation*, 790.

evil ruler/empire and to the promised land. God's enabling work to secure the victors' victory and enable their worship remains foundational.

Second, God is worshiped for who he is—almighty, sovereign, glorious, holy—and his great, marvelous, righteous, and true acts flow from his incomparable nature. In the end, all true worship finds its final home in the character of God. Third, Revelation anticipates a time when all nations will worship the Lord (e.g., 5:9; 7:9; 21:24–26; 22:2). It stops short of universalistic salvation since there are wicked nations that are deceived (e.g., 11:2, 9, 18; 13:7; 14:8; 16:19; 17:15; 18:3, 23; 20:3, 8; 21:27). But God's hope and intention remain clear—the nations were meant for worship and the hymn calls worshipers, gentiles included, to respond positively to God.

17.5.7 Revelation 16:5–7

This hymn of divine justice is sometimes referred to as a "judgment doxology."[90] It appears between the third and fourth bowl judgments in Rev 16 and serves as both a response to God's wrath (16:1–4) and a prelude to additional announcements of judgment (16:8–21). More specifically, verses 5–6 function as an "interpretive elaboration" of the third bowl, with blood being a symbol of persecution and martyrdom (cf. Isa 49:26).[91] The hymn in Revelation has two parts: (1) a declaration by the "angel of the waters" (Rev 16:5–6, NASB) and (2) the response by the altar (16:7). In Judaism and in Revelation angels are often connected to earthly realities (e.g., 7:1; 14:18), and here the earthly acclamation calls for a heavenly response in the voice from the altar.[92] Mounce observes that the "speaking altar is obviously a personification (cf. 9:13) . . . that represents the corporate testimony of the martyrs in 6:9 and the prayers of the saints in 8:3–5."[93]

The angel praises God using three descriptive titles: you are righteous, you who are and who were, the Holy One (ὁ ὅσιος). God's righteous, holy, and sovereign character stands as the basis for his just judgment of those who persecute his people (cf. 1:4, 8; 4:8; 6:10; 11:17). The two ὅτι clauses work together to explain God's judgment, as verse 6 elaborates on verse 5b. First, God has judged "these things," referring to some or all of the bowl judgments. Thus, God is righteous for having decreed these judgments.[94] God's judgment is just because the perpetrators deserve the judgment they are receiving since they have shed the blood of God's saints and prophets (v. 6). Second, God makes sure the punishment fits the crime with another example of *lex talionis* (the law of retribution) in Revelation—they shed or poured out the blood of God's people so God is pouring out their blood (cf. 2:23; 6:9–11; 11:5, 18; 14:8, 10; 18:5–7; 19:2; 20:12–13;

90. Aune, *Revelation 6–16*, 864; Peters, *Mandate of the Church*, 71.

91. Beale, *Revelation*, 817.

92. Smalley, *Revelation*, 402.

93. Mounce, *Revelation*, 295. He observes that except in 11:1 the altar is always connected with judgment (6:9; 8:3–5; 9:13; 14:18; 16:7).

94. Smalley, *Revelation*, 403.

Exod 21:23–25). The verb "shed" (ἐκχέω) is the same term used of the "pouring out" of the bowls (cf. Rev 16:1, 2, 3, 4, 8, 10, 12, 17) and intensifies the sense of God's justice.[95]

The altar then responds antiphonally, affirming God's power and his true and righteous judgments (v. 7). The response begins with a "Yes" (ναί), affirming the truth of the angel's words in 16:6 (cf. 1:7; 14:13; 22:20). The souls under the altar, the description of God as sovereign, holy, and true, and the theme of divine judgment link this hymn with the scene in 6:9–10. There God asks the martyrs to wait a little longer, implying that he will avenge their blood by judging the ungodly according to his timing (6:10–11). Thus, the trumpet and bowl judgments form part of God's answer to the martyrs' plea and the prayers of his people for justice in the face of persecution (see 8:3–5; 9:13).

Theologically, this hymn informs our understanding of worship in two primary ways. First, we see that God is worthy of worship because of his righteous, true, and holy character. His judgments are never arbitrary or reactionary. Rather, they flow out of his "true and righteous" nature. God's salvation, accomplished in part through his judgment of evil, reflects his divine integrity, in contrast to the erratic, capricious actions of pagan deities.[96] God's ways, including his judgments, are just, holy, and true because his nature is just, holy, and true. This divine reliability calls forth trust and praise from the worshiper.

Second, God is worshiped for judging the false and evil judgments of the ungodly against his people. We worship because God has answered the question, "How long, Sovereign Lord, holy and true, until you judge . . . ?" (6:10). For the churches reading John's Apocalypse and facing pressure for refusing to worship the emperor, Peters notes that "their prayers of worship at the altar of suffering and sacrifice will facilitate the process of divine justice."[97] While Christians might be tempted to seek revenge themselves, the hymn reminds us that worship is the primary response for believers—praise, trust, and hope that God will, in his time, bring justice (cf. Rom 12:17–19).[98]

17.5.8 Revelation 19:1–8

The final hymn in Revelation is set in the heavenly throne room and occurs at a crucial place in the narrative—between the judgment of Babylon in chapters 17–18 and the appearance of the New Jerusalem in chapters 21–22. The hymn serves as a pivot between God's judgment of evil and the beginning of his eternal reign. The focus shifts from pleading for God's justice to celebrating God's deliverance, yet both occasions are appropriate for worship (rejoicing and hallelujahs in 18:20; 19:1, 3, 4, 6). This presents John's readers with a significant choice regarding their allegiance—to Babylon, the

95. Osborne, *Revelation*, 583.
96. Smalley, *Revelation*, 402.
97. Peters, *Mandate of the Church*, 72.
98. Mangina, *Revelation*, 187.

dragon, and the beasts or to the New Jerusalem, God, the Lamb, and the Spirit. The groups making the respective choices are described as two women: the harlot who allies herself with evil, contrasted with the bride of the Lamb. This analogy serves to personalize and clarify the relational choice and its eternal consequences.

The hymn contains three sections: 19:1–3, 4–5, 6–8 with four uses of "Hallelujah!" (19:1, 3, 4, 6), the only occurrences of the word in the New Testament and only used here in Revelation.[99] The worshipers include the great multitude in heaven (19:1, 3, 6), the twenty-four elders and four living creatures (19:4), an anonymous voice from the throne (19:5), and all who are listening as they are urged by the multitude to join the heavenly chorus: "Let *us* rejoice and be glad and give him glory!" (19:7, emphasis added).

In the first section (19:1–3), the great multitude shouts praise to God: Hallelujah, salvation, power, and glory, with another Hallelujah in verse 3. God's "salvation" refers to his victory or triumph (cf. 7:10; 12:10).[100] God is praised for (ὅτι) his just and true judgments and, specifically, for (ὅτι) condemning the great prostitute. The harlot deserved God's judgment because she corrupted the earth with her adulteries (19:2; cf. 14:8; 17:2; 18:3, 9). He has avenged on Babylon the blood of his servants and the smoke from her goes up forever and ever (19:3). The martyrs' cry has been heard and answered at last (cf. 6:10). In many ways this hymn summarizes the previous hymns as the praise of God reaches a climax.

The second section (19:4–5) features a response from the elders and living creatures. They fall prostrate and worship God seated on his throne, crying out "Amen, Hallelujah!" (19:4). Then an unnamed voice from the throne calls all of God's people—those who fear him—to continue in praise of God (19:5). Unidentified "voices" from heaven are heard throughout the book and may belong either to Christ or to an angelic being (e.g., 9:13; 11:12, 15; 12:10; 14:13, 15, 18; 16:1, 17; 18:4; 21:3). The fear of the Lord is sometimes connected to worship in Revelation (11:18; 14:7; 15:4).

The final section forms an *inclusio* with the first section through the second reference to the great multitude and the fourth Hallelujah. The progression comes in 19:7–8 with the pivot away from God's judgment of Babylon toward the wedding of the Lamb. The unit is replete with sounds of worship—the sound of the great multitude, the roar of rushing waters, loud peals of thunder, and shouting of praise. The forceful sounds attest to the public and victorious nature of God's reign. The final hallelujah is shouted because or "for (ὅτι) our Lord God Almighty reigns." This title occurs seven times in the book (1:8; 4:8; 11:17; 15:3; 16:7; 19:6; 21:22) and symbolizes God's sovereign

99. Karrer, "God in the Book of Revelation," 207, notes that Revelation provides the earliest written documentation of the use of "Hallelujah" in Christianity. He concludes that John "wrote in Greek for Greco-Roman readers, and yet he implicitly reminds them that through the centuries the God, whom they revere, has a Semitic name: Yah(we) is the God mighty in wrath and grace, deserving of respect and praise" (p. 207).

100. Grabiner, *Revelation's Hymns*, 203.

control over all things.[101] The rejoicing, gladness, and giving glory are the result (ὅτι) of the arrival of the Lamb's wedding (19:7b). The preparation of the bride makes this a joyous occasion (19:8). The celebration continues with the fourth beatitude and an angelic warning about the true nature of worship (19:9–10).

Theologically, this final hymn repeats a central theme found throughout Revelation, that God will at last avenge the suffering of his people at the hands of evil powers, both earthly and cosmic. The people of God shout their praises and acclaim God as glorious and powerful for saving his people, specifically for condemning the prostitute who corrupted the earth and shed the blood of his servants (19:1–3). The seemingly all-powerful earthly prostitute that spread her immorality and idolatry abroad and persecuted God's people will face God's judgment fully and finally. God's righteous judgment of the wicked forms the basis of worship in this hymn (cf. 11:18). This is the victory song of God's righteous triumph over the forces of evil. A lingering question is how can God use violent power to bring about this victory without being any different from the dragon? A closer reading, however, reveals that God conquers through the slain Lamb, that victory comes through sacrificial death (cf. 5:5–6; 12:10–12).[102]

Similarly, worship is also a response to God beginning his eternal reign: "For our Lord God Almighty reigns" (19:6). The verb "reign" (ἐβασίλευσεν) is likely an ingressive aorist, referring to the initiation of God's full and final rule (cf. 11:15–18; 1 Chr 16:31).[103] As we noted before, the hymn shows that worship looks both backward to God's judgment of Babylon and forward to his reign over all creation, with both aspects stressing God's sovereignty over history.[104]

Continuing the forward-looking dimension of worship, the hymn stresses the specific occasion as the coming wedding of the Lamb and the readiness of the bride (19:7–8). As Schedtler observes, "The hymnic proclamation of the impending marriage looks forward to the final acts of God to establish God's kingdom upon a renewed earth (Rev 20–22)."[105] Worship is not only driven by justice but also by hope, a hope that returns the grand story back to the very beginning, but this time with a different outcome: God and his people living in harmony in the new creation.

Finally, this hymn reminds us that worship is a loud, public, responsive act. In 19:4–5 the twenty-four elders and the four living creatures respond to the hallelujahs of the great multitude by falling down in worship. Worship encourages a response of worship, and the antiphonal arrangement gathers the worshipers into a cosmic chorus shouting praises to God. Perhaps surprising is the bodily enthusiasm of the worshipers in this final hymn: a roaring shout (vv. 1, 3, 6), falling down in worship (v. 4), speaking

101. Bauckham, *Theology*, 30.

102. Grabiner, *Revelation's Hymns*, 210–12.

103. Grabiner, *Revelation's Hymns*, 208; Osborne, *Revelation*, 672; Beale, *Revelation*, 932. Mathewson, *Revelation*, 260, sees this as a present temporal or even a timeless term referring to the entire state of reigning rather than just the inauguration of his reign.

104. Fanning, *Revelation*, 479–80.

105. Schedtler, "Hymns in Revelation," 127.

praise (v. 5), rejoicing (v. 7), and giving glory (v. 7). There is nothing subtle or secret about worship here. Just as the first-century worshipers lived in a Roman setting where the emperor was worshiped publicly through parades, festivals, proclamations, and the like, so true worship is unashamed and bold and public in its proclamation of the worth of the one, true God.

17.6 OTHER ASPECTS OF WORSHIP

While the hymns in Revelation capture most of what worship entails, other aspects of worship deserve brief comment. First, special liturgical words of worship surface throughout. The term "Amen" (ἀμήν: 1:6–7; 3:14; 5:14; 7:12 [2x]; 19:4; 22:20) often serves as a confident confirmation or verification of what is true and reliable (1:6–7; 5:14; 7:12; 22:20). It can also serve as a word of praise (7:12; 19:4 with hallelujah). In 3:14 we even see it as a personal designation for Jesus, "the faithful and true witness" (cf. Isa 65:16). Here the term indicates "the one in whom perfect conformity to reality is exemplified."[106] A second term, "Hallelujah" (Ἁλληλουϊά, Rev 19:1, 3, 4, 6), occurs only in the final hymn, suggesting it is "a very special exclamatory word of worship—a word reserved for expressing unbridled jubilation at the work of God."[107]

Second, Revelation is a songbook and reflects the early Christian practice of singing in worship. Pliny the Younger notes in his description of Christians in Bithynia that "they were in the habit of assembling on a fixed day before dawn and singing a hymn to Christ as though he were a god."[108] In 5:9, 14:3, and 15:3 reference is made to singing (ᾄδω) a song (ᾠδή). In 5:9 the twenty-four elders and four living creatures sing a "new song" praising the Lamb for fulfilling God's salvation plan. In 14:3 the 144,000 sing a "new song" before the throne, the elders, and the living creatures, a song of the redeemed or purchased who did not defile themselves but instead followed the Lamb. In 15:3 victorious believers sing the song of Moses and of the Lamb, celebrating God's character and mighty works of deliverance. In connection with songs, musical instruments are found throughout Revelation. We see the seven angels with seven trumpets (σάλπιγξ), and harps (κιθάρα) also appear in worship scenes (5:8; 14:2; 15:2). The harps seem to accompany the singing and contribute to the volume of the celebration.

Third, in addition to the doxologies within hymns (4:9, 11; 5:12, 13; 7:10, 12; 12:10; 15:3; 16:7; 19:1–2, 7), we see a separate doxology in 1:5b–6 praising Jesus Christ, "the faithful witness, the firstborn from the dead, and the ruler of the kings of the earth": "To him who loves us and has freed us from our sins by his blood, and has made us to be a kingdom and priests to serve his God and Father—to him be glory

106. Mounce, *Revelation*, 108.
107. Archer, *'I Was in the Spirit on the Lord's Day'*, 322.
108. Pliny, *Ep.* 10.96 (my translation).

and power for ever and ever! Amen." Here Jesus is worshiped as the one who loves his people and demonstrated his love by giving his life on the cross. Furthermore, he transformed his people and made them into a kingdom of priests to God, who also is praised. This doxology immediately precedes a prophetic word about the second coming of Christ (1:7).

Fourth, in the hymn of 12:10–12 and in 18:20 the term "rejoice" (εὐφραίνω) is used to call God's people to praise him for his judgment of evil powers. In 12:12 heaven's joy comes from the announcement that Satan has been cast down. In 18:20 the saints are called to rejoice over God's judgment of Babylon: "Rejoice . . . rejoice . . . rejoice . . . for God has judged her with the judgment she imposed on you." In contrast, rejoicing is one of five aspects of life never to be found in the condemned city again (18:21–23—the music of harpists, musicians, pipers, and trumpeters), revealing the certainty and finality of God's judgment of Babylon.

Fifth, although the "prayers of God's people" (αἱ προσευχαὶ τῶν ἁγίων) are only mentioned three times (5:8; 8:3–4; cf. 6:9–10; 22:17, 20), they play an important role in worship. In 5:8 the twenty-four elders and four living creatures each hold harps and golden bowls full of incense, "which are the prayers of God's people" (cf. Ps 141:2). God hears the prayers of his people, and their prayers make a difference in the working out of God's salvation plan through the Lamb (Rev 5:9–10). Prayers and praises are both given to the Lamb in the act of worship. In 8:2–5 seven angels who stand before God are given seven trumpets. And another angel with a golden censer came and stood at the altar. He was given "much incense to offer, with the prayers of all God's people" (8:3) In the next verse the smoke of the incense and prayers of God's people ascend before God and fire from the altar descends to the earth (8:4–5). We see a strong connection between worshipful prayer and God's judgment.[109] Again, God answers the prayers of his people.

Sixth, worship is a bodily activity in the Apocalypse, displayed through prostration, encircling the throne, laying down crowns, wearing robes, and holding palm branches or harps (e.g., 4:10; 5:11, 14; 7:9, 11; 11:16; 15:2; 19:4). The chief bodily action in worship is falling down. As Kraybill notes, "Ten times John uses *proskyneō* as an index of worshiping God and/or the Lamb [4:10; 5:14; 7:11; 11:1, 16; 15:4; 19:4, 10b; 22:9]; eleven times he uses it to refer to worship of the dragon, the beast, or an image of the beast [9:20; 13:4 (2x), 8, 12, 15; 14:9, 11; 16:2; 19:20; 20:4]."[110] Thompson observes that "physical posture indicates the attitude and action of offering one's allegiance."[111] This conclusion is supported by John's experience of mistakenly worshiping an angel before

109. Brian J. Tabb, "Prayer in Apocalyptic Perspective," in *For It Stands in Scripture: Essays in Honor of W. Edward Glenny*, ed. Ardel B. Caneday with Anna Rask and Greg Rosaver (St. Paul, MN: University of Northwestern-St. Paul, 2019), 199–200; Peters, *Mandate of the Church*, 60.

110. Kraybill, *Apocalypse and Allegiance*, 151. In 3:9; 19:10; 22:8 John uses the verb to describe bowing before other entities.

111. Marianne Meye Thompson, "Worship in the Book of Revelation," 48.

being rebuked and told to "worship God" instead (19:10; 22:8). Those who prostrate themselves before God recognize his presence in worship. As Archer puts it, "*Spirited* worship is embodied worship."[112]

Seventh, on occasion the term "serve" is used as a synonym for "worship."[113] In 7:15 those who have come through the great tribulation and have washed their robes white in the blood of the Lamb are before God's throne and "serve [λατρεύω] him day and night in his temple." God, then, is said to "shelter [or tabernacle over] them with his presence" (7:15).[114] Likewise, in 22:3, the "throne of God and of the Lamb will be in the city, and his servants will serve [λατρεύω] him." Worship is the primary occupation of heaven as God's people worship him forever in the new creation.

Eighth, worship is a matter of the will as seen in the exhortation to repent and the admonition to listen to the Spirit. This can be seen clearly in the seven messages of Rev 2–3. The central exhortation given to the five problematic churches is "repent" (μετανοέω—2:5, 5, 16, 21 [2x], 22; 3:3, 19). Repentance in the mind and heart leads to a change of behavior. Throughout Revelation repentance is linked to worship—negatively, Jezebel refuses to repent (2:20–22), as do the inhabitants of the earth (e.g., 9:20–21; 16:9, 11). A willingness to repent, described more positively, brings an attentiveness to the voice of the Spirit (2:7, 11, 17, 29; 3:6, 13, 22).

Finally, the concept of "glory" (δόξα) connects to worship. The term shows up in numerous hymn-like sections where God and/or the Lamb are given glory in worship (1:6; 4:9, 11; 5:12, 13; 7:12; 19:1). At times, "glory" is used to describe God's glorious presence (15:8; 21:11, 13). At other times, we can speak of the "glory" or "splendor" of the redeemed nations (21:24, 26). Three times "glory" is directly connected to worship. In 11:13 following the severe earthquake the survivors "were terrified and gave glory to the God of heaven," indicating either genuine repentance and worship or forced acknowledgement of God's sovereignty and glory. In 14:7 an angel proclaiming the eternal gospel to those on earth says, "Fear God and give him glory, because the hour of his judgment has come. Worship him who made the heavens, the earth, the sea and the springs of water." Here "fearing God and giving him glory" is equivalent to worship. In 16:9 those seared by intense heat in the fourth bowl judgment curse the name of God and "refus[e] to repent and glorify him."

17.7 CONCLUSION

John receives his vision that is the book of Revelation while worshiping (1:10–11), and the book that opens in worship closes in worship with God's people "serving/

112. Archer, *'I Was in the Spirit on the Lord's Day'*, 319–20, emphasis added.

113. Peterson, "Worship in the Revelation to John," 72.

114. Duvall and Hays, *God's Relational Presence*, 310.

worshiping" him (22:3). Throughout, heavenly worship scenes and hymns are connected to the overall purpose of the book, recentering a struggling church with a transforming vision of God and the Lamb and the divine victory. As Archer puts it, "Revelation is at its heart a narrative about worship."[115]

The core quality of worship in Revelation centers around God and the Lamb. Jesus is deemed worthy to receive worship in the same way as God. As Creator and Redeemer, God and the Lamb are worshiped for who they are and for their mighty works of salvation and judgment. This all occurs despite God's people being surrounded by powers promoting counterfeit worship.

Worshipers come from the angelic ranks as well as from the redeemed multitude. Their embodied and wholehearted praise takes a variety of forms with hymns playing a central role. Worship recalibrates, reorients, and guides God's people on their pilgrimage through dangers, toils, and snares. As Eugene Peterson puts it, "Worship is centering."[116]

Along with worship bringing heaven to earth, it also anticipates eternal worship in the consummated kingdom. The hymns sung in heaven and on earth proclaim eschatological realities that will one day collapse heaven into earth for good.[117] In this sense worship is the most hopeful of all the church's earthly practices.

115. Archer, *'I Was in the Spirit on the Lord's Day'*, 298.
116. Peterson, *Reversed Thunder*, 59.
117. Leonard Thompson, *Book of Revelation*, 63. See his discussion of "Heavenly Worship and Eschatology" on pp. 63–69.

Chapter 18

"They Follow the Lamb Wherever He Goes": Discipleship

Bibliography

Aune, David E. "Following the Lamb: Discipleship in the Apocalypse." Pages 66–78 in *Apocalypticism, Prophecy and Magic in Early Christianity*. Grand Rapids: Baker Academic, 2006. **Averbeck, Richard E.** "Spirit, Community, and Mission: A Biblical Theology for Spiritual Formation." *JSFSC* 1 (2008): 27–53. **Barr, David L.** "Doing Violence: Moral Issues in Reading John's Apocalypse." Pages 97–108 in *Reading the Book of Revelation: A Resource for Students*. Edited by David L. Barr. RBS 44. Atlanta: Society of Biblical Literature, 2003. **Bauckham, Richard.** "Prayer in the Book of Revelation." Pages 252–71 in *Into God's Presence: Prayer in the New Testament*. Edited by Richard N. Longenecker. Grand Rapids: Eerdmans, 2001. **Beale, G. K.** *We Become What We Worship: A Biblical Theology of Idolatry*. Downers Grove, IL: IVP Academic, 2008. **Byassee, Jason, and Andria Irwin.** *Following: Embodied Discipleship in a Digital Age*. Grand Rapids: Baker Academic, 2021. **Chennattu, Rekha M.** *Johannine Discipleship as a Covenant Relationship*. Peabody, MA: Hendrickson, 2006. **Dalrymple, Rob.** *Revelation and the Two Witnesses: The Implications for Understanding John's Depiction of the People of God and His Hortatory Intent*. Eugene, OR: Wipf & Stock, 2011. **Deans, Graham D. S.** "Discipleship in the Book of Revelation." *BCW* 1 (2019): 9–18. **Duvall, J. Scott.** "Revelation: The Transforming Vision." Pages 255–77 in *The Story of Israel: A Biblical Theology*. Edited by C. Marvin Pate et al. Downers Grove, IL: InterVarsity Press, 2004. **Enroth, Anne-Marit.** "The Hearing Formula in the Book of Revelation." *NTS* 36 (1990): 598–608. **Fanning, Buist M.** "Witnesses for the Lamb: Discipleship in Revelation." Pages 283–98 in *Following Jesus Christ: The New Testament Message for Discipleship Today*. Edited by John K. Goodrich and Mark L. Strauss. Grand Rapids: Kregel Academic, 2019. **Fekkes, Jan, III.** "'His Bride Has Prepared Herself': Revelation 19–21 and Isaian Nuptial Imagery." *JBL* 109 (1990): 269–87. **Flemming, Dean.** "Following the Lamb Wherever He Goes: Missional Ecclesiology in Revelation 7 and 14:1–5." Pages 260–78 in *Cruciform Scripture: Cross, Participation, and Mission*. Edited by Christopher W. Skinner et al. Grand Rapids: Eerdmans, 2021. ———. "'On Earth as It Is in Heaven': Holiness and the People of God in Revelation." Pages 343–62 in *Holiness and Ecclesiology in the New Testament*. Edited by Kent E. Brower and Andy Johnson. Grand Rapids: Eerdmans, 2007. **Gundry, Robert H.** *The Church* *and the Tribulation: A Biblical Examination of Posttribulationalism*. Grand Rapids: Zondervan, 1973. **Homcy, Stephen L.** "'To Him Who Overcomes': A Fresh Look at What 'Victory' Means for the Believer according to the Book of Revelation." *JETS* 38 (June 1995): 193–201. **Johnson, Darrell.** *Discipleship on the Edge: An Expository Journey through the Book of Revelation*. Vancouver, BC: Regent College Publishing, 2004. **Kraybill, J. Nelson.** *Apocalypse and Allegiance: Worship, Politics, and Devotion in the Book of Revelation*. Grand Rapids: Brazos, 2010. **Ladd, George Eldon.** *The Blessed Hope: A Biblical Study of the Second Advent and the Rapture*. Grand Rapids: Eerdmans, 1956. **Marriner, Keith T.** *Following the Lamb: The Theme of Discipleship in the Book of Revelation*. Eugene, OR: Wipf & Stock, 2016. **McIlraith, Donal A.** "'For the Fine Linen Is the Righteous Deeds of the Saints': Works and Wife in Revelation 19:8." *CBQ* 61 (1999): 512–29. ———. *The Reciprocal Love Between Christ and the Church in the Apocalypse*. Rome: Columban Fathers, 1989. **Millar, J. Gary.** *Calling on the Name of the Lord: A Biblical Theology of Prayer*. NSBT 38. Downers Grove, IL: IVP Academic, 2016. **Miller, Kevin E.** "The Nuptial Eschatology of Revelation 19–22." *CBQ* 60 (1998): 301–18. **Newton, Jon K.** "Reading Revelation Romantically." *JPT* 18 (2009): 194–215. **Ng, Esther Y. L.** "Prayer in Revelation." Pages 119–35 in *Teach Us to Pray: Prayer in the Bible and the World*. Edited by D. A. Carson. Eugene, OR: Wipf & Stock, 1990. **Peters, Olutola K.** *The Mandate of the Church in the Apocalypse of John*. StBL 77. New York: Peter Lang, 2005. **Peterson, David G.** *Engaging with God: A Biblical Theology of Worship*. Downers Grove, IL: InterVarsity Press, 1992. ———. *Possessed by God: A New Testament Theology of Sanctification and Holiness*. Grand Rapids: Eerdmans, 1995. **Samra, James G.** "A Biblical View of Discipleship." *BibS* 160 (2003): 219–34. **Schüssler Fiorenza, Elisabeth.** "The Followers of the Lamb: Visionary Rhetoric and Social-Political Situation." Pages 144–65 in *Discipleship in the New Testament*. Edited by Fernando F. Segovia. Philadelphia: Fortress, 1985. **Segovia, Fernando F.,** ed. *Discipleship in the New Testament*. Philadelphia: Fortress, 1985. **Smalley, Stephen S.** "The Christ-Christian Relationship in Paul and John." Pages 95–105 in *Pauline Studies: Essays Presented to F. F. Bruce on his 70th Birthday*. Edited by D. A. Hagner and M. J. Harris. Grand Rapids: Eerdmans, 1980. **Stuckenbruck, Loren T.** "Revelation: Historical Setting and John's Call to Discipleship." *Leaven* 8 (2000): 27–31. **Tabb, Brian J.** "Prayer in Apocalyptic Perspective." Pages 191–208 in *For It Stands in Scripture: Essays in Honor of W. Edward Glenny*. Edited by Ardel B. Caneday. St. Paul: University of Northwestern Bernsten Library, 2019. **Talbert, Charles H.** "Divine Assistance and Enablement of Human Faithfulness in the Revelation of John Viewed within Its Apocalyptic Context." Pages 265–82 in *Getting 'Saved': The Whole Story of Salvation in the New Testament*. Edited by Charles H. Talbert and Jason A. Whitlark. Grand Rapids: Eerdmans, 2011. **Thomas, Rodney Lawrence.** *Magic Motifs in the Book of Revelation*. LNTS 416. New York: T&T Clark, 2010. **Trites, Allison A.** *The New Testament Concept of Witness*. Cambridge: Cambridge University Press, 1977. ———. "Witness and the Resurrection in the Apocalypse of John." Pages 270–88 in *Life in the Face of Death: The Resurrection Message of the New Testament*. Edited by Richard N. Longenecker. Grand Rapids: Eerdmans, 1998. **Wright, Christopher J. H.** *The Mission of God's People: A Biblical Theology of the Church's Mission*. Grand Rapids: Zondervan, 2010.

18.1 INTRODUCTION

We do not need to think for one minute that Revelation encourages eschatology apart from ethics. Just a few sentences into the book the opening beatitude makes a bold pronouncement: "Blessed is the one who reads aloud the words of this prophecy, and blessed are those who hear it and take to heart what is written in it, because the time is near" (1:3). In light of the eschatological urgency ("the time is near"), God promises a blessing on those who obey the prophecy or proclamation that is Revelation. This makes it clear that discipleship lies at the very heart of the book's purposes.

Revelation emphasizes discipleship to the Lamb in a variety of ways, some of which we explore in greater detail in other chapters (e.g., the role of the Spirit, the people of God, worship, new creation). Readers should expect overlap because discipleship relates to the lived experience of the Christian faith, a faith that touches on multiple areas—the Triune God, communities of faith, our response of worship, our experience of the Spirit, our enemies and spiritual challenges, the missional task, and the hope of resurrection and life in the new creation.

We begin by looking at the context of discipleship—suffering and trials—a context that flies in the face of most expectations held by contemporary Western Christians. But disciples are called to reject evil and any devotion to ungodly leaders or structures, to repent if needed, and to embrace a life of faithful endurance. Such a life includes holiness, obedience, and perseverance.

Because of all that God has done for his people in Christ, a response of worship is the only fitting response. This life is lived with a particular prophetic mission in mind, that of bearing witness to the Triune God and his kingdom truth. Because disciples are valued and treasured by the Lord as his bride, they live in hope that one day all things will be made new.[1]

18.2 THE CONTEXT OF SUFFERING

One of the most surprising discoveries regarding discipleship in Revelation is that it often assumes a context of trials and suffering.[2] As Mark Wilson says, persecution is

1. In *Reading Revelation Responsibly*, 176, Gorman sees a life of faithful discipleship along similar lines, perhaps with a more political flavor. He says that Revelation advances a spirituality that includes the following main elements: worship; discernment, vision, and imagination; faithfulness and prophetic resistance (to idolatry and injustice); self-criticism; cruciform, courageous nonviolent warfare; embodied communal witness and mission, including evangelization; and hope.

2. Loren T. Stuckenbruck, "Revelation: Historical Setting and John's Call to Discipleship," *Leaven* 8 (2000), 29, asks, "If it is correct at all that there is little real evidence that supports a political persecution sponsored by Domitian (not only of Christians but also of the senatorial class in Rome), then we are forced to ask what we are to make of references in Revelation to tribulation, persecution, beheading (20:4), conquering (2:7, 11, 17, 26; 3:5, 12, 21; 5:5; 12:11; 13:7; 15:2; 17:14), pouring out of blood (16:6), and death (2:13; 6:9, 11; 12:11; 20:6)." I find his answer unconvincing: "For the most part, passages frequently taken as allusions to harsh realities faced by John's readers are not descriptions of what was actually happening in their world."

the "historical exigence that gave rise to Revelation."[3] Perhaps this is only surprising for Christians who have not known opposition, while those who have endured such trials would consider it perfectly normal. Revelation mentions the general context of suffering along with specific types of ordeals, some that result in death. John notes particular sources of suffering, both human and demonic, and provides insight into why God's people should expect such trials. This is not to say that one must be constantly facing trials to be a follower of Jesus, but the sobering message remains: in Revelation, trials and tribulations are a common course for followers of the Lamb. Nevertheless, as the seven messages show, some situations are simply more difficult than others (e.g., Smyrna, Pergamum, Philadelphia).

John describes himself as a fellow companion with his audience "in the suffering (ἐν τῇ θλίψει) and kingdom and patient endurance that are ours in Jesus" (1:9). The term "suffering" refers to affliction or persecution or tribulation faced by believers as part of following Jesus. It is equated with "suffering" (πάσχω) and "trials" (πειράζω) in 2:10 when Jesus tells the church at Smyrna that he knows their "afflictions" and that they should expect additional "persecution" (both uses of θλῖψις in 2:8, 10). In 7:14 the great multitude clothed in white is described as those "who have come out of the great tribulation" (τῆς θλίψεως τῆς μεγάλης), likely meaning they have come through this ordeal and arrived victoriously in heaven (cf. the "hour of trial" or testing mentioned in 3:10).[4]

Two other images remind us of the general context of suffering in Revelation. First, the 144,000's being numbered according to tribes in 7:4–8 suggests a military census taking stock of battle readiness. This also explains the mention of adult males in 14:4 and why each tribe would contribute a certain number to engage in warfare. All this portrays the people of God as a messianic army ready for spiritual battle. Second, when the heavenly voice calls John to participate in his dramatic vision by eating the little scroll, it turns out to be a bitter-sweet experience (10:8–11). God's salvific plan will certainly come to fulfillment, but the bitterness of God's people suffering persecution in the process remains (cf. 6:9–11). As we note below, these trials come from multiple sources.

Revelation details specific types of suffering that followers of Jesus can expect. These include physical trials, such as imprisonment (2:10), poverty, and economic hardship (2:8; 13:16–17), even slavery and death (18:13). Although possibly metaphorical, the hunger, thirst, and scorching heat endured by the great multitude would also presume at least some background of physical sufferings (7:16). Trials included spiritual attacks

3. Wilson, *Victor Sayings*, 233, 235. I take this to be the case for both an early and a late date. See also Buist M. Fanning, "Witnesses for the Lamb: Discipleship in Revelation," in John K. Goodrich and Mark L. Strauss, eds., *Following Jesus Christ: The New Testament Message for Discipleship Today* (Grand Rapids: Kregel Academic, 2019), 288–90.

4. See Robert H. Gundry, *The Church and the Tribulation: A Biblical Examination of Posttribulationalism* (Grand Rapids: Zondervan, 1973), 53–61.

as well (e.g., the burdens or hardships of 2:3, the slander of 2:9, accusation in 12:10). We see this portrayed vividly in chapter 12 as the dragon attacks the woman by spewing a river of lies, deceit, false teaching, slander, and accusation her way in hopes of destroying her (12:13–17). Such suffering is portrayed symbolically in the lives of the two witnesses in chapter 11, figures who represent the witnessing church. The witnesses' enemies (11:5) attack, overpower, and kill them (11:7–10). Although a figurative depiction of the rejection and persecution encountered by God's people, the overall message that disciples/witnesses should expect opposition remains. At times, the trials become deeply personal as demonstrated through acts and emotions such as mourning, crying, and pain, realities entirely absent from the new creation (21:4; cf. 21:5–26; 22:1–3, 5). Finally, such opposition frequently results in physical death for the disciple (see below). Part of following Jesus involves facing rejection and judgment from the world system that opposed his lordship (18:20).

As noted above, Revelation does not shy away from reporting that disciples might be called upon to pay the ultimate price. The church at Smyrna is exhorted to remain faithful "even to the point of death" (2:10), and we find a named martyr in the letter to Pergamum: "Antipas, my faithful witness, who was put to death in your city" (2:13). At the opening of the fifth seal, John sees the souls under the altar "of those who had been slain because of the word of God and the testimony they had maintained" (6:9, 11). The beast kills the two witnesses (11:7) and wages war against and conquers God's holy people, a victory quite possibly including the death penalty (13:6–7, 15). In 20:4 John sees the souls of those beheaded because of their testimony about Jesus and the word of God, people who refused to worship the beast or its image and had not received its mark. The victors triumph by the blood of the Lamb, by the word of their testimony, and because "they did not love their lives so much as to shrink from death" (12:11). Discipleship might involve both captivity and death (13:9–10). While the second beatitude in 14:13 should not be restricted to martyrs, the context suggests it would certainly include them: "Blessed are the dead who die in the Lord from now on." Babylon is repeatedly held responsible for shedding the blood of God's holy people (16:6; 17:6; 18:24; 19:1–2).

The trials and suffering detailed above comes from particular enemies, both demonic and human.

Satan or the dragon is portrayed as the accuser of God's people who attacks the woman and her offspring (12:10, 12–16, 17). He is God's archenemy who works primarily through human agency to inflict suffering. At the end of the drama, the camp of God's people, the city he loves, is surrounded by Satan and an army of nations before the devil is thrown into the lake of burning sulfur for eternity (20:9). At times the human opposition to God's people is left more general (e.g., the vice lists of 9:20–21; 21:8; 22:15, or the gentiles who trample the unmeasured court in 11:1–2, or the ten horns or kings who wage war against the Lamb and his followers in 17:14). But usually, the human opposition is named as the two beasts and Babylon the Great. We understand the sea beast to symbolize political, military, social, and economic power in service of the dragon and the earth beast to represent pagan religious power or ideology that supports these wicked power structures and their leaders. Both beasts are sources of opposition for God's people, waging war against them (13:6–7, 16–17; 19:19), and even conquering them from a human perspective (13:1, 7; 20:4). Babylon represents any great center of pagan power in opposition to God and certainly plays a key role in pressuring and persecuting God's people (17:6; 18:20, 24; 19:1–2; cf. 11:18).

Occasionally Revelation states particular reasons why God's people suffer in the course of their discipleship to Jesus, and almost always these relate to a clash of kingdoms. Believers face opposition because their actions and words show an allegiance to God and the Lamb over against the kingdoms of this world. The term "testimony" (μαρτυρία) can refer to the words spoken and embodied by Jesus himself, especially through his faithful witness unto death (1:2 and perhaps 19:10b). Most often, though, the term points to the faithful witness of believers to Jesus (1:9; 6:9; 11:7; 12:11, 17; 19:10a; 20:4). Here it is often paired with the "word (or commands) of God" to describe the teachings of the Christian faith with a focus on the gospel (1:9; 6:9; 12:17; 20:4). Christians are those who have been faithful to believe, obey, and proclaim God's good news in Jesus (cf. 12:11). We see this primary reason for opposition highlighted especially in chapter 11 where the two witnesses "devour" and "torment" their enemies through speaking this same message (11:5, 10). The church also displays its allegiance by refusing to worship the image of the beast on pain of death (13:15; 20:4). Disciples live in a broken world that sometimes brings mourning, crying, pain, and death (21:4–5).

This first discipleship emphasis in Revelation regarding the context of suffering echoes Jesus's own words to his disciples the night before his crucifixion: "In this world you will have trouble [θλῖψις]. But take heart! I have overcome [νικάω] the world" (John 16:33). Revelation portrays Jesus as the crucified Messiah or the slain Lamb (Rev 1:7, 18; 5:6, 9) and echoes Jesus's warning to his disciples: "If the world hates you, keep in mind that it hated me first" or "If they persecuted me, they will persecute you also" (John 15:18, 20; cf. 2 Tim 3:12). The context of suffering repudiates an escapist or exemption theology of discipleship and serves to adjust disciples' expectations and prepares them to follow the slain-but-risen Lamb.

18.3 REJECTING EVIL

Revelation suggests that Christians are in a real spiritual battle on two fronts. First, opposition from a pagan world system and its demonic patrons may result in persecution and, for some, martyrdom. But the other battlefront is equally dangerous and perhaps even more common: the temptation to compromise with this same world system (and its demonic supporters), to switch allegiance from God's kingdom to rival kingdoms. This two-front war may be summed up in this way: opposition and temptation. Both were deadly threats for those first followers of Jesus and remain so. In this section we will explore the temptation side of the battle in more detail.

In general, the temptation to compromise consists of the constant pressure to fit into the surrounding culture, initially a culture permeated by the Roman imperial cult. Emperor worship gathered political, social, economic, and military influences into a single dominating religious force, featuring temples, priests, festivals, images, coins, statues, and the like as reinforcing images. The attendant idolatrous and immoral activities ran counter to the beliefs and practices of faithful followers of Jesus. Christians were pressured to participate in the imperial cult or face the consequences. To throw fuel on the fire, some false teachers in these Christian communities were saying one could be a committed follower of Jesus and join in the immoral and idolatrous imperial cult activities without spiritual consequence (e.g., 2:6, 14–15, 20–24). Throughout Revelation Jesus calls his followers to uncompromising devotion, and this involves saying "No!" to evil in its various forms.

For disciples, saying "No!" to evil includes the rejection of false teaching, false worship or idolatry, and false ethical behavior. The seven letters mention false teachers/leaders on several occasions. The Ephesian church has tested false apostles and found them false (2:2) and hates the practices of the Nicolaitans (2:6), a response Jesus supports. Jesus faults some in the Pergamum church for holding to Balaam's teaching, which endorsed idolatry and sexual immorality, along with the teaching of the Nicolaitans (2:14–15). And the church in Thyatira tolerates the prophetess Jezebel, who misleads believers into sexual immorality and idolatry (2:20), teaching advertised as "Satan's so-called deep secrets" (2:24). True discipleship to Jesus includes rejection of any false teaching that attempts to redefine the Christian faith in a way that allows believers to be fully accepted by, and perhaps even profit from, the prevailing pagan culture at the cost of their devotion to Jesus as Lord.

Rejection of false worship or idolatry is likewise part of a disciple's calling. Bauckham observes that distinguishing "the one true God and his righteousness from idolatry and its evils is the theme of true prophecy."[5] We see this call to reject idolatry in several messages to the churches as noted above. In addition, idolatry is also one of several sins that appears in every vice list in Revelation (9:20–21; 21:8; 22:15). It surfaces most visibly in the worship of the dragon, the beast, and the beast's image in Rev 13, as well as the temptation to commit adultery with the great prostitute in chapters 17–18. Throughout, materialism and power are often connected

5. Bauckham, *Theology*, 121.

to idolatrous practices. In Rev 13 those who refuse the mark of the beast suffer economically (13:16–17), the mark being a symbol of "ownership, identification and allegiance" (13:16–17), a figurative sign of idolatry evidenced through actions (right hand) and thinking (forehead).[6] Believers are consistently called to refuse worship of the dragon or the beast or its image and to refuse its mark (14:8–11; 15:2–4; 16:2; 20:4–6). In chapters 17–18 Christians are called to resist the seductive materialism of the great prostitute Babylon.[7] In 18:4 a heavenly voice calls God's people to come out of Babylon, to withdraw, to refuse to participate in her adulterous ways. Gorman observes, "The church is called to resistance in word and deed as the inevitable corollary of faithfulness to God, a call that requires the prophetic spiritual discernment provided by God's Spirit in true worship."[8]

At times the image of staining or soiling or polluting illustrates the threat of idolatry. The church in Sardis has a few who have not "soiled their clothes" (3:4, where it contrasts with white clothing). This term for "soil" or "stain" (μολύνω) is also used in 14:4 where disciples of the Lamb are characterized as "those who did not defile themselves with women." These metaphorical "virgins" have remained faithful to God and have refrained from idolatrous involvement with pagan powers (cf. 1 Cor 8:7 and μολυσμός ["defilement"] in 2 Cor 7:1).[9]

Rejecting evil also means saying "no" to ungodly behaviors. In addition to idolatry, three other vices— sexual immorality, magic arts, murders—are repeated in all three lists, and lying or deception is mentioned twice (see 9:20–21; 21:8; 22:15). Wilson notes a clear connection between the vices, the Ten Commandments, and the rest of Revelation.[10] Five forms of evil and wickedness surface repeatedly throughout the book: false worship, idolatry, sexual immorality, deception, and murder. All five are expressly prohibited in the Ten Commandments.

Followers of the Lamb are those who reject sexual immorality. The πορν- word group appears nineteen times in Revelation and thirty-six times in the rest of the New Testament.[11] While sexual immorality is often used in Revelation as a metaphor for idolatry (e.g., 14:8; 17:2, 4; 18:3, 9), this usually occurs in the context of those who commit adultery with the great prostitute. Literal sexual immorality is certainly in view in other contexts. In those cases it is normally associated with the false teaching

6. Duvall, *Heart of Revelation*, 188.

7. See Richard Bauckham's essay, "The Economic Critique of Rome in Revelation 18," in *Climax of Prophecy*, 338–83.

8. Gorman, *Reading Revelation Responsibly*, 182.

9. Aune, "Following the Lamb," 70; Beale, *Revelation*, 276. Spiritual unfaithfulness in the Old Testament is often described as adultery (e.g., Jer 3:2; 13:27; Ezek 16:15–58; 23:1–49; Hos 5:4; 6:10).

10. Mark Wilson, *Charts on the Book of Revelation*, 81, where he correlates the vice lists in Revelation with the Ten Commandments.

11. The noun πορνεία refers to Babylon's immorality or adultery (14:8; 17:2, 4; 18:3; 19:2) and to sexual immorality (2:21; 9:21). The verb πορνεύω refers also to Babylon's adultery, often partnering with the kings of the earth (17:2; 18:3, 9) and to sexual immorality (2:14, 20). The noun πόρνη refers to Babylon the prostitute (17:1, 5, 15, 16; 19:2). And the noun πόρνος refers to sexual immorality (21:8; 22:15). For an overview of the uses of this word group in Revelation, see Koester, *Revelation*, 288–89.

that encouraged Christians to participate in immoral pagan worship events with the assurance that such practices would not harm their faith. Revelation calls followers of Christ to embrace an embodied spirituality that rejects sexual immorality.[12]

Revelation also includes sorcery and murder several times in the lists of sinful behavior. Louw and Nida observe that the term φάρμακος means "to practice magic, to engage in sorcery" (21:8; 22:15), while the terms φάρμακον (9:21) and φαρμακεία (18:23) place the focus on the use of drugs or potions and the casting of spells upon people.[13] John links sorcery closely with murder (φόνος in 9:21 and φονεύς in 21:8; 22:15) and sexual immorality, perhaps as Koester says, "because some potions could kill people (*T. Ab.* 19:16; P.Oxy. 472.6), and others bewitched people into love relations, sometimes of an immoral sort (*Ant.* 15.93; *T. Reu.* 4:9)."[14] John calls Christians away from murder and the practice of magic arts, including the figurative use of magic as illicit religious behavior that has the power to deceive and destroy (cf. Isa 47:9).[15]

Revelation also highlights the evils associated with deception and lying. Throughout the book, the deceivers include Satan (12:9; 20:3, 8, 10), the beast of the earth (13:14; 19:20), Babylon (18:23), and Jezebel (2:20). Those who are deceived include the inhabitants of the earth (13:14), the nations (18:23; 20:3, 8, 10), the whole world (12:9), and those who receive the mark of the beast (19:20). Only in 2:20 are Christians said to be misled or deceived; every other instance refers to unbelievers. In chapter 14, the 144,000 are without deceit: "No lie was found in their mouths; they are blameless" (14:5). And believers are called to reject deception and lying and falsehood at various points (e.g., 21:8; 22:15). Richard Bauckham rightly concludes that "the most important contrast between the forces of evil and the army of the Lamb is the contrast between deceit and truth."[16]

Revelation most definitely calls disciples of Jesus to reject particular ways of thinking and living that run counter to God's kingdom. Discipleship in Revelation is not just about embracing the good. Specific attitudes, mindsets, and behaviors are identified as anti-Christian and must be abandoned and rejected. The vice lists (9:20–21; 21:8; 22:15) illustrate practices of people who refuse to pledge allegiance to the Lamb and, as a result, will be excluded from God's eternal presence (cf. also 21:25–22:5; 22:10–11). But Christians do not always live like they should and thus the need for the next section featuring a call to repentance.

12. For further reflection on embodied spirituality in the current age, see Jason Byassee and Andria Irwin, *Following: Embodied Discipleship in a Digital Age* (Grand Rapids: Baker Academic, 2021).

13. L&N 544, §§53.100, 101.

14. Koester, *Revelation*, 470.

15. For more background on sorcery, see Rodney Lawrence Thomas, *Magic Motifs in the Book of Revelation*, LNTS 416 (New York: T&T Clark, 2010), esp. 22–44 ("Sorcery Passages in the Revelation"); Aune, *Apocalypticism*, 347–420.

16. Bauckham, *Theology*, 91.

18.4 REPENTANCE

From the previous survey of how Christ-followers typically stand against evil and wickedness, one cannot help but notice that this is not always the case. At times, believers are led astray by false teachers into idolatry and immorality, or they compromise with the prevailing pagan culture in other ways. Another discipleship essential is the willingness to repent. This stands in contrast to unbelievers, who display a stubborn and sustained refusal to repent (2:21; 9:20, 21; 16:9, 11). Repentance involves a change of mind and heart that leads to a rejection of ungodly behavior and a redirection of future thinking and actions.

Christ gives the command to repent to five of the seven churches. Ephesus is told to repent by returning to its first deeds, implying a rekindling of love (2:5). Pergamum and Thyatira are commanded to repent by rejecting false teachings (2:16, 21). The church in Sardis will repent when it remembers and obeys what it has previously heard, a likely reference to the gospel (3:3). Repentance for Laodicea means abandoning its self-sufficiency in favor of dependence upon Christ (3:19). Often the commands to repent are tied to consequences for failure to repent: "If you do not repent . . ." (2:5), "Repent, therefore! Otherwise . . ." (2:16), "unless they repent . . ." (2:22), "if you do not wake up . . ." (3:3), and "So be earnest and repent" (3:19). These consequences involve Jesus's coming to the church in judgment.

In addition to these explicit commands to repent, Anne-Marit Enroth has demonstrated that the hearing formula—"Whoever has ears, let them hear what the Spirit says to the churches"—carries a paraenetic function in Revelation (2:7, 11, 17, 29; 3:6, 12, 22).[17] The formula may reinforce the need to repent (five of the seven churches) or challenge believers to maintain the faith (two of the seven). Noting the immediate background of the Synoptics and the ultimate background of Isa 6:9–10 (and perhaps Ezek 3:22–27), Beale observes how suitable the hearing formula is for warning churches struggling to survive in an idolatrous atmosphere.[18] The practical value of hearing the voice of the Spirit above competing voices cannot be overemphasized. The only other use of the hearing formula outside chapters 2–3 is in chapter 13 at the end of the vision of the beast rising out of the sea. The formula in this context does not call the church to repentance but rather exhorts believers to endure in faithful witness as 13:10 makes explicit.

Repentance is also related to the value of memory. Repentance normally involves an admission that something is lacking that needs to be restored or recovered (e.g., deeds,

17. Enroth, "Hearing Formula," 598–608. See also Peters, *Mandate of the Church*, ch. 4.

18. See G. K. Beale's *We Become What We Worship: A Biblical Theology of Idolatry* (Downers Grove, IL: InterVarsity Press, 2008), ch. 9.

first love, what was originally received, what remains and is about to die). Believers are sometimes encouraged to reflect upon or remember their history with the Lord, which in turn will convict them of present errors and lead to repentance. As Grant Osborne observes, "Remembering is the basis of repentance."[19] Aune notes that remembering was a device often used in both Old and New Testament contexts to encourage people to "live up to or recapture earlier moral and spiritual standards" and even to summon people to repentance.[20]

While Revelation never downplays the "no" of rejecting wickedness and the need for repentance at times, the focus rests upon the "yes" of what follows: enduring faithfulness, devotion to the mission, worship, hope, and relational communion with the Triune God. The "no" is essential, however, since it makes the "yes" possible. The final chapter of Revelation hints that the righteous do indeed repent—they have washed their robes, entered the city, and partaken of the tree of life (22:14); they have indeed come to Christ and quenched their thirst with the gift of the water of life (22:17).

18.5 Enduring Faithfulness

The "no" of rejecting evil and repenting leads to the "yes" of persevering in righteous living.[21] Discipleship in Revelation is firmly tied to a person's deeds or actions of obedience.[22] The entire book is enclosed with beatitudes stressing obedience, macarisms that stand in contrast to the curse formula concluding the book (22:18–19; emphasis added throughout):

1:3 "Blessed is the one who reads aloud the words of this prophecy, and blessed are those who hear it and *take to heart* what is written in it, because the time is near."

22:7 "Look, I am coming soon! Blessed is the one who *keeps* the words of the prophecy written in this scroll."

22:14 "Blessed are those who *wash their robes*, that they may have the right to the tree of life and may go through the gates into the city."

---

19. Osborne, *Revelation*, 117.

20. Aune, *Revelation 1–5*, 147.

21. For an insightful reflection on holiness and the people of God, see Dean Flemming, "'On Earth as It Is in Heaven': Holiness and the People of God in Revelation," in *Holiness and Ecclesiology in the New Testament*, ed. Kent E. Brower and Andy Johnson (Grand Rapids: Eerdmans, 2007), 343–62. Flemming concludes that the church's holiness must flow out of its vison of God's holiness, is communicated through the community's worship, has a strong communal emphasis, is a public call, and is wedded to hope.

22. See Charles H. Talbert, "Divine Assistance and Enablement of Human Faithfulness in the Revelation of John Viewed within Its Apocalyptic Context," in Charles H. Talbert and Jason A. Whitlark, eds., *Getting "Saved": The Whole Story of Salvation in the New Testament* (Grand Rapids: Eerdmans, 2011), 265–82, and Paul Decock, "The Works of God, of Christ, and of the Faithful in the Apocalypse of John," *Neot* 41 (2007): 37–66.

In this section we will focus our attention on the importance of righteous deeds, obedience, and perseverance for followers of Jesus. All three are closely related perspectives on the overall call to enduring faithfulness.

18.5.1 Righteous Deeds

Discipleship goes beyond mere reflection or contemplation and is firmly tied to a person's actions or behavior. The theme of righteous deeds appears consistently in the messages to the seven churches. In all but two churches, the risen Christ is said to know the deeds of his people (2:2, 19; 3:1, 8, 15). In the other two cases, he knows their afflictions and their difficult circumstances (Smyrna and Pergamum). He calls Smyrna to "be faithful, even to the point of death" (2:10) and commends Pergamum for remaining true to his name and not renouncing their faith in him, not even in the days of "Antipas, my faithful witness" (2:13). In Ephesus, deeds are further defined as "hard work and perseverance" (2:2). They have persevered and endured and have not grown weary (2:3). They must do the deeds they did at first, suggesting a return to the acts of love toward God and one another that early on characterized their community. Christ commends Thyatira for her deeds (as defined by four particular works: love, faith, service, and perseverance) and for doing more now than they did at first (2:19). They are challenged to hold on to what they have until Christ returns (2:25). He knows that the deeds of the church in Sardis are in fact dead deeds, meaning they are inadequate or incomplete (3:1). He calls on them to "wake up" and "strengthen what remains and is about to die, for I have found your deeds unfinished in the sight of my God" (3:2). He then charges them "Remember . . . what you have received and heard; hold it fast, and repent" (3:3). The complacency that marks the deeds of the Laodicean church makes him sick (3:15), whereas he has only praise for the deeds of the church in Philadelphia (3:8). They have kept his word and not denied his name (3:8), and they have fulfilled his command to endure patiently (3:10).

Throughout the book God's people are consistently referred to as "God's holy people" or "the saints" (τῶν ἁγίων)—5:8; 8:3, 4; 11:18; 13:7, 10; 14:12; 16:6; 17:6; 18:20, 24; 19:8; 20:9 (see Ch. 16 above). This description itself serves as a not-so-subtle reminder of the importance of righteous deeds for God's people. Their obedience is also conveyed through "righteous imagery." The color white and the image of cleanliness are often used to describe the deeds of God's people. For instance, a few in Sardis have not soiled their clothing, meaning they have refused to compromise. Their worthiness, represented here by wearing white, seems connected to their works, specifically to their loyalty to Christ. The Laodicean Christians need white clothing to cover their shameful nakedness (3:18). The great multitude described in chapter 7 is wearing robes made white by trusting in the finished work of Christ (7:9, 13–14; cf. 22:14). In Revelation 19, the bride of Christ makes herself ready and, as a result, is given fine linen to wear.

The fine linen, we are told, stands for the "righteous acts of God's holy people" (19:7–8). Just a few verses later we also read of the armies of heaven dressed in fine linen, bright and clean (19:14). The lists of vices noted earlier serve as a contrasting backdrop to these images of righteousness. The vices imply a contrasting set of virtues for the righteous who are allowed into the New Jerusalem, virtues such as love, purity, devotion, honesty, and so on.[23]

Revelation also warns of the importance of righteous deeds using the theme of judgment. Along with the rest of the New Testament, Revelation teaches judgment according to deeds (see, e.g., 2:23; 14:13; 20:12–13; 22:11–12; cf. Matt 12:36–37; 16:27; 25:34–36; John 5:28–29; Rom 2:6–10; 14:12; 1 Cor 3:12–15; 2 Cor 5:10; 11:15; 1 Pet 1:17). To the church in Thyatira, Jesus makes an interesting statement: "Then all the churches will know that I am he who searches hearts and minds, and I will repay each of you according to your deeds" (Rev 2:23; cf. Jer 17:10). We are told in Revelation 14:13 that those who die in the Lord are blessed and may rest from their labor because their deeds will follow after them. The specific deeds in view are patient endurance and faithful obedience (14:12). This same theme of judgment according to works appears clearly in 20:12–13 and 22:10–12, where it is tied to Jesus's return. John Stott reminds us that "deeds or works are never the ground or means of salvation, but they are the necessary evidence of it, and therefore they constitute an excellent basis for judgment."[24] Michael Gorman captures the idea well:

> If that sounds like what some Christians (especially certain Protestants) label "works righteousness," it is time for us to stop worrying about this concern and start realizing the seriousness of the call to covenant faithfulness in the Scriptures, including Revelation. Revelation sees death all around, especially in the evils of imperial cultures (whether ancient or modern) that promise life but deliver the opposite. The New Testament offers rescue from this culture of death in all its forms, but its offer of salvation is an offer of liberation from death *for a new way of life*. That is, salvation in the New Testament is as much about faithfulness (fidelity) as it is about faith (assent and trust). This is not, however, "works righteousness," for we do not earn our salvation—the Lamb did that for us by his death.[25]

Often when people hear the term "judgment" they assume it means punishment or condemnation. But it can, and often does in Revelation, refer to the rewards God has for the righteous. Although the warnings to the churches in chapters 2–3 are real, every letter ends on a positive note, holding out the eschatological rewards for the victorious.[26]

23. Wilson, *Victory Sayings*, 233.

24. John Stott, *What Christ Thinks of the Church: An Exposition of Revelation 1–3* (Grand Rapids: Baker Academic, 2003), 70.

25. Gorman, *Reading Revelation Responsibly*, 177, emphasis original.

26. Decock, "Works of God," 48.

In a sense, the phrase "reward according to works" seems especially appropriate. Jesus continues interacting with his people, challenging and encouraging them to persevere.[27] And we must always keep in mind that God is at work not only outside his people but also within them—the bride "was given" fine linen (righteous acts) to wear (19:8), the sealing, the measuring, the names being written in the Lamb's Book of life, and so on. As Talbert concludes, "Divine enablement supplies the resources to enable people to act out of gratitude and/or in line with the certainty of future judgment and rewards."[28]

18.5.2 Obedience

Revelation stresses the necessity and importance of obedience for God's people. Throughout the book, when believers are told to "hold fast to" or "do" or "keep" something, the consistent object is God's truth revealed in and lived out by Jesus Christ. The opening paragraph of the book reinforces this reading: "John, who testifies to everything he saw—that is, the word of God and the testimony of Jesus Christ. Blessed is the one who reads aloud the words of this prophecy, and blessed are those who hear it and take to heart what is written in it, because the time is near" (1:1b–3). For the church in Thyatira, the victorious one is the one who does Christ's will (or deeds) till the end (2:26). The church in Sardis is commanded to "remember what [they] have received and heard and hold it fast," likely an exhortation to obey the truth of the faith taught by Jesus and passed down by his apostles (i.e., the gospel; see 3:3). It is Jesus's word (3:8) or God's word (1:2, 9; 6:9) or God's commands (12:17; 14:12) that are to be obeyed by his people. Aune argues that the phrase "commands of God" refers specifically to the ethical commands of torah, especially to the second table of the Decalogue summed up in the love command.[29] Because the "commands of God" seems synonymous with Jesus's word or will, the expression goes beyond the ethical teachings of torah. More likely, the entire gospel is in view, which certainly includes Jesus's fulfillment of the Law through his teachings. The consistent pairing of "obeying God's word/commands" and "holding to the testimony of Jesus" confirms this conclusion (see 1:2, 9; 6:9; 12:17; 14:12; 19:9–13; 20:4). Then, at the end of the book, the angel who interacts with John identifies himself as a fellow servant with all who "keep the words of this scroll" (22:9). When seen alongside the other beatitudes, this exhortation reminds us that Revelation's goal is that God's people obey his word and receive the promised rewards as a result (cf. 14:13; 16:15; 19:9; 20:6; 22:14).

The most direct call to obedience is found in 14:4 where we have, in Aune's words, "a very simple, yet profound generic concept of discipleship—that is, those who are Jesus's disciples 'follow Jesus wherever he goes'" (cf. John 10:4–5, 27; 12:26; 21:19, 22).[30] This

27. Decock, "Works of God," 50.
28. Talbert, "Divine Assistance," 282.
29. Aune, "Following the Lamb," 74–76.
30. Aune, "Following the Lamb," 71.

single image pulls together much of what we find in Revelation related to the theme of obedience. As Aune observes, to "follow" Jesus means to adhere to his teachings *and* to promote his cause, even to the point of death.[31] Interestingly, the figurative meaning of the verb "follow" (ἀκολουθέω) is found only here outside the Gospels. Whatever else discipleship might include, one of the non-negotiables reinforced by Revelation is obedience to Jesus Christ and his teachings.

18.5.3 Perseverance

Revelation also calls Christians to persevere. Obedience and perseverance are in fact a single, inseparable reality, but one that can be viewed from different vantage points. Perseverance is obedience extended over time through even the toughest of circumstances. The term "perseverance" or "patient endurance" (ὑπομονή) appears seven times in the book (1:9; 2:2, 3, 19; 3:10; 13:1; 14:12). It refers to "the capacity to hold out or bear up in the face of difficulty, patience, endurance, fortitude, steadfastness, perseverance."[32] As Osborne notes, it always occurs in "the context of pervasive evil" and serves as "a comprehensive concept referring to a life of trust and patient steadfastness in hard times."[33] Jesus's instructions to Thyatira illustrate the idea of sustained obedience: "hold on to what you have until I come" (2:25). And in the very next verse, the one who is victorious is described as the "one who does my will [ἔργον, "work"] to the end" (2:26).

Perseverance is often depicted as "remaining faithful to" or "fearing" or "not denying" Jesus's name (e.g., 2:10, 13, 19; 3:8; 11:18; 13:10; 14:12; 15:4; 17:14; 19:5). Together, the terms "faith" (πίστις: 2:13, 19; 13:10; 14:12) and "faithful" (πιστός: 1:5; 2:10, 13; 3:14; 17:14; 19:11; 21:5; 22:6) appear twelve times in Revelation. Osborne sees faithfulness as providing the spiritual dimension to perseverance by "demanding that one refuse to give in to the temptations and demands of the world but instead remain true to God."[34]

The victor sayings of Revelation forcefully portray the call to perseverance.[35] The promises that Jesus makes to the victors in the seven churches function as exhortations to persevere. Overcoming is a process. Victory takes time and relates to how one lives and not just to how one dies. It also allows for the ebb and flow of struggle. Many of

31. Aune, "Following the Lamb," 70. In his commentary on Revelation, Aune writes of a Christian martyr named Vettius Epagathus who is described in Eusebius's *Ecclesiastical History* (5.1.10) as a "true disciple of Christ, following the Lamb wherever he goes" (*Revelation 6–16*, 813–14). At times true discipleship may involve martyrdom.

32. "ὑπομονή," BDAG 1039, §1.

33. Osborne, *Revelation*, 114. Interestingly, this is the only term (aside from the single use of βαστάζω in 2:3) from the semantic domain of "Patience, Endurance, Perseverance (25.167–25.178)" used in Revelation. See L&N 307, §25.177.

34. Osborne, *Revelation*, 44.

35. The definitive work here is Wilson's *Victor Sayings*. The term νικάω is used seventeen times in Revelation—in the seven messages as promises to those who are victorious (2:7, 11, 17, 26; 3:5, 12, 21) and in reference to Jesus's victory (3:21; 5:5; 17:14), to divine judgment (6:2, 2), to persecution of God's people (11:7; 13:7), and to the victor's triumph (12:11; 15:2; 21:7).

the churches are disobedient but the risen Christ exhorts them to change, knowing they can. To sum up, to overcome or triumph ties directly to the call to discipleship to Jesus and in the end involves "following the Lamb with one's whole life until the very end of one's life."[36]

The victor sayings also provide perspective on the nature of perseverance. The forces of evil will be allowed to "conquer" God's people by inflicting upon them persecution and, in some cases, even martyrdom (11:7; 13:7). Yet they follow Jesus, the Lion-Lamb, who through his death and resurrection has triumphed over evil (3:21; 5:5–6; 17:14). Exactly how believers conquer is spelled out in 12:11: "They triumphed over him by the blood of the Lamb and by the word of their testimony; they did not love their lives so much as to shrink from death." Victory comes by relying upon Christ's redemptive work and by remaining loyal to Christ even in the face of suffering. Ironically, then, believers conquer just as Christ conquered: by being "conquered" (12:11; 15:2; 21:7; Rom 8:35–37).[37]

The victor sayings, by pointing to the final outcome in cosmic battle, offer incentive for obedience in the present. Talbert notes that John participates in this type of motivation that appears regularly in other apocalyptic works. Revelation offers "a heavenly perspective on redemptive history," and as readers are immersed in John's "symbolic universe" they are motivated to obey "the commands of the Lord of history. If they know, they will do."[38]

Disciples of Jesus do find themselves in a spiritual battle. Holy war imagery permeates the Apocalypse (e.g., 7:2–14; 14:4–5; 17:14; 19:14).[39] Although the extent to which Christians in Asia Minor were facing widespread persecution continues to be debated, there is agreement that localized opposition was an issue for the original audience (or at least for one Antipas of Pergamum).[40] Yet for disciples of Jesus, the battle is fought differently than typical wars. Bauckham writes:

> Revelation makes lavish use of holy war *language* while transferring its *meaning* to non-military means of triumph over evil. . . . Human participation in the eschatological war is not rejected in Revelation but emphasized again and again. . . . To be faithful in bearing the witness of Jesus even to the point of death is not to become a helpless victim of the beast, but to take the field against him and win.[41]

36. Duvall, "Transforming Vision," 276.

37. For more on the irony of how believers "conquer," see Beale, *Revelation*, 269–72, and Bauckham, *Theology*, 90–94.

38. Talbert, "Divine Assistance," 276.

39. See the insightful essay by Bauckham, "The Apocalypse as a Christian War Scroll," in *Climax of Prophecy*, 210–37.

40. Responding to scholars like Adela Yarbro Collins and L. Thompson who downplay the presence of persecution of Christians under Domitian and afterward, Ben Witherington remarks: "We cannot say that we have no evidence of a systematic persecution of Christians by Roman officials in this period because we do have clear evidence of suffering, oppression, repression, suppression, and occasional martyrdom" (*Revelation*, NCBC [Cambridge: Cambridge University Press, 2003], 8).

41. Bauckham, *Climax of Prophecy*, 233, 235, emphasis original.

Perseverance includes a spiritual battle and fighting the battle involves "faithful, nonviolent action and speech, rooted in the life and witness of the Lamb. . . . *This combination of a cry for justice and a commitment to nonviolence may be the most significant feature of Revelation's liturgical theology and spirituality.*"[42]

Revelation does not suggest any sort of apocalyptic retreat from the world but instead promotes wholesale a lived, acted, behaved, practiced faith in the face of pressure and opposition from the anti-Christian world system. Righteous actions matter. Obedience matters. Perseverance matters. Revelation's theology of discipleship is not of the bunker variety, secluding Christians from engagement with the world. Rather, Revelation calls believers to a public and prophetic participation in the coming kingdom of God.[43]

18.6 DEVOTION TO THE PROPHETIC MISSION

The concept of witness plays a central role for believers in Revelation (see 16.2.6).[44] The foundation phrase "the witness/testimony of Jesus" (μαρτυρία Ἰησοῦ) occurs six times in the book (1:2, 9; 12:17; 19:10 [2x]; 20:4). In 1:2 the "testimony of Jesus" stands in apposition to everything John saw and represents the vision that is the book of Revelation, a vision centering upon the message from God and the witness from Jesus. In 1:9 we learn that John is on Patmos because of the word of God and the testimony of Jesus. In 12:17 the rest of the woman's offspring are identified as those who keep God's commands and hold fast to the testimony of Jesus. Believers are also identified as those who hold to the testimony of Jesus in 19:10, and in 20:4 we read about those who have been beheaded because of the testimony of Jesus and the word of God.

Translators and exegetes have wrestled with whether this foundational phrase should be understood as a subjective genitive (witness given by Jesus) or an objective genitive (witness about/to Jesus).[45] Allison Trites and others have argued that "witness of Jesus" in Revelation should always be taken as a subjective genitive, referring to the witness Jesus himself bore.[46] Most scholars, however, see both grammatical options at play throughout the book depending on the specific context. Beale even concludes that "it is perhaps best to see an intentional ambiguity and therefore [opt for] a 'general'

42. Gorman, *Reading Revelation Responsibly*, 184, emphasis original.

43. Bauckham, *Theology*, 161.

44. See Fanning, "Discipleship in Revelation," 290–94.

45. See Peters, *Mandate of the Church*, 82–84, for a summary of the famous "Μαρτυρία Debate" in a series of articles appearing in *Bible Translator* in the late 1980s and early 1990s.

46. Allison A. Trites, *The New Testament Concept of Witness* (Cambridge: Cambridge University Press, 1977). See also Trites, "Witness and the Resurrection in the Apocalypse of John," in *Life in the Face of Death: The Resurrection Message of the New Testament*, ed. Richard N. Longenecker (Grand Rapids: Eerdmans, 1998), 270–88. Bauckham, *Theology*, 72–73, concurs: "'The witness of Jesus' means not 'witness to Jesus', but the witness Jesus himself bore and which his faithful followers continue to bear. It is primarily Jesus' and his followers' witness to the true God and his righteousness, which exposes the falsehood of idolatry and the evil of those who worship the beast. The theme of witness is connected with Revelation's dominant concern with truth and falsehood."

genitive which includes both subjective and objective aspects."[47] Even if Trites is correct that all are subjective genitives, and this seems doubtful, Revelation calls on believers to be faithful in holding to this witness. As Trites himself says, "It is this wonderful testimony by Christ himself that has been committed to his people, the church. It is their solemn duty to preserve it and maintain it, however costly this may prove."[48] In the end, serving as a prophetic witness remains a crucial part of Christian discipleship. That much is clear.

In addition to the foundational expression "witness/testimony of Jesus," other occurrences of the μαρτ- word group help us grasp the witnessing responsibility of Jesus's followers. In 6:9 the souls under the altar have been slain because of the word of God and the testimony they had maintained. In 12:11 believers triumph over Satan by the word of their testimony. In 14:12, even though the term is not used, the parallel seems clear: God's people are called to endure and are identified as those who keep God's commands and remain faithful to Jesus. In 17:6 God's people are identified as those who bear witness to Jesus. A second occurrence in 19:10 identifies the witness of Jesus with the Spirit of the prophecy. And in 22:16 we read that Jesus sent his angel to give John "this testimony for the churches."

Throughout Revelation, bearing witness is often connected with obedience to God's word as a way of identifying Jesus's disciples (12:17; 14:12; 17:6; 19:10). In other words, Christians are those who hold fast their testimony about Jesus (or hold fast Jesus's testimony). The people of God are a prophetic, witnessing people. We also see that witnessing often brings about suffering for believers (1:9; 6:9; 20:4), yet through faithful suffering they overcome Satan (12:11). Now perhaps that enigmatic phrase in 19:10 makes more sense: "the testimony of Jesus is the Spirit of the prophecy," meaning that those who faithfully hold to their testimony about Jesus are being empowered by the Spirit in the same way that the Spirit has always empowered true prophets.[49]

In addition, Revelation stresses the prophetic role of disciples by what we might call the named witnesses and the two witnesses of Rev 11. From the beginning of the book, Jesus is identified as the "faithful witness" (1:5; 3:14), a reference to his faithfulness unto death.[50] Aune notes that "the victory achieved by Jesus through suffering and death becomes a central paradigm for discipleship in the Apocalypse."[51] Aside from John, who is early on identified as suffering exile due to his faithful testimony about Jesus (1:9), the only other named witness is Antipas, who is also described by Christ as

47. Beale, *Revelation*, 184. Wallace calls this the "plenary genitive." See Wallace, *Greek Grammar Beyond the Basics*, 119–21.

48. Trites, "Witness and Resurrection," 277–78.

49. See a similar conclusion in Osborne, *Revelation*, 678.

50. Around the time of Emperor Nero, the government began to distinguish between Judaism (a legal religion) and Christianity (a harmful new religious movement). As a result, Christians who lived and preached the gospel began to be persecuted as political enemies of the state. The terms for "witness" or "testimony" (*martys* and *martyria* most commonly) were not yet functioning as technical terms for "martyr," but the word group is associated in Revelation with Christians dying for the cause of Christ.

51. Aune, "Following the Lamb," 73.

"my faithful witness" (2:13). The connection between Jesus and Antipas is no doubt intentional. The rhetorical effect of these two being described as "faithful witnesses" perhaps has not been fully appreciated. The task of witnessing is no longer hypothetical for the churches of Asia since they now have concrete examples to imitate when it comes to faithfully testifying.

In his book *Revelation and the Two Witnesses*, Dalrymple presents a persuasive argument that the two witnesses in Rev 11 should be seen as a "corporate entity composed of the entirety of the people of God."[52] Not surprisingly, Dalrymple identifies witnessing as one of four primary themes that mark John's depiction of the two witnesses.[53] He also notes that John's focus on witness as one of the primary characteristics of Christians "greatly distinguishes Revelation's portrait of the people of God from that of the literature of ST [Second Temple] Judaism."[54]

If the two witnesses represent the witnessing church, then in some ways their mission becomes paradigmatic for disciples. Several aspects of this mission are worth noting. First, they are empowered by God to fight the spiritual battle, an empowerment that includes miraculous demonstrations of the Spirit's power and the courageous ability to speak God's truth to Empire (11:3, 5–6, 10). Second, they will encounter the opposition of Empire as the beast attacks and kills them and their bodies lay unburied, and their defeat is celebrated (11:7–10). Third, God's Spirit has the final word in this battle by raising them from the dead and ushering them into God's presence (11:11–12). Fourth, as the two olive trees and two lampstands (1:20; 11:4; cf. Zech 4:1–14; Rev 1:6; 5:10), they share powers attributed to Moses and Elijah and typify the church's service to the Lord as kings and priests. Fifth, there are two of them, signifying both the validity of their witness as well as the importance of the church as community.

All this leads to the conclusion that, as Bauckham says, the "essential form of Christian witness, which cannot be replaced by any other, is consistent loyalty to God's kingdom."[55] Allegiance to God's kingdom inevitably brings resistance to Empire and its ways of conquering. As the witnesses speak God's truth, cooperate with God's empowerment, face opposition, and hope for resurrection and eternal life in God's presence forever, their calling is essentially one of trusting, fearless proclamation of God's truth to Babylon.[56] As Gorman so beautifully puts it, Christian resistance is evangelical to the core:

> Christian resistance, like warfare, is not passive but active. It consists of the formation of communities and individuals who pledge allegiance to God alone; live in

52. Dalrymple, *Revelation and the Two Witnesses*, 36.

53. Dalrymple, *Revelation and the Two Witnesses*, 49–51, 87–89, 103, 113–14.

54. Dalrymple, *Revelation and the Two Witnesses*, 143. He observes that "the call to witness to the nations, however, is absent in the apocalypses of the ST period."

55. Bauckham, *Theology*, 163.

56. Osborne, *Revelation*, 56.

> nonviolent love toward friends and enemies alike; leave vengeance to God but bear witness to God's coming judgment and salvation; create, by God's Spirit, mini-cultures of life as alternatives to Empire's culture of death; and invite all who desire life with God to repent and worship God and the Lamb. The will of God is for all to follow the Lamb and participate in the present and coming life of God-with-us forever. A community that takes the spirituality of Revelation seriously will therefore be unashamedly evangelical, that is, proclaiming in word and deed "the eternal gospel" (14:6) and inviting others into the communion of the saints.[57]

As a result, God's people must "come out of" Babylon (18:4), not withdrawing as escapists, but pulling away spiritually from the kingdom of Empire that rejects Jesus as Lord. As Gorman says, "The church cannot be the church *in* Babylon until it is the church *out of* Babylon."[58] It is a matter of allegiance to the one true God and his everlasting kingdom. As resistance fighters in this spiritual battle, prophetic witness constitutes the church's chief "weapon," "the sword of the Spirit, which is the word of God" (Eph 6:17).

18.7 WORSHIP

In the book of Revelation, worship is central to Christian discipleship.[59] The contrast between heavenly worship and earthly worship stands out immediately. On earth we find the wicked worshiping demons, idols, the dragon, and the beast (9:20; 13:4, 8, 12, 15; 14:9, 11; 16:2; 19:20), while heavenly worship is led by angels and directed toward God and the Lamb (4:8, 11; 5:9–10, 12–13; 7:10, 12; 11:17–18; 14:3; 15:2–4; 16:5–7; 19:1–3, 6–8). Only a few times do we find believers on earth described as worshipers—the worshipers in the temple in 11:1, the angel calling the nations to worship God in 14:7, and the voice from the throne calling all God's servants to praise him in 19:5. But as believers on earth take in the grandeur and majesty of the heavenly worship, they are drawn to commune with God as if they were a part of the heavenly choir. Their affections turn away from the imperial imposters to the one true God and the Lamb.

Worship in Revelation involves speaking, singing, crying out, falling down, casting crowns, playing harps, and rejoicing. There are numerous hymns in Revelation.[60] God and the Lamb are praised for who they are, for what they have done, and for conquering evil. The book both begins and ends with worship, as John receives the vision in a

57. Gorman, *Reading Revelation Responsibly*, 184–85.

58. Gorman, *Reading Revelation Responsibly*, 185, emphasis original.

59. We explore the theme of worship more fully in Ch. 17 and will highlight here only a few elements related to discipleship. For a comprehensive look at worship in Revelation, see Kraybill, *Apocalypse and Allegiance*.

60. See Ch. 17 and Mark Wilson, *Charts on the Book of Revelation*, 74–75. By contrast, Kraybill, *Apocalypse and Allegiance*, 60, notes that "music was a prime index of praise in the emperor cult."

setting of worship (1:6, 10) and the book concludes with the final worship scene of the new heaven and new earth in 21:1–22:5. While it is true that the New Jerusalem does not feature a worship scene per se, the entire experience should be understood as one continuous worship experience with God's people communing with, serving, and worshiping him (λατρεύω in 7:15; 22:3).[61] True discipleship includes habits and practices that open believers' hearts to authentic communion with the Lord.

Worship in Revelation cannot be separated from matters of allegiance. Who should people follow as Lord: Jesus or Caesar? Who is on the throne: God or the emperor? It can only be one or the other—the Triune God or the Dragon, the beasts, and their human puppet rulers. Will it be truth or idolatry? The new heaven and new earth or the lake of burning sulfur? Revelation calls all nations to make this most important of choices. To choose one is to reject the other. As we have seen, there is a "no" and a "yes." And the making and living out of that fundamental choice we call worship. Revelation leaves no room for civil religion in Christian discipleship. Worship calls us to abandon the false promises, idolatry, and immorality of Babylon and follow the Lamb wherever he goes (14:4).

18.8 Hope

Christian discipleship is characterized by hope. Bauckham writes, "John's apocalypse . . . is exclusively concerned with eschatology: with eschatological judgment and salvation, and with the impact of these on the present situation in which he writes. The heavenly revelation he receives concerns God's activity in history to achieve his eschatological purpose for the world."[62]

Throughout the seven messages Jesus makes firm promises to the victors, and each one is eschatological (2:7, 10–11, 17, 26–28; 3:4–5, 11–12, 21). Present challenges are set against future rewards specifically tailored to the struggles of each church. In addition, there are other mentions of the victors and their rewards. Just as white robes are given to the victors in 3:4–5 and to the martyrs in 6:11, so the great multitude is wearing white robes and holding palm branches (7:9, 13–14), both symbols of victory. Their rich rewards are detailed in 7:15–17 and center on abundant life in God's presence. In 15:2 John sees a sea of glass, likely the sea before the throne (4:6), and beside the sea are those "who had been victorious over" the beast, its image, and the number of its name. They hold harps given them by God and sing the song of Moses and the Lamb. The victors are given places in God's presence as their reward. After describing the new heaven and new earth in 21:1–6, God on his throne tells John that "those who are victorious will inherit all this, and I will be their God and they will be my

61. Osborne, *Revelation*, 50.

62. Bauckham, *Theology*, 6.

children" (21:7). We are also told that Jesus is returning with his "reward" (μισθός) in 22:12 (cf. 11:18).

The promises made to God's people form the core of their eschatological hope. This hope consists of four primary realities: (1) Jesus's return, (2) God's coming judgment of evil, (3) the complete elimination of sin's curse, and (4) eternal life in God's presence.[63] The "blessed hope," as George Ladd puts it and the apostle Paul before him (Titus 2:13), is the second coming of Christ.[64] This monumental event bookends the entire work (Rev 1:3; 22:10). Without a doubt, Revelation grounds hope in the promised, always-near return of Jesus (e.g., 1:7; 2:25; 3:3; 3:11; 16:15; 19:7; 22:7, 12, 20). God even identifies himself in part as "the one who is to come" (1:4, 8; 4:8). Believers are called to prepare for his coming by being obedient to the Lord (e.g., 16:15).[65]

Another dimension of Christian hope is that God will bring final justice and deal a death blow to evil. Jesus promises the churches that he will right all wrongs, including requiring a public confession of those who have troubled his people (e.g., 3:9). When the martyrs cry out, "How long, Sovereign Lord, holy and true, until you judge the inhabitants of the earth and avenge our blood?" they are told to wait a little longer before the meting out of final justice (6:10–11). God's judgment is coming (14:7) when he will judge all Babylon-like powers (18:20; 19:2). Even the overall structure of the book in terms of seals, trumpets, and bowl judgments points toward God's commitment to judge evil in preparation for a final new-exodus salvation.[66] Disciples need not worry that evil will get away with it.

More positively, hope means there will be "no more" of the old as disciples experience God's loving comfort and protection. The great multitude, having endured the great tribulation, will never again hunger or thirst or face scorching heat or lack of water, all symbols of suffering. Instead, the Lamb will shepherd them to springs of living water and God will wipe away every tear (7:16–17). There will be no more fear of the second death (20:6). No more death, mourning, crying, or pain (21:4). No more night or threat of intruders (21:25). The one seated on the throne says, "I am making everything new!" (21:5). So that "God may be all in all" (1 Cor 15:28), Revelation promises believers a hope that includes not only ushering in the new but ridding creation of all sin, death, and evil (Rev 21:4). Part of hope is the anticipation that God will do just that.

Ultimately a disciple's hope rests upon God's promise of life and presence. Revelation affirms the coming resurrection of believers to eternal life. The two witnesses are raised to life and escorted into God's presence (11:11–12). The fifth beatitude blesses those who share in the first resurrection since they will not be affected by the second death

63. These themes are dealt with in more detail in Chs. 19–20.

64. George Eldon Ladd, *The Blessed Hope: A Biblical Study of the Second Advent and the Rapture* (Grand Rapids: Eerdmans, 1956).

65. The return of Christ also forms the basis of Christian hope in the Synoptic Gospels. See Duvall and Hays, *God's Relational Presence*, 215–20.

66. See Tabb, *All Things New*, ch. 7.

(20:4–6). Resurrection life is the initial step toward eternal life in God's presence, a reality Revelation stresses numerous times in various ways. God provides living water for his people (7:17; 21:6; 22:17). God provides eternal light in his new creation (21:23; 22:5). God provides citizenship in the Holy City for his redeemed people (21:24, 26; 22:14). God provides the right to the tree of life (22:1–3, 14). In the end, God himself becomes the dwelling place and temple and city for his people (7:15; 21:3, 22; 22:3). At this point the symbols and figures and images offer us but a glimpse of what is to come.

Perhaps the intimacy of God's relational presence among his people offers the reason why wedding imagery is used throughout to depict the hope of Christ's followers. Maybe another reason is that there is likely no human image so joyous and hopeful as that of a wedding/marriage. The wedding of the Lamb along with the bride's preparation is announced in 19:6–8, leading to the fourth beatitude, blessing those invited to the wedding banquet of the Lamb in 19:9. In the description of the new creation in 21:1–8, the Holy City, the new Jerusalem comes down out of heaven from God, "prepared as a bride beautifully dressed for her husband" (21:2). The details of this bride city are revealed to John in what follows (21:9–22:5). Discipleship to Jesus means growing in this hope so that God's age-to-come promises transform our choices and priorities in this age.

18.9 Love Relationship

Revelation is a story that ends with a wedding.[67] This book moves beyond the obligations and responsibilities of discipleship to stress the personal and relational aspects. In the Apocalypse discipleship is rooted in biblical love. Four emphases stand out. First, disciples are in a personal love relationship with the Lord. Both the opening greeting and the closing sentence highlight God's grace or unmerited favor (1:4; 22:21). The greeting gives way to doxology that ascribes glory and power to "him who loves us and has freed us from our sins by his blood and has made us to be a kingdom and priests" (1:5b–6). The people of God are even defined in 20:9 as "the camp of God's people, the city he loves."

This theme also runs through the seven messages. In spite of the Ephesian church's deeds, hard work, perseverance, doctrinal purity, and endurance of hardships, Jesus calls them to return to their first love: "Yet I hold this against you: You have forsaken the love you had at first" (2:4). Such love likely includes both love for God and love for one another. Thyatira, on the other hand, is commended for their "love and faith" along with their "service and perseverance" (2:19).

67. Jon K. Newton, "Reading Revelation Romantically," *JPT* 18 (2009): 194. See also McIlraith, *Reciprocal Love*.

Jesus promises to make those who are opposing the Philadelphian church "come and fall down at your feet and acknowledge that I have loved you" (3:9). Jesus has such strong words of rebuke for the Laodicean church because he loves them: "Those whom I love I rebuke and discipline. So be earnest and repent" (3:19).[68] This love is reaffirmed through the standing invitation to table fellowship in 3:20.

Revelation also uses "the name" (ὄνομα) of Jesus or God to highlight this personal love relationship with disciples. Several churches are commended for enduring trials for the sake of Jesus's name or for remaining faithful to his name (2:3, 13; 3:8). To the victors he promises to write on them the divine name (3:12; 14:1; 22:4). The "name" represents the person and stresses the secure, permanent, personal love relationship disciples have with the Lord. This is affirmed in 22:4, where seeing God's face and having his name written on the disciples' foreheads runs parallel.

Similarly, Revelation uses the phrases "in Jesus" (1:9; 14:13) or "in the Lord" to identify this personal union. In 1:9 John describes the "suffering and kingdom and patient endurance that are ours in Jesus" and refers in 14:13 to the blessing that comes to those who "die in the Lord." Smalley says this language depicts "the intimate relationship with Jesus experienced by the believer."[69] The shared community of the faithful is based upon a personal love relationship with the Lord.

A second emphasis relates to God's protection, provision, and comfort for his people. Numerous times Revelation stresses that God will protect his people spiritually even though they may suffer physical persecution. Jesus promises protection through the coming hour of trial (3:10). The "seal of the living God" indicates both ownership and spiritual protection.[70] Only those who are sealed can withstand God's coming wrath (6:16–17; 7:2–4), and the scorpion locusts can only harm those who have not been sealed (9:4–7). God's people are also "measured" or protected spiritually from demonic powers. Talbert concludes, "The *measuring*, just as the *sealing*, speaks of God's enablement of Christian faithfulness, an enablement that is something more than the provision of a certain knowledge. It involves the empowering of persons."[71]

The wilderness provides yet another image of God's protection of his people. The woman flees into the wilderness to a place prepared by God where he takes care of her (τρέφω), an image depicting spiritual nourishment and protection (12:6, 16). The description of the great multitude as those who have come through the great tribulation underscores God's protection and comfort: they are before his throne being sheltered

68. The Greek term for in 3:19 is φιλέω (also in 22:15), another reminder that this term is often used synonymously with ἀγάπ- forms (ἀγαπάω in 1:5; 3:9; 12:11; 20:9 and ἀγάπη in 2:4, 19).

69. Smalley, *Revelation*, 49. See also Stephen S. Smalley, "The Christ-Christian Relationship in Paul and John," in *Pauline Studies: Essays Presented to F. F. Bruce on His 70th Birthday*, ed. D. A. Hagner and M. J. Harris (Grand Rapids: Eerdmans, 1980), 95–105.

70. Duvall, *Revelation*, 114.

71. Talbert, "Divine Assistance," 278, emphasis original.

(σκηνόω) in his presence (7:15). They will never hunger or thirst again, nor will they experience scorching heat, for the Lamb will be their shepherd and lead them to springs of living water (7:17–16), and God will wipe away every tear (7:17). These followers of the Lamb have been called and chosen (17:14), redeemed and purchased and offered as firstfruits (14:3–5), and their names have been written in the Lamb's book of life (13:8; 21:27). Images of protection, security, provision, and comfort abound.

Third, disciples will experience God's intimate, relational presence eternally.[72] Revelation depicts this experience in a variety of ways, and many are introduced in the promises to the victors, which are all eschatological in nature: for example, the right to the tree of life (2:7), immunity from the second death (2:11), inclusion in the book of life (3:5), a permanent place in God's temple (3:12), the experience of table fellowship (3:20), the right to sit with Jesus on his throne (3:21). The promise of God's presence continues throughout the book. Believers are assured a place God's temple, before God's throne (7:15). The cube shape of the city reflects the inner sanctuary of the temple and portrays God's presence filling the celestial city (21:16). In fact, the entirety of the new creation is God's city and temple with his people being his dwelling place (13:6–7; 21:22–23). This fulfills the long-standing tripartite promise that God would one day live among his people and be their God and they would be his people (21:3, 7; cf. Lev 26:11–12; Ezek 37:26–28; Zech 2:10–11). The goal of Rev 21–22 is to describe the communion disciples will have with their Triune God. As Duvall and Hays conclude, "This final vision represents the fulfillment of the promises to those who overcome (chaps. 2–3), the full realization of the worship in the throne room (chaps. 4–5), the answer to the martyrs' prayer (6:9–11), the goal of the judgments (chaps. 6–16), and the outcome of the final conflict with evil (chaps. 17–19)."[73] God's people will live in his presence, see his face, and serve/worship/reign as kings and priests (1:6; 3:21; 5:10; 20:4, 6; 22:4–5).

Fourth, the relational nature of discipleship is made even more personal with the bride/wedding imagery.[74] This is the dominant image for God's relationship to his people in the final section of the book. The Old Testament prophets speak often about Israel as Yahweh's wife (e.g., Isa 49:18; 54:5–6; 62:5; Jer 2:2; Ezek 16:15–63; Hos 2:14–23), and throughout Scripture marriage imagery consistently portrays the intimacy of God's relationship with his people (e.g., Isa 54:5–7; Jer 2:2; Hos 2:16, 19–20; Matt 25:1–13). The wedding of the Lamb is announced in Rev 19:6–10, along with a declaration of the bride's readiness through both gift and response (19:7–8): "'For the wedding of the Lamb has come, and his bride has made herself ready. Fine linen, bright and clean, was

72. Duvall and Hays, *God's Relational Presence*, 318–22. In this section we will hit the high points and save the more detailed analysis for Ch. 20.

73. Duvall and Hays, *God's Relational Presence*, 319.

74. See Duvall, *Revelation*, 250–54; Fekkes, "His Bride Has Prepared Herself"; Kevin E. Miller, "The Nuptial Eschatology of Revelation 19–22," *CBQ* 60 (1998): 301–18.

given her to wear.' (Fine linen stands for the righteous acts of God's holy people)."[75] This is immediately followed by the fourth beatitude blessing those invited to the wedding supper of the Lamb (19:9). As chapter 21 opens, the heavenly city comes down out of heaven "as a bride beautifully dressed for her husband" (21:2) as God prepares to dwell among his people eternally (21:3). John is carried away in the Spirit and given a tour of the heavenly city in 21:10–22:5, a city introduced as "the bride, the wife of the Lamb" (21:9). The language of marriage communicates God's perfect love for his people and anticipates the joyous, intimate, personal nature of the discipleship relationship for eternity. God and his people will now spend eternity as husband and wife.[76]

18.10 CONCLUSION

The theme of discipleship in Revelation embraces numerous aspects of what it means to follow the Lamb. Suffering and trials will be a common experience for most believers, and those unfamiliar with such opposition should adjust their expectations and prepare to persevere. Enemies could be human or demonic, and the conflict is necessary because disciples are called to allegiance to God's kingdom even when it means conflict with the kingdoms of this world.

It is tempting for believers to compromise under pressure in order to avoid opposition and/or profit from the world system. Yet, disciples are challenged to say "No!" to evil by rejecting false teaching, abandoning false worship, and abstaining from ungodly behavior. The three vice lists (9:20–21; 21:8; 22:15) provide examples of the wickedness disciples are called to forsake. When they do compromise, however, they are called to repentance: "Whoever has ears, let them hear what the Spirit says to the churches." Remembering previous spiritual experiences and standards paves the way for repentance and for saying "Yes!" to God. Such faithfulness involves three major areas: righteous or holy living, obedience to God's truth, and perseverance.

Disciples are also called to a prophetic mission of bearing witness to Jesus, even to the point of "coming out of Babylon" and suffering the consequences. More positively, worship stands central to Christian discipleship. Worship is grounded in the church's eschatological hope: Jesus's return, the judgment and total eradication of evil, and eternal life in God's presence. In the end, faithful discipleship calls believers into a love relationship with their Creator, an eternal marriage between God and his people that includes love, protection, provision, comfort, and an intimate experience of God's relational presence in the new creation.

75. See Donal McIlraith, "'For the Fine Linen Is the Righteous Deeds of the Saints': Works and Wife in Revelation 19:8," *CBQ* 61 (1999): 512–29.

76. Osborne, *Revelation*, 748.

Chapter 19

"SOVEREIGN LORD, HOLY AND TRUE": GOD'S JUDGMENT OF EVIL

BIBLIOGRAPHY

Barr, David L. "Doing Violence: Moral Issues in Reading John's Apocalypse." Pages 97–108 in *Reading the Book of Revelation: A Resource for Students*. RBibSt 44. Edited by David L. Barr. Atlanta: Society of Biblical Literature, 2003. ———. "Violence in the Apocalypse of John." *OHBR* 291–305. **Bates, Matthew W.** *Salvation by Allegiance Alone: Rethinking Faith, Works, and the Gospel of Jesus the King*. Grand Rapids: Baker Academic, 2017. **Bauckham, Richard.** "Judgment in the Book of Revelation." Pages 55–79 in *The Book of Revelation*. Edited by Garrick V. Allen, Ian Paul, and Simon P. Woodman. WUNT 411. Tübingen: Mohr Siebeck, 2015. ———. "Prayer in the Book of Revelation." Pages 252–71 in *Into God's Presence: Prayer in the New Testament*. Edited by Richard N. Longenecker. Grand Rapids: Eerdmans, 2001. **Block, Daniel I.** *The Book of Ezekiel, Chapters 25–48*. NICOT. Grand Rapids: Eerdmans, 1998. **Callahan, Allen D.** "Babylon Boycott: The Book of Revelation." *Int* 63.1 (2009): 48–54. **Decock, Paul.** "The Works of God, of Christ, and of the Faithful in the Apocalypse of John." *Neot* 41.1 (2007): 37–65. **De Villiers, Pieter G. R.** "Prime Evil and Its Many Faces in the Book of Revelation." *Neot* 34 (2000): 57–85. ———. "The Violence of Nonviolence in the Revelation of John." *OpenTh* 1 (2015): 189–203. **Duvall, J. Scott.** "A Synchronic Analysis of the Indicative-Imperative Structure of Pauline Exhortation." Ph.D. diss., Southwestern Baptist Theological Seminary, 1991. **Glasson, T. Francis.** "The Last Judgment—in Revelation 20 and Related Writings." *NTS* 28 (1982): 528–39. **Harris, Dana M.** "John and Punishment: Did He Delight in Violence?" Pages 68–86 in *The Apocalypse of John among Its Critics: Questions and Controversies*. StScrBT. Edited by Alexander E. Stewart and Alan S. Brady. Bellingham, WA: Lexham, 2023. ———. "Understanding Images of Violence in the Book of Revelation." Pages 148–64 in *Encountering Violence in the Bible*. Edited by Markus Zenhder and Hallvard Hagelia. BMW 55. Sheffield: Sheffield Phoenix, 2013. **Hylen, Susan E.** "Metaphor Matters: Violence and Ethics in Revelation." *CBQ* 73.4 (2011): 777–96. **Kio, Stephen H.** "The Exodus Symbol of Liberation in the Apocalypse and Its Relevance for Some Aspects of Translation." *BT* 40.1 (1989): 120–35. **Klassen, William.** "Vengeance in the Apocalypse of John." *CBQ* 28.3 (1966): 300–311. **Koester, Craig R.** *Revelation and the End of All Things*. 2nd ed. Grand Rapids: Eerdmans, 2018. **Lambrecht, Jan.** "Final Judgments and Ultimate Blessings: The Climactic

Visions of Revelation 20,11–21,8." *Bib* 81 (2000): 361–85. **Lane, Tony.** "The Wrath of God as an Aspect of the Love of God." Pages 138–67 in *Nothing Greater, Nothing Better: Theological Essays on the Love of God.* Edited by Kevin J. Vanhoozer. Grand Rapids: Eerdmans, 2001. **Longman, Tremper, III.** "The Divine Warrior: The New Testament Use of an Old Testament Motif." *WTJ* 44 (1982): 290–307. **Mathewson, David L.** "A Re-examination of the Millennium in Rev 20:1–6: Consummation and Recapitulation." *JETS* 44.2 (2001): 237–51. ———. *Uncovering the Treasures of the Apocalypse: Keys to Unlocking the Mysteries of the Book of Revelation.* Eugene, OR: Cascade, 2022. **McCall, Thomas H., Caleb T. Friedeman, and Matt T. Friedeman.** *The Doctrine of Good Works: Reclaiming a Neglected Protestant Teaching.* Grand Rapids: Baker Academic, 2023. **Metzger, Bruce M.** *Breaking the Code: Understanding the Book of Revelation.* Nashville: Abingdon, 1993. **Middleton, J. Richard.** *A New Heaven and a New Earth: Reclaiming Biblical Eschatology.* Grand Rapids: Baker Academic, 2014. **Middleton, Paul.** *The Violence of the Lamb: Martyrs as Agents of Divine Judgement in the Book of Revelation.* LNTS 586. London: T&T Clark, 2018. **Morris, Leon.** *The Biblical Doctrine of Judgment.* Eugene, OR: Wipf & Stock, 2006. **Moyise, Steve.** "Does the Lion Lie Down with the Lamb?" Pages 181–94 in *Studies in the Book of Revelation.* Edited by Steve Moyise. Edinburgh: T&T Clark, 2001. **Osborne, Grant R.** "Theodicy in the Apocalypse." *TrinJ* 14 (1993): 63–77. **Schnabel, Eckhard J.** "John and the Future of the Nations." *BBR* 12.2 (2002): 243–71. **Shogren, Gary S.** "Hell, Abyss, Eternal Punishment." *DLNT* 459–62. **Skaggs, Rebecca, and Thomas Doyle.** "Violence in the Apocalypse of John." *CurBR* 5.2 (2007): 220–34. **Sprinkle, Preston,** ed. *Four Views on Hell.* 2nd ed. Grand Rapids: Zondervan, 2016. **Stevenson, Gregory.** *A Slaughtered Lamb: Revelation and the Apocalyptic Response to Evil and Suffering.* Abilene, TX: Abilene Christian University Press, 2013. ———. "Perspectives on Evil in the Book of Revelation." *OHBR* 275–89. **Tabb, Brian J.** "Prayer in Apocalyptic Perspective." Pages 191–208 in *For It Stands in Scripture: Essays in Honor of W. Edward Glenny.* Edited by Ardel B. Caneday. Saint Paul, MN: University of Northwestern Berntsen Library, 2019. **Tonstad, Sigve.** *Saving God's Reputation.* LNTS 337. London: T&T Clark, 2006. **Woodman, Simon P.** "Fire from Heaven: Divine Judgment in the Book of Revelation." Pages 175–91 in *The Book of Revelation.* Edited by Garrick V. Allen, Ian Paul, and Simon P. Woodman. WUNT 411. Tübingen: Mohr Siebeck, 2015. **Yarbro Collins, Adela.** "Persecution and Vengeance in the Book of Revelation." Pages 729–49 in *Apocalypticism in the Mediterranean World and the Near East.* Edited by David Hellholm. Tübingen: Mohr Siebeck, 1989.

19.1 INTRODUCTION

"Revelation is a war story," writes Gregory Stevenson, with the language of warfare permeating the entire book (e.g., make war/battle, victory, kill/slaughter, sword, army).[1]

1. Gregory Stevenson, "Perspectives on Evil in the Book of Revelation" *OHBR* 276. Although warfare remains an important emphasis throughout, we stop short of concluding with Stevenson that "warfare functions as the governing metaphor that structures the book's narrative world" (p. 276). As we will see, judgment is a means to the end of salvation.

Indeed, it is. Most people could probably tell you that judgment is an important theme of John's Apocalypse, but they might be surprised to learn exactly how dominant it really is. Revelation is thoroughly consumed with judgment, yet these judgments are essential if the world is to be made right. As Mathewson puts it, "God's judgments are necessary if he is to offer a world free of injustice, evil, pain and death. He must remove anything and anyone who would oppose and attempt to destroy such a world."[2] God's ultimate purpose is not judgment, however, but salvation (see Chs. 15 and 20).[3] Thus, judgment is a prelude to full and final salvation. God opposes evil because it threatens his grand salvation project. As Gorman rightly observes, "in the book of Revelation, divine judgment is not an end in itself. It is God's 'Plan B' when humanity persists in evil rather than repenting. It then becomes a means—a necessary means, to be sure, but still only a means—to the fulfillment of God's plan to heal the nations and create space for all people to flourish in harmony with one another before God."[4] Similarly, Flemming concludes that "the overarching purpose of God's judgment in Revelation is not *revenge* or *retribution* but *repentance* and *restoration*."[5] Flemming's statement brings us to the heart of God. Mapping out the specifics is the task of this chapter.

John sets the scene early on with this judgment-salvation interaction: "I, John, your brother and companion in the suffering and kingdom and patient endurance that are ours in Jesus, was on the island of Patmos because of the word of God and the testimony of Jesus" (1:9). The experience of John and all faithful disciples is this dynamic interaction between suffering, kingdom, and patient endurance or, to put it differently, it is an experience of salvation through judgment.[6] This plays out not only through the entire metanarrative of Scripture but also in key passages throughout Revelation, as we will see.[7]

Revelation features certain terms for judgment: ὀργή ("anger" or "wrath"—6:16, 17; 11:18; 14:10; 16:19; 19:15), θυμός ("fury" or "wrath"—14:10, 19; 15:1, 7; 16:1, 19; 19:15), κρίνω ("judge" or "condemn"—6:10; 11:18; 16:5; 18:8, 20; 19:2, 11; 20:12, 13), κρίσις ("judgment"—14:7; 16:7; 18:10; 19:2), and κρίμα ("punishment" or "judgment"—17:1;

2. David L. Mathewson, *Uncovering the Treasures of the Apocalypse: Keys to Unlocking the Mysteries of the Book of Revelation* (Eugene, OR: Cascade, 2022), 64.

3. Richard Bauckham, "Judgment in the Book of Revelation," in *The Book of Revelation*, ed. Garrick V. Allen, et al., WUNT 411 (Tübingen: Mohr Siebeck, 2015), 67; also a repeated emphasis in Middleton, *New Heaven and a New Earth*, e.g., 110, 121–22, 125–28, 209–10.

4. Gorman, *Reading Revelation Responsibly*, 153.

5. Flemming, *Foretaste of the Future*, 128, emphasis original.

6. James Hamilton captures this dynamic in the title of his book, *God's Glory in Salvation through Judgment: A Biblical Theology* (Wheaton, IL: Crossway, 2010).

7. Dana M. Harris, "Understanding Images of Violence in the Book of Revelation," in *Encountering Violence in the Bible*, ed. Markus Zehnder and Hallvard Hagella (Sheffield: Sheffield Phoenix, 2013), 157–63. From her very brief overview of the biblical metanarrative she identifies three key themes that are essential for understanding Revelation's take on judgment (p. 156): (1) the Bible consistently portrays God as good, holy, just, and loving, (2) God is a Divine Warrior who "fights for his people against evil and against his people when they reject him for evil," and (3) there is the future expectation of the eradication of evil.

18:20; 20:4).[8] These terms highlight key aspects of judgment throughout the book: God (and the Lamb) as the ultimate source of judgment, God's character (holy, just, faithful, true, etc.) as the only worthy Judge, the coming great day of God's wrath, God's judgment of the wicked and rebellious (e.g., Babylon the Great, beast worshipers), three series of judgments allowing time to repent, and the impartial nature of God's judgments based on allegiance demonstrated through actions. To be sure, Revelation's theology of divine judgment moves beyond a survey of key terms, but even these capture the basic elements of God's judgment of evil.

This chapter focuses on a more comprehensive evaluation of Revelation's theology of judgment. We begin with a brief sketch of the judgment texts in Revelation to get a feel for the scope of judgment. Then we consider the source of judgment—the Triune God—and what Revelation says about his character and purposes as Judge. The three series of judgments reveal much about the outworking of divine judgment. Next, we pay close attention to the enemies of God, those powers and people facing divine judgment, before investigating Jesus's return and the final judgment. Finally, we highlight the justice of God's judgments and then reflect on the surprising role of God's people in judgment.

19.2 Overview of Judgment Texts in Revelation

Gorman is correct when he cautions that we should take the judgment scenes seriously if for no other reason than they account for approximately half of the book.[9] In this section we get a bird's-eye view of the judgment sections of Revelation to give context and perspective. From the beginning Jesus is connected to judgment as "the faithful witness, the firstborn from the dead, and the ruler of the kings of the earth" (1:5), meaning the one who was faithful unto death now stands victorious over death and all earthly rulers and kingdoms. The judgment passages repeatedly ask and answer the important question, "Who is Lord of the universe?" Jesus, the ruler of all, has also made his people into a kingdom and priests (1:6). The Lord God is described as the "Almighty" (παντοκράτωρ), an intentional trumping of the oft-used title for Ceaser, αὐτοκράτωρ. The divine warrior theme appears in 1:12–18 using imagery drawn from Dan 7 and 10 to depict the risen Jesus as glorious, powerful, and sovereign. He stands among the churches as the Lord of life and death. No competing ruler, whether human or demonic, can claim such power. As a result, he alone is worthy of worship and allegiance.

8. In addition, Stevenson, "Perspectives," 276, notes that terms for "evil" (κακός in 2:2; 16:2 and πονηρός in 16:2) are used rarely in Revelation, and the usual term for "good" (καλός) does not appear. He concludes: "Given the paucity of such terminology, one might question whether categories of 'good' and 'evil' are the best way to characterize John's vision. However, though the terminology is not pervasive, the concepts of good and evil are interwoven into the very fabric of Revelation's narrative, impacting and being impacted by virtually all aspects of the text."

9. Gorman, *Reading Revelation Responsibly*, 140.

Jesus confronts his people in the seven messages of Rev 2–3. The descriptions of Jesus emphasize his presence, power, sovereignty, and compassion. The churches that are found faithful are encouraged to persevere, while those that are complacent or compromising are warned and called to repentance. Judgment occurs not only on the last day but in the here and now as God's people make ongoing decisions. These churches are called to wake up and realize their true spiritual condition and, when necessary, to repent. The warnings that accompany the calls to repentance, however, are redemptive in purpose, either by protection through the storm or preliminary judgment encouraging repentance.[10]

The heavenly throne room vision of chapters 4–5 stresses God's glory, majesty, and sovereignty. The absolute holiness of the Lord God Almighty is front and center (4:8, 11). But John's anguish at not finding anyone worthy to break the seals and open the scroll of judgment is relieved upon hearing about the Lion who has triumphed and then turning to see the slain Lamb standing at the center of the throne (5:5–6). God's message: victory comes through the sacrificial suffering of the Lamb. God and the Lamb are praised for redeeming a people from every nation and making them into a kingdom and priests who will reign on the earth (5:9–10). As a result, we see that God's judgment comes through the sacrifice he himself provides.

In chapters 6–16 we see the unfolding of divine judgments as the means of conquering the evil powers. In three sets of seven judgments—seals, trumpets, and bowls—God judges evil and urges people to repent. The series overlap and recapitulate but also intensify and progress toward final judgment. The number seven represents completeness and fullness. The message is clear: God will defeat the evil powers. He has won and will win! Interspersed among these series are interludes that reveal the situation faced by God's people and remind them that their hope is firm and steadfast—the 144,000 and the great multitude (7:1–17), John's recommissioning and the two witnesses (10:1–11:14), and the cosmic war between God and the forces of evil (12:1–14:20). Particularly in this third interlude of chapters 12–14 we see multiple allusions to the cosmic war and God's judgment of evil: the heavenly war (12:7–12), the earthly war (12:13–13:18), and the two visions of judgment (14:6–20).

The fall of Babylon the Great occurs in chapters 17–18. The Roman Empire (and future ungodly empires) is portrayed as a shameless prostitute, bloodthirsty for worship, power, violence, and luxury. She blasphemes God and stands in contrast to the glorious bride of Christ appearing in chapter 19 (e.g., her gaudy apparel vs. the fine linen, bright and clean, worn by the bride). Her arrogance and sinful offences are well documented. Harris notes that "Rome epitomized opposition to the True God at every level: it glorified itself, indulged itself in every possible way, exploited human beings and the rest of

10. Harris, "Understanding Images of Violence," 159.

creation, and violently suppressed its opponents."[11] God's judgment of the harlot queen occurs suddenly and decisively, emphasizing God's sovereign power over all earthly powers. God's people are called out of Babylon (18:4) and are also called to worship God for his just judgment of her (18:20). The famous "Hallelujah Chorus" of chapter 19 is the heavenly response to God's true and just judgment of the great prostitute (19:2).

God's judgment of evil culminates in the return of Christ to conquer the two beasts and their followers (19:11–21), the final judgment of Satan (20:1–10), and the final judgment of wicked humanity (20:11–15). Although chapters 19–20 have been read in a variety of ways, the view from afar indicates that the coming of Christ brings complete and total victory over all of God's enemies, paving the way for the emergence of the new creation in chapters 21–22. Chapters 19–20 reinforce several important aspects of divine judgment. Christ returns as the Warrior Messiah to judge evil justly (see the description of the rider on the white horse in 19:11–16). There is no doubt about God's commitment to rid all creation of evil. And while the stage is set for an epic battle, no such battle actually occurs. Jesus simply wins by his appearing: "But the beast was captured, and with it the false prophet" (19:20). So much for the much-advertised battle of Armageddon in popular eschatology. Jesus judges by his word (19:15, 21). Harris notes that the "army" that accompanies Christ is "dressed in fine linen, suggesting that they are prepared for the marriage banquet and not for war," indicating that God alone executes judgment.[12] Whatever one makes of the millennium, there is no doubt that it takes place within the context of the judgment of Satan. God's people are raised and vindicated while Satan continues his descent toward final judgment. The judgment of 20:11–15 is most likely the judgment of unbelievers and perhaps another perspective on the final battle narrated in 19:11–21 (see 11.6.6).

19.3 DIVINE CHARACTER AS THE BASIS OF JUDGMENT

Revelation clearly and forcefully stresses God's anger and wrath against evil. Beast worshipers will be made to "drink the wine of God's fury, which has been poured full strength into the cup of his wrath. They will be tormented with burning sulfur in the presence of the holy angels and of the Lamb. And the smoke of their torment will rise for ever and ever. There will be no rest day or night for those who worship the beast and its image, or for anyone who receives the mark of its name" (14:10–11). The seven last plagues, described as "the seven bowls of God's wrath" (16:1), are necessary to complete God's wrath (15:1, 6–8). With the final bowl judgment God remembers Babylon the Great and gives her "the cup filled with the wine of the fury of his wrath" (16:19). Jesus, the rider on the white horse, "treads the winepress of the fury of the wrath of

11. Harris, "Understanding Images of Violence," 162.

12. Harris, "Understanding Images of Violence," 162–63.

God Almighty" (19:15). In the end God's judgment falls on the devil, the two beasts, Babylon the Great, wicked humanity, and death and Hades.

Although the imagery is no doubt quite violent at times, we do well to notice how God's character grounds these judgments. What does the text tell us about God's nature in the context of the judgments? Seven character qualities appear in relation to the Triune God that must inform our understanding of the judgments overall. The first three are closely related. First, God is all-powerful or almighty. The title "Almighty" (παντοκράτωρ) occurs nine times in the book (1:8; 4:8; 11:17; 15:3; 16:7, 14; 19:6, 15; 21:22) and speaks to God's "unrivaled power over all things and therefore his supremacy over the course of historical events."[13] In 11:17 and 19:6 God's power is linked to his reign, in 15:3 to his "great and marvelous deeds," to his victorious judgments in 16:7, 14; 19:15, and to his powerful presence in the new creation in 21:22.

Second, God is the sovereign ruler over history (see 12.3). He is "the Lord" or "Lord God" (1:8; 4:8, 11; 11:4, 15, 17; 15:3, 4; 16:7; 18:8; 19:6; 21:22; 22:5, 6; used of Jesus in 11:8; 14:13; 17:14; 19:16; 22:20, 21), "King" (15:3; of Jesus in 1:5; 17:14; 19:16), the "Alpha and the Omega" (1:8; 21:6; 22:13), the "Beginning and the End" (21:6; 22:13), "the First and the Last" (22:13; cf. used of Jesus in 1:17; 2:8), and the one "who is, and who was, and who is to come" (1:8; 4:8; 11:17). In addition to specific terms such as these, we find images of sovereignty used throughout (e.g., the throne of God, Jesus among the lampstands).

Third, God is the eternal Creator (see 12.3.1). In the grounding vision of chapters 4–5 God is worshiped as the one who "created all things," and by his will "they were created and have their being" (4:11). It is "God's creation" (3:14), and it was he who "created the heavens and all that is in them, the earth and all that is in it, and the sea and all that is in it" (10:6). Every creature is summoned to "fear God and give him glory, because the hour of his judgment has come. Worship him who made the heavens, the earth, the sea, and the springs of water" (14:7). As the all-powerful, sovereign Creator, God alone deserves to be the Judge.

Fourth, God is perfectly holy. "Holy, holy, holy," cry the four living creatures (4:8). The martyrs under the altar cry out for justice to the "Sovereign Lord, holy and true" (6:10). Jesus, the "holy and true" One, speaks to the churches (3:7). God's judgments flow out of his holy character. They are not biased or partial or corruptible. They are holy judgments because God is holy. Even God's people are known as the "holy ones" (ἁγίων; e.g. 5:8; 8:3–4; 11:18; 13:7, 10; 14:12; 16:6; 17:6; 18:20, 24; 19:8; 20:9; 22:11). Those who share in the first resurrection are "holy" (20:6). The New Jerusalem, God's eternal home with his people, is described as "the Holy City" (21:2, 10; 22:19).

Fifth, God is true. Again, part of the martyrs' cry for justice is based on God's

13. Bauckham, *Theology*, 30.

character as the "true" God (6:10). Part of the song of Moses and of the Lamb in chapter 15 praises God for his "just and true ways" (15:3). His ways include his judgments, which are also described as "true and just" by the altar (16:7) and by the great multitude (19:2). God's words, including his judgments, are "trustworthy and true" (21:5; 22:6). In addition, Jesus is described as the "faithful and true witness" (3:7, 14) and as the one who is called "Faithful and True" (19:11). All this is to say that truth plays a vital role in divine justice and in John's theodicy, in strong contrast to the lies and deceit of the evil one. *Justice should never be divorced from truth!*

Sixth, God is just or righteous (the δικ- word group). Thus, God's judgments are just, fair, and true to reality. God is praised with a new song because his ways are "just and true" (15:3) and because his "righteous acts have been revealed" (15:4). In the third bowl judgment the angel proclaims, "You are just in these judgments, O Holy One, you who are and who were; for they have shed the blood of your holy people and your prophets, and you have given them blood to drink as they deserve" (16:5–6). And the heavenly altar affirms God's justice: "Yes, Lord God Almighty, true and just are your judgments" (16:7). The great multitude shouts praise to God: "Salvation and glory and power belong to our God, for true and just are his judgments. He has condemned the great prostitute who corrupted the earth by her adulteries. He has avenged on her the blood of his servants" (19:1–2). Here we see God giving back to the evildoers exactly as they have given to his people. The Roman legal principle of *lex talionis* (law of retribution) surfaces here and at other places in Revelation. In addition, at Jesus's return, he judges and wages war "with justice" (19:11). The war that Jesus wages is best understood as his just and true judgment of humanity, including those who cannot be brought to justice in a human court (cf. 2:16; 19:15).

Finally, God's character is loving and compassionate. To begin with, God cares enough to create, and the primary characterization of God in the grounding vision is that of Creator: "You are worthy, our Lord and God . . . for you created all things" (4:11). Next, as Creator, Revelation stresses God's relationship with his creation. The entire story of Scripture recounts God's devotion to his people, and Revelation highlights the incarnation of the Lamb of God, the Lamb who was slain for their salvation. The risen Jesus also walks among the churches, and the Spirit speaks to them the words of the risen Christ. God's compassion also shines through the progression and intensification of the judgments. He patiently calls them to repentance, and they repeatedly reject his love (2:20–22; 9:20–21; 16:9, 11, 21).

Another subtle indication of God's love as one aspect of his character that grounds his judgments is his relation to these judgments.[14] Although God is clearly ultimately

14. See Bauckham, "Judgment in the Book of Revelation," 59–65, on how God and Jesus relate to the judgments.

responsible for the judgments, he usually does not directly command or execute them. Instead, they are indirect and mediated, commonly using the passive voice (e.g., "was given," "were thrown," "was burned"). This is what Bauckham calls a "reverential circumlocution," a device that is completely abandoned when the talk shifts to God's actions in salvation; in that case, God is the stated subject.[15] In other words, "The book of Revelation distances God from his judgments—both linguistically and actually (by the intermediation of angelic agents)—but not from his acts of salvation. . . . It is clear that for Revelation God is not related in the same way to judgment as he is to salvation."[16] This is surely because God's judgments are not an end but a necessary means.[17] And they are a means because although God's love has been perfectly demonstrated in the person and work of Jesus, the slain and resurrected Lamb, the unrepentant do not receive or reciprocate his love. Thus, what God had planned for the wicked, the future his love intended for them, must be abandoned in their case since it has been rejected.

The brief survey of the divine character that forms the basis of judgment makes it clear that God will judge justly and righteously, truthfully and lovingly.[18] Whatever else may be said about God's judgments, we must begin with the consistent and widespread depiction of God as holy and righteous, true and loving. Here we follow Harris who makes an important distinction between "justice" that flows from the Triune God who is holy, just, good, and loving and occurs in response to human injustice, and "violence" that appears in conjunction with human sinful actions.[19] Klassen concurs when he insists that we need to "differentiate between the wrath of God and human desire for vengeance."[20] God's central concern is to redeem and save and deliver his people from evil. Another important part of this distinction lies in the symbolic nature of language in the Apocalypse, a topic we will address below in our discussion of the three series of judgments.

19.4 THE THREE SERIES OF JUDGMENTS—SEALS, TRUMPETS, BOWLS

Revelation is organized around a series of judgments alternating with a series of interludes (7:1–17; 10:1–11:14; 12:1–14:20; see Ch. 9). The two realities of judgments and

15. Bauckham, "Judgment in the Book of Revelation," 60.

16. Bauckham, "Judgment in the Book of Revelation," 61.

17. Gorman, *Reading Revelation Responsibly*, 153.

18. Some raise the issue of theodicy at this point, meaning the question of how God can be both good and loving as well as all-powerful and sovereign in light of the reality of evil. See the helpful exploration of this topic in Osborne, "Theodicy in the Apocalypse," 63–77. See also the insightful discussion by Stevenson, *A Slaughtered Lamb*, chs. 2–3. See esp. pp. 40–49, where he deals with the problems of theodicy and with viewing Revelation as a modern theodicy. Revelation's primary concern is not with sustaining a systematic, rational explanation of evil, but with calling God's people to follow the Lamb in faithful witness.

19. Harris, "Understanding Images of Violence," 149–51.

20. William Klassen, "Vengeance in the Apocalypse of John," *CBQ* 28.3 (1966): 304.

interludes in some ways represent two contrasting stories—the story of God's judgment of his enemies and the story of God's salvation of his people and creation:[21]

Seal Judgments (6:1–17)
  Interlude (7:1–17)
    Transition (8:1–6)
Trumpet Judgments (8:7–9:21; 11:15–19)
    Transition (11:15–19)
  Interlude (10:1–11:14)
  Interlude (12:1–14:20)
    Transition (15:1–8)
Bowl Judgments (16:1–17)

As for these series of judgments, in addition to providing a contrasting story to that featured in the interludes, each series ends in the day of the Lord and the culmination of history—6:12–17; 11:15–19; 16:17–21. To some degree there is repetition and overlap, but there is also progression, moving from one-fourth to one-third to one, and from more general judgments to more specific. Most see this intensification as an example of God's patience and forbearance, allowing more time for the faithful to bear witness and for humanity to repent and worship the true God.[22]

The first four seal judgments represent preliminary judgment-like conditions of a fallen world, reminding readers that God is not taken by surprise or thrown off his game by ongoing human depravity: conquest, war, famine, and death. As Stevenson concludes, "The larger theological message of these seals asserts that the existence of suffering and violence in the world by no means nullifies the sovereignty of God over his creation."[23] The fifth seal does not depict judgment against evil so much as the world's judgment against God's people and the important question of when God will do something about it. This scene depicts the souls of martyrs under the altar crying out to God for justice: "How long, Sovereign Lord, holy and true, until you judge the inhabitants of the earth and avenge our blood?" (6:10). God tells them to wait until others have born witness and paid the ultimate price, perhaps another example of his longsuffering love. Seal judgment six brings us to the last day and final judgment (6:16–17), and the seventh seal provides a literary transition (8:1).

The intensity increases with the trumpets and then even more with the bowl judgments (e.g., no fractions and no interlude between numbers six and seven). Of particular significance is that both series of judgments are patterned after the plagues

21. Bauckham, "Judgment in the Book of Revelation," 63. John uses transition units to connect these two contrasting stories: 8:1–6; 11:15–19; 15:1–8; 19:6–10; 21:1–8; 22:6–9 (see 9.3.5).

22. Bauckham, "Judgment in the Book of Revelation," 63.

23. Stevenson, *Slaughtered Lamb*, 143.

in the exodus event.[24] In that Old Testament context, the immediate purpose of these judgments was to liberate God's people from slavery (e.g., Exod 3:20; 4:21–23; 6:1), while the ultimate purpose was that people would know that Yahweh is God (e.g., Exod 7:5; 10:1–3; 11:1–3).[25] The phrase "I am the LORD your God, who brought you out of Egypt" (or some variation) is repeated throughout the Old Testament. Revelation uses Exodus imagery to send the clear message that God is God above all gods and that he will save his people through the judgment of his/their enemies.

To read Revelation responsibly means we take seriously the nature of its symbolic language, and this certainly applies to these series of judgments. While some who appreciate Revelation's metaphorical language deny that any referent is ever in view, this probably pushes a good thing too far.[26] Surely Babylon represents the Roman Empire as well as future oppressive centers of power, and the rider on the white horse symbolizes the risen and victorious Christ returning in glory. Claiming that judgments never play out in human history undermines the integrity of God's character and his redemptive story. On the other hand—and this is by far the more common misstep—looking at every detail of this judgment imagery in an attempt to discover what it represents in the real world moves too far in the opposite direction. Will the sea and rivers and springs become literal blood (16:3–4)? Will the great city literally be split into three parts (16:19)? While the "never-a-referent" solution is not the answer, pushing too hard to find the "exact referent in every case" has multiple problems as well. We must take seriously Revelation's metaphorical language, seeing a referent when it is clearly supported from the context and focusing on the rhetorical impact on the hearer otherwise.[27] Metzger's appraisal hits the target: "The descriptions are not descriptions of real occurrences, but symbols of the real occurrences."[28]

The more common misreading is to take a literalistic approach when trying to discern the meaning of these series of judgments. Yet, taking them literally in all cases often results in outright contradiction. Bauckham uses the example of the judgment of Babylon to make the point.[29] Babylon is destroyed by an earthquake in 16:17–21, then Babylon is a harlot who is stripped, eaten, and burned in 17:16, and finally it/

24. Mark Wilson, *Charts on the Book of Revelation*, 80; Beale, *Revelation*, 809–10; Tabb, *All Things New*, 154.

25. Stephen H. Kio, "The Exodus Symbol of Liberation in the Apocalypse and Its Relevance for Some Aspects of Translation," *The Bible Translator* 40.1 (1989): 122.

26. David L. Barr, "Violence in the Apocalypse of John," *OHBR* 302, seems sympathetic to this view: "The actions and images recounted there do not refer to something else; neither future events nor timeless truths are figured."

27. Harris seems to support this both/and approach to metaphorical language. See Dana M. Harris, "John and Punishment: Did He Delight in Violence?" in *Apocalypse of John among Its Critics*, StScrBT, ed. Alexander E. Stewart and Alan S. Bandy (Bellingham, WA: Lexham Academic), 76–78. See also the contribution by Susan E. Hylen, "Metaphor Matters: Violence and Ethics in Revelation," *CBQ* 73.4 (2011): 777–96, who reminds us that we must take into consideration the multiple metaphors that Revelation uses to communicate theological truth (e.g., Lion and Lamb). Rather than dismiss the violent images, we should notice how John limits or modifies the violent images with other non-violent metaphors.

28. Metzger, *Breaking the Code*, 92. See also Stevenson, *Slaughtered Lamb*, 195–98, on "Metaphor and Judgment."

29. Bauckham, *Theology*, 20–21.

she is overtaken with plagues and consumed with fire from the Lord God (18:8). A literal reading of these images results in nonsense. John is using repeated images of destruction and judgment on the city of man, the center of rebellion against God. That is the point. They are "symbols rather than depictions," using Gorman's words.[30] And powerful symbols they are. When reading these series of judgments, we do well to focus on the rhetorical and theological impact of these images on the hearers, including the warnings they pose to churches living in rebellion.

Again, the primary theological point of these judgment series is that God is the one true God above all gods and that he will judge his enemies as part of saving his people (see 12.3; 12.6). Bauckham notes a clue to this overarching purpose in the formula first found in 4:5a: "From the throne came flashes of lightning, rumblings and peals of thunder."[31] The phrase appears again at the opening of the seven seals (8:5), the sounding of the seven trumpets (11:19), and the pouring out of the seven bowls (16:18–21). This formula that stresses God's holiness expands as the book progresses so that, in the end, it signals final judgment.

The outworking of God's perfect justice stems from his character as loving and holy. All in all, it demonstrates God's commitment to judge evil. This purpose of the series of judgments is confirmed by warfare imagery appearing also in the interludes that represent the story of God's people, a story that includes God's judgment of evil (e.g., the 144,000 in 7:1–8, the two witnesses of chapter 11, the heavenly war in 12:7–12, the earthly war in 12:13–13:18, and the two visions of judgment in 14:6–20). Nevertheless, we must remember in all this talk of warfare and judgment that God and God's people win the victory (see 19.8 below). We turn now to look more carefully at the enemies of God and the threat they pose.

19.5 THE ENEMIES OF GOD

God's enemies include diabolical powers and wicked humanity living in rebellion. One such power is the power of sin and death/Hades. Interestingly, this particular foe bookends the entire Apocalypse. Jesus is the "firstborn from the dead" who "loves us and has freed us from our sins by his blood" (1:5). He is "the Living One" who was dead and is now "alive for ever and ever," the one who holds "the keys of death and Hades" (1:17–18). Then, at the conclusion of the book, after death has done its damage throughout, we read that "death and Hades were thrown into the lake of fire" (i.e., the second death; cf. 20:14; 21:8) so that there is no longer any curse of sin (20:13–14; 22:3). In the end God will wipe away every tear, announcing that "there will be no more death or mourning or crying or pain" (21:4). In the central part of this prophetic

30. Gorman, *Reading Revelation Responsibly*, 138.

31. Bauckham, "Judgment in the Book of Revelation," 59.

letter, the last enemy, death, is dealt a fatal blow by Jesus, the slain but resurrected Lamb (5:6, 9, 12; 7:14; cf. 1 Cor 15:26; 2 Tim 1:10). The crucifixion/resurrection of Jesus is God's judgment of sin and death until the time when sin and death/Hades will be permanently destroyed.

Revelation describes wicked humanity extensively and from multiple angles. To begin with, they do bad things. Several vice lists illustrate their acts of rebellion. In contrast to the victorious stands "the cowardly, the unbelieving, the vile, the murderers, the sexually immoral, those who practice magic arts, the idolaters and all liars" (21:8). In contrast to those whose names are written in the Lamb's book of life stands anyone who is "impure" or "does what is shameful or deceitful" (21:27). John is told not to seal up the words of the prophecy because there will continue to be wrongdoers and vile people (22:11). In contrast to those who "wash their robes" and have permission to enter the eternal city and partake of the tree of life are those outside—"the dogs, those who practice magic arts, the sexually immoral, the murderers, the idolaters and everyone who loves and practices falsehood" (22:15; cf. 22:19). One especially diabolical vice in Revelation is that of false and deceptive teaching. Some claim to be apostles but are not (2:2). Some claim to be Jews but are instead a synagogue of Satan (2:9; 3:9). We read of the Nicolaitans, those who hold to the teachings of Balaam, and the false prophetess Jezebel and her followers. These vices are relationally destructive—Jesus's crucifixion (1:7; 5:6, 9, 11), John's exile to Patmos (1:9), the killing of God's people (6:9–11), the persecution and death of the two witnesses (11:5, 12), the beheading of the saints (20:4). The naming of particular sins certifies and verifies the evil actions of those who reject God's rule. They are repeatedly described as falling under the judgment of God (e.g., 2:12, 16, 22–23; 21:8; 22:19).

The wicked are also devoted to ungodly empires and anti-Christian powers rather than God. These rulers and kings and ungodly nations and earth dwellers are mentioned throughout as various groups that pledge allegiance to the beast and seek to harm God's people. They kill the two witnesses and trample the holy city (11:1–14). They follow the beast (e.g., 13:3–4, 7–8, 12; 14:9, 11; 16:2), who amasses an army from among wicked humanity (e.g., 16:12–16; 17:2, 12–14, 18; 18:3, 9–10; 19:19). They receive the beast's mark and worship its image (14:9; 19:20). Revelation depicts the wickedness of humanity at a corporate and not just an individual level. Although it is ultimately unsuccessful, evil temporarily forges partnerships in its assault on God and his people. Part of God's judgment is to allow the selfish agendas and interests of the wicked to run wild and bring self-destruction (e.g., 17:15–18).

In the end, wicked humanity stubbornly refuses to repent. Early in the book, the false prophetess Jezebel is characterized by her unwillingness to repent of her immorality and idolatry (2:20–21).

Following the devastation of the sixth trumpet, "the rest of mankind who were not killed by these plagues still did not repent. . . . Nor did they repent of . . ." (9:20–21). The vice list here illustrates the refusal of the wicked to turn back to God. After the fourth bowl judgment, those seared by the intense heat curse God and refuse to repent and give him glory (16:8–9). Following the fifth bowl judgment of darkness, people again curse God because of their pains and sores but refuse to repent of their actions (16:10–11).

The wicked do not bear the seal of the living God (9:4–6) and do not have their names written in the Lamb's book of life (13:8; 17:8; 20:15; cf. 21:27). Throughout Revelation they are portrayed as the ones who will face God's judgment. Jesus fights against the false teachers with the sword of his mouth (2:12, 16). Jesus gives his people authority over the rebellious nations (2:26–27). The earth destroyers will be destroyed (11:18). God justly judges those who have judged his people (16:5–7). They are judged by the word of Christ (19:15, 21) and their ultimate fate is the lake of burning sulfur or the second death (20:15; 21:8), an image depicting the permanent removal of the wicked from God's life-giving presence. This is what it means to suffer the wrath of God (14:9–11). In fact, Revelation uses three graphic images for the ultimate fate of the wicked: (1) they will be "outside" the new Jerusalem (22:15; 21:27), meaning they will be excluded from experiencing the new creation and all that entails; (2) they will experience the "second death" (2:11; 20:6, 14; 21:8), meaning they will not be raised to eternal life; and (3) their final destination is the "lake of fire" (14:10; 19:20; 20:10, 14, 15; 21:8), referring to their final destruction.[32]

Closely related to wicked humanity are two symbols of collective power set against God: the two beasts and Babylon the Great. The two beasts are described in Rev 13. The beast from the earth represents political, social, military, and economic power used in the service of Satan (13:1–2).[33] Often such power is personified in a single wicked leader (e.g., Nero or Domitian in first-century Rome). Traditionally, the final evil eschatological leader has been identified with this beast and referred to as "the antichrist," although Revelation never uses this term. The beast from the earth or "false prophet" represents ungodly religious power in service of the first beast (13:11–12). This figure promotes the worship of the first beast and can be identified with the priesthood of the imperial cult in the first century, that religious system that promoted the worship of the Roman emperor and other pagan deities.[34] Along with the dragon or Satan, these two evil agents constitute the "unholy trinity." The first beast "slanders"

32. Bauckham, "Judgment in the Book of Revelation," 75–79. For the larger theological debate regarding the nature of hell—e.g., eternal conscious torment or annihilation—see Preston Sprinkle, ed., *Four Views on Hell*, 2nd ed. (Grand Rapids: Zondervan, 2016). As Shogren observes, "the real issue is whether God's punishment is consciously experienced by the wicked for eternity or whether it is everlasting in its permanence but not in its infliction of torment"; see Gary S. Shogren, "Hell, Abyss, Eternal Punishment," *DLNT* 461.

33. Duvall, *Revelation*, 311.

34. Duvall, *Revelation*, 311.

and "conquers" the saints through persecution and martyrdom (13:7–10), while the second uses deception and falsehood in an attempt to lead people into false worship that carries serious economic consequences (13:13–17; 16:13; 19:20).

Both beasts will face God's sure and certain judgment. We are told that the first beast will "go to destruction" (ἀπώλεια; 17:8, 11; cf. Dan 7:11, 26). When the beast and the kings of the earth gather to wage war against Christ, the rider on the white horse and his army (19:19), the battle is certainly anticlimactic: "But the beast was captured, and with it the false prophet who had performed the signs on its behalf. With these signs he had deluded those who had received the mark of the beast and worshiped its image. The two of them were thrown alive into the fiery lake of burning sulfur" (19:20). In the end, the dragon joins them in the fiery lake, where "they will be tormented night and day for ever and ever" (20:10). God allows both beasts to operate for a time to accomplish his sovereign purposes and even "conquer" the saints through persecution and martyrdom (13:7), yet, in the end, the saints conquer the unholy trinity through faithful endurance (12:11; 15:2).

A second corporate power is Babylon the Great, an image symbolizing wicked empires—Rome in the first century and subsequently any great center of pagan power in rebellion against God (chs. 17–18). Perhaps much to the surprise of Rome's citizens who were familiar with images of *Dea Roma* (Goddess Rome) and *Roma Aeterna* (Eternal Rome), Revelation portrays her as a seductively dangerous and self-absorbed whore. This portrait contrasts sharply with the purity of Christ's treasured bride (19:8). As a self-glorifying city, Babylon stands in contrast to the city of God (i.e., the woman of ch. 12 and the bride of Christ in chs. 19–22). *Porn*-words occur multiple times in Rev 17–19, sending the clear message that this prostitute/empire leads the rebellion against God and his people (πόρνη in 17:1, 5, 15, 16; 19:2; πορνεία in 17:2, 4; 18:3; 19:2; πορνεύω in 17:2; 18:3, 9; cf. the false teachers in 2:14, 20). Babylon's sins are many—self-glorification, luxury, pride (18:7, 14), opulent wealth (18:3, 16–17, 19), human slavery (18:13), deceiving and misleading the nations (18:23), corrupting the earth with her adulteries (17:4–5; 18:3; 19:2), forming ungodly partnerships (17:2), and shedding the blood of God's people (17:6; 18:24), to name a few.[35]

God's judgment of Babylon the Great begins with an announcement of her coming judgment: "'Fallen! Fallen is Babylon the Great,' which made all the nations drink the maddening wine of her adulteries" (14:8; 18:2). So certain is her "punishment" or judgment (17:1) that the verdict is announced prior to its fulfillment, and in Rome's

35. Gorman, *Reading Revelation Responsibly*, 145–46, identifies seven features of Empire: (1) a system of domination that seduces the powerful, (2) territorially grand and ideologically expansive with blasphemous self-promotion, (3) masks abominations with pseudo beauty, (4) always opposed to the true God and his people, (5) grows because the conquered comply, (6) eventually dies of self-inflicted wounds as its subjects revolt, and (7) is an incarnation of something more powerful and permanent (i.e., Empire).

case, at the height of her power. Her sins are many. They are "piled up to heaven" (18:5). Her downfall will be sudden and sure: "in one day her plagues will overtake her: death, mourning and famine. She will be consumed by fire, for mighty is the Lord God who judges her" (18:8; cf. 18:10, 17, 19). Like a heavy milestone, she is "thrown down, never to be found again" (18:21). "Never again" (repeated six times in 18:21–23) will Babylon play host to music, trade and business, light, and bridegroom and bride. Using another metaphor of judgment, she is burned to the ground and completely consumed (18:9, 18; 19:3). God's judgment of her is indeed just and true. She is paid back fully for what she has done (18:6), given "as much torment and grief as the glory and luxury she gave herself" (18:7). Recalling the principle of *lex talionis*, we are told that "God has judged her with the judgment she imposed on you" (18:20), for she shed "the blood of the prophets and of God's holy people, of all who have been slaughtered on the earth" (18:24). God's justice is an occasion for praise (19:1–3), for finally the cries of the martyrs have been heard and answered (6:10).

Revelation moves beyond God's judgment of wicked humanity and systems to his judgment of the satanic powers behind them. In the seven messages we see examples of how Satan stands behind the false teaching and persecution threatening God's people. Jesus identifies those in the Smyrnaic and Philadelphian contexts who claim to be Jews but are not as a synagogue of Satan instead (2:9; 3:9). In Smyrna the devil is the source of the imprisonment and persecution of some believers (2:10). Pergamum is identified as the place where "Satan has his throne" (2:13), another indication that Satan ultimately empowers the opposition faced by believers in this city (cf. Eph 6:11–12).[36] In Thyatira the false teachings of Jezebel are labeled "Satan's so-called deep secrets" (Rev 2:24). These instances in the seven messages demonstrate that Satan's activity manifested itself in the immoral and idolatrous activities of evil empires and false teachers.

In Rev 12–13 we see the church in cosmic conflict with God's archenemy, the dragon, and his two chief assistants—the beast from the sea and the beast from the earth. In contrast to the great sign of the pregnant woman, "another sign," an enormous red dragon with seven heads, seven crowns, and ten horns sweeps one-third of the stars in heaven to earth and stands in front of the woman, ready to devour her child (12:1–4). God protects both the woman and her son (12:5–6), while the dragon and his angels finds themselves in a heavenly battle with Michael and his angels, a battle they lose (12:7–8). As a result of this defeat (whether primordial or at the cross/resurrection of Jesus or both), the dragon forfeits his place in heaven and is cast down to earth (12:9, 10, 13): "The great dragon was hurled down—that ancient serpent called the devil, or Satan, who leads the whole world astray. He was hurled to the earth, and his angels with him" (12:9). God's judgment of Satan displays a succession of downfalls (from

36. Weima, *Sermons to the Seven Churches*, 95.

heaven to earth to the fiery lake). The war in heaven becomes a war on earth, but believers are reassured that they can triumph over the evil one by the finished work of Christ and their faithful perseverance (12:11). The wounded devil recognizes his defeat and furiously attempts to inflict any damage he can on God's people (12:12–17). Largely this takes the form of a river of deception and false teaching illustrated in the seven messages, in addition to the diabolical ministries of the two beasts depicted in chapter 13. Having failed to terminate the woman or her son or her other offspring, the dragon calls forth two evil agents to continue his ill-fated mission of blaspheming God, persecuting his people, and deceiving the nations. The dragon gives these beasts his power, throne, and authority (13:1–2, 4, 11). They assemble an army of rebels but are decisively defeated at the last battle (16:13–14).

The final judgment of Satan occurs in Rev 20 (see 11.6.5–11.6.6). His judgment occurs in two stages: the imprisonment of "the dragon, that ancient serpent, who is the devil, or Satan," in the abyss for a limited time (20:1–3), followed by his release to be defeated and destroyed in the final battle (20:7–10) where "the devil, who deceived them, was thrown into the lake of burning sulfur, where the beast and the false prophet had been thrown. They will be tormented day and night for ever and ever" (20:10). The judgment of Satan provides the context of the millennium, emphasizing the contrast between the judgment of the dragon with the vindication of the saints he so relentlessly persecuted.[37] The three and one-half years, forty-two months, 1,260 days of suffering are set against the one-thousand years of the saints' reign.[38]

In God's judgment of his enemies, the martyr's question of 6:10 receives a full and final answer. The final judgment scenes of Rev 19–20 feature a series of removals. Mathewson writes, "Everything that stands in the way of the establishment of God's holy, just, and righteous kingdom and his people's enjoyment of it, is removed in judgment"—including Babylon (ch. 18), the wicked nations (19:11–21), the two beasts (19:20), Satan (20:10), and everything that stands in the way of God's new creation to come (20:11–15).[39]

19.6 JESUS'S RETURN AND THE FINAL JUDGMENT

God's preliminary judgment of evil occurs throughout the book, leading to the climactic judgment at the return of Christ and the great day of God Almighty. We catch reminders of this promised coming along the way. The parousia announcement in 1:7 conflates Dan 7:13 and Zech 12:10 (cf. Matt 24:30) to emphasize the coming judgment of the nations, although some take "mourning" here to refer to the repentance of the

37. Mathewson, *Companion to the Book of Revelation*, 112.
38. Mathewson, *Companion to the Book of Revelation*, 113.
39. Mathewson, *Uncovering the Treasures of the Apocalypse*, 76–77.

nations.[40] It is possible that John is intentionally ambiguous in this case.[41] Jesus tells the churches at Ephesus, Pergamum, and Sardis that unless they repent he will come to them in judgment (Rev 2:5, 16; 3:3; cf. 2:22–23, 25). He sometimes uses the image of a stealthy thief to stress that his coming with be sudden and surprising (3:3; 16:15). The book closes with repeated promises of Christ to return—"I am coming soon" (22:7, 12, 20; cf. 22:17). In addition, God is often described as "the one who is coming" (1:4, 8; 4:8; cf. 11:17; 16:5).

Christ's "coming" results in the final judgment of evil, a theme repeated throughout. At long last the martyrs' plea for justice will be answered (6:10–11). At the opening of the sixth seal, the great day of the wrath of the Lamb and him who sits on the throne has come, and only his people can withstand it (6:16–17). At the seventh trumpet the Lord God Almighty has taken his great power and begun to reign (11:17). His wrath has come as the destroyers of the earth are destroyed and God's people rewarded (11:18). The eternal kingdom has finally arrived in full (11:15). Those who worship the beast "will drink the wine of God's fury, which has been poured full strength into the cup of his wrath," suffering torment that is verified by the Lamb and his holy angels (14:10). The earth is harvested (14:15–16). The grapes are gathered and thrown into the great winepress of God's wrath, where they are trampled (14:19–20). With the seventh bowl judgment, the "battle on the great day of God Almighty" has arrived (16:14). God gives the city of man "the cup filled with the wine of the fury of his wrath" (16:19). The Lamb will triumph over those who wage war against him "because he is Lord of lords and King of kings" (17:14). In this case, the triumph comes about as God causes the beast and the ten horns to turn against the prostitute, leaving her destitute (17:16–17). The schemes and purposes of the evil parties become self-destructive under the sovereign rule of God.

Christ's return leading to final judgment is expressed most clearly in 19:11–21 (see 11.6.3). Christ, the rider on the white horse, is called "Faithful and True," and he judges and wages the war against evil with justice (19:11). He is followed by the "armies of heaven" and strikes down the wicked nations with the sharp sword coming out of his mouth (19:15).[42] As King of kings and Lord of lords, he "treads the winepress of the fury of the wrath of God Almighty" (19:15–16). The beast and the false prophet are captured and "thrown alive into the fiery lake of burning sulfur" (19:20). Their armies are killed. Although battle language is used, the emphasis on waging war with

40. See the summary in Fanning, *Revelation*, 86.

41. Osborne, *Revelation*, 69, who notes that "this ambiguity continues throughout the book, as the conversion of the nations and the judgment of the nations develop side by side."

42. Gorman puts into perspective the power of God's word in judgment (*Reading Revelation Responsibly*, 152): "Revelation should be understood as portraying *symbolically* what God does *actually* with a divine performative utterance, an effective word not unlike the word that spoke creation into existence. It is a word of *new* creation. Revelation's symbolic language uses the only kinds of realities known to humans to approximate the universality and finality of God's eschatological dealing with evil. What, after all, is more comprehensive and permanent in human experience than total destruction?" (emphasis original).

justice (19:11), the rider's penetrating vision and many crowns (19:12), his name "the Word of God" (19:13), his army following rather than fighting (19:14), the sword coming out of his mouth (19:15, 21), and the lack of an actual battle scene (i.e., "the beast was captured" in 19:20) all point to the reality of this being a judgment scene rather than a literal battle. Rev 20:11–15 offers yet another angle on final judgment (cf. 16:12–16; 19:11–21; 20:1–10). This last scene of final judgment focuses on the judgment of unbelievers, whereas 19:11–21 portrays the judgment of the two beasts and 20:1–10 the judgment of Satan. Those condemned here do not have their names written in the Lamb's book of life, and their deeds are not enough to cover their sin and gain them entrance into the new creation. Their destiny is the lake of fire, meaning the "second death" (20:14–15 contrasting with 20:6).[43]

Regrettably, judgment has usually been construed as strictly negative, meaning God's judgment of evil. But judgment may also involve a positive outcome, which it surely does for God's people. As all teachers know, some students will pass the exam and even do extremely well. Some believers persevere in faithful obedience to the Lord. Revelation has much to say about the rewards God has in store for his faithful people.[44] Here we sketch an overview of the rewards awaiting those who receive a favorable judgment from God (see Ch. 20 for more detail). Revelation clearly states that God's people will be rewarded when the kingdom of this world becomes the kingdom of the Lord God Almighty and his Messiah (11:15–17): "The time has come for judging the dead, and for rewarding your servants the prophets and your people who revere your name" (11:18). Jesus says, "Look, I am coming soon! My reward is with me, and I will give to each person according to what they have done" (22:12). These passages echo Isa 40:10 (cf. also Isa 62:11; Jer 17:10; Matt 16:27) and show that God and the Lamb will reward their people with the blessings of eternal life in the presence of the Triune God.[45]

These rewards are described throughout the book, beginning with the promises to the victors. The images, such as eating from the tree of life (2:7), wearing a victor's crown (2:10), receiving hidden manna and a white stone with a new name (2:17), receiving authority over the nations and the morning star (2:26–28), being made a pillar in God's temple and bearing God's name (3:11–12), and sitting with Jesus on his throne (3:21) are colorful ways of expressing the blessings of life in God's presence. More plainly, the victors will not be hurt by the second death (2:11) since they will

43. Throughout Rev 19–20 John draws on Ezek 38–39, which describes Gog's invasion of Israel and God's destruction of these enemies. This suggests that the final battle is described in Revelation from multiple angles: 16:12–16; 19:11–21; 20:7–10, 11–15. See Daniel I. Block, *The Book of Ezekiel, Chapters 25–48*, NICOT (Grand Rapids: Eerdmans, 1998), 424; Tabb, *All Things New*, 132–33.

44. Decock, "Works of God," 45–48.

45. See Smalley, *Revelation*, 572; Osborne, *Revelation*, 787–88. Cf. also Barn. 21.3: "The day is near when everything will perish together with the evil one. 'The Lord, and his reward, is near.'" Holmes, *Apostolic Fathers*, 325.

be resurrected to new life and will walk with Jesus in the full life of the new creation (3:4–5). Likewise, many of the seven beatitudes echo similar eschatological rewards that await God's people—eternal rest (14:13), an invitation to the wedding supper of the Lamb (19:9), a share in the first resurrection and immunity from the second death (20:6), the privilege of serving as kings and priests in the new creation (20:6), and the right to enter the heavenly city and partake of the tree of life (22:14).

Aside from the specific promises to the victors and the beatitudes, rewards are mentioned throughout that include the blessings and responsibilities of life in the new creation. The great multitude that endured the great tribulation is rewarded with life in God's presence: shelter, abundant provision, protection, shepherding by the Lamb, living water, and God's personal comfort (7:14–17). These are reemphasized in the final chapters of the book: God's presence (21:3) and comfort (21:4), the water of life (21:6; 22:1), and "all this" (21:7) are spelled out in the vision of the New Jerusalem (21:9–22:5; see Ch. 20). In addition to God's abundant, eternal blessings we see God's people rewarded with responsibilities and meaningful work. They will "serve" and worship God (7:15; 22:3). They will reign in the new creation as kings and priests (1:6; 5:10; 20:4, 6; 22:5) and carry authority to judge (3:21; 20:6).

The greatest reward of all is resurrection from the dead (11:11–12; 20:4–5) and eternal life in the presence of the Triune God (chs. 21–22). In Rom 8:1 the apostle Paul encourages his readers with the truth-promise that "there is now no condemnation (κατάκριμα) for those who are Christ Jesus." Believers have moved from death to life, from condemnation to the forgiveness and freedom of life in relationship with God through Christ. Revelation spells out especially in chapters 21–22 what this eternal life looks like using the rich, powerful imagery of a new garden city (see Ch. 20).

19.7 THE JUSTICE OF GOD'S JUDGMENTS

God's judgments are not arbitrary, capricious, or vindictive; they are not about getting revenge or demonstrating superior power. God, the universal Judge, delivers perfect justice in his judgments. And as Bauckham says, "Justice is about exposing the truth of things. God's judgments are true in that they correspond to reality. They establish truth, sweeping away the lies and illusions in which evil cloaks itself."[46] As a result, Flemming is correct to note that "God's just judgment represents the flip side of God's missional love" and Revelation "preserves both the perfect justice and the lavish love of a missional God."[47] Truth and love (John 1:14) belong together. Revelation highlights three aspects of the justice of God's judgments.

First, Revelation stresses the larger biblical teaching that judgment will be

46. Bauckham, "Judgment in the Book of Revelation," 55–56.

47. Flemming, *Foretaste of the Future*, 128.

according to a person's actual works or deeds (e.g., Ezek 7:8; 24:14; 36:19; Matt 16:27; 25:31–46; Rom 2:5–16; 1 Cor 3:8; 1 Pet 1:17).[48] We see this pattern throughout the book. Jesus tells the church in Thyatira that he will judge Jezebel and those who commit adultery with her unless they repent and "then all the churches will know that I am he who searches hearts and minds, and I will repay each of you according to your deeds" (Rev 2:23). In the second beatitude, the heavenly voice tells John to write, "Blessed are the dead who die in the Lord from now on. 'Yes,' says the Spirit, 'they will rest from their labor, for their deeds will follow them'" (14:13). Again, judgment according to deeds should not be understood to be necessarily negative. In this case the righteous deeds of those who die "in the Lord" attest to their faithful life, a life blessed by God. In the warning to God's people about the coming judgment of Babylon, we are told that "God has remembered her crimes" (18:5) and his agents of judgment are called upon to "give back to her as she has given" (18:6), suggesting judgment according to her unrighteous works. At the great white throne judgment, a judgment we understand to include only unbelievers (see 11.6.6), those whose names are not found in the book of life are called to account for their unrighteous actions (20:12–13):

> And I saw the dead, great and small, standing before the throne, and books were opened. Another book was opened, which is the book of life. *The dead were judged according to what they had done as recorded in the books.* The sea gave up the dead that were in it, and death and Hades gave up the dead that were in them, *and each person was judged according to what they had done.* [emphasis added]

Jesus once again encourages his people with a reminder that he is coming soon to reward them: "Look, I am coming soon! My reward is with me, and I will give to each person according to what they have done" (22:12; cf. 11:18). Judgment according to works may be either a positive or a negative experience, depending on a person's relationship to God. Revelation captures the tension between faith in Jesus and the outworking of that faith in the course of a person's actions.[49] Judgment according to works discerns a person's true allegiance and demonstrates God's perfect justice.

A second aspect of God's justice is the principle of *lex talionis* or "law of retribution." This suggests that "what you do to others God will do to you" and appears repeatedly in the Old and New Testaments (Pss 28:4; 61:13; 62:12; Prov 24:12; Isa

48. Leon Morris, *The Biblical Doctrine of Judgment* (Eugene, OR: Wipf & Stock, 2006), 66–67; Decock, "Works of God," 37–65.

49. See Duvall, "Synchronic Analysis." More recently, see Matthew W. Bates, *Salvation by Allegiance Alone: Rethinking Faith, Works, and the Gospel of Jesus the King* (Grand Rapids: Baker Academic, 2017); Thomas H. McCall, Caleb T. Friedeman, and Matt T. Friedeman, *The Doctrine of Good Works: Reclaiming a Neglected Protestant Teaching* (Grand Rapids: Baker Academic, 2023).

3:11; Jer 17:10; Lam. 3:64; Obad 15; Matt 16:27; Rom 2:6; 14:12; 1 Cor 3:12–15; 2 Cor 5:10; 1 Pet 1:17).[50] God's justice demands that the punishment fit the crime.[51] There are at least three examples of God's rewards for the righteous matching their deeds (Rev 11:18; 14:13; 22:12), but most instances relate to his judgment of the wicked. The basic principle is that God will give to each according to the life they have given to God displayed by their actions (2:23). Along with rewarding his servants the prophets and those who revere his name, God will destroy "those who destroy the earth" (11:18; cf. 19:2 for similar language explicitly applied to Babylon; Jer 51:25), a sure example of the punishment fitting the crime. Babylon the Great made the nations drink "the maddening wine of her adulteries" (Rev 14:8) and those who participate with her will be forced to drink "the wine of God's fury" (14:10). Judgment entails sinners drinking the wine of God's passion (θυμός) in reward for drinking the wine Babylon's passion (θυμός).[52] Likewise, the angelic beings and the great multitude worship God day and night (4:8; 7:15), while the unholy trinity and their followers will find no rest day or night, only torment (12:10; 14:11; 20:10).[53] Similarly, Babylon is repeatedly condemned using this principle. She should receive in judgment what she has dished out in persecution (18:6).[54] Her torment and grief should match the glory and luxury she gave herself (18:7). God "has judged her with the judgment" she imposed on God's apostles and prophets (18:20; cf. 19:2). The principle is made especially clear in 16:5–6: "You are just in these judgments, O Holy One, you who are and who were; for they have shed the blood of your holy people and your prophets, and you have given them blood to drink as they deserve." The crime of shedding blood is met with the punishment of drinking blood.[55] In the final warning against adding to or subtracting from the book, the principle also appears (22:18–19).

Finally, and closely related to the previous aspect, is the idea that God's justice is demonstrated by allowing evil to consume itself. The first four seal judgments in 6:1–8 focus on human sinfulness, showing that "God simply allows human sin to come full circle, turn in upon itself, and self-destruct."[56] This is akin to what Paul is saying in Rom 1:18–32 when he talks about God handing people over to their sinful, self-destructive behavior. Commenting on the seal, trumpet, and bowl judgments, Bauckham observes, "We should probably not think of the majority of the judgments in Revelation as special divine interventions. They are simply the regular evils of human history, escalated over the course of the three septenaries to exceptional

50. Osborne, *Revelation*, 40.
51. Bauckham, "Judgment in the Book of Revelation," 56.
52. Bauckham, "Judgment in the Book of Revelation," 78.
53. Bauckham, "Judgment in the Book of Revelation," 78.
54. Bauckham, "Judgment in the Book of Revelation," 57, rightly observes that the usual translation of "pay her back double" is probably wrong with the idea being that Babylon will receive exactly what her sin deserves—the "exact equivalent."
55. Tabb, *All Things New*, 156–57.
56. Osborne, *Revelation*, 272.

proportions."[57] Of course, God can and does intervene directly in judgment as he wishes, but Revelation reinforces the truth that often God's judgment consists of allowing evil to run its course. At the sounding of the fifth trumpet (9:1–6), for example, out of the Abyss come scorpion-like locusts told to harm only those people without the seal of the God (i.e., unbelievers). In 17:15–17, God allows the beast to attack and destroy the harlot, fulfilling God's promise to punish the prostitute (17:1). God's judgment of evil is just in allowing evil powers to taste their own medicine, to turn on each other and self-destruct.

19.8 The Role of God's People in Judgment

Does Revelation assign a role to God's people when it comes to divine judgment? Several factors come into play when answering this question. To begin with, Revelation makes it clear that the saints are protected from God's wrath to come. The emphasis in the grounding vision of chapter 5 is that the Lamb was slain to purchase for God people from every nation who will reign on earth as kings and priests (5:6, 9–10, 12). The Lamb's blood has cleansed them and empowered them to endure the great tribulation (7:14). They have been sealed and will be protected spiritually through trials (7:1–8; cf. 9:4). As God's temple they are both unmeasured or vulnerable to persecution (11:2, 7–10), but measured or protected from divine wrath and empowered to persevere in faithful witness (11:1, 11–12).

Nevertheless, God's people are regularly confronted with the need to repent in order to demonstrate their allegiance to God. Although many of the images of judgment pertain to evil empires, the primary audience remains the people of God, who are warned against compromise and called to repentance when necessary (e.g., 2:5, 16, 22–23; 3:3, 16). Readers/hearers are encouraged to see the judgment scenes as warnings to those who are complicit with the evils of Babylon and who worship the beast.[58] As Gorman puts it, the judgment visions "create a literary, rhetorical, and emotional experience of shock and awe. The primary purpose, however, is not to instill fear but to provide a wake-up call for those who are sleeping, not merely through life, but through Empire."[59] As a result, God's people are called to faithful perseverance (14:12), to leave Babylon-like empires so as not to receive their punishment (18:4).

God's people also participate in divine judgment through their prayers.[60] There are

57. Bauckham, "Judgment in the Book of Revelation," 62; Osborne, "Theodicy in the Apocalypse," 71; Gorman, *Reading Revelation Responsibly*, 140; Metzger, *Breaking the Code*, 79; Flemming, *Foretaste of the Future*, 135–36.

58. Bauckham, "Judgment in the Book of Revelation," 79; Dana M. Harris, "John and Punishment," 85–86.

59. Gorman, *Reading Revelation Responsibly*, 141.

60. See Richard Bauckham, "Prayer in the Book of Revelation," in *Into God's Presence: Prayer in the New Testament*, ed. Richard N. Longenecker (Grand Rapids: Eerdmans, 2001), 252–71; Brian J. Tabb, "Prayer in Apocalyptic Perspective," in *For It Stands in Scripture: Essays in Honor of W. Edward Glenny*, ed. Ardel B. Caneday (Saint Paul, MN: University of Northwestern Berntsen Library, 2019), 191–208.

three prayers in the main body of the book (5:8; 6:9–10; 8:3–4), as well as prayers for Christ to return (22:17, 20) and a closing benediction in the epilogue (22:21). In 5:8 the four living creatures and the twenty-four elders fall down before the Lamb and each elder is given a harp and a golden bowl full of incense, which are "the prayers of God's people." The elders are priestly representatives of the saints, suggesting the saints have access to God in his heavenly temple. The depiction of the prayers as incense perhaps also shows a close connection between prayer and sacrifice and offerings (e.g., Ps 141:2).[61] In the earthly temple the golden bowls full of incense were placed on the table of the bread of the Presence (e.g., Exod 25:29; Lev 24:7) and are likely mentioned here to emphasize their role in the coming of God's kingdom (cf. Matt 6:10).[62] Golden bowls are mentioned again only in Rev 15:7, a reference to the bowl judgments where God's wrath is poured out on wicked humanity (cf. 9:13–14; 14:18–20).

The prayers in 5:8 link with 8:3–4 and the opening of the seventh seal, where an angel with a golden censer is given incense along "with the prayers of all God's people" to offer on the golden altar in front of the throne. The result is that "the smoke of the incense, together with the prayers of God's people, went up before God from the angel's hand" (8:4). Verse 5 reveals the answer to the saints' prayers: "Then the angel took the censer, filled it with fire from the altar, and hurled it on the earth; and there came peals of thunder, rumblings, flashes of lightning and an earthquake."

The seven trumpet judgments follow. The thunderstorm theophany also appears in 4:5; 11:19; and 16:18–21 with an emphasis on divine judgment. The prayers of God's people for justice play some role in judgment as God hears and answers the imprecatory prayers of his people, many of whom have been martyred.

In 6:9–11 the martyred saints under the altar have been sacrificed or "slaughtered" (6:9; cf. 18:24 and Jesus being "slain" in 5:6, 9, 12; 13:8). They now plead with God for vindication: "How long, Sovereign Lord, holy and true, until you judge the inhabitants of the earth and avenge our blood?" (6:10). This is a prayer for God's justice to win the day rather than a pursuit of revenge. The answer of justice is delayed, perhaps so that their witness may multiply and the nations may turn to Christ.[63] As every believer knows, sometimes God's answer is "not yet," but there is divine compassion and purpose in the delay.

The final prayers occur in the epilogue. At least twice and perhaps three times John prays for Christ to return (22:17, 20), and we have a closing benediction (22:21) in the epilogue. Likely most of the imperatives in 22:17 are invitations to respond positively to Christ, but the second one probably refers to a prayer for the parousia: "And let the one who hears say, 'Come!'" Jesus has promised his coming seven times in Revelation

---

61. Tabb, "Prayer in Apocalyptic Perspective," 192.
62. Bauckham, "Prayer in the Book of Revelation," 254–55.
63. Bauckham, "Prayer in the Book of Revelation," 265; Flemming, *Foretaste of the Future*, 137.

(2:5, 16; 3:11; 16:15; 22:7, 12, 20), and in response to this climactic seventh promise, John responds in solidarity with all God's people: "Amen. Come, Lord Jesus" (22:21). These prayers reveal an expectation and yearning on the part of the saints for Christ to return and make all things right and new (cf. Matt 6:10; Luke 11:2). As Bauckham reminds us, "It is in the *parousia* of Jesus that God himself is coming to his creation" and "the prayer for the *parousia* in 22:20b, therefore, encompasses and completes all other prayers."[64] The book itself closes with a final benediction of grace for God's people who will continue to persevere in their mission to the nations. Meanwhile, they cry for and wait for divine justice.

One final way in which God's people participate in divine judgment relates to how they fight. At first reading one might think that Revelation encourages the saints to take up arms in the war against evil, as is often depicted in popular eschatological fiction. After all, fire comes from the mouths of the two witnesses and devours their enemies (11:5) and they strike terror into the hearts of their opponents (11:11). Yet a careful reading points to the fire-from-the-mouth image as the power of prophetic witness rather than armed combat, and terror is the result of God's resurrection of the witnesses, an action belonging to God alone. In addition, in the account of the final battle in 19:11–21, we read of "the armies of heaven" following the rider on the white horse (19:14; cf. 17:14; 19:8). The portrayal of God's people (and perhaps also angels) as an "army" leads to the assumption that they will engage in battle with the forces of evil. Yet surprisingly, they never fight; they only follow. Or, perhaps better, they fight *by* following! They wear "fine linen, white and clean," a far cry from combat gear. Koester captures the essence of how God's people participate in this final battle scene:

> Revelation does call Christians to take an uncompromising stand against sin and evil, but this militancy takes the form of faithful resistance against corrupt religious practice and greed. Moreover, in the cataclysmic battle of Revelation 19, what do the heavenly armies do? Nothing, according to John's account. All the action belongs to Christ: "in righteousness *he* judges and makes war" (19:11); "from *his* mouth comes a sharp sword with which to strike down the nations, and *he* will rule them with a rod of iron; *he* will tread the wine press of the fury of the wrath of God the Almighty" (19:15). John's vision of the great battle does not show the Christian community taking up arms against the nations of the world, but it identifies Christ himself as the agent of God's victory. The one weapon that is mentioned is the sword of the word that comes from Christ's mouth.[65]

64. Bauckham, "Prayer in the Book of Revelation," 269–70.

65. Koester, *Revelation and the End of All Things*, 174, emphasis original.

Interestingly, John's vision also shows the army of the 144,000 in 7:1–8 becoming a great worshiping community in 7:9–17.

Again, God's people "fight" by following. Their role in God's ongoing judgment of evil is to "follow the Lamb wherever he goes" (14:4). They are to "come out of Babylon" rather than joining in the wickedness of Empire (18:4). They overcome evil by relying on the finished work of Christ and by the word of their testimony (12:11). They will play some role in eschatological judgment (20:4), but this is most likely an acknowledgment of God's just judgments rather than an initiation or carrying out of the judgments themselves.

19.9 CONCLUSION

God's ultimate purpose is the redemption of his people and his creation, but because of the presence and persistence of evil, his judgments are necessary. The judgment scenes comprise about half of the book and should not be ignored or downplayed. God's judgment of evil stands as an essential part of the grand story of Scripture. Following our overview of the judgment texts in Revelation, we turned our attention to God's character, which forms the basis of judgment. His holy and true and loving character also explains his longsuffering and patience when it comes to judgment. He acts out of his loving, true, and holy character as the book demonstrates through the three prolonged series of judgments.

But God's enemies persist and must be dealt with. In the end, Christ returns and brings final judgment on those who have pledged allegiance to evil. Although unpleasant to read about, God's judgments are just and necessary if the world is to be made right and new. They also serve as a warning to his people, calling them to repentance and obedience. Through their faithful perseverance and their prayers, the saints participate with God in judgment. Although described as an "army," they never fight a physical battle but rather engage in warfare through discipleship to the Lamb. And Revelation will not let us lose sight of the positive side of divine judgment—that God will reward his people with his presence and life in the new creation. The anticipation of hearing "Well done, good and faithful servant!" motivates God's people to overcome (Matt 25:23).

Chapter 20

"I SAW A NEW HEAVEN AND A NEW EARTH": NEW CREATION

BIBLIOGRAPHY

Alexander, T. Desmond. *The City of God and the Goal of Creation.* SSBT. Wheaton, IL: Crossway, 2018. ———. *From Eden to the New Jerusalem: An Introduction to Biblical Theology.* Grand Rapids: Kregel, 2008. **Beale, Gregory K.** *The Temple and the Church's Mission: A Biblical Theology of the Dwelling Place of God.* NSBT 17. Downers Grove, IL: InterVarsity Press, 2004. **Brannon, M. Jeff.** *The Hope of Life After Death: A Biblical Theology of Resurrection.* ESBT. Downers Grove, IL: IVP Academic, 2022. **Den Dulk, Matthijs.** "The Promises to the Conquerors in the Book of Revelation." *Bib* 87 (2006): 516–22. **Deutsch, Celia.** "Transformation of Symbols: The New Jerusalem in Rv 21:1–22:5." *ZNW* 78 (1987): 106–26. **Du Rand, J. A.** "The Imagery of the Heavenly Jerusalem (Revelation 21:9–22:5)." *Neot* 22 (1988): 65–86. ———. "The New Jerusalem as Pinnacle of Salvation: Text (Rev 21:1–22:5) and Intertext." *Neot* 38 (2004): 275–302. **Dumbrell, William J.** *The End of the Beginning: Revelation 21–22 and the Old Testament.* Eugene, OR: Wipf & Stock, 2001. **Duvall, J. Scott, and J. Daniel Hays.** *God's Relational Presence: The Cohesive Center of Biblical Theology.* Grand Rapids: Baker Academic, 2019. **Fekkes, Jan, III.** "'His Bride Has Prepared Herself': Revelation 19–21 and Isaian Nuptial Imagery." *JBL* 109 (1990): 269–87. **Giblin, Charles H.** "The Millennium (Rev 20:4–6) as Heaven." *NTS* 45 (1999): 553–70. **Gundry, Robert H.** *Matthew: A Commentary on His Literary and Theological Art.* Grand Rapids: Eerdmans, 1982. ———. "The New Jerusalem: People as Place, Not Place for People." *NovT* 29 (1987): 254–64. **Heide, Gale Z.** "What Is New about the New Heaven and the New Earth? A Theology of Creation from Revelation 21 and 2 Peter 3." *JETS* 40.1 (1997): 37–56. **Huber, Lynn R.** *Like a Bride Adorned: Reading Metaphor in John's Apocalypse.* New York: T&T Clark, 2007. **Köstenberger, Andreas J.** *A Theology of John's Gospel and Letters: The Word, the Christ, the Son of God.* BTNT. Grand Rapids: Zondervan Academic, 2009. **Lee, Pilchan.** *The New Jerusalem in the Book of Revelation: A Study of Revelation 21–22 in Light of Its Background in Jewish Tradition.* WUNT 129. Tübingen: Mohr Siebeck, 2001. **Malina, Bruce J.** *The New Jerusalem in the Revelation of John: The City as Symbol of Life with God.* Collegeville, MN: Liturgical Press, 2000. **Mathewson, David L.** "The Destiny of the Nations in Revelation 21:1–22:5: A Reconsideration." *TynBul*

53 (2002): 121–42. ———. "New Exodus as a Background for 'The Sea Was No More' in Revelation 21:1c." *TrinJ* 24 (2003): 243–58. ———. *A New Heaven and a New Earth: The Meaning and Function of the Old Testament in Revelation 21.1–22.5*. JSNTSup 238. New York: Sheffield Academic, 2003. **McDonough, Sean M.** "Revelation: The Climax of Cosmology." Pages 178–88 in *Cosmology and New Testament Theology*. Edited by Jonathan T. Pennington and Sean M. McDonough. LNTS 355. London: T&T Clark, 2008. **Middleton, J. Richard.** *A New Heaven and a New Earth: Reclaiming Biblical Eschatology*. Grand Rapids: Baker Academic, 2014. **Miller, Kevin E.** "The Nuptial Eschatology of Revelation 19–22." *CBQ* 60 (1998): 301–18. **Och, Bernard.** "Creation and Redemption: Towards a Theology of Creation." *Judaism* 44 (1995): 226–43. **Robinson, Andrea L.** *Temple of Presence: The Christological Fulfillment of Ezekiel 40–48 in Revelation 21:1–22:5*. Eugene, OR: Wipf & Stock, 2019. **Rossing, Barbara R.** *The Choice between Two Cities: Whore, Bride, and Empire in the Apocalypse*. Harrisburg, PA: Trinity Press International, 1999. **Russell, David M.** *The "New Heavens and New Earth": Hope for the Creation in Jewish Apocalyptic and the New Testament*. SBAL 1. Philadelphia: Visionary, 1996. **Schellenberg, Ryan S.** "Seeing the World Whole: Intertextuality and the New Jerusalem (Revelation 21–22)." *PRSt* 33 (2006): 467–76. **Stephens, Mark B.** "Creation and New Creation in the Book of Revelation." *OHBR* 257–73. **Thomas, John Christopher.** "New Jerusalem and the Conversion of the Nations: An Exercise in Pneumatic Discernment—Revelation 21:1–22:5." Pages 228–45 in *The Spirit and Christ in the New Testament & Christian Theology: Essays in Honour of Max Turner*. Edited by I. Howard Marshall, Volker Rabens, and Cornelis Bennema. Grand Rapids: Eerdmans, 2012. **Tõniste, Külli.** *The Ending of the Canon: A Canonical and Intertextual Reading of Revelation 21–22*. LNTS 526. London: T&T Clark, 2016. **Turner, David L.** "The New Jerusalem in Revelation 21:1–22:5: Consummation of a Biblical Continuum." Pages 264–92 in *Dispensationalism, Israel, and the Church: The Search for Definition*. Edited by Craig Blaising and Darrell Bock. Grand Rapids: Zondervan, 1992. **Villeneuve, André.** *Nuptial Symbolism in Second Temple Writings, the New Testament and Rabbinic Literature: Divine Marriage at Key Moments of Salvation History*. Leiden: Brill, 2016. **Walls, Jerry L.** "Heaven." Pages 399–412 in *The Oxford Handbook of Eschatology*. Edited by Jerry L. Walls. Oxford: Oxford University Press, 2008. **Wright, N. T.** *Surprised by Hope: Rethinking Heaven, the Resurrection, and the Mission of the Church*. New York: HarperOne, 2008. **Zimmermann, Ruben.** "Nuptial Imagery in the Revelation of John." *Bib* 84 (2003): 153–83.

20.1 INTRODUCTION

God's final word is not judgment, but a new creation![1] Here we see the positive side of divine judgment. We behold God's ultimate purpose in creation—the redemption of his

1. See the chapter on creation and new creation in John's Gospel by Andreas J. Köstenberger, *A Theology of John's Gospel and Letters: The Word, the Christ, the Son of God*, BTNT (Grand Rapids: Zondervan Academic, 2009), 336–54, featuring the motifs of word, light, and life.

people and transformation of his world, all to the praise of his glory. In Gorman's words, in this final vision of hope fulfilled we come to the "*climax of the book of Revelation, the New Testament, the entire Bible, the whole story of God, and also the story of humanity.*"[2] Revelation touches on this final outcome throughout, but it comes to center stage in chapters 21–22. As a result, the thread of God's final victory runs through chapters 1–20 (e.g., promises to the victors in chs. 2–3, the throne room vision of chs. 4–5, the seventh trumpet in 11:15–19, the Lamb and the 144,000 in 14:1–5, the vision of final victory in 19:6–20:15). But in chapters 21–22 the portrait of final redemption is put on full display.

Revelation portrays the new creation using multiple interconnected images. First, the new creation is a place—"a new heaven and a new earth." We are looking at the total transformation of the material creation. Revelation does not encourage an escape from materiality or its destruction but a radically transformed, renewed material world. Ultimately, salvation is restoration and that includes the restoration of the place of God's eternal dwelling. Second, the new creation is people, those followers of the Lamb who belong to God and have persevered in faithfulness. They are true citizens of the Holy City and constitute God's holy temple in the new creation. Third, the new creation includes God's rich provision. God is with his people as the One who meets all their needs and desires so that in God they find ultimate satisfaction and fulfillment. Fourth, the new creation is also missing some things, things that have always prevented human beings from flourishing as intended. As a result, Revelation features a series of "no more" declarations to reassure readers that the new creation will be safe and secure, totally without threat from sin and evil. Finally, the new creation is a place where God's people experience their ultimate provision—God's relational presence. Using a variety of powerful images Revelation reassures readers and motivates them to trust in God's sure and certain plan to defeat evil and live forever with his creation in unhindered fellowship.

20.2 OVERVIEW OF NEW CREATION

20.2.1 Revelation 1–20

Jesus's words to the seven churches in Rev 2–3 include promises to the victors that are almost all eschatological in nature. The rewards fall into several categories, but the imagery is relational and, as a result, often extends to more than one category (e.g., the divine names of 3:12 could fall under provision or presence).[3] Nevertheless, the categories remain a helpful way to grasp at least one important aspect of the promise.

2. Gorman, *Reading Revelation Responsibly*, 163, emphasis original.

3. Mark Wilson, *Victory through the Lamb*, 41–46, observes that the promises fall into categories of "provision," "place," and "person." See Weima, *Sermons to the Seven Churches*, for more detail on each image.

First, there are promises of provision. These include the tree of life (2:7), the crown or victor's wreath (2:10), hidden manna and a white stone (2:17), the responsibility of ruling (or judging) the nations (2:26–27), the acknowledgment (rather than blotting out) of one's name before God (3:5), and the three names (3:12). It is common in each case for the reward or blessing to compare to or contrast with the local situation (e.g., those rejected in the seven cities will be accepted and find their eternal citizenship in the heavenly city, or those who have not denied the Lord's name will be blessed with three names).

Second, some rewards relate to the new creation as place. The victors are promised the "paradise of God," a new Eden complete with the tree of life (2:7). They will be made pillars in God's temple and citizens of the New Jerusalem (3:12). They will sit with Christ on his heavenly throne (3:21).

Third, Christ acknowledges the absence of certain realities in the new creation. There will be no second death to harm God's people (2:11), only life. Jesus promises never to blot their names from the book of life but to acknowledge their names before the Father and his angels (3:5). In other words, their citizenship in God's kingdom is assured and there are no non-citizens in the heavenly kingdom. The new creation is also a place void of unrighteousness and wickedness, as the white garments symbolizing ethical purity indicate (3:5).

Fourth, the new creation is where God's people experience his relational presence. They will receive the "morning star," later explicitly identified with Jesus himself (2:28; 22:16). They will bear God's name, conveying the promise that they will belong to and live with God eternally (3:12). They will renew fellowship with Christ, a fellowship that will continue forever (3:20). And Christ's promise that his people will share his throne in 3:21 indicates both presence and some future responsibility in the new creation.

The heavenly throne room vision of Rev 4–5 reflects how God-centered the new creation will be. Heaven is not just about one of God's many blessings. It is first and foremost about the God of the blessings. God and the Lamb on the throne (4:2, 9–10; 5:1, 6, 7), along with the Spirit blazing in front of (4:5) and going out from the throne (5:6), constitute the very center of ultimate reality. These chapters portray the Triune God in all his glory (4:3), receiving a new song of worship from all creation (4:8, 10–11; 5:9–10, 12–13; cf. 14:3). God as Creator (4:11), the Lamb as Redeemer (5:5, 9–10), and the Spirit as Empowering Presence (4:5; 5:6) form the center of the grounding vision of the Apocalypse. The salvific work of Christ has made his people into a kingdom of priests who will serve God and reign on the earth in the new creation (5:9–10; cf. 20:4, 6; 22:5).

The vision of the great multitude in 7:9–17 has much to say about the new creation. This uncountable multitude is drawn from "every nation, tribe, people and language" (7:9). They are before the throne and the Lamb, wearing white robes and holding palm branches, robes made white by the red blood of the Lamb and palm branches indicating victory through the great tribulation (7:9, 14). Along with a great multitude of angels, they cry out in worship (7:10–12) as they live in God's presence, serving and worshiping him continually (7:15). These suffering but now victorious believers will be sheltered by God himself (7:15), who will wipe away every tear from their eyes (7:17). Never again will they experience hunger, thirst, or scorching heat (7:16). In addition to God's comforting presence, the Lamb will shepherd his sheep and lead them to springs of living water, a likely reference to the Spirit's life-giving provision (7:17).

In Rev 11:1–14 we see God's eschatological care for his missional people, symbolized by the temple and the two empowered witnesses who will suffer opposition and even martyrdom in this world (11:2, 7–10). But God will defeat this last enemy, death, and raise his people to life and bring them to heaven (11:11–12). The account of the two witnesses reminds persecuted and pressured readers that bodily resurrection from the dead is God's trump card in the battle against sin and Satan and death. In the sounding of the seventh trumpet that follows (11:15–19), we have a prelude to God's heavenly kingdom. The new creation will be the time when God's kingdom is consummated and the Lord and his Messiah will reign for ever and ever (11:15, 17). There will be no remaining threats to God's sovereign reign over creation. God will receive worship (11:16) and the saints will receive rewards (11:18).

The battle of Rev 13 gives way to the victory recounted in chapter 14 as the Lamb stands victorious on Mount Zion with his faithful followers (14:1–5). The name of the Lamb and the Father written on the foreheads of the 144,000 conveys the reality that God's people belong to him and that he protects them from spiritual harm (14:1). The victorious saints then sing a new song of praise to God (14:2–3). The redeemed are God's pure bride, spiritually faithful to their divine husband (14:4). They are devoted disciples of the Lamb consecrated by God and purchased by the Lamb with his blood (14:3–5). They reject the lies and deceit of this world system and embrace unreserved faithfulness to Jesus their Redeemer (14:5). They are people of wholehearted devotion and ethical integrity (14:5).

The final two episodes of chapters 1–20 that relate to the new creation are the announcement of the wedding of the Lamb in 19:6–10 and the millennial reign described in 20:4–6. Chapter 19 features a string of "Hallelujahs" at Babylon's downfall (19:1, 3, 4, 6). The final "Praise Yahweh!" (translation of "hallelujah") in verse 6 begins the account of the great multitude shouting thunderous praises to our Lord God Almighty who reigns (19:6). God's people rejoice and give him glory for the arrival of the wedding of the Lamb (19:7). The marriage of the Lamb has arrived, and the bride is described as "God's holy people" (19:7–8). She has made herself ready for the marriage (19:7) and is dressed in "fine linen, bright and clean," which "was given to her to wear," with the "fine linen" representing her righteous acts (19:8). God's people are portrayed here as both the bride and those invited to the wedding supper of the Lamb (19:9). Their blessing is an eternal one.

In 20:4–6 we see God's people seated on thrones and given authority to judge (20:4). This most likely represents the martyr church, meaning those who have proven faithful in their testimony about Jesus and their devotion to the word of God in spite of opposition (20:4). God's people participate in the "first resurrection" (20:5–6), that is, they experience resurrection from the dead and assume the privilege of reigning with Christ as priests of God and of Christ (20:4, 6). The second death has no power over them (20:6).

20.2.2 Revelation 21–22

To begin with, the transitional summary vision of 21:1–8 places the emphasis on the new creation as a new place: "a new heaven and a new earth" (21:1), where all things have been made new (21:5). The new heaven or sky and the new earth or land indicate a whole new world. The new creation is portrayed as a city, "the Holy City, the new Jerusalem" (21:2), that comes down from heaven as a gift from God (21:2). The city is also depicted as a bride, the bride of Christ, "beautifully dressed for her husband" (21:2).

As we will see throughout, the place is also people; not only people, but also people.[4] God dwells among his people in the new creation (21:3), fulfilling his age-old promise to one day live among his people (e.g., Lev 26:11–12; Ezek 37:26–28). God will live among them, and they will belong to him, and he will be their God (Rev 21:3). God will live forever among those now affectionately described as "his children" (21:7). And God not only lives among them but provides for and sustains them. Their inheritance is God's presence in a new creation and all that he gives (21:7). To the thirsty God "will give water without cost from the spring of the water of life" (21:6), a likely allusion to God the Spirit.

Certain things will be missing from the new creation. There will no longer be any sea (21:1), often used as a symbol of evil or chaos as well as the origin of the beast and the means by which Babylon led astray the nations. There will also be no more tears of sorrow and no more "death or mourning or crying or pain" (21:4), for the old order of things has passed away. Nor will there be any wicked in the city, since they are not citizens. Instead, their destiny is divine judgment (21:8). God living among his people as Father with his children and as Husband with his wife apart from any trace of sin and evil shows that his divine mission has been accomplished (21:3, 7). God then announces, "It is done. I am the Alpha and the Omega, the Beginning and the End" (21:6).

4. Thomas R. Schreiner, *The Joy of Hearing: A Theology of the Book of Revelation* (Wheaton, IL: Crossway, 2021), 157–58, also opts for a both/and answer to the question about whether the new creation is people or place.

In the rest of chapters 21–22 (excluding the epilogue) we see the new creation described in more detail as a Holy City (21:9–21), a temple city (21:22–27), and a garden city (22:1–5), although the images overlap considerably. In 21:9–21 the focus is on the new creation as place, people, and presence. The place is the "Holy City, Jerusalem, coming down out of heaven from God" (21:10). The great city has high walls with twelve gates and twelve foundations (21:12–15). But the place is also people as the city is also portrayed as "the bride, the wife of the Lamb" (21:9). On the gates are written the names of the twelve tribes of Israel (21:12) and on the foundations are written the names of the twelve apostles of the Lamb (21:14), indicating God's one people consisting of Jewish and gentile followers of Jesus. The emphasis of this section falls on God's presence reflected in the city's architecture. The city "shone with the glory of God" and its brilliance was like a precious jewel (21:11, 18–21). The entire city, laid out as a cube, constitutes not only God's temple but the holy of holies within that temple, the place where God's presence dwelt among his people (21:16).

Revelation 21:22–27 highlights the new creation as God's heavenly temple. As a devout Jew, John would certainly have expected a temple in the heavenly city, but he does not find one because "the Lord God Almighty and the Lamb are its temple" (21:22). God's glorious presence also provides the light needed for the new creation, so the sun and moon are absent (21:23). In this section, the people are identified precisely as the redeemed nations and kings, meaning only those whose names are written in the Lamb's book of life (21:27). These redeemed peoples will walk by the light of God's presence and bring their glory and honor into the city as tribute to the Triune God (21:24, 26). Along with the absence of earthly lights, in the temple city the gates will never shut and there will be no night, pointing to the absence of danger and darkness and implying the presence of safety and light (21:25). In addition, nothing impure will enter the city, including those who practice what is shameful or deceitful (21:27).

John describes the celestial garden city in 22:1–5. By this point, the reader understands that the city implies place, people, and presence. The garden is a city, and the city is a garden, combining the best of human culture and natural creation. The river of the water of life (again, the Spirit) flows from the throne of God and of the Lamb down the middle of the great street of the city which is surrounded and sustained by the tree(s) of life, bearing fruit continually (22:1–2). The garden city flourishes with God's provisions of water, fruit, light, and healing. God's people are described as nations, servants, and those who reign or kings (22:2, 3, 5). Perhaps most importantly, they will be healed by God, serve him, see his face, have his name written on their foreheads, and reign with him as vice-regents (22:2–5). The garden city will know no curse (22:3) and will no longer need created sources of light since there will be no night and God himself will light the new world (22:5).

Surprisingly, the epilogue of 22:6–21 features many of the new creation themes mentioned earlier. With regard to place, the city is a Holy City (22:14, 19). The city includes the "tree of life" (22:14, 19). The people of God are described as "the churches" (22:16), "the bride" (22:17), and "God's people" (22:21). In this section of reassurance and warning, the saints are also depicted as those who do right and continue to live holy lives (22:11) and those who "wash their robes" that they might have the right to the tree of life (22:14). God's provision is reemphasized—the prophetic vision from God (22:6), the free gift of eternal life (22:17), a share in the tree of life and citizenship in the Holy City (22:19), and the sustaining grace of the Lord Jesus until the last day (22:21). What is missing from the new creation is also noted: those who do wrong and are vile (22:11), along with the vice list depicting those excluded from the heavenly city: "Outside are the dogs, those who practice magic arts, the sexually immoral, the murderers, the idolaters and everyone who loves and practices falsehood" (22:15; cf. 9:20–21; 21:8). Finally, there is the warning for those who hear the word of this prophecy and add to it or take away from it (22:18–19). This conclusion emphasizes God's presence throughout. It is the Lord God who inspires the prophets (22:6). Jesus, the One who is coming soon (22:7, 10, 12, 17), is also the Alpha and the Omega, the First and the Last, the Beginning and the End (22:13). He is the Root and Offspring of David, the bright Morning Star (22:16). Meanwhile, the Spirit empowers the church in calling the nations to Christ (22:17). In the rest of this chapter we will explore in more detail the new creation as place, people, provision, absence, and presence. Again, overlap is to be expected in light of the splendor and grandeur of the subject matter.

20.3 NEW CREATION AS PLACE

To begin with, the new creation is a place, and the place is a new creation, "a new heaven and a new earth" (21:1; cf. Isa 65:17; 66:22; 2 Pet 3:13). To say "new creation" raises the question about the relationship between the present creation and the one to come. Although some biblical passages can be read to suggest complete destruction of the present creation and total replacement by the new, John most likely envisions a radical transformation and renewal of the present creation (cf. Rom 8:20–22).[5] Mathewson rightly concludes that "the final destiny of God's people is a thoroughly physical, earthly existence, albeit transformed and renewed (Rev 21:5)."[6] As Gorman puts it, "This eschatological reality is not an *escape* from the materiality of existence, but the

5. Gale Z. Heide rightly compares the new creation to what we can expect from our resurrection bodies to come—"transformation and renewal rather than a re-creation *ex nihilo*." See "What Is New about the New Heaven and the New Earth? A Theology of Creation from Revelation 21 and 2 Peter 3," *JETS* 40.1 (1997): 55. Writing in the early part of seventh century, Andrew of Caesarea cross-references Rom 8:21 and Ps 102:26 in concluding, "This passage does not speak of the obliteration of creation but of its renewal into something better." See Oecumenius and Andrew of Caesarea, *Greek Commentaries*, 195.

6. Mathewson, *Companion to the Book of Revelation*, 118. Similarly, Flemming, *Foretaste of the Future*, 192–95; Middleton, *New Heaven and a New Earth*, 209–37.

very *fulfillment* of material existence."[7] Revelation 21–22 is all about place, a new place, a new world.[8] N. T. Wright has made the case powerfully for a wider audience: "It is not we who go to heaven, it is heaven that comes to earth. . . . This is the ultimate rejection of . . . every worldview that sees the final goal as the separation of the world from God, of the physical from the spiritual, of earth from heaven."[9] The structure of 21:1–5 also points in the direction of radical transformation rather than replacement with the new-creation *inclusio*:[10]

A (v. 1a) coming of the new heaven and new earth
  B (v. 1b) transformation of the first heaven and earth
    C (v. 1c) no more sea; no more curses
    C′ (v. 4a) no more tears, death, mourning, crying, or pain; removal of curses
  B′ (v. 4b) transformation of the first things (the first heaven and earth)
A′ (v. 5) making all things new (new heaven and earth)

What is more, the new creation, and more specifically the Holy City, comes down out of heaven *from God*, as a divine gift (21:1, 10; 3:12; Heb 11:10). This speaks volumes both about the heart of God as loving and about God's sovereignty displayed through the magnitude of his salvation. This is more than saving individual souls; this is about the cosmic scope of God's eschatological salvation.[11]

More specifically with reference to place, the new creation is a Holy City, a temple city, and a garden or paradise city (see 20.2.2). The new creation is described as a city, a Holy City. What stands out from the beginning is the contrast between the New Jerusalem, the city of God, and Babylon, the city of man. Even their introduction in Revelation speaks to the contrast:

- "Then the angel carried me away in the Spirit into a wilderness. There I saw a woman sitting on a scarlet beast that was covered with blasphemous names" (17:3).

7. Gorman, *Reading Revelation Responsibly*, 164, emphasis original.

8. Gundry, who stresses that the New Jerusalem is "people as place, not place as people," admits the importance of the new creation as place: "The New Jerusalem is a dwelling place, to be sure; but it is God's dwelling place in the saints rather than their dwelling place on earth. The new earth—the whole of it so far as we can tell, not just a localized city . . . —is the saints' dwelling *place*." See Gundry, "The New Jerusalem," 256.

9. Wright, *Surprised by Hope*, 104.

10. See Pilchan Lee, *The New Jerusalem in the Book of Revelation*, WUNT 129 (Tübingen: Mohr Siebeck, 2001), 267. Lee (p. 268) notes that the Greek term καινός indicates a "radical change from the old world to the new" but simultaneously indicates "newness in nature or in quality." Therefore, John "does not mean the emergence of a cosmos totally other than the present one in origin or time, but the creation of a universe which, though it has been gloriously and radically renewed in quality or nature, stands in continuity with the present one."

11. Stephens, "Creation and New Creation," 257.

- "And he carried me away in the Spirit to a mountain great and high, and showed me the Holy City, Jerusalem, coming down out of heaven from God" (21:10).

Revelation creates a symbolic world for hearers/readers to enter where they are transformed and their allegiance redirected to God and his kingdom and away from the kingdom of this world. In short, the book helps believers "come out of Babylon" (18:4).[12] Bauckham notes many ways that the New Jerusalem contrasts with Babylon in this symbolic world: bride vs. harlot, honoring God vs. exploiting the earth; nations walk by its light vs. corrupting and deceiving the nations; kings bringing glory into the Holy City vs. Babylon ruling over the kings of the earth; water of life and tree of life for healing vs. Babylon's wine that makes the nations drunk; life and healing vs. slaughter; and God's people entering the Holy City vs. God's people exiting Babylon.[13] In addition, the image of the bride dressed in fine linen (19:7) contrasts with the prostitute adorned with blasphemous names and drunk on the blood of the saints (17:3–6). Babylon is adorned with "gold, precious stones, and pearls" (17:4; 18:6), as is the Holy City: gold (21:18), precious stones (21:19–20), and pearls (21:21a).[14] The Holy City has "no more" of what corrupts the earthly city (see 20.6 below).

The location and construction of the city also announces it as a Holy City. John's vantage point to watch the Holy City descend was "a mountain great and high " (21:10; cf. 14:1), a traditional image of God's holy dwelling place (e.g., Ps 48:1–2; Isa 2:2; 11:9; 24:23; Ezek 40:2; Joel 3:17; Mic 4:1–2; Zech 8:3).[15] The city is constructed of precious stones and metals (Rev 21:18–21), reflecting not only the city's purity and beauty but ultimately God's holiness and glory.[16] While "glory" conveys the reality of God's glorious presence (see 20.7 below), it also connotes holiness, especially when connected to the image of light. The city shines with the glory of God, and its brilliance is like jasper (21:11). Jasper receives special attention perhaps because it has already been connected to God's holy presence in 4:3: "And the one who sat there had the appearance of jasper and ruby" (cf. 21:18–19). The city was pure gold with a great street of gold, as pure as glass (21:18, 21). It does not need the sun or moon for God's glory gives it light and the Lamb is its lamp (21:23).

The city's architecture features walls, gates, foundations, and the great street (21:12–25; 22:2). While walls and gates are usually in place to protect against enemies, there are no more enemies in the new creation and the gates never close (21:25). The walls

12. Bauckham, *Theology*, 129.

13. Bauckham, *Theology*, 131–32. See also Celia Deutsch, "Transformation of Symbols: The New Jerusalem in Rv 21:1–22:5," *ZNW* 78 (1987): 123; Alexander, *From Eden to the New Jerusalem*, 175–87.

14. Mathewson, *New Heaven and a New Earth*, 150.

15. Bauckham, *Theology*, 132–33; Robinson, *Temple of Presence*, 122–28.

16. See Mathewson, *New Heaven and a New Earth*, ch. 5: "Precious Stones and Divine Presence in Revelation 21:18–21."

and gates could represent the safety and security of the city but could also symbolize the boundary between the clean and unclean, particularly in light of John's insistence that nothing unclean will enter the city (21:27; cf. 21:8). Robinson is on target when she concludes, "The walls delimit the holy from that which is unholy."[17] The larger purpose of both the gates and the foundation stones with the names of the twelve tribes and the twelve apostles of the Lamb probably relates more directly to divine presence (see 20.7 below). Yet the mention of the twelve precious stones alludes to the high priest's breastplate (Exod 28:17–20) and provides "a contextual link with the author's portrayal of the entire city-people as a holy of holies and as priests who enjoy continual, uninhibited access to God" (Rev 21:19–20).[18] Perhaps the most significant architectural element is the perfect cubic shape of the city, which recalls the holy of holies in the temple (21:16; cf. 1 Kgs 6:20; Ezek 41:4).

In addition to being a holy city, the new creation is a temple city, an appropriate dwelling place for God's priestly people (Rev 1:6; 5:9–10; 20:6).[19] Mathewson shows how the following three phrases in 22:3–4 highlight the priestly identity and role of God's people living in the new temple city: "his servants will serve him," "they will see his face," and "his name will be on their foreheads" (cf. 3:12).[20] Although Ezekiel had anticipated the building of a new temple (Ezek 40–48), John says that he saw no physical temple in the heavenly city, "because the Lord God Almighty and the Lamb are its temple" (Rev 21:22). He saw an entirely different kind of temple, still a place, but a place where "God with us" is the entire cosmic temple. John presents God and the Lamb as "the true substance of Ezekiel 40–48."[21] As mentioned before, the city is described as a cube (21:16), meaning the entire city is the holy of holies as God's presence fills the eschatological temple that is the new creation.[22] For this reason, the whole city is said to be filled with God's glory (21:11, 23).[23] Just as the Spirit has indwelt God's people while on earth, they now live in the heavenly temple which is the Triune God. This fulfills Christ's promise to make his people "pillars in the temple of my God" (NLT) or pillars in the "temple that is my God" (3:12; cf. 7:15).[24] This fulfills the temple language of 21:3: "Look! God's dwelling place is now among the people, and he will dwell with them. They will be his people, and God himself will be with them and be their God" (Exod 29:45–46; Lev 26:11–12). Beale sums it up well:

17. Robinson, *Temple of Presence*, 138.

18. Mathewson, *New Heaven and a New Earth*, 139.

19. For more on the New Jerusalem as the new temple, see Mathewson, *New Heaven and a New Earth*, ch. 4; Beale, *Temple and the Church's Mission*, chs. 10, 12; Koester, *Dwelling of God*, ch. 6; William J. Dumbrell, *The End of the Beginning: Revelation 21–22 and the Old Testament* (Eugene, OR: Wipf & Stock, 2001), 35–71.

20. Mathewson, *New Heaven and a New Earth*, 205–10. He also notes that 1:6 and 22:3–5 form a kind of priestly *inclusio* to the entire vision (p. 215).

21. Robinson, *Temple of Presence*, 164.

22. Middleton, *New Heaven and New Earth*, 172.

23. Gundry, "New Jerusalem," 261.

24. Gundry, "New Jerusalem," 262, who takes this phrase as a genitive of apposition.

> Consequently, the new creation and Jerusalem are none other than God's tabernacle, the true temple of God's special presence portrayed throughout chapter 21. It was this divine presence that was formerly limited to Israel's temple and has began [sic] to expand through the church, and which will fill the whole earth and heaven, becoming coequal with it. Then the eschatological goal of the temple of the garden of Eden dominating the entire creation will be finally fulfilled (so Rev. 22:1–3). Hence, eschatology not only recapitulates the protology of Eden but escalates it."[25]

And this brings us to the city as a garden or paradise city, complete with the tree of life and water of life (Gen 2:9–10; 3:22, 24; Rev 22:1–2). Alexander notes how two acts of creation frame the entire canon of Scripture: the creation of the heavens and the earth, including the garden of Eden (Gen 1:1; 2:8–17), and the creation of the new heavens and new earth, the garden city (Rev 21:1; 22:1–5)—a garden and a garden city where God and humans relate face to face (Gen 2:8–9; 3:8; Rev 22:4).[26] The end of Revelation portrays paradise once lost but now restored. The fact that the new creation is a garden city also speaks of the full and complete integration of nature, human civilization, and culture:[27]

> The image of a garden combines culture and nature in a way that makes vivid the beauty and bounteous delights of creation and our ability to participate in them. Sometimes these images have been combined, either by depicting the perfect city at the center of a garden, or by describing paradise restored within the walls of the new Jerusalem. However these images are deployed, they capture the human longing for a return to Eden, for an unbroken relationship with God, with other persons, and with the world of nature.[28]

As an ideal garden city, the New Jerusalem features "the water of life" (21:6; 22:1–2, 17) and the "tree of life" (2:7; 22:2, 14, 19). In Ezekiel the water flows from the temple (Ezek 47:1–6), but in the new creation the river originates from the throne of God and the Lamb (Rev 22:1). If, as we conclude, the water of life symbolizes the life provided by the Holy Spirit, then the image conveys the reality that the Triune God infuses the entire garden city with his eternal, life-giving presence (cf. a similar use of light in 21:23; 22:5; see 14.8.3). The garden also features the tree(s) of life that surrounds the water of life (22:2, 14, 19; Ezek 47:12). The tree(s) represents God's life that sustains his people continually rather than just seasonally since the tree bears fruit all year

25. Beale, *Temple and the Church's Mission*, 368.
26. Alexander, *City of God*, 16–17.
27. Bauckham, *Theology*, 135.
28. Jerry L. Walls, "Heaven," in *The Oxford Handbook of Eschatology*, ed. Jerry L. Walls (Oxford: Oxford University Press, 2008), 402. Flemming, *Foretaste of the Future*, 195, concludes that the "New Jerusalem represents not an escape from human history and human community but their *fulfillment*" (emphasis original).

round (Rev 22:2). What the original garden was expected to provide is now surpassed by the perfect provision of God in the eternal garden city. And the tree(s) does not just supply nourishment but also eternal life and healing: "the leaves of the tree are for the healing of the nations" (22:2). The healing in view is most likely physical and spiritual salvation, a permanent liberation from the curse itself (22:3).[29] In the garden city, God's servants will serve him, see his face, and bear his name (22:3–4). Lee points out that this should be seen in terms of the reversal of the curse of the first garden. Seeing God's face reverses the shameful hiding from God's face by Adam and Eve (Gen 3:9–11) and the banishment of Cain from God's presence (Gen 4:10–14), all due to their sin.[30]

20.4 NEW CREATION AS PEOPLE

John uses covenantal language to describe God's relationship to his people. The loud voice from the throne proclaims, "Look! God's dwelling place is now among the people, and he will dwell with them. They will be his people, and God himself will be with them and be their God" (21:3).[31] As we have noted before, this fulfills God's long-standing tripartite covenant promise to dwell among his people (Lev 26:11–12; Ezek 37:26–28; Zech 2:10–11; 8:8; John 1:14; 2 Cor 6:16; Rev 21:22). Goldsworthy comments on the significance of God's keeping his promise:

> This one verse could be said to sum up and to contain the entire message of the Bible. The whole of the history of the covenant and of redemption lies behind this glorious affirmation. Every aspect of the hope of Israel—covenant, redemption, promised land, temple, Zion, Davidic prince, new Eden—is woven into this one simple and yet profound statement.[32]

God's dwelling place, his throne, is now among the people (22:3). Whatever else we might say about the new creation, the central thing is that God's people will now experience his presence. The goal of the entire salvation project is not just God's deliverance of his people from sin and Satan but the deliverance of his people to himself.[33]

Revelation also stresses that God's new covenant people, the church, stand in continuity with God's first covenant people, Israel (see 16.2.4). The gates of the city are inscribed with the names of the twelve tribes of Israel (21:12; Ezek 48:30–34), while

29. Beale, *Revelation*, 1108; Thomas and Macchia, *Revelation*, 388; Robinson, *Temple of Presence*, 175. Again, as Schnabel, "John and the Future of the Nations," 268–71, reminds us, only the redeemed nations are in view here. Otherwise, the book of life as the registry of authentic citizens becomes meaningless.

30. Lee, *New Jerusalem in the Book of Revelation*, 292.

31. Tõniste, *Ending of the Canon*, 149, suggests that this tripartite statement could even be viewed as a wedding vow since it often occurs in the prophetic writings alongside wedding imagery.

32. Graeme Goldsworthy, *The Goldsworthy Trilogy* (Eugene, OR: Wipf & Stock, 2000), 313.

33. Duvall and Hays, *God's Relational Presence*, 318–22, 334–36.

the twelve foundations of the wall feature the names of the twelve apostles of the Lamb (21:14). The people among whom God dwells is one people, not two separate peoples: the New Testament church comprised of redeemed Jews and gentiles (symbolized by the twelve apostles), fulfilling faithful Israel (depicted by the twelve tribes).[34] The now familiar number 144,000 (12 tribes × 12 apostles × 1,000 for completeness) depicts the ultimate fulfillment and unity of God's one people (7:4; 14:1–5).

The people of God are people who belong to God and who are citizens of the New Jerusalem. They are members of God's eternal kingdom. Several promises in the seven messages stress the importance of belonging and membership. Jesus promises the victors the "right to eat from the tree of life, which is in the paradise of God" (2:7), a promise that assumes admittance into the new Jerusalem and the rights and privileges of official citizens. Similarly, in the message to Sardis, Jesus promises to never blot out the name of the victors from the book of life but to acknowledge their names before the Father and his angels (3:5). In the Pergamum letter, Jesus promises "hidden manna and a white stone" to the victors (2:17). While various interpretations of these particular images have been proposed, perhaps the most reasonable is to see them connected to admission to the messianic banquet with all its attendant blessings. The new name inscribed on the stone "personalizes the admission token and ensures that it cannot be used by anyone other than the one bearing that name."[35] In the Philadelphian letter Jesus promises to make the victors "a pillar in the temple of my God" and they will never again leave it (3:12). In addition, as pillars or permanent fixtures in God's presence, they are inscribed with "the name of my God and the name of the city of my God, the new Jerusalem, . . . and I will also write on them my new name" (3:12). These two acts, Weima suggests, "reassure the oppressed believers in Philadelphia that they have both an honored and a guaranteed place in the kingdom of God."[36]

We see this citizenship/membership emphasis continue in chapters 21–22, primarily through a contrast between those included and those excluded. In 21:7 we see that the victors will inherit the new creation described in 21:1–6, but the unfaithful will be excluded and suffer a fate of death rather than life (21:8). In 21:25–27 the faithful (including the redeemed nations—see 16.2.5) are allowed to enter the Holy City, while nothing impure nor anyone who does what is shameful or deceitful is allowed to enter. The citizens all have their names written in the Lamb's book of life. In 22:2–3 the city of pure life with the river of the water of life and the tree of life with its never-ending supply of fruit and healing leaves is said to be curse-free. In 22:14–15 those who wash their robes will have the right to the tree of life and be admitted into the city, while evildoers are kept outside the city. Finally, the warning in 22:18–19 implies a contrast

34. Lee, *New Jerusalem in the Book of Revelation*, 280.

35. Weima, *Sermons to the Seven Churches*, 118. See his discussion of the options on pp. 112–18.

36. Weima, *Sermons to the Seven Churches*, 214.

between those who hear the prophecy and obey it and those who hear the prophecy and add to or take away from it. This second group will forfeit membership in the Holy City. Rossing is on target when she concludes that "access into the New Jerusalem is not unrestricted. . . . The lamb's book of life functions as a register of citizens who may enter. . . . While Revelation 21–22 makes important changes to universalize and open up the vision of Ezekiel 40–48 to all 'nations,' Revelation does not make access universal."[37]

As we have discussed earlier (see 16.2.9 and 20.3), God and the Lamb are the temple in the Holy City (21:22), and God's people live in this holy temple who is the Triune God (cf. 3:12). This is confirmed by the cubic shape of the new Jerusalem (21:16). What Jesus initiated in his incarnation (John 1:14) we now see fully realized in the new creation as God's people become his eternal temple (Rev 11:1–4).[38] In addition, God's people are "a kingdom" and "priests" who will rule on the earth (1:6; 5:10; 20:6; see 16.2.4). They have already begun to reign (1:6; 5:10a), yet they await their eschatological reign to come (5:10b; 20:6; cf. 2:26–27; 3:21; 20:4; 22:5).[39] God's original charge to human beings to rule over God's creation (Gen 1:26) is now fulfilled. They will worship/serve him (Rev 22:3–4) and share in his reign as kings (22:5).[40]

Using the most intimate, personal picture known to human beings, Revelation portrays God's eternal relationship with his people as that of a marriage (see 16.2.8). The image of the saints as the bride or wife of Yahweh in the prophetic tradition (e.g., Isa 49:18; 54:5–8; 61:10–62:5; Jer 2:2; 3:14; 31:32; Ezek 16; Hos 2:14–20) and the depiction of Christ as the bridegroom of the church, his bride, in the New Testament (e.g., Matt 9:14–17; 25:1–13; John 3:22–30; 2 Cor 11:2; Eph 5:25–27, 32) culminates in the marriage of God and his people in Revelation (18:23; 19:6–9; 21:2, 9–10; 22:17). Fekkes observes that in 19:7–9 we have the marriage announcement and the preparation of the bride, in 21:2 we have the grand entry of the bride, and in 21:9–21 we have a full description of the bride.[41]

This eschatological marriage is what Du Rand rightly calls the climax of soteriology in Revelation.[42] Already those who "follow the Lamb wherever he goes" are described as "virgins," raising the expectation that "the goal of their chastity was faithful union with the Lamb."[43] Then, in the end, the "virgins" become the bride as the marriage is consummated in the new creation.

37. Rossing, *Choice between Two Cities*, 154–55.

38. For additional discussion, see Beale, *Temple and the Church's Mission*, chs. 10–11; Robinson, *Temple of Presence*; Lee, *New Jerusalem in the Book of Revelation*, 281–85.

39. Weima, *Sermons to the Seven Churches*, 151–55, makes a good case for understanding "rule" (ποιμαίνω) in 2:27 in the negative sense of "judging" or "destroying" rather than the positive sense of "shepherding."

40. Bauckham, *Theology*, 137–38. Middleton, *New Heaven and New Earth*, 139–54, perceptively observes the crucial connection between resurrection and earthly rule.

41. Fekkes, *Isaiah and Prophetic Traditions*, 232.

42. Du Rand, "Soteriology in the Apocalypse," 476.

43. Pattemore, *People of God in the Apocalypse*, 208.

At the macro level, Revelation stresses the contrast between God's people as bride (chs. 19–22) and the harlot Babylon (chs. 17–18).[44] Huber also demonstrates that the vision of the church's relationship to God and the Lamb as bride to husband stands in contrast to the dominant cultural narrative that portrayed the imperial family as the ideal family.[45] Along with contrasting God's people with those who reject God and the Lamb, the nuptial imagery sends a strong personal message: God loves his people in the most deeply intimate way possible and anticipates spending eternity in fellowship with them. The virgin is now the wife, and she will no longer be tempted to play the unfaithful spouse or to join in Babylon's harlotry.

20.5 New Creation as Provision

There is much overlap between this category and the categories of place, people, and presence. But it deserves its own mention, albeit brief. Much like human children need not only the parents' presence but also their provision, so God's people need God's provision. God is not just with his people; he is with them as the One who meets all their needs and godly desires perfectly. The expression in 21:7 that "those who are victorious will inherit (κληρονομέω) all this" gets at the idea (cf. Matt 24:34; Heb 6:12). Similarly, Paul talks of inheriting the kingdom (1 Cor 6:9–10; 15:50; Gal 5:21; Eph 5:5), while Peter and the writer of Hebrews speak of inheriting salvation (1 Pet 1:3–9; Heb 1:14; 6:12; 9:28). Revelation describes in grand terms our promised inheritance of God's presence in a transformed cosmos.

Our inheritance includes many of the blessings promised to the victors in Rev 2–3 and often repeated or recast in chapters 21–22. These include life-sustaining water (7:17; 21:6; 22:1, 17; cf. John 4:10), access to the tree of life in God's paradise (Rev 2:7; 22:2, 14), exemption from the second death (2:11; 20:6), hidden manna and a white stone with a new name, suggesting a sharing in the messianic banquet (2:17), the morning star and authority over the nations, implying participation in God's justice (2:26–27; 20:4–6; 22:16), white garments and permanent citizenship, pointing toward eschatological acquittal in God's lawcourt and participation in Christ's victory (3:5; 7:15; 19:14; 20:12), an eternal place in God's temple-presence with new names to indicate they truly belong (3:12; 21:9–27; 22:14), and a share in Christ's rule over creation (3:21; 20:4; 22:5). Even when these images symbolize or represent a different reality (e.g., a pillar in God's temple in 3:12), they communicate something significant about how God will provide for his people (e.g., a permanent place in God's eternal presence in 3:12).[46]

44. Ruben Zimmermann, "Nuptial Imagery in the Revelation of John," *Bib* 84 (2003): 178–82; Fekkes, "His Bride Has Prepared Herself," 283–87.

45. Lynn R. Huber, *Like a Bride Adorned: Reading Metaphor in John's Apocalypse* (New York: T&T Clark, 2007), 182.

46. Again, to gain a contextual grasp on the meaning of these images, see the older work by Hemer, *Letters to the Seven Churches*, and the more recent contribution by Weima, *Sermons to the Seven Churches*.

20.6 New Creation as Absence

Revelation makes it clear that certain people and things will not be present in the new creation. Along with the "new" language we find plenty of "no more" references. In this sense, we should note that one dimension of Revelation's new creation theology is a theology of absence.[47] Gorman offers insight:

> The necessary correspondence to the absolute divine presence is the absence of all that is anti-God. The series of negations ("no this, no that") used to describe the eschatological reality in Revelation 21–22 does not imply something essentially negative or unpleasant, much less something incomplete. On the contrary, this series of negations means the *removal of all that prevents human flourishing in community before God* and the *presence of all that permits and promotes that flourishing.* In this reality, people have all that they need, expressed in the concrete realities of light and water.[48]

The "no more" language reassures readers that in the new creation evil of any kind will be completely and totally absent since it has been removed. Anything that hinders the perfect fellowship of the Triune God with his creation and diminishes the life and full flourishing of that creation in God's presence will not be present. As the loud voice from the throne announces, "the old order of things has passed away (τὰ πρῶτα ἀπῆλθαν). . . . I am making everything new!" (21:4–5; cf. Isa 65:16–17). There are at least seven things that will not be allowed into the new creation.

First, there will be "no more sea" (21:1). In Revelation the "sea" is often associated with evil powers such as the dragon standing on the shore of the sea calling forth the beast from the sea (12:18; 13:1) or the prostitute sitting on many waters (17:1) or the (likely wicked) dead arising from the sea (20:13).[49] Rossing also observes that in Revelation the sea is directly related politically and economically to Babylon's maritime trade, another aspect of injustice and evil.[50] This association of the sea with evil and chaos and God's opposition to the hostile sea runs throughout the Old Testament as well (e.g., Job 7:12; 26:12; Pss 18:15; 29:3; 74:13–14; 77:16; 89:9–10; Isa 51:9–10; Jer 5:22; 51:36; Dan 7:2–3; Nah 1:4; Hab 3:8; Zech 10:10–11). In essence, the "sea metaphorically represents the entire scope of trouble and afflictions suffered by the

47. Mathewson, *Companion to the Book of Revelation*, 119–121, is one of few scholars who formally acknowledges this "theology of absence" playing a key role in the new creation. See also David L. Mathewson, "New Exodus as a Background for 'The Sea Was No More' in Revelation 21:1c," *TrinJ* 24 (2003): 243–58.

48. Gorman, *Reading Revelation Responsibly*, 165, emphasis original.

49. Tõniste, *The Ending of the Canon*, 143, views the sea as a synonym for the "abyss" and concludes that "every evil creature in Revelation rises from the sea."

50. Rossing, *Choice between Two Cities*, 146.

people of God" in connection with their being under the "old order of things."[51] The removal of the sea sends the clear message that God will be totally victorious over the forces of evil. He will eliminate evil and chaos and any other threat to his people. Bauckham concludes that God is making creation "eternally secure from any threat of destructive evil."[52] In removing the sea of evil and chaos God prepares the way for a new exodus for his people on their way to the promised land.[53]

Second, death and all the pain it causes (mourning, crying, pain) will be no more (Rev 20:14; 21:4). This fulfills Isa 25:8: "He will swallow up death forever. The Sovereign LORD will wipe away the tears from all faces; he will remove his people's disgrace from all the earth. The LORD has spoken" (cf. Isa 35:10; 51:11). The explanation for the removal of death and its painful consequences is that "the old order of things has passed away" (Rev 21:4; cf. Isa 65:17; 43:18). The old order, including Satan and his demonic forces, along with sin and its consequences, has been removed. Lee sees the eschatological blessings such as comfort and no more death, grieving, and pain as the opposite of the covenantal curses (e.g., Isa 65:20–25).[54] The saints begin to experience these blessings now, but the full experience comes with the new creation. In addition, believers are also promised exemption from the "second death" or eschatological death (Rev 2:11; 20:6, 14; 21:8).

Third, there will be no more wicked humanity (21:8; 22:15, 19).[55] Access into the new creation is not unrestricted but limited to redeemed humanity, including the redeemed nations. Nothing impure nor anyone who does what is shameful or deceitful will enter the new creation (21:27). The white garment attire of the righteous represents ethical and spiritual purity (3:4–5, 18; 6:11; 7:9, 13–14; 19:8, 14; cf. 21:2; 22:14). These blameless citizens of the new creation stand in contrast to those who lie and pledge allegiance to the beast (14:5, 11; 20:4). This particular "no more" means that there will be no room "for anyone or anything that would cause harm, evil, pain, injustice, and destruction of life or bring impurity in God's just and perfect world."[56] Instead of no more death, wicked humanity will experience much more death, the second death, and separation from God's presence.

Fourth, there is no physical temple in the new creation because the Lord God and the Lamb will now live among the people (21:22). The entire creation is holy unto the Lord (indicated by the cube shape of this new holy of holies world in 21:16).[57] This fulfills Ezekiel's vision in an unexpectedly wonderful way: "THE LORD IS THERE"

51. Mathewson, "New Exodus as Background," 246; Robinson, *Temple of Presence*, 168.

52. Bauckham, *Theology*, 53.

53. Mathewson, "New Exodus as Background."

54. Lee, *New Jerusalem in the Book of Revelation*, 273–74. See also, Aune, *Revelation 17–22*, 1125.

55. Keener, *Revelation*, 489–91, identifies the specific list of those excluded from the New Jerusalem: cowardly, unbelieving, vile, murderers, sexually immoral, those who practice magic arts, idolaters, and liars.

56. Mathewson, *Companion to the Book of Revelation*, 119–20.

57. Duvall and Hays, *God's Relational Presence*, 318–22.

(Ezek 48:35). The unmediated, personal presence of the Triune God engulfs the entire creation so there is no need for a particular place like the temple to mediate his presence. As Mathewson puts it, "The symbol has given way to the reality, so a further physical temple would be redundant."[58]

Fifth, there will be no need for the sun or moon or a lamp or any other kind of created or artificial light since the glorious presence of the Lord God and the Lamb will give it light (Rev 21:23; 22:5; cf. Zech 14:7).[59] The light of God's presence will make the natural light sources obsolete (esp. Isa 60:19). Babylon, in contrast, will exist in unending darkness (Rev 18:23; cf. 16:10), a symbol of evil and judgment.[60] All of Rev 21:23–26 draws on Isa 60 where the gates of the city will never shut, the wealth of the nations will be brought into it, and God's glorious presence will replace natural light (Isa 60:3, 5, 11–12, 19–20).

Sixth, and closely related, there will be no night or darkness (Rev 21:25; 22:5). The gates will no longer shut even at night because there will be no darkness, spiritual or physical, and thus no threat of attack or harm.[61] Throughout Revelation darkness is associated with judgment and the kingdom of evil (e.g., 6:12; 8:12; 9:2; 16:10). The open gates and lack of darkness suggests that the Holy City will be perfectly safe and secure.

Seventh, there will no longer be any curse (22:3). The term for "curse" (κατάθεμα) can be understood to mean "that which is devoted to or given over to a deity, i.e. under a curse."[62] This new world will no longer be under a curse or fear of destruction (cf. Gen 3:14–17; Rom 8:18–25). In a broader sense, the restoration of the new creation involves the reversal of the covenantal curses (e.g., Isa 65:20–25).[63] Zechariah's promise that Jerusalem will never again be destroyed but will be secure is fulfilled in the new Jerusalem (14:11). In essence this means the new creation will experience the permanent removal of sin and evil, never fear destruction by enemies, and live in eternal peace and security.[64]

20.7 NEW CREATION AS GOD'S RELATIONAL PRESENCE

Much of what we have discussed under Place, People, Provision, and Absence above touches on God's relational presence. In the end, what makes the new creation new or

58. Mathewson, *Companion to the Book of Revelation*, 120.

59. Aune, *Revelation 17–22*, 1181, observes that 4 Ezra 7:38–42 lists "twenty-seven things that will no longer exist in the day of judgment (*sun, moon, stars*, cloud, thunder, lightning, wind, water, air, darkness, evening, *morning*, summer, spring, heat, winter, frost, cold, hail, rain, dew, *noon*, night, *dawn, shining, brightness*, and *light*), 'but only the splendor of the glory of the Most High, by which all shall see what has been determined for them.'" The italicized elements are original and relate to the theme of light.

60. See "Darkness" in Leland Ryken et al., *DBI* 191–193; Kuykendall, *Lions, Locusts, and the Lamb*, 85–86.

61. On the open gates in the New Jerusalem, see Schnabel, "John and the Future of the Nations," 265–68.

62. "κατάθεμα," BDAG, 517.

63. Lee, *New Jerusalem in the Book of Revelation*, 273. Robinson, *Temple of Presence*, 175, adds that the presence of the tree of life indicates the removal of the curse; the "previous separation and enmity between God and humankind is now completely removed."

64. Kuykendall, *Lions, Locusts, and the Lamb*, 333; Mathewson, *New Heaven and a New Earth*, 201–3.

holy or glorious or anything else good and beautiful and true is that the Triune God dwells there. God lives in and among the people; the people live in God's presence. To get at the profound significance of God's presence, Revelation uses multiple images and metaphors, many of which we have touched upon earlier.[65]

To begin with, the image of a sacred marriage, complete with a wedding feast, portrays God's presence in the new creation.[66] One reason God is to be praised is that "the wedding of the Lamb has come, and his bride has made herself ready" (19:7). The fourth beatitude pronounces a blessing on those "invited to the wedding supper of the Lamb!" (19:9). When the Holy City, the new Jerusalem descends from God, she does so "prepared as a bride beautifully dressed for her husband" (21:2), and subsequently John is invited by one of the seven angels to tour the Holy City: "Come, I will show you the bride, the wife of the Lamb" (21:9). The nuptial imagery conveys God's intimate, perfect love for his people and anticipates their joyous experience of God's personal presence for eternity.[67] As the divine husband, God plans a lavish banquet celebrating his defeat of his enemies and abundant provision for his people, the bride (e.g., Isa 25:6–9).[68] This image conveys God's final union with his people in the new creation, including "the deep relational and emotional significance of life in God's presence."[69]

Using the imagery of the tabernacle/temple, we are assured that "God's dwelling place (σκηνή) is now among the people" (Rev 21:3; cf. 21:16, 22).[70] Mathewson notes that coupling the bride-city with God's dwelling place in 21:2–3 leads the reader to conclude that the bride-city is God's tabernacle.[71] The relational nature of God dwelling among his people is made explicit in 21:22 when John admits, "I did not see a temple in the city, because the Lord God Almighty and the Lamb are its temple." It is difficult to escape Flemming's conclusion that "at its heart, New Jerusalem represents the unfiltered *presence* of the Triune God with his people."[72] What Jesus explicitly began with his incarnation—the Lamb as the new temple (John 1:14; 2:19–21; Mark 14:58)—now comes to fulfillment with God and the Lamb as the new temple. The main feature of the temple's architecture noted in Revelation confirms this conclusion. The cubical

65. What Middleton, *New Heaven and New Earth*, 71–72, says about the role of "heaven" in the biblical plot is spot on: "Heaven was never part of God's purposes for humanity in the beginning of the story and has no intrinsic role as the final destiny of human salvation. Indeed, there is not a single reference in the entire biblical canon (Old and New Testaments) to heaven as the eternal destiny of the believer."

66. Many have written on the nuptial imagery in Revelation. See, e.g., Fekkes, "'His Bride Has Prepared Herself'"; Huber, *Like a Bride Adorned*; Miller, "The Nuptial Eschatology of Revelation 19–22," *CBQ* 60 (1998): 301–18; André Villeneuve, *Nuptial Symbolism in Second Temple Writings, the New Testament and Rabbinic Literature: Divine Marriage at Key Moments of Salvation History* (Leiden: Brill, 2016); Zimmermann, "Nuptial Imagery in the Revelation of John."

67. Duvall and Hays, *God's Relational Presence*, 318–19. The marriage metaphor occurs throughout Scripture to depict God's intimate relationship with his people (e.g., Isa 54:5–7; Jer 2:2; Hos 2:16, 19–20; Matt 25:1–13).

68. Duvall and Hays, *God's Relational Presence*, 319. Jesus also speaks of such a wedding banquet (e.g., Matt 8:11; 22:1–14; 25:1–13; 26:29; Luke 13:29; 14:16–24).

69. Duvall and Hays, *God's Relational Presence*, 335.

70. Mounce, *Revelation*, 383.

71. Mathewson, *New Heaven and a New Earth*, 55.

72. Flemming, *Foretaste of the Future*, 188, emphasis original.

shape (Rev 21:16) indicates that the whole of the New Jerusalem is the holy of holies, filled by the "unrestricted presence of God and the Lamb (21:22)."[73] By implication, God's people are then priests who enjoy "continual, uninhibited access to God."[74]

An underrated image of God's relational presence is that of God as Father and his people as his children. Although the term "Father" is primarily used for God's relationship to Jesus in Revelation (e.g., 1:6; 2:28; 3:5, 21; 14:1), on several occasions we find the reality that God is a Father to his people stated or implied (7:17; 21:4, 7). God is certainly said to be the Father to his people elsewhere in the New Testament (e.g., Matt 6:9; Luke 11:2; John 20:17; Rom 1:7; 8:19; 1 Cor 1:3; 1 Pet 1:17; 1 John 3:2). In Rev 21:7 the victors will "inherit all this, and I will be their God and they will be my children (υἱός)." What is sometimes lost in the translation "children" is the adoption language of sonship and the inheritance rights involved.[75] In 2 Sam 7:14 God says about the heir to David's throne, "I will be his father, and he will be my son," a text used primarily for the Messiah but also extended to Israel and the Christian community (e.g., 2 Cor 6:18).[76] Perhaps the most powerful aspect of this familial image in Revelation occurs in 7:17 and 21:4—that of God as a loving Father. John draws on Isa 25:8 to depict the coming restoration in language every parent or caring adult can relate to—tenderly wiping away tears from the face of a crying child.[77] Duvall and Hays conclude:

> In 21:4 God is portrayed as a tender, compassionate Father who wipes away every tear from the eyes of his children and whose presence means the absence of all that is evil and disruptive to *shalom*: tears, death, mourning, crying, and pain. Finally, in 21:7 the victors are assured that they will inherit the new creation and will live as God's children in his presence forever. Familial imagery stresses God's relational presence in a manner that plumbs the depths of human emotion.[78]

Three garden-city images powerfully convey the reality of God's relational presence in the new creation: the river of the water of life, the throne of God, and the tree of life. We have discussed these images previously (see 20.3), so here we simply stress their specific connection to God's relational presence. The link between the Spirit and water imagery in John's Gospel has been explored (e.g., John 1:32–33; 3:5–6; 4:10–14, 21–24; 7:37–39; cf. Isa 44:3; Ezek 36:25–27; 1 John 5:7–8).[79] In Rev 7:17 the Lamb

73. Bauckham, *Theology*, 140; cf. Duvall and Hays, *God's Relational Presence*, 322; Gundry, "New Jerusalem," 261; Lee, *New Jerusalem in the Book of Revelation*, 281–85; Beale, *Temple and the Church's Mission*, 368–69.

74. Mathewson, *New Heaven and a New Earth*, 139.

75. Paul, *Revelation*, 345, writes, "the more common English translations of 'my children' or 'my sons and daughters' miss the cultural significance by which it is sons who inherit, so believers of either sex are inheriting 'sons' (Rom. 8:17)."

76. Koester, *Revelation*, 800.

77. Beale, *Revelation*, 443.

78. Duvall and Hays, *God's Relational Presence*, 320–21.

79. See 14.8.3 for more detail. See esp. Wilson, "Water of Life."

shepherds his people and guides them to "springs of living water," an allusion to the "eternal presence of God"[80] mediated by the Spirit (cf. Isa 49:10; John 14:15–17; 16:13).[81] Similarly, in Rev 21:6 God provides "water without cost from the spring of the water of life" to the thirsty, water that proceeds from the throne of God and the Lamb (22:1), another indication of God's trinitarian presence in the new creation (cf. John 7:38–39; Ezek 47:1–2). Smalley concludes that the concept of living water denotes "the eternal, spiritual vitality which flows from God in Christ and through the Spirit" and is used in the New Testament solely in John's Gospel and Revelation.[82] The book concludes with an invitation to come experience this "free gift of the water of life" (22:17).

Bauckham notes that the divine throne is "the central symbol of the whole book" (see 12.3.3).[83] The throne image is often connected with God's presence with the sevenfold Spirit before the throne (1:4), the seven lamps representing the sevenfold Spirit blazing in front of the throne (4:5), the Lamb standing at the center of the throne with seven eyes that are "the seven spirits of God" or the Holy Spirit (5:6), and the river of the water of life flowing from the throne (22:1). In addition, in the new creation the great multitude stands before the throne and before the Lamb (7:9) where they serve God, reign with Christ (3:21), and are sheltered by (7:15; cf. 22:3) and nourished in (7:17) God's presence. Likewise, the 144,000 sing a new song before the throne (14:3). It is God's voice from the throne that announces the accomplishment of salvation (16:17) and the arrival of his eternal, immediate presence among his people (21:3). Bauckham perceptively observes that "Revelation's final use of its central image of God's throne (22:3b–5) frees it of all the associations of human rule, which must always have subjects, and makes it a pure symbol of the theocentricity of its vision of human fulfilment."[84]

The final of the garden-city images is that of the tree of life (see 11.7.3.3), a symbol of "immortal life in the full presence and intimate fellowship of God" (see 2:7; 22:2, 14, 19).[85] As the ultimate fulfillment of the original garden tree(s) in Eden (Gen 2:9) and the prophetic trees of life in Ezek 47:12, this tree(s) of life depicts the never-ending provision of God's eternal presence. The victors are promised the right to eat from the tree of life (Rev 2:7; 22:14), a tree that brings nourishment and healing (22:1–2). In contrast, the wicked will be denied access to the tree (22:19). In essence, the tree of life represents "participation forever in the blessedness of the end time when God and humankind and the whole creation again experience the perfect fellowship and peace that existed before the fall."[86]

God's presence is also portrayed through the closely related images of glory and light

80. Mounce, *Revelation*, 167.

81. Thomas and Macchia, *Revelation*, 174.

82. Smalley, *Revelation*, 562.

83. Bauckham, *Theology*, 141–42; cf. Middleton, *New Heaven and New Earth*, 170, who notes that "the center of God's governance of the cosmos from now on will be permanently established on a renewed earth."

84. Bauckham, *Theology*, 143.

85. Kuykendall, *Lions, Locusts, and the Lamb*, 77.

86. Weima, *Sermons to the Seven Churches*, 49.

(see 14.8.2).[87] The call goes out to rejoice and be glad and glorify God, for the eschatological wedding of the Lamb has finally arrived and the bride has prepared herself (19:7). The new Jerusalem is said to shine "with the glory of God," and its brilliance is like the precious jewel jasper and like gold as pure as glass (21:11, 18–19, 21). The city is adorned with precious stones throughout as an additional reflection of God's glorious presence.[88] The theme of light serves as a complementary theme: the glory of God and the Lamb provides the light and, as a result, there is no night (21:23–25; 22:5). The incarnate Son displayed God's glorious presence (John 1:14) and now eschatological life in the new creation is marked by, in the words of Gorman, "God's *perpetual perceptible presence*—a state of permanent incarnation, so to speak."[89] According to Mathewson, "the presence of light and glory in the final visionary drama of Revelation (21.11, 23) functions as the climax to all previous references, as God's luminous glory now comes down to fill the new creation and new Jerusalem."[90] The entire city is enlightened by the glorious presence of God and the Lamb (21:23–27; 22:5).[91]

While "name" (ὄνομα) in Revelation can refer to people, to a proper name, or to a person's reputation, it can also signify the personal presence of God. In the seven messages, Jesus commends the church at Ephesus for persevering and enduring hardships "for my name," meaning they have stayed loyal to the person of Christ (2:3). Similarly, Pergamum is applauded for staying loyal to Christ's name or person (2:13), as is Philadelphia for not denying his name or person (3:8). God's people may be described as those who revere his name (11:18) and bring glory to his name (15:4), in contrast to those who blaspheme God and slander (13:6) or curse his name (16:9). These are all responses to the personal presence of God and/or Christ.

The victors are promised the reward of a "white stone with a new name" (2:17), likely referring to a permanent place of residence in God's eternal presence. Similarly, Jesus also promises to make the victors a "pillar in the temple of my God," never again to leave it, and to write on them "the name of my God and the name of the city of my God . . . and I will also write on them my new name" (3:12; cf. Isa 56:5; 62:2; 65:15). The threefold inscription emphasizes that believers belong to God and Christ and have permanent citizenship in the heavenly city. They will never leave God's presence and should fear no possible separation by natural disaster or enemies, human or demonic.

We see this promise come to fruition with the portrait of the 144,000 standing

87. Duvall and Hays, *God's Relational Presence*, 321.

88. Mathewson, *New Heaven and a New Earth*, ch. 5, explores the relationship between precious stones and divine presence. Bauckham, *Theology*, 141, is certainly correct to note that the city's adornment with glory and light images suggests that "creation has thus a moral and religious goal—its dedication to God fulfilled in God's holy presence—and also an aesthetic goal—its beauty fulfilled in reflecting the divine glory."

89. Gorman, *Reading Revelation Responsibly*, 165, emphasis original.

90. Mathewson, *New Heaven and a New Earth*, 163.

91. The presence of God the Spirit is more indirect. For example, we notice it is God, the Lamb, and *light* in 21:23; God, the Lamb, and *the water of life* in 22:1; and God, the Lamb, and *his name* in 22:3–4, perhaps images pointing to the Spirit's role in God making his presence known.

on Mount Zion with the Lamb, having his name and his Father's name written on their foreheads (Rev 14:1; cf. 7:2–3; 9:4; 22:4, in contrast to the mark of the beast in 13:16–17; 14:9; 20:4 and the name of Babylon on her forehead in 17:5). Beale concludes that the "OT background suggests that the divine name written on believers is a figurative way of speaking of God's presence with his people, which protects them."[92] In 22:4 we read that God's people "will see his face, and his name will be on their foreheads." Mathewson has detected a connection to the name the high priest wore on his forehead when he served in the temple—"Holy to the LORD" (Exod 28:36)—and sees the emphasis in 22:4 on God's priestly people serving him in the new creation temple where God's presence is completely unrestricted.[93]

The image of "God's face" complements his name in depicting God's relational presence among his people. The face signifies the person, so "to see God's face will be to know who God is in his personal being."[94] Seeing God's face is a firm eschatological hope in both Testaments (e.g., Pss 11:7; 17:15; 24:6; 42:2; Isa 60:1–2; Matt 5:8; 1 Cor 13:12; Heb 12:14; 1 John 3:2–3).[95] There is a clear connection between "face" and God's presence throughout the New Testament (e.g., 2 Cor 4:6; 2 Thess 1:9; Heb 9:24; 1 Pet 3:12).[96] Aune writes, "The phrase 'seeing the face of God' is a metaphor in Judaism and early Christianity for a full awareness of the presence and power of God."[97] In this unparalleled intimacy between God and his people, we find not only the climax to the grand story of Scripture but also the epicenter of the new creation as God's priestly people encounter the living God face to face.

20.8 CONCLUSION

It is fitting that, before the conclusory Chapter 21, the final chapter in this volume on the biblical theology of the final book of the Bible concerns the new creation to come. The end of Revelation spells out the primary goal and theme of the whole of Scripture: God's relational presence among his people in the new creation.

> This final vision represents the fulfillment of the promises to those who overcome (chaps. 2–3), the full realization of the worship in the throne room (chaps. 4–5), the answer to the martyrs' prayer (6:9–11), the goal of the judgments (chaps. 6–16), and the outcome of the final conflict with evil (chaps. 17–19). The final vision is actually a doublet: 21:1–8 summarizes what is later explained in more glorious detail in 21:9–22:5 . . . God's relational presence among his people.[98]

92. Beale, *Revelation*, 733.
93. Mathewson, *New Heaven and a New Earth*, 208–10.
94. Bauckham, *Theology*, 142.
95. Mathewson, *New Heaven and a New Earth*, 206; Duvall and Hays, *God's Relational Presence*, 322.
96. Duvall and Hays, *God's Relational Presence*, 322.
97. Aune, *Revelation 17–22*, 1179.
98. Duvall and Hays, *God's Relational Presence*, 319.

Revelation speaks of this new creation using multiple overlapping and mutually reinforcing images. The new creation is a place where God and his people will spend eternity. But this Holy City, this new Jerusalem, is also a people, in and among whom God will dwell eternally. The chief image of the bridegroom and bride anticipates the personal, intimate, joyous time of fellowship that God plans to enjoy with his people for eternity. He will love, care for, and provide for his people. They will lack nothing. What is more, nothing will exist in all this new creation that will threaten their relationship—no evil, no chaos, no wicked empires, no enemies demonic or human. Only true citizens may enter and inhabit the Holy City, and they will live in absolute safety and security, totally without fear.

The final novel in C. S. Lewis's *The Chronicles of Narnia* series is appropriately titled *The Last Battle*. In the penultimate chapter Lewis depicts the characters' experience of Narnia being transformed into new Narnia. As he says, "It was the Unicorn who summed up what everyone was feeling":

> He stamped his right fore-hoof on the ground and neighed, and then cried: "I have come home at last! This is my real country! I belong here. This is the land I have been looking for all my life, though I never knew it till now. The reason why we loved the old Narnia is that it sometimes looked a little like this. Bree-hee-hee! Come further up, come further in!"[99]

And then Lewis concludes the book and the entire series with a reflection on what the characters were certainly thinking and feeling:

> And for us this is the end of all the stories, and we can most truly say that they all lived happily ever after. But for them it was only the beginning of the real story. All their life in this world and all their adventures in Narnia had only been the cover and the title page: now at last they were beginning Chapter One of the Great Story which no one on earth has read: which goes on forever: in which every chapter is better than the one before.[100]

Further up and further in indeed. The new creation, more than anything, fulfills Ezekiel's prophetic vision: "The Lord is There" (Ezek 48:35). It is the place where God's people will experience the glorious presence and eternal kingdom of the Triune God forever.

---

99. C. S. Lewis, *The Last Battle* in The Chronicles of Narnia series (1956; repr., Harper Collins. Kindle Edition), 114.

100. Lewis, *The Last Battle*, 119.

Part 5

FINAL MATTERS

Chapter 21

CONCLUSION

WE COME TO the end of a long journey through the mysteriously wonderful and captivating world that is the book of Revelation. Wow! What an amazing book! The rich historical, literary, theological, and spiritual layers of John's Apocalypse make me keenly aware of my own inadequacies as an interpreter and writer, like a novice art student staring at a masterpiece and trying to communicate its magnificence. I feel like I should begin all over again. Yet, my hunch is that even after multiple trips through this book, I would probably come to the same conclusion: I have learned so much, but there is still so much left to learn. Nevertheless, I hope and pray that I have allowed the text of Revelation to speak loudly and clearly and that I have provided a faithful reading of Revelation's complex and profound theology.

This is a theology of the book of Revelation, not primarily a Johannine theology or a New Testament theology. The plan has been, after Part 1 introducing the topic, to provide a historical framework for reading Revelation in Part 2 by exploring questions of authorship, date, occasion, and purpose. We built on this by exploring in Part 3 the literary-theological foundations for Revelation's theology. Here we considered the genre, text, canonicity, grammar, symbolic language, use of the Old Testament, literary structure, and interpretive guidelines for grasping the message of Revelation. We completed this section with an extensive literary-theological reading of the entire book. Parts 2 and 3 provide the groundwork for Part 4—a survey of the primary theological themes of Revelation.

We began Part 4 by considering Revelation's theology proper: What does the book tell us about God himself? Quite a lot, as it turns out. God is the central character in the entire narrative. God creates, speaks, rules, receives worship, loves, and judges, among other things. God is on the throne of the universe. Next, we considered Revelation's portrait of Jesus, the Lamb-Lion also seated on the throne, now walking among the churches, and one day to return in glory. We observed that a neglected aspect of Revelation's theology is the person and work of the Holy Spirit, the one who moves out from the throne as God's personal presence to carry out his mission in this world.

The people of God are the primary beneficiaries of this rock-solid theology, sky-high Christology, and empowering pneumatology. They are portrayed as God's pilgrim people faithfully following the Lamb through dangers, toils, and snares. They journey on to vindication and restoration. Next, we embraced Revelation as principally a worship story, recalibrating God's people and anticipating the renewal to come. Little surprise here that the main text on worship in the New Testament features a multitude of hymns. Revelation sings! In the next two chapters we explored what Revelation teaches about discipleship to Jesus and about God's plan to save—to destroy evil, rescue his people, and restore creation. The Apocalypse concludes in dramatic fashion with God's judgment of his persistent and diabolical enemies and his restoration of creation. We are back to the beginning, but this time to a restored garden city that is God's cosmic temple, and this time to paradise without a poisonous snake. Yet, as Boring famously puts it, "God does not make 'all new things,' but 'all things new' (Rev 21:5)."[1] The prophetic visions of Scripture find their ultimate fulfillment in the final vision of Revelation with its depiction of God's triune, relational presence among his people in the transformed creation. That is the kind of theology you would expect from the closing chapter of the Christian canon.

Especially since the publication of the first edition of Robert Mounce's commentary on Revelation in the New International Commentary on the New Testament series in 1977, the secondary literature on Revelation in the modern period from a non-dispensational perspective has expanded rapidly.[2] Today we are spoiled by a wealth of interpretive resources and wisdom to grasp clearly the message of this canonical capstone, a message today's church desperately needs. Tõniste has helped us see that as a canonical ending Revelation builds on the rest of the story and especially mirrors the story's beginning, reveals the full meaning of what went before, resolves the crisis, shows what the characters have learned, provides closure, and sends the reader into action.[3] Amen! What a final chapter to the grand story![4]

To close this volume, I leave you with a few surprises I have found along the way—not an exhaustive list, just the ones that stand out—along with a few accompanying prayers. First, although I know God is God, Revelation makes that one hundred percent explicit, no doubts remaining. I did not fully realize how pervasive theology really is. Revelation's theology truly affects every other aspect of life. I pray that the contemporary church will find all the solutions it is looking for in God himself. Second, I

1. M. Eugene Boring, "Revelation 19–21: End Without Closure," *PSBSup* 3 (1994): 74–75.

2. Evangelical interpreters have been influenced greatly not only by Mounce, but by the many valuable contributions that followed, esp. Bauckham, *Theology* (1993) and *Climax of Prophecy* (1993); Beale, *Revelation* (1999); Osborne, *Revelation* (2002); and Smalley, *Revelation* (2005).

3. Tõniste, *The Ending of the Canon*, 132–38.

4. In *Cradle, Cross, and Crown*, 992, Köstenberger, Kellum, and Quarles anticipate the theological contribution of Revelation to the New Testament (see 1.2), highlighting worship, Christ, discipleship, God's judgment of evil, and Christ's anticipated return and ultimate victory followed by the restoration of all things in the new creation. Although only a summary, this hits the target as far as it goes. See also the insightful conclusions by Gorman, *Reading Revelation Responsibly*, 163–68, 176–86; Flemming, *Foretaste of the Future*, 208–26.

knew the Christology was high but did not expect it to be this high. Revelation offers a "re-presentation" of God that leaves no room for a merely respectful view of Jesus while denying his full divinity. None! I pray today's church will move against the cultural grain of seeing Jesus as one of many paths to God and see him as the incarnate Son of God. Third, enough of ignoring the presence of the Spirit in Revelation. May the Spirit himself open our eyes to see the many ways he plays a crucial role in the book. Revelation is thoroughly trinitarian.

Fourth, God's people are very, very important to him. It is mindboggling the trouble God goes to for this relationship. May Christians who claim no need of church see how valuable the church is to God and respond accordingly. Fifth, may our entire understanding and practice of worship be overhauled and transformed. Something C. S. Lewis once said sums up how far we have to go when it comes to experiencing God-centered worship:

> Our Lord finds our desires not too strong, but too weak. We are half-hearted creatures, fooling about with drink and sex and ambition when infinite joy is offered us, like an ignorant child who wants to go on making mud pies in a slum because he cannot imagine what is meant by the offer of a holiday at the sea. We are far too easily pleased.[5]

Sixth, when our worship gets right, I expect our missional discipleship will follow. This also ties directly into our understanding of salvation. I pray our grasp of God's salvation will grow higher and deeper and longer and wider as we move from placing ourselves in the center to seeing the Triune God as the center of reality. May we come to see salvation as more than a transaction for an individual but as God's plan to destroy evil, rescue his people and restore his creation. May we truly be willing to follow the Lamb wherever he goes. Seventh, may we not lose heart in our struggle against Satan and sin. In Christ, God has landed the death blow to his enemies. But we live between the already and the not fully, where life is often difficult and trying. May the future God has planned come into sharper focus and may this bring great hope. May God give us grace to persevere faithfully. Finally, may our whole understanding of "heaven" be baptized in Scripture so that it moves from the periphery to the center, from a side trip, a mere place, to a primary destination of ultimate personhood in fellowship with God. May the Lord open our eyes to see why he created in the first place, to grasp the depth of his costly, redemptive love, and to anticipate what he has in store for those who love him (1 Cor 2:9; 13:12).

5. C. S. Lewis, *The Weight of Glory* (1980; repr., New York: HarperCollins. Kindle Edition), 27.

While much of Revelation studies is oriented toward the past, some is directed toward the future as the book dictates. It is not often that we get to reflect and write on events still future. I guess one day we will see just how on (or off) target I have been with these reflections. I doubt seriously, however, that we will be sitting around reading theology books. As Paul said, "Now we see only a reflection as in a mirror; then we shall see face to face" (1 Cor 13:12).

For now, there will be times when we cry out as the martyr church, "How long, Sovereign Lord?" (Rev 6:10). But may there also be times when we boldly confess our hope: "Come, Lord Jesus. The grace of the Lord Jesus be with God's people. Amen." (22:20–21). *Soli Deo gloria!*

BIBLIOGRAPHY

Aland, Barbara, and Klaus Wachtel. "The Greek Minuscule Manuscripts of the New Testament." Pages 43–60 in *The Text of the New Testament in Contemporary Research: Essays on the* Status Quaestionis." Edited by Bart Ehrman and Michael W. Holmes, Studies and Documents. Grand Rapids: Eerdmans, 1995.

Alexander, T. Desmond. *The City of God and the Goal of Creation*. SSBT. Wheaton, IL: Crossway, 2018.

———. *From Eden to the New Jerusalem: An Introduction to Biblical Theology*. Grand Rapids: Kregel Academic, 2008.

Alexander, T. Desmond, and Simon Gathercole, eds. *Heaven on Earth: The Temple in Biblical Theology*. Waynesboro, GA: Paternoster, 2004.

Alexander, T. Desmond, and Brian S. Rosner, eds. *NDBT*. Electronic ed. Downers Grove, IL: InterVarsity Press, 2000.

Allen, Garrick V. "The Apocalypse in Codex Alexandrinus: Exegetical Reasonings and Singular Readings in New Testament Greek Manuscripts." *JBL* 135 (2016): 859–80.

———. *The Future of New Testament Textual Scholarship: From H. C. Hoskier to the Editio Critica Maior and Beyond*. WUNT 417. Tübingen: Mohr Siebeck, 2019.

———. "Scriptural Allusions in the Book of Revelation and the Contours of Textual Research 1900–2014: Retrospect and Prospects." *CurBR* 14 (2016): 319–39.

———. "The Son of God in the Book of Revelation and Apocalyptic Literature." Pages 53–71 in *Son of God: Divine Sonship in Jewish and Christian Antiquity*. Edited by Garrick V. Allen et al. University Park, PA: Eisenbrauns; Pennsylvania State University, 2019.

———. "Textual Pluriformity and Allusions in the Book of Revelation: The Text of Zechariah 4 in the Apocalypse." *ZNW* 106.1 (2015): 136–45.

Allen, Garrick V., Ian Paul, and Simon Woodman, eds. *The Book of Revelation*. WUNT 411. Tübingen: Mohr Siebeck, 2015.

Allen, Michael. *Grounded in Heaven: Recentering Christian Hope and Life on God*. Grand Rapids: Eerdmans, 2018.

Allert, Craig D. *A High View of Scripture: The Authority of the Bible and the Formation of the New Testament Canon*. Grand Rapids: Baker Academic, 2007.

Allison, Gregg R., and Andreas J. Köstenberger. *The Holy Spirit*. ThPG. Nashville: B&H Academic, 2020.

Archer, Melissa L. *"I Was in the Spirit on the Lord's Day": A Pentecostal Engagement with Worship in the Apocalypse*. Cleveland, TN: CPT, 2015.

Archer, Melissa, and Robby Waddell. "The Spirit in John's Apocalypse: Vision, Prophecy, Discernment." *Pneuma* 43 (2021): 553–66.

Arnold, Clinton E. "Magic and Astrology." *DLNT* 701–5.

———. "Satan, Devil." *DLNT* 1077–82.

Aune, David E. "The Apocalypse of John and the Problem of Genre." Pages 65–96 in *Early Christian Apocalypticism: Genre and Social Setting*. Edited by Adela Yarbro Collins. Semeia 36. Atlanta: Society of Biblical Literature, 1986.

———. "Apocalypse Renewed: An Intertextual Reading of the Apocalypse of John." Pages 43–70 in *The Reality of the Apocalypse: Rhetoric and Politics in the Book of Revelation*. Edited by David L. Barr. SBLSymS 39. Atlanta: Society of Biblical Literature, 2006.

———. *Apocalypticism, Prophecy, and Magic in Early Christianity*. Grand Rapids: Baker Academic, 2008.

———. "Following the Lamb: Discipleship in the Apocalypse." Pages 66–78 in *Apocalypticism, Prophecy and Magic in Early Christianity*. Grand Rapids: Baker Academic, 2006.

———. "The Form and Function of the Proclamations to the Seven Churches (Revelation 2–3)." *NTS* 36 (1990): 182–204.

———. "The Influence of Roman Imperial Court Ceremonial on the Apocalypse of John." *BR* 28 (1983): 5–26.

———. *Prophecy in Early Christianity and the Ancient Mediterranean World*. Grand Rapids: Eerdmans, 1983.

———. *Revelation 1–5*. WBC 52A. Dallas: Word, 1998.

———. *Revelation 6–16*. WBC 52B. Dallas: Word, 1998.

———. *Revelation 17–22*. WBC 52C. Dallas: Word, 1998.

Aune, David E., T. J. Geddert, and Craig A. Evans. "Apocalypticism." Pages 45–58 in *DNTB*. Downers Grove, IL: InterVarsity Press, 2000.

Averbeck, Richard E. "Spirit, Community, and Mission: A Biblical Theology for Spiritual Formation." *JSFSC* 1 (2008): 27–53.

Bandstra, Andrew J. "'A Kingship and Priests': Inaugurated Eschatology in the Apocalypse." *CTJ* 27 (1992): 10–25.

Bandy, Alan S. "The Hermeneutics of Symbolism: How to Interpret the Symbols of John's Apocalypse." *SBTJ* 14.1 (2010): 46–58.

———. "The Layers of the Apocalypse: An Integrated Approach to Revelation's Macrostructure." *JSNT* 31.4 (2009): 469–99.

———. "Persecution and the Purpose of Revelation with Reference to Roman Jurisprudence." *BBR* 23.3 (2013): 377–98.

———. *The Prophetic Lawsuit in the Book of Revelation*. NTMon 29. Sheffield: Sheffield Phoenix, 2010.

———. "Should John's Apocalypse Be in the Canon?" Pages 9–35 in *The Apocalypse of John Among Its Critics: Questions & Controversies*. Edited by Alexander E. Stewart & Alan S. Bandy. StScrBT. Bellingham, WA: Lexham Academic, 2023.

Bandy, Alan S., and Alexander E. Stewart, eds. *The Apocalypse of John among Its Critics: Questions and Controversies*. StScrBT. Bellingham, WA: Lexham, 2023.

Barclay, John M. G. *Jews in the Mediterranean Diaspora from Alexander to Trajan (323 BCE–117 CE)*. Edinburgh: T&T Clark, 1996.

Barnard, L. W. "Clement of Rome and the Persecution of Domitian." *NTS* 10 (1964): 251–60.

Barnett, Paul W. *Apocalypse Then and Now: Reading Revelation Today*. South Sydney: Aquila, 2004.

Barr, David L. "The Apocalypse of John as Oral Enactment." *Int* 40 (1986): 243–56.

———. "Doing Violence: Moral Issues in Reading John's Apocalypse." Pages 97–108 in *Reading the Book of Revelation: A Resource for Students*. Edited by David L. Barr. RBibSt 44. Atlanta: Society of Biblical Literature, 2003.

———. "The Lamb Who Looks Like a Dragon? Characterizing Jesus in John's Apocalypse." Pages 205–20 in *The Reality of the Apocalypse: Rhetoric and Politics in the Book of Revelation*. Edited by David L. Barr. Symposium Series 39. Atlanta: Society of Biblical Literature, 2006.

———. *Tales of the End: A Narrative Commentary on the Book of Revelation*. 2nd ed. Salem, OR: Polebridge, 2012.

———. "Violence in the Apocalypse of John." *OHBR* 291–305.

Bateman, Herbert W., IV, ed. *Three Central Issues in Contemporary Dispensationalism: A Comparison of Traditional and Progressive Views*. Grand Rapids: Kregel, 1999.

Bates, Matthew W. *Salvation by Allegiance Alone: Rethinking Faith, Works, and the Gospel of Jesus the King*. Grand Rapids: Baker Academic, 2017.

Bauckham, Richard J. *The Climax of Prophecy: Studies in the Book of Revelation*. London: T&T Clark, 1993.

———. *Jesus and the Eyewitnesses: The Gospels as Eyewitness Testimony*. Grand Rapids: Eerdmans, 2006.

———. "Judgment in the Book of Revelation." Pages 55–79 in *The Book of Revelation*. Edited by Garrick V. Allen, Ian Paul, and Simon P. Woodman. WUNT 411. Tübingen: Mohr Siebeck, 2015.

———. "The List of the Tribes in Revelation 7 Again." *JSNT* 42 (1991): 99–115.

———. "Prayer in the Book of Revelation." Pages 252–71 in *Into God's Presence: Prayer in the New Testament*. Edited by Richard N. Longenecker. Grand Rapids: Eerdmans, 2001.

———. "The Role of the Spirit in the Apocalypse." *EvQ* 52.2 (1980): 66–83.

———. *The Theology of the Book of Revelation*. Cambridge: Cambridge University Press, 1993.

———. "The Worship of Jesus in Apocalyptic Christianity." *NTS* 27 (1981): 322–41.

Baynes, Leslie. *The Heavenly Book Motif in Judeo-Christian Apocalypses, 200 B.C.E.–200 C.E. JSJSup* 152. Leiden: Brill, 2012.

Beagley, Alan J. *The "Sitz im Leben" of the Apocalypse with Particular Reference to the Role of the Church's Enemies.* BZNW 50. Berlin: de Gruyter, 1987.

Beale, G. K. "Afterward: Thirty-Five Years of Research on John's Use of the Old Testament in Revelation." Pages 188–246 in *The Apocalypse of John among Its Critics: Questions and Controversies.* Edited by Alan S. Bandy and Alexander E. Stewart. StScrBT. Bellingham, WA: Lexham, 2023.

———. *The Book of Revelation: A Commentary on the Greek Text.* NIGTC. Grand Rapids: Eerdmans, 1999.

———. *Handbook on the New Testament Use of the Old Testament: Exegesis and Interpretation.* Grand Rapids: Baker Academic, 2012.

———. *John's Use of the Old Testament in Revelation.* LNTS 166. London: T&T Clark, 2015.

———. *A New Testament Biblical Theology: The Unfolding of the Old Testament in the New.* Grand Rapids: Baker Academic, 2011.

———. "Revelation." Pages 318–36 in *It is Written: Scripture Citing Scripture.* Edited by D. A. Carson and H. G. M. Williamson. Cambridge: Cambridge University Press, 1988.

———. "Solecisms in the Apocalypse as Signals for the Presence of Old Testament Allusions: A Selective Analysis of Revelation 1–22." Pages 421–46 in *Early Christian Interpretation of the Scriptures of Israel: Investigations and Proposals.* Edited by Craig A. Evans and James A. Sanders. JSNTSup 148. Sheffield: Sheffield Academic, 1997.

———. *The Temple and the Church's Mission: A Biblical Theology of the Dwelling Place of God.* NSBT 17. Downers Grove, IL: InterVarsity Press, 2004.

———. *The Use of Daniel in Jewish Apocalyptic Literature and in the Revelation of St. John.* Eugene, OR: Wipf & Stock, 1984.

———. *We Become What We Worship: A Biblical Theology of Idolatry.* Downers Grove, IL: IVP Academic, 2008.

Beale, G. K., and D. A. Carson, eds. *Commentary on the New Testament Use of the Old Testament.* Grand Rapids: Baker Academic, 2007.

Beale, G. K., and Benjamin L. Gladd. *The Story Retold: A Biblical-Theological Introduction to the New Testament.* Downers Grove, IL: IVP Academic, 2020.

Beale, G. K., and Sean M. McDonough. "Revelation." Pages 1081–1161 in *Commentary on the New Testament Use of the Old Testament.* Edited by G. K. Beale and D. A. Carson. Grand Rapids: Baker Academic, 2007.

Beasley-Murray, G. R. *The Book of Revelation.* NCB. London: Oliphants, 1974.

Beckwith, I. T. *The Apocalypse of St John: Studies in Introduction with a Critical and Exegetical Commentary.* New York: Macmillan, 1919.

Beitzel, Barry, ed. *Lexham Geographic Commentary on Acts through Revelation.* Bellingham, WA: Lexham, 2019.

Belcher, Kimberly Hope. "Early Trinitarian Hymns (East and West)." Pages 95–105 in *An Introduction to the History of Hymns.* Edited by Benjamin K. Forest, Mark A. Lamport, and Vernon M. Whaley. Eugene, OR: Cascade, 2019.

Bell, A. A. "The Date of John's Apocalypse: The Evidence of Some Roman Historians Reconsidered." *NTS* 25 (1979): 93–102.

Blackwell, Ben C., John K. Goodrich, and Jason Maston, eds., *Reading Revelation in Context: John's Apocalypse and Second Temple Judaism.* Grand Rapids: Zondervan, 2019.

Blaising, Craig A. and Darrell L. Bock. *Progressive Dispensationalism.* Grand Rapids: Baker, 1993.

Block, Daniel I. *The Book of Ezekiel, Chapters 25–48.* NICOT. Grand Rapids: Eerdmans, 1998.

———. *For the Glory of God: Recovering a Biblical Theology of Worship.* Grand Rapids: Baker Academic, 2014.

Bloesch, Donald G. *The Holy Spirit: Works and Gifts.* ChrF. Downers Grove, IL: InterVarsity Press, 2000.

Blomberg, Craig L. *A New Testament Theology.* Waco TX: Baylor University Press, 2018.

Blomberg, Craig L., and Sung Wook Chung, eds. *A Case for Historic Premillennialism: An Alternative to "Left Behind" Eschatology.* Grand Rapids: Baker Academic, 2009.

Blomberg, Craig L., and Darlene M. Seal. *From Pentecost to Patmos: An Introduction to Actsthrough Revelation.* 2nd ed. Nashville: B&H Academic, 2021.

Blount, Brian K. *Revelation: A Commentary.* NTL. Louisville: Westminster John Knox, 2009.

Böcher, Otto. "Johanneisches in der Apokalypse des Johannes." *NTS* 27 (1981): 310–21.

Bock, Darrell L. *Three Views on the Millennium and Beyond.* Grand Rapids: Zondervan, 1999.

Boring, M. Eugene. "Narrative Christology in the Apocalypse." *CBQ* 54 (1992): 702–23.

———. *Revelation*. Interpretation. Louisville: Westminster John Knox, 1989.

———. "Revelation 19–21: End Without Closure." *PSBSup* 3 (1994): 57–84.

———. "The Theology of Revelation: 'The Lord Our God the Almighty Reigns.'" *Int* 40.3 (1986): 257–69.

Boxall, Ian. *Patmos in the Reception History of the Apocalypse*. Oxford: Oxford University Press, 2013.

———. "Reading the Apocalypse on the Island of Patmos." *ScrB* 40 (2010): 22–33.

———. "Reception History and the Interpretation of Revelation." *OHBR* 377–93.

———. *The Revelation of Saint John*. BNTC. Peabody, MA: Hendrickson, 2006.

Brannon, M. Jeff. *The Hope of Life After Death: A Biblical Theology of Resurrection*. ESBT. Downers Grove, IL: IVP Academic, 2022.

Briggs, Robert A. *Jewish Temple Imagery in the Book of Revelation*. SBL 10. New York: Peter Lang, 1999.

Brighton, Louis A. "Christological Trinitarian Theology in the Book of Revelation." *ConJ* 34 (2008): 292–97.

Bruce, F. F. "The Spirit in the Apocalypse." Pages 333–44 in *Christ and the Spirit in the New Testament: In Honour of Charles Francis Digby Moule*. Edited by Barnabas Lindars and Stephen S. Smalley. Cambridge: Cambridge University Press, 1973.

Bruner, Frederick Dale, and William Hordern. *The Holy Spirit: Shy Member of the Trinity*. Eugene, OR: Wipf & Stock, 2001.

Burge, Gary M. *The Anointed Community: The Holy Spirit in the Johannine Tradition*. Grand Rapids: Eerdmans, 1987.

Byassee, Jason, and Andria Irwin. *Following: Embodied Discipleship in a Digital Age*. Grand Rapids: Baker Academic, 2021.

Caird, G. B. *The Language and Imagery of the Bible*. Grand Rapids: Eerdmans, 1980, 1997.

———. *The Revelation of St. John the Divine*. Harper's New Testament Commentaries. New York: Harper & Row, 1966.

Callahan, Allen Dwight. "Babylon Boycott: The Book of Revelation." *Int* 63.1 (2009): 48–54.

———. "Language of the Apocalypse." *HTR* 88 (1995): 453–70.

Campbell, Constantine R. *Basics of Verbal Aspect*. Grand Rapids: Zondervan, 2008.

———. *Verbal Aspect and Non-Indicative Verbs: Further Soundings in the Greek of the New Testament*. SBG 15. New York: Peter Lang, 2008.

———. *Verbal Aspect, the Indicative Mood, and Narrative: Soundings in the Greek of the New Testament*. SBG 13. New York: Peter Lang, 2007.

Campbell, W. G. *Reading Revelation: A Thematic Approach*. Cambridge: James Clarke, 2012.

Carey, Greg. "The Book of Revelation as Counter-Imperial Script." Pages 157–76 in *In the Shadow of Empire: Reclaiming the Bible as a History of Faithful Resistance*. Edited by Richard A. Horsley. Louisville: Westminster John Knox, 2008.

Carnegie, David R. "Worthy is the Lamb: The Hymns in Revelation." Pages 243–56 in *Christ the Lord: Studies in Christology Presented to Donald Guthrie*. Edited by Harold H. Rowdon. Downers Grove, IL: InterVarsity Press, 1982.

Carroll, Scott T. "Patmos (Place)." *ABD* 5:178–79.

Carson, D. A., and Douglas J. Moo, *An Introduction to the New Testament*. 2nd ed. Grand Rapids: Zondervan, 2005.

Charles, Elizabeth Rundle. *The Book of Unveiling: Studies in the Revelation of St. John the Divine*. London: SPCK, 1892.

Charles, R. H. *A Critical and Exegetical Commentary on the Revelation of St. John*. 2 vols. ICC. Edinburgh: T&T Clark, 1920.

———. *Studies in the Apocalypse*. Edinburgh: T&T Clark, 1923.

Chennattu, Rekha M. *Johannine Discipleship as a Covenant Relationship*. Peabody, MA: Hendrickson, 2006.

Chesterton, G. K. *Orthodoxy*. New York: John Lane Company, 1909.

Chilton, Bruce. *Visions of the Apocalypse: Receptions of John's Revelation in Western Imagination*. Waco, TX: Baylor University Press, 2013.

Chilton, David. *Days of Vengeance: An Exposition of the Book of Revelation*. Tyler, TX: Dominion, 1987.

Chung, Sung Wook, and David Mathewson. *Models of Premillennialism*. Eugene, OR: Cascade, 2018.

Clouse, Robert G., ed. *The Meaning of the Millennium*. Downers Grove, IL: InterVarsity Press, 1977.

Cole, Graham A. *He Who Gives Life: The Doctrine of the Holy Spirit*. FET. Wheaton, IL: Crossway, 2007.

Collins, John J. "Introduction: Towards the Morphology of a Genre." *Semeia* 14 (1979): 1–20.

Comfort, Philip W. *Encountering the Manuscripts: An Introduction to New Testament Paleography and Textual Criticism*. Nashville: B&H Academic, 2005.

Cook, John Granger. *Roman Attitudes Toward the Christians: From Claudius to Hadrian*. WUNT 261. Tübingen: Mohr Siebeck, 2010.

Culy, Martin M. *The Book of Revelation: The Rest of the Story*. Eugene, OR: Pickwick, 2017.

Daley, Brian E. *The Hope of the Early Church: A Handbook of Patristic Eschatology*. Grand Rapids: Baker Academic, 2002.

Dalrymple, Rob. *Follow the Lamb: A Guide to Reading, Understanding, and Applying the Book of Revelation*. Wooster, OH: Weaver, 2017.

———. *Revelation and the Two Witnesses: The Implications for Understanding John's Depiction of the People of God and His Hortatory Intent*. Eugene, OR: Wipf & Stock, 2011.

Daniels, T. Scott. *Seven Deadly Spirits: The Message of Revelation's Letters for Today's Church*. Grand Rapids: Baker Academic, 2009.

Danker, Frederick W., Walter Bauer, William F. Arndt, and Wilbur Gingrich. *A Greek-English Lexicon of the New Testament and Other Early Christian Literature*. 3rd ed. Chicago: University of Chicago Press, 2000.

Davis, D. Mark. *Left Behind & Loving It: A Cheeky Look at the End Times*. Eugene, OR: Cascade, 2011.

De Jonge, Henk Jan. "The Apocalypse of John and the Imperial Cult." Pages 127–41 in *KYKEON: Studies in Honour of H. S. Versnel*. Edited by H. F. J. Horstmanshoff. Leiden: Brill, 2002.

De Smidt, J. C. "The Holy Spirit in the Book of Revelation—Nomenclature." *Neot* 28 (1994): 229–44.

De Smidt, Kobus. "Hermeneutical Perspectives on the Spirit in the Book of Revelation." *JPT* 14 (1999): 27–47.

De Villiers, Pieter G. R. "Prime Evil and Its Many Faces in the Book of Revelation." *Neot* 34 (2000): 57–85.

———. "The Violence of Nonviolence in the Revelation of John." *OpenTh* 1 (2015): 189–203.

Deans, Graham D. S. "Discipleship in the Book of Revelation." *BCW* 1 (2019): 9–18.

Decker, Rodney. *Temporal Deixis of the Greek Verb in the Gospel of Mark with Reference to Verbal Aspect*. SBG 10. New York: Peter Lang, 2001.

Decock, Paul B. "Scriptures in the Book of Revelation." *Neot* 33 (1999): 373–410.

———. "The Works of God, of Christ, and of the Faithful in the Apocalypse of John." *Neot* 41.1 (2007): 37–65.

Deissmann, Adolf. *Light from the Ancient East: The New Testament Illustrated by Recently Discovered Texts of the Graeco-Roman World*. 2nd ed. Translated by Lionel R. M. Strachan. London: Hodder & Stoughton, 1911.

Den Dulk, Matthijs. "The Promises to the Conquerors in the Book of Revelation." *Bib* 87 (2006): 516–22.

DeSilva, David A. *Discovering Revelation: Content, Interpretation, Reception*. DBT. Grand Rapids: Eerdmans, 2021.

———. "Honor Discourse and the Rhetorical Strategy of the Apocalypse of John." *JSNT* 71 (1998): 79–110.

———. *An Introduction to the New Testament: Contexts, Methods and Ministry Formation*. Downers Grove, IL: IVP Academic, 2004.

———. "Rhetorical Features in the Book of Revelation." *OHBR* 69–83.

———. *Seeing Things John's Way: The Rhetoric of the Book of Revelation*. Louisville: Westminster John Knox, 2009.

———. "The Social Setting of the Revelation to John: Conflicts Within, Fears Without." *WTJ* 54 (1992): 273–302.

———. *Unholy Allegiances: Heeding Revelation's Warning*. Peabody, MA: Hendrickson, 2013.

———. "X Marks the Spot? A Critique of the Use of Chiasmus in Macro-Structural Analyses of Revelation." *JSNT* 30 (2008): 343–71.

Deutsch, Celia. "Transformation of Symbols: The New Jerusalem in Rv 21:1–22:5." *ZNW* 78 (1987): 106–26.

Dixon, Sarah S. U. *The Testimony of the Exalted Jesus in the Book of Revelation*. LNTS 570 London: Bloomsbury T&T Clark, 2017.

Downing, F. Gerald. "Pliny's Prosecutions of Christians: Revelation and 1 Peter." *JSNT* 11 (1988): 105–23.

Du Rand, Jan A. "The Imagery of the Heavenly Jerusalem (Revelation 21:9–22:5)." *Neot* 22 (1988): 65–86.

———. "The New Jerusalem as Pinnacle of Salvation: Text (Rev 21:1–22:5) and Intertext." *Neot* 38 (2004): 275–302.

———. "'Now the Salvation of Our God Has Come . . .': A Narrative Perspective on the Hymns in Revelation 12–15." *Neot* 27.2 (1993): 313–30.

———. "Soteriology in the Apocalypse of John." Pages 492–95 in *Salvation in the New Testament: Perspectives on Soteriology*. Edited by Jan G. van der Watt. Leiden: Brill, 2005.

Duff, Paul B. *Who Rides the Beast? Prophetic Rivalry and the Rhetoric of Crisis in the Churches of the Apocalypse*. Oxford: Oxford University Press, 2001.

Dumbrell, William J. *The End of the Beginning: Revelation 21–22 and the Old Testament*. Eugene, OR: Wipf & Stock, 2001.

Dunn, James D. G., ed. *Jews and Christians: The Parting of the Ways, 70–135 A.D.* Grand Rapids: Eerdmans, 1999.

Duvall, J. Scott. "Following the Lamb: Spiritual Formation in the Book of Revelation." Paper presented at the annual meeting of the ETS. San Francisco, November 2011.

———. *The Heart of Revelation: Understanding the 10 Essential Themes of the Bible's Final Book*. Nashville: B&H Academic, 2019.

———. *Revelation*. TTC. Grand Rapids: Baker Books, 2014.

———. "Revelation: The Transforming Vision." Pages 255–77 in *The Story of Israel: A Biblical Theology*. Edited by C. Marvin Pate et al. Downers Grove, IL: InterVarsity Press, 2004.

———. "A Synchronic Analysis of the Indicative-Imperative Structure of Pauline Exhortation." Ph.D. diss., Southwestern Baptist Theological Seminary, 1991.

Duvall, J. Scott, and J. Daniel Hays. *God's Relational Presence: The Cohesive Center of Biblical Theology*. Grand Rapids: Baker Academic, 2019.

———. *Grasping God's Word: A Hands-On Approach to Reading, Interpreting and Applying the Bible*. 4th ed. Grand Rapids: Zondervan Academic, 2020.

———. *Living God's Word: Discovering Our Place in the Great Story of Scripture*. 2nd ed. Grand Rapids: Zondervan Academic, 2021.

Elgvin, Torleif. "Priests on Earth as in Heaven: Jewish Light on the Book of Revelation." Pages 257–78 in *Echoes from the Caves: Qumran and the New Testament*. Edited by F. García Martínez. Leiden: Brill, 2009.

Elliott, J. K. "Recent Work on the Greek Manuscripts of Revelation and the Consequences for the *Kurzgefasste Liste*." *JTS* 66 (2015): 574–84.

Elwell, Walter A. *Evangelical Dictionary of Biblical Theology*. Baker Reference Library. Grand Rapids: Baker Books, 1996.

Enroth, Anne-Marit. "The Hearing Formula in the Book of Revelation." *NTS* 36 (1990): 598–608.

Eusebius. *Eusebius: Church History, Life of Constantine the Great, and Oration in Praise of Constantine*. In vol. 1 of *NPNF*². Edited by Philip Schaff and Henry Wace. 14 vols. Repr., Peabody, MA: Hendrickson, 1994.

Evans, Craig A., and James A. Sanders, eds. *Early Christian Interpretation of the Scriptures of Israel: Investigations and Proposals*. JSNTSup 148. Sheffield: Sheffield Academic, 1997.

Fanning, Buist M. *Revelation*. ZECNT. Grand Rapids: Zondervan Academic, 2020.

———. *Verbal Aspect in New Testament Greek*. Oxford: Clarendon, 1990.

———. "Witnesses for the Lamb: Discipleship in Revelation." Pages 283–98 in *Following Jesus Christ: The New Testament Message for Discipleship Today*. Edited by John K. Goodrich and Mark L. Strauss. Grand Rapids: Kregel Academic, 2019.

Fee, Gordon D. *Revelation*. NCC. Eugene, OR: Cascade, 2011.

Fee, Gordon D., and Douglas Stuart. *How to Read the Bible for All Its Worth*. 4th ed. Grand Rapids: Zondervan, 2014.

Fekkes, Jan, III. "'His Bride Has Prepared Herself': Revelation 19–21 and Isaian Nuptial Imagery." *JBL* 109 (1990): 269–87.

———. *Isaiah and Prophetic Traditions in the Book of Revelation: Visionary Antecedents and Their Development*. JSNTSup 93. Sheffield: Sheffield Academic, 1994.

Ferguson, Sinclair B. *The Holy Spirit*. CCT. Downers Grove, IL: InterVarsity Press, 1996.

Flemming, Dean. "Following the Lamb Wherever He Goes: Missional Ecclesiology in Revelation 7 and 14:1–5." Pages 260–78 in *Cruciform Scripture: Cross, Participation, and Mission*. Edited by Christopher W. Skinner et al. Grand Rapids: Eerdmans, 2021.

———. *Foretaste of the Future: Reading Revelation in Light of God's Mission*. Downers Grove, IL: IVP Academic, 2022.

———. "'On Earth as It Is in Heaven: Holiness and the People of God in Revelation." Pages 343–62 in *Holiness and Ecclesiology in the New Testament*. Edited by Kent E. Brower and Andy Johnson. Grand Rapids: Eerdmans, 2007.

———. "Revelation and the *Missio Dei*: Toward a Missional Reading of the Apocalypse." *JTI* 6 (2012): 161–78.

Fletcher, Michelle. "Apocalypse Noir: How Revelation Defined and Defied a Genre." Pages 115–34 in *The Book of Revelation*. WUNT 411. Edited by Garrick V. Allen, Ian Paul, and Simon Woodman. Tübingen: Mohr Siebeck, 2015.
Ford, Josephine M. Massyngberde. "The Christological Function of the Hymns in the Apocalypse of John." *AUSS* 36 (1998): 207–29.
———. *Revelation*. AB 38. Garden City, NY: Doubleday, 1975.
Forsyth, P. T. *The Work of Christ*. London: Hodder & Stoughton, 1910.
Franke, John R. *Missional Theology: An Introduction*. Grand Rapids: Baker Academic, 2020.
Frey, Jörg. "Erwägungen zum Verhältnis der Johannesapokalypse zu den übrigen Schriften des Corpus Johanneum." Pages 326–429 in *Die johanneische Frage: Ein Lösungversuch*. Edited by Martin Hengel. Tübingen: Mohr Siebeck, 1993.
Friesen, Steven J. *Imperial Cults and the Apocalypse of John: Reading Revelation in the Ruins*. Oxford: Oxford University Press, 2001.
———. "Satan's Throne, Imperial Cults and the Social Settings of Revelation." *JSNT* 27.3 (2005): 351–73.
———. *Twice Neokoros: Ephesus, Asia and the Cult of the Flavian Imperial Family*. Leiden: Brill, 1993.
Gallagher, Edmon L., and John D. Meade. *The Biblical Canon Lists from Early Christianity: Texts and Analysis*. Oxford: Oxford University Press, 2017.
Gallusz, Laszlo. *The Throne Motif in the Book of Revelation*. LNTS 487. London: Bloomsbury T&T Clark, 2014.
Gentry, K. L. "A Preterist View of Revelation." Pages 37–92 in *Four Views on the Book of Revelation*. Edited by C. Marvin Pate. Grand Rapids: Zondervan, 1998.
Gentry, Peter J. "The Meaning of 'Holy' in the Old Testament." *BSac* 170 (2013): 400–417.
Gentry, Peter J., and Stephen J. Wellum. *God's Kingdom through God's Covenants: A Concise Biblical Theology*. Wheaton, IL: Crossway, 2015.
Giblin, Charles H. *The Book of Revelation: The Open Book of Prophecy*. Collegeville, MN: Liturgical Press, 1991.
———. "The Millennium (Rev 20:4–6) as Heaven." *NTS* 45 (1999): 553–70.
———. "Revelation 11.1–13: Its Form, Function, and Contextual Integration." *NTS* 30 (1984): 433–59.
Gladd, Benjamin L. *From Adam and Israel to the Church: A Biblical Theology of the People of God*. ESBT. Downers Grove, IL: IVP Academic, 2019.
Gladd, Benjamin L., and Matthew S. Harmon. *Making All Things New: Inaugurated Eschatology for the Life of the Church*. Grand Rapids: Baker, 2016.
Glasson, T. Francis. "The Last Judgment—In Revelation 20 and Related Writings." *NTS* 28 (1982): 528–39.
Gloer, W. H. "Worship God! Liturgical Elements in the Apocalypse." *RevExp* 98 (2001): 35–57.
Goldingay, John E. *Biblical Theology: The God of the Christian Scriptures*. Downers Grove, IL: IVP Academic, 2016.
———. *Daniel*. WBC 30. Dallas: Word, 1989.
Goldsworthy, Graeme. *According to Plan: The Unfolding Revelation of God in the Bible*. Downers Grove, IL: InterVarsity Press, 2002.
———. *The Goldsworthy Trilogy*. Eugene, OR: Wipf & Stock, 2000.
———. *The Son of God and the New Creation*. Wheaton, IL: Crossway, 2015.
Goppelt, Leonhard. *Theology of the New Testament*. 2 vols. Edited by Jürgen Roloff. Translated by John E. Alsup. Grand Rapids: Eerdmans, 1981–1982.
Gorman, Michael J. *Reading Revelation Responsibly: Uncivil Worship and Witness: Following the Lamb into the New Creation*. Eugene, OR: Cascade, 2011.
Grabiner, Steven. *Revelation's Hymns: Commentary on the Cosmic Conflict*. LNTS 511. London: Bloomsbury T&T Clark, 2015.
Green, Bernard. *Christianity in Ancient Rome in the First Three Centuries*. New York: T&T Clark, 2010.
Gruenwald, Ithamar. *Apocalyptic and Merkavah Mysticism*. AGJU 14. Leiden: Brill, 1980.
Guffey, Andrew R. *The Book of Revelation and the Visual Culture of Asia Minor: A Concurrence of Images*. Lanham; London: Lexington Books; Fortress Academic, 2019.
Gundry, Robert H. *The Church and the Tribulation: A Biblical Examination of Posttribulationalism*. Grand Rapids: Zondervan, 1973.
———. *Matthew: A Commentary on His Literary and Theological Art*. Grand Rapids: Eerdmans, 1982.
———. "The New Jerusalem: People as Place, Not Place for People." *NovT* 29 (1987): 254–64.
Gunther, John J. "The Elder John, Author of Revelation." *JSNT* 11 (1981): 3–20.

Gurry, Peter J. "How Your Greek NT Is Changing: A Simple Introduction to the Coherence-Based Genealogical Method (CBGM)." *JETS* 59 (2016): 675–89.

Guthrie, Donald. "The Christology of Revelation." Pages 297–409 in *Jesus of Nazareth: Lord and Christ: Essays on the Historical Jesus and New Testament Christology*. Edited by Joel B. Green and Max Turner. Grand Rapids: Eerdmans, 1994.

———. "The Lamb in the Structure of the Book of Revelation." *VE* 12 (1987): 64–71.

———. *New Testament Introduction*. 4th rev. ed. Downers Grove, IL: InterVarsity Press, 1996.

———. *New Testament Theology*. Downers Grove, IL: InterVarsity Press, 1981.

Hall, Mark Seaborn. "The Hook Interlocking Structure of Revelation: The Most Important Verses in the Book and How They May Unify Its Structure." *NovT* 44.3 (2002): 278–96.

Hamilton, James M., Jr. *God's Glory in Salvation through Judgment: A Biblical Theology*. Wheaton, IL: Crossway, 2010.

———. *Revelation: The Spirit Speaks to the Churches*. PW. Wheaton, IL: Crossway, 2012.

Hanson, Paul D. "Apocalypses and Apocalypticism: The Genre." *ABD* 1:279–80.

———. *The Dawn of Apocalyptic*. Philadelphia: Fortress, 1975.

Harland, Philip A. "Honouring the Emperor or Assailing the Beast: Participation in Civic Life among Associations (Jewish, Christian and Other) in Asia Minor and the Apocalypse of John." *JSNT* 22 (2000): 99–121.

Harrington, W. J. *Revelation*. SacPag 16. Collegeville, MN: Liturgical Press, 2008.

Harris, Dana M. "John and Punishment: Did He Delight in Violence?" Pages 68–86 in *The Apocalypse of John among Its Critics: Questions and Controversies*. Edited by Alan S. Bandy and Alexander E. Stewart. StScrBT. Bellingham, WA: Lexham, 2023.

———. "Understanding Images of Violence in the Book of Revelation." Pages 148–64 in *Encountering Violence in the Bible*. Edited by Markus Zenhder and Hallvard Hagelia. BMW 55. Sheffield: Sheffield Phoenix, 2013.

Harris, W. Hall. "A Theology of John's Writings." Pages 167–242 in *A Biblical Theology of the New Testament*. Edited by Roy B. Zuck and Darrell L. Bock. Chicago: Moody, 1994.

Hays, J. Daniel. *From Every People and Nation: A Biblical Theology of Race*. NSBT 14. Downers Grove, IL: IVP Academic, 2003.

———. *The Temple and the Tabernacle: A Study of God's Dwelling Places from Genesis to Revelation*. Grand Rapids: Baker Academic, 2016.

Hays, J. Daniel, J. Scott Duvall, and C. Marvin Pate. *An A-to-Z Guide to Biblical Prophecy and End Times*. Grand Rapids: Zondervan, 2007.

Hays, Richard B. *Echoes of Scripture in the Letters of Paul*. New Haven: Yale University Press, 1989.

———. "Faithful Witness, Alpha and Omega: The Identity of Jesus in the Apocalypse of John." Pages 69–83 in *Revelation and the Politics of Apocalyptic Interpretation*. Edited by Richard B. Hays and Stefan Alkier. Waco, TX: Baylor University Press, 2012.

———. *The Moral Vision of the New Testament: A Contemporary Introduction to New Testament Ethics*. New York: HarperSanFrancisco, 1996.

Hays, Richard B., and Stefan Alkier, eds. *Revelation and the Politics of Apocalyptic Interpretation*. Waco, TX: Baylor University Press, 2012.

Head, Peter M. "Editio Critica Maior: An Introduction and Assessment." *TynBul* 61 (2010): 131–52.

Heide, Gale Z. "What Is New about the New Heaven and the New Earth? A Theology of Creation from Revelation 21 and 2 Peter 3." *JETS* 40.1 (1997): 37–56.

Helmbold, Andrew. "A Note on the Authorship of the Apocalypse." *NTS* 8 (1961): 77–79.

Helyer, Larry R. *Exploring Jewish Literature of the Second Temple Period: A Guide for New Testament Students*. Downers Grove, IL: InterVarsity Press, 2002.

———. *The Witness of Jesus, Paul and John: An Exploration in Biblical Theology*. Downers Grove, IL: InterVarsity Press, 2008.

Hemer, Colin J. *The Letters to the Seven Churches of Asia in Their Local Setting*. BRS. Grand Rapids: Eerdmans, 2001.

Hengel, Martin. *The Johannine Question*. London: SCM, 1989.

Herms, Ronald. *An Apocalypse for the Church and for the World: The Narrative Function of Universal Language in the Book of Revelation*. BZNW 143. Berlin: de Gruyter, 2006.

———. "πνευματικῶς and Antagonists in Revelation 11 Reconsidered." Pages 135–46 in *The Book of Revelation:*

Currents in British Research on the Apocalypse. Edited by Garrick V. Allen, Ian Paul, and Simon P. Woodman. WUNT 2.411. Tübingen: Mohr Siebeck, 2015.

Hernández, Juan, Jr. "The Apocalypse in Codex Alexandrinus: Its Singular Readings and Scribal Habits." Pages 341–58 in *Scripture and Traditions: Essays on Early Judaism and Christianity in Honor of Carl R. Holladay*. Edited by Patrick Gray and Gail R. O'Day. NovTSup 129. Leiden: Brill, 2008.

———. "The Greek Text of Revelation." *OHBR* 343–60.

———. "Nestle-Aland 28 and the Revision of the Apocalypse's Textual History." Pages 71–81 in *Studies of the Text of the New Testament and Early Christianity: Essays in Honor of Michael W. Holmes*. Edited by Daniel M. Gurtner, Juan Hernández Jr., and Paul Foster. NTTSD 50. Leiden: Brill, 2015.

Hieke, Thomas. "The Reception of Daniel 7 in the Revelation of John." Pages 47–67 in *Revelation and the Politics of Apocalyptic Interpretation*. Edited by Richard B. Hays and Stefan Alkier. Waco, TX: Baylor University Press, 2012.

Hill, Charles E. "The Interpretation of the Book of Revelation in Early Christianity." *OHBR* 395–411.

Hill, David. "Prophecy and Prophets in the Revelation of St John." *NTS* 18 (1972): 401–18.

Holmes, Michael William. *The Apostolic Fathers: Greek Texts and English Translations*. Updated ed. Grand Rapids: Baker, 1999.

Holtz, Traugott. *Die Christologie der Apokalypse des Johannes*. 2nd ed. Berlin: Akademie-Verlag, 1971.

Holwerda, David E. "The Church and the Little Scroll (Revelation 10, 11)." *CTJ* 34 (1999): 148–61.

Homcy, Stephen L. "'To Him Who Overcomes': A Fresh Look at What 'Victory' Means for the Believer according to the Book of Revelation." *JETS* 38 (June 1995): 193–201.

Horn, Stephen N. "Hallelujah, the Lord Our God, the Almighty Reigns: The Theology of the Hymns of Revelation." Pages 42–54 in *Essays on Revelation: Appropriating Yesterday's Apocalypse in Today's World*. Edited by Gerald L. Stevens. Eugene, OR: Pickwick, 2010.

Hoskins, Paul M. *The Book of Revelation: A Theological and Exegetical Commentary*. North Charleston, SC: ChristoDoulos Publications, 2017.

Howard-Brook, Wes, and Anthony Gwyther. *Unveiling Empire: Reading Revelation Then and Now*. Maryknoll, NY: Orbis Books, 1999.

Huber, Konrad. "Imagery in the Book of Revelation." *OHBR* 53–67.

———. "Jesus Christus—der Erste und der Letzte: Zur Christologie der Johannesapokalypse." Pages 435–72 in *Die Johannesapokalypse: Kontexte–Konzepte–Rezeption*. Edited by J. Frey, J. Kelhoffer, and F. Toth. WUNT 287. Tübingen: Mohr Siebeck, 2012.

Huber, L. R. *Like a Bride Adorned: Reading Metaphor in John's Apocalypse*. ESEC 10. New York: T&T Clark, 2007.

Hurtado, Larry W. "Revelation 4–5 in the Light of Jewish Apocalyptic Analogies." *JSNT* 25 (1985): 105–24.

Hylen, Susan E. "Metaphor Matters: Violence and Ethics in Revelation." *CBQ* 73.4 (2011): 777–96.

Jauhiainen, Marko. "The Minor Prophets in Revelation." Pages 155–71 in *The Minor Prophets in the New Testament*. Edited by Maarten J. J. Menken and Steve Moyise. LNTS 377. London: T&T Clark, 2009.

———. *The Use of Zechariah in Revelation*. Tübingen: Mohr Siebeck, 2005.

Jeske, R. L. "Spirit and Community in the Johannine Apocalypse." *NTS* 31 (1985): 452–66.

Jobes, Karen H. *1 Peter*. BECNT. Grand Rapids: Baker Academic, 2005.

Johns, Loren L. "Jesus in the Book of Revelation." *OHBR* 223–39.

———. *The Lamb Christology of the Apocalypse of John: An Investigation into Its Origins and Rhetorical Force*. WUNT 2.167. Tübingen: Mohr Siebeck, 2003. Repr., Eugene, OR: Wipf & Stock, 2015.

Johnson, Alan F. "Revelation." Pages 571–789 in *Hebrews–Revelation*. The Expositor's Bible Commentary 13. Rev. ed. Grand Rapids: Zondervan, 2005.

Johnson, Andy. *Holiness and the Missio Dei*. Eugene, OR: Cascade, 2016.

Johnson, Darrell. *Discipleship on the Edge: An Expository Journey through the Book of Revelation*. Vancouver, BC: Regent College Publishing, 2004.

Johnson, David R. *Pneumatic Discernment in the Apocalypse: An Intertextual and Pentecostal Exploration*. Cleveland, TN: CPT, 2018.

Jones, Brian W. *The Emperor Domitian*. London: Routledge, 1992.

Karrer, Martin. "God in the Book of Revelation." *OHBR* 205–22.

Keener, Craig S. *The IVP Bible Background Commentary: New Testament*. 2nd ed. Downers Grove, IL: IVP Academic, 2014.

———. *Revelation*. NIVAC. Grand Rapids: Zondervan, 1999.

Kelly, Balmer H. "Revelation 7:9–17." *Int* 40.03 (2001): 288–95.

Kennedy, David. "Roman Army." *ABD* 1:789–98.

Kiddle, Martin. *The Revelation of St. John*. London: Hodder & Stoughton, 1940.

Kimble, Jeremy M., and Ched Spellman. *Invitation to Biblical Theology: Exploring the Shape, Storyline, and Themes of Scripture*. ITSS. Grand Rapids: Kregel Academic, 2020.

Kio, Stephen H. "The Exodus Symbol of Liberation in the Apocalypse and Its Relevance for Some Aspects of Translation." *BT* 40.1 (1989): 120–35.

Klassen, William. "Vengeance in the Apocalypse of John." *CBQ* 28.3 (1966): 300–311.

Klauck, Hans-Josef. "Do They Never Come Back? Nero Redivivus and the Apocalypse of John." *CBQ* 63 (2001): 683–98.

Klink, Edward W., III, and Darian R. Lockett. *Understanding Biblical Theology: A Comparison of Theory and Practice*. Grand Rapids: Zondervan, 2012.

Knight, Jonathan. "The Enthroned Christ of Revelation 5:6 and the Development of Christian Theology." Pages 43–50 in *Studies in the Book of Revelation*. Edited by Steve Moyise. Edinburgh: T&T Clark, 2001.

Koch, Klaus. *The Rediscovery of Apocalyptic*. London: SCM, 1972.

Koester, Craig R. "The Distant Triumph Song: Music and the Book of Revelation." *WW* 12.3 (1992): 243–49.

———. *The Dwelling of God: The Tabernacle in the Old Testament, Intertestamental Jewish Literature, and the New Testament*. CBQMS 22. Washington, DC: Catholic Biblical Association of America, 1989.

———. "On the Verge of the Millennium: A History of the Interpretation of Revelation." *WW* 15.2 (1995): 128–36.

———. *Revelation: A New Translation with Introduction and Commentary*. AB. 38A. New Haven: Yale University Press, 2014.

———. *Revelation and the End of All Things*. 2nd ed. Grand Rapids: Eerdmans, 2018.

———. *Symbolism in the Fourth Gospel: Meaning, Mystery, Community*. Minneapolis: Fortress, 1995.

———, ed. *The Oxford Handbook of the Book of Revelation*. Oxford: Oxford University Press, 2020.

Kooy, V. "The Apocalypse and Worship—Some Preliminary Considerations." *RefR* 30 (1976): 198–209.

Korner, Ralph J. "'And I Saw . . .': An Apocalyptic Literary Convention for Structural Identification in the Apocalypse." *NovT* 42 (2000): 160–83.

———. *The Origin and Meaning of Ekklēsia in the Early Jesus Movement*. AJEC 98. Leiden: Brill, 2017.

Köstenberger, Andreas J. *A Theology of John's Gospel and Letters: The Word, the Christ, the Son of God*. BTNT. Grand Rapids: Zondervan Academic, 2009.

Köstenberger, Andreas J., and Gregory Goswell. *Biblical Theology: A Canonical, Ethical and Thematic Approach*. Wheaton, IL: Crossway, 2023.

Köstenberger, Andreas J., L. Scott Kellum, and Charles L. Quarles. *The Cradle, the Cross, and the Crown: An Introduction to the New Testament*. 2nd ed. Nashville: B&H Academic, 2016.

Kovacs, Judith L. "The Purpose of the Millennium: Perspectives Ancient and Modern on Revelation 20:1–6." Pages 367–75 in *New Perspectives on the Book of Revelation*. Edited by Adela Yarbro Collins. Leuven: Peeters, 2017.

Kovacs, Judith, and Christopher Rowland. *Revelation: The Apocalypse of Jesus Christ*. BBC. Oxford: Blackwell, 2004.

Kowalski, Beate. "Transformation of Ezekiel in John's Revelation." Pages 279–311 in *Transforming Visions: Transformations of Text, Traditions, and Theology in Ezekiel*. Edited by W. A. Tooman and M. A. Lyons. Cambridge: James Clark, 2010.

Kraybill, J. Nelson. *Apocalypse and Allegiance: Worship, Politics, and Devotion in the Book of Revelation*. Grand Rapids: Brazos, 2010.

———. *Imperial Cult and Commerce in John's Apocalypse*. JSNTSup 127. Sheffield: Sheffield Academic, 1996.

Kreitzer, Larry J. "Apocalyptic, Apocalypticism." *DLNT* 55–68.

Krodel, Gerhard A. *Revelation*. ACNT. Minneapolis: Fortress, 1990.

Kruger, Michael J. *Canon Revisited: Establishing the Origins and Authority of the New Testament Books*. Wheaton, IL: Crossway, 2012.

———. "The Reception of the Book of Revelation in the Early Church." Pages 159–74 in *Book of Seven Seals*. Edited by Thomas J. Kraus and Michael Sommer. WUNT 363. Tübingen: Mohr Siebeck, 2016.

———, ed. *A Biblical–Theological Introduction to the New Testament: The Gospel Realized*. Wheaton, IL: Crossway, 2016.

Kuykendall, Michael. "An Expanded Role for the Spirit in the Book of Revelation." *JETS* 64.3 (2021): 527–44.

———. *Lions, Locusts, and the Lamb: Interpreting Key Images in the Book of Revelation*. Eugene, OR: Wipf & Stock, 2019.

Labahn, M., and O. Lehtipuu, eds. *Imagery in the Book of Revelation*. Leuven: Peeters, 2011.

Ladd, George Eldon. *The Blessed Hope: A Biblical Study of the Second Advent and the Rapture*. Grand Rapids: Eerdmans, 1956.

———. *A Commentary on the Revelation of John*. Grand Rapids: Eerdmans, 1972.

———. *A Theology of the New Testament*. Edited by Donald A. Hagner. Rev. ed. Grand Rapids: Eerdmans, 1993.

———. "Why Not Prophetic-Apocalyptic?" *JBL* 76 (1957): 192–200.

LaHaye, Tim. *Revelation Unveiled*. Grand Rapids: Zondervan, 1999.

Lambrecht, Jan. "Final Judgments and Ultimate Blessings: The Climactic Visions of Revelation 20,11–21,8." *Bib* 81 (2000): 362–85.

Lane, Tony. "The Wrath of God as an Aspect of the Love of God." Pages 138–67 in *Nothing Greater, Nothing Better: Theological Essays on the Love of God*. Edited by Kevin J. Vanhoozer. Grand Rapids: Eerdmans, 2001.

Laws, Sophie. *In the Light of the Lamb: Imagery, Parody, and Theology in the Apocalypse of John*. Wilmington, DE: Glazier, 1988.

Lee, Hee Youl. *A Dynamic Reading of the Holy Spirit in Revelation: A Theological Reflection on the Functional Role of the Holy Spirit in the Narrative*. Eugene, OR: Wipf & Stock, 2014.

Lee, Pilchan. *The New Jerusalem in the Book of Revelation: A Study of Revelation 21–22 in Light of Its Background in Jewish Tradition*. WUNT 129. Tübingen: Mohr Siebeck, 2001.

Leithart, Peter J. *Revelation*. ITC. London: Bloomsbury T&T Clark, 2018.

Lembke, Markus, Darius Müller, and Ulrich B. Schmid with Martin Karrer, eds. *Text und Textwert der griechischen Handschriften des Neuen Testaments VI: Die Apokalypse; Teststellenkollation und Auswertungen*. ANTF 49. Berlin: de Gruyter, 2017.

Lewis, C. S. *The Great Divorce*. 1945. Repr., New York: HarperSanFrancisco, 1973.

———. *The Last Battle: The Chronicles of Narnia*. 1956. Repr., Harper Collins. Kindle Edition.

———. *The Weight of Glory*. 1980. Repr., HarperCollins. Kindle Edition.

Linton, Gregory L. "Reading the Apocalypse as Apocalypse: The Limits of Genre." Pages 9–41 in *The Reality of the Apocalypse: Rhetoric and Politics in the Book of Revelation*. Edited by David L. Barr. SBLSymS 39. Atlanta: Society of Biblical Literature, 2006.

Lioy, D. *The Book of Revelation in Christological Focus*. StBL 58. New York: Peter Lang, 2003.

Lister, J. Ryan. *The Presence of God: Its Place in the Storyline of Scripture and the Story of Our Lives*. Wheaton, IL: Crossway, 2015.

Longman, Tremper, III. "The Divine Warrior: The New Testament Use of an Old Testament Motif." *WTJ* 44 (1982): 290–307.

———. *Revelation through Old Testament Eyes*. Grand Rapids: Kregel Academic, 2022.

Louw, Johannes P., and Eugene A. Nida. *Greek-English Lexicon of the New Testament: Based on Semantic Domains*. New York: United Bible Societies, 1996.

Lucas, Ernest C. *Daniel*. AOTC 20. Downers Grove, IL: InterVarsity Press, 2002.

Lupieri, Edmondo F. *A Commentary on the Apocalypse of John*. Grand Rapids: Eerdmans, 1999.

Maier, Gerhard. *Die Johannesoffenbarung und die Kirche*. WUNT 25. Tübingen: Mohr Siebeck, 1981.

Maier, Harry O. *Apocalypse Recalled: The Book of Revelation after Christendom*. Minneapolis: Fortress, 2002.

Malik, Peter. *P.Beatty III (P47): The Codex, Its Scribe, and Its Text*. NTTSD 52. Leiden: Brill, 2017.

Malina, Bruce J. *The New Jerusalem in the Revelation of John: The City as Symbol of Life with God*. Collegeville, MN: Liturgical Press, 2000.

Malone, Andrew S. *God's Mediators: A Biblical Theology of Priesthood*. NSBT 43. Downers Grove, IL: InterVarsity Press, 2017.

Maloney, Francis J. *The Apocalypse of John: A Commentary*. Grand Rapids: Baker Academic, 2020.

Mangina, Joseph L. *Revelation*. BTCB. Grand Rapids: Brazos, 2010.

Marriner, Keith T. *Following the Lamb: The Theme of Discipleship in the Book of Revelation*. Eugene, OR: Wipf & Stock, 2016.

Marshall, I. Howard. "Church and Temple in the New Testament." *TynBul* 40 (1989): 203–22.

———. *New Testament Theology: Many Witnesses, One Gospel*. Downers Grove, IL: InterVarsity Press, 2004.

Martin, Ralph P. *Worship in the Early Church*. Grand Rapids: Eerdmans, 1974.

Martin, Ralph P., and Peter H. Davids, eds. *Dictionary of the Later New Testament and Its Developments.* Edited by Downers Grove, IL: InterVarsity Press, 1997.

Mathews, Mark D. *Riches, Poverty, and the Faithful: Perspectives on Wealth in the Second Temple Period and the Apocalypse of John.* SNTSMS 154. Cambridge: Cambridge University Press, 2013.

Mathewson, David L. "Assessing Old Testament Allusions in the Book of Revelation." *EvQ* 75:4 (2003): 311–25.

———. *A Companion to the Book of Revelation.* Eugene, OR: Cascade, 2020.

———. "The Destiny of the Nations in Revelation 21:1–22:5: A Reconsideration." *TynBul* 53 (2002): 121–42.

———. "Isaiah in Revelation." Pages 189–210 in *Isaiah in the New Testament.* Edited by Steve Moyise and Maarten J. J. Menken. London: T&T Clark, 2005.

———. "New Exodus as a Background for 'The Sea Was No More' in Revelation 21:1c." *TrinJ* 24 (2003): 243–58.

———. *A New Heaven and a New Earth: The Meaning and Function of the Old Testament in Revelation 21.1–22.5.* JSNTSup 238. Sheffield: Sheffield Academic, 2003.

———. "A Note on the Foundation Stones in Revelation 21.14, 19–20." *JSNT* 25.4 (2003): 487–98.

———. "A Re-examination of the Millennium in Rev 20:1–6: Consummation and Recapitulation." *JETS* 44.2 (2001): 237–51.

———. *Revelation: A Handbook on the Greek Text.* Waco, TX: Baylor University Press, 2016.

———. "Revelation in Recent Genre Criticism: Some Implications for Interpretation." *TrinJ* 13 (1992): 193–213.

———. "Revelation's Use of the Greek Language." *OHBR* 101–14.

———. *Uncovering the Treasures of the Apocalypse: Keys to Unlocking the Mysteries of the Book of Revelation.* Eugene, OR: Cascade, 2022.

———. "Verbal Aspect in the Apocalypse of John: An Analysis of Revelation 5." *NovT* 50 (2008): 58–77.

———. *Verbal Aspect in the Book of Revelation: The Function of Greek Verb Tenses in John's Apocalypse.* LBS 4. Leiden: Brill, 2010.

Matthews, Kenneth A. *Genesis 1–11:26.* NAC 1A. Nashville: B&H, 1996.

Mayo, Philip L. *"Those Who Call Themselves Jews": The Church and Judaism in the Apocalypse of John.* PTMS 60. Eugene, OR: Pickwick, 2006.

Mazzaferri, F. D. *The Genre of the Book of Revelation from a Source-Critical Perspective.* BZNW 54. New York: de Gruyter, 1989.

McCall, Thomas H., Caleb T. Friedeman, and Matt T. Friedeman. *The Doctrine of Good Works: Reclaiming a Neglected Protestant Teaching.* Grand Rapids: Baker Academic, 2023.

McCaulley, Esau. *Reading While Black: African American Biblical Interpretations as an Exercise in Hope.* Downers Grove, IL: IVP Academic, 2020.

McDonald, Lee Martin. *The Biblical Canon: Its Origin, Transmission, and Authority.* Peabody, MA: Hendrickson, 2007.

McDonough, Sean. "Revelation: The Climax of Cosmology." Pages 178–88 in *Cosmology and New Testament Theology.* Edited by Jonathan T. Pennington and Sean M. McDonough. LNTS 355. London: T&T Clark, 2008.

———. *YHWH at Patmos: Rev. 1:4 in Its Hellenistic and Early Jewish Setting.* WUNT 2.107. Tübingen: Mohr Siebeck, 1999. Reprint, Eugene, OR: Wipf & Stock, 2011.

McGowan, Andrew B. *Ancient Christian Worship: Early Church Practices in Social, Historical, and Theological Perspective.* Grand Rapids: Baker Academic, 2014.

McGrath, James F. *The Only True God: Early Christian Monotheism in Its Jewish Context.* Urbana, IL: University of Illinois Press, 2009.

McIlraith, Donal A. "'For the Fine Linen Is the Righteous Deeds of the Saints': Works and Wife in Revelation 19:8." *CBQ* 61 (1999): 512–29.

———. *The Reciprocal Love Between Christ and the Church in the Apocalypse.* Rome: Columban Fathers, 1989.

McKay, K. L. *A New Syntax of the Verb in the New Testament.* SBG 5. New York: Peter Lang, 1994.

McKelvey, R. J. *The New Temple: The Church in the New Testament.* OTM. Oxford: Oxford University Press, 1969.

McKinnon, James W. *Music in Early Christian Literature.* Cambridge: Cambridge University Press, 1987.

McKnight, Scot, with Cody Matchett. *Revelation for the Rest of Us: A Prophetic Call to Follow Jesus as a Dissident Disciple.* Grand Rapids: Zondervan Reflective, 2023.

McNicol, Allan. "Revelation 11:1–14 and the Structure of the Apocalypse." *ResQ* 22 (1979): 193–202.

Mealy, J. Webb. *After the Thousand Years: Resurrection and Judgment in Revelation 20.* JSNTSup 70. Sheffield: JSOT Press, 1992.

———. *New Creation Millennialism*. J. Webb Mealy, 2019.
Metzger, Bruce M. *Breaking the Code: Understanding the Book of Revelation*. Nashville: Abingdon, 1993.
———. *The Canon of the New Testament: Its Origin, Development, and Significance*. Oxford: Clarendon, 1987.
———. *A Textual Commentary on the Greek New Testament*. 2nd ed. New York: United Bible Societies, 1994.
Metzger, Bruce M., and Bart D. Ehrman, *The Text of the New Testament: Its Transmission, Corruption, and Restoration*. 4th ed. Oxford: Oxford University Press, 2005.
Michaels, J. Ramsey. *Interpreting the Book of Revelation*. GNTE. Grand Rapids: Baker Books, 1992.
———. "Old Testament in Revelation." *DLNT* 850–55.
———. *Revelation*. IVPNTC. Downers Grove, IL: InterVarsity Press, 1997.
Middleton, J. Richard. *A New Heaven and a New Earth: Reclaiming Biblical Eschatology*. Grand Rapids: Baker Academic, 2014.
Middleton, J. Richard, and Michael J. Gorman. "Salvation." *NIDB* 5:45–61.
Middleton, Paul. "Male Virgins, Male Martyrs, Male Brides: A Reconsideration of the 144,000 'who have not dirtied themselves with women' (Revelation 14:4)." Pages 193–208 in *The Book of Revelation: Currents in British Research on the Apocalypse*. Edited by Garrick V. Allen, Ian Paul, and Simon P. Woodman. WUNT 2.411. Tübingen: Mohr Siebeck, 2015.
———. *The Violence of the Lamb: Martyrs as Agents of Divine Judgement in the Book of Revelation*. LNTS 586. New York: Bloomsbury T&T Clark, 2018.
Millar, J. Gary. *Calling on the Name of the Lord: A Biblical Theology of Prayer*. NSBT 38. Downers Grove, IL: IVP Academic, 2016.
Miller, Kevin E. "The Nuptial Eschatology of Revelation 19–22." *CBQ* 60 (1998): 301–18.
Milligan, W. *The Revelation of St. John*. 2nd ed. London: Macmillan, 1887.
Moltmann, Jürgen. *The Spirit of Life: A Universal Affirmation*. Systematic Contributions to Theology. Minneapolis: Fortress, 2001.
Montague, George T. *The Holy Spirit: Growth of a Biblical Tradition*. New York: Paulist, 1976.
Morales, Jon. *Christ, Shepherd of the Nations: The Nations as Narrative Character and Audience in John's Apocalypse*. LNTS 577. London: T&T Clark, 2018.
Morris, Leon. *Apocalyptic*. London: Tyndale, 1973.
———. *The Biblical Doctrine of Judgment*. Eugene, OR: Wipf & Stock, 2006.
Morton, Russell. "Glory to God and to the Lamb: John's Use of Jewish and Hellenistic/Roman Themes in Formatting his Theology in Revelation 4–5." *JSNT* 83 (2001): 89–109.
———. *One upon the Throne and the Lamb: A Tradition Historical/Theological Analysis of Revelation 4–5*. New York: Peter Lang, 2007.
———. "Revelation 7:9–17: The Innumerable Crowd Before the One upon the Throne and Lamb." *ATJ* 32 (2000): 1–11.
Moule, C. F. D. *The Holy Spirit*. Grand Rapids: Eerdmans, 1978.
Mounce, Robert H. *The Book of Revelation*. Rev. ed. NICNT. Grand Rapids: Eerdmans, 1997.
Mowry, L. "Revelation 4–5 and Early Christian Liturgical Usage." *JBL* 71.2 (1952): 75–84.
Moyise, Steve. "Does the Lion Lie Down with the Lamb?" Pages 181–94 in *Studies in the Book of Revelation*. Edited by Steve Moyise. Edinburgh: T&T Clark, 2001.
———. "Genesis in Revelation." Pages 166–79 in *Genesis in the New Testament*. Edited by Maarten J. J. Menken and Steve Moyise. LNTS 466. London: T&T Clark, 2012.
———. "The Language of the Old Testament in the Apocalypse." *JSNT* 76 (1999): 97–113.
———. *The Old Testament in the Book of Revelation*. JSNTSup 115. London: Bloomsbury T&T Clark, 2015.
———. *The Old Testament in the New: An Introduction*. 2nd ed. London: Bloomsbury T&T Clark, 2015.
———. "The Psalms in the Book of Revelation." Pages 231–47 in *Psalms in the New Testament*. Edited by Steve Moyise and Maarten J. J. Menken. London: T&T Clark, 2004.
———, ed. *Studies in the Book of Revelation*. Edinburgh: T&T Clark, 2001.
Mucha, Robert. "Ein flavischer Nero: Zur Domitian-Darstellung und Datierung der Johannesoffenbarung." *NTS* 60.1 (2014): 83–105.
Mühling, Markus. *T&T Clark Handbook of Christian Eschatology*. London: Bloomsbury T&T Clark, 2015.
Mulzac, Kenneth. "The 'Fall of Babylon' Motif in the Books of Jeremiah and Revelation." *JATS* 8.1–2 (1997): 137–49.
Mussies, G. *The Morphology of Koine Greek as Used in the Apocalypse of St. John: A Study in Bilingualism*. NovTSup 27. London: Brill, 1971.

Naylor, M. "The Roman Imperial Cult and Revelation." *CurBR* 8 (2010): 207–39.

Neville, David J. *A Peaceable Hope: Contesting Violent Eschatology in New Testament Narratives*. Grand Rapids: Baker Academic, 2013.

Newton, Jon K. "Reading Revelation Romantically." *JPT* 18 (2009): 194–215.

Nichols, Terence. *Death and the Afterlife: A Theological Introduction*. Grand Rapids: Brazos, 2010.

Nicklas, Tobias. "The Early Text of Revelation." Pages 225–38 in *The Early Text of the New Testament*. Edited by C. E. Hill and M. J. Kruger. Oxford: Oxford University Press, 2012.

Ng, Esther Y. L. "Prayer in Revelation." Pages 119–35 in *Teach Us to Pray: Prayer in the Bible and the World*. Edited by D. A. Carson. Eugene, OR: Wipf & Stock, 1990.

O'Rourke, J. J. "The Hymns of the Apocalypse." *CBQ* 30 (1968): 399–409.

Och, Bernard. "Creation and Redemption: Towards a Theology of Creation." *Judaism* 44 (1995): 226–43.

Oecumenius and Andrew of Caesarea. *Greek Commentaries on Revelation*. Edited by Thomas C. Oden and Gerald L. Bray. Translated by William C. Weinrich. ACT. Downers Grove, IL: IVP Academic, 2011.

Osborne, Grant R. "Recent Trends in the Study of the Apocalypse." Pages 473–504 in *The Face of New Testament Studies: A Survey of Recent Research*. Edited by Scot McKnight and Grant R. Osborne. Grand Rapids: Baker Academic, 2004.

———. *Revelation*. BECNT. Grand Rapids: Baker Academic, 2002.

———. "Theodicy in the Apocalypse." *TrinJ* 14 (1993): 63–77.

Ozanne, C. G. "The Language of the Apocalypse." *TynBul* 16 (1965): 3–9.

Parker, D. C. *An Introduction to the New Testament Manuscripts and Their Texts*. Cambridge: Cambridge University Press, 2008.

Pate, C. Marvin, ed. *Four Views on the Book of Revelation*. Grand Rapids: Zondervan, 1998.

Pate, C. Marvin, J. Scott Duvall, J. Daniel Hays, E. Randolph Richards, W. Dennis Tucker Jr., and Preben Vang. *The Story of Israel: A Biblical Theology*. Downers Grove, IL: InterVarsity Press, 2004.

Pattemore, Stephen. *The People of God in the Apocalypse: Discourse, Structure and Exegesis*. SNTSMS 128. Cambridge: Cambridge University Press, 2004.

Paul, Ian. "The Book of Revelation: Image, Symbol and Metaphor." Pages 131–47 in *Studies in the Book of Revelation*. Edited by Steve Moyise. Edinburgh: T&T Clark, 2001.

———. "The Genre of Revelation." Pages 36–50 in *The Apocalypse of John among Its Critics: Questions & Controversies*. Edited by Alexander S. Stewart and Alan S. Bandy. StScrBT. Bellingham, WA: Lexham Academic, 2023.

———. *Revelation: An Introduction and Commentary*. TNTC. London: InterVarsity Press, 2018.

———. "The Trinitarian Dynamic in the Book of Revelation." Pages 85–108 in *Trinity Without Hierarchy: Reclaiming Nicene Orthodoxy in Evangelical Theology*. Edited by Michael F. Bird and Scott Harrower. Grand Rapids: Kregel, 2019.

———. "The Use of the Old Testament in Revelation 12." Pages 256–76 in *The Old Testament in the New Testament: Essays in Honour of J. L. North*. Edited by Steve Moyise. JSNTSup 189. Sheffield: Sheffield Academic, 2000.

Paulien, Jon. "Armageddon (Place)." *ABD* 1:394–95.

———. "Criteria and Assessment of Allusions to the Old Testament in the Book of Revelation." Pages 113–29 in *Studies in the Book of Revelation*. Edited by Steve Moyise. Edinburgh: T&T Clark, 2001.

Perry, Peter S. "The People of God in the Book of Revelation." *OHBR* 325–40.

———. *The Rhetoric of Digressions: Revelation 7:1–17 and 10:1–11:13 and Ancient Communication*. WUNT 2.268. Tübingen: Mohr Siebeck, 2009.

Peters, Olutola K. *The Mandate of the Church in the Apocalypse of John*. StBL 77. New York: Peter Lang, 2005.

Peterson, David G. *Engaging with God: A Biblical Theology of Worship*. Downers Grove, IL: InterVarsity Press, 1992.

———. *Possessed by God: A New Testament Theology of Sanctification and Holiness*. Grand Rapids: Eerdmans, 1995.

———. "Worship in the New Testament." Pages 51–91 in *Worship: Adoration and Action*. Edited by D. A. Carson. Grand Rapids: Baker, 1993.

———. "Worship in the Revelation to John." *RTR* 47 (1986): 67–77.

Peterson, Eugene H. *Reversed Thunder: The Revelation of John & the Praying Imagination*. New York: HarperSanFrancisco, 1988; repr., 1991.

Hubler, J. Noel, trans. "Iezekiel." Pages 947–85 in *A New English Translation of the Septuagint (Primary Texts)*. Edited by Albert Pietersma and Benjamin G. Wright. New York; Oxford: Oxford University Press, 2007.

Piper, O. "The Apocalypse of John and the Liturgy of the Ancient Church." *CH* 20.1 (1951): 10–22.

Porter, Stanley E. *How We Got the New Testament: Text, Transmission, Translation.* Grand Rapids: Baker Academic, 2013.

———. "The Language of the Apocalypse in Recent Discussion." *NTS* 35 (1989): 582–603.

———. *Verbal Aspect in the Greek of the New Testament, with Reference to Tense and Mood.* SBG 1. New York: Peter Lang, 1989.

Porter, Stanley E., and A. K. Gabriel. *Johannine Writings and Apocalyptic: An Annotated Bibliography.* JohSt 1. Leiden: Brill, 2013.

Portier-Young, Anathea E. *Apocalypse against Empire: Theologies of Resistance in Early Judaism.* Grand Rapids: Eerdmans, 2011.

Powery, Luke A. "Painful Praise: Exploring the Public Proclamation of the Hymns of Revelation." *ThTo* 70 (2013): 69–78.

Poythress, Vern S. "Genre and Hermeneutics in Rev 20:1–6." *JETS* 36.1 (1993): 41–54.

Price, Simon R. F. *Rituals and Power: The Roman Imperial Cult in Asia Minor.* Cambridge: Cambridge University Press, 1984.

Rainbow, Paul. *Johannine Theology: The Gospel, the Epistles and the Apocalypse.* Downers Grove, IL: InterVarsity Press, 2014.

———. *The Pith of the Apocalypse: Essential Message and Principles for Interpretation.* Eugene, OR: Wipf & Stock, 2008.

Ramsay, William M. *The Letters to the Seven Churches.* Edited and updated by Mark Wilson. Peabody, MA: Hendrickson, 1994.

Reddish, Mitchell G. "The Genre of the Book of Revelation." *OHBR* 21–34.

———. *Revelation.* SHBC. Macon, GA: Smith & Helwys, 2001.

Resseguie, James L. "Narrative Features of the Book of Revelation." *OHBR* 37–52.

———. *The Revelation of John: A Narrative Commentary.* Grand Rapids: Baker Academic, 2009.

Reynolds, Benjamin E. *John among the Apocalypses: Jewish Apocalyptic Tradition and the 'Apocalyptic' Gospel.* Oxford: Oxford University Press, 2020.

Ribeira, Franciscus. *In sacram Beati Ioannis Apostoli.* EAC. Ludguni: Ex Officina Iuntarum, 1593.

Richards, E. Randolph. *Paul and First-Century Letter Writing: Secretaries, Composition and Collection.* Downers Grove, IL: InterVarsity Press, 2004.

Rissi, Mathias. *The Future of the World: An Exegetical Study of Rev. 19:11–22:15.* SBT 23. London: SCM, 1972.

Robinson, Andrea L. *Temple of Presence: The Christological Fulfillment of Ezekiel 40–48 in Revelation 21:1–22:5.* Eugene, OR: Wipf & Stock, 2019.

Robinson, John A. T. *Redating the New Testament.* London: SCM, 1976.

Rojas-Flores, Gonzalo. "The Book of Revelation and the First Years of Nero's Reign." *Bib* 85.3 (2004): 375–92.

Ross, Allen P. *Recalling the Hope of Glory: Biblical Worship from the Garden to the New Creation.* Grand Rapids: Kregel Academic, 2006.

Rossing, Barbara R. *The Choice between Two Cities: Whore, Bride, and Empire in the Apocalypse.* Harrisburg, PA: Trinity Press International, 1999.

———. *The Rapture Exposed: The Message of Hope in the Book of Revelation.* Boulder, CO: Westview, 2004.

Rowland, Christopher. "The Lamb and the Beast, the Sheep and the Goats: 'The Mystery of Salvation' in Revelation." Pages 181–192 in *A Vision for the Church: Studies in Early Christian Ecclesiology in Honor of J. P. M. Sweet.* Edited by Markus Bockmuehl and Michael B. Thompson. Edinburgh: T&T Clark, 1997.

———. *Open Heaven: A Study of Apocalyptic in Judaism and Early Christianity.* Eugene, OR: Wipf & Stock, 1982.

Royalty, Robert. *The Streets of Heaven: The Ideology of Wealth in the Apocalypse of John.* Macon, GA: Mercer University Press, 1998.

Ruiz, Jean-Pierre. "Revelation 4:8–11; 5:9–14: Hymns of the Heavenly Liturgy." *SBLSP* 34 (1995): 216–19.

Russell, D. S. *The Method and Message of Jewish Apocalyptic.* London: SCM, 1964.

Russell, David M. *The "New Heavens and New Earth": Hope for the Creation in Jewish Apocalyptic and the New Testament.* SBAL 1. Philadelphia: Visionary, 1996.

Ryken, Leland, James C. Wilhoit, Tremper Longman III, Colin Duriez, Douglas Penney, and Daniel G. Reid, eds. *DBI.* Downers Grove, IL: InterVarsity, 2000.

Samra, James G. "A Biblical View of Discipleship." *BSac* 160 (2003) 219–34.

———. "Hymns and Credal Worship in the New Testament." Pages 3–15 in *An Introduction to the History of Hymns*. Edited by Benjamin K. Forest, Mark A. Lamport, and Vernon M. Whaley. Eugene, OR: Cascade, 2019.

Sandy, D. Brent. *Plowshares & Pruning Hooks: Rethinking the Language of Biblical Prophecy and Apocalyptic*. Downers Grove, IL: InterVarsity Press, 2002.

Sandy, D. Brent, and D. M. O'Hare. *Prophecy and Apocalyptic: An Annotated Bibliography*. IBR Bibliographies. Grand Rapids: Baker Academic, 2007.

Saucy, Robert L. *The Case for Progressive Dispensationalism*. Grand Rapids: Zondervan, 1993.

Saunders, S. "Revelation and Resistance: Narrative and Worship in John's Apocalypse." Pages 119–22 in *Narrative Reading, Narrative Preaching*. Edited by Joel B. Green and M. Pasquarello III. Grand Rapids: Baker Academic, 2003.

Schedtler, Justin P. Jeffcoat. *A Heavenly Chorus: The Dramatic Function of Revelation's Hymns*. WUNT 2.381. Tübingen: Mohr Siebeck, 2014.

———. "The Hymns in Revelation." *OHBR* 115–30.

Schellenberg, Ryan S. "Seeing the World Whole: Intertextuality and the New Jerusalem (Revelation 21–22)." *PRSt* 33 (2006): 467–76.

Scherrer, Steven J. "Signs and Wonders in the Imperial Cult: A New Look at a Roman Religious Institution in the Light of Rev 13:13–15." *JBL* 103 (1984): 599–610.

Schimanowski, Gottfried. "'Connecting Heaven and Earth': The Function of the Hymns in Revelation 4–5." Pages 67–84 in *Heavenly Realms and Earthly Realities in Late Antique Religions*. Edited by Ra'anan S. Boustan and Annette Yoshiko Reed. Cambridge: Cambridge University Press, 2004.

Schlatter, Adolf. *New Testament Theology: The History of the Christ and the Theology of the Apostles*. Translated by Andreas J. Köstenberger. Grand Rapids: Baker, 1997, 1999.

Schmid, Josef. *Studies in the History of the Greek Text of the Apocalypse: The Ancient Stems*. Edited and translated by Juan Hernández Jr., Garrick V. Allen, and Darius Müller. Atlanta: Society of Biblical Literature, 2018.

Schmidt, Daryl D. "Semitisms and Septuagintalisms in the Book of Revelation." *NTS* 37 (1991): 592–603.

Schnabel, Eckhard J. *40 Questions about the End Times*. Grand Rapids: Kregel, 2011.

———. "John and the Future of the Nations." *BBR* 12.2 (2002): 243–71.

———. "The Persecution of Christians in the First Century." *JETS* 61 (2018): 525–47.

Schnelle, Udo. *Theology of the New Testament*. Translated by M. Eugene Boring. Grand Rapids: Baker Academic, 2007.

Schreiner, Thomas R. *The Joy of Hearing: A Theology of the Book of Revelation*. Wheaton, IL: Crossway, 2021.

———. *The King in His Beauty: A Biblical Theology of the Old and New Testaments*. Grand Rapids: Baker Academic, 2013.

———. *New Testament Theology: Magnifying God in Christ*. Grand Rapids: Baker Academic, 2008.

———. *Revelation*. BECNT. Grand Rapids: Baker Academic, 2023.

Schüssler Fiorenza, Elizabeth. *The Book of Revelation: Justice and Judgment*. 2nd ed. Minneapolis: Fortress, 1998.

———. "The Followers of the Lamb: Visionary Rhetoric and Social-Political Situation." Pages 144–65 in *Discipleship in the New Testament*. Edited by Fernando F. Segovia. Philadelphia: Fortress, 1985.

———. "Redemption as Liberation: Apoc 1:5f. and 5:9f." *CBQ* 36 (1974): 220–32.

———. *Revelation: Vision of a Just World*. PC. Minneapolis: Fortress, 1991.

Scobie, Charles H. H. *Ways of Our God: An Approach to Biblical Theology*. Grand Rapids: Eerdmans, 2002.

Scott, Kenneth. *The Imperial Cult under the Flavians*. New York: Arno, 1975.

Segovia, Fernando F., ed. *Discipleship in the New Testament*. Philadelphia: Fortress, 1985.

Shanks, Monte A. *Papias and the New Testament*. Eugene, OR: Pickwick, 2013.

Shogren, Gary S. "Hell, Abyss, Eternal Punishment." *DLNT* 459–62.

Siew, Antonius King Wai. *The War between the Two Beasts and the Two Witnesses: A Chiastic Reading of Revelation 11:1–14:5*. London: T&T Clark, 2005.

Skaggs, Rebecca, and Thomas Doyle. "Lion/Lamb in Revelation." *CurBR* 7 (2009): 363–75.

———. "Violence in the Apocalypse of John." *CurBR* 5.2 (2007): 220–34.

Slater, Thomas B. "On the Social Setting of the Revelation to John." *NTS* 44 (1998): 232–56.

Smalley, Stephen S. "The Christ-Christian Relationship in Paul and John." Pages 95–105 in *Pauline Studies: Essays Presented to F. F. Bruce on His 70th Birthday*. Edited by D. A. Hagner and M. J. Harris. Grand Rapids: Eerdmans, 1980.

———. "John's Revelation and John's Community." *BJRL* 69 (1987): 549–71.

———. "The Paraclete: Pneumatology in the Johannine Gospel and Apocalypse." Pages 289–300 in *Exploring the Gospel of John*. Edited by R. Alan Culpepper and C. Clifton Black. Louisville: Westminster John Knox, 1996.

———. *The Revelation to John: A Commentary on the Greek Text of the Apocalypse*. Downers Grove, IL: InterVarsity Press, 2005.

———. *Thunder and Love: John's Revelation and John's Community*. Eugene, OR: Wipf & Stock, 1994.

Smith, Brandon D. "The Identification of Jesus with YHWH in the Book of Revelation: A Brief Sketch." *CTR* 14.1 (2016): 67–84.

———. *The Trinity in the Book of Revelation: Seeing Father, Son, and Holy Spirit in John's Apocalypse*. SCDS. Downers Grove, IL: IVP Academic, 2022.

Smith, Christopher R. "The Portrayal of the Church as the New Israel in the Names and Order of the Tribes in Revelation 7.5–8." *JSNT* 39 (1990): 111–18.

———. "The Structure of the Book of Revelation in the Light of Apocalyptic Literary Conventions." *NovT* 36 (1994): 373–93.

Smith, Morton. "On the History of ΑΠΟΚΑΛΥΠΤΩ and ΑΠΟΚΑΛΥΨΙΣ." Pages 9–20 in *Apocalypticism in the Mediterranean World and the Near East*. Edited by David Hellholm. Tübingen: Mohr Siebeck, 1983.

Smith, Robert S. "Songs of the Seer: The Purpose of Revelation's Hymns." *Them* 43.2 (2018): 193–204.

Song, Seung-In. *Water as an Image of the Spirit in the Johannine Literature*. StBL 171. New York: Peter Lang, 2019.

Spilsbury, Paul. *The Throne, the Lamb & the Dragon: A Reader's Guide to the Book of Revelation*. Downers Grove, IL: InterVarsity Press, 2002.

Sprinkle, Preston, ed., *Four Views on Hell*. 2nd ed. Grand Rapids: Zondervan, 2016.

Stephens, Mark B. "Creation and New Creation in the Book of Revelation." *OHBR* 257–73.

Stevens, Gerald L. *Revelation: The Past and Future of John's Apocalypse*. Eugene, OR: Pickwick, 2014.

———, ed. *Essays on Revelation: Appropriating Yesterday's Apocalypse in Today's World*. Eugene, OR: Pickwick, 2010.

Stevenson, Gregory M. "Conceptual Background to Golden Crown Imagery in the Apocalypse of John (4:4, 10; 14:14)." *JBL* 114/2 (1995): 257–72.

———. "Perspectives on Evil in the Book of Revelation." *OHBR* 275–89.

———. *A Slaughtered Lamb: Revelation and the Apocalyptic Response to Evil and Suffering*. Abilene, TX: Abilene Christian University Press, 2013.

Stewart, Alexander E. "Ekphrasis, Fear, and Motivation in the Apocalypse of John." *BBR* 27 (2017): 227–40.

———. *Reading the Book of Revelation: Five Principles for Interpretation*. Bellingham, WA: Lexham, 2021.

———. *Soteriology as Motivation in the Apocalypse of John*. GBS 61. Piscataway, NJ: Gorgias, 2015.

Stewart, Alexander E., and Alan S. Brady, eds. *The Apocalypse of John among Its Critics: Questions and Controversies*. StScrBT. Bellingham, WA: Lexham, 2023.

Stott, John R. W. *What Christ Thinks of the Church: An Exposition of Revelation 1–3*. Grand Rapids: Baker Academic, 2003.

Stuckenbruck, Loren T. *Angel Veneration and Christology: A Study in Early Judaism and in the Christology of the Apocalypse of John*. WUNT 2.70. Tübingen: Mohr Siebeck, 1995.

———. "Revelation: Historical Setting and John's Call to Discipleship." *Leaven* 8 (2000): 27–31.

Svigel, Michael J. "The Apocalypse of John and the Rapture of the Church: A Reevaluation," *TrinJ* 22 (2001): 23–74.

Sweet, John. *Revelation*. TPI New Testament. Philadelphia: Trinity Press International, 1990.

Swete, H. B. *The Apocalypse of St. John*. 3rd ed. London, England: Macmillan, 1909.

Swete, J. P. M. "Maintaining the Testimony of Jesus: The Suffering of Christians in the Revelation of John." Pages 101–17 in *Suffering and Martyrdom in the New Testament: Studies Presented to G. M. Styler*. Cambridge: Cambridge University Press, 1981.

Tabb, Brian J. *All Things New: Revelation as Canonical Capstone*. NSBT 48. Downers Grove, IL: IVP Academic, 2019.

———. "Prayer in Apocalyptic Perspective." Pages 191–208 in *For It Stands in Scripture: Essays in Honor of W. Edward Glenny*. Edited by Ardel B. Caneday with Anna Rask and Greg Rosaver. St. Paul, MN: University of Northwestern—St. Paul, 2019.

Talbot, Charles H. *The Development of Christology During the First Hundred Years: And Other Essays on Early Christian Christology*. Leiden: Brill, 2011.

———. "Divine Assistance and Enablement of Human Faithfulness in the Revelation of John Viewed within Its Apocalyptic Context." Pages 265–82 in *Getting 'Saved': The Whole Story of Salvation in the New Testament*. Edited by Charles H. Talbert and Jason A. Whitlark. Grand Rapids: Eerdmans, 2011.

Tavo, Felise. "The Structure of the Apocalypse: Re-examining a Perennial Problem." *NovT* 47 (2005): 47–68.

Thielman, Frank S. *Theology of the New Testament: A Canonical and Systematic Approach*. Grand Rapids: Zondervan, 2005.

Thiselton, Anthony C. *The Holy Spirit—In Biblical Teaching, through the Centuries, and Today*. Grand Rapids: Eerdmans, 2013.

Thomas, John Christopher. "New Jerusalem and the Conversion of the Nations: An Exercise in Pneumatic Discernment—Revelation 21:1–22:5." Pages 228–45 in *The Spirit and Christ in the New Testament & Christian Theology: Essays in Honour of Max Turner*. Edited by I. Howard Marshall, Volker Rabens, and Cornelis Bennema. Grand Rapids: Eerdmans, 2012.

———. "Revelation." Pages 257–66 in *A Biblical Theology of the Holy Spirit*. Edited by Trevor J. Burke and Keith Warrington. Eugene, OR: Cascade, 2014.

———. "The Spirit in the Book of Revelation." *OHBR* 241–55.

Thomas, John Christopher, and Frank D. Macchia. *Revelation*. THNTC. Grand Rapids: Eerdmans, 2016.

Thomas, Robert L. *Revelation 1–7: An Exegetical Commentary*. Chicago: Moody, 1992.

Thomas, Rodney Lawrence. *Magic Motifs in the Book of Revelation*. LNTS 416. New York: T&T Clark, 2010.

Thompson, Leonard L. *The Book of Revelation: Apocalypse and Empire*. Oxford: Oxford University Press, 1990.

Thompson, Marianne Meye. "The Breath of Life: John 20:22–23 Once More." Pages 69–78 in *The Holy Spirit and Christian Origins: Essays in Honor of James D. G. Dunn*. Edited by Graham N. Stanton, Bruce W. Longenecker, and Stepen C. Barton. Grand Rapids: Eerdmans, 2004.

———. "Worship in the Book of Revelation." *ExAud* 8 (1992): 45–54.

Thompson, Steven. *The Apocalypse and Semitic Syntax*. SNTSMS 52. Cambridge: Cambridge University Press, 1985.

Tõniste, Külli. *The Ending of the Canon: A Canonical and Intertextual Reading of Revelation 21–22*. LNTS 526. London: T&T Clark, 2016.

Tonstad, Sigve. *Revelation*. Paideia. Grand Rapids: Baker Academic, 2019.

———. *Saving God's Reputation*. LNTS 337. London: T&T Clark, 2006.

Trail, Ronald L. *An Exegetical Summary of Revelation 1–11*. 2nd ed. Dallas: SIL International, 2008.

———. *An Exegetical Summary of Revelation 12–22*. 2nd ed. Dallas: SIL International, 2008.

Treier, Daniel J., and Walter A. Elwell, eds. *Evangelical Dictionary of Theology*. 3rd ed. Grand Rapids: Baker Academic, 2017.

Trites, Allison A. *The New Testament Concept of Witness*. Cambridge: Cambridge University Press, 1977.

———. "Witness and the Resurrection in the Apocalypse of John." Pages 270–88 in *Life in the Face of Death: The Resurrection Message of the New Testament*. Edited by Richard N. Longenecker. Grand Rapids: Eerdmans, 1998.

Turner, David L. "The New Jerusalem in Revelation 21:1–22:5: Consummation of a Biblical Continuum." Pages 264–92 in *Dispensationalism, Israel, and the Church: The Search for Definition*. Edited by Craig Blaising and Darrell Bock. Grand Rapids: Zondervan, 1992.

Turner, Nigel. *Grammatical Insights into the New Testament*. Edinburgh: T&T Clark, 1966.

———. *Style*. Vol. 4 of *A Grammar of New Testament Greek*. Edinburgh: T&T Clark, 1976.

Ureña, Lourdes García. *Narrative and Drama in the Book of Revelation: A Literary Approach*. SNTS 175. Cambridge: Cambridge University Press, 2019.

VanderKam, James C., and William Adler, eds. *The Jewish Apocalyptic Heritage in Early Christianity*. CRINT. Minneapolis: Fortress, 1996.

Verbrugge, Verlyn D. *A Not-So-Silent Night: The Unheard Story of Christmas and Why It Matters*. Grand Rapids: Kregel, 2009.

Victorinus of Petovium et al. *Latin Commentaries on Revelation*. Edited by Thomas C. Oden. Translated by William C. Weinrich. ACT. Downers Grove, IL: IVP Academic, 2011.

Villeneuve, André. *Nuptial Symbolism in Second Temple Writings, the New Testament and Rabbinic Literature: Divine Marriage at Key Moments of Salvation History*. Leiden: Brill, 2016.

Voorwinde, Stephen. "Worship, the Key to the Book of Revelation?" *VR* 63 (1998): 3–35.

Vos, Geerhardus. *Biblical Theology: Old and New Testaments*. Grand Rapids: Eerdmans, 1948. Repr., Eugene, OR: Wipf & Stock, 2003.

Waddell, Robby. *The Spirit of the Book of Revelation*. JPTSup 30. Blandford Forum: Deo, 2006.

Wai-yee Ng. *Water Symbolism in John: An Eschatological Interpretation*. SBL 15. New York: Peter Lang, 2001.

Wainwright, A. W. *Mysterious Apocalypse: Interpreting the Book of Revelation*. Nashville: Abingdon, 1993.

Walker, P. W. L. *Jesus and the Holy City: New Testament Perspectives on Jerusalem*. Grand Rapids: Eerdmans, 1996.

Wall, Robert W. "Apocalypse of the New Testament in Canonical Context." Pages 274–98 in *The New Testament as Canon: A Reader in Canonical Criticism*. Edited by Robert W. Wall and Eugene E. Lemico. JSNTSup 76. Sheffield: JSOT Press, 1992.

Wallace, Daniel B. *The Basics of New Testament Syntax*. Grand Rapids: Zondervan, 2000.

———. *Greek Grammar beyond the Basics: An Exegetical Syntax of the New Testament*. Grand Rapids: Zondervan, 1996.

Walls, Jerry L. "Heaven." Pages 399–412 in *The Oxford Handbook of Eschatology*. Edited by Jerry L. Walls. Oxford: Oxford University Press, 2008.

Walvoord, John F. *The Revelation of Jesus Christ: A Commentary*. Chicago: Moody, 1966.

Warden, Duane. "Imperial Persecution and the Dating of 1 Peter and Revelation." *JETS* 34.2 (1991): 203–12.

Watt, Jonathan M. "Some Implications of Bilingualism for New Testament Exegesis." Pages 9–27 in *The Language of the New Testament: Context, History, and Development*. Edited by Stanley E. Porter and Andrew W. Pitts. LBS 6. Leiden: Brill, 2013.

Waymeyer, Matthew. "The First Resurrection in Revelation 20." *MSJ* 27 (2016): 3–32.

Webster, Douglas D. *Follow the Lamb: A Pastoral Approach to The Revelation*. Eugene, OR: Cascade, 2014.

Weima, Jeffrey A. D. *The Sermons to the Seven Churches of Revelation: A Commentary and Guide*. Grand Rapids: Baker Academic, 2021.

Weinrich, William C., ed. *Revelation*. ACCS 12. Downers Grove, IL: InterVarsity Press, 2005.

Wendland, Ernst R. "The Hermeneutical Significance of Literary Structure in Revelation." *Neot* 48.2 (2014): 447–76.

Wenkel, David H. *Shining Like the Sun: A Biblical Theology of Meeting God Face to Face*. Bellingham, WA: Lexham, 2016.

Westermeyer, Paul. "The Book of Revelation in Music and Liturgy." *OHBR* 431–46.

Whale, Peter, "The Lamb of John: Some Myths about the Vocabulary of the Johannine Literature." *JBL* 106 (1987): 289–95.

White, J. R. "The 144,000 in Revelation 7 and 14: Old Testament and Intratextual Clues to Their Identity." Pages 179–97 in *From Creation to New Creation: Biblical Theology and Exegesis: Essays in Honor of G. K. Beale*. Edited by D. M. Gurtner and B. L. Gladd. Peabody, MA: Hendrickson 2013.

Wilcox, Max. "Text Form." Pages 193–203 in *It Is Written: Scripture Citing Scripture*. Edited by D. A. Carson and H. G. M. Williamson. Cambridge: Cambridge University Press, 1988.

Williams, Jarvis J. *Redemptive Kingdom Diversity: A Biblical Theology of the People of God*. Grand Rapids: Baker Academic, 2021.

Williams, Peter J. "P[115] and the Number of the Beast." *TynBul* 58 (2007): 151–53.

Wilson, J. Christian. "The Problem of the Domitianic Date of Revelation." *NTS* (1993): 587–605.

Wilson, Mark. *Biblical Turkey: A Guide to the Jewish and Christian Sites of Asia Minor*. 4th ed. Istanbul: Ege Yayinlari, 2020.

———. *Charts on the Book of Revelation: Literary, Historical, and Theological Perspectives*. Grand Rapids: Kregel Academic, 2007.

———. "The Early Christians in Ephesus and the Date of Revelation, Again." *Neot* 39.1 (2005): 163–93.

———. "John of Ephesus: A Case of Multi-Personality Identification Disorder." Paper presented at the ETS annual meeting, New Orleans, November 19, 2009.

———. "Revelation." Pages 244–383 in *Hebrews to Revelation*. Vol. 4 in ZIBBC. Edited by Clinton E. Arnold. Grand Rapids: Zondervan, 2002.

———. Review of *The Spirit of the Book of Revelation*, by Robby Waddell. *JEPTA* 27.2 (2007): 153–160.

———. "The Spirit in Revelation: Explorations in Imagery and Metaphor." *CTR* 17.1 (2019): 83–96.

———. *The Victor Sayings in the Book of Revelation*. Eugene, OR: Wipf & Stock, 2007.

———. *Victory through the Lamb: A Guide to Revelation in Plain Language*. 2nd ed. Bellingham, WA: Lexham, 2014.

———. "The Water of Life: Three Explorations into Water Imagery in Revelation and the Fourth Gospel." *Scriptura* 118 (2019): 1–17.

Witherington III, Ben. *Revelation*. NCBC. Cambridge: Cambridge University Press, 2003.

Wong, Daniel K. K. "The Two Witnesses in Revelation 11." *BSac* 54 (July 1997): 344–54.

Woodman, Simon P. "Fire from Heaven: Divine Judgment in the Book of Revelation." Pages 175–91 in *The Book of Revelation*. Edited by Garrick V. Allen, Ian Paul, and Simon P. Woodman. WUNT 411. Tübingen: Mohr Siebeck, 2015.

Wright, Brian J. *Communal Reading in the Time of Jesus: A Window into Early Christian Reading Practices*. Minneapolis: Fortress, 2017.

Wright, Christopher J. H. *The Mission of God: Unlocking the Bible's Grand Narrative*. Downers Grove, IL: IVP Academic, 2006.

———. *The Mission of God's People: A Biblical Theology of the Church's Mission*. BTL. Grand Rapids: Zondervan Academic, 2010.

———. *Salvation Belongs to Our God: Celebrating the Bible's Central Story*. Downers Grove, IL: IVP Academic, 2007.

Wright, N. T. *The New Testament and the People of God*. Minneapolis: Fortress, 1992.

———. *Revelation for Everyone*. Louisville: Westminster John Knox, 2011.

———. *Surprised by Hope: Rethinking Heaven, the Resurrection, and the Mission of the Church*. New York: HarperOne, 2008.

Yarbro Collins, Adela. *The Apocalypse*. NTM 22. Wilmington, DE: Glazier, 1979.

———. *The Combat Myth in the Book of Revelation*. Eugene, OR: Wipf & Stock, 2001.

———. *Crisis and Catharsis: The Power of the Apocalypse*. Philadelphia: Westminster, 1984.

———. "Introduction: Early Christian Apocalypticism." *Semeia* 36 (1986): 1–11.

———. "Numerical Symbolism in Jewish and Early Christian Apocalyptic Literature." *ANRW* II/21/2 (1984): 1221–87.

———. "Pergamon in Early Christian Literature." Pages 163–84 in *Pergamon: Citadel of the Gods*. Edited by Helmut Koester. Harrisburg, PA: Trinity Press International, 1998.

———. "Persecution and Vengeance in the Book of Revelation." Pages 729–49 in *Apocalypticism in the Mediterranean World and the Near East*. Edited by David Hellholm. Tübingen: Mohr Siebeck, 1989.

Yarbrough, Robert W. "The Date of Papias: A Reassessment." *JETS* 26 (1983): 181–91.

Yarnell, Malcolm B., III. *God the Trinity*. Nashville: B&H Academic, 2016.

Zimmermann, Ruben. "Nuptial Imagery in the Revelation of John." *Bib* 84 (2003): 153–83.

Zuck, Roy B. *A Biblical Theology of the New Testament*. Electronic ed. Chicago: Moody, 1994.

Scripture Index

Proverbs

Ecclesiastes

Isaiah

JEREMIAH

Hosea

Joel

Amos

Obadiah

Micah

EXTRABIBLICAL SOURCES INDEX

SUBJECT INDEX

AUTHOR INDEX